The Selected Papers of Margaret Sanger

VOLUME 1

THE WOMAN REBEL

1900–1928

THE SELECTED PAPERS OF MARGARET SANGER

Volume 1: The Woman Rebel, 1900–1928

Edited by Esther Katz

Assistant Editors

Cathy Moran Hajo and Peter C. Engelman

UNIVERSITY OF ILLINOIS PRESS
URBANA AND CHICAGO

First Illinois paperback, 2007

∞ This book is printed on acid-free paper.

The Library of Congress cataloged the cloth edition as follows:
Sanger, Margaret, 1879–1966.
[Selections. 2003]
The selected papers of Margaret Sanger / edited by Esther Katz ; assistant editors, Cathy Moran Hajo and Peter C. Engelman.
v. cm.
Includes bibliographical references and index.
Contents: v. 1: The woman rebel, 1900–1928.
ISBN 0-252-02737-X (cloth : acid-free paper)
1. Sanger, Margaret, 1879–1966.
2. Sanger, Margaret, 1879–1966—Correspondence.
3. Birth control—United States—History—20th century.
4. Women's rights—United States—History—20th century.
I. Katz, Esther. II. Hajo, Cathy Moran. III. Engelman, Peter. IV. Title.
HQ764.S3A25 2003
363.9'6'09730904—dc21 2001005959

Paperback ISBN 9780252074608

In memory of my parents,
Rose (Ruzena) and Harry (Chaim Moshe) Katz,
survivors, for their courage, honor, and loving support
—Esther Katz

Contents

Acknowledgments

We are indebted to the many talented people who helped make this volume possible. At New York University, the principal sponsor of the project, we are grateful to all those in the Department of History who made it a comfortable and creative environment in which to work. Professor Emeritus Carl E. Prince, former codirector of the project and past chair of the Department of History, ensured the project's survival during its early days and continues to be an unfailing source of strength and guidance. Chairs Jerrold Seigel and Mary Nolan have continued that support. We specially thank NYU's dean of research, Joseph Juliano, for his assistance and encouragement; Martha Dunne and Tim Kirby of the Office of Sponsored Programs for helping us negotiate the minefield of federal grant support; and Peter Wosh, director of the Department of History's Program in Archival Management and Historical Editing, for his consistent support and fellowship. The staff at NYU's Bobst Library was essential to our work; we particularly thank the interlibrary loan staff, the archivists at the Tamiment Library and Robert F. Wagner Labor Archives, and Claire Gabriel and Jennifer Schwartz, librarians for U.S. and world history, who helped us secure essential research materials.

Preparation of this volume would not have been possible without the generous cooperation of the Sophia Smith Collection at Smith College. Sherrill Redmon, head of the collection, and her staff showed us commitment, patience, and generosity and provided a warm, supportive environment for our years of ongoing work in the collection. We are grateful to Smith's Neilson Library reference staff for pointing us in the right direction so many times. We also thank all the repositories that granted us permission to publish their materials, particularly the Sophia Smith Collection and others from which we selected a substantial number of documents: the British Library, the Rauner Special Collections Library at Dartmouth College, and the Library of Congress.

We are deeply indebted to many other archivists and librarians who aided us in our research, particularly Lesley Hall at the Wellcome Institute for the History of Medicine; Caroline Duroselle-Melish at the New York Academy of Medicine; Susan Fagan at the Newberry Library; Sue Hanson at Special Collections, Kelvin Smith Library, Case Western Reserve University; Gary Jones at the Onondaga County Public Library, Syracuse, New York; Jennifer Peters at the Archives of the Episcopal Church, Austin, Texas; Edward Skipworth at Special Collections and University Archives, Rutgers University; Edward C. Weber, curator of the Labadie Collection, University of Michigan; Patricia Willis, curator of the Yale Collection of American Literature, Beineke Rare Books and Manuscript Library; Thomas M. Whitehead at Special Collections, Temple University Libraries; and the staffs of the Schlesinger Library, Radcliffe College; the Brooklyn Collection of the Brooklyn Public Library; the Long Island Division of the Queens Borough Public Library; the Manuscripts Division of the New York Public Library; the reference department at the Multnomah County Library, Portland, Oregon; the National Archives Northeast Region, New York City; and the New York City Municipal Archives.

We are especially grateful to the family of Margaret Sanger for providing us with full access to Margaret Sanger's papers and for sharing their personal knowledge and reflections. Our particular thanks go to Alexander C. Sanger, whose support, insights, and generosity have been invaluable; and to Margaret Sanger Lampe, whose door has always been open to us. We would also like to thank Mabel Purcell Higgins, Nancy Purcell Higgins Dooley, and Joan Sanger Hoppe.

Many students have worked side by side with us at our NYU offices. We especially thank our Department of History graduate research assistants, Jasmine Mir, Kirsten Fermaglich, Angela Cotten-Harris, and Kate Culkin; and student assistants, Shelley Matthews, Tawana Youngblood, Jordan Pascoe, Tricia Khan, Kristina Wertz, Liz Joseph, Lisa Patel, Susan Haacke, Katie Redfield, Christina Nelson, Lia Araujo, Meghan Horvath, Pilara Brunson, Elizabeth Vayda, and Meghan Duffy. The project has also benefited from the excellent work of many unpaid interns: Bernadette Boucher, Anastasia Curwood, Chris Nardi, Holly Piscopo, Heather Davis, Sarah Habich, Amy Hay, Carli Crozier Schiffner, Franck Dubois, Leigh Fought, Rosanna Gabriele, Ivy Klenetsky, Jon S. Middaugh, Emily Osborne, Zivah Perel, and Natalie Whittaker.

We are grateful to Dr. Stacy K. Sewell, a fellow at the National Historical Publications and Records Commission, for her productive year with us. We would also like to acknowledge the research assistance of Doris Kinney, who volunteered to research Sanger's Hudson County, New York, doings and proofread the volume; Michael T. Meier and J. Dane Hartgrove of the National Historical Publications and Records Commission, who located records for us at the National Archives and the Library of Congress in Washington, D.C.; Professor Paul Avrich, Queens College, City University of New York, who provided invaluable knowledge and insights on anarchism, as well as assistance in locating the records of many of Sanger's anarchist associates; and Kevin E. McClearey, associate dean at Southern Illinois University, Edwardsville, who shared with us his research on Sanger's 1916 tour. We also thank Lawrence Lader and George and Ellen Rublee for giving us access to their private collections of Sanger materials.

Securing adequate financial support is one of the most critical tasks of any editorial project. This endeavor would not have been possible without the endorsement and support of the National Historical Publications and Records Commission (NHPRC) and the National Endowment for the Humanities (NEH). We are grateful for the assistance and encouragement of their respective staffs, particularly Mary Giunta, Tim Connelly, Roger Bruns, and Ann Newhall at the NHPRC and Elizabeth Arndt, Dan Jones, and Margot Backus at NEH. In addition, the following private foundations provided essential assistance: the Mary Duke Biddle Foundation; New York University Research Challenge Fund; the Blanchette Hooker Rockefeller Fund; the Samuel Rubin Foundation; the Helen Clay Frick Foundation; the Albert and Mary Lasker Foundation; and several anonymous donors. Preparation of this volume would not have been possible without the contributions of Anna Clark, David Clark, Elizabeth Miner Fosdick, Carol Lebworth, Frances Moss, Brooke Neidich, Daniel Neidich, Frances Garber Pepper, Alexander C. Sanger, David Solomon, Ellen Violett, and the hundreds of other individuals whose personal contributions ensured its survival and impressed both federal and private funders with the reach of our work.

We have been fortunate in being able to call on a distinguished advisory board: Debra E. Bernhardt, Ellen Chesler, Elizabeth Fee, Gloria Feldt, Linda Gordon, Sarah Pritchard, Sherrill Redmon, James Reed, Allan Rosenfield, Alexander Sanger, Stuart Sanger, Jill Sheffield, Avabai B. Wadia, and Faye Wattleton.

We would also like to acknowledge the support, assistance, and fellowship of other editors and scholars, particularly Charlene Bickford, Alex Baskin, Ellen Chesler, Elaine F. Crane, Martin Duberman, Ann D. Gordon, Barry Patemon, and Elizabeth Hall Witherell. Special thanks are due Elaine F. Crane and Mary Giunta, who are responsible for the birth of this project; our editor, Joan Catapano, for her patient support for so many years; Stephen Crane, Grace Engelman, Kendall Engelman, Waverley Engelman, Meg Hajo, Nabil Hajo, Tamar March, and Eli Zal for their encouragement and uncommon patience; and Terry Collins for her diverse and immeasurable contributions to the manuscript and many years of unwavering support.

Introduction

In 1916, just two years after she helped coin the term *birth control,* Margaret Sanger told a reporter, "I have been called in turn a vile female, a person with a barnyard philosophy, a God-send, the greatest woman of the century, the counterpart of Abraham Lincoln and a horrible creature. . . . Rather conflicting epithets, but I go on doing what I believe to be right, carrying a message of help, as I believe it to be."[1] She would balance such insults with accolades for the next five decades as she dedicated herself to making birth control safe, available, legal, and respectable. This four-volume edition of selected papers traces the life and career of Margaret Sanger, from her efforts to escape the working-class insecurity and small-town parochialism of her childhood through her rise as the international leader of one of the most controversial and fundamental social movements of the twentieth century.

Controversy was central to Margaret Sanger's life, as it is among those who try to capture that life. Was she a moderate reformer or a revolutionary; an immoral libertine or a radical feminist; a tool of fanatical eugenics or a sincere proponent of scientific breeding; a working-class heroine or a social climber; self-sacrificing or self-obsessed? To a greater or lesser degree, she was all these things and more. Bolder than her delicate features and diminutive frame implied, she was a complex woman driven by a staunch sense of public duty, ruled by a restless spirit, yet committed to those she felt were ignored or abandoned. But she was guided, always, by the radical, irreducible belief that every woman must have both the knowledge and right to practice birth control—a conviction that demanded compromises and conversions.

To a large extent, Sanger carefully crafted her own image. In her two autobiographies, *My Fight for Birth Control* (1931) and *Autobiography* (1938), she embraced the role of David fighting the Goliath of Victorian morality and Catholic repression. Intended as propaganda tools, these narratives of her life were structured as prelude to and product of her epiphanous discovery of birth control. But the complexities, nuances, and contradictions of Margaret Sanger, in public and private, along with her real achievements, were muted or omitted. They must be found elsewhere—in her letters, diaries, journals, articles, and speeches—the daily record of her life and the raw materials of her work.

These papers unmask a woman in a constant process of self-discovery and self-definition, sometimes introspective and self-aware and at other times remarkably blind to the impact of her words and deeds. They offer a polychromatic portrait of an activist who overcame illness and insecurity with ego and spirited optimism, as well as talent and intelligence. What emerges is a woman with a sexual allure that affected both men and women, as much as her speaking and writing inspired them to join her struggle. Her papers also reveal a curiously eccentric interest in psychic and spiritual phenomenon seemingly at odds with her reverence for science and positivist logic. And her letters and journal entries lay open her struggle to balance her roles as mother, wife, lover, and friend against her all-consuming crusade.

"I seem to have no life and no history apart from the birth control movement," Sanger wrote in 1938.[2] But in fact she was thirty-five years old when she began fighting for a woman's right to decide whether and when to have children. A consumptive, a suburban wife, and a mother of three, she was also a nurse, a journalist, an activist passionately committed to socialism and anarchism, and a veteran of several militant labor struggles. Sanger was anything but an innocent with a disposable past when she first started laying the groundwork for the birth control movement.

In this volume, covering the years 1900 to 1928, Sanger traverses many worlds, from the picket lines of striking textile workers to lavish English country estates, from the Queens County Penitentiary to the presidency of the nation's most successful birth control organization. Starting with her nurses training, it traces her early work treating desperate immigrant women on the Lower East Side, her volunteer efforts for New York's Socialist Party, and her emergence as an activist in the liberating radical salons of prewar Greenwich Village. Here, amidst intense debates over economic liberation and women's sexual equality, Sanger recognized birth control as the issue that would most effect fundamental social change. It became for her the undeniable focal point of all revolutions. She came to believe that women's political and economic liberation depended on their ability to free themselves from the shackles of unplanned and unwanted pregnancy. And she was among the few prewar bohemians to actualize her beliefs by quietly and privately living out the subtext of her birth control agenda—women's sexual equality and liberation—making her one of the most daring and unorthodox of feminists. Drawing ideas, strategy, and inspiration from other radicals, she advanced the birth control movement through the tactics of direct action and agitation, not only managing publicity but daring to seek it.

Sanger's initial goal was to bring birth control out of what she referred to as the "gutter" of indecency and immorality, to fight the censorship that banned women's access to contraception and make it available to any woman who wanted it. But toward the end of World War I, Sanger began to steer the birth control movement away from the radical margins to mainstream respectability. The second half of the volume follows her gradual turn to organization building and legislative reform. Seeking acceptance from and alliances with upper- and middle-class women, the medical profession, and the eugenics movement, she spoke less frequently about the free speech implications of her work and more about strengthening the human race. During these same years, public life in the United States was being purged of its most radical discourse, while popular interest in eugenics increased dramatically. Coalescing around the grief of war, many argued that with millions of "fit" young men lost to combat, the less desirable and often biologically "unfit" were left to further the race. In a Western world demoralized by war and obsessed with race regeneration, Sanger offered birth control as the answer.

With little formal education but a hunger for knowledge and ideas, Sanger embraced postwar eugenics discourse but not without outside inspiration and guidance. She sought and found a series of mentors—men of learning who advanced her education and provided her with a coherent scientific and social rationale for her belief. Her intellectual and class-based insecurities may have left her reluctant to challenge their views or the moral toll of the "scientific studies" on which they were based, but she never failed to keep the interests and needs of all women at the forefront of her crusade.

By 1928, as many Americans sought to put the radical turmoil of the previous decades behind them by throwing themselves into a search for personal liberation—adopting new social and sexual mores and the ethic of mass consumption—while others fought for a return to prewar traditionalism, Sanger's "barnyard philosophy" had become part of the public debate. Her life is a story of modernity.

Margaret Louise Higgins was born in Corning, New York, on September 14, 1879, the sixth of eleven children. Her parents, Anne Purcell (1848–99) and Michael Hennessey Higgins (1845–1926), married in 1869 and drifted from Brooklyn to Ohio and then to New Jersey before settling in the small industrial city of Corning, in western New York. There Michael Higgins, a first-generation Irish American and a veteran of the Union Army, set up a stonecutting business in the mostly Irish Catholic community of artisans and laborers revolving around the prosperous Corning Glass Works. He became a vocal advocate for socialist ideas and a critic of the Catholic church—thereby alienating his customer base. Along with Higgins's passion for politics, his indulgence of liquor further limited his employment, and he made little money. He was eventually forced to take a menial job at the Corning Glass Works and later had to rely on his children for income. The resourceful Anne Higgins, a second-generation Irish American resigned to economic uncertainty and plagued by bouts of tuberculosis, persevered through more than a dozen pregnancies to raise and nurture a remarkably robust family of ten surviving children. Margaret's parents' marriage was a precarious union of a consumptive in a state of nearly perpetual pregnancy and a faithful but erratic husband. The third daughter and middle child of the family, Margaret was watched over by two older sisters: Mary, by all accounts charming, poised, and skilled at domestic work from cooking to carpentry; and the more studious and ambitious Anna (Nan), who aspired to write but was forced to postpone her scholarly endeavors and take a job. The two older sisters left home to earn money as domestic workers before their younger sister reached adolescence. Margaret and her younger sister, Ethel, were left to carry on the housework when their mother ailed or another baby brother came into the world. The older brothers, Joseph, John, and Thomas, took unskilled positions at the Corning Glass Works as soon as they were able. The additional income sent home by the older children improved the lot of the others, but Margaret remembered her childhood as "one of longing for things that were always denied."[3]

By Margaret's own admission, her father had the greatest impact on her education. He opened the Higgins house to a range of charismatic characters and serious debate and encouraged his sons and daughters alike to express themselves on any issue. Margaret came to share his politics and ideals, among them a belief in economic and sexual equality, advocacy of free education, and disdain for Catholic dogma. Despite her father's impiety, her mother was a practicing Catholic. Through her mother's influence and probably against her father's wishes, Margaret attended a parish school at St. Mary's Catholic Church and was baptized at age thirteen. She was confirmed there in 1894 but left in 1896, a few weeks prior to graduation. With help from her older sisters, young Margaret finished her formal education at a private boarding school. Margaret Sanger's early years, unorthodox and difficult, left her angry and frustrated over the injustices and inequities experienced by working-class families, particularly the burden carried by women like her mother, yet she was inspired by her father's idealism. What she sought was a place to channel her energy and impatience, a place to leave her mark.[4]

NOTES

1. *Portland Oregonian,* June 17, 1916.
2. MS to W. W. Norton, Sept. 21, 1938 (*MSM* C6:896).
3. MS, *My Fight,* 4–8, 9 (quote); MS, *Autobiography,* 11–19.
4. According to MS, her decision came after a teacher humiliated her for being late. (MS, *My Fight,* 22–23; MS, *Autobiography,* 20–23; Chesler, *Woman of Valor,* 29.)

Editorial Method

Selection

Margaret Sanger left a voluminous archive of over 120,000 letters, speeches, diaries, and organizational and legal records documenting her long and eventful life.[1] Our goal in creating this volume is to highlight Sanger's distinctive voice and illuminate the multiple narratives of her life and work. Our choices were governed by our desire to document critical events, major themes, and central issues of Sanger's life from 1900 to 1928 and to reveal her thought processes and modes of expression. Some 80 percent of the documents selected for this volume consist of letters, augmented by articles, speeches, and selections from Sanger's pamphlets, journals, and diaries. We have focused on letters written by Sanger, generally limiting incoming letters to those that provide indispensable context that cannot be adequately summarized or offer critical information about Sanger and her agenda, particularly when Sanger's outgoing letters have not been preserved. We have included a representative selection of letters written to Sanger by those seeking birth control advice. All but a few of the vast number of organizational and legal documents have been excluded. Documents are printed in their entirety with the exception of pamphlets, diaries, and journals (entries were selected from the larger document) and testimony and newspaper interviews (we have included only Sanger's contribution).

Margaret Sanger not only led the American movement but also sought to globalize birth control by organizing international conferences and cultivating contacts among scientists, economists, social reformers, and population control leaders around the world. Much of her international work was, by design, conducted independent of her leadership of the U.S. movement. We have therefore omitted documents relating to her international work from this and the two subsequent volumes of this edition and will gather them in a separate (fourth) volume.

Establishing Text

The majority of source texts used for this edition are unique, but when there are multiple versions of letters, the recipient's copy is used. In the case of multiple drafts of Sanger's speeches or articles, we generally chose the one that most closely resembles the final version. Occasionally a composite text was created from various incomplete versions (for example, incomplete drafts of speeches with additional portions from published sources). Exceptions to these guidelines are noted in the headnotes or endnotes. Variant versions of documents are cited in the source notes.

Organization and Format of the Volume

Documents in this volume are grouped in chronological chapters. Because this is such a highly selective edition, we have sought to provide narrative and chronological links in brief essays introducing each chapter. Each document is preceded by a header identifying the author, recipient, or title. Headnotes sometimes appear above documents to provide context or explain issues or events relating to their creation. Documents are arranged in chronological order. Documents written on the same day are placed in the order in which they were written or, in the case of journal articles, in the order in which they appeared in the journal. Otherwise they are placed in alphabetical order by author. Letters dated only by month and year are placed at the end of that month, though journal articles appear at the beginning of the month. An unnumbered source note follows each document providing an abbreviation to describe the physical characteristics of the source text and its provenance, followed by its microfilm location, information on variant versions, notes on enclosures, anything notable about its physical condition (for example, water stains or ink blots), and other identifying information (letterhead, Sanger's return address, and the like).

Transcription

Our transcription goal was to retain the authorial voice, color, and tone of the original by reproducing the source text as accurately as possible. Original spelling, punctuation, paragraph division, abbreviations, ampersands, superscript, and other idiosyncrasies have been preserved, as have underlining and double underlining for emphasis (though text underlined more than twice is rendered as double underline). Authors' use of initial capitals and capitalization as a means of emphasis has also been preserved. When capitalization could not be determined, we have adopted standard usage. Terminal punctuation rendered as long dashes or periods has also been retained. However, when sentences are terminated by the use of extra spaces or when terminal punctuation is missing, we have silently supplied terminal periods.

For words or parts of words that are illegible or missing in the source text, we supplied, wherever possible, entire words in italics within square brackets. When the supplied information is conjecture, we have followed that portion with a question mark. If the information cannot be supplied, the missing portion is rendered as [*illegible*] or [*pages missing or torn*].

To ensure a more readable text, we have standardized the following elements: the first letter of each sentence, unless it appears in a postscript, is always capitalized; new paragraphs are always indented; the complimentary closing is run into the last paragraph of letters; and signatures are always placed at the right margin beneath the text. In typed, signed letters, the handwritten signature is indicated by [*signed*] or [*initialed*] following the name. The place/date lines are always located flush to the right margin; the salutation, flush to the left margin. Document dates and places written or typed by the author are rendered as they appear on the original, though in place lines, street addresses and county names have been omitted. For missing or incomplete dates, we have supplied the missing portion in standardized form. Dates or places added to the documents by the recipient or a third party have been omitted.

In letters written by Sanger, home and hotel addresses have been retained but appear in the source notes. Since Sanger often used whatever paper or stationary was at hand, we have determined that letterhead alone is not sufficient to identify the place of origin. In these cases, Sanger's location has been verified, and the missing place is supplied in standardized form. For all letters written to Sanger, places of origin derived from the letterhead are accepted and rendered without italics and brackets. Places of origin do not generally appear in speeches and published writings; if a place is associated with such a document, it is provided in the source note.

Typographical errors and obvious slips of the pen have been silently corrected, and closing quotation marks or parentheses have been silently supplied. Canceled text, interlineations, and other corrections and additions to the text by the author have been retained and indicated through symbols. Interlineations in the text are rendered within up and down arrows (↑↓); author insertions or intended interlineations that appear elsewhere on the original (in the margins or on the reverse, often with an arrow or other mark directing its intended placement in the text) are placed at the appropriate location in the text.

Insertions that can be linked only to a paragraph are placed at the end of that paragraph, with an endnote indicating its location on the original. When an author's insertion or marginalia cannot be linked to a specific point in the document, it is placed below the signature, preceded by an editorial note describing its location on the original. Marginalia written by someone other than the author are described in the endnotes if they are linked to a specific portion of the text, otherwise, in the source note. Because the originals are available on microfilm, general routing notes (including stamps, collection names, dates, etc.) and marks by archivists, researchers, or others made well after the document was created have been omitted.

Annotation

Source notes are followed, when needed, by one or more numbered endnotes that identify persons (and correct or identify partial names, nicknames, initials, and misspelled names); places; organizations; technical, medical, or legal terms; publications (with bibliographic reference); abbreviations; and archaic and foreign words or phrases. They also explain textual complexities in transcription and contextualize events that are not explained elsewhere in the document, chapter essay, or headnote. Notes may also point the reader to related material in the microfilm edition and summarize documents excluded from the volume in order to furnish context (when quotes are used in headnotes and endnotes, we have inserted ellipses to indicate omissions). We have tried to identify every person mentioned in the text, generally at the first full mention in a document. Location of the first biographical identification is noted in the index. We have not indicated when people or places are unidentified, though unidentified events and documents are noted.

NOTE

1. The full corpus of Sanger documents can be found in the two-series microfilm *The Margaret Sanger Papers: Smith College Collections* and *Collected Documents Series* (Bethesda, Md.: University Publications of America, 1996, 1997); and in the Papers of Margaret Sanger, microfilm, Library of Congress, Washington, D.C.

Abbreviations

MS Margaret Sanger

Document Descriptions

AD	Autograph Document
ADf	Autograph Draft
AL	Autograph Letter
ALI	Autograph Letter Initialed
ALS	Autograph Letter Signed
TDcy	Typed Document, Carbon Copy
TDf	Typed Draft
TEL	Telegram
TFL	Typed Form Letter
TL	Typed Letter
TLcy	Typed Letter Carbon Copy
TLcyS	Typed Letter Carbon Copy Signed
TLI	Typed Letter Initialed
TLS	Typed Letter Signed
TM	Typed Memo
TRcy	Transcribed Copy
TRcyI	Transcribed Copy Initialed

Microfilm Editions

When citing documents in a microfilm edition, the microfilm abbreviation is followed by the reel and frame numbers. When a Sanger document appears in this volume, we have replaced the microfilm citation with the word *herein.*

EGPM	*The Emma Goldman Papers: A Microfilm Edition,* edited by Candace Falk, Ronald Zboray, and Daniel Cornford (Alexandria, Va., 1990)
LCM	Margaret Sanger Papers Microfilm (1977), Library of Congress
MSM	*The Margaret Sanger Papers [Microfilm],* edited by Esther Katz, Peter C. Engelman, Cathy Moran Hajo, and Anke Hubbard (Bethesda, Md., 1996–97). Reels starting with "S" are from *The Smith College Collection Series;* those starting with "C" are from *The Collected Documents Series.*
MWDPM	*Women's Studies Manuscript Collections from the Schlesinger Library, Radcliffe College [Microfilm], Series 3: Pt. B: The Papers of Mary Ware Dennett and the Voluntary Parenthood League* (Bethesda, Md., 1994)

Standard References

ANB	*American National Biography*
BCR	*Birth Control Review*
CA Death Index	California Death Index, 1940–97
DAB	*Dictionary of American Biography*
DNB	*Dictionary of National Biography*
DSB	*Dictionary of Scientific Biography*
ENYC	*Encyclopedia of New York City*
NatCAB	*National Cyclopedia of American Biography*
OED	*Oxford English Dictionary*
SSDI	Social Security Death Index
WWW America	*Who Was Who in America*
WWW England	*Who Was Who in England*

Manuscript Collections

ABCLR	American Birth Control League Records, Houghton Library, Harvard University, Cambridge, Mass.
ACLUR	American Civil Liberties Union Records, Mudd Library, Princeton University, Princeton, N.J.
CBDP	Charles B. Davenport Papers, American Philosophical Society, Philadelphia, Pa.
CBP	Charles Francis Brush Papers, Kelvin Smith Library, Case Western Reserve University, Cleveland, Ohio

CCR	Records of Claverack College, Claverack Free Library, Claverack, N.Y.
CZP	Carl Zigrosser Papers, Department of Special Collections, Annenberg Rare Book and Manuscript Library, University of Pennsylvania, Philadelphia
EHMP	Edith How-Martyn Papers, privately held by Hilary Frances, Harrogate, North Yorkshire, UK.
FBP	Frederick A. Blossom Papers, State Historical Society of Wisconsin, Madison.
FPAA	Family Planning Association Archive, Wellcome Institute for the History of Medicine, London, England
FRP	Florence Rose Papers, Sophia Smith Collection, Smith College, Northampton, Mass.
GHP	Granville Hicks Papers, Department of Special Collections, Syracuse University Library, Syracuse, N.Y.
GTP	Gertrude Traubel Papers, Special Collections Department, Temple University Library, Philadelphia, Pa.
JRP	Juliet Barrett Rublee Papers, Dartmouth College Library, Hanover, N.H.; and Sophia Smith Collection, Smith College, Northampton, Mass.
Labadie	Labadie Collection, Harlan Hatcher Library, University of Michigan, Ann Arbor
Lader	Lawrence Lader Papers, privately held
LJCP	Leon J. Cole Papers, University Archives, University of Wisconsin Memorial Library, Madison
MHP	Morris Hillquit Papers, Robert F. Wagner Archives and Tamiment Library, New York University, New York City
MSP	Margaret Sanger Papers, Sophia Smith Collection, Smith College, Northampton, Mass., and Manuscripts Division, Library of Congress, Washington, D.C.
MSRBR	Margaret Sanger Research Bureau Records, Sophia Smith Collection, Smith College, Northampton, Mass.
MS Unfilmed	Margaret Sanger Papers, Unfilmed Portion, Sophia Smith Collection, Smith College, Northampton, Mass.
MWDP	Mary Ware Dennett Papers, Arthur and Elizabeth Schlesinger Library on the History of Women in America, Radcliffe College, Harvard University, Cambridge, Mass.
NBB	Nancy Brush Pearmain Bowditch Papers, Archives of American Art, Smithsonian Institution, Washington, D.C.
NCMHR	National Committee on Maternal Health Records, Countway Library of Medicine, Harvard Medical School, Cambridge, Mass.

NCWCR	National Catholic Welfare Council/United States Catholic Conference Collection, Department of Archives, Manuscripts, and Museum Collections, Catholic University of America, Washington, D.C.
NFP	Norris Family Papers, Bancroft Library, University of California, Berkeley
POR	Records of the U.S. Postmaster, National Archives, Washington, D.C.
PPFAR	Records of Planned Parenthood Federation of America, Sophia Smith Collection, Smith College, Northampton, Mass.
PPLMR	Records of Planned Parenthood League of Massachusetts, Sophia Smith Collection, Smith College, Northampton, Mass.
RCB	Records of the U.S. Children's Bureau, National Archives, Washington, D.C
RGP	Ralph Ginzburg Papers, State Historical Society of Wisconsin, Madison
RHR	Records of the House of Representatives, National Archives, Washington, D.C.
RKP	Rockwell Kent Papers, Archives of American Art, Smithsonian Institution, Washington, D.C.
RLWP	Ray Lyman Wilbur Collection, Box 123, Hoover Institution Archives, Stanford University, Stanford, Calif.
RNBP	Roger N. Baldwin Papers, Mudd Library, Princeton University, Princeton, N.J.
Rockefeller	Records of the Office of the Messrs. Rockefeller General Files, Medical Interests Series, Rockefeller Archive Center, Sleepy Hollow, N.Y.
RPP	Raymond Pearl Papers, American Philosophical Society, Philadelphia, Pa.
RPSP	Rose Pastor Stokes Papers, Sterling Library, Yale University, New Haven, Conn.
RSSC	Rochester Socialist Scrapbook Collection, 1910–19, Rush Rhees Library, University of Rochester, Rochester, N.Y.
SCR	Records of the U.S. Supreme Court, RG 267, National Archives, Washington, D.C.
SHP	Stephen Haweis Papers, Butler Library, Columbia University, New York, N.Y.
SPLL	Records of the Socialist Party (U.S.), Local New York, Robert F. Wagner Archives and Tamiment Library, New York University, New York City
Stopes	Marie Stopes Papers, British Library, London, England

TSP	Theodore Schroeder Papers, Southern Illinois University Library, Carbondale
USP	Upton Sinclair Papers, Lilly Library, Indiana University, Bloomington.
WJFP	William J. Fielding Papers, Robert F. Wagner Archives and Tamiment Library, New York University, New York City

Repositories (listed according to their **Library of Congress National Union Catalog** *designations)*

CST-H	Hoover Institution Archives, Stanford University, Stanford, Calif.
CtY-S	Sterling Library, Yale University, New Haven, Conn.
CU-B	Bancroft Library, University of California, Berkeley
D-ArA	Archives of American Art, Smithsonian Institution, Washington, D.C.
DCU	Catholic University of America Archives, Washington, D.C.
DLC	Library of Congress Manuscripts Division, Washington D.C.
DNA	National Archives, Washington D.C.
ICU	University of Chicago, Chicago, Ill.
InU	Lilly Library, Indiana University, Bloomington
MdBe	National Library of Medicine, Bethesda, Md.
MH-H	Houghton Library, Harvard University, Cambridge, Mass.
MH-S	Arthur and Elizabeth Schlesinger Library on the History of Women in America, Radcliffe College, Harvard University, Cambridge, Mass.
MN-SSC	Sophia Smith Collection, Smith College, Northampton, Mass.
NhD	Dartmouth College Library, Hanover, N.H.
NjP-M	Mudd Library, Princeton University, Princeton, N.J.
NNC	Butler Library, Columbia University, New York, N.Y.
NNC-HSL	A. C. Long Health Science Library, Columbia University, New York, N.Y.
NNU-T	Robert F. Wagner Archives and Tamiment Library, New York University, New York, N.Y.
NRU	University of Rochester, Rochester, N.Y.
PPAmP	American Philosophical Society, Philadelphia, Pa.
PU	Annenberg Rare Book and Manuscript Library, University of Pennsylvania, Philadelphia
UK-BL	British Library, London, England
UKW-MRC	Modern Records Centre, University of Warwick, Warwick, England
WHi	State Historical Society of Wisconsin, Madison

WU	University Archives, University of Wisconsin Memorial Library, Madison

Organizations

ABCL	American Birth Control League
CRB	Clinical Research Bureau
IWW	Industrial Workers of the World
NBCL	National Birth Control League
NYBCL	New York Birth Control League
NYWPC	New York Women's Publishing Company
VPL	Voluntary Parenthood League

Chronology

1879	Sept.	Margaret Higgins born
1896	Sept.	Enters Claverack College and Hudson River Institute
1900	Mar.?	Enters White Plains Hospital Nursing Program
1902	Aug.	Marries William Sanger
1903	Nov.	Stuart Sanger born
1908	July	Grant Sanger born
1910	May	Margaret (Peggy) Sanger born
1911	Oct.	"What Every Mother Should Know" begins publication in *New York Call*
1912	Jan–Mar.	Lawrence, Massachusetts, silk strike
1912	Nov.	"What Every Girl Should Know" begins publication in *New York Call*
1913	Feb.	"What Every Girl Should Know" article suppressed; Hazleton, Pennsylvania, and Paterson, New Jersey, strikes begin
	Apr.	Arrested in Hazleton for picketing
	June	Paterson Strike Pageant
1914	Mar.	The *Woman Rebel* begins publication
	Aug.	Federal indictment for the *Woman Rebel*
	Oct.	*Family Limitation* published
	Nov.	Flees the United States
1915	Jan.	William Sanger arrested for distributing *Family Limitation*
	Feb.	*English Methods of Birth Control* published
	Apr.	*Dutch Methods of Birth Control* published
	Aug.	*Magnetation Methods of Birth Control* published
	Sept.	William Sanger's trial and imprisonment

	Oct.	Returns from European exile
	Nov.	Peggy Sanger dies
1916	Feb.	*Woman Rebel* charges dropped
	Apr.–June	First national speaking tour
	June	Arrested in Portland, Oregon, for selling *Family Limitation*
	Oct.	Brownsville Clinic opened and closed; Committee of 100 formed
	Dec.	New York Birth Control League founded
1917	Jan–Feb.	Brownsville Clinic trials
	Feb.	*Birth Control Review* begins publication; sentenced and imprisoned on *Brownsville* case
	Mar.	Released from prison
	May	*The Case for Birth Control: A Supplementary Brief and Statement of the Facts* published
1918	Jan.	*Crane* decision, appeal of *Brownsville* case
1919	Feb.	New York Women's Publishing Company founded
1920	Aug.	*Woman and the New Race* published
1921	Oct.	Divorces William Sanger
1921	Nov.	First American Birth Control Conference (New York City); Town Hall raid and arrests; American Birth Control League founded
1922	May	*The Pivot of Civilization* published
	Sept.	Marries J. Noah Slee
1923	Jan.	Clinical Research Bureau founded
	Oct.	Middle Western States Birth Control Conference (Chicago)
1925	Mar.	Sixth International Neo-Malthusian and Birth Control Conference (New York City)
1926	June	*Happiness in Marriage* published
1927	Aug.	World Population Conference (Geneva)
1928	June	Resigns from the American Birth Control League

The Selected Papers of Margaret Sanger

VOLUME 1

THE WOMAN REBEL

1900–1928

ONE

A Nurse's Education

In the spring of 1896, Margaret Higgins resisted her family's attempts to return her to her eighth-grade class at St. Mary's, a Catholic parochial school. During the summer, the sixteen-year-old Margaret considered finding a job but was persuaded by her parents and older sisters to attend a two-week program of lectures and cultural activities at the Chautauqua Institute, an experience that convinced her to continue her education. She expressed an interest in medicine and apparently shared with family her ambition to attend Cornell University and possibly its medical school. A good preparatory school presented the best means of achieving this goal, but in Corning most working-class daughters married Corning Glass factory workers, and few moved on. Determined to help their younger sister break free of this pattern, Anna and Mary Higgins pulled together enough money to pay at least a year's tuition to extend Margaret's education.

That fall Margaret Higgins began a three-year term at Claverack College and Hudson River Institute, a private coeducational school located in the Catskill mountains near the town of Hudson, New York. Founded in 1854, Claverack College was a respected coeducational institution whose goal was to promote "thorough and systematic education to young men and women, and at the same time furnish them a comfortable, cultured Christian home."[1] Claverack proved to be a socially and intellectually liberating experience for Margaret, who quickly formed several close friendships. She became particularly fond of the elegant Esther Farquharson, an aspiring actress who left after a year to pursue that dream. Following Esther's lead, Margaret briefly considered leaving Claverack to become an actress and even prepared an application and photographs for a New York acting school. She dismissed the idea only when she received a request for her physical measurements.[2] While at Claverack, Margaret entered into a secret engagement with her fellow student Corey Albertson, one among many suitors. Another student, Amelia Stewart, remembered Margaret as "one of the most popular girls in school; I would be inclined to say the most popular, with both the girls and the boys. . . . How proficient she was. She could sew as well as cook, . . . dance divinely; excel in her classes without becoming a book-worm."[3]

Claverack gave Margaret her only formal secondary school education. She earned her room and board by working in the school's kitchen during her first two years, but when her sisters could not meet the tuition payment for her third year, she was forced to leave her congenial life at school and find work. Margaret took a position in the fall of 1898 teaching English to foreign-born first graders in a southern New Jersey public school. By her own admission, she was not "suited by temperament" to the teaching profession, and family circumstances intervened to disrupt any thoughts she may have had of returning to school.[4] Anne Higgins's fragile health deteriorated, compelling Margaret to return home during the winter of 1898–99 to nurse her mother and tend the household. During this time, Margaret contracted tuberculosis of the adrenal glands and suffered from fatigue and other symptoms. On March 31, 1899, Anne Higgins died of tuberculosis at the age of fifty, having borne eleven children and suffered an indeterminate number of miscarriages.

While caring for her mother confirmed Margaret's interest in medicine, her early withdrawal from Claverack and lack of income compromised her chances of success. "Cornell College still called to me," she later wrote, "but I could not bridge the gap between my life and the long journey fitting one for the medical profession." Although she may have harbored a vague notion of someday becoming a doctor, like so many women who wished to enter the medical field, the twenty-year-old Margaret Higgins turned to nursing. In the spring of 1900, she arranged through Esther Farquharson's family to be admitted to the newly established nurse's training program at the White Plains Hospital, outside of New York City.[5]

The training program at White Plains consisted of a three-year curriculum. In addition to attending lectures, students were trained in making dressings, sterilizing equipment, and preparing medical solutions. Margaret later described her training as "severe as only it can be in a small hospital where the equipment is less modern." Because of her fragile health, the long hours and overnight shifts were especially draining. The young women lived in small quarters located at the hospital. In their second year, student nurses continued their training at area hospitals and were often sent out on private cases, including obstetrical ones, and Margaret sometimes delivered babies when physicians did not arrive on time.[6] During her second year, Margaret had a brief stint as a nursing intern at the Manhattan Eye and Ear Infirmary, where at an informal dance in the spring of 1902 she met a young draftsman and artist named William Sanger (1873–1961). Born in Berlin, William had immigrated to the United States with his parents and sister in 1878 and had studied architecture and art at the Cooper Union for the Advancement of Science and Art in New York. Although it is unclear where William Sanger was working when he first encountered Margaret Higgins, he boasted to her of his potential as a provider. He pursued her for several months until she agreed to a hastily arranged marriage in 1902. Shortly thereafter, she abruptly ended her medical training.[7]

NOTES

1. 1889 Claverack College Brochure, MS Unfilmed.

2. On her acting career, see MS Diary, "Girlhood," LCM 2:864; MS, *My Fight*, 24–25.

3. Quoted in Hersey, "Margaret Sanger," 61.

4. MS, *Autobiography*, 41.

5. MS, *My Fight*, 32.

6. "A Brief Sketch of White Plains Hospital," *Kirmess and Spielkartenfest*, Nov. 1902, 8–11; MS, *Autobiography*, 47–55; MS, *My Fight*, 32–33 (quote on 32).

7. MS, *Autobiography*, 56; Hersey, "Margaret Sanger," 82–85; A. C. Sanger, "Margaret Sanger," 8–20.

1. To Mary B. Higgins[1]

White Plains, New York.
June 20—[*1900*]

My dear Mary:-

Anna[2] sent me your address today and I am so sorry I could not have seen you before you sailed[3] but I had left Esther's on Columbus Ave.[4] and have been here ever since as train nurse so did not get your "special"[5] until the day of sailing. I am only on probation until July 1—and then <u>if I am accepted</u> I shall continue to take the three year course consisting of four lectures by different Doctors a week and training by our head nurse who is an unusually capable woman.[6] I had my first patient die a young man came on Monday died Tuesday in the most awful agony Wednesday we went to the postmortem Thursday morning at five a baby boy came and in the afternoon an operation. Now talk about work! I slept just four hours out of 74—and about ten hours all last week. Nan said she had been home and everything is the same. Ethel was a very brave girl she said and did nicely,[7] and how very delightful for you to go abroad. When you return you must come up to see me. If I am here I may be accepted but I can not tell until July 1—when I will be accepted which I hope I will. The work is very interesting and hard. When you write me tell me all about your trip. I suppose you will take in a great deal of the world and tho' you may feel strange, you will probably have a delightful time.

Corey[8] came up to spend Saturday and Sunday with me, he is the same old boy. When do you expect to return? Were you sea sick? Who else is with you? besides the family? I shall write you more when I am not so busy.

AL MSP, MN-SSC (*MSM* S1:15–17). Return address: "#36 Lexington Ave."

1. Mary Higgins (1870–1926), the oldest Higgins child, was a housekeeper for George L. Abbott (1845–1923) and Nellie Houghton Abbott (1854–?), whose family had founded the Corning Glass Works, where George Abbott worked as an executive. (Leaming, *Katharine Hepburn*, 5–8; Office of the Town Clerk, Hamburg, N.Y.)

2. Anna (Nan) Higgins (1874–1943), the third Higgins child, had worked as a governess in Corning before taking a job as a commercial secretary in Buffalo in the 1890s. (Chesler, "Interview with Grant Sanger," 35; Chesler, *Woman of Valor*, 27.)

3. Mary Higgins, who accompanied the Abbotts on family trips, traveled with them to Europe in the summer of 1900. (Leaming, *Katharine Hepburn*, 5–8.)

4. She remained close friends with Esther Farquharson [Barker] (1878–1930). After the death of her mother, MS lived briefly with the Farquharson family on Manhattan's stylish Upper West Side. (MS, *My Fight*, 26; 1895 Claverack Register [CCR].)

5. The letter or telegram was not found.

6. Anna M. Gasz (1863–?) was superintendent of the White Plains Hospital. (U.S. Bureau of the Census, *Twelfth Census of the United States, 1900* [Washington, D.C., 1901–2].)

7. Ethel Higgins Byrne (1883–1955), the youngest of MS's sisters, eloped around this time with Jack Byrne, a factory worker at the Corning Glass Works. (Van Voris, "Olive Byrne Richard Interview," 1–2.)

8. William Corey Albertson (1878–1944), MS's school beau, graduated from Claverack in 1898 and then worked at his father's livery stable in Southold, New York. (1898 Claverack College Register, [CCR]; correspondence between editors and family members.)

2. *To Mary B. Higgins*

[*White Plains, N.Y.*]
July 15, [*1900*]

My dear Mogs:—

This is some time after having written you the inclosed,[1] but I am so busy now I have time really for nothing.

I have been accepted for the three year course in training and no doubt shall be such an angel at the end of that time that I shall fly heavenward.

Nan wrote me yesterday[2] you were now in Paris. I hope you will come up to see me when you arrive let me know the time you expect to arrive and I shall meet you and bring you up with me to spend as long as you can.

Have not heard from home in some time Ethel wrote me about three weeks ago.[3]

We have a wonderful case just now. It surpasses all the doctors experiences. A man brought in unconscious struck by lightening first 48 hours no signs of consciousness but after that said the word "I". Now he is nearly well, Can speak intelligently on every subject but does not know who he is or what his name is. He is an author of short stories, knows Harold Frederick & Richard Harding Davis[4] and a few other men personally. Can discuss every subject but can not remember who he is. He knows his name is Will.

We had a baby case. I was private nurse now I am head nurse of the womans ward[5] and indeed I feel complimented to think they feel I am capable.

Do write me when you can. As ever

Margaret

ALS MSP, MN-SSC (*MSM* S1:18–20). Return address: "36 Lexington Ave." Year at the top of the first page was added by an unidentified author; month and day were added by MS at a later date.

1. She may have been referring to her letter to Mary Higgins, June 20, 1900, herein.
2. The letter was not found.
3. The letter was not found.
4. Harold Frederic (1856–98) was the London correspondent for the *New York Times* and the author of *Damnation of Theron Ware* (1896) and *Gloria Mundi* (1898). Richard Harding Davis (1864–1916) was a journalist and the author of many books, including *Soldiers of Fortune* (1897), and several plays. (*ANB; DAB*)
5. White Plains Hospital had two separate six-bed wards, one for men and one for women, as well as three private rooms. ("History of White Plains Hospital," *Kirmess,* Oct. 16–20, 1900.)

3. *To Mary B. Higgins*

White Plains New York
June 2—1901.

My dear Mary:—

Before I try to copy my lectures I want to drop you a word or two. It is really wonderful the condition I am in since the operation[1] but only today one of the Doctors took me aside & told me he would speak only to <u>my interest</u> & he [*knew*] I would always be troubled more or less unless I gave up living in doors.

You see I am having a fight if I can only get through the three years I can go out & nurse in the west where the animals cannot exist (Colorado for instance)[2] Miss Gasz would not have me give up the profession for anything & I am doing all I can to be well but in a place where there are so many girls it is hard for them to see [*one*] going out two or three hours every day where they have "strictly one" & I hate to have it like that: but Miss Gasz does not know that Dr de Hart[3] spoke to me or she would not like it. Now about vacations. I expect to go to Buffalo[4] for four days & then down to Corning. Make the engagement with Dr Wilbur[5] for the second week: I am very anxious to go home & see all the people. I do hope I can see you. Esther will spend a few days: & as I have not decided to remain long there Corey does not know if he will go or not. I guess he wanted me to take the whole vacation where he could be but as I did not ask him [*home*] he feels it. So you are soon to be in Cloverbank. A fine description of the trip! Whose dress was the sample? Surely not yours![6]

An operation soon on a man: & oh how can I stand the smell of ether!

Mary I wish either you or Nan would write to Drs Knapp & Sherman[7] for the family & thank them: Sherman is the operator or Surgeon & poor Dr Knapp had to do all the dressings and take all the back talk from me. I was a <u>perfect</u> <u>tarter.</u> Simply all the nurses dreaded to be near me think of it!

Dr L P. Knapp White Plains & Dr W. H Sherman Yonkers NY.

I really think they have been so kind that a word of thanks from the family is due them: what do you think?

The people are coming from church so Good night. Love to all Lovingly

Margaret.

ALS MSP, DLC (LCM 6:17–23). Return address: "#36 Lexington Ave."

1. MS underwent two operations in the spring of 1901 to remove tubercular lymph nodes in her neck, but she was left with a draining sinus that debilitated her for the next twenty years. (Chesler, "Interview with Grant Sanger," 19; MS, *Autobiography,* 48.)

2. "Animals" is a reference to the tuberculosis bacteria. Her doctors recommended that MS live in a drier climate, which was less hospitable to the bacterium, and spend more time outdoors, advice consistent with studies done by leading tuberculosis authorities at the time, including Edward L. Trudeau and Robert Koch. (Robert Koch, "The Suppression of Tuberculosis," *Living Age,* Aug. 31, 1901, 529–40.)

3. Henry Garrett Voorhees DeHart (1849–1914) was the attending physician at White Plains Hospital. (Bio. files, NNC-HSL.)

4. MS probably planned to visit her sisters: Anna, in Buffalo, and Mary, whose employers spent summers in Cloverbank, outside of Buffalo.

5. W. Cuttins Wilbur (1860–?) was a Corning, New York, dentist who treated several members of the Higgins family. (Wilbur to MS, Aug. 30 and Oct. 12, 1936 [*MSM* S11:496 and 686].)

6. The letter from Mary Higgins was not found.

7. William H. Sherman (1859–1908), a consulting surgeon at White Plains Hospital and local tuberculosis expert, performed lymph node surgery on MS, assisted by Lewis Palmer Knapp (1872–1902), an assistant surgeon at White Plains Hospital who also suf-

fered from tuberculosis. (Yale College, *History of the Class of 1880* [New Haven, Conn., 1910], 242–43; *White Plains Directory, 1901–1902* [New York: 1902], 189; Bio. file, UP-PA.)

4. From William Sanger

[*New York, N.Y.*]
Wednesday May [*?, 1902*]

Dearest—

Did you get my letters—I sent them all to the hospital—

I sent you a letter enclosing a copy of the one I got from father and also the long letter of 10 pages.[1] The reason I mention the ↑long↓ one is that I am [*not*] sure that I sent it to the right address—[2]

I have written a reply to Fathers letter but have not [*mailed?*] as yet thinking that perhaps I might see you today (Wedsey) but your letter came—telling me that it would be impossible for us to meet, so I will send it away tonight dear and let you see a copy when I come up—[3] You have too much enthusiasm or to much—[*good*] nature or something—I [*don't know*] what keeps you on your feet all night!— I don't see how you can stand dearest its surely heroic—and I mean it when I say it— I've worked 18 hours on a stretch—but I must have at least 6 hours sleep and you have none at all!! ~~night~~

Now I don't want to discourage you in this particular case you have on hand[4]—but you have given up the best time of your life in your present professional vocation—and I thank God that I came that our souls met—and that you will give up this strenous life—in very short order— If its in my power to do so— Just as quick as I can get myself on a proper financial standing everything will be changed and you will be able to have all the leasure and enjoy life—

Im laying tracks for a lot of work—yes we will soon be on "easy" street[5]—dear one—

I have made further inquiries for the book—The Three Empresses[6]—but have not been able to get it.

A home with [~~*illegible*~~] ↑you↓ as presiding Queen dearest. A real home—with love the necessary household utensil as father puts it to shed it light upon our life—

The little home nestled among the trees—we shall build it of course we shall! With infinite love—goodnight

William

ALS MSP, DLC (LCM 7:452–58).

1. The letter from MS's father, Michael Higgins, was not found. This is the only surviving correspondence between William Sanger and MS prior to 1913.

2. He may have sent the letter to the Manhattan Eye and Ear Infirmary at Forty-first Street and Park Avenue, where MS was staying, rather than to the White Plains Hospital.

3. The letters were not found.

4. No information on the specific cases to which MS was assigned was found.

5. William Sanger worked as a freelance draftsman for several New York City architectural firms, possibly including McKim, Mead and White. It is not known what project(s) he was working on at this time, but he appears to have been looking for a permanent position. (A. C. Sanger, "Margaret Sanger," 19–31.)

6. This was a reference to Caroline Gearey's *Three Empresses: Josephine, Marie-Louise, Eugenie* (London, 1893).

5. *To Mary B. Higgins*

[*White Plains, N.Y.*]
Sunday 12 [*May ?, 1902*]

My dear Mary—

Yours came yesterday and as usual your letters are always interesting.[1]

I have no picture of Sanger Lad—to let you see, they are coming later on—but enclosed you will find a letter of his to me[2]—he writes everyday & telephones between—comes out Wednesday & Sunday when I am not too busy to see him.

I wish you would write him[3]—he would be delighted I know and as father never ever said I was a good daughter (after all the washings & scrubbing I did too) I will expect to hear you tell him he is getting the best woman in the world—excepting one—yourself— It is my duty you know to make him think that—always—his home address is #631 East 136th St. New York and I forget his down town number—father has it. By the way his people are going to have an "at home" for me as soon as I can get away—oh ye gods I dread to meet them. I wonder if they will have long noses—and own flashy diamonds[4]—by the [*way*] again—I am going to have one— I wrote Nan last week about our trip—[5] I do not know yet that I can afford it—my feet are such an expense—shoes ten dollars a pair—and five dollars for the ~~pl~~ order— I fear future trouble—

I wonder if I can see you this summer—I have not seen you a day in almost years— Are you going to Cloverbank? I wish Mrs A[6] would ask me to spend a few days with you if you are there—

You see there are so many things to have your advice on that I really could not dispense with such a valuable sister—

If I can go to the mts I will love to—but if not then I must go home—Esther wants me to spend my vacation with her—and I wish I could—I really can not decide yet—until I know if I will have money enough— You speak of debts— The only ones I owe are Miss Johnson and I owe Dr Wilbur some—

if he would just send in the bill—he has not yet and I asked him twice to do it—but his bill is not much about ten dollars I guess.

I straightened myself all out this last year thank the Lord—

You see if I graduate in June—I have a month to make up from my two operations and then too it takes some money— I am not prepared to marry anyone—and if I could get two or three good cases[7]—it would start me off nicely—and then too—I must get some clothing made— I hate long engagements myself but I would rather finish training[8]—and when I think of all the hard work—the bitter tears I shed night after night for the old training—the lonesome nights I passed waiting for some old tramp to die—then when it is finished—without a laurel to get married—then I want to stop it all— I would love one year of private nursing—and get some money—and then if any one wants me all right—but the Lad does not care about waiting longer than six months—he is working like mad he adores father all ready—both socialists[9]—oh heavens—the conversations they will hold!— I want you to see his picture or face—and just as soon as he gets one you may have it—

There is so much to think of—it takes a year—brides maids the time, the place—the dress—and the trip—and everything— I suppose it had better take place at home have we a <u>house</u> or a <u>barn?</u> it was somewhat of a barn when I saw it last— It must be a small affair—only families admitted and all my dear friends Miss Johnson—Edna Bushnell Amelia Stewart—Esther and [*Minerva*][10]—all must be left out—because I am poor— I think a good way to save expense would to have him on the "verge of death" and I can nurse him & insist on a death bed marriage—or do like Ethel did[11] but I prefer the former—I do not like secret marriges they are so liable to cause comment & doubtful smiles.

Don't you think an evening wedding at the house pretty—it is not so swell as High noon—or as practical as the morning—but it is pretty. Tell me what you think about it— I suppose it is <u>our place</u> to give the "spread" which ever it will be—isn't it—he has a married sister & he is the only boy[12]—so no best men from his side & unless he has someone he wants I think Jack would be a dear don't you. But I am dying to see his people—and will tell you all about them—

He sent me a beautiful copy of "Crankisms"[13] yesterday have you read it?

Write again soon— I wonder if this excitement will pass away. Lovingly

Margaret

Lad & I laughed ourselves sick when he told me how father said at the phone—not "hollo" at all but "<u>What do you want</u>"! oh poor Lad was thrown off his feet and did not know what he had wanted: Just like father—

M:

ALS MSP, DLC (LCM 6:38–46).

1. The letter was not found.

2. She was possibly referring to the preceding letter, William Sanger to MS, May 1902.

3. William Sanger wrote to Mary Higgins on July 27, 1902, and August 18, 1902 (LCM 7:619 and 6:24), in which he thanked Mary for her recent letters (not found) to him. There is no other extant correspondence between them.

4. This anti-Semitic reference was one of the few times MS referred to the fact that both her in-laws were German Jewish immigrants. Edward Elias Sanger (1824–1903) was a wool merchant, and the family lived in generally poor neighborhoods; yet in her autobiographies, MS claimed that he was a wealthy sheep rancher from Australia who came to the United States during the gold rush and that his wife, Henrietta Wolffberg Sanger (1836–1932), "a lovely person—artistic, musical, and highly cultured," was a mayor's daughter from a northern German town. (Edna Greenwald, "Sanger Family History" [1995] and "Sanger Family Genealogy" [MN-SSC]; MS, *Autobiography,* 56 [quote]; Chesler, *Woman of Valor,* 50–51.)

5. MS was probably referring to a June 1902 trip she took with her father to Lake Placid, New York. The letter to Anna Higgins was not found. (See MS to Mary Higgins, June 1902 [LCM 7:459].)

6. Mrs. A was Nellie Houghton Abbott.

7. Very little is known about MS's cases, but one source that provides at least a fictionalized look at her private nursing experience is "The Unrecorded Battle," a melodramatic short story she wrote, most likely in the early 1910s. (LCM 131:87.)

8. While no specific injunction against marriage at White Plains Hospital has been found, all the nursing students were single, and the residential nature of the program would have been complicated by marriage.

9. Michael Higgins was a follower of the ideas of the freethinker Robert Ingersoll and the single-tax enthusiast Henry George. He organized the Corning chapter of the Knights of Labor and played an important role as labor organizer during the 1890 Corning Glass Works strike, but there is no evidence to suggest that he was an active socialist or party member. No information was found on William Sanger's politics at this time, though by 1910 he was a Socialist Party member. (Hersey, "Margaret Sanger," 8–26, 92; Chesler, *Woman of Valor,* 23–27; A. C. Sanger, "Margaret Sanger," 8–11.)

10. Miss Johnson was possibly a teacher; the rest were MS's Claverack classmates: Edna Jeanette Bushnell (Wicks) (1875–1949); Amelia B. Stewart (Michell) (1880–1954), who followed MS to the White Plains nursing program; Esther Farquharson; and probably Minerva L. Goodwin. (CCR)

11. Ethel Higgins eloped with Jack Byrne.

12. William's younger sister was Cecilia Sanger (Nadle) (1875–1962). His younger brother, Heinrich, died in 1882 at age six. (Greenwald, "Sanger Family History" and "Sanger Family Genealogy.")

13. "Crankisms" probably refers to collections of witticisms and eccentric proverbs. MS may have been referring either to Lisle de Vaux Matthewman's *Crankisms* (Philadelphia, 1901), which parodied male and female behavior, or to James B. Gifford's *Crankisms; or, Random Thoughts Written in Rhyme* (Salem, Mass., 1900).

6. To Anna E. Higgins

New York City [*N.Y.*]
[*August 20–24?, 1902*]

Nan—dearest:

Here I am no longer a Higgins—we were married Monday by the Rev Dr Norris of 144th St.[1] That man of mine simply carried me off—he made me marry him 'now or never' he said I only had two hours off duty—and we drove around the Park[2] arguing on the subject until four oclock—then he turned in and made me get out—and we were married at ten minutes past—and I was due here at four thirty. I vow I will not live with such a beast of a man. I can not give up my Training and he wants me to take an apartment uptown for the winter and until he can build in the spring but I am going to go on in Training School not let any one know I am married and keep house in the fall of [*1903*].[3]

I wrote father[4] and told him I am to be home next month— William gave me a beautiful gold watch & chain he is such a dear fellow crazy—that's all— He is collecting furniture—[*casts*] pictures vases—old rugs—and vows we shall have an ideal home—you must know Nan he is jealous—beastly insanely jealous—and was afraid I would marry a Doctor— He is so happy and so am I—although I won't see him—he sends me flowers—flowers—books—and now jewelry—a marquis ring today—(turquois) and yet I won't go out—he hangs on the corner after three oclock to wait. Forgive me Nan—I do hate this kind of a thing—but it was very unexpected for me he had everything arranged the witnesses—the ring the minister, and a boy to hold the horse—& I came out for a walk a constitutional in a horrid blue dress—oh such a bride.

I am sure I could not have a better husband—he is my ideal in many ways—but I wanted to wait I shall write Mary & tell her—[5]

Nan would you not like to spend your vacation with Esther? She is going to some cheap place to rest for three weeks—before taking up her Dramatic course—and wants me to spend some time where she is—of course she does not care where she goes if it is only cheap: What do you say. You would have a quiet time but such a resting time with Esther—she likes you so much.

Perhaps you have made other plans I have not told her of you yet but I am sure she—

Esther just came in to see me and has decided to go to Chicago to see her brother & wife—

William is jealous of Esther oh such a man.

Write me Nan when you are able and with much love to your dear self—write to William will you— #631 East 136th St. City lovingly

Margaret

ALS MSP, DLC (LCM 5:1207–12). Return address: "770 St. Nicholas Ave." The words "marriage August 1902" were added at the top of the first page, possibly by MS.

1. They were married on August 18, 1902, by Jacob Norris, a Presbyterian minister, at his residence at 539 West 144th Street. (State of New York, Borough of Manhattan, Marriage Certificate #15290, Aug. 18, 1902.)

2. This was possibly St. Nicholas Park in Upper Manhattan.

3. MS continued her nurse's training at White Plains for at least a few weeks following her marriage, but she succumbed to pressure from William to resign in order to preserve her health and set up their new household. (William Sanger to Mary Higgins, Aug. 18, 1902 [LCM 6:24].)

4. The letter was not found.

5. For a very similar, though briefer description of the marriage, see MS to Mary Higgins, Aug. ?, 1902 (LCM 6:38).

TWO

A Radical in Bohemia

LESS THAN SIX MONTHS after her August 1902 marriage, Sanger had turned from her pursuit of a nursing career to housekeeping and starting a family. She joined her new husband in New York City and in the late fall of 1902 moved into an apartment on St. Nicholas Avenue and 149th Street, an ethnically mixed, working- and middle-class neighborhood in Upper Manhattan. The Sangers had envisioned a comfortable, predictable family life that neither partner had previously known, but Margaret's poor health interrupted the new marriage and delayed their plans to build a home in suburban Westchester County, New York. Her pregnancy in the spring of 1903 aggravated her tuberculosis, forcing her to spend the summer taking a cold cure at the Trudeau Adirondack Cottage Sanitarium at Saranac Lake, New York. She returned to New York City only briefly to have her first child, Stuart, in November 1903. The difficult birth caused her fragile health to deteriorate further. This time taking her baby and a wet nurse, Margaret returned to the mountains and spent most of the following year in a small farmhouse near Saranac Lake. There she followed the prescribed diet for consumptives (including daily doses of creosote capsules and large quantities of eggs and milk) and kept close to her bed. Lonely, showing no sign of improvement, and concerned for Stuart's health, Margaret fled the sanitarium district early in 1905.[1]

She rejoined William in Yonkers, New York, and in 1906 the couple moved to nearby Hastings-on-Hudson. They settled in the Locust Hill development, along with a number of Columbia University professors and other New York professionals, where William Sanger designed and built a three-story house in the style of an Italian villa. No longer treated like an invalid, Margaret regained her health and helped her husband with the building project. On February 19, 1908, their first night in the new house, a fire broke out in the basement furnace. The Sangers escaped unharmed, but most of the house and its contents went up in flames. They rebuilt in time for the birth of their second child, Grant, in the summer of 1908. Less than two years later, in May 1910, Margaret Sanger gave birth to her only daughter, Margaret Louisa (Peggy).[2]

During Margaret's five years in Hastings, she focused on her three young children. In a 1930 letter, she recalled that her life "seemed to begin & end in their development & growth. . . . Owing to ill health, I had spent much time with them, planning their lives, reading & playing with each in his turn. . . . Stuart . . . was sturdy, active, athletic, reasoning, daring & logical— He seemed like one who had been born into life to <u>test</u> and <u>prove</u> himself. Grant . . . was the artist type—loving, affectionate, original. . . . Peggy—the most independent child I ever knew . . . was positive, accurate, truthful, mischievous, laughing— She was born to do, to act, to lead."[3] Even as a young suburban mother, she made an impression. As one of her Hastings friends recalled, "Of course, Margaret Sanger was lovely to look at, with her bright rippling reddish hair and laughing eyes, but much of her charm was in her voice and manner. . . ."[4] However, she felt restless in this suburban enclave; following the chaotic drama of her nurse's training and her battle to save her life and her health, she experienced domesticity as "spiritual stagnation" and became embittered by complacency.[5] Apart from a small women's literary club that she founded, Sanger's only intellectual outlet was through her husband and his involvement in the burgeoning New York radical scene.

William Sanger, who belonged to the Yonkers branch of the Socialist Party and had joined the Industrial Workers of the World (IWW), surely discussed his socialist views with his wife. But he claimed she ignored his radical leanings until one day in 1910, when she talked to the foreman of a road crew repairing the street outside her house. The foreman gave her some labor leaflets, and that night Margaret peppered her husband with questions on labor and socialism. More likely, if this chance meeting actually took place, it only reignited a passion for radical ideas that Margaret had been developing through exposure to her father's freethinking opinions, school debates on suffrage and free silver, her own experiences nursing the poor, and possibly her battle with ill health, certain to generate sympathy for the underdog. All combined to feed her outrage over economic and social inequities. She also claimed the traumatic house fire taught her to disdain material things. Though mired in middle-class suburbia, Margaret Sanger had grown up among the working classes, her intellectual development dominated by both father and husband—two freethinking socialists. At age thirty-one, she had the makings of a radical.[6]

By 1910, William Sanger was determined to become an artist and gradually abandoned his vocation as a draftsman, a move that strained the family's budget. Early in 1911, the Sangers decided to sell their Hastings house and move to a railroad flat at West 135th Street in the Washington Heights section of northern Manhattan, a neighborhood that housed mostly working-class Jewish and Greek immigrants. The couple wanted to be closer to the prewar bohemian culture of the city, particularly its experiments in art, politics, and education. A move to the city also offered them free child care (Bill's mother moved in with them) and an opportunity for Margaret to return to work as a part-time nurse.[7]

Though it is not clear how frequently Margaret Sanger worked in this period, she joined a visiting nurse's association and took obstetrical patients for two-week stints. Most of her cases brought her to the tenement districts of New York's Lower East Side, where she encountered desperately poor women recovering from the ill effects of multiple pregnancies or unhygienic abortions. Sanger later claimed that her patients begged for contraceptive information, but the only methods she knew of at the time, condoms and withdrawal, entrusted the husband with all the responsibility.[8] The women ridiculed these methods as utterly insufficient and untrustworthy. Whether Sanger knew about other means of conception control or not, she was prohibited by law from sharing this information and warned by doctors to remain silent. Increasingly, she became frustrated by her inability to help these women.

Once settled in New York, the Sangers immersed themselves in the city's Socialist Party. Bill Sanger established himself as a leader of Upper Manhattan's Branch Five; he helped organize strike-related protest meetings and ran unsuccessfully for the board of aldermen as the Socialist candidate from the Twenty-first Assembly District. Margaret Sanger became a paid organizer and lecturer for the Socialist Party's Women's Committee.[9]

Socialist politics ushered the Sangers into the eclectic crowd of anarchists, socialists, syndicalists, single-taxers, and civil libertarians who came together at several gathering places and institutions in Greenwich Village. They participated in the Liberal Club, an intellectual center for radicals, and the Ferrer Center, a cultural hub for activists and artists. William Sanger's painting introduced the couple to the New York art world, including the social realists of the "ashcan" school and a growing modernist movement inspired by the Parisian assault on traditional art forms, as exhibited in New York at the 1913 Armory Show. Many of the leading names in this cornucopia of spirited self-expression and cultural rebellion were brought together by Mabel Dodge, patron of the radical chic, at her 23 Fifth Avenue salon. Dodge recalled Margaret Sanger as "the Madonna type of woman, with soft brown hair parted over a quiet brow, and crystal-clear light brown eyes. Eyes that were of a one-toned brown, not fusing and mixing with other shades as in the case of more complex natures. She had a husband, Bill Sanger, who tried to paint, and two children."[10] At Dodge's salon, the Sangers listened to and participated in discussions about free love, paganism, psychology, and cubism with the likes of such writers as Upton Sinclair, Mary Heaton Vorse, and Hutchins Hapgood; the anarchists Emma Goldman, Alexander Berkman, and Hippolyte Havel; and the artists John Sloan, John Marin, and Marsden Hartley. The Sangers' small apartment also became a gathering place, as Margaret later recalled, "where liberals, anarchists, Socialists, and I.W.W.'s could meet. These vehement individualists had to have an audience, preferably a small, intimate one. They really came to see Bill; I made the cocoa."[11]

If Margaret Sanger was ever the diminutive artist's wife, it was short-lived. By 1912, she had resigned as a Socialist Party organizer in favor of the direct action tactics of the IWW. Founded in 1905 by a group of radical leaders that included William "Big Bill" Haywood, Daniel DeLeon, and Eugene Debs, the IWW, or Wobblies, as they were known, countered the trade-based, multiunion structure of the American Federation of Labor by seeking one broad-based union, organized by industry and open to unskilled workers, immigrants, African Americans, and women. To Margaret Sanger, the IWW exhibited a vigor the Socialist Party lacked, and she was impressed with its willingness to use sabotage and violent protest when needed. She became friends with organizers Haywood, the former Utah mine worker who was the most well-known and charismatic IWW leader, and Elizabeth Gurley Flynn, known for her passionate and eloquent speeches. They, in turn, recognized her strengths as a communicator and encouraged her participation in worker revolts in Lawrence, Massachusetts; Hazleton, Pennsylvania; and Paterson, New Jersey.[12]

As a lecturer for the Socialist Party and a strike organizer for the IWW, Sanger often met with groups of women and increasingly incorporated issues of health and sex education into informal talks, drawing on her nursing experiences in New York. She also launched a brief journalistic career, writing articles for the *New York Call,* the Socialist Party's daily, which gave her an outlet to express the problems of working-class women, including sexual exploitation and excessive childbearing—issues that the anticapitalist organizations generally ignored.

The sexual awakening and experimentation pursued by the Village crowd challenged traditional notions of heterosexual marriage and monogamy and contributed to the increasingly fragile state of the Sanger marriage; Margaret Sanger carried on at least one affair before the family retreated to Provincetown on Cape Cod in the summer of 1913, joining other intellectuals, artists, and activists. Both William and Margaret Sanger turned to their own interests that summer, he focusing on painting, she on accumulating information on sex hygiene and possibly on what was then referred to as family limitation. The Sangers also found themselves increasingly at odds over their marital expectations.[13]

Perhaps to escape the emotional distractions that imperiled their relationship and to satisfy both their callings, they packed up the children and sailed to Europe in October 1913. They first stopped at Glasgow, where the *Call* had assigned her to write a series of articles on socialism in that city. The family then went to Paris, where Margaret explored the Continental life and investigated the open trade in contraception, while William devoted himself to art. They rented an apartment on the Boulevard St. Michel, put Stuart in school, and lived off the income generated by the sale of their Hastings house. Margaret Sanger met with such Paris-based radicals as the Hindu nationalist Shyamaji Krishnavarma and Victor Dave (1847–1922), the Flemish-born anarchist, writer, and leader of the French syndicalist movement whose deep roots in European radicalism and interest in neo-Malthusianism made him an indispensable contact. She explored the city with the IWW activists Jessie Ashley and Bill Haywood, who were also staying there. Later she recalled that she and Haywood visited the shops and stalls of the city's working-class districts, purchased all available contraceptive devices, and discussed contraceptive techniques with doctors, druggists, and midwives.[14]

While the Parisian sojourn was enlightening for Sanger—who would soon use the information she acquired to draft a birth control manual—her marriage continued to disintegrate. At the end of December 1913, she left her husband in his Paris studio and returned home with the children, with plans to write a book on Malthusian ideas and sex hygiene. But her sudden departure may have had more to do with her wish to separate from William, who remained to paint, and to rejoin her circle of anarchist free lovers in New York.

Few incoming letters survive for the years 1903–10, partly because of the Hastings fire, but the absence of outgoing correspondence suggests that Sanger seldom corresponded in this period. What has survived are published writings that reveal Sanger's intellectual and ideological development as she transformed herself from suburban housewife to militant radical activist.

NOTES

1. MS, *Autobiography*, 58–59.
2. A. C. Sanger, "Margaret Sanger," 21–25; unidentified newspaper, Feb. 20, 1908 (LCM 135:171).
3. MS to Blakely Hall, July 24, 1930 (*MSM* S5:727).
4. Julia Emerson House quoted in Hersey, "Margaret Sanger," 91–92.
5. MS, *My Fight*, 40.
6. Hersey, "Margaret Sanger," 91–92; MS, *My Fight*, 42.
7. Chesler, *Woman of Valor*, 55.
8. MS, *Autobiography*, 86–87.
9. A. C. Sanger, "Margaret Sanger," 31; Hersey, "Margaret Sanger," 91–92; *New York Call*, Nov. 6 and 17, 1911; Gordon, *Woman's Body*, 213.

10. Rebecca Zurier, *Art for the Masses* (Philadelphia, 1988), 102; Luhan, *Movers and Shakers,* 69 (quote).

11. Reed, *Birth Control Movement and American Society,* 75–77; MS, *Autobiography,* 70.

12. MS, *Autobiography,* 79–85; Haywood, *Bill Haywood's Book,* 268.

13. MS, *My Fight,* 58–59.

14. Max Nettlau, "Victor Dave, 1847–1922," vertical files (Labadie); MS to Amelia Michell, July ?, 1913, herein; William Sanger to MS, Jan. 11 and 23, 1914 (*MSM* S1:71 and 95).

7. "Impressions of the East Side, Part I"

When the Sangers moved to New York City in 1911, Margaret began working as a visiting nurse on Manhattan's Lower East Side. The neighborhood stretched from Broadway to the East River, serving as home to generations of new arrivals to America. In 1911, most residents were recent immigrants from Italy and eastern Europe.

[*September 3, 1911*]

When you walk through the streets of the much talked about East Side you come away with the feeling that you have seen all of it you wish to see. When you pass through Cherry street and emerge from its depths with fish scales and fruit stains on your clothing, you feel quite satisfied with the glimpse you have had of it, and with both hands up exclaim "Never again!"

But the East Side thus seen from the outside is nothing compared to the living hell within its walls. To eat with its people, to sleep with them, to buy where they buy, to listen to their quarrels, gossip, tales of sorrow, sickness and fears, is to see them as they are in their daily life.

Everything is thrown out of the windows; garbage is rolled up in newspapers and thrown into the courts, when there is one; if not, then into the streets. A piece of meat is eaten and the bone thrown out of the window; so are dead rats, dead cats, decayed vegetables. And in cases where the toilets are in use by the many families on the same floor, the mother allows the children to use paper as toilet receptacles, and that, too, is thrown out of the window.

In very clean places the courts are cleaned once a month, but where the windows overlook so-called sheds, these are cleaned only when conditions become so vile that the tenants threaten to leave.

Everybody complains of this filthy habit of throwing things out of the windows, and every one denies having any part in doing it!

Then the vermin. In one of the small flats, the kitchen was swarming with, not thousands, but millions of roaches. They were piled four layers high in places and in corners they were stacked up several inches high. Cobwebs hung from the ceiling, and touched your head as you entered. Bed bugs, too, are everywhere, and on the hot nights the moaning and crying of the little children show how their sleep is disturbed by the vermin. It is pitiful to hear the cries of often ten or more children all at once as the houses are so near, it of course keeps every one near by awake, and shouts of "Shut up" issue forth from the men who must get their night's rest in order to keep their jobs.

After the poverty and filth, the next thing which leaves its lasting impression on you is the ignorant cruelty with which the people of the East Side treat their children. Everybody strikes the children, parents, neighbors, sisters, boarders; in fact, every one seems to take a slap at the children, for any trifling thing, and yet every parent thinks himself a model parent. It is most common to see a father strike his 6 or 8-year-old boy with the same force he would strike at a man. "I'll smash you," he says, but fortunately the little fellow has learned how to dodge.

Thousands of mothers leave their little children in the care of the older boy or girl (usually not over 9 years old), and go to work early in the morning in the factories or work shops to return at night to do the work of the family. First, the mother does the washing which takes until 2 in the morning; the next night she irons, which takes the same time, and so on with the scrubbing, cleaning, and mending. Then it is time to do the washing again, and so on, in this terrible existence, day after day this worn out and half-famished mother continues her burden of life. The Woman who does not do this work at night, being too tired or half sick, is considered "lazy" by the neighbors, and all her misfortune is summed up in her "laziness."

With the food that one gets at even the "rich" families it is difficult to continue work until noon without stocking up again, so little do they understand combinations of food or the requirements of the human system. It is a common sight, too, to see a workingman, working on the streets, stop at the noon hour and with the hunk of bread which he brought with him, go to a nearby stand and buy a penny's worth of watermelon.

Some of the mothers close the house all day, and give the children bread and tea to stay in the parks until night time. Others give over the responsibility to the oldest child and let them run in and out as they choose, with no guidance, no care or instruction. Is it not marvelous that they continue meek and docile?

One of the greatest blessings of the East Side came when the milk stations were instituted.[1] The milk is prepared at the stations by trained nurses, for special ages, and it is increased according to age. Should the child not thrive and the parent think it is not doing well, the mother takes it to the station where it is examined by physicians, and either barley water or a different preparation is given for the child, all without extra cost. They give nine bottles with two and a half ounces of milk for an infant (and that is all they can have), at 1 cent a bottle. Later on, when the quantity of milk is increased, the charges are a little more, but the fact that the bottles are washed, sterilized, and sealed by trained hands almost insures the life of the child against disease. The infant at least has the proper food, for even when the mother is in the factory the children go for the milk, give the name of the child and receive the milk and give it to the baby during the day. Every individual child is registered and has its special milk.

Again, one of the terrible sights which meets your gaze is the army of little pale-faced children which come into the streets at night to play. Accustomed to seeing the children, although ragged and filthy at least browned by the sun, playing about in the day time, your attention is attracted to these white and drawn faces, and you inquire about them. You are told that these little children, anywhere around 10 years of age, are products of the sweatshops. There they work all day, sometimes in cellars, picking over old rags, and sometimes in "shops" carrying huge bundles from place to place.[2]

The very thought is nauseous, that where there are thousands of able-bodied men willing and glad to work, these little pale-faced girls with shoulders already bent, should spend their childhood days struggling for an existence. The parents of these little ones are loathe to send them to work, but each added baby makes it harder for them to fight off starvation, and anything which offers relief from worry and debt is acceptable to even the most loving parents. And as they watch these little toilers join hands with the other children and sing "Sweet Land of Liberty"[3] the hope springs up in their breasts that perhaps some "luck" will come to them, and the children be able to go to school again.

The younger generation of women are no more anxious than their uptown sisters to have large families, and these young women are easy victims for the many fake and quack physicians who inhabit the East Side. One Woman aged 72, said she would gladly have another baby if nature were willing, but her daughters and sons, who had endured poverty and neglect, remembering what a nightmare their childhood had been, preferred risking imprisonment and death, rather than bearing children and have them go through what they lived through.

(To be concluded.)[4]

New York Call, Sept. 3, 1911, 15.

1. Public concern over the high infant mortality rate led charities and the city to establish summertime milk stations as early as 1892. The New York Milk Committee opened eight milk stations in 1908 and was running thirty-one by 1911. (Harvey Levenstein, "'Best for Babies' or 'Preventable Infanticide'? The Controversy over Artificial Feeding of Infants in America," *Journal of American History* 70 [June 1, 1983]: 75–94.)

2. Estimates of the number of child sweatshop workers were notoriously unreliable because so many worked in private homes manufacturing artificial flowers and hats;

finishing clothing, linens, and neckwear; and shelling nuts. (National Child Labor Committee, *New York Child Workers in the Tenements* [New York, 1912], 11.)

3. This is the second line of "My Country 'Tis of Thee," written by the clergyman Samuel Francis Smith in 1831.

4. In part 2, published in the September 10, 1911, issue of the *New York Call*, MS focused on the problems of ignorance and greed bred by poverty. It was, she wrote, "the aim and ambition of everybody to bleed everybody else, including doctors, lawyers and pharmacists who charge far more than is paid anywhere else." Though she asserted that socialism was "almost a household word" among immigrants, they were too hungry and demoralized to do more than dream about it.

8. To Julius Gerber[1]

On October 31, 1911, Sanger was hired as a paid organizer by the Woman's Committee for Propaganda, Socialism and Suffrage of the local New York branch of the Socialist Party of America. For fifteen dollars a week, she visited the various local branches, persuading them to open their headquarters one day a week to women and helping orchestrate special women's days. She also organized street meetings, distributed literature, and supervised the Socialist Suffrage clubs.

New York City [*N.Y.*]
[*December 9?, 1911*]

My dear Comrade Gerber:—

I tried to get you on the phone this afternoon but could not catch you in so I left a message, asking you first—if you could get us some speakers for next week open air at noon[2]— The Womans Committees[3] wish you not to send Frost or Phillips.[4] We have been having excellent success at the meetings, people coming up and asking for both literature & application blanks.

I also left word for you that we are out of literature. Could you rush that order of The New York Woman[5] and have five thousand sent directly to my home. Also I wish you would send me some general literature of your own suggestion. You know what kind is best suited to out door crowds.

As I am visiting all branches[6] & starting literature distributions by the women—would it not save time & money to send five thousand of The NY Woman leaflets to each branch?—

We need speakers so badly and I do hope you can get some who understand the Woman question.[7]

I trust I am not giving you too much trouble. Fraternally

Margaret H. Sanger

ALS SPLL, NNU-T (*MSM* C1:20–23). Return address: "235 West 135 St." The return address was repeated at the end of the page, followed by "Phone 2950 Morningside."

1. Julius Gerber (1872–1956) was a Latvian-born sheet metal worker who was the executive secretary for the Socialist Party's Local New York from 1911 to 1922. (Solon De Leon, *American Labor Who's Who* [New York, 1925], 84; *New York Times,* July 18, 1956.)

2. This was possibly a reference to an open-air meeting sponsored by the Committee on Propaganda among Women held at noon on the corner of Broad and Wall streets on December 14. The scheduled speakers were Lena Morrow Lewis and Luella Twinning. (*New York Call,* Dec. 14, 1911.)

3. With the emergence of women wage earners as a political force, a conscious effort was made to boost the Socialist Party's appeal to women. At the party's 1908 national convention, delegates sanctioned the formation of the Woman's National Committee to employ female organizers and encourage women to join. Women's branches of the Socialist Party sprang up in urban areas in 1907–8 to recruit women into the regular mixed locals. (Buhle, *Women and American Socialism,* 133–38, 155–57, 305.)

4. J. C. Frost was the vice-chair of Branch 5 of Local New York; I. Phillips was a member of Branch 6 of Local New York in 1912. (Minutes of the Convention of Local New York, Nov. 26, 1911 [SPLL].)

5. This was possibly one of the leaflets produced by the Woman's National Committee of the Socialist Party.

6. The party's New York local had eleven regular and seven foreign-language branches. (Minutes of the Convention of Local New York, Nov. 26, 1911 [SPLL].)

7. She was referring to the issue of how Socialists reconciled their commitment to liberating the working class with demands for women's rights. (Buhle, *Women and American Socialism,* xiv, 147–52.)

9. "What Every Mother Should Know: Conclusion"[1]

Sanger was asked to write a series of articles on sex education aimed at young children for the New York Call; *it was published as a booklet,* What Every Mother Should Know or How Six Little Children Were Taught the Truth, *in 1913. In the booklet's preface, Sanger wrote, "The following articles were put into story form for the mother so as to enable her to make the truth and facts just as interesting to a child's imagination as possible. The idea is that a child be taught the process of reproduction and absorb such knowledge without realizing he has received any 'sex' instruction." These pieces were based on discussions and lessons Sanger had developed around 1908–9 for her son Stuart and neighboring children in Hastings, New York. What follows is the last of the eight articles that ran from October 29 to December 17, 1911. (LCM 131:273.)*

[*December 17, 1911*]

The great object which Bobby's mother[2] had in mind was to make these teachings of such a nature that the children would be impressed with the truth that they are only PART of nature's great and wonderful plan.

They were reminded again and again of the stages of life—plants, frogs, birds and mammals; of the millions of years it took to bring about these wonderful creatures and that at the top of the list, perfect, intelligent and supreme, stands man. Man, the most complex of all and the most perfect. What responsibilities are at his door!

It was most natural for the children to consider nutrition and reproduction as the two most important essentials of any form of life.

Up to this point this was quite sufficient. The animals had instincts to nourish their bodies and also to procreate their offspring. This seemed their life object, but since man being [*the*] more intelligent, there must, of course, be other and broader outlets for this great intelligence. Their own bodies was a subject%hich took months to cover in study. They were shown charts of the human figure (both sexes) and all parts of the body were named in the same way as parts of the flower were named. Parts of the organs of reproduction were called by their names in telling of the works each part performed. No special stress was laid on the naming of these parts, but simply, casually, as one would speak of the various parts of the eye, or any other organ. In the same manner they were told of the harm done to their bodies in handling or touching any one part unnecessarily. If the eye, ear or nose was dug into, we would surely greatly injure ourselves, perhaps losing the use of that organ for the rest of our lives. The generative organs are no exception in this. To tamper with this most wonderful part of nature's machinery, means not only sickness, dullness of intellect, stupidity, physical and mental weakness, but oftimes disables a little child for life.[3]

In order to grow into perfect manhood or womanhood, all parts of the body must be developed naturally. If a little bud of a flower were to be roughly opened, it fades and dies long before it can carry out the great object of its life, namely, to develop the baby seeds within it.

So with a boy or girl who carries within their bodies the making of a human life. How terrible to cause that little life to be shattered, just through ignorance and neglect.

The children were taught that there was one beautiful time to come to them—to look forward to and to hope for that time when they can look into a tiny baby face, clasp two tiny baby hands and feel this wonderful and beautiful creation a part of their being—the expression of their souls.

They were told to keep in mind this time which should come, and to keep their minds and bodies clean for this wonderful gift.

As all the children were still too young to go into the details of either menstruation or venereal diseases, it was considered best to dwell on the early tribes of man on up to marriage, and wait for future developments before going further. The tree dwellers and cave dwellers were already familiar stories to them. The fact that people lived together very closely; that the Woman had great freedom in choosing the man whom she wished to be the father of her child, even as freely as the animals chose their mates; that in this freedom great mistakes were often made, such as that for a period some mothers chose their sons or brothers, or fathers to be the father of the new little one; that after a time it was found that this was very injurious to this new little child, for he often could not walk, or talk, and was weak, and sometimes a cripple—and more often died very young.

So the chiefs of these tribes got together and said this must not be, for if this continued there would be no strong young men or women to till the soil or fight off the animals, wild beasts or the enemy. Then a law was made that only those of the different tribes or families should choose each other for the parents of the future children, and here the lesson of the Buttercups came in[4]—that often Mrs. Buttercup would reject the pollen from the stamen in her own house, but would accept the pollen from another buttercup house and become fertilized with that.

The part the two sexes took in different ways to strengthen and develop the race seemed of great interest to the children.

The work of hunting and fishing was left to the men of the family, while equally important work, that of cleaning and cooking the food, was for the women. Men spent much time in making tools and weapons. They were able to save much time and energy when the bow and arrow was invented, for, instead of taking all the time to creep upon a beast or enemy with a knife or sharp stone, he could remain at a distance and do the same work. Thus, men got a little more leisure time. With every new invention their labor and energy was saved, but it took much longer for labor-saving inventions for the women to come into use.

Gradually the marriage form came into existence, as these new tools and weapons became more valuable. Men wanted these to go to their very own children, so a law was passed that the man could choose any Woman he wanted to have for the mother of his children by getting consent from the captain or chief of the tribe. If he received this consent, then she, the Woman, must live with him, love him, honor him (no matter what he did), and obey him in everything. Absolute submission was the law for the wife. If she objected to this and ran away she was cast out and was beaten. Other tribes had the same laws and dared not take her in, so she was left to die. If she did not like her husband and took another for the father of her child she was often not only cast into prison, but either stoned to death or burned at the stake.

Naturally, after years of this treatment, she became submissive and so dependent on man for her living that she dared not express herself aloud, merely as her husband allowed her to do so. If she was very beautiful she was not made to work, but the prisoners of other tribes who had been captured were made to work for her. Often the captain or chief had several wives, but the wife was allowed only one husband.

As the children had been taught the lives of the mother flowers, frogs, birds, bees and mammals, there was no reason why the history of Woman should not be taken up until they were ready for older work.

They loved to hear about this, and it seemed just as interesting to them as the other stories.

It is important that mothers teach children the true history of the race, and get the seed of truth planted for future cultivation.

The marriage laws have had many changes for the man, they were told, but few as far as the Woman is concerned. The different customs of women in different countries can be told them, and the general development of both men and women can occupy a great deal of time until the children are more ready to understand the true or real significance of the studies to be later dwelt on.

The children were never talked "AT," but always "WITH." They were allowed to talk freely and once or twice when the older children seemed a little conscious on taking up the matter of their own bodies, yet after a few minutes as the other children joined in the conversation they, too, forgot or overcame the embarrassment and all went well.

The children were told frankly that some mothers did not like their children to know these things, that like the fairy tales and the story of Santa Claus, the mothers liked their children to believe that the stork brought them, or some other fairy tale. They were told that these things are NOT TO BE TALKED ABOUT WITH OTHER CHILDREN, and any time any child wished to know any thing about himself or any question whatever to come to the mother or father, but NEVER to other boys or girls. These children were taught the necessities for the excretions of the body—that in order to have good health this used up waste food must pass out of the body or it would become poison and the boy or girl become sick and die. There was no hurry in telling anything to the children. Most of this information was told on walks in the woods, or at times when they seemed to want to know. One story leads to another, and before long the children's questions will bring everything from you which you wish to tell.

The result of these teachings has been commented on by the school teachers of these children, who say they are so truthful, clean-minded, frank and open about all things that it is a pleasure to know them.

Every mother can teach her children the truth if she only knows it herself, and has the right attitude toward it. She can elaborate on this plan or outline as much as she wishes, but she must get down to the child's world in order to make her teachings impressive and successful. The one unpardonable sin on the part of a mother is to let her children learn the truth elsewhere than from her own lips.

New York Call, Dec. 17, 1911, 15 (*MSM* C19:453–54). The series was subtitled "How Six Little Children Learned the Truth." Anita Cahn Block, editor of the "Woman's Sphere" column of the *Sunday New York Call,* added a note to the end of the article announcing that MS was preparing a series of similar articles for older children and requested that readers send in questions they wanted her to address: "We shall all feel much better satisfied if we know that we are meeting some REAL PROBLEMS that mothers are struggling with along the lines of sexual education. All communications on this subject will be treated by the editor in STRICTEST CONFIDENCE."

1. This article was rewritten as chapter 7, "Man's Development," when the series was republished as a booklet, followed by chapter 8, "Conclusion." (For the booklet version, see LCM 131:275.)

2. Bobby was the five-year-old boy who in a previous article, "The Flowers: Mr. and Mrs. Buttercup, Their Home and Children," asked, "Mother, where did I come from?" (*New York Call,* Nov. 5, 1911.)

3. Introduced in the eighteenth century, the theory that masturbation caused disease and insanity gained popularity in nineteenth-century America when much of the medical advice literature directed toward young men concentrated on the dangers of masturbation and how to control it. By the early twentieth century, sex education advocates dismissed the link between masturbation and insanity yet continued to discourage the practice on the grounds that it weakened the nervous system and indirectly affected general health. (D'Emilio and Freedman, *Intimate Matters,* 68, 206.)

4. See also "Mr. and Mrs. Buttercup, Their Home and Family—Concluded," *New York Call,* Nov. 12, 1911.

10. "Dirt, Smell and Sweat"

[*December 24, 1911*]

Editor Woman's Sphere:

At a meeting of the Woman's Suffrage party of the 27th Assembly District a few days ago[1] a tall, beautiful and charming Woman named Mrs. Weeks,[2] acted as chairman of the meeting. In what was called her maiden speech, she mentioned among other things that the men who objected to Woman's voting because she would be obliged to bump against the dirty, smelly and sweaty man at the polls, evidently did not object to her bumping against them at other times; they objected only on Election Day and at the ballot box. Then she offered the following suggestion as a cure for this objection: "TO REMOVE THE DIRTY, SMELLING, SWEATY MEN FROM THE POLLS," so that she and her class could vote undisturbed.

But what about the women who are liable to be just as dirty, smelly and sweaty as their working brothers? Are they, too, to be removed? Dirt is dirt, smell is smell, and sweat is sweat, no matter on whom these unfortunate afflictions happen to be. And if the chairman and her class object to the smell of the workingman, so will they object to the smell of the working Woman.

Throughout the meeting the atmosphere was laden with class arguments. Such nice and polite and kind arguments in favor of the women in the home, who need the ballot to get CLEAN milk, clean streets and fresh air. Not one word about the millions of women driven out of the home into the factories and shops. Never a word about the women who cannot give any kind of milk to their children, but give them black tea and coffee and sell the milk and cream to her own class. These women and these conditions have not been considered by the Woman's Suffrage party, and it is doubtful if they will consider them until the working Woman stands shoulder to shoulder with her working brother for the emancipation of her class.

The only thing which seems to concern this chairman and her followers is POLITICAL FREEDOM. No other kind of freedom enters into their arguments. For instance, she spoke of the men who say the women who are suffragists smoke cigarettes. This she hotly denied by saying it is the anti-suffragist who smokes! Did she stop to ask why any Woman, suffragist or anti-suffragist, should not smoke as well as a man if she cared to? Not she. The idea of emancipating Woman from any of the narrow conventionalities of the dark ages has not yet dawned upon the minds of these women.

The idea of making Woman's sphere "unlimited, unbounded," as the Socialist women are striving for, has so far scarcely entered their craniums.

The working women evidently are not aware that POLITICAL FREEDOM does not mean INDUSTRIAL FREEDOM and it is the object and desire of Socialist women to show the working Woman that Socialism stands not only for her political freedom, but for her industrial freedom and her intellectual freedom. All three with one stroke of the pen can be gained and given to her by the Socialist party.

When the workingman shall be paid the full value of his labor he can then emancipate himself from dirt, smell and sweat. If he had the full product of his labor he would have the time and place to get and keep clean. If he were not robbed of the product of his toil by the master class, to which the chairman of that meeting belongs, he could have a clean coat, instead of wearing one either already bought second-hand or given him by the charity organizations. No wonder it is smelly.

Let any Woman who labors for her bread enter any of these meetings and see what there is in this movement for her benefit, and she will be made to realize that there is no more for her in political freedom alone than there has been for her brother who has had his political rights for some time.

Unless the women will use their political rights in the interest of their class, they will be no more free from dirt, smell and sweat than their brothers in the working class, and will find themselves liable to the same treatment at the hands of their "sisters" of the upper class.

MARGARET H. SANGER.

New York Call, Dec. 24, 1911, 15.

1. The meeting was probably held on December 18, 1911, at the Twenty-seventh Assembly District headquarters on Seventh Avenue. The New York City Woman's Suffrage Party (NYC-WSP) deployed members into the city's various electoral districts and lobbied for a referendum to bring the question of woman suffrage to a state vote. (*ENYC; Woman Voter,* Dec. 1911, 33.)

2. Anna Ross Weeks (1867–1941), suffragist and wife of New York City deputy fire commissioner W. Holden Weeks, was the leader of the Twenty-seventh Assembly District of the NYC-WSP. (*New York Times*, Jan. 30, 1941; *Woman Voter*, Nov. 1911, 33; see also *Woman Voter*, Jan. 1912, 8, 26–30.)

11. Testimony on the Strike at Lawrence, Mass.[1]

By 1912, Sanger was increasingly drawn to the work of the IWW and in February accepted her first assignment for the Wobblies, helping to evacuate the children of the Lawrence, Massachusetts, strikers to homes outside the city. The strikers' representatives argued that the evacuations would ensure the well-being of the children, but opponents charged that it was a propaganda device and that some children were being removed without their families' permission. Sanger helped peacefully lead the first group of children out on February 9, but on February 24, with strike opponents urging city officials to prevent another exodus, the Lawrence police pulled some forty children and their escorts from the Lawrence train station, loaded them onto a truck, and ordered them held. The police action led to widespread condemnation of the Lawrence police and city officials and a call by Victor Berger, a Socialist congressman from Wisconsin, for an investigation of the strike and police actions. While the strike continued in Lawrence, the House of Representative's Committee on Rules heard testimony on conditions in the mills and the lives of the workers. Sanger was one of the IWW representatives called to testify, along with more than a dozen Lawrence children and others who participated in the evacuations. Her testimony was significant; as a nurse, she alone among the witnesses could speak to the physical condition of the children. She was questioned by congressmen William Pou (1863–1934), a Democrat from North Carolina; Martin David Foster (1861–1919), a Democrat from Illinois; Augustus Owsley Stanley (1867–1958), a Democrat from Kentucky; Robert Lee Henry (1864–1931), a Democrat from Texas and chair of the House Rules Committee; William Warfield Wilson (1868–1942), a Republican from Illinois; Irvin Luther Lenroot (1869–1949), a Republican from Wisconsin; and Thomas William Hardwick (1872–1944), a Democrat from Georgia.

The hearings had an immediate impact. Mill owners, fearful that publicity would result in a reduction of the tariff that protected their industry, capitulated. On March 12, they offered a relatively generous settlement that included an across-the-board 5 percent rate increase for all piece workers. Two days later, the Lawrence workers accepted the proposal and returned to work. The strike marked the IWW's biggest victory to date.

[*March 5, 1912*]

STATEMENT OF MISS MARGARET SANGER.

MR. POU. You are from New York, are you?

MISS SANGER. Yes.

MR. POU. You were instrumental in taking a number of children away from Lawrence, were you not?

MISS SANGER. Yes.

MR. POU. I will be obliged to you if you will just go ahead and state in your own way what took place.

MISS SANGER. Well, I helped to take the first section of children, when there was no difficulty in getting them away. We brought them to New York and gave them supper; we took them to the Labor Temple,[2] where people were waiting to take them to their homes; there they had a supper and they were distributed, and that was all there was to that.

MR. POU. How long was that before the day we have been talking about, the 24th of February, I think it was?

MISS SANGER. I think that was two weeks.

MR. POU. How many of the children were taken to New York?

MISS SANGER. One hundred and nineteen at this time and 92 a week afterwards.

MR. POU. Altogether that would be something over 200?

MISS SANGER. Yes, sir.

MR. POU. Well, you had no trouble with the police?

MISS SANGER. No; we had no trouble.

MR. POU. They had not decided to prevent the children from leaving when you took these away?

MISS SANGER. No; not at this time.

MR. POU. Did you talk with those children about their manner of living in Lawrence and about the food they got?

MISS SANGER. Yes, sir. I am a trained nurse, and I was especially interested in the condition of the children.

MR. POU. Now, as a rule, is it true that the children of the working people in Lawrence—the class we are investigating now—only got meat once a week.

MISS SANGER. Those were the assertions of not only the children but of the parents that I interviewed.

MR. FOSTER. How long were you in Lawrence?

MISS SANGER. I was only there one night.

MR. FOSTER. You arrived in Lawrence in the evening and left the next morning?[3]

MISS SANGER. Yes.

MR. FOSTER. You did not visit any of the homes of the strikers?

MISS SANGER. No. When the people brought the children to the hall[4] the next morning to be taken away I inquired of some of the parents about the children.

MR. FOSTER. You say you are a trained nurse?

MISS SANGER. Yes, sir.

MR. FOSTER. And what was the physical appearance of these children that you took to New York? You know something about how they should look; were they properly nourished?

MISS SANGER. Well, the condition of those children was the most horrible that I have ever seen.

MR. FOSTER. Tell the committee something about how they looked.

MISS SANGER. In the first place, there were four little children who had chicken pox that we kept there; we would not allow them to go away; and then one of the children had just gotten over chicken pox, and the father begged us to let the child come; he had one 2 years old and another 3½ years old, I believe, and he begged us to let those children come, because he was a widower and had no wife or anyone to take care of these children; he left them with the neighbors during the day. So I took these little children, and we isolated them on the way to New York, and when we got there they were placed under the doctor's care. All of these children were walking about there apparently not noticing chicken pox or diphtheria; one child had diphtheria and had been walking around, and no attention paid to it at all, and had been working up to the time of the strike. Out of the 119 children four of them had underwear on, and it was the most bitter weather; we had to run all the way from the hall to the station in order to keep warm; and only four had underwear.

MR. FOSTER. You say only four had underwear?

MISS SANGER. Yes.

MR. FOSTER. What was the character of their outer clothing; was it woolen?

MR. STANLEY. Were the people working in a woolen mill?

MISS SANGER. Yes, sir.

MR. STANLEY. Where they make underwear?

MISS SANGER. Yes, sir.

MR. FOSTER. How about the outer clothing?

MISS SANGER. It was almost in rags; their coats were eaten off as though they were simply worn to shreds.

MR. FOSTER. Was it woolen clothing?

MISS SANGER. No, sir; I do not think any one of them had on any woolen clothing; that is, to my own knowledge.

MR. FOSTER. What was their color? Did they seem to be well nourished?

MISS SANGER. They were very much emaciated; every child there showed the effects of malnutrition, and all of them, or almost all of them, according to the doctor's certificate that night, had adenoids and enlarged tonsils. They were all examined at the station. We had a little time in the morning, and they were examined before they left.

MR. FOSTER. They all looked thin and pale?

MISS SANGER. Yes. I would like to say that when they had this supper it would bring tears to your eyes to see them grab the meat with their hands and eat it.

MR. FOSTER. They ate the meat as though they really enjoyed it?

MISS SANGER. Yes; decidedly.

MR. FOSTER. And you say that there were only four out of 119 that had any underclothing?

Miss Sanger. Yes, sir; and it was the bitterest weather we have had this year.

Mr. Foster. And the outer clothing was ragged?

Miss Sanger. In rags. I think perhaps 20 of them had overcoats.

Mr. Foster. What kind of shoes did they have?

Miss Sanger. Almost on the ground, except some of the older girls, who had been working in the mills; they had better shoes; but the little ones, who had to depend on others, were in a most deplorable condition.

Mr. Foster. Did they have on woolen stockings?

Miss Sanger. I do not think any of them had a bit of wool on their bodies.

Mr. Foster. And yet working in woolen mills?

Miss Sanger. Yes, sir.

The Chairman. Kindly read the letter I now hand you to the committee.

Mr. Foster. May I ask Miss Sanger what organization she represents in New York City.

Miss Sanger. I was previously the Woman organizer of the Socialist Party.[5] <Reading:>

> New York, February 1, 1912.[6]
>
> *To whom it may concern:*
>
> We, undersigned Italian doctors invited to make a preliminary physical examination of the Lawrence strikers' children, verified that all children were of poor physical build, defective, and underfed. The majority of them had enlarged glands, throat, nose, eyes, defective, and affected. All were poorly clad even against the rigor of the season.
>
> (And signed by six physicians.)

The Chairman. Can you read their names?

Miss Sanger. Diamede Petilex, M.D., 56 Mulberry Street; Dr. Exore Jeseau, 175 Worth Street; Dr. Alfredo De Filipi, 56 Mott Street; Dr. Rocco Bellantoni, 373 Broome Street; Dr. J. Loquito, 200 Grand Street, New York City.

The Chairman. Does that refer to the same children of whom you have been speaking?

Miss Sanger. Yes, sir.

Mr. Wilson. Where did those doctors live?

Miss Sanger. They were physicians of the Italian federation of New York City,[7] who volunteered their services to take charge of the children while in New York.

Mr. Lenroot. Have you had an opportunity to become familiar with the condition of children of other workers in other places?

Miss Sanger. Yes; I have.

Mr. Lenroot. Can you give the committee any information as to how the condition of these children compared with that of other children in similar circumstances of life?

MISS SANGER. Yes; I have been brought up in a factory town where there are glassblowers and children of glassblowers,[8] and I must say that I have never seen in any place children so ragged and so deplorable as these children were. I have never seen such children in my work in the Italian districts of New York City; in the slum districts, I must say, there are always a few of them who are fat and rugged, but these children were pale and thin.

THE CHAIRMAN. Have you any other statement you would like to make to the committee?

MISS SANGER. I would like to refute the statement that has been made that the children appeared in New York at a mass meeting. That is not so.[9]

THE CHAIRMAN. You may make any statement you deem proper about that.

MISS SANGER. That is not so. I was on the children's committee for both consignments of children, and they have never appeared on a platform in New York City, except the second time; when the children came to New York, in order to prevent the terrible rush when they were going for their dinner, we crossed over at Union Square on a little platform to get ahead of the rush, so they could get into Arlington Hall[10] before the rush and mob came. That was the only appearance they ever made on a platform, in crossing from one side to the other.

THE CHAIRMAN. Speaking for myself, I do not think that needs any apology. I think if they wanted to parade them before the public they had a constitutional right to do so.

[Editors' Note: We have omitted a short conversation between the chairman and Hardwick over whether the committee should express itself on the constitutional right to parade the children.]

MR. HARDWICK. Is it true or not—I am not expressing an opinion one way or the other, although I have an opinion on that subject, the same as my colleague, but I do not care express myself at present—that these children were in any way exhibited to the public during their stay in New York?

MISS SANGER. Only from the time they left the Grand Central Station until they went to hall where they were to have their supper.

MR. HARDWICK. When they went to the hall, of course, there was a crowd there, and was that a public affair?

MISS SANGER. No.

MR. HARDWICK. How many people were there?

MISS SANGER. Well, no one was allowed there except the committee who were to take charge of the children and to give them their food.

MR. HARDWICK. I have seen some statements in the New York papers[11] about these things, and you have probably read them, too. I was under the impression that one of those statements was to the effect that these children were taken to some mass meeting of either the Socialist Party or some labor organization. Is that true in point of fact or not?

MISS SANGER. No; that is not true. They have never been taken to a public meeting in New York.

MR. HARDWICK. They never were?

MISS SANGER. No, sir.

MR. HARDWICK. When they came to the station natural curiosity brought a great crowd to see them?

MISS SANGER. Yes; and they wrapped their coats about these little children; the men took their coats right off and carried them on their shoulders to their place of destination.

MR. HARDWICK. Just the natural curiosity to see these little suffering children?

MISS SANGER. Yes, sir.

MR. HARDWICK. And outside of the usual publicity that attends such a thing as this there was no attempt to give it purposeful publicity?

MISS SANGER. No; I do not think there was any special attention given to that; they were simply taken from one place to another—from the Grand Central Station to their place of destination.

MR. HARDWICK. They were not used at any public place or at a mass meeting?

MISS SANGER. No; there was no attempt to exploit these children, as the papers stated.

MR. HARDWICK. I am very glad to hear you say that this is incorrect.

MISS SANGER. That is absolutely untrue.

THE CHAIRMAN. Will you explain a little further about the index cards or identification cards[12] so we may understand about them exactly?

MISS SANGER. We first had an application blank made out in printed form. Any applicant who desired to have a child would make this application, stating that at a specified time, or whenever the parents desired, the child would be returned to them, or whenever the strike committee asked that the child be returned. Then there was another identification card; on one side was the child's name. Its parents' names, the place of residence and nationality, and on the opposite side of the card was the child's tutor or guardian. Those cards were signed by the committee from Lawrence. A special committee came with each nationality; the Polish people sent a Polish delegate, the French people sent a delegate representing their nationality, and so on, so that all of the children were placed in families where they could learn to speak their own language. And those cards were signed, and we kept them together.

THE CHAIRMAN. In other words, you had a perfect system of identification?

MISS SANGER. A very good system; yes.

MR. HARDWICK. Those children are still in New York, you say?

MISS SANGER. Yes, sir.

MR. HARDWICK. You are taking good care of them?

MISS SANGER. Yes, sir.

MR. HARDWICK. Treating them nicely?

MISS SANGER. Yes, sir.

MR. HARDWICK. And they are enjoying their vacation?

MISS SANGER. They have enjoyed it very much.

MR. HARDWICK. And their physical condition has improved very much?

MISS SANGER. We have a number of letters from the people who have the children saying that they have noticed an improvement in their physical condition.

MR. HARDWICK. You seem to be very thoroughly familiar with the details of this thing, so far as the New York end of it is concerned. I want to ask you a plain question and I want a candid answer to it, and I believe you will give it to me: Was the purpose in carrying these children to New York single or was it twofold? Was it single in that its only purpose was that of taking care of the children and helping the strikers, or was it twofold in that it was not only for the purpose I have just mentioned, but also for the purposes of aiding the strikers and helping break down the opposition of the bosses?

MISS SANGER. The main purpose in my estimation was that it was going to help them—

MR. HARDWICK (interposing). Win the strike?

MISS SANGER. Yes; win the strike. For instance, a father that I have in mind sent five boys with me: I said to him, "Is this going to help you?" He said, "God, I do not know what I would have done with the five children if you had not taken them," and so on. The people all expressed themselves in the same way—that this was going to be of great assistance to them.

MR. STANLEY. You mean they could weather the storm if they did not have to provide for the children?

MISS SANGER. Yes, sir.

MR. HARDWICK. As this is a new departure in American strike warfare I want to see what it means. Was it also the idea that by sending these children to other cities it would excite the sympathy of the people and aid the strikers in their warfare?

MISS SANGER. I think it is having a great deal to do with it.

MR. HARDWICK. I thought you would answer frankly. I am not expressing any opinion one way or the other.

MISS SANGER. I think it has.

THE CHAIRMAN. Personally, was it your purpose to aid the strikers or to give the children a home.

MISS SANGER. I was first interested in it as soon as I heard the children were coming to New York, when I telegraphed that I desired to take care of the children; that was my first interest.

THE CHAIRMAN. That was your main purpose?

MISS SANGER. Yes, sir.

THE CHAIRMAN. Personally?

MISS SANGER. Yes, sir.

Thereupon a recess was taken until 2:30 o'clock p.m.

AFTER RECESS.

The committee met, pursuant to the taking of recess, at 2:30 o'clock p.m., Hon. Robert L. Henry (chairman) presiding.

THE CHAIRMAN. The committee will be in order. Miss Sanger, will you take the stand again?

STATEMENT OF MISS MARGARET SANGER—Resumed.

THE CHAIRMAN. Miss Sanger, it has been stated that it would have been cheaper to have kept the children in Lawrence than to pay the railroad fare to New York. What about that?

MISS SANGER. Yes, that phase of the subject was considered by the New York committee before the final arrangements were made to bring them there. I myself went about among a number of people who had volunteered through the press, their request for the children, and I came to the committee with an assurance of about $100 that the people would send to those homes in Lawrence. But after the committee figured out the number of children there to be taken care of, it was asserted that there would take something like a hundred thousand or a couple of hundred thousand dollars to care for the children there, and it was decided that it would not be as beneficial to the children as to bring them to New York and put them in these families.

MR. WILSON. May I ask you a question?

MISS SANGER. Certainly.

MR. WILSON. You stated this morning that four of the children out of the one hundred and nineteen had on underclothing. It was suggested during the noon hour by individuals, to me, that the rest of the children were possibly in the habit of wearing underclothing during the cold weather, but that it had been taken off to create a little more sympathy, or excite a little more sympathy. Do you know whether or not these children were in the habit of wearing underclothing?

MISS SANGER. My candid opinion is that the first consignment of children were not in the best condition, because they were simply picked out of their homes without any preparation, and I do not believe that is true. They were simply taken out of their homes, being told the night before that they had to start on the early train. Some of the fathers and mothers brought them to the station with their own clothing wrapped around them to keep them from the cold.

MR. WILSON. Do you think that these same children, when going to New York, wore their poorest clothing, thinking that they would be replenished when they got in New York by your friends, and that they left their better clothing at home for the purpose of getting more out of it than if they had taken their other clothing?

MISS SANGER. I thought of that at the time, and I asked the children if they had any better clothing, and not one of them had. They wore the best clothing they had. They all tried to look their very best. The girls wore their best ribbons.

THE CHAIRMAN. You may stand aside.

House Committee on Rules, *The Strike at Lawrence, Mass.*, 62d Congress, 2d sess., Mar. 2–7, 1912, H. Doc. 671, 226–33. RHR, DNA (*MSM* C15:19–27).

1. The Lawrence strike began on January 11, 1912, when 23,000 woolen mill workers walked off the job to protest reductions in wages and increased workloads and speed. The IWW quickly sent the organizers Joseph Ettor and Arturo Giovannitti, who led strikers in demanding a 15 percent wage hike. They kept the strike fairly orderly and peaceful until January 29, when they were arrested as accessories in the murder of a bystander during a police-led break-up of a strike march. Their arrests brought national publicity and increased support for the IWW, which sent in a new contingent of strike organizers, notably William Haywood, Elizabeth Gurley Flynn, and Carlo Tresca.

2. The Labor Temple was a meeting hall run by the mostly German American Workmen's Educational Association. (Federal Writers' Project, *New York Panorama: A Companion to the WPA Guide to New York City* [1938; reprint, New York, 1984], 100; *New York Call*, Feb. 7, 1912.)

3. She arrived in Lawrence on February 9, 1912. The next day, she and the children took a train to New York City via Boston. (*New York Times*, Feb. 11, 1912; *New York Call*, Feb. 10, 1912.)

4. This was possibly a reference to the headquarters of the Central Labor Union of Lawrence, which housed a relief station that distributed food and clothing to strikers and maintained a trained nurse. (*Report on Strike of Textile Workers in Lawrence*, 64–65.)

5. MS had resigned as a paid Socialist Party organizer in January 1912. (Gordon, *Woman's Body*, 213.)

6. This date was probably a misprint of February 10, the day the children arrived in New York City; the original letter was not found.

7. This was probably the Italian Socialist Federation. (Dubofsky, *We Shall Be All,* 250.)
8. MS's hometown housed the Corning Flint Glass Company factory.
9. The IWW's intent was clearly to create a spectacle, for the Lawrence Strike Committee had announced, "It is the object of the Committee to make the reception of strikers' children in New York the most dramatic and significant event in labor history." A large crowd had gathered to wait for the children, with a large rally planned. However, because MS and the children missed their train from Boston and arrived at Grand Central Station much later, the children were greeted by a smaller crowd before going directly to the Labor Temple. (*New York Call,* Feb. 10, 1912 [quote]; *New York Times,* Feb. 11, 1912; "Children of a Strike.")
10. Arlington Hall was a trade union meeting hall on St. Mark's Place. (Moses King, ed., *King's Handbook of New York City,* 2d ed. [New York, 1893], 832.)
11. See, for example, the *New York Times,* February 11, 1912.
12. For a sample identification card, see *Report on Strike of Textile Workers in Lawrence,* 52–53.

12. To Nancy Brush Pearmain[1]

[*New York, N.Y.*]
Monday Nov. 4—[*1912*]

Dear, dear Nancy:

Pardon me for not writing you before to thank you for the money for the boys,[2] but I've been so, busy trying to keep house and also, write some articles which begin next Sunday in Normans Page.[3] I have no one to help me and it is some week! Then the children are so full of life and fun that I am almost beside myself to keep them quiet.

The two dollars came in pretty fine for the boys. I am going to try to get a regular fund of a couple of dollars a month to help them for a while, until they can get on their feet. I really feel awful to have treated your mattress so,[4] but I'll get you something else you need when you want it, if you will say the word.

Did you see Solidarity?[5] They had a notice of Robert's death in it this week.[6] I'll send it on to you. Mr. Berkman's new book, "The Prison Memoirs of an Anarchist" is just out.[7] They gave a dinner for him last Monday night[8] at the Café Boulevard, and when the speakers were relating various chapters of the book, I could scarcely control myself, so strongly did I think of Robert. You must read it Nancy. They say you can not ever feel the same after reading it. The "Girl" in it is Emma Goldman.[9] All radicals are talking about it. I'll send one up to you as soon as I get down to the Mother Earth Office[10] and read it. It will take you so close to Robert's ideas of Anarchy, and the justification of them.

I hope you will get into New York this winter to see us all, and stay with me as long as you can. I am dying to organize the houseworkers into a big union,[11] and oh so long for Robert to help me which he would do I know. Bill is very busy in the Syndacalist League, which he and a few others have launched,[12] so I can not depend on his help in this—but if I can get it going it will be great.

My kindest regards to your dear kind father, Mr. Brush,[13] and tell Jane and Thea,[14] Stuart and Grant[15] talk of them very often and send their love.

My dearest love to Polly[16] and yourself.

Write when you can and thanks again for the "boys".

Margaret (Sanger)

TRcy NBB, D-ArA. The source of the transcription was not identified; no original was found.

1. Nancy Brush Pearmain (Bowditch) (1890–1979) was a painter, playwright, and costume and set designer. (D-ArA.)

2. This was a reference to the trial of the IWW organizers Ettor and Giovannitti. They were acquitted on November 26, 1912. (Dubofsky, *We Shall Be All,* 254–55.)

3. A mistranscription of "Woman's Page," a weekly section in the Sunday *New York Call.* MS was preparing her series "What Every Girl Should Know." The first article appeared on November 17, 1912. (*MSM* C16:24.)

4. The Sanger family spent the summer of 1912 at a farmhouse in Dublin, New Hampshire, owned by Nancy Pearmain's father, the artist George De Forest Brush. (A. C. Sanger, "Margaret Sanger," 43.)

5. *Solidarity* was the IWW weekly published in New Castle, Pennsylvania, and edited by Ben H. Williams from 1909 to 1917. (Dubofsky, *We Shall Be All,* 144–45.)

6. William Robert Pearmain (1888–1912) was an affluent painter and socialist. After the Sangers introduced him to radical labor leaders in 1911, Pearmain decided to work as a general laborer, attempting to organize workers in Pittsburgh; he died of leukemia on September 28. A brief notice of his death appeared in *Solidarity* on November 2, 1912. ("A Short Biography of William Robert Pearmain, 1888–1912," 1975, 12–13, [NBB]; Traxel, *American Saga,* 76.)

7. Alexander Berkman (1870–1936) was a Russian-born anarchist and journalist who in 1892 attempted to assassinate the industrialist Henry Clay Frick, for which he served fourteen years in prison. He began writing *Prison Memoirs of an Anarchist* upon his release from prison in 1906. (*DAB*)

8. The dinner, held on October 28, was attended by some 250 "anarchists, near-anarchists, and all kinds of Socialists." The printer Harry Kelly presided, and speeches were made by Emma Goldman, Hippolyte Havel, and William English Walling, among others. (*New York Call,* Oct. 29, 1912.)

9. Emma Goldman (1869–1940), a Russian-born anarchist and feminist, was the editor of *Mother Earth* (1906–17) and author of *Anarchism and Other Essays* (1911). In *Prison Memoirs,* Berkman depicted her as the "sole personification of revolutionary persistence" and his most loyal supporter (344). (*DAB*)

10. Launched by Goldman in 1906, *Mother Earth,* an influential anarchist monthly featuring essays on labor politics, feminism, and literature, was located at 55 West Twenty-

eighth Street in New York City. (Buhle, Buhle, and Georgakas, *Encyclopedia of the American Left.*)

11. There is no evidence that MS pursued efforts to organize houseworkers.

12. The Syndicalist Educational League was a short-lived propaganda organization founded in October 1912 by Havel and Kelly in New York City. Influenced by European syndicalism, which aspired to overthrow capitalism through the direct action of organized workers, the league's organizers chose to remain outside of the mainstream labor movement for fear of compromising their anarchist ideals. William Sanger was organizing the league's first mass meeting, scheduled for November 14 in New York City. (Brissenden, *I.W.W.*, 274–75; Harry Kelly, "A Syndicalist League" and "The Syndicalist Education League," *Mother Earth*, Sept. 1912, 218–33, and Nov. 1912, 307–8.)

13. George De Forest Brush (1855–1941) was a traditionalist figure artist known for his paintings of idealized Native Americans and a series of "mother and child" paintings. A socialist, Brush had been interviewed by MS for the *New York Call.* (*DAB; New York Times,* Apr. 25, 1941; MS's interview, "An Evening with George De Forest Brush," was published in the Aug. 4, 1912, issue.)

14. These were Nancy Pearmain's younger sisters, Jane Brush (Coates) (1900–1987) and Thea Brush (Cabot) (ca. 1903–88). (Nancy Bowditch, *George De Forest Brush: Recollections of a Joyous Painter* [Peterborough, N.H., 1970], 61, 72.)

15. She was referring to MS's sons, Stuart (1903–95) and Grant (1908–89), ages eight and four.

16. Mary Alice (Polly) Pearmain (Marlowe) (1911–?) was the only child of William and Nancy Pearmain.

13. "*What Every Girl Should Know: Sexual Impulses—Part II*"[1]

This was the seventh of a twelve-part series of articles on sex education published in the Woman's Sphere column of the New York Call, *from November 17, 1912, to March 2, 1913. "Sexual Impulses, Part I" appeared on December 22, 1912, and dealt with the temptations and dangers of masturbation. The last article, "Some Consequences of Ignorance and Silence—Part III," was to appear in the February 9 issue, but it was suppressed by post office authorities. In place of it, the* Call *ran a blank column with the heading, "What Every Girl Should Know; NOTHING! By Order of the Post Office Department." The full article was published in the March 2 issue.*

[*December 29, 1912*]

In the first part of this article we learned that the sexual impulse is a combination of the two impulses, the one which impels the discharge of ripe sex cells, strongest in the boy, and the other which impels the individual to touch or caress an individual of the opposite sex, strongest in the girl.

Every girl has in mind an ideal man. This ideal begins to form sometime in the early adolescent age. He is usually distinct in her mind as to his physical qualities, such as dark or light hair, or brown or blue eyes. He is always a certain physical type, and often remains an ideal to her through life. At the forming period of the type she will be attracted toward many men who seem to answer the ideal type, but as she reads and develops through the various stages of the adolescent period, the ideal changes and grows with her. As she reaches the romantic stage the ideal must be brave, daring, courteous. If she is inclined toward out-door sports he must be athletic. And so it goes on until the twenty-third year, when the average girl has a fairly settled idea of the man who would suit her as a mate through life.

When the sexual impulse makes itself felt strongly in the adolescent boy or girl, they, feeling satisfied with the physical beauty and perfection of the other, marry, they are unconscious that the incentive to love when based on physical attraction alone is soon destroyed. For sickness, poverty or disease will affect even the most seemingly perfect physical attraction.

Let us not confuse the sexual impulse with love, for it alone is not love, but merely a necessary quality for the growth of love.

No sexual attraction or impulse is the foundation of the beautiful emotion of love. Upon this is built respect, self-control, sympathy, unity of purpose, many common tastes and desires, building up and up until this real love unites two individuals as one being, one life. Then it becomes the strongest and purest emotion of which the human soul is capable.

There is no doubt that the natural aim of the sexual impulse is the sexual act, yet when the impulse is strongest and followed by the sexual act without love or any of the relative instincts which go to make up love, the relations are invariably followed by a feeling of disgust. Respect for each other and for one's self is a primary essential to this intimate relation.

In plant and animal life the reproductive cell of the male is the active seeker of the passive female cell, imbued with the instinct to chase and bodily capture the female cell for the purpose of reproduction.

This instinct man, as he is today, has inherited, and, as with the lower forms of life, the senses are intensely involved. It is kept alive by the sense of sight, sound and smell, and reaches its highest development through the sense of touch. It is heightened by touching smooth and soft surfaces—which is said to account for the pleasure of kissing.

In the early part of this article I spoke of the desire to touch being stronger in girls than in boys. This desire leads a girl to kiss and fondle a man without any conscious desire for the sexual act; whereas in the man, to be touched and caressed by the girl for whom he has a sexual attraction, stimulates the accumulation of sex cells, and the desire for the sexual act becomes paramount in his mind. Many a young girl bubbling over with the joy of living, innocent of any serious consequences, is oft-times misjudged by men on account of these natural actions. But she soon puts on her armor of defense, and stifles and represses any outbursts of affection.

Society, too, condemns the natural expression of Woman's emotion, save under certain prescribed conditions. In consequence of this, women suppress their maternal desires and today direct this great force into other channels, participating in the bigger and broader movements and activities in which they are active today.

This is one reason why the type of the so-called "old maid," so characteristic of the generation past, has disappeared. These great maternal powers are being used up in the activities of modern life. Instead of allowing it to remain dormant and make her odd and whimsical, the modern Woman turns her sexual impulse into a big directing force.

That the male creature is the pursuer of the female in all forms of life, there is no question, but that the female has the choice of selection and uses fine discrimination in her choice, cannot be denied either. This instinct of selection seems to lie dormant in women of today, for at puberty nature calls to every girl to make a selection suitable to her nature. Yet few girls follow this instinct on account of the specter of economic insecurity which looms up before them. Instead of asking themselves: "Are we matable and sympathetic?" they ask: "Shall we have enough food, clothing and shelter?"

Indeed, girls, this system increases our degradation, and places us in ideals lower than the animals. All over the civilized world today girls are being given and taken in marriage with but one purpose in view; to be well-supported by the man who takes her. She does not concern herself with the man's physical condition: his hereditary taints, the cleanliness of his mind or past life, nor with the future race.

There will no doubt be a great change in Woman's attitude on this subject in the next few years. When women gain their economic freedom they will cease being playthings and utilities for men, but will assert themselves and choose the father of their offspring. As Bernard Shaw tells of her in one of his greatest plays, she will hunt down her ideal in order to produce the Superman.[2]

There seems to be a general tendency on the part of the Woman who is demanding political freedom, to demand sexual freedom also. When a girl reaches the age nearing thirty her natural development tends toward sexual freedom. It seems as though nature, knowing the time of reproduction is drawing to a close, calls with all the fury of her strength to complete its development and procreate.

It is at this age where physicians claim a Woman awakens to the sexual desire, and it is at this age that women seek affection, or gratification with a "lover." To her there is nothing to say; she is mature, developed and can judge for herself where best her happiness lies.

But to the young girl at the age of say twenty, or even younger, immature, mentally undeveloped, there is something she should know, and that is that every physical impulse, every sensual feeling, every lustful desire will come to her whitewashed with the sacred word LOVE.

Neither the boy nor the girl knows the difference between the sexual impulse and love. A boys meets a girl, he feels a great attraction for her, he feels the sexual impulse throbbing within him, he is full of this life giving current he feels it throughout his being, he walks lighter and straighter, he feels it in his voice, in his laughter, he grows tenderer within himself, and to women. He feels all this and is sure it is a love that will never die. If there is an attraction on the girl's part there is no difficulty in persuading her that this feeling IS love.

But it is not love; it is the creative force of sexual impulse scattered through his being and the sexual act brings it to its climax.

If motherhood comes to the girl through this relation, she has developed and the experience has enriched her life. But today the girl has an idea she has escaped the greatest disgrace when she has avoided motherhood. If the relation was based on physical attraction, a few abortions and the monotony of every day life soon remove this, and the man goes elsewhere in search of this wonderful sensation which he felt at first, but did not know how to keep or how to use.

The girl, however, has become a new being, sexually awakened and conscious of it. But ignorant of the use of the forces she possesses, she plunges forth blindly, with social and economic forces against her, and prostitution beckoning at every turn. So she soon passes with the crowd on the road to the Easiest Way. This is the story of thousands of young girls living in prostitution.

Women should know that the creative instinct does not need to be expended entirely on the propagation of the race. Though the sex cells are placed in a part of the anatomy for the essential purpose of easily expelling them into the female for the purpose of reproduction there are other elements in the sexual fluid which are the essence of blood, nerve, brain and muscle. When redirected into the building and strengthening of these we find men or women of the greatest endurance and greatest magnetic power. A girl can waste her creative powers by brooding over a love affair to the extent of exhausting her system, with results not unlike the effects of masturbation and debauchery.

Of course the sexual impulse is natural. It is natural in animals, degenerates, and in normal man. But in man it is mixed with other essentials which, together, are termed love. These essentials are derived from man's power of reasoning by which he is known as a higher species and through which he differs from the animals.

When man emerged from the jungle and stood upright on his hind legs, the shape of his head and his face changed from the long jaw and flat head of the animal to the flat face and high head of the man. All progress from that time forward was made along mental lines. According to the universal law then in existence he should have been limited to a geographical area and killed by the extreme heat or cold or starved for one kind of food if it were not obtained, but against all these he fought, because he became endowed with such attributes as reason, knowledge and will-power. Instead of using his creative powers solely in hunting food and reproducing his species, he used this force in making plans for his self-preservation. He built rafts and boats to cross rivers and streams, he devised methods of clothing himself against extreme heat and cold and discovered various ways of preparing food for different climates suitable for his various needs. In other words he conserved his creative force and redirected it into channels which have resulted in giving him precedence over all other living creatures. For man has developed a CONSCIOUS MIND which asserts itself by reasoning, which in turn has developed his brain-power.

It is said a fish as large as a man has a brain no larger than the kernel of an almond. In all fish and reptiles where there is no great brain development, there is also no conscious sexual control. The lower down in the scale of human development we go the less sexual control we find. It is said that the aboriginal Australian, the lowest known species of the human family, just a step higher than the chimpanzee in brain development, has so little sexual control that police authority alone prevents him from obtaining sexual satisfaction on the streets.[3] According to one writer, the rapist has just enough brain development to raise him above the animal, but like the animal, when in heat knows no law except nature which impels him to procreate whatever the result.[4] Every normal man and Woman has the power to control and direct his sexual impulse. Men and women who have it in control and constantly use their brain cells in thinking deeply, are never sensual.

It is well to understand that the natural aim of the sexual impulse is the sexual act and the natural aim of the sexual act is reproduction, though it does not always result in this. It is possible for conception to take place without love, it is even possible that there is no conscious knowledge to procreate before or during the act, yet this does not disprove the fact that nature has designed it for the purpose of reproduction, no matter what uses man has put it to today. This subject of procreation we shall discuss next.

Every girl should know that to hold in check the sexual impulse; to absorb this power into the system until there is a freely conscious sympathy, a confidence and respect between her and her ideal; that this will go toward building up the sexual impulse and will make the purest, strongest and most sacred passion of adult life, compared to which all other passions pale into insignificance.

(To Be Continued.)[5]

New York Call, Dec. 29, 1912, 15 (*MSM* C16:46–48).

1. For the full series, see *MSM* C16:24–62; for the suppressed article, see C16:59–62.

2. This was a reference to George Bernard Shaw's 1905 play, *Man and Superman,* which justifies a woman's efforts to select her mate on the grounds of positive eugenics.

3. It was a commonly held notion in the late nineteenth century and early twentieth that Australian aborigines ranked lowest on the scale of physical measurements designed to test mental ability. Francis Galton, for example, in his rankings of the natural abilities of nations and races, noted, "The Australian type is at least one grade below the African negro." Another popular assumption was that limited mental abilities led to excessive sexuality. (Francis Galton, *Hereditary Genius: An Inquiry into Its Laws and Consequences,* rev. ed. [New York, 1871], 339; see also Stephen Jay Gould, *The Mismeasure of Man* [New York, 1981], 85–87; and Kevles, *In the Name of Eugenics,* 107.)

4. The exact author was not identified, but theories such as this were popularized in the late nineteenth century by the Italian anthropologist Cesare Lombroso (1835–1909) and his followers, who argued that criminality was inherited, that hereditary criminals could be identified by facial features and other physical characteristics, and that habitual criminals were atavistic throwbacks to an earlier stage of human development. By the time MS wrote this article, such beliefs were already being challenged and were eventually displaced by theories that linked criminality to environmental factors. (Ysabel Rennie, *The Search for Criminal Man* [Toronto, 1978], 68–75.)

5. The next article in the series was "Reproduction—Part I." (Jan. 12, 1913 [*MSM* C16:51].)

14. "With the Girls in Hazleton Jail"

Early in April of 1913, Sanger arrived in Hazleton, a town thirty-five miles northeast of Allentown, Pennsylvania, where some twelve hundred workers from the Duplan Silk Mill had walked off the job on February 7, 1913. The strikers, many of them the daughters of Italian American coal miners, protested low wages and the imposition of fines. The strike was led by IWW organizers, but by early March, the United Textile Workers (UTW), an American Federation of Labor (AFL) affiliate, challenged the IWW leadership and mediated a settlement. On April 2, despite lobbying by the IWW, a majority of the strikers accepted the offer, and by April 3, partial work had resumed at the mills. Nevertheless, IWW leaders led a small but vociferous group of strikers on the picket lines. The IWW sent Sanger to Hazleton to join the remaining strikers.

[*April 20, 1913*]

When eighteen girls of the Duplin Silk Mill of Hazelton,[1] Pa., were put into a patrol wagon and thrown into filthy cells a week ago last Tuesday morning, we all questioned ourselves closely to think what we had done. We had been on the picket line, walking along quietly, when two mounted policemen called out to us: "Stop!" Then they added: "We'll take them all in."[2]

The acting Mayor[3] tried the cases, and charged us with "loitering on the streets." The officer said we had loitered after he had told us to stop. However, we all took our time to serve from three to eight days—those walking with me got five days, like myself, while second offenders got eight days.[4]

We were placed in filthy cells, two and three together.

The cells are about eight feet long and five feet wide. Half of the length is taken up with a sheet-iron bench on which the inmate sleeps. In the corner is a toilet, which is flushed once a day. The walls are sheet-iron, covered with paint.

Through the bars every morning at 11 o'clock comes the lone loaf of bread, which must serve until the next morning at the same time. Two cups of water must serve as washing and drinking water. No basin is provided for washing purposes; no blankets or covering of any kind; no comb, brush, soap, towel or anything for the ordinary decency of the prisoner is allowed her. Nor may any food from outside be carried within.

Before being tried before the judge, we were all thrown together in the cell corridor. The girls pounded on the gates for a drink of water. The keeper gave a pitcher of water to the girls and they all drank it hastily, until one of them spied a large dead roach in the bottom of the pitcher. Closer examination showed the pitcher to be filthy inside as well as outside.

One girl held it high over her head and said:

"Girls, do we drink from a pitcher like this?"

"No!" shouted the rest in chorus.

Bang! on the stone floor went the pitcher, crashing into dozens of pieces.

The spirit of the girl was beyond everything ever known in that town before for cheerfulness and defiance. Heretofore, it has been a terrible disgrace to go to the "lock up." But all this has changed in these few weeks, and the girl who serves her time on bread and water is considered a full-fledged fellow worker.

All night long, the boys and girls pounded upon the iron walls of their cells and sang revolutionary songs for the benefit of the Mayor, police and political bosses, who lounge about in the adjoining room.

They did not miss their mark, either, for the papers printed glaring accounts of the abusive and revolutionary language of the prisoners.[5]

An influential lawyer was now called upon in Wilkes-Barre. No lawyer in Hazelton would take the strikers' case, except a socialist lawyer,[6] and the authorities ignored his every act. When the tools of the mill bosses heard this, they decided to keep their dirty work hidden by freeing all those who had been arrested.[7]

Before doing so, McKelvey, the political boss, detective and Alderman in one,[8] went to the girls and boys to ask if their fathers were voters and said he was using all his influence to have them freed. (He is up for Mayor.) But the girls told him they wanted none of his mercy, nor influence, and preferred to serve their time out rather than accept favors from him.

For that they were kept in the cells a few hours longer. In fact, they refused to come out until the lawyer came in for them and said they had committed no offense and were freed.

The next morning they were on the picket line again at 6 o'clock, but the authorities don't want them in jail again: they want money, and that is what the boys and girls won't give.[9]

While we were locked up, the stench from the toilets became so strong that the girls called to an officer to flush them. He refused to do this, and so the prisoners decided to let the loungers in the adjoining room have some of the odors. They, accordingly, emptied the toilets with the assistance of their tin cups into the cell corridors which all run into the Mayor's office. The officers came running in and asked what in heaven's name they were up to now! Several officers at once cleaned out the place, scrubbed and disinfected the floors, and those of the girls who could sleep in the sheetiron beds turned in for the night.

Roaches and bugs infest the cells, and as you are about to get friendly with these a huge rat comes upon the scene to fight it out with you about that loaf of bread.

The girls decided they'd rather be friends with the rats and give up [*their*] bread than show any fear to the officers. Nevertheless, a rat is a rat [*to*] a Woman.

The fight is still on.[10] The girls [*know*] they have learned more in eight weeks than they learned in all their lives before, and they are not going to stop learning. Life in the silk mill was heretofore a bore and work was drudgery. It will not be so again. The girls say they see now that there is a fight on for the working class, and, they are in that fight. There is something now to work for, to live for. It is the fight to emancipate the worker from wage slavery.

New York Call, Apr. 20, 1913, 15 (*MSM* C16:65).

1. MS misspelled the name of the mill (Duplan) and the town (Hazleton).
2. On Tuesday, April 8, after some of the strikers ignored calls to return to the mill, the police arrested twenty-six picketers, among them MS. (*Hazleton Daily Standard*, Apr. 8 and 10, 1913; *Solidarity*, Apr. 19, 1913; Golin, *Fragile Bridge*, 44.)
3. The reference was to Henry Heidenreich, who replaced Mayor Charles Bruch sometime in late March or early April.
4. MS, along with a number of other picketers, was found guilty and fined five dollars, but she refused to pay and was sentenced to five days in jail. (*Hazleton Daily Standard*, Apr. 10 and 11, 1913; *Solidarity*, Apr. 19, 1913; see also Lynch, "Pennsylvania Anthracite," 131–32.)
5. The local papers gave detailed accounts of the arrests of the strikers, including MS who, according to the April 11, 1913, *Hazleton Daily Standard*, declared "she believed in

the doctrines of the I.W.W. that of direct action for the reason that she did not believe there was any law, nor courts where political action existed."

6. The IWW engaged an attorney named Shea (unclear if he was from Wilkes-Barre or Hazleton), who phoned Mayor Heidenreich on April 9 and pleaded with him to release the remaining strikers. (*Hazleton Daily Standard,* Apr. 10 and 11, 1913.)

7. Heidenreich released MS on April 9, hoping she would leave town. Most of the strikers were released on the same afternoon, the day after their arrest, after agreeing not to repeat their crime. (*Hazleton Daily Standard,* Apr. 10 and 11, 1913.)

8. Daniel McKelvey (1886–1946), an alderman, was also doing police duty at the mill. (U.S. Bureau of the Census, *Thirteenth Census of the United States, 1910,* Pennsylvania.)

9. Several of those arrested were not released immediately because they would not promise to go back to work. When they were finally freed, they returned to the picket line. MS rejoined them and was arrested again on April 11. This time she claimed that as she was being arrested, McKelvey called her a "New York Bowery Bum." Angered, she demanded that police arrest him too, but the officer she appealed to claimed not to have heard McKelvey's remark. According to the local papers, MS became enraged and tried to strike McKelvey, but "as she attempted to land a blow, McKelvey dodged and had her sent to the lockup in the patrol." At her arraignment, MS denied she had assaulted McKelvey. This time she was not jailed. (Lynch, "Pennsylvania Anthracite," 135–36 [first quote]; *Hazleton Daily Standard,* Apr. 11, 1913 [second quote].)

10. Despite MS's optimistic words, the IWW was unable to sustain the strike, which effectively collapsed by April 19. (Golin, *Fragile Bridge,* 44.)

15. *From John Rompapas*[1]

[*New York, N.Y.?*]
Monday 12—noon [*July? 1913*][2]

Dearest Margaret: —

Six days of real suffering were enough to make me feel that to suffer for you it is not suffering. It is the sweetest feeling. It is life. And I live only for you and with you.

I am not any longer myself. I have died long ago and I am reborn with a combined self, in which you are the leading part.

From the minute you left me I felt the emptyness of my existence alone. I felt the impossibitily of life without your [~~*illegible*~~] love. I am suffering. I am unhappy alone and I can not see the possibility of life without you. Once we lose our individuality and we live with a combined self we isolate our lives from the rest of the world as individuals.

Although I am sure of your love, the fact that we could apart even for a short period created in me a fear, a strong fear, and while I am glad we did not elope and thus we will have no reason of regret, in reality I am sorry I did not force you to run away. For I wanted you. Yes, dearest, I want you and I am sorry I have knowledge of future feelings through certain acts.

I do not see how I can live without you. I was an individual free from any care and free from conditions. Nothing could crush me. Nothing could interest me. I had a dream of perfect love and equal lover, but I thought that even love was a step bellow my individuality.

I could never compromise in feelings and the minute I was attracted to a person, that minute or the following minutes were with a feeling of self freedom. I was free, for the persons, who attracted me then were not my equals or my little superiors. If Big Bill[3] or any one else could not see real love, equal and mutual, and they only know how to give advices, to me it does not matter. I can never expect from such people high class ~~of~~ feelings. The coward free lovers ought to know the real and only responsibility of attraction. The natural one and not the socially accepted responsibility.

My life in past was in part a flourising garden of self contentement, a complete individual existence. And while I felt the weakness of every person who attracted me I kept forming a clearer view of my Ideal lover. My dreams were a part of my life.

One day I met you. Did I fall in love with you? No, I did not and I am glad I did not have a sexual attraction then for you. You were more then sex. Subconsciously I wanted to tell you (right then if I could) all about me and all about my life. And I looked around (in the dancing hall) to see you. The individual who cared for nothing had a desire to tell you something even if that something was nothing. That was a strange desire.

When I was at a meeting for the Social War, someone told us you did not care to have anything to do with an anti-political paper & [*illegible*] because you wanted to keep in good terms with S. P.[4] This ought to be a shock to me even if I misunderstood the statement. It was the time that I should have stopped thinking of you and regain control of my absolute freedom. It was a chance to form a stronger Ideal lover in me. Instead of this the next minute was with a desire to know you better. The evolution of my feelings ~~are~~ is known to you and I am sure you know that I can give more and more.

Yet, I do not dream of more love from your part. I am completelly satisfied.

Dear love I have no other desire exept your love, I am not hoping to live with you in the future in order to gain happiness. To hope is not a present feeling of real life. I am in love with you and you perfectly fulfil all my dreams and desires. I can not live and have you live away from me. Yet, I can not even imagine the possibility of losing you, your love. No matter what you do I know the reasons and I justify your acts. But, dear heart I realy want to kill you with love in order to have you always near me, where you will not be able to move. Then I, a slave before your feet, to sing the eternal song of love, of equal love.

If we can live all our lives in a forest, isolated from the world, just you and me, away from everything, it will be Ideal and I will miss nothing from conditional life, for I care for nothing else but you, there is no other person, who could creat in me the feeling that "you are not capable of big, strong, everlasting love." So, there will never come the minute of dissapointement in me. Even if you tell me "you do not love me" you can not free me from your love, because I am not capable of dreaming of a stronger lover than you. I feel you are my Ideal lover and we can love only once and good. As long as I felt that you love me and I love you equally that ended my dreams for another perfect love. Even if you tell me, "You can not look any more in my eyes unless you are free", I can not change my conception of our love that we are free. Even if you will tell me that my eyes do not effect you any longer I can not free myself from your attraction. I will try to interest you then as a blind lover. I am living with you for you and by your dear heart. It is too late, dear lover, and if in future I can not attract you I will gladly be blind in order to accept a charity love from you.

I do not think I will end my life through force, because I suffer for you. That is not my view of love. I prefer to suffer for you and my life will be a sweet existence to suffer for real love. Yet, I am not weak, for to suffer for my Ideal lover is not a state of weakness. It is a pleasure of life even though I am crushed. If I had another desire in life I could survive. Fortunately now I can not think of such a possibility because already I feel a self creation in me. The knowledge (the inward knowledge) that there existed a period of equality ~~you~~ with you abolished all dreams of new attractions and I am glad I have no other desire.

I do respect your "resolve" and gladly I suffer by it. From the minute I read it, I felt the isolation of my life from other people and because of that feeling your resolve did not take the pleasure of my life away. Yet it is killing a little by little my life. Willingly I give in for I have not another desire but to see you. I want you so much that I can start now, or any minute, to come where ever you are, to see you, to love you, to hear a word from you, to receive life.

I could never imagine that I would not see you again, yet a black pall covers this minute the future. I do not try to survive in life. I do not care. I love you and I feel you are free. You have been free and I am right to feel that that resolve is not right. Can not last. It is impossible to last very long. I have one purpose in life and you hold in your heart my whole life, myself. You are my Ideal lover and no matter how I try to justify or not our love or your resolve I come to one conclusion that you are my Ideal lover.

In my past life every minute of attraction was followed by a period of indefference, with your attraction I feel complete equality and it is just right when I say and feel that you are my first & last lover. If you will try to run above or bellow me, I will follow you. I will keep our equality no matter what it happens. I will use all my strenght to keep you, my love, for I can live only with you.

I want to see you. I do want to see you even for a moment. Nothing else in this world interests me.

I [*packed*] nicely Boxes & Barrels and my thoughts were on you. Everything I tuched was a sweet memory. I was just happy. To day I will go for the records of music.

I want to be your slave. I hate every person, who cares for you and I feel strong enough to fulfill your dreams of life.

I am not only a dreamer. I am the best of lovers and I can feel that very strongly. Love me dearest and you will discover every day in me your Ideal lover, your strong Ideal lover, the stronger, the strongest.

By telephone I received your telegram.[5] I am glad to take the Books in my place, because you will have to send me another sweet mesage in order to take them back. I am selfish! oh! Dear heart! what all this mean? You killed my individuality or rather you give me yours and now I can not live but only with you. Willingly and gladly I accept your half self and I am happy to realize the [*fact*].

Do not do anything you don't want to do. I understand all. I am happy to feel that I know you. have your way and love me.

Yeânnis[6]

ALS MSP, MN-SSC (*MSM* S60:60–79). A note written by MS at the top of the first page reads, "The rival."

1. John Nicholas Rompapas (1878–?), a Macedonian-born writer and tobacco importer, immigrated to the United States in 1903. He founded the Rabelais Press, published radical tracts, and owned a Greenwich Village bookshop. An anarchist, he financed the *Revolutionary Almanac* and was a regular at the Ferrer Center. In 1914, Rabelais Press published *A Book of My Life,* Rompapas's rambling meditation on love and revolution. Mabel Dodge described Rompapas as having "a handsome head on a handsome body. Black hair and the darkest brown eyes far apart in his strong face." He probably met MS at a socialist dance hall and saw her regularly at Dodge's salon. They began a love affair in the spring of 1913, which may have continued that summer in Provincetown and sporadically in 1914. (Petitions for Naturalization, New York State Supreme Court, New York County, vol. 142, 36; Avrich, *Modern School Movement,* 117, 124; Avrich, *Anarchist Voices,* 201; *New York Times,* Apr. 4, 1915; William Sanger to MS, Dec. 8, 1914 [*MSM* S1:305]; Luhan, *Movers and Shakers,* 60–66 [quote on 61]; Patricia R. Everett, ed., *The History of Having a Great Many Times Not Continued to Be Friends: The Correspondence between Mabel Dodge and Gertrude Stein* [Albuquerque, 1996], 185.)

2. This letter was probably written after the Sangers had moved to Provincetown.

3. This was a reference to William Dudley ("Big Bill") Haywood (1869–1928), the radical labor leader and cofounder of the IWW, who kept his love life private. Separated

but never divorced from his wife, Nevada Jane Minor, Haywood had liaisons with several women. (*ANB*)

4. *Social War,* published in New York City in 1913 by Robert Lee Warwick, was, according to its masthead, "A Revolutionary Weekly Advocate of Free Communism." It was edited by Edward Mylius (a former London correspondent for the *Liberator* [Paris] and probably another of MS's lovers) and the outspoken Greenwich Village anarchist Hippolyte Havel; Rompapas apparently also worked on the journal. "S.P." refers to the Socialist Party. (Avrich, *Modern School Movement,* 117, 373; *New York Times,* Dec. 24, 1912; *Social War,* Mar. 26, 1913 [WHi].)

5. The telegram was not found.

6. Yeânnis is a Greek version of John.

16. To Amelia Stewart Michell[1]

Provincetown, Mass.
[*July ?, 1913*][2]

Amelia—dear old love.

Why have I not followed my impulses again & again & written to you. Always putting things off. However it is not because I have not tho't of you but the terrible lack of time has driven me to leave all the tender things I would love to do undone. I am sending you a little treatise on What Every Girl Should Know[3] and trust you may agree with it enough to pass it on to those who may need the knowledge it contains.

We have been here since July 1st. Bill is painting these days and we go to Paris for the winter. We sail from Boston Oct 16th and take all the kids along—of course we may have to walk back but who cares—

Ill write you again dear— Let me know your present address & Ill never do like this again. Are you interested in the movement:

I was asked to lecture at Schnectady by the Y.P.S.L.[4] in Oct. can't do it.

Love from Bill to you both. My best love to Clarence too. Lovingly, devotedly as ever

Margaret

ALS MSP, MN-SSC (*MSM* S1:24–27).

1. Amelia Stewart left the White Plains nursing school to marry her Claverack classmate Clarence Michell (1879–1974). They settled in Schenectady, New York, where he took a job with General Electric. (CCR; MS to Mabel Michell Pyott, June 1, 1954 [*MSM* S43:887].)

2. The Sangers rented a small cottage on the outskirts of Provincetown. While MS spent a good deal of the summer in Boston libraries, she also socialized in Provincetown with other Greenwich Village denizens, including the socialist writer Mary Heaton Vorse and her husband, Joseph O'Brien, as well as the writers Hutchins Hapgood and Neith Boyce. (MS, *My Fight,* 58–59; Tripp, *I.W.W. and the Paterson Strike,* 154.)

3. This was a reference to MS's sex education series, republished as a booklet early in 1914 by Rompapas's Rabelais Press. (For several published versions, see LCM 131:136–219.)

4. Young People's Socialist Leagues began forming in 1907, with the largest chapters in Rochester, Buffalo, and Schenectady, which in 1911 had elected a Socialist mayor. (Arthur McDowell, "The Socialist Youth Movement," *American Socialist Quarterly* 3 [Summer 1934]: 43; David A. Shannon, *The Socialist Party of America: A History* [New York, 1955], 13, 164.)

17. "The Paterson Strike"

On February 24, a few weeks after the Hazleton strike broke out, a larger strike of silk workers began in Paterson, New Jersey. Sanger participated as a speaker at special meetings for women and children and as a member of the Children's Committee, which was charged with organizing children's evacuations. In Paterson, the strikers faced more vigorous opposition from mill owners and municipal authorities than had the Lawrence strikers. As the strike dragged on, strike leaders, supporters, and IWW organizers divided over strategies and tactics. Bill Haywood and some other strike leaders repudiated the IWW's earlier violent confrontations in favor of passive resistance, refusing to promote sabotage by Paterson strikers or urge them to fight back against police. Others, such as Sanger, sought more militant action designed to incite confrontations with authorities. The Paterson strike was also significant for tearing apart the alliance between the radical labor movement and the Greenwich Village intelligentsia. This was most obvious after the Paterson Strike Pageant, held on June 7, 1913, to publicize the strike and to fill the strike fund's depleted coffers. Not only did the pageant fail to raise sufficient funds for the strikers' relief, but also some workers accused pageant leaders of stealing the profits, despite the fact that many involved in the production, including the Sangers (who hosted several pageant meetings at their small Uptown apartment), John Reed, Mabel Dodge, and Jessie Ashley, had loaned money for the event and were not repaid.

When the Paterson strike ended in failure in August 1913, the IWW was seriously damaged. Among the IWW's most notable critics was Sanger, who voiced her objections in the following article, published early in 1914. (For views on the strike, see Haywood, Bill Haywood's Book, *267; Steve Golin, "Defeat Becomes Disaster: The Paterson Silk Strike of 1913 and the Decline of the IWW,"* Labor History *24 [Spring 1983]: 229; Golin,* Fragile Bridge, *7, 143, 207–8, 228–29; Tripp,* I.W.W. and the Paterson Strike, *37; and Martin Green,* New York, 1913: The Armory Show and the Paterson Strike Pageant *[New York, 1988], 196–97.)*

[*September? 1913*]

When the Lawrence strikers returned to work victorious, after a struggle of three months duration, their victory caused the capitalists to recognize the strength and revolutionary character of the Industrial Workers of the World, and also caused a general dissatisfaction among the workers in the East, for it gave to some of them a historical vision of their class and its relation to present day society.

After this victory a general strike fever permeated the New England States, as well as New York, Pennsylvania and New Jersey, calling upon the

I.W.W. for organizers, and showing a desire to form a revolutionary organization as well as a willingness to use revolutionary weapons.[1]

The Little Falls strike followed and was almost at its height when twenty-five thousand silk workers of Paterson arose in revolt and struck.[2]

For years previous to this strike, Paterson had been called by the capitalists "the hot bed of anarchy;" special laws had been passed to prosecute anyone advocating anarchistic principles; those laws were revived and came in most advantageously when the bosses found that the strike had been called by the Industrial Workers of the World.[3]

It is true that the Italian anarchists had been working among the silk workers for years, sowing the seeds of dissatisfaction and rebellion against their slavery, and when the strike was called this small minority formed the backbone of the strike, which gave to it most of its revolutionary momentum.

While there was this small revolutionary element, most ably led and advised by Carlo Tresca,[4] the larger part of the workers had just emerged from the conservative American Federation of Labor, which accounts for many of the inconsistencies shown throughout the strike.[5]

Had the conservative element co-operated with the revolutionists, they would have had not only Paterson, but all Northern Jersey aflame in revolt, for workers in this vicinity were found to be surprisingly sympathetic.

The New York Silk Workers, including College Point, Hoboken, Long Island City and other towns, added over twelve thousand men and women to the ranks of the Paterson strikers.[6] Though not generally recognized, nor given much publicity, they really occupied a most strategic position, for their return to work would have enabled the manufacturers to fill their orders in the New York mills, which would have meant absolute defeat for their Paterson comrades.

There is no doubt that the capitalists in America had become alarmed at the radical trend the labor movement in general had taken, and the I.W.W. in particular. This knowledge caused the National Manufacturers Association to concentrate their efforts in the Paterson strike situation.[7] They realized that the growth of this organization which had for its slogan "the abolition of the wage system" must be fought and checked at all costs, for its growth meant absolute ruin, and subsequent control of the industries by the workers.

Accordingly they armed themselves to the hilt in preparation for a fight, expecting a repetition of the spirit prevalent in all previous I.W.W. fights. They controlled the press both local and general; intimidated the smaller manufacturers to hold out; indicted the leaders, Wm. D. Haywood,[8] Carlo Tresca, Elizabeth Gurley Flynn,[9] Adolph Lessig[10] and Frederick Sumner Boyd;[11] confiscated the "Passaic Weekly" and arrested its editor, Alexander Scott because he criticised the Paterson police. He was tried and sentenced to imprisonment for a term of seven years.[12] They denied the workers the rights of free speech and assemblage (through their tools, the police and courts), arrested the strikers in numbers while doing picket duty, on the slightest pretext, and finally closed the halls which the strikers had used for their meeting places.

They used any weapon they found necessary to accomplish their ends.

On the other hand the silk workers did not use their best weapons, they aimed to have a peaceful strike, and took the advice of the leaders who told them they could win their strike "by keeping their hands in their pockets," thereby keeping the "mills idle." They avoided many clashes with the police which might have brought out the militia, thereby intensifying the situation by burdening the taxpayer so that pressure be brought upon the bosses and an earlier settlement made.

They also delegated to lawyers[13] the task of regaining their rights of free speech and assemblage, instead of fighting directly to regain them, which action nullified (as far as Paterson is concerned) the work of the I.W.W. and all that it has fought for in its free speech fights in the West.

The veteran free speech fighters sent word they were ready to back up the Paterson workers if called upon—they were not called.[14] In the early work of the strike, thugs and detectives were sent into Paterson to help the police, and in one encounter in the vicinity of the mills, a man named Valentino Modestino, not a striker but a sympathizer, was shot and killed by the detectives as he sat on his door-step looking on. The strikers came out in mass and joined the funeral procession and followed their comrade to the grave. In passing it is interesting to note that this body of workers, belonging to a most revolutionary organization, entered the Roman Catholic Church for the funeral service, and, using the statues of the saints and Virgin Mary as racks for their hats, quietly passed out again.[15]

At the grave Carlo Tresca delivered the funeral oration in Italian, in a part of which he called upon the working class to "take blood for blood and life for life."

After this arrangements were made to send the children of the strikers to friends and sympathizers in New York to be cared for until the strike was over. About two hundred and fifty little ones left their parents, and in large motor trucks were brought singing and shouting to what they called their "strike mothers," and were tenderly cared for until the parents returned to work.[16]

The great psychological moment came when the police refused the strikers entrance to their regular meeting places, Turn and Helvetia Halls. That day the strike was lost (though it lasted months longer) for when Patrick Quinlan, one of the leaders, swung to the front and shouted, "On to Haledon boys," they went, followed like sheep.[17]

Haledon is a nearby village under Socialist administration which of course willingly allowed meetings to be held in the open air, but the fact remains that the I.W.W., an organization advocating direct action, had to flee for protection to political Socialism for free speech and assemblage when it should have taken and held them in Paterson where the twenty-five thousand workers toiled and lived. Had the leaders not advocated the "hands in your pockets" programme they might have done it.

Up to this time the police and press of Paterson as well as the bosses and capitalists elsewhere were anxious and feared the strength and tactics of the I.W.W., but here they found an army of twenty-five thousand sturdy men and women against one hundred police who practiced passive resistance. They were no longer feared.

Although large and enthusiastic meetings were held each Sunday at Haledon, these meetings really weakened the strike for they transferred the centre of interest from industrial Paterson to political Haledon and prevented the strikers from depending on their own force for their victory.

Had there been a definite trap set for the purpose of deferring the I.W.W. from its principles, it could not have been better planned. It is here that leadership if it means anything to the workers should have counted. Had they been clear in their methods or visions, they would not have complicated and confused the issues by pandering to that dead letter thing—public opinion, for, according to the I.W.W. preamble, "The Working Class and the Employing Class have nothing in common,"[18] then surely their opinion means nothing to the workers, and should be ignored. Again, had the leaders awakened the workers to the use of their economic power, and injected in them the spirit of revolt against all powers of oppression, they would have acted otherwise.

The strike committee was fully as cautious, fearing lest public opinion be against them, and when Frederick Sumner Boyd spoke on the Stars and Stripes, and told them that the stars on the flag meant the badges of the policemen's uniforms, and the stripes were symbols of the prison bars, he was requested by the committee not to speak again. He also was arrested and indicted and sentenced to from one to seven years.[19]

There was a splendid spirit of solidarity among these workers; they did everything in large numbers; they picketed by the thousands; were arrested by the hundreds, filling the jails and refusing to pay fines; organized their own orchestras and bands; whenever there was anything occurring which concerned the strikers they turned out by the thousands.

There were various nationalities among them, Italians, German, Polish, etc., a very large percentage being English speaking. These nationalities vied with each other in their loyalty to their cause and each prided itself that it would not be the first to break the ranks.

Nothing could break them, not even the A.F. of L. who sent organizers into Paterson with rosy promises of an easy settlement. These were hooted and laughed out of town.

There was a meeting held at the armory by the A.F. of L. organizers, John Golden and Sarah Conboy.[20] The strikers filled the place and laughed at their promises until the police entered and cleared the place. It filled again with the same result, but Golden and Conboy could not break that solidarity.

One of the most beautiful demonstrations ever seen in Paterson was the May Day Parade with the women strikers and children dressed in bright red or in white with red sashes and caps. It was one procession of brilliancy, while here and there among the men was the red flag.

On the 7th of June a thousand men and women strikers came from Paterson to New York to produce the scenes at Madison Square Garden in the form of a Pageant. This was the first time a strike had been presented in the form of a pageant in America. There had been no rehearsing of the parts. These men and women portraying their lives as they lived them; there was a spirit among them not to be forgotten and the enthusiasm of the audience which filled the Garden to its fullest capacity was tremendous.[21] After five months they made individual settlements, some making slight gains, while others gained nothing.[22]

At the Tom Mann meeting in New York shortly after the striker's return to work, Wm. D. Haywood, one of the prominent leaders stated that the strike was not lost, but had just begun.[23] This has been so in the past I.W.W. strikes, for the propaganda at the time of strikes has been of the kind that never dies, and it is sincerely to be hoped that the Paterson strikers have given the hands-in-your-pockets fallacy and passive resistance tactics their last chance, and understand that if a general strike were possible in the textile industries of the country, then to keep the mills idle would be sufficient violence to do all that was necessary to win a strike, but when the workmen know that there is no dearth of their own production visible in the markets, if realized there were numerous silk mills working whose location was unknown, then the time comes for tactics of a different character; they should then aim to make the strike swift in action and of short duration, or return to work for the purpose of sabotage or carrying on intermittent strikes.

The I.W.W. has for its object the building of a new society. It is not merely a labor organization aiming only at a fatter pay envelope and a shorter working day, but it is a historical movement of the workers toward their own emancipation from all slavery. It is an effort to create a new society based on their industries alone, where state or government control shall not exist, but instead a voluntary co-operation of industrial unions creating a new psychology, new literature, new art, and relegating to the junk heap all present day symbols of their slavery.

The Revolutionary Almanac, 1914, 47–49 (*MSM* C16:68–70).

1. The IWW had supported successful strikes in Lowell and New Bedford, Massachusetts, as well as Hazleton, Pennsylvania, and its threat to launch additional strikes helped textile workers win wage hikes in Salem and Fall River, Massachusetts. (Tripp, *I.W.W. and the Paterson Strike,* xi, 34–35; Golin, *Fragile Bridge,* 44, 206–7.)

2. Since the Little Falls, New York, strike ended on January 4, 1913, almost two months before the Paterson workers struck, MS may have been referring to the Hazleton strike, which began early in February 1913. (Robert E. Snyder, "Women, Wobblies and Workers' Rights: The Textile Strike at Little Falls, New York," in *At the Point of Production: The Local History of the I.W.W.,* ed. Joseph R. Conlin [Westport, Conn., 1981], 27–48.)

3. Paterson's reputation as a radical center stemmed from the large number of Italian anarchists who settled there to escape political persecution in the 1890s, among them Gaetano Bresci, who in 1900 assassinated King Humbert of Italy. Antiradical, nativist feelings in Paterson intensified after a 1902 walkout by Italian dye workers led to violent rioting. This resulted in the passage of a 1902 statute aimed at anarchists, making it a crime to malign the state or federal government, which was used against IWW leaders during the 1913 strike. (James D. Osborne, "Paterson: Immigrant Strikers and the War of 1913," in *At the Point of Production,* ed. Conlin, 68–69; Golin, *Fragile Bridge,* 13–15; Tripp, *I.W.W. and the Paterson Strike,* 127.)

4. Carlo Tresca (1879–1943) was a well-born Italian radical socialist, labor activist, and journalist who immigrated to the United States in 1904. Tresca was involved in a number of IWW strikes. In Paterson, he played a critical role in controlling and maintaining discipline among the traditionally militant Italian dye helpers, one of the key striking groups. (*ANB;* Golin, *Fragile Bridge,* 28–29.)

5. The more conservative American Federation of Labor (AFL) had earlier attempted to organize Paterson's broad-silk weavers and incorporate them into the United Textile Workers (UTW), but the weavers rejected AFL leadership and turned to the IWW. MS attributed the lack of militancy among Paterson strikers to the AFL's influence. (Golin, *Fragile Bridge,* 28, 84–87, 141–42, 207–8.)

6. Approximately 12,000 silk workers struck in sympathy with the Paterson strikers, including some 6,000 ribbon workers from New York and some 6,000 workers from the Schwarzenbach-Huber Company (Hoboken, West Hoboken, and Union Hill, N.J.). (Golin, *Fragile Bridge,* 45; *New York Times,* May 3, 1913; Tripp, *I.W.W. and the Paterson Strike,* 71–72, 92.)

7. The National Association of Manufacturers, organized in 1895, sought to offset the growth of organized labor by combining to fight both collective bargaining and union recognition. (Samuel B. Hays, *The Response to Industrialism, 1895–1914,* 2d ed. [Chicago, 1995], 89–90.)

8. William Haywood arrived in Paterson on March 7, 1913, to reinforce solidarity among the strikers. He was arrested on March 30, along with Adolph Lessig, and charged with unlawful assembly and disorderly conduct. He was released on April 5, but was rearrested on April 29 for inciting to riot. (Tripp, *I.W.W. and the Paterson Strike,* 99–100; Carlson, *Roughneck,* 193–200; *New York Call,* Apr. 8, 1913; *New York Times,* Mar. 30, Apr. 6, and Apr. 29, 1913; Golin, *Fragile Bridge,* 41, 53, 80.)

9. Elizabeth Gurley Flynn (1890–1964), who had first worked with MS during the Lawrence strike, was arrested in Paterson on February 25, along with Carlo Tresca and others, on charges of "inciting to riot." Their arrests outraged the fifteen hundred strikers

waiting outside; police responded to their protests by clubbing hundreds of them. Flynn was arrested again at the end of April, along with Haywood, Tresca, and Patrick Quinlan. Unlike Haywood, Flynn did try to spur the strikers into confronting authorities, hoping this would produce the same results it had in Lawrence, though she, too, refused to overtly encourage violence. (*NAW; New York Times,* Feb. 26, 1913 [quote]; Tripp, *I. W. W. and the Paterson Strike,* 68–77, 158, 164–5; Golin, "Defeat Becomes Disaster," 228–31.)

10. Adolph Lessig (1872–1935), a German-speaking broad-silk weaver and strike leader, warned Paterson strikers of the risks of violent confrontation. He was arrested with Haywood and Carlo Tresca on March 30. (*New York Times,* Aug. 13, 1935; Golin, *Fragile Bridge,* 40, 53–55, 213–14, 246; Dubofsky, *We Shall Be All,* 277; Tripp, *I. W. W. and the Paterson Strike,* 85–86.)

11. Frederick Sumner Boyd (ca. 1885–1937), a British-born socialist street speaker and labor organizer, joined the IWW during the 1912 Lawrence strike. He was arrested on June 14, 1913, during a police crackdown on outside agitators. (Granville Hicks, *John Reed: The Making of a Revolutionary* [New York, 1936], 111; Tripp, *I. W. W. and the Paterson Strike,* 101–5; Mercedes Boyle to Granville Hicks, Mar. 25, 1937 [GHP].)

12. The *Passaic Weekly Issue,* edited by Alexander Scott, was the official organ of the Passaic County Socialist Party and the only paper that supported the strikers. On February 28, 1913, after one of Scott's editorials branded the police "a bunch of drunken cossacks," the paper's offices were raided, and Scott was arrested and charged with criminal libel. He was arrested again on May 18, 1913, for another editorial condemning government actions and charged with violating New Jersey's 1902 anti-anarchist statute. He was convicted on June 3, fined $250, and given a stiff sentence of one to fifteen years. The conviction was later overturned. ("Conviction of Alexander Scott," 10–11; *New York Times,* Mar. 1, May 18, and July 4, 1913, and Apr. 21, 1914; *New York Call,* June 4, 1913; Tripp, *I. W. W. and the Paterson Strike,* 69–72, 165–66.)

13. Among the lawyers who defended Alexander Scott were Henry Marelli, Gustave A. Hunziker, and Henry Carless, a socialist attorney from Newark who appealed Scott's conviction on the grounds that it violated free speech and freedom of the press. ("Conviction of Alexander Scott," 10–11; *New York Call,* June 4, 1913; Tripp, *I. W. W. and the Paterson Strike,* 127–28.)

14. The IWW had become nationally known beginning in 1909, when it launched a series of "free speech fights" in the West and attacked local laws passed to silence radical propaganda. The "veteran free speech fighters" were not identified. (Joseph R. Conlin, *Bread and Roses Too: Studies of the Wobblies* [Westport, Conn., 1969], 3–8; Tripp, *I. W. W. and the Paterson Strike,* 35.)

15. Modestino Valentino (1888?–1913), whose name was variously recorded in the press, was shot on April 17 during an altercation between private detectives and strikers. The IWW turned Valentino's April 22 funeral into a political statement; a procession of 5,000–15,000 strikers marched to the Laurel Grove Cemetery and deposited red carnations on his grave. (Ellis Island Passenger Ship Database, <www.ellisisland.org>; Golin, *Fragile Bridge,* 79–81; Tripp, *I. W. W. and the Paterson Strike,* 89, 109–10; *Paterson Evening News,* Apr. 23, 1913.)

16. The first group of fifty children was led out of Paterson on May 1, 1913, by MS, Frederick Sumner Boyd, and Jessie Ashley and placed with foster parents. In the following weeks, additional groups were evacuated, but because Paterson police did not try to block

their departure, as the Lawrence police had, the children's crusade did not garner the same level of publicity. (*New York Times,* May 1 and 6, 1913; Tripp, *I. W. W. and the Paterson Strike,* 118–19; Golin, *Fragile Bridge,* 133–35.)

17. Patrick L. Quinlan (1883–1948), an Irish-born socialist and IWW representative, was arrested on February 25, along with Tresca and Flynn, for inciting a riot. On March 2, 1913, after city officials decided to enforce Paterson's blue laws banning Sunday meetings and outlaw outdoor rallies, the first of what would become weekly Sunday mass rallies was held in the nearby town of Haledon, then headed by a Socialist mayor. (John Nicholas Beffel, "Obituary," *Industrial Worker,* Mar. 22, 1948, 4; Tripp, *I. W. W. and the Paterson Strike,* 84–85; Golin, *Fragile Bridge,* 152–53.)

18. This was a quote from the first sentence of the 1905 preamble to the IWW constitution. (Brissenden, *I. W. W.,* appendix 2, 349.)

19. The Central Strike Committee protested Frederick Sumner Boyd's inflammatory March 31, 1913, speech, which encouraged strikers to commit acts of sabotage in the mills, and demanded that he stop speaking to workers. However others, including Flynn and Tresca, defended his right to free speech. On May 23, 1915, after his appeals were denied, Boyd began serving his sentence in Trenton State Prison. Within a few days, he appealed for clemency by denouncing his radicalism. Though his appeal was again denied, Boyd had made serious enemies of his former friends and associates, notably Flynn, who accused him of being an agent provocateur of the government. (Tripp, *I. W. W. and the Paterson Strike,* 101–4.)

20. John Golden (1863–1921), UTW president, tried to break IWW-led strikes in Lawrence and Hazleton; and Sarah McLaughlin Conboy (1871–1928), UTW general organizer, led an AFL-sponsored meeting designed to break the Paterson strike on April 21, 1913. When IWW leaders were denied a platform to speak in rebuttal, the audience voiced its disapproval. Police arrived and forced Haywood, Flynn, and Tresca to leave, but the angry audience refused to listen to Golden and Conboy. (*New York Times,* June 10, 1921, and Apr. 22, 1913; Golin, *Fragile Bridge,* 82–93; Tripp, *I. W. W. and the Paterson Strike,* 113–14.)

21. The pageant was a publicity event dreamed up in April 1913 when a depressed William Haywood told a gathering of intellectual supporters that the strike was deadlocked and that the public was unaware of the struggle. Organized by John Reed, the pageant was staged at Madison Square Garden and consisted of scenes reenacting highlights of the strike, including the May Day parade and the evacuation of the strikers' children. While reaction to the pageant as an artistic production was positive and helped give the strike national publicity, many papers criticized its radical political content. (*New York Times,* May 22, June 8–9, June 24–25, and June 27, 1913; Tripp, *I. W. W. and the Paterson Strike,* 138–54.)

22. The strike began to peter out in July 1913 after the Central Strike Committee held a vote on whether to push for a shop-by-shop settlement instead of adhering to the IWW strategy of holding out for a general agreement. While the majority voted down the shop-by-shop proposal, many of the strikers, tired and hungry, were ready to yield. On July 18, the highly skilled ribbon weavers became the first group to repudiate the Central Strike Committee and accept less than the original demands. Soon other shops joined them. On July 22, the dyer helpers and finishers, the group most loyal to the IWW, returned to work, and the strike was over. (Philip S. Foner, *History of the Labor Movement*

in the United States, vol. 2 [New York, 1965], 367–69; Tripp, *I. W. W. and the Paterson Strike,* 158–62, 171–80.)

23. Tom Mann (1856–1941), a British syndicalist and founder of the British Workers' Union, visited the United States in 1913. In August, he and Haywood spoke to Paterson workers at IWW headquarters on Water Street in New York City. Though supportive of the strike at the time, Mann later published an article in the January 1914 issue of the *International Socialist Review* highly critical of the IWW's focus on economic revolution instead of union organization. (*New York Times,* Mar. 14, 1941; Tripp, *I. W. W. and the Paterson Strike,* 204–5; for Haywood's statement, see the *New York Call,* Aug. 4, 1913, and *Solidarity,* Aug. 9, 1913.)

18. From William Sanger

The Sangers sailed from Boston to Scotland on October 16, spending approximately two weeks in Glasgow before moving on to Paris. Margaret and the children left France on December 24, 1913, leaving William in Paris. He sent at least fifteen handwritten letters to his wife, many of them long, painful, sometimes incoherent expressions of his anguish and bewilderment over the dissolution of their marriage. He also became obsessed with Sanger's affair with Rompapas and her circle of anarchist friends in New York City and in January wrote that she had "advanced sexually—you once said that you would be in different relations as a service for the woman of your time—to all this I have no answer." (See William Sanger's letters to MS [MSM *S1:53–145*]*; for quote, see Jan ?, 1914* [MSM *S1:130*]*.)*

[*Paris, France*]
6th Friday Feb[*y*]—19[14]

Sweetheart

I sort of hesitated in writing the contents of this letter but you ought to know how I feel— I must tell you that I have been working under a terrific mental strain, one thought seems crowding in everlasting and that is when you will finish up with the Greek.[1]

You wrote that you & he were invited out the Hapgood place[2]—thats strange. Why you and he— Is it a fact that you seem to be coupled with his personality— I tell you I must be frank dear heart I know [*their*] ↑(the anarchists)↓ games & thats always to first associate one with one of theirs—& then finally get [*them*] by association.

The same thing might have happened to me when during the last trial of that Spaniard,[3] they tried to get [*that?*] Becky[4] to trot along with me but I soon made them understand that I would have none of their underhand work.

I feel they are playing with your personality, you write that you were invited to "stay over night" with a notorious free lover.[5] I would liked to have read that you wanted to come home rather than you had to come home.

I repeat that ever since your departure this has weighed heavily on my mind—when you told me that this free lover sent over $10[00] for the children[6] I sort of suspected what would occur, and I have not been deceived, and bet that he has played the same cards as last summer when we experienced that chapter of unhappiness & spoiled our stay in Provincetown.[7] He is again—ferreting his way into my family relations—trying to break down, everything I have built up & hold so dear.

You say that you hate to meet people yet you receive his devotion—as your personality is being [*associated*] more & more—as time rolls by.

In the final sum [~~*illegible*~~] ↑up it↓ is you dear heart that can end it once & for all. You told me yourself that he would not care to press his attentions unless they were wanted.

My stay here looks rosy doesnt it, but owing to this ~~black~~ personality [*coming?*] in your life, it has overshadowed the joy of the working here, and many times I retrench my self here alone with my thoughts & myself.

The thought of getting back—into that hell hole of free love promiscuity & prostitution appalls me. I hate all their isms— Perhaps you do not realize dear heart [~~*have keen*~~] ↑how keen↓ has been the mental anguish at times. I cannot change! My family life is in me not an external symptom. As long as their personalities hover around you, they will constantly endeavor to break—to disintegrate our family life—the contradiction we have lived—in trying to mix in with out & out free lovers & expect our relations to remain intact ↑is apparent↓— I know I shall experience the same hell for I am of the family & they don't want that, they want you—your body—to, h—l with our relations—

Here in Paris they wont stand for Prostitution masquerading under the mantle of Revolution—but in N.Y. anything goes. The Havel affair[8] ought to be a lesson. Where was Ethel compromised but in their Den 30 Charles St. where all free love starts, (which has been the scene of most of the Mavro Daphne brawls, [*the atelier?*]).[9]

When my term[10] [*to?*] ends here I shall go. I don't care [*where?*] even before. I might as soon as I have my entries for the Salon[11] in March 15—I cant work under this uncertainty. I rather walk the streets any time— But you [~~*wont*~~] must tell me whether I am really wanted. And if I go home, then it will be a home ↑(which you can make)↓—with you & and the kids—

I'd rather accomplish less & be with you for I cannot live with out you will believe me dear one I know.

The sexual yearning with in me has been strong since your departure—even heightened by the atmosphere all around—the strain at times is terrific—but I have decided to weather it all— Its easy when I think of you. Just think of you & your dear self. If we ever see each other again you will find me the same just the same spiritually & physically.

Do I love you a wee bit? Yes I do. More than a wee bit—sometimes more than you really want— I cannot love but one & built by nature to love just one woman. I feel isolated—when you chill at times I [*mostly?*] feel you are confiding in telling me about these various trips etc—but whether you tell me or not I <u>feel</u> them [*thats?*] all. You are a world Lover who can take recourse to most people. I am <u>not</u>—I am a single Lover—one that has created the [*current?*] anguish which knows no confiding but must be born in silence—I love too deep & not broad enough.— Oh dear love. It cant be just written! I close—dear heart how I could just whisper [*sweetly?*] to you—

Bill

ALS MSP, MN-SSC (*MSM* S1:146–51).

1. He was referring to John Rompapas.
2. None of MS's letters to William Sanger in this period was found. Hutchins Hapgood (1869–1944), a Chicago-born journalist/writer noted for his exercise in bohemian journalism, *The Spirit of the Ghetto* (1910), and his wife, the writer Neith Boyce (1872–1951), were part of the prewar Greenwich Village literary circle with which the Sangers associated. In 1911, the couple settled in Dobbs Ferry, New York, where MS probably visited them in January 1914. (*ANB*)
3. He was referring to a mass meeting held in New York City on December 1, 1912, to protest the trial and imprisonment of Alexander Aldamas, a member of the Marine Firemen's Union, who was arrested for shooting two police officers and a strikebreaker in July 1912. (*New York Call,* Dec. 2, 1912.)
4. This was probably Rebecca (Becky) Edelsohn (Plunkett Crawford) (ca. 1893–1973), a fiery young anarchist who at age fifteen had an affair with Alexander Berkman and became part of Emma Goldman's inner circle. (Avrich, *Modern School Movement,* 189–98, 332; Wexler, *Emma Goldman,* 134; correspondence between editors and Paul Avrich, Nov. 7, 1999.)
5. This was probably another reference to Rompapas. "They" most likely refers to Greenwich Village anarchists and free lovers (whom William Sanger indicts interchangeably), such as Hapgood and Boyce, or more specifically those closely associated with the *Social War* and the *Revolutionary Almanac,* including Rompapas and Mylius. These sexual bohemians sought to free themselves from Victorian moral constraints and the separate sexual standards for men and women.
6. The three Sanger children were then living with MS on Post Avenue in Upper Manhattan. William's decision to devote himself to painting left his family without a steady source of income. (William Sanger to MS, Feb. 25 and Dec. 25, 1914 [*MSM* S1:183 and 349].)
7. During the Sangers' 1913 stay in Provincetown, Rompapas had apparently asked MS to live with him. The move to Paris was, in William Sanger's mind, partly an attempt to save their marriage. He wrote to his wife in early 1915 that "you should have lived with him (J. R.) if it were not for the d—n Catholic tradition you were brought up in. . . ." (William Sanger to MS, Dec. 8, 1914, and Jan. 10, 1915 [*MSM* S1:305 and 371].)
8. This was a reference to Hippolyte Havel (1869–1950), who in 1913 was living with Polly Holladay, owner of Polly's Café, a popular Greenwich Village restaurant. Havel,

though a free love proponent, was jealous and sometimes violent when he found Holladay involved with other men. (Watson, *Strange Bedfellows,* 209; Avrich, *Modern School Movement,* 117–33, 237–38.)

9. 30 Charles Street was Rompapas's Greenwich Village residence in 1913–14. It is not clear what happened to Ethel Byrne, though William Sanger later refers to "the slur put on Eth." Byrne had abandoned her husband and children in Corning, New York, in 1906 to enroll in nursing school at Mt. Sinai Hospital in New York City, where she subsequently worked as a nurse. She never regained custody of her children, who lived with her in-laws, even after the death of her husband in 1913. Mavro Daphne is a sweet Greek wine that Rompapas imported and shared with his friends. Mabel Dodge remembered that Rompapas sent her "cases of delicious, sweet, yellow, Greek wine." (William Sanger to MS, Jan. 22, 1914 [*MSM* S1:90]; Chesler, *Woman of Valor,* 62; Van Voris, "Olive Byrne Richard Interview," 1–2; Luhan, *Movers and Shakers,* 65.)

10. This was probably the lease on his Paris studio.

11. *Le Penseur,* the one painting he entered in the Salon des Artistes Français, was rejected. (William Sanger to MS, Mar. 13 and Apr. 2, 1914 [*MSM* S1:209 and 236].)

19. From William Sanger

Paris [*France*]
March 12, 1914.

Peg Dear Heart

Your two letters arrived[1]—indeed they were epoch-makers in our lives—you stated in clear unmistakable language—what has only heretofore been vaguely expressed—but now is a stern reality both in thought as well as in action—the struggle—yes more than a struggle a soul-combat at Provincetown[2] we had—has grown—to a relation which ~~is~~ ↑favors↓ somewhat of the Platonic—

Somehow I remember you calling my attention to a remark Bill Haywood made last Summer that he didnt care for the personal love—of any body? or just B-[3] I don't know which—however you remember how you somewhat recoiled from the very idea of it—the personal equation you thought must be a part of two lives—linked together so only after less than a year you have changed,—and now—you care not for ~~personal~~ the communion of close personalities—and yet I sent you a little bunch of violets—Oh they will be gone when they arrive—& the note— I shall not recall it!—

Your letters stagger me—I reread them several times today—[*and?*] after it all—I feel queer——and cant just get my bearing in many things on life—but this I know that after eleven years you have arrived where I was—when I first saw your lovely self— I came under the rays of your sunshine basked in the beauty of your mind—revelled in your vivacity your intellect your womanlyness, your very feminine qualities without being effeminate—and to give me the climax of it all—the three precious little ones that I too call my own you have given me—as they grew I came under the only ~~f~~ real family life I ever knew experienced the first home ties— and above it all I saw the sweet & tender aspects of ↑your↓ motherhood—Dear Heart Dear Heart if I came under the spell of your lovely self you as a mother & a helpmate if I became a family man—If came to love children—well—dear it was thru you—your personality set~~s~~ its die deep across my soul—I don't want to erase it—we cannot erase of things that are worth while—in life—

Oh how I hunger to linger in the past our first meeting—the Farquarsons[4]—White Plains & the Hospital—Dusenberry Hill[5]—Hopatkong[6]—and the years after—oh—they were sweet years—and they are beyond recall!!—but sweetheart lets not forget those days—lets ~~sit~~ ↑sit↓ by the road side of life—& linger in those happy hours after all life is tragic as you say—& lets not crush the sweet & the tender they are only too few—

But now you have arrived—you are now to express your self—to [*New York?*] but dear here I am—in the family life altho in Paris—I love to [*illegible*] my thoughts are ever in the bosom of my family—you at the head of the table & with our little ones clustered around—Yes, I pray for you to be the ↑big↓ woman of our generation—& I know you will—that you must be released from the family [*care?*] I know— Dear I want you to have freedom [*free?*] of thought. ↑Indeed you will take it!↓ Oh let your wings of thought flap to the very skies—there is no intellectual height you cannot reach.

I realize that my love has been personal indeed I have adapted myself to your wish as you grew. ~~I came too~~—today I realize that this love you have outgrown—& its either a different love—or a process of further adaptation to your lifes work—In this you can always count on—indeed—I shall always be with you in everything you do for the betterment of your individuality & you're the work—of the Paper—[7] Indeed I shall consider it always a priceless privilege to sit beside you spiritually—that you might express the best that is in your [*expedient?*]. There will be times when it will be trying & hard to stand I know that time will come but it is Just ~~that~~ these times one must weather.

Look at Social War—↑(my baby)↓ how I felt I could have made it hum! at one time in my life—it was dragged down by individuals who were not serious with themselves or any body else. It was used as the personal organ of the Libeler of the King[8]—finally——I return his letters cheerfully—quite cordially.

I said I would send over the Dunes[9] I have no money for it ↑express↓ so must wait until I do. At this writing I am living on borrowed money— That stiff—Fishel[10]—has [*simply?*] taken three months.

You advise me to stay— I have decided to do so—so have not given the city a notice that I will move. I have obligated myself [*to*] at least three months—so if Fishels doesnt come to by the receipt of this letter let me know the facts.

This place is too small for the mine scene which I intend to make 18 feet long—& expect to make the Salon D'Autumne in November with it.[11] However if Lascari[12] goes to Brittany in the Summer it might be that I might use his place.

I am working on another Cartoon[13] for you—but I expect to hear from you on how you like the first one before I send—

How are my babies—I have sent a few things with Samuels[14]—

How is my little flaxen hair Peggy Lou. Does she still "speak French in Paris" & my sweet boy—with his soulful eyes, & Sunny Jim—he doesnt care whether Dad ever came back![15]

I have sent Grant some modelling wax & 3-tools. I could have sent him a small modelling stand—but it was too much ↑to↓ ~~of~~ ask of Samuels.

Do take care Dear Heart—of your self now You are too precious to all of us. Love as ever—

Bill

[*Written by William Sanger along left margin of fifth page*] P.S. Cant just locate this letter and send next letters[16]

ALS MSP, MN-SSC (*MSM* S1:203–8).

1. The letters were not found.

2. Greenwich Village bohemia in the prewar years was imbued with not only psychological jargon but also a mysticism preoccupied with the soul, and it was quite common to find references to "soul mates," "soul fights," "soul struggle," and, in this case, "soul combat" to describe marital conflict. (Keith Richwine, "The Liberal Club: Bohemia and the Resurgence in Greenwich Village, 1912–1918," Ph.D. diss. University of Pennsylvania, 1968, 60.)

3. This was probably B. Shostac, a Greenwich Village schoolteacher whose New York City apartment Bill Haywood shared early in 1913. (Carlson, *Roughneck,* 210–11, 221–23; Watson, *Strange Bedfellows,* 403.)

4. This was a reference to MS's friend Esther Farquharson [Barker], who had moved to San Diego in 1908. (MS to Juliet Rublee, Oct. 21, 1929 [*MSM* C4:1104].)

5. Dusenbery Hill (now called Purdy Hill) was a scenic area in White Plains that had been the site of one of George Washington's encampments. (John Rösch, *Historic White Plains* [Harrison, N.Y., 1976], 45.)

6. Lake Hopatcong was a popular resort in Sussex County, New Jersey, about fifty miles from New York City.

7. In early February, when he first learned of MS's plan to publish a radical journal, he had offered to be a "roving correspondent" or to come back to New York City and work alongside her. Though MS apparently rejected his proposals to collaborate, she

enlisted his help in locating Malthusian, suffrage, socialist, and sex hygiene publications and establishing contacts with Malthusians and fertility-control advocates in Europe. (William Sanger to MS, Feb. 5, 1914 [*MSM* S1:1381].)

8. This was a reference to Edward (Ned) Frederick Mylius (1878–?), a Belgian-born British journalist who fled to the United States after serving a year in an English prison for libeling King George V. He changed his name to E. J. Boskin in 1924. (Avrich, *Modern School Movement,* 117, 373; *New York Times,* Dec. 24, 1912; Mylius to MS, Nov. 30, 1924 [*MSM* S2:824].)

9. William Sanger first painted *Dunes* in Provincetown during the summer of 1913. He worked on several versions of the painting while in Paris in 1914 and sent three of them back to New York later that spring. (William Sanger to MS, Feb. 8 and Mar. 19, 1914 [*MSM* S1:152 and 219].)

10. William Fishel, a furniture dealer, purchased the Sangers' Hastings house sometime in 1911–12. The Sangers held his mortgage and depended on this money to fund their 1913 trip to Europe. (William Sanger to MS, Jan. 11, Mar. 3, Mar. 5, and May 25, 1914 [*MSM* S1:171, 187, 199, and 255]; Gray, *Margaret Sanger,* 36, 48.)

11. William Sanger intended to submit *Mine Scene,* also called *The Night Scene* or *Avalanche,* to the Salon d'Automne, an annual exhibition founded in 1903 as an alternative to the official salon, but he either changed his mind or missed the deadline. (William Sanger to MS, Jan. 5 and Feb. 3, 1914 [*MSM* S1:59 and 132]; Ian Chilvers and Harold Osborne, eds., *The Oxford Dictionary of Art* [Oxford, 1997], 500–501.)

12. Salvatore Lascari (1884–1967) was an American portrait painter and muralist who studied with George De Forest Brush. He befriended the Sangers in Paris in the fall of 1913. (*New York Times,* Mar. 14, 1967; Peter H. Falk, *Who Was Who in American Art* [Madison, Conn., 1985], 317.)

13. He drafted several cartoons to be used in the *Woman Rebel,* but MS opted to publish the paper without illustrations. (William Sanger to MS, Feb. 14 and Mar. 19, 1914 [*MSM* S1:158 and 219].)

14. Arthur Samuels, a friend from the Ferrer School, where he served as treasurer from 1913 to 1915, carried gifts to New York City from William Sanger to his children. He may also have delivered British suffragist and radical papers to MS. (William Sanger to MS, Feb. 14, Mar. 3, and Mar. 5, 1914 [*MSM* S1:163, 187, and 199]; Avrich, *Modern School Movement,* 131.)

15. These were references to Peggy, Grant, and Stuart. "Sunny Jim" was a nickname often used as an informal term for a young man.

16. He was referring to letters from Edward Mylius to MS, possibly including one on February 24, 1914 (*MSM* S1:181); the other letters were not found.

THREE

The Woman Rebel

In March 1914, Margaret Sanger published the first issue of the *Woman Rebel,* an eight-page "monthly paper of militant thought," designed and written from her New York apartment.[1] In a series of declarations and imperatives strung together into short editorials, Sanger urged women to fight gender oppression, prodding her readers to "look the whole world in the face with a go-to-hell look in the eye; to have an ideal; to speak and act in defiance of convention."[2] The paper included articles by a variety of contributors on labor strife, marriage, prostitution, and notable woman rebels of the past. It was fiery, aggressively defiant, and frequently sarcastic and vindictive. The *Masses* editor Max Eastman wrote critically of the first number: "The Woman Rebel has fallen into that most unfeminist of errors, the tendency to cry out when a quiet and contained utterance is indispensable."[3]

After the defeat at Paterson in August 1913, Sanger, like so many associated with that strike, was frustrated, angry, and casting about for a place to channel her passion and energy for radical social change. By 1914, she was ready to speak directly to working women, who she decided held the key to working-class empowerment. The axiomatic conclusion that uncontrolled fertility oppressed working-women was an idea she derived from other radicals, notably the anarchists Emma Goldman and Victor Dave. Her belief that women had little reproductive choice because of their limited access to contraceptive information stemmed from her experiences as a nurse, socialist, and labor organizer. But these were part of a more systematic argument informed by her associations with anarchists and leftist radical activists. For Sanger, the smooth functioning of capitalism, the state, and its institutions—the factory, the public school, the insane asylum—depended on the unregulated breeding of the masses. The most revolutionary act for an individual woman was to control her own reproduction and thus limit the number of children she fed into the capitalist state.[4]

Sanger probably conceived of the *Woman Rebel* shortly after she returned to New York, effectively postponing her plans to write a book on sex hygiene. She met with Edward Mylius, John Rompapas, and other anarchist friends, many of whom had significant experience in publishing radical journals and pamphlets. By May or June, they had coined the term *birth control* as an alternative to the more passive expressions commonly used to describe contraception, such as *family limitation.*[5]

Determined to use the paper to spark a revolution among working-class women, Sanger fired off lists of women's rights; endorsed direct action tactics, including violent labor strikes; and compiled anecdotes to illustrate capitalist gluttony and worker enslavement. While Sanger endorsed birth control in the early issues of the *Woman Rebel,* it was not until the summer of 1914, following repeated attempts by the post office to suppress the publication for its advocacy of birth control, that she decided to wage a free speech battle and test the laws that prevented the distribution of birth control information. Ensuing issues of the *Woman Rebel* included pieces on birth control, neo-Malthusianism, motherhood, sexual liberation, and abortion, as well as censorship. Sanger also revived her 1913 plan to write a book on sex hygiene and began drafting *Family Limitation,* a sixteen-page pamphlet that contained the kind of explicit birth control information she had withheld from the *Woman Rebel.*[6]

Although years later she claimed the *Woman Rebel* was a one-woman endeavor—and it was emphatically Margaret Sanger's paper—she was aided by her close circle of radical friends, particularly Mylius; the birth control activist Otto Bobsien, who wrote short pieces for the *Woman Rebel* and most likely assisted her in its production; and John Rompapas, who probably helped fund it. She also received considerable guidance from Victor Dave and William Sanger, both in Paris.[7] Dave, who had been closely associated with leading anarchist publications in Europe, advised Margaret Sanger (via William Sanger's letters to his wife) to publish the *Woman Rebel* as a monthly rather than a weekly journal of international scope. He put her in touch with leading European Malthusians who advocated population control through contraception, as well as women's rights agitators and anarchist sympathizers. William Sanger, who helped collect European materials on sex hygiene and birth control, advised his wife to proceed cautiously, warning her that she would be "put away" for discussing "new Malthusianism" and "prevention of conception."[8]

Margaret Sanger published seven issues of the *Woman Rebel*, six of which were suppressed by the post office. Despite these actions (or more likely because of them), the *Woman Rebel* quickly gained a widespread national audience among feminists and leftists. It achieved a subscription base of about two thousand through notices in radical publications, leaflets (a year's subscription cost $1.00; $.50 for six-months), and large bundles sent to radical groups, labor organizations, and individuals for distribution at meetings and rallies. In August 1914, the federal government indicted Sanger for publishing obscene material, and in October, fearing conviction, she abandoned the journal and fled the country. Nevertheless, the *Woman Rebel* gave Sanger a forum to experiment with rough-hewn radical ideas and test the strength of her own commitment to a single issue—birth control—that ultimately transcended class. This chapter contains several of Sanger's *Woman Rebel* editorials and articles as well as her response to the efforts of authorities to suppress it.

NOTES

1. For a facsimile edition of the *Woman Rebel*, see Alex Baskin, ed., *Margaret Sanger, the Woman Rebel* (New York, 1976), or *MSM* C16:515–63.
2. MS, "Aim"; MS, "Why the Woman Rebel?" Mar. 1914, herein; MS, "A Woman's Duty," *Woman Rebel*, Mar. 1914, 1, 8 (*MSM* C16:515, 522).
3. Max Eastman, "The Woman Rebel," *Masses*, May 1914, 1.
4. MS, "Why the Woman Rebel?" Mar. 1914, herein.
5. Otto Bobsien to MS, Oct. 25, 1953 (*MSM* S41:956).
6. MS, "Aim," 1.
7. William Sanger to MS, Feb.–Mar. 1914 (*MSM* S1:138–87).
8. William Sanger to MS, Mar. 3, 1914 (*MSM* S1:187).

20. "Why the Woman Rebel?"

This article was published on the last page of the first issue of the Woman Rebel.

[*March 1914*]

Because I believe that deep down in woman's nature lies slumbering the spirit of revolt.

Because I believe that woman is enslaved by the world machine, by sex conventions, by motherhood and its present necessary child-rearing, by wage-slavery, by middle-class morality, by customs, laws and superstitions.

Because I believe that woman's freedom depends upon awakening that spirit of revolt within her against these things which enslave her.

Because I believe that these things which enslave woman must be fought openly, fearlessly, consciously.

Because I believe she must consciously disturb and destroy and be fearless in its accomplishment.

Because I believe in freedom, created through individual action.

Because I believe in the offspring of the immigrant, the great majority of whom make up the unorganized working class to-day.

Because I believe that this immigrant with a vision, an ideal of a new world where liberty, freedom, kindness, plenty hold sway, who had courage to leave the certain old for the uncertain new to face a strange new people, new habits, a strange language, for this vision, this ideal, certainly has brought to this country a wholesome spirit of unrest which this generation of Americans has lost through a few generations of prosperity and respectability.

Because I believe that on the courage, vision and idealism of the immigrant and the offspring does the industrial revolution depend.

Because I believe that through the efforts of the industrial revolution will woman's freedom emerge.

Because I believe that not until wage slavery is abolished can either woman's or man's freedom be fully attained.

Because I have six months' time to devote to arousing this slumbered spirit in the working woman, and if within this time I shall have succeeded in arousing my own laggard self I shall have succeeded sufficiently to continue this paper until all the slumbered spirits have awakened to its assistance or its destruction.

Woman Rebel, Mar. 1914, 8 (*MSM* C16:522).

21. "The Prevention of Conception"

[*March 1914*]

Is there any reason why women should not receive clean, harmless, scientific knowledge on how to prevent conception? Everybody is aware that the old, stupid fallacy that such knowledge will cause a girl to enter into prostitution has long been shattered. Seldom does a prostitute become pregnant. Seldom does the girl practicing promiscuity become pregnant.[1] The woman of the upper middle class have all available knowledge and implements to prevent conception. The woman of the lower middle class is struggling for this knowledge.[2] She tries various methods of prevention, and after a few years of experience plus medical advice succeeds in discovering some method suitable to her individual self. The woman of the people is the only one left in ignorance of this information. Her neighbors, relatives and friends tell her stories of special devices and the success of them all. They tell her also of the blood-sucking men with M.D. after their names who perform operations for the price of so-and-so.[3] But the working woman's purse is thin. Its far cheaper to have a baby, "though God knows what it will do after it gets here." Then, too, all other classes of women live in places where there is at least a semblance of privacy and sanitation. It is easier for them to care for themselves whereas the large majority of the women of the people have no bathing or sanitary conveniences. This accounts too for the fact that the higher the standard of living, the more care can be taken and fewer children result. No plagues, famines or wars could ever frighten the capitalist class so much as the universal practice of the prevention of conception. On the other hand no better method could be utilized for increasing the wages of the workers.

As is well known, a law exists forbidding the imparting of information on this subject, the penalty being several years' imprisonment.[4] Is it not the time to defy this law? And what fitter place could be found than in the pages of the WOMAN REBEL?[5]

Woman Rebel, Mar. 1914, 8 (*MSM* C16:522).

1. The prevailing view on this matter rested on supposition, not science. Regarding prostitutes, Dr. William W. Sanger (no relation), a nineteenth-century researcher who investigated the reasons women entered the sex trade, wrote, "It is generally imagined that the excessive action of the generative organs interferes with the power of procreation in common women." Although the hypothesis was challenged during this period, it was neither definitively nor popularly debunked. (William W. Sanger, *The History of Prostitution: Its Extent, Causes and Effects* [New York, 1858, 1937], 213.)

2. MS's assertion that upper- and middle-class women had greater access to contraception than working-class women is borne out by the dramatic decline in middle- and upper-class family size after 1850. Moreover, contraceptive advertisements and informational literature, which proliferated openly in early nineteenth-century newspapers, periodicals, and circulars, became more narrowly circulated, less direct, and more confusing after 1873 as advertisers and publishers sought to circumvent the Comstock laws. Information on the safest methods, pharmacological ingredients, and devices remained available to those with resources or access to physicians willing to prescribe them. While the vast majority of all women continued to rely on traditional male-controlled forms of contraception, such as withdrawal and condoms, middle- and upper-class women were more likely to use safer and more effective methods (pessaries, douches, and sponges), methods more likely to fail among those in the poorer classes who lacked indoor plumbing, proper hygiene, and privacy. (Gordon, *Woman's Body,* 60–70; Brodie, *Contraception and Abortion,* 190–94, 281–88.)

3. After the nineteenth-century campaign to criminalize abortion led to the passage of anti-abortion laws in almost every state, midwives and lay practitioners were driven out of the field, and fewer physicians were willing to risk prosecution for performing the procedure. Many who did were either elderly and uninformed about new techniques or young and inexperienced. In either case, many physicians were now so poorly trained in abortion procedures that their patients ran increased risks of complications, such as

perforated uteruses and septicemia. Women were increasingly forced to rely on these marginal physicians or turn to the unlicensed and increasingly unqualified professional abortionists. (Shorter, *History of Women's Bodies,* 207; James C. Mohr, *Abortion in America: The Origins and Evolution of National Policy* [New York, 1978], 95.)

4. In 1873, Congress passed Section 211 of the U.S. Criminal Code (the Comstock Act), which revised the prohibitions on mailing obscene materials and included in that category "matter of a character tending to incite arson, murder, or assassination," as well as articles and information "designed, adapted or intended for preventing conception or producing abortion." Violations of the Comstock Act were misdemeanors punishable by one to ten years of hard labor for each offense. (*U.S. Code of Laws,* 259–60.)

5. Although she advocated birth control, MS never provided specific contraceptive information in the *Woman Rebel.*

22. *From Edward M. Morgan and Thomas F. Murphy*[1]

Under Section 480 of the Postal Laws and Regulations regarding obscene materials, local postmasters were required to contact the assistant attorney general for the Post Office Department for a ruling on whether specific matter deposited in the mail was obscene under Section 211 of the U.S. Criminal Code and therefore unmailable. The assistant attorney general could suppress individual issues of a publication, as in the case of the Woman Rebel, *or he could shut down an entire publication.*

New York, New York
April 2, 1914

Dear Madam:

In accordance with advice from the Assistant Attorney General for the Post Office Department,[2] you are informed that the publication entitled "The Woman Rebel", for March 1914, is unmailable under the provisions of Section 211 of the Criminal Code as amended by the Act of March 4, 1911.[3]

Copies of the March 1914 issue found in the mail are held at Washington Bridge Station of the New York Post Office where they may be obtained by calling for the same and exhibiting this letter.[4] Very respectfully,

E. M. Morgan [*stamped*]
Postmaster
Per Th. F. Murphy [*signed*]
Assistant Postmaster

TLS MSP, DLC (LCM 11:198). Letterhead of the Office of the Postmaster, U.S. Post Office. Addressed to "Publisher of 'The Woman Rebel,' 34 Post Avenue, New York, N.Y."

1. Edward M. Morgan (1855–1925) and Thomas F. Murphy were appointed to the positions of postmaster and assistant postmaster, respectively, in New York City in 1907. (*New York Times,* July 13, 1921, and Jan. 9, 1925.)

2. On March 28, 1914, the New York City post office confiscated several copies of the March issue of the *Woman Rebel.* Morgan referred the journal, with offending portions marked, to William Lamar (1859–1921), the assistant attorney general for the Post Office Department, for a ruling. Lamar declared the issue unmailable on March 31, 1914. It appears that Postmaster Morgan hoped to suppress the entire publication, but Lamar was reluctant to do so. (*WWW America;* see Morgan to Lamar, Mar. 28, May 29, and Aug. 14, 1914, and Lamar to Morgan, Mar. 31 and June 2, 1914 [POR].)

3. The revised provisions of Section 211 added to the prohibition on distributing contraceptive information by also banning efforts to promote the use of contraception or abortion or to provide any information about where or how abortions and contraception could be obtained. (*U.S. Code of Laws,* 486–87.)

4. Bertram Wolfe, a former postal employee, recalled being ordered one day in April 1914 to hold up to the light all second- and third-class mail, as well as newspapers and magazines in circular wrappers, to see if another piece of mail was enclosed. He was told by his supervisor, "We're looking for copies of an eight-page sheet called *The Woman Rebel.* . . . The solicitor has declared it obscene and unmailable . . . , but the bitch who edits it, name of Margaret Sanger, . . . has been trying to fool us by mailing it wrapped up in respectable newspapers and magazines. . . . *Don't let any get through!*" (Bertram Wolfe, *A Life in Two Centuries* [New York, 1981], 27.)

23. *From Emma Goldman*[1]

Chicago, [*Ill.*]
April the Ninth, 1914.

My dear Margaret:—

So the thing has happened before you have at all started on the way! But, then, we might have expected it, from the stupidity of the postal department. I only hope that it will prove a false alarm, because the law pertaining to "obscene" literature embraces almost every channel of distribution—the express and freight, and also those who circulate or sell so-called objectionable matter. Therefore, it would be almost impossible for you to continue the "Woman Rebel," if the authorities place their damnable seal upon it. However, meanwhile, I am pushing the paper all I can.[2]

By the way, the first bundle contained only 37, and not 50 copies.

Let me know what your agent's prices are. You can send me another hundred by express to this city, and if you have sufficient copies on hand you may ship 200 to Denver to Julia May Courtney, 617 Fourteenth St.[3]

It is too bad that you did not get out a very large edition of the first number,[4] as we would at least have been able to circularize the first attempt, and thus arouse enough sympathy and interest.

I know you will be amused to learn that most of the women are up in arms against your paper; mostly women, of course, whose emancipation has been on paper and not in reality.[5] I am kept busy answering questions as to your "brazen" method. They would not believe me when I told them that you were a little, delicate woman, refined and shrinking, but that you did believe in the daring and courage of woman in her struggle for freedom.

I am having good and interesting meetings and shall stay in this city all of next week. Write me again soon. I am keeping posted about the brutalities in New York.[6] One so long in the revolutionary struggle as I have been is no longer surprised at anything that the police will do, but it is a pity that our boys must always be the victims. With much love.

Emma [*signed*]

TLS MSP, DLC (LCM 8:877). Letterhead of the Lexington Hotel. A marginal note at the top left added by an unidentified author reads, "200 copies sent to Denver." Addressed to "34 Post Ave., New York City."

1. One of the earliest advocates of family limitation, Goldman exerted a strong influence on MS's growing conviction that family limitation was a critical tool for working-class empowerment. MS met the notable anarchist at Mabel Dodge's Greenwich Village salon around 1911–12. (MS, *Autobiography,* 72–73; Wexler, *Emma Goldman,* 201.)
2. Goldman promoted and sold copies of the *Woman Rebel* during her April–August 1914 national lecture tour. (Wexler, *Emma Goldman,* 211.)
3. Julia May Courtney (Wey) (1873–1951), a chiropractor and poet, was part of Goldman's Denver circle of friends. (*Denver Post,* Apr. 27, 1951.)
4. The subscription list for the *Woman Rebel* numbered several hundred names before the first issue went to the printers, but it is not clear how many copies were printed or how many were confiscated by postal authorities. (MS, *Autobiography,* 109.)
5. In addition to the many nonsocialist suffragists who recoiled at MS's radicalism, some women on the left resented her indictment of "new feminists," including such groups as the Feminist Alliance in New York City, which she claimed were bound by "bourgeois convention" and were indifferent to the working class. The first issue of the journal also advocated violence as indispensable to achieving economic liberation and called for nothing less than a social revolution to fully liberate women—radical ultimatums that undoubtedly antagonized even many socialist readers. (MS, "New Feminists.")
6. She was most likely referring to an April 4 Union Square rally held by the Central Federation of Labor, at which over six thousand IWW activists demonstrated. Police clubbed the demonstrators and arrested nine ringleaders. (*New York Times,* Apr. 5, 1914.)

24. "HUMBLE PIE"

[*April 1914*]

The Postmaster did not like the first number of the WOMAN REBEL. He even took the trouble to tell the WOMAN REBEL so. He advised her not to send any more copies through the United States mails. He said the WOMAN REBEL was unmailable under Section 211 of the Criminal Code, as amended by the act of March 4, 1911.[1] Of course the Postmaster was acting within his rights. He is empowered by the federal government to stop the circulation of any printed expression of honest convictions. It is a crime to have honest convictions in these United States. It is a crime to express them publicly. It is a crime to send them through the mails. Therefore the WOMAN REBEL has not yet been informed which of her views were so displeasing to the Postmaster, but whatever they were, she hastens to agree with the Postmaster that she was absolutely mistaken in these views.[2] She realizes that the Postoffice is always "right," since it has the monopolized POWER to enforce that "right." Therefore the WOMAN REBEL, humbled and repentant, curtseys coyly to the Postmaster and apologizes for the expression of any opinion that is unmailable under Section 211 of the Criminal Code as amended by the act of March 4, 1911.

The WOMAN REBEL has decided to be patriotic. It pays, you know. If, last month, the WOMAN REBEL suggested "race control" the daily papers discreetly expressed the problem, this month she switches over for large families, like Mr. Roosevelt.[3] This great and glorious country needs children—to uphold its great and glorious industrial system, its great and glorious public schools, its great and glorious silk mills and mush factories, its great and glorious, its magnificently equipped, and efficiently conducted asylums for the insane and feeble-minded, its reformatories and juvenile courts, its noble slums. Let us sing "My Country, 'Tis of Thee!" And "My Country 'Tis of Thee" is mailable under Section 211 of the Criminal Code as amended by the act of March 4, 1911.

In order to comply with the rules and regulations of the government, the WOMAN REBEL may be forced to become indecent and to advocate a total ignorance of Sexual Hygiene for woman. As the purpose of the WOMAN REBEL is to stimulate her readers **to think for themselves,** and to act according to their own convictions, let them be not surprised or dismayed at her mildness and meekness this month. Mildness and meekness, the attributes of a feeble mentality, are mailable according to Section 211 of the Criminal Code as amended by the act of March 4, 1911. This suppression may not be as important to you as to us, for you are not suppressed. Do not forget that you have a voice to protest and fight against a censorship that is busy suppressing scientific truths that the working people are demanding.

Woman Rebel, Apr. 1914, 9 (*MSM* C16:523).

1. See Morgan and Murphy to MS, Apr. 2, 1914, herein; see also Morgan to MS, Apr. 7, 1914 (LCM 11:197).

2. MS apparently sent a letter to postal authorities asking them to specify which articles violated the law. Only a draft of this letter exists, written on the back of Morgan's April 2 letter, possibly drafted for MS by Leonard Abbott on April 4 and mailed April 5. Officials would not provide her with this information. (Morgan to MS, Apr. 7, and MS to Morgan, Apr. 4, 1914 [LCM 11:197 and 199].)

3. Theodore Roosevelt (1858–1919), the twenty-sixth president of the United States (1901–9), was one of the better-known proponents of "race suicide," which linked declining birthrates among the white middle class to the dilution of white stock and characterized middle-class white women who used contraceptives as selfish and decadent. The father of six children, Roosevelt recommended that unless families produced at least four children, the "whole race will disappear in a very few generations." (*ANB;* Gordon, *Woman's Body,* 136–42; Theodore Roosevelt, "A Premium on Race Suicide," *Outlook,* Sept. 27, 1913, 164; Roosevelt, "Race Decadence.")

25. *"No Gods"*[1]

[*July 1914*]

"Alas, brethern, that God whom I created was man's work and man's madness, like all gods. Far too many are born. For the superfluous was the State created. Behold how it devoureth them. . . . . Aye, it findeth out even you, ye conquerors of the old God. Ye got wearied in battle and now your weariness serveth new idols."

Friedrich Nietzsche.[2]

From the dawn of civilization man made the gods in his own image and likeness. He crouched before the creature of his imagination and the incarnations of his spirit; before idols of wood and stone, of flesh and blood. Often he became heartily ashamed of his creations.

Before the conventional lies of Society and the superstitions of Science, democracy is now on its knees, offering its daily happiness at the shrines of petty idols, vainly struggling to rise unashamed, fearless and free. The State, the Flag, Law, Justice, Progress, Precedent and Large Families each in turn receive the service and homage of the masses.

In this country the social position of woman has undergone a remarkable change. The rich man places his wife on a pedestal and serves her with docility in order that she may be admired, and he, envied. He has raised her to the rank of queen. This deified woman is one of the new idols at whose feet plundering plutocracy lays the shining gold wrung from the sweat and blood of the toiling long-suffering masses.

But the rich woman is not happy. Her sensibilities have been crushed, and her mind impoverished by her parasitical position. Working women do not realise these facts. While man gazes upon his idol with admiration and desire, the woman worker tamely follows the beaten path. Instead of seeking elsewhere for a free and joyous existence, she struggles in competition to attain or to imitate that costly and dependent life which involves dresses, diamonds and expensive dinners. The prizes are few and the victims many.

Plutocracy makes it its business to support the priesthood. The common people must have "gods" to keep them in subjection. And so, before the vision of the workers is flashed the ideal of a grossly material existence, and by appeals to vanity and worldly ambition, the free slaves of society are lured into the domain of the lower senses. And, for the reason that civilization is what it is, working women are taking the same wrong turn, missing the ideal and forgetting that one ever existed.

The road of Happiness lies open to all, but it will not be found until we workers cease to immolate ourselves on the alter of man-made idols. For beneath the cruelty and the filthy cynicism of our commercial system, we women workers are being dehumanised. Our womanhood is being shamefully destroyed. The woman rebel wants to destroy the tyranny. The priests and profit-mongers want to destroy the womanhood.

This silly subjugation by woman to the conduct and habits of man; this surrender and supplication to his gods, is all part and parcel of the programme of the master class. Working women even more than men share in the idolatry which throws fictitious glory on the "defenders of country"; the soldier and marine. Romantic liars in the press sedulously foster the idea that the military or naval serf as a type possesses in battle—Courage, Patriotism and Chivalry.

The truth is, as was recently shown at Vera Cruz,[3] that the marine's nerves go to pieces after three hours under fire, and that he prefers food to fighting.

The only logical cure for all this is our assertion of a human ideal. If we do not strike the fetters off ourselves we shall be knocked about until we forget the fetters. To our society apologists, and to their plausible excuses for modern impression, the only adequate answer is—we have done with your civilization and your gods. We will organize society in such a way as to make it certain for all to live in comfort and leisure without bartering their affections or their convictions. Let us turn a deaf ear to the trumpet-tongued liars clamoring for Protection, Patriotism, Prisons, Police, Workhouses and Large Families. Leave them to vomit their own filth and let us take the good things mother earth daily offers unheeded, to us her children.

Woman Rebel, July 1914, 40 (*MSM* C16:554).

1. The masthead of the *Woman Rebel* contained the slogan, "No Gods, No Masters," which MS drew from a placard carried by IWW representatives during the 1912 strike at Lawrence that read "Arise!! Slaves of the World!!!! No God! No Master! One for all and all for one." (Brissenden, *I.W.W.,* 292.)

2. This was a quote from Friedrich Nietzsche's *Thus Spoke Zarathustra* (1883). The first lines were taken from "First Part: On the Afterworldly"; the last was from "First Part: The New Idol."

3. In April 1914, U.S. Navy and Marine units were dispatched to Vera Cruz, Mexico, to interdict German arms shipments and force Mexican president Victoriano Huerta to accept U.S. hegemony in the region. Four marines were killed, along with at least a dozen other American civilians.

26. To Stephen Haweis[1]

The New York City post office confiscated two hundred copies of the May issue of the Woman Rebel *and on May 29, following Section 480 of the Postal Laws, asked for a ruling on the publication's mailability. On June 2, 1914, Assistant Attorney General Lamar ruled that the issue was unmailable. The specific articles that triggered the suppression were "Open Discussion," by Ethel Cole; "Can You Afford to Have a Large Family," by Elizabeth Kleen; and "Abortion in the United States," by Margaret Sanger. The June issue was not suppressed. (See indictments,* MSM *C15:29; for a transcribed version of the suppression letter, see "Your Liberty," in the June issue of the* Woman Rebel [MSM *C16:546]; and Edward Morgan to William Lamar, May 29, 1914, and Lamar to Morgan, June 2, 1914 [POR].)*

[*New York, N.Y.*]
July 21 [*1914*]

Dear Stephen [*Haweis*]—

Your nice long letter[2] came some time ago. I shall not attempt to answer it, but if you will let me come down to see your work some afternoon next week when you are not very busy and we shall discuss these things together—

I sent the Woman Rebel out last Thursday but so far no one has received a copy so it looks to me I am in for trouble—I have an article on The Defense of Assassination[3] which shall cause me to be "pinched" perhaps—but———

Let me know when I may come to see you—Fraternally

Margaret H Sanger

ALS SHP, NNC (*MSM* C1:32–33). Letterhead of the *Woman Rebel,* 34 Post Avenue.

1. Hugh (Stephen) Haweis (1877–1969) was a British-born painter who, along with his wife, Mina Loy, met MS through Mabel Dodge, most likely shortly before this letter was written. (Glenn M. Opitz, ed., *Mantle-Fielding's Dictionary of American Painters, Sculptors and Engravers* [Poughkeepsie, N.Y., 1986], 385.)
2. The letter was not found.
3. "A Defense of Assassination" was written by Herbert A. Thorpe, a radical free speech activist from Jersey City, New Jersey. He argued that because the working classes did not have the power to make laws or determine working conditions, they had the right to defend themselves against oppression by greedy capitalists using "whatever other means of defense may be at its disposal, such as the strikes, boycott, sabotage or assassination." Quoting the abolitionist Wendell Phillips, Thorpe asserted that, as in the American Revolution, violence was justified to resist tyranny. (*Woman Rebel,* July 1914, 33–34 [*MSM* C16:547]; Thorpe to MS, June 23, 1915 [LCM 10:750].)

27. To Theodore Schroeder[1]

As Sanger anticipated, the July issue was suppressed for her articles "Birth Control League" and "Are Preventive Means Injurious," along with "The Marriage Bed" by Alice Groff and

Thorpe's "Defense of Assassination." (See indictments, MSM C15:29; and "Confiscated," in the August issue of the Woman Rebel *[MSM C16:562].)*

[*New York, N.Y.*]
Aug 19—1914

Dear Theodore Schroeder,

Im so mad that I missed you last Saturday. Yesterday two P.O. inspectors came here to see me and talk over my "impropoganda."[2] They made it quite clear to me that the case will come before the Grand Jury in a few days for decision.[3] They were also anxious to get the information who my attorneys are and if it is to be a test case. I gave them as little information as to my plans as possible, because I really have no definite ones. That is legal plans I mean.[4] They are making preparations to go ahead on the suppressed issues, which in my mind will not hold water, and told them so. I told them not to hurry, that there will be plenty of good material if they wait a little.[5] They sort of hoped I would promise to be good, Finding I had no intention of doing so they advised me to get the best advice and go ahead. I was so amused, yet I am preplexed, what can it mean?

The shadow is called off,[6] is nowhere to be seen. Write me if you will be so kind, and let me come to talk to you for a few minutes.

Margaret H Sanger [*signed*]

TLS RGP, WHi (*MSM* C1:35). Date and return address "34 Post Ave" added by hand.

1. Theodore Schroeder (1865–1953), an attorney and psychologist, led the effort to incorporate the Free Speech League in 1911. A leading civil libertarian, Schroeder took many cases on behalf of those who challenged government suppression of alleged obscenity. (*ANB*)

2. In her two autobiographies, MS asserted that during this meeting she argued the merits of birth control with the post office inspectors for nearly three hours, convincing them and her own father, who sat in the next room, of the virtues of her crusade. (MS, *My Fight,* 90; MS, *Autobiography,* 114–15.)

3. The grand jury considered MS's case on August 25, 1914, and returned indictments against articles published in the March, May, and July issues. She pled not guilty. (For indictments, see *MSM* C15:29; for criminal docket see *MSM* C15:39.)

4. MS contacted Schroeder and his Free Speech League associates, the attorneys Gilbert Roe and Leonard Abbott, soon after the post office suppressed the first issue. Although neither attorney formally represented her, she met Schroeder periodically at the Liberal Club, where he gave her legal advice. MS saw Roe a few days after she wrote this letter and was still "undecided whether or not to have any lawyer in her case at all." MS jotted Abbott and Schroeder's telephone numbers on the April 2 letter from Morgan and Murphy. (MS, *Autobiography,* 112; Roe to Schroeder, Sept. 28, 1914 [quote] [*MSM* C15:59]; Rabban, *Free Speech,* 69.)

5. This was probably a reference to *Family Limitation,* a pamphlet on specific contra-

ceptive methods that MS pieced together in April or May 1914 from materials she collected during her 1913 trip to Europe. By August, she had finally secured a printer. (MS, *Autobiography,* 112, 121.)

6. MS was probably followed by agents of Anthony Comstock (1844–1915), an anti-vice crusader who in 1873 had successfully lobbied Congress for the federal statute banning the mailing of obscene, lewd, or indecent material. Shortly thereafter, he was appointed special inspector of the Post Office Department to enforce this "Comstock law." He also served as secretary for the New York Society for the Suppression of Vice. (*ANB*)

28. *From Edward M. Morgan and Thomas F. Murphy*

New York, New York
August 27, 1914.

Dear Madam:

You are hereby notified that the Solicitor for the Post Office Department has decided that "The Woman Rebel" for August 1914 is unmailable under Section 480, Postal Laws and Regulations.[1] Very respectfully,

E. M. MORGAN [*stamped*]
Postmaster.
Per Th. F. Murphy [*signed*]
Assistant Postmaster.

TLS MSP, DLC (LCM 11:200). Letterhead of the U.S. Post Office. Addressed to "Editor, 'The Woman Rebel,' 34 Post Avenue, New York, N.Y."

1. Morgan sent a copy of the August issue to Solicitor (previously Assistant Attorney General) Lamar, enclosing a request for suppressing the entire journal "in view of the fact that several issues of this publication have been declared unmailable and that the matter of the mailing of such issues is in the hands of the United States Attorney for this District." Lamar ruled only on the August issue. It is unclear why this issue was banned under Section 480 of the Postal Code and the March and May issues under Section 211 of the U.S. Criminal Code; the texts of the two laws are identical, carrying the same ability to fine and imprison offenders. The New York City post office confiscated the final issue, dated September–October, and on October 14, Lamar ruled it unmailable under Section 211. (Morgan to MS, Apr. 2, 1914; Morgan to Lamar, Aug. 14 and Oct. 10, 1914; and Lamar to Morgan, Aug. 25 and Oct. 14, 1914 [POR]; *Postal Laws and Regulations of the United States of America* [Washington, D.C., 1913].)

29. *From James F. Morton Jr.*[1]

[*New York, N.Y.*]
Sept. 8, 1914.

Dear Comrade,—

I have been studying over the matter a little, and comparing notes with others. If my office ties did not absolutely cut me off from court work, I would like nothing better than to fight the case to a finish; for I am honestly afraid of some features of it, if you plead for yourself. There are technical aspects that these old fogies of the bench and jury will trip you up on, just for lack of a little legal experience, and so prevent you from getting a full and fair hearing and decision on the principles involved. Of course, a lawyer with no interest in the principle would be of little help for what you most want; but if you can get one who will fight on the right line, and use technicalities only so far as necessary to force a full hearing and decision on the basic principle, you will have a far better chance than by pleading alone. I know you are not afraid of the sentence they could give you; but if you are choked off without getting a hearing for the real issue, the cause gains nothing, and you lose your liberty for no real good. Besides, as I think I suggested, the judges of the higher courts are much more decent and likely to do justice and to understand the larger principles, than those of the lower or than the ordinary bourgeois jury; and so you might be cheated of justice at the trial, but win it on appeal. To lay a foundation for appeal, certain technical forms have to be strictly observed at the trial; and the prosecutor and judge would take advantage of your inexperience to head you off from putting yourself in a position to appeal, while they could not fool or hinder a lawyer who had your case in hand. Besides, courts are bound largely by precedent; and if injustice is done in one case, that decision is quoted when the next case of the kind comes up, even if years afterward; and the court holds itself bound by the earlier decision to decide in the same way. So, if by not fighting your case in the most effective manner, you lose it, it is not only you who must pay the penalty, but other comrades who may at any future time be arrested on a similar charge, and who will be condemned just because you were. It is horrible, but it is true. Our courts are both better and worse than outsiders, especially radicals, believe. They are less deliberately corrupt than they are often accused of being; but they are more automatic and slavish worshipers of the mistakes of the past than is easy to believe. They are often willing to do justice, if only their ceremonial fetich is propitiated by the observance of the technical forms, which are often very puerile and ridiculous; but they would expect the world to come to an end, should they pretermit one of those forms, to accomplish the larger end of justice. That is why lawyers are necessary, to trace the path through the labyrinth of forms to the central point where the real issue can at last be reached and fought out.

In the main, you ought to win over the enemy at the very start; but there are one or two ticklish points where I think you would be safer (and through you other radicals on whom the beast will lay its claws in future) to have expert assistance. The only difficulty was to get some one who would use technicalities only as a means to the end, and not as the issue itself. I have been thinking it over, and have one young lawyer in mind, who is enough of a convinced radical not to betray your trust in this regard. He is a good and vigorous fighter, and would seek to win for the principle, and not just to keep you out of prison; and he is thoroughly competent and with enough experience to be all right. Both Schroeder and I would of course work with him, even if Schroeder will not and I cannot go into court to take part in the trial.[2] His name is Robert Ferrari,[3] and his address 327 East 116th St. Can you not communicate with him, and at least talk the matter over? I have already explained the case to him, and he is much interested, and in thorough sympathy with you and with the principle involved. If you would prefer, I could arrange an appointment with him for some evening, where we could all three meet, and discuss the whole proposition, and then you could finally decide whether to use his services or to carry out your original plan of pleading your own case. It is needless to say that whatever method you adopt, I will do all that is in my power to help. Sincerely yours,

James F. Morton, Jr. [*signed*]

TLS MSP, DLC (LCM 9:736–38). A handwritten note by MS at the top center of the first page reads, "answered."

1. James F. Morton Jr. (1870–1941) was a lawyer, journalist, civil rights activist, and editor of such radical and anarchist journals as *Free Society* and the *Demonstrator.* In 1914, he was associate editor of the *Truth Seeker,* a journal devoted to free thought. (*New York Times,* Apr. 13, 1914; Avrich, *Modern School Movement,* 71.)

2. Schroeder made it a practice never to serve as attorney of record in free speech litigation. He believed his independent writings more effectively influenced the courts, and he recognized that his contentious and voluble personality was better suited for the court of public opinion. Schroeder may also have disapproved of MS's strategy of allowing the *Woman Rebel* to be the test case. MS recalled that Schroeder had warned her that if she kept publishing the monthly, the post office would wear her down and that she would eventually "have to take the consequences." (Rabban, *Free Speech,* 53–54; MS, *Autobiography,* 112–13.)

3. Robert Joseph Ferrari (1881–1975?) was a self-employed lawyer. (U.S. Bureau of the Census, *Thirteenth Census of the United States, 1910;* SSDI.)

30. To Upton Sinclair[1]

[*New York, N.Y.*]
Sept 23—1914

Dear Comrade Sinclair—

Keep the copies do.[2] I am glad to have you have a set just to see what foolishness has possessed the P.O. officials. Following are the articles on which I am indicted. "Prevention of Conception" (March) "Open Discussion," "Can you Afford to have a Large family"? "Abortion in U.S." (May).

"Marriage Bed" "Are preventive Means Injurious" "Birth Control League" and the "Defense of Assassination" in July issue— Aug issue held up on Birth Control League.[3] If you should care to read them—you will be highly amused— I 'specially requested the inspectors to wait, a few weeks ↑so↓ that I could give them something to really indict me on— Thank you for your interest. Fraternally

Margaret H. Sanger

ALS USP, InU (*MSM* C1:39–40). Letterhead of the *Woman Rebel.*

1. Upton Beall Sinclair (1878–1968), a naturalistic writer, socialist, and muckraker, was best known for *The Jungle,* his 1906 exposé of the Chicago stockyards. MS most likely met him in New York City in 1911. (*ANB*)
2. The letter from Sinclair was not found.
3. With the exception of Herbert Thorpe's "Defense of Assassination," all of the indicted articles discussed birth control and abortion or were critical of marriage. Notices announcing the formation of the Birth Control League of America appeared in both the July and August issues. (For complete texts, see *MSM* C15:522–61.)

31. *To the Editor of the* Woman Rebel

Sanger received a number of letters commending her for the Woman Rebel *and requesting specific information on how to prevent conception. Six such letters were printed for the first time in the September–October number, the final issue. The originals have not been found.*

Chicago, Ill.
[*September? 1914*]

Woman Rebel:—

I am the mother of six children. I am not well enough to have any more, and hardly strong enough to work for these. My husband is sick too, had an operation a month ago, will not be able to work for some time yet. With Winter coming on it is awful. Will you please send me the information you speak of in your paper, so I can prevent me having another child. Your doing a noble work for women.

Mrs. J. S.

Woman Rebel, Sept.–Oct. 1914, 55, published as part of the column "Some Letters" (*MSM* C16:569). This letter may have been edited for publication.

32. *From H. Snowden Marshall*[1]

New York [*N.Y.*]
October 7, 1914.

Madam:

The three indictments returned in this District against you for violations of Section 211 of the U.S. Criminal Code were on the calendar for October 5, 1914, and you were duly notified to appear at that time. When your case was called, there was no response on your behalf.[2] Accordingly, Judge Foster[3] set the cases for October 13, 1914, at 10:30 o'clock in the forenoon, in Room 331, and you are hereby notified to appear at that time.

You will recollect that when you were arraigned for pleading, Judge Hazel[4] released you without bail and upon your own recognizance, which is not customary in criminal cases. Respectfully,

H. Snowden Marshall [*signed*]
U.S. Attorney.

TLS MSP, DLC (LCM 11:201). Letterhead of the U.S. Attorney's Office. A handwritten note at the top left by an unidentified author reads, "replied to 9 Oct."[5] Case citation typed at the top left reads, "H.A.C./ 11053." Addressed to "34 Post Ave., New York, N.Y."

1. Hudson Snowden Marshall (1870–1931) was the U.S. attorney for New York's Southern District (1913–17). (*New York Times,* May 30, 1931.)
2. The notification was not found. MS later claimed that she failed to appear on October 5 because she had not received any notice. (MS, *Autobiography,* 117.)
3. Warren W. Foster (1859–1943) served on the court of special sessions from 1899 to 1914. (*New York Times,* Aug. 10, 1943.)
4. MS was arraigned before Judge John Raymond Hazel (1860–1951) on August 25, 1914. Hazel, a Buffalo-based U.S. district judge for western New York, likely heard MS's case under a provision of the 1913 Lacombe bill, which permitted the Southern District to draw on judges from other districts to handle the overflow of New York City cases. (Charles Merrill Hough, *The U.S. District Court for the Southern District of New York* [Staten Island, N.Y., 1934], 32.)
5. The reply was not found.

33. *To Elmer Swanson*[1]

[*New York City, N.Y.*]
Oct 9—1914.

Dear Comrade—

My trial is coming up in a few days— Shall let you know definitely about date of speaking— Don't advertise yet. I had inside information I am to get the limit.[2] Your kind letter[3] is greatly appreciated.

I shall let you know next week definitely if Nov 29th will be OK. also regarding fare etc. Thank you hurriedly but Fraternally

Margaret H Sanger.

ALS RSSC, NRU (*MSM* C1:43–44). Letterhead of the *Woman Rebel.*

1. Elmer Swanson was secretary for the Rochester, New York, Labor Lyceum. (RSSC; MS incorrectly addressed him as Elmer Sulansin in her Sept. 23, 1914, letter [*MSM* C1:43].)
2. It is unclear where or how MS received this information. She later indicated only that "from the Post Office Department I received roundabout word that my conviction had already been decided on." (MS, *Autobiography,* 118.)
3. The letter was not found, but it is clear from MS's September 23 response that Swanson had invited her to speak at the Labor Lyceum on November 29, 1914.

34. *Excerpt from* Family Limitation: "A Nurse's Advice to Women"

Family Limitation, *Sanger's sixteen-page pamphlet written for working men and women, contained explicit contraceptive information, including an illustration of how to insert a pessary, recipes for suppositories, suggestions for douching, and information on how to obtain pessaries, condoms, and sponges. It also provided advice on sex and sexual hygiene and included statements on working-class exploitation. The pamphlet was written in the spring of 1914 and printed in the fall by Sanger's Ferrer School friend Bill Shatoff, a Russian-born labor organizer and Linotype operator in New Jersey. She appealed to Theodore Schroeder for support to pay for the printing and later claimed that Schroeder, who administered a fund established by the birth control advocate and civil libertarian Edward Bond Foote, refused to release money to her unless she went through six weeks of psychoanalysis to clarify her motives. When he told her he did not believe she would want to continue the fight after those six weeks, Sanger refused to be analyzed. Schroeder, nevertheless, gave her enough money to fund the printing of 10,000 copies. Sanger later asserted that a first edition of 100,000 copies was printed, though there is no indication of where she acquired the extra funds to do so. She bundled the pamphlets and addressed them to labor groups, radical organizations, and workers at mills and mines across the country and then divided them among a small group of friends to be distributed at the appropriate time. Over the next twenty years, at least eighteen English-language editions of* Family Limitation *were published; it was also translated into many other languages. Other editions, both authorized and unauthorized, were reprinted by labor organizers, socialists, and other birth control sympathizers. The pamphlet was also hand copied and passed from woman to woman. "A Nurse's Advice to Women" follows the introduction in the first edition. (MS,* Autobiography, *112–22; MS,* My Fight, *86–88. For copies of numerous editions, including the first, see* MSM, *S76:898–1085.)*

[*October 1914*]

Every woman who is desirous of preventing conception will follow this advice:

Don't wait to see if you do *not* menstruate (monthly sickness) but make it your duty to see that you *do.*

If you are due to be "sick" on the eighth of August, do not wait until the eighth to see, but begin as early as the fourth to take a good laxative for the bowels, and continue this each night until the eighth.

If there is the slightest possibility that conception may have taken place, take on these same nights before retiring, five or ten grains of quinine, with a hot drink.[1] The quinine in capsule form is considered fresher, but if this is taken do not use alcoholic drinks directly after, as it hardens the capsules, thus delaying the action of the quinine.

By taking the above precautions you will prevent the ovum from making its nest in the lining of the womb.

Women of intelligence who refuse to have children until they are ready for them, keep definite track of the date of their menstrual periods. A calendar should be kept, on which can be marked the date of the last menstruation, as well as the date when the next period should occur.

Women must learn to know their own bodies, and watch and know definitely how regular or irregular they are: if the period comes regularly every twenty-eight days (normal) or every thirty days as in the case of many young girls.

Mark it accordingly on your private calendar; do not leave it to memory or guess work.

Only ignorance and indifference will cause one to be careless in this most important matter.

A very good laxative (though it is a patent medicine) is Beechams Pills. Two of these taken night and morning, four days before menstruation, will give a good cleansing of the bowels, and assist with the menstrual flow.[2]

The American physician's may object to this advice because Beechams Pills are a patent medicine. But until they are willing to give open advice on this subject, we must resort to such as the least harmful, until such time as they do.

If a woman will give herself attention BEFORE the menstrual period arrives, she will almost never have any trouble, but if she neglects herself and waits to see if she "comes around," she is likely to have difficulty.

It takes quinine from four to six days to bring about the desired results, and if one finds a longer time has elapsed and the flow is not brought on, then the only remedy is an abortion. When once one has been convinced that an abortion is necessary, do not indulge in medicines of any kind. They only weaken the system, and require a much greater length of time to recuperate. Never allow a pregnancy to run over a month.

If you are going to have an abortion, make up your mind to it in the first stages, and have it done. On the other hand, there is often a feeling of the strongest desire to continue with the pregnancy. It is for each woman to decide this for herself, but act at once, whichever way you decide.

There is current among people an idea that conception can take place only at certain times of the month.[3] For instance: ten days after the menstrual period, and ten or fourteen days before the next period. This is not to be relied upon at all, for it has been proven again and again that a woman can conceive at any time in the month. Do not depend upon this belief, for there is no reliable foundation for it. There is also the knowledge that nursing after childbirth prevents the return of the menstrual flow for several months and conception does not take place. It is well not to depend upon this too much, especially after the fifth or sixth month, for often a woman becomes pregnant again without having "seen anything" or without her realizing that she has become pregnant. She thus finds herself with one at the breast and another in the womb. Use some preventive.

Again, it is believed that conception cannot take place if the woman lies upon her left side at the time of the act. It makes no difference which side she lies upon; she can become pregnant if the semen is not prevented from entering the womb.

Perhaps the commonest preventive excepting the use of the condom is "coitus interruptus," or withdrawal of the penis from the vagina shortly before the ejaculation of the semen. No one can doubt that this is a perfectly safe method; and it is not considered so dangerous to the man as some authorities have formerly viewed it,[4] but it requires a man of the strongest will-power to be certain that he has withdrawn before any of the semen has been deposited in the vagina. It is very difficult to determine exactly whether this has been done. The greatest objection to this is the evil effect upon the woman's nervous condition. She has not completed her desire, she is under a highly nervous tension, her whole being is perhaps on the verge of satisfaction. She is then left in this dissatisfied state, which is far from humane. This does her injury. A mutual and satisfied sexual act is of great benefit to the average woman, the magnetism of it is health giving, and acts as a beautifier and tonic. When it is not desired on the part of the woman and she has no response, it should not take place. This is an act of prostitution and is degrading to the woman's finer sensibility, all the marriage certificates on earth to the contrary notwithstanding. When a woman desires the sexual act, and is completely satisfied, her whole being is built up and beautified through it, her form develops, her eyes become brighter, her health improves, color comes into her cheeks. All life is changed for her and would continue thus if it were not for the fact that she allows intercourse when she has no natural desire for it, and then allowing it, she is without means for prevention of conception, and is so throughout the act conscious and fearful of its consequences. Withdrawal on the part of the man should be substituted by some other means that does not injure the woman.

Family Limitation, 1914, 4–7 (*MSM* S76:852–53).

1. Quinine, best known in the nineteenth century as an antimalaria powder, was also rumored to be useful in stimulating the uterus. By the 1870s, research suggested it was effective in initiating labor and strengthening uterine muscles in animals, supporting its use as an abortifacient. By the end of World War I, as it became a popular remedy for unwanted pregnancy, questions arose about its dangers. In small doses, quinine increases uterine contractions, but large doses can become poisonous and paralyze the uterus. (Shorter, *History of Women's Bodies,* 213–14.)

2. Laxatives were sometimes used as abortifacients, though without scientific basis. MS deleted this reference in the 1920 version and all subsequent editions of the pamphlet. (For MS's explanation on the inclusion of laxatives as a contraceptive method, see MS to Howard Lindeman, Feb. 16, 1923 [LCM 117:482].)

3. The "safe period" or "rhythm" method of birth control relies on the premise that women are infertile at certain times of each month. However, until the 1930s, most physicians and birth control advocates advised women seeking to avoid pregnancy to have intercourse just when a woman's egg was released—their most fertile period. While the "rhythm method" remains highly unreliable, experts on fertility now advise that conception is less likely to take place in the few days immediately following the menstrual period and then approximately fifteen days after menses cease. (McLaren, *History of Contraception,* 187; Planned Parenthood Federation of America, *Ways to Chart Your Fertility Pattern* [New York, 1996].)

4. Also known as "onanism," "interrupted intercourse," "taking care," and "withdrawal," the practice was common despite its unreliability. Nineteenth-century experts, such as Enoch Heinrich Kisch and Auguste Henri Forel, believed that coitus interruptus caused nervous and mental ailments in both men and women, but by the early twentieth century most criticized the method for forcing women to rely on their husband's self-control, making it difficult to achieve sexual satisfaction themselves. (Cooper, *Technique of Contraception,* 105–7.)

35. *To Comrades and Friends*

Sanger's trial was rescheduled to begin on October 13, 1914. In her Autobiography, *she indicated that she appeared in court that morning and asked for a postponement but that Harold Content, the assistant U.S. attorney, objected, saying, "Every day's delay means that her violations are increased." Judge Hazel agreed and told her to return after lunch with a lawyer. Sanger returned with the attorney Simon Pollack, whose request for a postponement was also denied. The trial was on the calendar to begin October 20, but Sanger did not appear. She later claimed to have sent both Hazel and Content copies of* Family Limitation *along with letters announcing her intention to leave the country "until I made ready my case," but the letters were not found. (H. Snowden Marshall to MS, Oct. 7, 1914, herein; MS,* Autobiography, *118–20;* New York Call, *Oct. 20, 1914.)*

New York [*N.Y.*]
Oct. 28th 1914

Comrades and Friends

Every paper published should have a message for its readers. It should deliver it and be done. The Woman Rebel had for its aim the imparting of information of the prevention of conception. It was not the intention to labor on for years advocating the idea, but to give the information directly to those desired it. The March, May, July, August, September and October issues have been suppressed and confiscated by the Post Office. They have been mailed regularly to all subscribers. If you have not received your copies, it has been because the U.S. Post Office has refused to carry them to you.

My work on the nursing field for the past fourteen years has convinced me that the workers desire the knowledge of prevention of conception. My work among women of the working class proved to me sufficiently that it is they who are suffering because of the law which forbids the imparting of this information. To wait for this law to be repealed would be years and years hense. Thousands of un-wanted children may be born into the world in the meantime. Thousands of women made miserable and unhappy.

Why should we wait?

Shall we who have heard the cries and seen the agony of dying Women respect the law which has caused their death?

Shall we watch in patience the murdering of 25000 women, who die each year in U.S. from criminal abortion?[1]

Shall we fold our hands and wait until a body of sleek and well fed politicians get ready to abolish the cause of such slaughter?

Shall we look upon a piece of parchment as greater than human happiness greater than human life?

Shall we let it destroy our womanhood, and hold millions of workers in bondage and slavery? Shall we who respond to the throbbing pulse of human needs concern ourselves with indictments, courts and judges, or shall we do our work first and settle with these evils later?

This law has caused the perpetuation of quackery. It has created the fake and quack who benefits by its existence.

Jail has not been my goal. There is special work to be done and I shall do it first. If jail comes after I shall call upon all to assist me. In the meantime I shall attempt to nullify the law by direct action and attend to the consecquences later.[2]

Over 100000 working men and women in U.S. shall hear from me.

The Boston Tea Party was a defiant and revolutionary act in the eyes of the English Government, but to the American Revolutionist it was but an act of courage and justice. Yours Fraternally

Margaret H. Sanger

TDf MSP, DLC (LCM 129:2).

1. MS's figure of 25,000 abortion-related maternal deaths cannot be substantiated and differs markedly from her "lowest estimate" of 6,000, which she included in "Abortion in the United States," *Woman Rebel,* May 1914 (*MSM* C16:535).

2. MS took a train to Montreal the next day, October 29, to avoid prosecution. She arranged to have *Family Limitation* distributed once on board the England-bound RMS *Virginian* in early November.

Margaret Higgins with friend Esther Farquharson at Claverack, ca. 1899 (photograph by Sullivan Brothers, Margaret Sanger Papers, Sophia Smith Collection, Smith College).

Margaret Higgins at White Plains Hospital, ca. 1901 (photograph by Boyce, Margaret Sanger Papers, Sophia Smith Collection, Smith College).

Portrait of Margaret Higgins, July 9, 1902 (Margaret Sanger Papers, Sophia Smith Collection, Smith College).

William Sanger, n.d. (Margaret Sanger Papers, Sophia Smith Collection, Smith College).

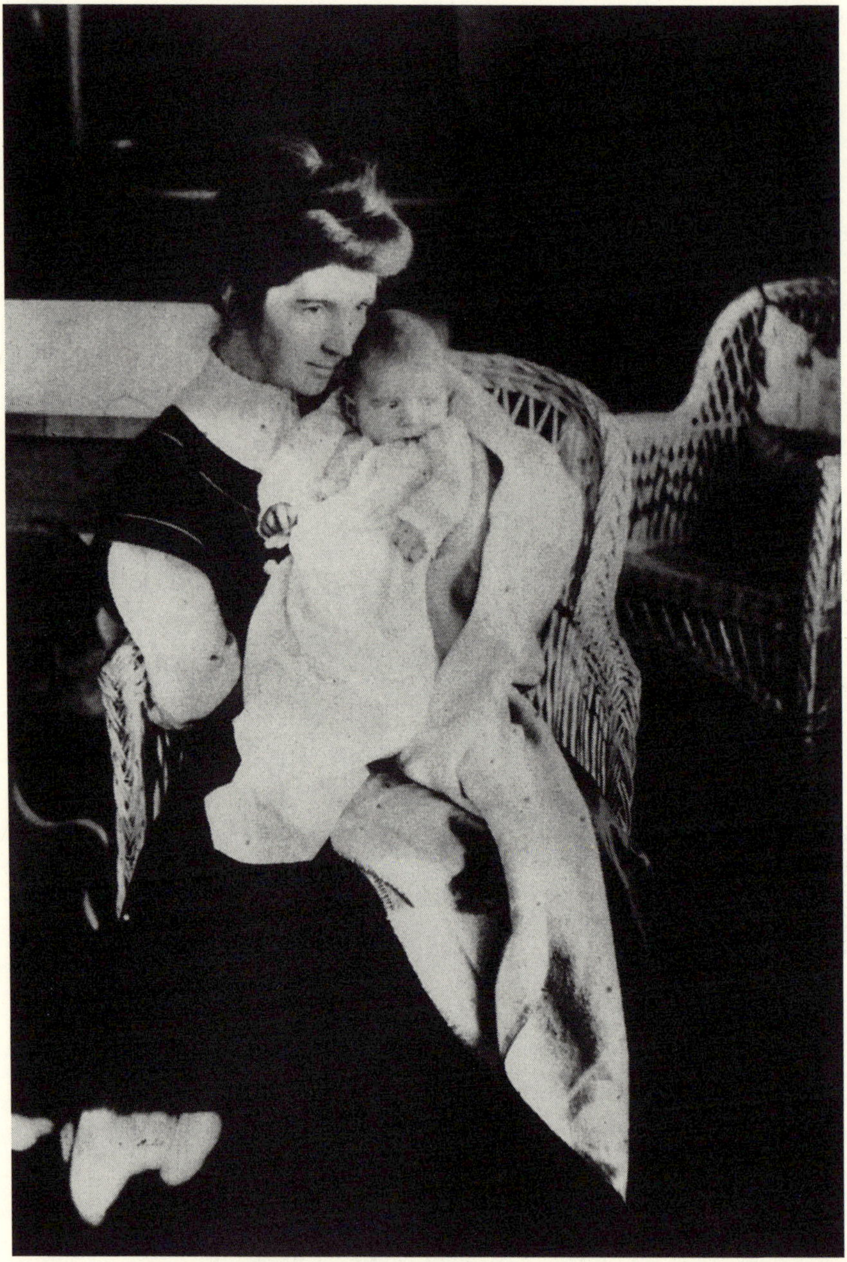

Margaret Sanger with second son, Grant, 1908 (Margaret Sanger Papers, Sophia Smith Collection, Smith College).

Margaret Sanger and sister Ethel Byrne, with their children (*left to right*) Stuart Sanger, Olive Byrne, and Jack Byrne at Coney Island, August 3, 1910 (photograph by Dreamland Postcard, Margaret Sanger Papers, Sophia Smith Collection, Smith College).

Paterson strike leaders (*left to right*): Patrick Quinlan, Carlo Tresca, Elizabeth Gurley Flynn, Adolph Lessig, and William ("Big Bill") Haywood, 1913 (Walter P. Reuther Library, Wayne State University).

Peggy Sanger, age three, at Cape Cod, summer 1913 (Margaret Sanger Papers, Sophia Smith Collection, Smith College).

Sanger's 1915 passport under the alias "Bertha Watson" (Margaret Sanger Papers, Sophia Smith Collection, Smith College).

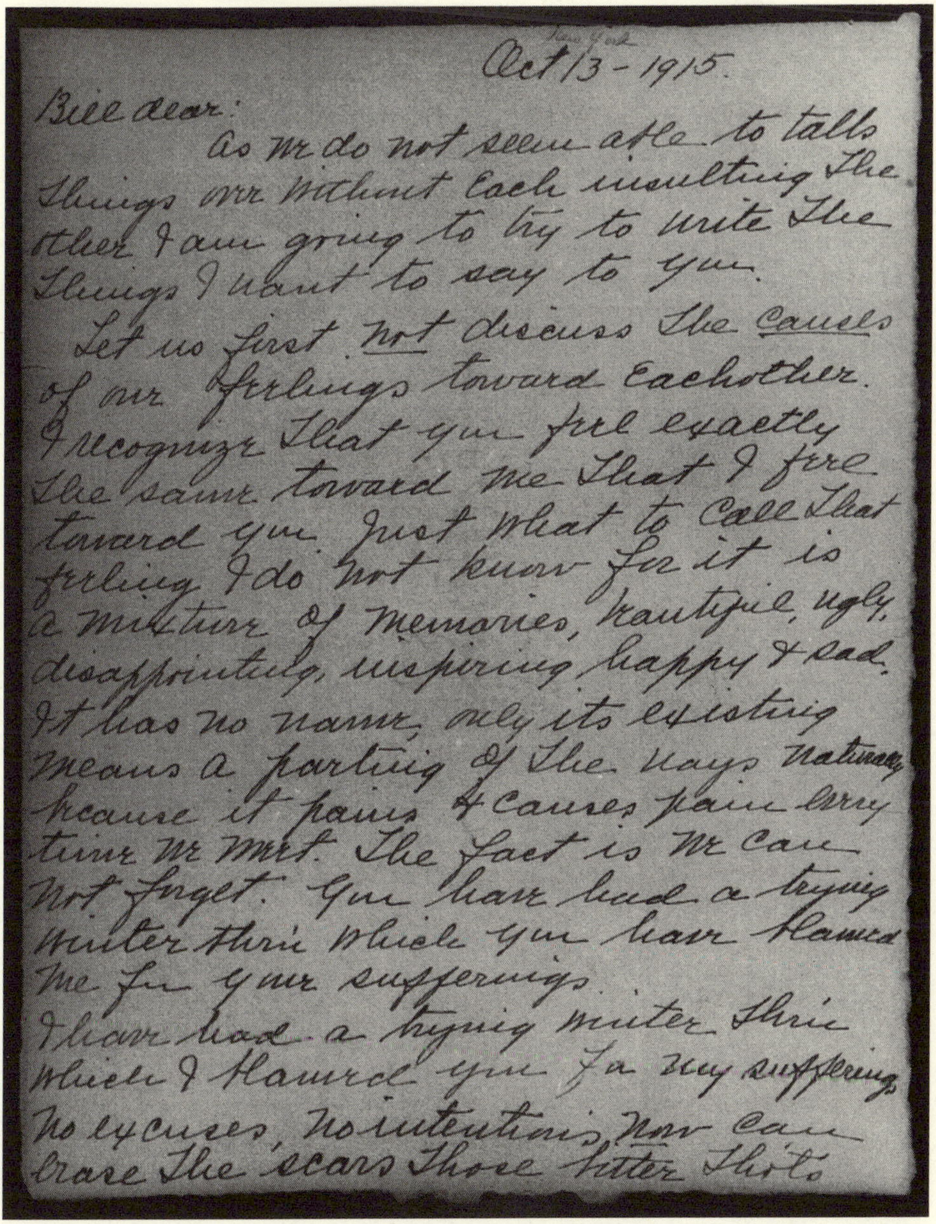

New York
Oct 13 - 1915.
Bill dear:
As we do not seem able to talk
things over without each insulting the
other I am going to try to write the
things I want to say to you.
Let us first not discuss the causes
of our feelings toward eachother.
I recognize that you feel exactly
the same toward me that I feel
toward you. Just what to call that
feeling I do not know for it is
a mixture of memories, beautiful, ugly,
disappointing, inspiring, happy & sad.
It has no name, only its existing
means a parting of the ways naturally,
because it pains & causes pain every
time we meet. The fact is we can
not forget. You have had a trying
winter thru which you have blamed
me for your sufferings.
I have had a trying winter thru
which I blamed you for my suffering.
No excuses, no intentions, now can
erase the scars those bitter thots

Margaret Sanger letter (page one) to William Sanger, October 13, 1915 (Margaret Sanger Papers, Sophia Smith Collection, Smith College).

Rose Pastor Stokes, Margaret Sanger, and Ethel Byrne at hearings for the *Woman Rebel*, January 18, 1916 (© Corbis/Bettmann).

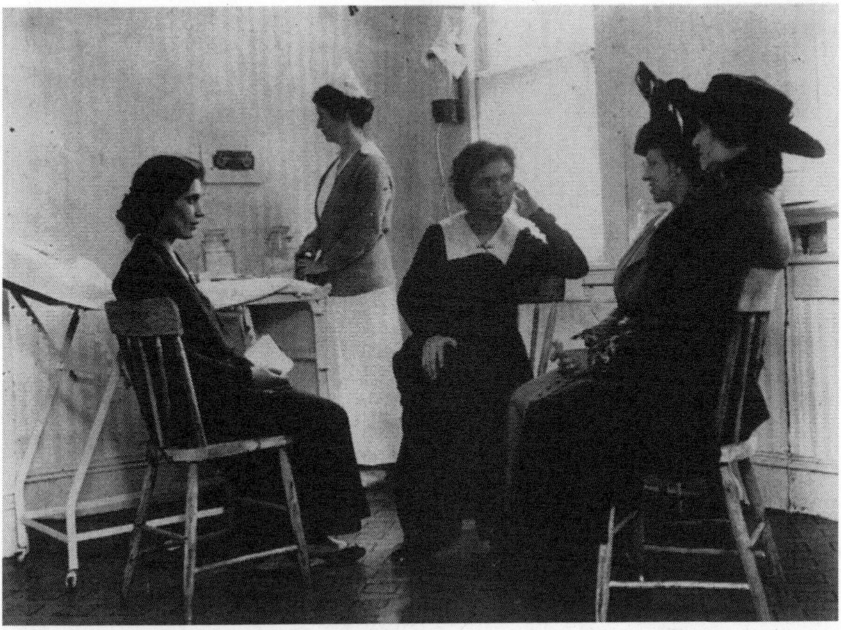

Interior of the Brownsville Clinic, October 1916. *Left to right:* Fania Mindell, Ethel Byrne (standing), Margaret Sanger, and two clients (Cleveland Public Library/Newspaper Enterprise Association).

Margaret Sanger, ca. 1916 (Margaret Sanger Papers, Sophia Smith Collection, Smith College).

Poster advertising meeting on the eve of the Brownsville trial (Margaret Sanger Papers Project).

Leaving the courthouse during the Brownsville Clinic trials, *from left:* unidentified, Ethel Byrne, Lillian Fassett, unidentified, Margaret Sanger, and the attorney Jonah J. Goldstein, Jan. 1917 (Margaret Sanger Papers, Sophia Smith Collection, Smith College).

Havelock Ellis, ca. 1910, from photo used in the *Birth Control Review,* February 1919 (Margaret Sanger Papers, Sophia Smith Collection, Smith College).

Juliet Barrett Rublee, n.d. (Margaret Sanger Papers, Sophia Smith Collection, Smith College).

FOUR

Exile and Renewal

MARGARET SANGER arrived in Liverpool on November 13, 1914, a fugitive from the law, lonely and homesick, and with little money. She was seeking a safe place to rest while she gathered her thoughts and energy, but she also wanted to explore new intellectual ground. Curious and impressionable, she was eager to learn more about European approaches to contraception, sexual liberation, and social reform. What Sanger found during the next eleven months was a community of reformers, philosophers, and writers who would help her clarify and refine her promotion of birth control—a crusade she had not yet fully conceived but was beginning to understand could potentially transcend class, race, and geography.

With references provided by American and Canadian socialist friends, she approached local Fabian socialists in Liverpool and, on their advice, made her way to London. There she contacted leaders of the Malthusian League, the first organization in the world to advocate the use of contraception and the only group in England pressing the cause at a time when the European war dominated most agendas. The Malthusian League based its work on the theory of the British economist Thomas Malthus (1766–1834), who argued that without checks, population growth would exceed the food supply. The founders of the league disagreed with Malthus's solution of controlling population growth through abstinence or delayed marriage. Instead, these neo-Malthusians advocated the use of artificial contraception and campaigned among the middle class to win the support of doctors, feminists, politicians, and the clergy, who, in turn, would convince the lower classes to use birth control.[1]

At first glance, it would seem that Sanger, the working-class outlaw running in anarchist circles, had little in common with the academic, socially conservative British Malthusians who rejected reforms that would give power or voice to the working class. Their views contrasted sharply with those of French and Dutch Malthusians, who sought to make contraception immediately available to the poor as a means of liberation. The British league's elitism and antisocialist views limited its appeal to other advocates of contraceptive use, particularly among Fabian socialists and trade unionists. But when dealing with non-British proponents of family limitation, the league's leaders looked past political differences, joining in international conferences with socialist-inspired European leagues and welcoming such radicals as Emma Goldman and Victor Dave.

Like a growing minority of British Malthusians, Sanger was critical of the league's strategy of "educating the educators." As she argued in the *Woman Rebel,* the working classes' interest in family limitation was in simply getting access to effective contraception. Despite their differences in approach, the league's program presented Sanger with new possibilities for broadening interest in birth control by applying a more extensive range of scientific, economic, and academic arguments. Unlike Sanger's narrower radical economic rationale and incendiary rhetoric, the league's approach promised wider appeal; it could effectively counter medical opponents of legalized birth control and appease middle-class fears of social unrest and race decline.[2]

A web of personal connections formed early in her exile helped Sanger develop her ideas. Charles Drysdale, Bessie Drysdale, Binnie Dunlop, and Alice Vickery, all leaders of the league, warmly welcomed Sanger. They invited her into their homes, escorted her to lectures and teas, and buoyed her spirits during a time when she was battling depression and anxious over her separation from her children. Their attention and support contrasted starkly with what Sanger perceived as indifference to her work in the United States. She recalled in her *Autobiography,* "Instead of heaping criticism and fears upon me, they offered all the force of an international organization as well as their encyclopedic minds to back me up."[3] Her Malthusian League contacts introduced Sanger to their associates, both in England and abroad, many of whom became indispensable to the international movement Sanger would build in the next decade. They also encouraged her to meet the man who would become her most important mentor, Havelock Ellis, one of the pioneers of sexual modernism.

Sanger was already familiar with the work of Ellis, the author of the monumental *Studies in the Psychology of Sex* (1897–1928), but after they met, Ellis profoundly influenced her intellectual and emotional growth. Over the next year, as they formed a complex and intimate intellectual and physical bond, Ellis functioned as Sanger's teacher, advising her on what to read, how to write, whom to meet, and where to go. He also served as her cultural guide, taking her to concerts, lectures, and museums. In effect, Ellis gave Sanger what she had been deprived of in her abbreviated tenure at school—an education in the liberal arts.[4]

Ellis also legitimized Sanger's commitment to birth control: her conviction that women could find fulfillment in their own sexuality, as well as freedom from the oppression of male desire, by liberating themselves from the fear of unwanted pregnancy. While Ellis's theories were based in scientific inquiry, he also emphasized the romantic and spiritual importance of mutually pleasurable sexual relations. Under his tutelage, Sanger reformed and expanded her belief that through the use of birth control, women could acknowledge their own eroticism, men could help fulfill it, and together they could produce children by mutual consent.

Sanger also explored her growing interest in eugenics with Ellis who, like the Malthusians, believed that a scientific approach to reproduction and the use of contraception would regenerate the human race. But for Ellis, the poor were not the problem; rather it was class-based social institutions and Victorian sexual morality that suppressed both a sensible population policy and sexual liberation. While the logic of the Malthusians was informed by fears of economic scarcity and social instability, Ellis's views were rooted in the belief that social order and responsible eugenics were inextricably connected to individual happiness and fulfillment. After months of studying with Ellis, Sanger was able to construct a eugenic argument in which birth control became the critical tool for the betterment of the individual and the race.

Though she began to temper some of her more radical impulses and associated mainly with moderate reformers in England, Sanger also established ties with British socialists and anarchists. She met the utopian socialist and sex theorist Edward Carpenter and formed friendships with Stella Browne, the socialist sore thumb of the Malthusian League; Guy Aldred and Rose Witcop, the socialist/anarchist publishing couple; and many of their associates. She also embarked on an intense romance with Lorenzo Portet, a Spanish anarchist teaching at the University of Liverpool.

Despite the dangers of traveling abroad in the midst of World War I, Sanger managed lengthy trips to Wales, France, and Spain. She also made a brief trip to Holland, where she met Dr. Johannes Rutgers, who introduced her to the small but effective network of doctor-supervised contraceptive dispensaries in major Dutch cities. Sanger's exposure to the Dutch system of birth control clinics and its emphasis on providing women with personal instruction would inform her strategy for the movement.

While Sanger used her time abroad to study, write, and travel, birth control in the United States was catapulted into the public eye by the arrest in January 1915 of her estranged husband for distributing a copy of *Family Limitation.*

William Sanger's much-postponed trial and conviction nine months later thrust the issue into the newspapers, galvanized support for reform of the Comstock laws, and acted as a catalyst for the formation of the first viable birth control organization, the National Birth Control League (NBCL). New interest in family limitation also prompted a series of influential magazine articles in the spring and summer of 1915, and in May the prestigious New York Academy of Medicine discussed birth control for the first time.

Her husband's case was exactly what Margaret Sanger had hoped hers would be—a clear free speech issue that would bring birth control to center stage. She became increasingly restive as events in the United States seemed to pass her by. When she finally returned to New York in October 1915, ready to stand trial, birth control had become a cause célèbre. "At the first newsstand I passed, my attention was caught by the words 'Birth Control' printed boldly on the cover of the Pictorial Review," Sanger reported. "It was a queer sensation to be welcomed, not by friends or relatives, but by a phrase of one's own creation on the cover of a magazine, by the words which had sent me into exile."[5]

Sanger was poised for a dramatic court battle in the late fall of 1915, when she suffered a monumental personal loss—the death of her youngest child. Government prosecutors, in an attempt to deflate the pro-Sanger publicity that now surged even higher, abruptly backed off. Denied the platform of a trial, Sanger set off on a national tour to bring her message directly to the public.

People were captivated by the woman and her message. As one reporter wrote, "The audience saw a young-looking woman, in a very feminine outfit of blue foulard and chiffon with pearl beads and a tiny chained locket at the throat. When she spoke, the audience heard not a strong masculine utterance, but a musical voice like that of a woman who might sing mezzo-soprano. And they saw no gestures—she spoke from behind a desk and most of the time rested her hands on it, half clinched. Her diction, though marked by frank words at times, was never vulgarized—it never dropped into slang."[6] Another reporter described her as "a mild-looking woman to have braved the lions of the Federal law in the advocacy of birth control. Sitting in her apartment at the Palace Hotel today, her rich coppery-brown hair, brushed back from a pale forehead, beneath which glowed dark gray eyes, separated by a delicately modeled nose, smiling a sane smile over even white teeth, Mrs. Sanger presented anything but the expected radical appearance."[7] Her stump speech, given scores of times in twenty cities from coast to coast, reflected her newly acquired sophistication about how to make the case for birth control and, perhaps, a new detachment from her previous identification with working-class women; they now became the objects rather than the instigators of reform.[8]

Sanger returned from her tour in July 1916 having proved her ability to ignite passions and generate publicity. With a renewed willingness to do whatever it took to keep birth control on the front pages, Sanger positioned herself to seize command of the issue.

NOTES

1. Ledbetter, *Malthusian League,* xiii–xiv, 89–90.
2. MS, *My Fight,* 99 (quote); MS, "The Prevention of Conception," Mar. 1914, herein; Ledbetter, *Malthusian League,* 97–99.
3. MS, *Autobiography,* 129.
4. Chris Nottingham, *The Pursuit of Serenity: Havelock Ellis and the New Politics* (Amsterdam, 1999), 147–60; McCann, *Birth Control Politics,* 35–36, 106–7, 153.
5. MS, *My Fight,* 123. See also the cover of the *Pictorial Review,* Oct. 1915.
6. "900 Give Pledges to Birth Control League in Detroit," *Detroit Journal,* May 3, 1916.
7. "Birth Control Her Plea," *San Francisco Bulletin,* June 7, 1916.
8. For drafts of Sanger's speech, see "Birth Control," ca. Apr. 1916, and "Condemnation Is Misunderstanding," ca. Apr. 1916 (LCM 129:12 and 32).

36. Sailing to England Journal

Fearing imprisonment, Sanger decided she could not risk standing trial on the Woman Rebel *indictments. On October 29, she boarded a train for Montreal, where she acquired false papers under the alias "Bertha L. Watson." She sailed for England on the evening of November 2. What follows is a journal entry written on her first day at sea; for the rest of the journal (November 4–6), see* MSM *S70:17–23.*

R.M.S. Virginian
Nov 3rd 1914

First day out—

The ability to break away gracefully from a conversation that drags or bores—is a real art— A certain type of English woman is interesting—buoyant, frank, fearless—yet considerate. Her face is fair & lovely—abundant hair coiled at the back of her head. The slight framed, peked faced, youth who startles one by saying he is a cattle dealer—his talk is much of profits & the way of profit makers. He has one good idea—that he will <u>not</u> go to war. Lives at Chester parents keep the Albion Hotel there—five sisters—fifty-eight times across—buys cattle from Argentine.

My few days with the Bains at Montreal has left such a glow of love and good fellowship over my mind that I am forgetful of the trip. Frank is one of the Christs of the day—love of the virile kind ooses from him. Kind in acts—frank in his expression happy—glorious—loyal & adoring Horace Traubel.[1] They all do—all who come in contact with him, all who come within the radiance of his personality—

The trip reminds me of the trip a year ago when we left from Boston for Glasgow— Dear Peggy how my love goes out to you—I could weep from lonliness for you—just to touch your soft chubby hands—but work is to be done dear—work to help to make your path easier—& those who come after you.[2]

United States—what stupidity controls thy destiny—to drive from your shores those who can contribute to the happiness of its down trodden people. Who can enlighten the ignorant—& help to raise the standards of knowledge. Fortunately there is no feeling that I am leaving my Country—I know I have never had a country—for the landlord comes to my door in New York just as he comes in Montreal. And if there is nothing to give him in New York I have learned that there is no room for me there— Any country where one can pay their rent is yours—

I want to let the U.S. know that I am alive— May my invisible guardians help me to do so—& to do it well.

AD MSP, MN-SSC (*MSM* S70:13–16). Letterhead of the Canadian Pacific Railway Ocean Services. A handwritten note by MS at the top of the first page reads, "MS Personal Thots Sailing to England as Bertha Watson."

1. From October 30 to November 2, MS stayed with the socialists Frank W. Bain (1875–1959) and Mildred Jackson Bain (1875–?), close friends of the journalist Horace Traubel (1858–1919), Walt Whitman's intimate friend and literary executor. (Bain to Traubel, Oct. 30 and Nov. 3, 1914 [GTP]; James Hart, ed., *Oxford Companion to American Literature* [New York, 1983], 771.)

2. The Sanger children had spent the summer of 1914 away from their mother. Grant, age six, and Peggy, age four, stayed with friends in Woodstock, New York, and Stuart, age ten, was at a camp in Maine. In the fall, MS left Grant and Peggy with her sister Ethel, while Stuart entered Winnwood, a boarding school run by Christian Scientists in Ronkonkoma, Long Island. William Sanger, who had returned from Paris in the late summer, only sporadically cared for his children during his wife's absence. (William Sanger to MS, Jan. 21, 1915, herein; MS, *My Fight*, 90.)

37. *Diary Entry*

[*Liverpool, England*]
[*November 13–15, 1914*]

Arrived at the Adelphia Hotel 11am. <u>no trouble</u> at Customs[1] as I had only one bag. Mr Girling[2] helped me to a cab, and I found myself winding thru dirty streets greatly like all streets surrounding docks in all cities.

The Adelphia is a palace fairy like plus exceeding comfort. It rained all day—the wind blew, the sound of its howling came thru the windows & down the chimney, until homesickness crept over me like my first days at boarding school. I knew it would not do to "set & think" as the Quakers say so I set off to find the Clarion Café—advertised in Blatchford's Clarion.[3]

I found it at 30 Lord St but no one to be there until 6 PM. in the meantime I wandered about the business sections & tried to adjust my mind to the prices of clothing marked in the windows so that I might have some idea of the dollars & cents I was likely to deal in clothing prices very much the same as N.Y. shoes, hats etc all the same. Not any cheaper.

At 6 PM I went again to the Clarion Café & found the Fabians[4] have their Club room there & meet every Friday night for discussion. I was invited to tea with several of the members & remained for the discussion. The speaker an I.L.P. Man spoke on "After the war".[5] John Edwards a good Fabian was chairman[6]—a splendid fellow—written much & is the speaker here I think. Looked over the register & found Big Bill's[7] name, here Tom Mann, Jim Larkin G. B. Shaw H. G. Wells[8] & many other thinkers—

The Club is cozy and homelike the Comrades welcome us all. Elsie Hickling offered to assist me in getting a cheaper place for the few days I am to remain. Am now at the "Allendale" #18 Canning St. a very comfortable place with nice gentle middle class people. 30S[9] with breakfast & dinner—per week.

No mail for me yet, but I trust some shall arrive tomorrow to give me an idea of how Peggy & Grant are—

Liverpool is a quaint & clean city—its lovely tapestry brick houses I like there is an evenness and quiet & settled feeling about the place as if the people expected to remain where they are for time everlasting. The people seem comfortable not over dressed or stylish.

The poor look poor all over—out of their very souls poverty speaks—so far I have not seen the many like I saw at Glasgow,[10] but later I shall go into these districts.

War talk is every where— It is a relief to read the frank sane statement made by Ramsey McDonald M.P.[11] also by Clifford Allen on "Is Germany Right & Britain Wrong"?[12]

Today Nov 15th Lord Roberts is reported dead.[13]

This City is not greatly affected by the war—business is said to be slow, but things assume the same appearance as usual—

Women all back to knitting socks, mitts etc again—

One finds the English very polite in speech & actions very tolerant in listening too. A dark day—rainy this—Sunday too I walked about to see Church Architecture. The Cathedral which is not expected to be finished for 50 years did not look so splendid.[14] As all about it is closed I could not tell.

Much talk here of German spy system—[15] I wonder if it is not more the general characteristics of the German to always observe & remember to be accurate in detail etc which naturally makes his information valuable, without an intention of being a spy or even an intention of using such information. They do the same in U.S. yet no one thinks of calling them spies.

AD MSP, DLC (LCM 1:3–8).

1. MS, who was using an assumed name, Bertha Watson, probably feared being stopped at customs due to war-related security measures. (MS, *Autobiography,* 96–97; for passports and visa, see *MSM* S83:917–24.)

2. This was probably Arthur Girling, who lived in Ipswich. (MS, Address Book, n.d. [MS Unfilmed].)

3. Robert Peel Glanville Blatchford (1851–1943), a British author, journalist, and socialist, cofounded the Independent Labour Party (ILP) and edited the *Clarion,* a popular socialist paper (1891–1932). The Clarion Café was one of a number of sites set up by followers of Blatchford and the ILP, who also started Clarion publications, clubs, and other associations. (*DNB;* William Hamling, *A Short History of the Liverpool Trades Council, 1848–1948* [Liverpool, England, 1948], 31–33.)

4. The Fabian Society was a British socialist organization founded in London in 1884 by a group of intellectuals, including George Bernard Shaw, H. G. Wells, Beatrice Webb, and Sidney Webb. Rejecting strict Marxism and violent class struggle, they sought instead to promote collective ownership and democratic control of resources through education and propaganda. The Fabians joined trade unionists to form the British Labour Party in 1900.

5. The ILP, which supported socialist internationalism, opposed Britain's entry into World War I on the grounds that workers were being exploited by capitalists of every nationality. It worked closely with pacifist groups, the No Conscription Fellowship (NCF), and the Union of Democratic Control (UDC) to call for an end to forced service and secret diplomacy. This stance, unpopular with many patriotic trade unions, resulted in the imprisonment of many ILP members.

6. John Edwards (?–1922) was the first president of the Liverpool Fabian Society and the editor of the Liverpool *Labour Chronicle* (1894–1901). (*Liverpool Post and Mercury,* Feb. 15–16, 1922.)

7. William "Big Bill" Haywood toured the British Isles in November and December 1913. (Carlson, *Roughneck,* 223.)

8. The British syndicalist Tom Mann was closely associated with the ILP and the East London Fabians; James Larkin (1876–1947) was an Irish labor leader, socialist, and ILP member; George Bernard Shaw (1856–1950), the Irish-born playwright and critic, was the author of a number of socialist tracts and a member of the Fabian Society executive committee (1884–1911); and H. G. Wells (1866–1946), the British novelist and social critic, was an active member of the Fabian Society from 1903 to 1908. (*DNB*)

9. "30S" was circled.

10. For MS's unpublished "Impressions of Glasgow," 1913, see LCM 129:668.

11. James Ramsay MacDonald (1866–1937), a Scottish socialist politician and British prime minister (1924, 1929–35), was one of the founders of the UDC. Made up largely of Liberals and ILP members, the UDC was extremely unpopular, often characterized as pro-German or antiwar. However, it did not support the anticonscription movement

and tried to focus its criticism on British policy rather than on the war itself. MS is likely referring to MacDonald's August 8, 1914, *Leicester Pioneer* article in which he blamed the anti-German bias of the British Foreign Office for Britain's involvement in the war. (*DNB;* Blanche Cook, "Democracy in Wartime: Antimilitarism in England and the United States, 1914–1918," in *Peace Movements in America,* ed. Charles Chatfield [New York, 1973], 52–62.)

12. Clifford Allen (1889–1939) was a British socialist, journalist, ILP member, and one of the founders of the NCF, the largest antiwar group in Britain. He was among its many members imprisoned for refusing to serve in the military. In the pamphlet, Allen criticized the Labour Party and the Trade Union Congress for supporting the war effort and claimed that Germany was not solely to blame for the outbreak of war. (Clifford Allen, *Is Germany Right and Britain Wrong?* 2d ed. [London, 1914]; F. M. Leventhal, *Twentieth-Century Britain* [New York, 1995], 11–12.)

13. Frederick Sleigh (Lord) Roberts (1832–1914), who headed the British army from 1900 to 1904, died in France while en route to India. (*DNB*)

14. Construction on Liverpool's Gothic-style Anglican Cathedral Church of Christ, the largest church in England, began in 1904 and was completed in 1978.

15. Since mid-October, England had been gripped by "spy-fever," inflamed by speeches and press reports on German atrocities in Belgium, resulting in riots against England's German-born population. (Panikos Panayi, *Enemy in Our Midst: Germans in Britain during the First World War* [New York, 1991], 155, 226.)

38. Diary Entry

London [*England*]
Dec 13—1914—

I came to London Nov 25th remained at the Metropole[1] a day or so—Guy Aldred promptly answered my letter & came to invite me out to the little nest where Rose Witcop & he have lived in a free union for several years.[2] Henry Sara lives there too—a tall, fine chap mind & ways like our S.L.P. boys in U.S. same way of thinking.[3] Guy might have made a splendid I.W.W. boy were he not tainted with the morality of an Early parson training.[4] Rose is different too. Tall, slender & dark with straight black hair combed low over the forhead & ears & caught at the nape of the neck. Slow in her movements not entirely freed th'o from the influence of the boys—nor in conventional ties.

I met Malatesta[5]—small dark personage—with splendid head & eyes which looks thru' one— It must have been difficult for him to understand my English— He is a silent reticent one, with a feeling of suspicion hovering over him. How different from the Spanish Portet—full of vigor, confident—quick to understand—[6]

In Liverpool I went to hear a lecture on Nietzsche and was simply inspired & enthused.[7] It was given by a young minister at the Unitarian Church at Hope St. The most splendid & understandable rendering of Nietzsche I ever heard.

In London to the British Museum each day.[8] To the National Art Gallery on Sunday, but so few pictures being exhibited closed off & stored away.[9]

On Dec 10th H. came.[10] On the 11th the picture fell from the wall & the glass smashed into thousands of pieces—a voice that father had died was heard or rather not heard, but seemed to be an inner voice within myself queer thing this—the first time it ever occurred to me & I am anxious to know what has happened.[11]

On the 10th I called at the Malthusian League[12] Queen Annes Chambers to see Dr Drysdale—[13] Mrs Drysdale[14] was there Dr B. Dunlop[15]—Mrs Stella Brown[16] & a few others. We had tea together & talked of this work & the consequences. Mrs Drysdale is charming. It did seem to me I had known them both & seen them often—

No mail for nearly two weeks. One from Nan[17] that Ethel & Rob. Gertrude & John[18] all live together—that group should be very congenial. I hope to get up a lecture on Individualism soon[19]—as soon as I get this next work off—a pamphlet.[20] What a queer thing is faith. To have faith in one—what does it mean—simply that that person shall remain stationary in a certain idea or thought or emotion—that he shall not progress further but remain stagnant in that one particular thing in which we have our faith. How easily to upturn all these old words upon which so much false sentiment has been built.

It seems almost good to be alone—there is time to get acquainted with ones self, to reflect, to meditate to dream, there is so little time these days for memories it's a luxury to have time for anything but work.

AD MSP, DLC (LCM 1:10). Return address: "67 Torrington Sq."

1. The Metropole was a London hotel on Northumberland Avenue, near Charing Cross.

2. Guy Aldred (1886–1963), a British socialist and later a communist, was the editor of such monthly journals as the *Spur* (1914–21). Rose Witcop (1890–1932), a Ukrainian-born anarchist and writer, contributed to the *Freewoman*, a feminist journal. Witcop and Aldred met in 1906 and lived together until 1926, when they finally married to prevent Witcop's deportation. The letter to which she referred was not found. (Caldwell, *Come Dungeons Dark*, 287; Banks, *Biographical Dictionary of British Feminists*, 221–22.)

3. Henry Sara (1886–1953), a British socialist and antiwar activist, shared a commitment to industrial unionism with the American Socialist Labor Party (SLP), which, under the leadership of Daniel DeLeon, was well known for its militant labor activities. (Sara Papers finding aid [UKW-MRC].)

4. As a youth, Aldred had studied theology and church history but refused to be ordained in the Church of England, choosing instead to become a radical evangelical preacher. By 1904, he had rejected the church as he embraced socialism and atheism. (Caldwell, *Come Dungeons Dark*, 12–21, 35–36.)

5. Errico Malatesta (1853–1932) was an Italian anarchist and journalist who instigated insurrections in the Middle East, South America, eastern Europe, and other areas. Exiled from Italy in 1878, he spent much of his time in London. (*New York Times*, July 26, 1932.)

6. Lorenzo Portet (1870–1917) was a Spanish anarchist, educator, and close associate of the Spanish revolutionist and educational reformer Francisco Ferrer. Following Ferrer's 1909 execution in Spain, Portet led a mass protest in Paris, resulting in his arrest. He fled to England and took a teaching position in Liverpool. Anointed as Ferrer's successor, Portet headed the Casa Editorial Publicacciones de la Escuela Moderna, the publishing house of Ferrer's Modern School movement. MS met Portet at the Clarion Café in Liverpool. (MS, "Portet and Ferrer.")

7. Friedrich Nietzsche (1844–1900), the German philosopher, poet, and classical philologist, castigated Western bourgeois society as decadent and corrupt for its over dependence on rational thought and Christianity. He created the concept of the *overman* or superman, who is liberated from all traditional values save those he deems valid. No information was found on the minister who gave the lecture. (Jackson Spielvogel, *Western Civilization*, 2d ed. [Minneapolis, 1994], 876.)

8. MS was studying the demographics of European nations to investigate their approach to population problems and eugenics. (MS, *Autobiography*, 142.)

9. Growing fears about possible attacks on British public and cultural institutions by German aliens probably led the National Gallery to limit its hours and the number of objects on exhibition. (Haste, *Keep the Home Fires Burning*, chaps. 5–6.)

10. "H" was possibly Harold Brainerd Hersey (1894–1956), a poet, writer, and pulp magazine editor who was MS's close friend and possible lover. (*New York Times*, Mar. 19, 1956; MS, Biographical Note, June 13, 1947 [*MSM* S83:615].)

11. Michael Higgins did not die until 1926.

12. The Malthusian League, founded in 1877 by Charles Robert Drysdale (1829–1907) and Alice Vickery (1849–1929), published the *Malthusian*, a monthly that reported on the activities of the league and its international branches. (Ledbetter, *Malthusian League*, 62–65, 78–80.)

13. Charles Vickery Drysdale (1874–1961) was the son of Charles Robert Drysdale and Alice Vickery. An electrical engineer, he took over as Malthusian League secretary upon his father's death and edited its journal until 1921. He expanded the league's activities to include publishing and distributing pamphlets on contraception and opening birth control clinics, but he alienated many potential supporters with his intense hostility to socialism. (Soloway, *Birth Control*, 174, 87–88; Ledbetter, *Malthusian League*, 57–58, 219.)

14. Bessie Ingham Drysdale (1871–1950) was a teacher and suffragist who, along with husband Charles Vickery Drysdale, served as secretary of the Malthusian League (1911–23). Though noted for her antisocialist and antilabor stance, Bessie Drysdale was more pragmatic than her husband about accepting support from socialists. (Benn, *Predicaments of Love*, 191, 216–18.)

15. Binnie Dunlop (1874–1946) was a Scottish physician who investigated social and economic problems. Dunlop joined the Malthusian League in 1910 and probably wrote its 1913 pamphlet *Hygienic Methods of Birth Control*. (Ledbetter, *Malthusian League*, 206–9; Charles Vickery Drysdale, "Binnie Dunlop," *Eugenics Review* 38 [Oct. 1946]: 146.)

16. Frances Worsley Stella Browne (1882–1955) was a Canadian-born socialist/feminist who supported women's reproductive freedom and sexual liberation. She served as a link between the Malthusian League and socialists by lecturing and writing articles on labor issues for the *Malthusian.* (Sheila Rowbotham, *New World for Women: Stella Browne—Socialist Feminist* [London, 1977], 7, 18.)

17. The letter from Anna Higgins was not found.

18. Robert Allerton Parker (1889–1970), a writer and editor, lived in New York City with MS's younger sister, Ethel Byrne, from the 1910s through the early 1920s. A drama critic for such journals as *Current Opinion* and the *Literary Digest,* he also helped MS formulate plans for the publication of the *Woman Rebel* in 1914 and is credited by some with coining the term *birth control.* Parker later served as MS's editor and sometime ghostwriter on speeches, articles, and books. "Gertrude and John" were not identified. (*New York Times,* June 15, 1970; MS, *Autobiography,* 252; Van Voris, "Olive Byrne Richard Interview," 18; Chesler, *Woman of Valor,* 197.)

19. Individualism was a social and political philosophy that emphasized the freedom of the individual, self-reliance, privacy, and minimal government involvement in human lives. MS was familiar with anarchist conceptions of radical individualism, as put forth by the nineteenth-century anarchist Ezra Heywood and by Emma Goldman, who trusted in a natural moral order that made government unnecessary. She probably also read or heard other discussions on individualism, such as Havelock Ellis's 1912 article on its relation to socialism, and incorporated elements into various speeches, but there is no evidence that she ever lectured specifically on this topic. (Martin H. Blatt, *Free Love and Anarchism: The Biography of Ezra Heywood* [Chicago, 1989], 175–76; Havelock Ellis, "Individualism and Socialism," *Contemporary Review* 101 [Apr. 1912]: 519–28.)

20. This was probably *English Methods of Birth Control,* published in February 1915.

39. *From Havelock Ellis*[1]

[*London, England*]
15 Dec/14.

My dear Miss "Watson,"

Thank you for telling me about your sad experiences in conflict with the relics of so-called "Puritanism."[2] I should be glad to know more about it, & to have an opportunity of seeing any papers on the case. The ferocious antagonism (in theory only!) to anything so simple, human & necessary as the regulation of conception is a perpetual puzzle to me.

I should be most pleased to see you & to hear more about the matter. This week I am rather occupied; could you call some morning or afternoon next week?

Thank you for your kind words about my work. I am always very pleased to find that my books have been of any little help in this direction for that has been my aim from the outset. Sincerely yours

Havelock Ellis

I hope you can send me or bring me some copies of the "Woman Rebel," which I would carefully return.

ALS MSP, DLC (LCM 4:3–6).

1. Havelock Ellis (1859–1939), the British physician, psychologist, prominent author, and widely known proponent of post-Victorian modernism, emerged as one of the preeminent new European sex theorists. (*DNB*)

2. On the advice of the Drysdales and Stella Browne, MS had written a letter (not found) introducing herself, in which she probably recounted her persecution by Anthony Comstock. (Grosskurth, *Havelock Ellis,* 242–43.)

40. *From Eugene V. Debs*[1]

Terre Haute, Ind.
Dec. 16th., 1914.

Dear Comrade Sanger:—

Your good letter of the 8th. ult. came while I was in the Southwest, followed me for a time and has just been returned here.[2] I note with deep interest all you say about yourself and your work and your prospects. It is a burning shame that you had to leave here as a fugitive for trying to be of service, by the most humane and enlightened means possible, to the working class. But I doubt not your temporary exile will have its compensation. You will do your work all the same and I cannot think that when you return here the cave men in authority would dare lay their hands on you. And yet we have reason to know that they dare do anything to keep the workers in chains.

But if they do attempt to railroad you we have now some means of defense and we can call a pretty good-sized bunch of revolutionists to arms.

I have but little time here, so little that I can write no letters in answer to the many that are here until I get back again. I shall soon be off for the Pacific coast[3] where I am booked for a speaking tour that will cover a couple of months.

Allow me to wish you all success in your work and the fullest realization of your dreams and aspirations. Faithfully your comrade,

E. V. Debs [*signed*]

TLS MSP, DLC (LCM 8:146). Letterhead of the Office of Theodore Debs.

1. Eugene V. Debs (1855–1926) was a railroad worker, labor organizer, writer, lecturer, founder of the Socialist Party of America, and five-time Socialist Party candidate for president. (*ANB*)

2. The letter was not found. Debs was lecturing in the Southwest under the auspices

of the *National Rip-Saw,* a St. Louis–based Socialist Party paper. (Nick Salvatore, *Eugene V. Debs: Citizen and Socialist* [Chicago, 1982], 273.)

3. Debs toured the Pacific Coast from January 10 to February 17, 1915. (Robert J. Constantine, ed., *Letters of Eugene V. Debs* [Chicago, 1990], 129*n*5.)

41. Diary Entry

[*London, England*]
Dec 17th [*1914*]

Last night I went to hear Annie Kinnie speak in Kingsway Hall on her trip to U.S. Mrs Pankhurst was in the chair—[1]

Her tone was good, Her intellect clear & someway she reminded me of Charlotte Perkins Gillman—[2]

She seems like a good General & a maker of good generals. I wonder at her "patriotism" & have a sneaking suspicion it is a tactic rather than a feeling—[3]

What splendid looking girls in the making she has around her—faces bright, jaws well set, determined. Even the free stride many of them have in walking shows their trend of mind.

Many of them dainty of dress & frail of body, but nearly all I saw had conviction & courage & determination on their faces— Of course Mrs Pankhurst is their God—but perhaps its too early to take from them all things which give them support, but it will come later if not this generation perhaps the next. Women & men must be a god unto themselves, they must cease worshiping at the shrine of other egos & look into their own & develop & nourish it.

In the afternoon I went to a lecture of the International Womens Franchise ~~Asso~~ League[4] where Dr Chas V. Drysdale spoke on the causes of the War—[5]

He spoke freely & full of his subject, laughs a great deal in his address which is good. Proved the growing population of Germany demanded an outlet, & the war had to come— Russia is the next to be feared he said & when her population begins to decrease then & only then will there be signs of Internationalism. Dr Dunlop took me to the Hall to hear Kinney & Pankhurst.

How lonely it all is—could any prison be more isolated could one be more alone or more lonely in "solitary" than wandering about the world—separated from the little ones you love, from their childish prattle, caresses, whisperings & quarrels, & also from the other ones & things & friends one loves & one understands—

It is not only the language which separates "Comrades" it is psychology—

I burn & long to get to work on a lecture on Nietzsche. I believe a message to the workers of his teachings is the next greatest step to take.[6]

Yesterday I sent a letter to Bill S—parting the ways of our life together—He will not be surprised I know for the past year he has been prepared for it.[7] Only I am very slow in my decisions—I can not separate myself from my past emotions quickly all breeches must come gradually to me. It took me so long to get a Church out of my system then Socialism—bougueoise Society etc etc so in everything.

AD MSP, DLC (LCM 1:14–15).

1. Annie Kenney (Taylor) (1879–1953), a radical British suffragist, had recently toured the western United States, speaking at trade union and suffrage meetings. Kenney, Emmeline Pankhurst (1858–1928), and her daughter Christabel, founders of the Women's Social and Political Union (WSPU), were known for their militant tactics on behalf of woman suffrage. All three were repeatedly arrested and imprisoned. (Crawford et al., *Europa Biographical Dictionary of British Women*, 317–18.)

2. Charlotte Perkins Gilman (1860–1935) was a feminist writer and lecturer who published *Women and Economics* (1898), the notable short story "The Yellow Wallpaper" (1890), and the utopian novel *Herland* (1915). MS heard Gilman speak at the February 1914 mass meeting of the Feminist Alliance in New York City. (*ANB;* MS, "New Feminists.")

3. British suffragists were divided over the war. While Christabel and Emmeline Pankhurst, Annie Kenney, Millicent Fawcett of the National Union of Woman Suffrage Societies (NUWSS), and others supported the British war effort, many opposed it. By February 1915, the NUWSS had split over the issue, with some members forming the Women's International League for Peace and Freedom. MS, along with many American suffragists and socialists, opposed U.S. entry into the war and was critical of the zealous patriotism of the prowar suffragists. (Jill Liddington and Jill Norris, *One Hand Tied behind Us: The Rise of the Women's Suffrage Movement* [London, 1990], 252–57.)

4. No official organization by this name was found. MS probably attended a meeting of the Woman's Freedom League (WFL), organized by Alice Vickery, Bessie Drysdale, and others who split off from Pankhurst's WSPU in 1907 to remain allied with England's Labour Party. In addition to working for woman suffrage, the WFL opposed the war, urging members not to pay taxes and to support birth control as a means of depopulating England and denying the war machine. (Andro Linklater, *An Unhusbanded Life: Charlotte Despard* [London, 1980], 168–73.)

5. The Malthusian League escaped divisive conflict over the war, focusing solely on demographic issues. Members believed that unrestricted breeding in Germany and the Central Powers had created population pressures resulting in aggression, but they argued that nations with a lower birthrate (such as France and England) produced higher quality soldiers and would ultimately be victorious. However, such arguments were unpopular because they countered the prevailing sentiment in favor of producing "war babies" to replace those dying at the front. When the Drysdales criticized this notion as

economically and eugenically irresponsible, they were accused of being pro-German. (Soloway, *Birth Control,* 160–65, 173–74; *Malthusian,* Aug. 15 and Dec. 15, 1914.)

6. MS found a justification for her own actions and ideals in the philosophy of Nietzsche, whose works she was then reading. Sometime in 1915, she did draft a lecture on Nietzsche in which she observed that he taught her that "the individual is the original source and constituent of all value." (MS, "Frederick Nietzsche" [LCM 130:356].)

7. The letter was not found.

42. Diary Entry

[*London, England*]
Dec 22—1914

Today I went to Brixton to call on Havelock Ellis—[1] Tall, lovely, simple man with the most wonderful head & face & smile. He opened the door in answer to my knock.[2] We had no difficulty in feeling comfortable. It was four oclock & he lighted two candles on the mantle. These threw a soft light on to his features which gave him the look of a seer. We had tea which he prepared & carried into the room his work shop where we sat by the open fire & talked.

Wonderful mind, with an easy, not in a hurry rush at all, such a relief to find. It seems to be the men who do the most creative & productive work who are the simplest & easiest to meet & understand.

He talked of the trial on his book Inversions[3]—gave me a copy to read also his copy of Karazza[4] to take. Thinks the method advised in Karazza splendid if man is able to do it, spoke openly & freely on the subject which was a relief.

There is a shyness & reticence about him of the student & the simplicity of a great soul & mind.

I count this a glorious day to have conversed with the one man who has done more than anyone in this Century toward giving women & men a clear & sane understanding of their sex lives & of all life.

I am wondering what the kiddies are doing—its nearly christmas eve.[5] I sit here alone by the dying fire & thing of them & wonder & dream—

AD MSP, DLC (LCM 1:16–17).

1. With his wife on an American lecture tour, Ellis was living alone. In his autobiography, in which he carefully muted his relationship with MS, he wrote of their first encounter: "On me this first meeting simply left a pleasant impression which, aided by sympathy with her lonely situation in a strange city far from husband and children, induced me to invite her to come again. . . . An American of Irish origin, she attractively united the good points of both nationalities." (Ellis, *My Life,* 520.)

2. MS recalled her first impression of Ellis "in that sordid apartment in Brixton" in a 1952 letter to his biographer: "He opened the door for me, as he always did for his guests—and with his great white lovely head and flowing beard he was truly God-like." (MS to Vincent Brome, July 16, 1952 [*MSM* S38:731].)

3. Ellis's *Sexual Inversions* was England's first sympathetic and comprehensive treatment of homosexuality. Unable to find an English publisher, Ellis first published the book in a German translation in 1896. An English edition, finally issued by Watford University Press in 1898, was suppressed after the freethinker George Bedborough sold a copy to a detective. At his obscenity trial, Bedborough argued that *Sexual Inversions* was a scientific study. Ellis did little to defend his book or assist Bedborough, who was eventually convicted and fined. *Sexual Inversions* remained banned in England, but a second edition, revised and renumbered as volume 2 in Ellis's six-volume *Studies in the Psychology of Sex,* was published in the United States in 1901. In December 1914, Ellis was working on a revised third edition, published in the United States in 1915. (Grosskurth, *Havelock Ellis,* 179–85, 191–200, 471.)

4. Alice B. Stockham's *Karezza: Ethics of Marriage* (1898) describes *coitus reservatus,* a method of male continence whereby the male does not ejaculate during vaginal intercourse and, ideally, withdraws after detumescence. Though Stockham focused on Karezza as a technique to heighten sensual and spiritual awareness, it was used as a contraceptive method at Oneida and other utopian communities and was popular among nineteenth-century free love advocates in England and the United States. MS described Karezza and similar methods in her 1915 pamphlet *Magnetation Methods of Birth Control.* (Himes, *Medical History of Contraception,* 269–70.)

5. The three children spent the Christmas holiday with their father in his Manhattan studio. (William Sanger to MS, Dec. 25, 1914 [*MSM* S1:349].)

43. *Diary Entry*

[*London, England*]
Christmas Eve Dec 24—1914

What a fog! I could not see two feet ahead of me tonight as I came out of Rose Witcops house where I spent a few hours. Lorenzo Portet was with me until his train left.[1]

London is like every other place on Christmas. Many women drunk, but strong husky men taking them home. I have a furious headache and feel I am getting some kind of rheumatism.

I have such an amount of clothing on that I can scarcely walk & yet Im cold. Just a year ago tonight we left Havre for N.Y. The three children & I—ah what a year this has been!

I saw E. P. C. Haynes today gave me several letters of introduction—[2] Seems a good sort. Said American puritanism was like flowers on a rotting corpse. What has this next year in store for me I wonder. Each day must be lived full—& strong & powerfull then it will bring results unheard of.

Salvation Army singing Christmas Carrolls 12 PM in streets.

AD MSP, DLC (LCM 1:18).

1. Portet was probably returning to his family either in Liverpool or Barcelona for the holidays.

2. Edmund Sidney Pollack Haynes (1877–1949), a British solicitor, author, and expert on marriage law who traveled in intellectual circles that included the Drysdales, Havelock Ellis, and H. G. Wells, was a vice-president of the Malthusian League. The letters of introduction were not found. (*WWW England;* Smith, *H. G. Wells,* 365.)

44. From Havelock Ellis

After their initial meeting, Sanger and Ellis found themselves quickly becoming close friends, with Ellis later noting, "I had rarely known a more charming and congenial companion, and I have never found one so swiftly." (Ellis, My Life, *520.)*

[*London, England*]
26 Dec/14

Dear Woman Rebel,

A line to thank you for yours[1] & to say that, if nothing prevents, I expect to be at the Reading Room[2] on Monday between 11 & 1 & that if I do not arrive at L. I hope you will call at 9. 9 or 10 or thereabouts.

It was "What Every Mother Should Know" that I specially like, though I am quite in sympathy with the [*longer*] book which ought to be very useful.[3] I should like to see anything else you may have written.

I hope to hunt up & bring the Noyes pamphlets.[4] I will bear in mind, also, your questions. I should be pleased if I can suggest any reading; I can do this better when I know more of what you are feeling after.

As to me, I am not at all anxious for the scientific world to take its hat off to H. E. (not that there is any danger!) & am quite content to be allowed to follow quietly my own path—so long as I am helping rather than injuring others.

I had not noticed that your visit was long & I hope you will feel inclined to repeat it.

I was wondering if you had many friends here but in any case it is lonely to be in a strange city & away from all those you care for most, & especially at Xmas—always a hateful time, I think. I am more alone—though not without friends—then I have been at this season for a great many years ↑and my father has lately died,[5] which makes one feel old.↓ [*interlined in left margin*] So

I fall back on my Xmas habit when in Australia long ago & went to High Mass at the Catholic Cathedral![6]

Yours very sincerely

Havelock Ellis.

ALS MSP, DLC (LCM 4:11–15).

1. The letter was not found.
2. Ellis was referring to the British Museum Library, where he offered to advise MS on relevant books and materials on birth control in Europe, and for several weeks they regularly met there. (Grosskurth, *Havelock Ellis,* 243.)
3. The "longer book" is probably *What Every Girl Should Know.*
4. These were various editions of *Male Continence; or, Self Control in Sexual Intercourse,* first published in 1866 by John Humphrey Noyes (1811–86), a religious reformer and utopian socialist. (*ANB*)
5. Edward Peppen Ellis (1827–1914), a British merchant sea captain, died in the autumn of 1914. (Brome, *Havelock Ellis,* 171.)
6. Ellis lived in Australia from 1876 to 1879. Reared as an Anglican, he had converted to Evangelicalism and considered studying for the clergy. However, Ellis was tormented by doubts, until 1878 when a mystical religious experience in Australia led him to recapture his faith and reconcile it with his interest in science and medicine. (Grosskurth, *Havelock Ellis,* 20–47.)

45. *Diary Entry*

[*London, England*]

Dec 28—1914.

At the Br Museum today Havelock Ellis & I had a few minutes talk & went out to lunch together in Soho. The more one sees of him the ↑the more↓ bigness of the man grows upon one. The charm is that he does not paste words all about him or try to impress one at all—he's just natural—

Knows Carpenter[1] & tells me he will invite me to see Carpenter when he is in London again. Read his Impressions & Comments & find my self in H. E. presence talking over these things with him.[2] There is no doubt that the men & women who are thinking today are going on the road toward Individualism.

AD MSP, DLC (LCM 1:19).

1. Edward Carpenter (1844–1929) was a British writer, poet, and social reformer. A homosexual and a Fabian socialist who rebelled against social and religious conventions, he was a follower of William Morris, who asserted that genuine love could exist only among equals. Carpenter's book *Love's Coming-of-Age* (1896), extremely popular among American radical intellectuals, explored sexual relations and sexual differences between

men and women, as well as feminism, free love, and social reform. (*DNB;* Fishbein, *Rebels in Bohemia,* 94–95, 132.)

2. *Impressions and Comments,* First Series, 1912–13 (London, 1914) was the first of Ellis's series of essays, poems, vignettes, and other fragments recording events and his random thoughts.

46. From Havelock Ellis

[*London, England*]
30 Dec/14.

Dear Rebel,

I am pleased you like my book. It is such a personal sort of book that I am never sure whether people will like it or dislike,—though I certainly think that if they don't violently dislike it they ought to violently like it![1]

I don't see any reason why you should want to burn your own books. I quite understand that you have been [*mainly*] occupied with direct action, and I don't know that you have a special gift for writing (you may have, I am not sure) but your way of writing is so direct & sincere, & so much yourself, that I enjoy it, & hope you will write more.

I enjoyed our luncheon & hope you will be inclined for another meeting soon.— I expect to be in the Reading Room tomorrow morning. Sincerely yours

H. E.

ALI MSP, DLC (LCM 4:16–17).

1. Ellis called his *Impressions and Comments* volumes "the most intimately personal, the most spontaneous and the most deliberately moulded, of my writings." (Ellis, *My Life,* 162.)

47. From Havelock Ellis

[*London, England*]
Tuesday Morning [*January 5, 1915*]

Dear Margaret,

I have your letter[1] & will begin at the beginning. Like you, I feel suspicious about the idea that to have inter course with many men prevents the prostitute from becoming pregnant. I don't deny the possibility, but at present it is merely a vague idea.[2] There is a far better reason than that why prostitutes should not become pregnant. Nearly every prostitute must very soon get gonorrhea (even though she may not know it) & there is no cause of sterility in women so common as the inflammation arising from gonorrhea.[3] I doubt if one needs any other reasons.

Next, as regards coitus interruptus, what I say in "Sex~~ual~~ in Relation to Society" (Vol. VI of the Studies), p. 551 is "Coitus interruptus, since it involves sudden withdrawal on the part of the man without reference to the stage of excitement which his partner may have reached, cannot fail to produce frequently an injurious nervous effect on the woman."[4] Will that quotation suit you?

I find your writing perfectly easy to read. If your writing is a torture to read, what must my scrawl be!![5] I feel that I ought never to write to you again!!!

As things stand at present, I expect you here on Wednesday— Say about 5 (before the rush begins). If Thursday suits you better, that would also suit me.

Yes, you "just sensed" something—I knew you did—I sensed that you sensed it! But what you sensed was not really any disapproval whatever of the special combination of these two fascinating qualities in you. It had more reference to me. What I felt, & feel, is that by just being your natural spontaneous self you are giving me so much more than I can hope to give you. You see, I am an extremely odd, reserved, slow, undemonstrative person, whom it takes years & years to know. I have two or three very dear friends who date from 20 or 25 years back (& they like me better now than they did at first) & none of recent date. I'm not the least good for gobbling up rapidly—really don't [*repay*] the trouble! And I don't feel a bit anxious to be gobbled up, while the gobbler is already unwinding her scarf to wave to someone else![6]

I fear this sounds very rude & horrid & not at all as it is meant. But I am obliged to write rapidly as I am expecting a visitor.

I look forward to seeing you. Affectionately yours

Havelock

ALS MSP, DLC (LCM 4:20–24).

1. The letter was not found.

2. MS had asserted in March 1914, "Seldom does a prostitute become pregnant. Seldom does the girl practicing promiscuity become pregnant." It is unclear what research she had done that now prompted her to question this assumption. ("The Prevention of Conception," Mar. 1914, herein.)

3. Gonorrhea is a sexually transmitted disease caused by gonococcal bacteria that affect the mucous membranes of the genito-urinary tract and may cause sterility in both sexes. There are no firm statistics on sterility rates among prostitutes, but both Ellis and his contemporary sex researcher Iwan Bloch found high rates of venereal disease among prostitutes who participated in studies. (John Walton et al., eds., *Oxford Medical Companion* [New York, 1994], 330; Ellis, *Sex in Relation to Society,* 329–33; Bloch, *Sexual Life,* 396.)

4. The complete sentence read, "It is undoubtedly true that coitus interruptus, since

it involves sudden withdrawal on the part of the man without reference to the stage of sexual excitement which his partner may have reached, cannot fail to produce frequently an injurious nervous effect on the woman, though the injurious effect on the man, who obtains ejaculation, is little or none" (551). MS reflected Ellis's position in "Excerpt from *English Methods of Birth Control,* 'Are Preventive Means Injurious to Health?'" January–February 1915, herein.

5. Ellis did have an almost indecipherable handwriting.

6. MS had spent New Year's Eve with Ellis, who later wrote, "I have begun this new year at the stroke of midnight with a new kiss." MS may have "sensed" Ellis's fear they were too quickly becoming intimate. (Ellis, *Impressions and Comments,* Second Series, 1914–20 [London, 1921], 64; Grosskurth, *Havelock Ellis,* 224.)

48. *From William Sanger*[1]

[*New York, N.Y.*]
21st Jan. 1915

Peg:

The last three letters you sent me were opened and resealed by the post office.[2] The letters as you know were important as they gave your plans most fully and right good meat for the authorities to identify me and B—— and with the F.L. etc.[3] It would have been better if we had agreed as originally to have your mail to me to go to someother place than my studio. But that is all past now. It would be better if some other place than my studio address for the addressing of any further mail to me. Now as to business (this is one of the terms that you used in one of your letters.) On December the 18th last a party came into my studio and left his card, a Mr Hallock. He claimed to be a seller of rubber goods and etc. Not seeing me he called the next day about 8 a.m. and said, "I am Mr Hallock."[4] He said he had heard of your books, stated that he was personally acquainted with you, and wanted one of the pamphlets. I told him that I had no pamphlets that I knew of. Thinking that he was Hallock[5] of the S.P. whom you met[6] and being very early in the morning and being rather sleepy and in my pajamas and he further stating that it was for his own use personally, finally to get rid of him, I went to the library table and in it were your English and French pamphlets ~~a~~ and your own pamphlet.[7] I gave him the first one that I found. I thought no more of it until the same man called last Tuesday, January, the 19th and wanted to know where your <u>books</u> could be bought. I told him Meisel on Grand Street.[8] A few minutes after a grey haired, side ~~w~~ whiskered, ~~six~~ ↑Five↓ foot ass presented himself. He said "I am Mr Comstock, I have a warrant out for your arrest."[9] He was followed by that man Hallock.[10] Having a search warrant, he proceeded to search the studio and found two other pamphlets.[11] I had to submit to two searches, one by the pimp and one by the ass. I was taken to Yorkville Court.[12] But I want to say that before we left the studio Comstock said that I would be given every opportunity to prove my innocence which I ignored. He seemed eager for me to enter into a discussion of the case, saying that any statement that I made would not be used against me. I refused to say any thing claiming that I wished to consult my attorney. He replied that lawyers are expensive and only aggrevate the case, patting me on the shoulder he said he advised me like a brother to plead guilty and he would recommend to the court that I be given a suspended sentence. I refused to entertain any such plea. I told him that although I was in Europe at the time that the pamphlet was written and circulated ~~and that~~ I believed in the principle of family limitation. He then asked me whether we were living together or separated. I flatly told him that I would give him no information. When going out he asked me where Mrs Sanger could be found. I replied that I did not intend to tell and that he or no other official of any kind a right to ask me. That ended the interview and we proceeded to the police court. I was ~~brought~~ arraigned and my bail was fixed at $500. Meanwhile my studio collegue, Mr Ben Benn[13] started to look up Abbott and Roe[14] to get bail. No one seemed anxious to go on my bail and it was not until [*Wednesday*] night at ten O'clock that bail was procured for me through Roe and Abbott through a surety company. It was the general opinion that I would skip the bail. However I am out ↑on Bail now↓ but the prison soujourn although short was hell. I lived a year in thirty-six hours. The case comes up next Wednesday for preliminary examination. It will then be sent down the Court of Special Sessions and tried before a jury if possible.[15] It will come up sometime in February. I am liable to get the limit of one year and $1000. fine. I shall try to have the case tried on the principle of family limitation and free speech. But as far as I can see the case as a whole is a preliminary to the case that you will fight on your return. Yet at the same time I do not intend to show the white feather as a radical never-the-less, for my own personal satisfaction. ~~Independent of what you m~~ Of course my getting involved is entirely accidental.

The work is primarily a womans work and Your work and I would much more have liked it by a damn sight ↑for you to have↓ been here to take up the work from the start although I would not have ~~wi~~ wished you to go through the humility of being arrested by Comstock and thrown into a filthy jail. Most people seem to think that I will be acquited; Roe thinks that I am liable to get the limit. In going over the case with him to-day the question of your return was brought up. Although he did not advise me to advise you to stay in England he did however state that your coming before my case is settled would aggravate it, I think it would better for you to stay until April or until my case is cleared up one way or the other. ↑In case you thought of returning earlier.↓ In regard to your case in going up to jail that day with Comstock, I flatly asked him what he would do with the author of a pamphlet like yours and he said he would recommend that such a party be given the limit, five years at hard labor. I only mention this, perhaps it is a dream only of Comstock's. You know best what to do. Some body mentioned that if I would give the whereabouts of you I would be acquited and I replied not even if hell froze up would that occur. I understand now that you can be extradited.

The children are well. In fact Miss Pratt's house is a perfect haven for childhood.[16] They have a lovely room with separate beds and fine kindergarten program althrough the day. I have taken Grant from public school after Miss Pratt has convinced me that he was actually running behind younger children at her school. He looks better and learns better all along the line and his drawing is being brought out very well. I feel a great burden has been taken off my mind and it would be needless for me to write you at great length about their care because that is quite unnecessary only of course you would want to know from time to time how they are, which I will do. Another important point is that the letters that I sent over to you especially ~~for those~~ ↑of those people↓ asking for information I would not reply to if you can help it.[17] It would involve extended correspondence on your pamphlet and family limitation in general as replies would come back to my studio address.

Among all those letters sent to you I would not reply to except those you consider <u>most important</u>. There would be no use corresponding with individuals as you must consider that your mail comes to my studio now. Send all your letters to me, not in my name. Address the envelope to Helen Marot, 206 West 13th Street and she will know they are for me and hand them over without opening them.

Bill

The reason this was type written I wanted to be sure that you could read it.— [*Handwritten*] This case will be a free speech & F-L. case to the limit. Twenty women headed by Helen Marot have already banded together to fight—[18]

They will no doubt write you. All seem to think that you should remain in Europe until my case is disposed of.

B. [*initialed*]

TL MSP, MN-SSC (*MSM* S1:401–4). Handwritten interlineations and corrections were by William Sanger; interlineations and additions by an unidentified author are indicated in the endnotes.

1. William Sanger continued to paint and work as a freelance draftsman at a studio on East Fifteenth Street.

2. The letters were not found. Postal agents were monitoring William Sanger's mail to discover her whereabouts.

3. He was referring to MS's alias "Bertha Watson" and her pamphlet *Family Limitation.*

4. "Heller" was interlined over "Hallock." "Heller" was the alias used by Charles J.

Bamberger (1872–1947), an agent for the New York Society for the Suppression of Vice from 1894 to 1940. (Boyer, *Purity in Print,* 251.)

5. "Heller" was interlined over "Hallock."

6. It is unclear whether Hallock or Heller was a member of the Socialist Party.

7. The "French and English" pamphlets were probably reference materials MS had gathered while writing *Family Limitation.*

8. Max N. Maisel (1872–1959) owned a New York City bookshop, where he published and sold Yiddish and leftist materials, including MS's two booklets *What Every Mother Should Know* and *What Every Girl Should Know.* (Hersey, "Margaret Sanger," 119.)

9. Using aliases or sending out undercover agents, Comstock often entrapped his victims into sending or distributing criminalized material.

10. "Heller" was interlined over "Hallock."

11. These were additional copies of *Family Limitation* or other pamphlets MS had gathered for her research.

12. Located at 207 East Thirty-second Street, the courthouse served New York City's Fourth Municipal District.

13. Ben Benn (1884–1983) was a Ukrainian-born Cubist painter. (*New York Times,* Jan. 11, 1983.)

14. Leonard Dalton Abbott (1879–1953) was a British-born writer, literary editor, and socialist. Influenced by Emma Goldman, among others, Abbott became an ardent anarchist, pacifist, and free speech advocate, serving as president of the Free Speech League. Gilbert E. Roe (1865–1929) was a lawyer, author, and former law partner and political adviser of the Progressive Wisconsin senator Robert La Follette. After moving to New York City, Roe joined his law school classmate Theodore Schroeder in handling Free Speech League cases, including William Sanger's, often charging no fee. (*New York Times,* Mar. 20, 1953, and Dec. 23, 1929; Avrich, *Modern School Movement,* 41–42, 165–70; *DAB;* Abbott, "Conviction of William Sanger," 268–69.)

15. William Sanger was arrested for violating New York State Penal Law, Section 1141, subdivision 1 ("uttering an advertisement purporting to give information where, how, when, of whom, and by what means an article purporting to be for immoral use, could be obtained"). On Comstock's advice, Sanger agreed, without counsel present, to appear before the court of special sessions in which specific cases were tried before three judges appointed by the mayor. Roe tried twice to have the trial moved to General Sessions (where cases were heard by a jury), arguing that Comstock had violated his client's rights, but the requests were denied. (William Sanger appeal, July 9, 1915 [*MSM* C15:44]; *New York Globe and Commercial Advertiser,* Mar. 4, 1915.)

16. Caroline Pratt (1867–1954) was an educator and founder of the Greenwich Village City and Country School, a progressive kindergarten. Shortly after MS left for Montreal, William Sanger arranged for Peggy and Grant to stay with Pratt and her life companion, Helen Marot (1865–1940), a socialist labor reformer and executive secretary of the New York Women's Trade Union League (1903–13). Grant joined Peggy at Pratt's private school. (John F. Ohles, *Biographical Dictionary of American Educators* [Westport, Conn., 1978; *NAW;* William Sanger to MS, Dec. 25, 1914 [*MSM* S1:349].)

17. He was referring to additional letters from women seeking birth control information.

18. Mary Ware Dennett and Clara Gruening Stillman were also among those who attended informal meetings to raise defense funds for William Sanger. In March 1915, members of this defense fund, along with Jessie Ashley, Otto Bobsien, Lincoln Steffens, James Morton Jr., and others, organized the National Birth Control League (NBCL). (*Survey,* Apr. 3, 1915, 5; Chen, *Sex Side of Life,* 180.)

49. *Excerpt from* English Methods of Birth Control: "Are Preventive Methods Injurious to Health?"

While in England, Margaret Sanger decided to supplement the information provided in Family Limitation *in a series of three pamphlets. She claimed these would also fulfill her financial obligation to* Woman Rebel *subscribers. She released* English Methods of Birth Control *in February 1915, followed by* Dutch Methods of Birth Control, *probably in March or April, and* Magnetation Methods of Birth Control, *issued in August.* English Methods *provided instruction in basic sex education, with sections on the safety of and need for birth control methods, the dangers of abortion, and the impact of birth control on the labor movement. Sanger also included the portions of the Malthusian League's* Hygienic Methods of Family Limitation *(1913) that advocated male conception control through withdrawal or condoms.* Dutch Methods, *a translation of the Dutch Neo-Malthusian League's* Means of Preventing Large Families *(1890?–98), provided a history of the Dutch Neo-Malthusian League (Nieuw-Malthusiaansche Bond), traced the connection between contraceptive use and lower infant mortality and illegitimacy rates, and offered contraceptive advice. The Dutch league's most highly recommended method was the Mensinga occlusive pessary, a diaphragm designed to cover the cervix to prevent the entry of sperm.* Magnetation Methods *summarized French contraceptive techniques and included anonymous testimonials and illustrations of contraceptive devices available in France. It also contained a theoretical and practical discussion of the practice of male continence. All three pamphlets were printed in England and shipped to the United States for distribution, and though they clearly violated the Comstock Act, charges were never brought against Sanger.*

[January–February 1915]

One of the questions quite commonly asked by women and men who are fearful of using preventives is: "Will preventive methods injure the health of either the man or the woman?"

A prominent authority, Wille (as quoted by Kisch), maintains "that the continued fear of pregnancy will in most cases do more injury to the feminine system than all the preventive measures in the world."[1]

It is further claimed by some physicians that to a nervously weak woman a preventive method is almost necessary, and even helpful in regaining her health; but that much depends upon the kind of method employed is not doubted.

One of the most directly injurious methods to the woman is the use of *strong* solutions of antiseptics for the douche. If these are above the proper strength, they are liable to injure the delicate membraneous lining of the parts. The same solutions in weaker proportions will act as a cleanser, and are seldom injurious.[2]

But as each person is susceptible in a greater or less degree to all drugs, I advise the use of salt solution as a douche, as not only the least injurious and the cheapest, but as most beneficial.

Another question which has arisen in late years is the possibility that preventive methods have caused cancer. There is very little foundation for this assertion.

The constant use of the pessary, worn from month to month, or the "uterus button," worn by women in the Western States,[3] or any mechanical means worn constantly, might give rise to an irritation which could lead to the growth of cancer. But the temporary use of either of these would without doubt be quite harmless. By temporary use, I mean the use of either only when needed, followed by their removal.

In employing any preventive measures there is almost no danger to the man at all, even the habit of "coitus interruptus," or withdrawal, which is the most common method practised everywhere, is not considered as dangerous to the man's health, as some authorities formerly viewed it; but, on the other hand, is considered by the most prominent authorities as injurious to the woman's nervous system. The following are some of the best known men who look upon the practice as not beneficial to the woman: August Forel, Heinrich Kisch, Von Krafft-Ebing, Mensinga, Hirt, Freud, Löwenfeld, Elischer, Havelock Ellis, and many others.[4]

In the preceding pamphlet on "Family Limitation," I have explained this habit and the effects it has upon women, and shall not dwell upon it here.[5] It is sufficient to say that "coitus interruptus" is considered as the cause of nervous disturbances and other serious conditions of the generative organs in woman by many prominent medical authorities of the day.

"The lack of sexual satisfaction," concludes Kisch, "aggravates nervous and hysterical trouble in women, while suitably regulated intercourse with mutual satisfaction has an actively beneficial effect."[6]

There has been among men a common idea that woman had little or no sex desire or interest, and that marriage sanctioned a union which made of woman a recipient but not a mutual partner in the sex life. Fortunately this idea is giving way, and men of ideals and fine temperaments dislike the idea of the relation when it is not mutual.[7] That is one of the reasons that the use of preventive measures has come to play so important a part in the lives of both men and women, and why it must sooner or later receive the fullest attention from the medical profession, as well as from society at large.

Tolstoy was opposed to the use of preventives because they liberate men from the cares and sorrows of having children, which he thought must be regarded as the penance to be paid for sensual love.[8] One might naturally ask why the children should be made to suffer; and if sensual love is a degraded love, why not prevent children being born in it?

I think we, who have in view a new race, do not desire that race to be the penance of previous generations' sins.

There are only a few authorities to-day who look upon the use of preventive measures as either immoral or injurious;[9] it is more generally regarded as a rise in the physical and moral standards of the people who use them.

English Methods of Birth Control, 1915, 5–7 (*MSM* S76:880).

1. Bruno Wille (1860–1928), a German freethinker and socialist, used the phrase "in most instances," whereas MS used "in most cases." Enoch Heinrich Kisch (1841–1918) was a Czechoslovakian physician who argued that women risked neurasthenia and cardiac problems using coitus interruptus. (The Wille quote was from Kisch, *Sexual Life of Woman*, 280; Vernon L. Lidtke, "Naturalism and Socialism in Germany," *American Historical Review* 79 [Feb. 1974]: 19; Walther Killy and Rudolf Vierhaus, *Deutsche Biographische Enzyklopädie* [Munich, 1997].)

2. Using a douche to rinse sperm out of the vagina after intercourse was a common contraceptive method. Douching solutions varied from cold water and vinegar to such commercial disinfectants as Lysol, a creosol-based solution introduced as a household disinfectant in the nineteenth century. Astringents, such as bicarbonate of soda, alum, and saline solutions, were believed to constrict vaginal membranes and prevent sperm from passing through. Alkalines, found in a variety of soap products, were also used to inhibit sperm motility. Though widely used, contraceptive douches, as MS correctly noted, had a high rate of failure, and the use of strong solutions often resulted in vaginitis and cervicitis. (Brodie, *Contraception and Abortion*, 68–75.)

3. Pessaries, a generic term for intravaginal devices, took many forms. The "uterus button" was a stem pessary, most likely an intracervical device made of gold, silver, or hard plastic, that was inserted by a physician to plug the entrance to the cervix. Another stem pessary was the wishbone, or gold spring pessary, which extended into the uterus. Stem pessaries were left in place until menstruation, at which time they were removed. These devices were more common in continental Europe; MS's assertion that they were popular in the western United States cannot be confirmed. Occlusive pessaries and cervical caps, usually made of soft rubber and available in several sizes, covered the opening of the cervix to prevent the entry of sperm. To be certain of effectiveness, MS and others recommended that these pessaries be kept in place overnight and that the woman douche before and after use. (MS, *Family Limitation* [*MSM* S76:862], 13; Stopes, *Contraception*, 171–73; Cooper, *Technique of Contraception*, 67–68.)

4. In addition to Kisch and Ellis, who opposed the use of coitus interruptus, claiming it caused nervous and mental disorders in both men and women and interfered with sexual gratification, she was referring to the work of Auguste Henri Forel (1848–1931), a Swiss physician specializing in entomology, neurology, and social hygiene, in *The Sexual Question* (1905); Richard Freiherr von Krafft-Ebing (1840–1902), a German neuropsychiatrist, in *Pyschopathia Sexualis* (1886); Wilhelm Peter Johann Mensinga (1836–1910),

a German physician and inventor of the vaginal diaphragm, quoted in Albert Eulenburg, ed., *Real-Encyclopädie der Gesammten Heilkunde* (1891–98); Ludwig Hirt (1844–1907), a German physician, in *Diseases of the Nervous System* (1899); Sigmund Freud (1856–1939), the Austrian psychiatrist and founder of psychoanalysis, in "The Aetiology of Neuroses, Draft B" (1893); and Leopold Löwenfeld (1847–1924), a German physician and author of books on sexuality, psychology, and hypnotism, probably in *Sexualleben und Nervenleiden* (Wiesbaden, 1914). MS was also most likely referring to Julius (Gyula) Elischer Sr. (1846–1909), a Hungarian gynecologist and radiologist, but his work on coitus interruptus was not identified. (*DSB; New York Times,* Dec. 23, 1902; Stopes, *Contraception,* 74; James Strachey and Anna Freud, *Pre-Psycho-Analytic Publications and Unfinished Drafts: Standard Edition of the Complete Works of Sigmund Freud* [London, 1966], 181–83; Hans-Albrecht Koch, *Deutsches Biographisches Archiv* [New York, 1986]; Kisch, *Sexual Life of Women,* 278; P. Fürbringer, "Sexual Hygiene in Married Life," in *Health and Disease in Relation to the Married State,* ed. H. Senator and S. Kaminer [New York, 1929], 235.)

5. See the final paragraph of "Extract from *Family Limitation:* A Nurse's Advice to Women," October 1914, herein.

6. This was probably from Kisch's *Sexual Life of Woman,* though the exact quote was not located. It is possible MS paraphrased Kisch's statement that "moderate and regular indulgence in sexual intercourse is unquestionably advantageous to woman both physically and mentally, regulating all the functions of the body, and tending to produce a contented and cheerful frame of mind" (172).

7. In the nineteenth century, Victorians created the fiction that women were defined by and valued for their reproductive functions but were assumed to lack sexual feelings or desires. By the early twentieth century, sexual theorists, including Ellen Key, Havelock Ellis, and Edward Carpenter, challenged this notion of passionless womanhood and advocated mutual sexual expression. They promoted sexual indulgence and linked sexuality (both female and male) to individual self-definition and both moral and physical health. (See Gordon, *Woman's Body,* 186–97; and D'Emilio and Freedman, *Intimate Matters,* 223–25.)

8. Leo Tolstoy (1828–1910), the renowned Russian writer who was notable for his moral beliefs and Christian revisionism, propagated his views on spiritual love and abstinence in his 1889 *Kreutzer Sonata* (*The Kreutzer Sonata and Other Stories,* ed. Richard F. Gustafson and J. D. Duffy; trans. Louise and Aylmer Maude [New York, 1997]). In an 1890 afterword to that story, he noted, "It is not good to employ means to prevent the birth of children, in the first place because this frees people from the care and labour over children which serves as an expiation from carnal love, and secondly, because this is something quite close to an act most offensive to the human conscience—murder" (165).

9. While almost all European sex theorists advocated contraceptives, many physicians opposed birth control on the grounds that it not only was immoral but also caused cancer and gynecological ailments. (Gordon, *Woman's Body,* 181–83.)

50. *Excerpt from* English Methods of Birth Control: "Are Preventive Measures Certain?"

[*January–February 1915*]

It is difficult to say that anything is certain in its results, but there is every reason to believe that if directions are carefully followed in preventive methods, some means are quite certain.

A surgeon would not succeed with an operation was he not most particular to take every precaution and insist that his directions be followed out. It is the same in using preventive measures; care must be taken in douching after intercourse; attention given to adjusting the pessary correctly (or the cot or condom);[1] attention given to the date of the menstrual period, and a laxative taken four days before the time expected.[2] If these attentions and suggestions are applied before the date, there will seldom be any difficulty after.

The educated classes have been practising the methods of prevention for nearly a half-century, and have found them certain and safe.[3] If a woman is indifferent or too indolent to take precautions, then nothing will be certain; but I recommend the following as safe and harmless:—

The use of the Mezpah pessary[4] (not to be left in the vagina longer than twenty-four hours without cleansing).

The use of a salt solution before and after the removal of the pessary; two level tablespoonsful of salt to a pint of water: use two quarts for a thorough cleansing.

5 or 10 grains of quinine two or three nights preceding the date of menstruation, to eject any semen escaping into the uterus.

The pessary may be left in the vagina over night, which does away with the necessity of getting up in cold rooms to douche. It may be removed the following day at leisure; better in the morning, if possible, before it gets out of place by standing much on the feet.

There is no doubt that the use of the pessary and the use of the cot or condom are both safe and certain, if they are used intelligently.

English Methods of Birth Control, 1915, 7 (*MSM* S76:880).

1. Condoms ("cots" to the British) were sheaths made of animal membranes or rubber that encased the penis to prevent semen from entering the vagina. At the time, they were the most popular artificial means of contraception and were widely used in World War I to prevent venereal disease. (Cooper, *Technique of Contraception,* 50.)

2. This was a reference to the safe period or rhythm method of contraception. (See "Excerpt from *Family Limitation:* A Nurse's Advice to Women," Oct. 1914, note 3, herein.)

3. In western Europe and North America, middle-class fertility rates began to decline rapidly after 1850. Most historians attribute this to a deliberate effort to limit family size

in relation to the changing social and economic conditions brought on by urbanization and industrialization. Working-class fertility rates dropped later and at a slower rate, not approaching middle-class levels until the 1930s. The "educated classes" represented those middle-class families who employed barrier methods, such as diaphragms and condoms. These costlier methods were more effective than the non-mechanical methods of withdrawal and abstinence, and safer than abortion. (McLaren, *BC in 19th C. England,* 244–246; John R. Gillis, Louise A. Tilly, and David Levine, "The Quiet Revolution," in *The European Experience of Declining Fertility, 1850–1970,* ed. John R. Gillis [Cambridge, 1992], 5.)

4. The Mizpah pessary, an American rubber diaphragm, was constructed in two parts—a dome and a rim—which, its adherents argued, fit more closely to the cervix. (Cooper, *Technique of Contraception,* 56–57.)

51. To Comrades and Friends

This letter was probably enclosed with Sanger's English Methods of Birth Control.

London, England
February 4, 1915.

Comrades and Friends,—

I take this opportunity of expressing to you my thanks and appreciation for the many letters of encouragement received since the publication of the pamphlet "Family Limitation." I regret that I cannot comply with the numerous requests made for this pamphlet, but the supply, enormous as it was, is entirely exhausted. It is to be hoped that comrades who have a printing press equipment will reprint it in whole or in part, and continue its distribution among the workers.

Comrades are also urged to be careful into whose hands this propaganda is placed, as a letter to-day from New York tells me that William Sanger was arrested and his studio searched by Anthony Comstock, because they claim one of the pamphlets on Family Limitation was given to a U.S. Government spy. His case comes up for trial sometime in February, and there is the possibility of his getting sentenced to one year's imprisonment and $1,000 fine. The fact that Bill Sanger was in Europe when the pamphlet was written and circulated, and that I was most particular to keep not only him, but all my closest friends, ignorant of the work connected with the pamphlet, so that responsibility should fall upon no one else but me, is well known among the comrades. There is no doubt his arrest is but a trap of the Government, set to secure my return to U.S.A., as well as to frighten the advocates, and silence the propaganda of birth control or family limitation. But we who have hatred and contempt in our hearts for these authorities whose high-handed officialism is running riot in America, are not to be deterred from our cause nor trapped in our work because of sentiment; and just as I refused to go meekly like a lamb to slaughter when I saw that the Court was prejudiced against me, so now do I refuse to be tricked into rushing to the side of my comrade and pal,[1] or to the aid of my three little ones, who will be left unprotected by his imprisonment, until I have finished this work which I began to do. The sufferings of one who is loved by me could be no more deeply burned in my soul than the sufferings and anguish of thousands of other women's loved ones, left alone in sorrow by death which has been caused by abortion. Nor could the loneliness of my children be any greater, or their orphanage more tragic, than those thousands of little ones left motherless through deaths caused by the same tricky Government, through its ignorance and cruelty.

Comrades, this fight and cause is yours as well as mine. We are in it to the end, and your help is needed to spread this knowledge as well as to make public the outrageous suppression of free press and free speech by the Post Office authorities.

If comrades who in the past have ordered bundles of the *Woman Rebel* and books "What Every Girl and Mother Should Know," will kindly remit to me for those which have been sold,[2] it will help in this most trying time toward the continuation of the propaganda and the fight for the downfall of Comstockery. Fraternally yours,

MARGARET H. SANGER.

TFL MSP, DLC (LCM 129:3).

1. Though she carefully avoided referring to William Sanger as her husband, they were still legally married.

2. Many copies of the *Woman Rebel* and her pamphlets were distributed nationwide through a network of birth control supporters, labor organizers, and radical leaders, but MS rarely received proceeds from sales; many copies were also given away for free.

52. *To Anna E. Higgins*[1]

Sanger arrived at The Hague on February 9, 1915, and went to Amsterdam on February 14. (MS Diary [LCM 1:19].)

[*Amsterdam, The Netherlands*]
Feb 22 1915.

My dear Nan

Here I am tied up tight in Holland and can not tell when I can get away—[2]
I came to the Hague to study the latest methods adopted by the Dutch League ~~of~~ ↑on↓ Neo-Malthusian principles. I found dear little Doctor Rut-

gers most charming & cordial— He gave me a course of instruction & held a special clinic for my practice. I feel quite set up with the knowledge.[3]

I went for a day to Delft & found it such a dear & quaint place I wondered if you had ever been there. Then of course I spent a day at Haarlem where Frans Halls pictures & statue are—[4]

I have not heard from USA since the 19th of Jan and naturally I am anxious to know the results of the case of B. S.[5]

It is much worse than going to Atlanta[6]—this being away from all so many misunderstandings, so many ready with tongues of gossip to put the knife in your back—and so many to mis-interpit every action & word. But on the other hand these trials are soul developers, they teach us to depend only on that within us which is strongest & not to look for strength or comfort or courage on others. We must find it all ourselves.

I met Edward Carpenter,[7] Havelock Ellis, Dr Van Eeden,[8] & Olive Schrienter[9] & Dr Rutgers—a goodly number worthy of an ocean voyage any day.

Im going to try to get to London in a cargo boat & if so—then I shall begin to prepare for my trip to U.S.A. in April (4th or 6th).[10]

Have you seen the kiddies? Write me about them Nan please do. With love to you ever

Peg.

ALS MSP, DLC (LCM 5:1213–14). Letterhead of the Victoria Hotel.

1. Anna Higgins was working in New York City as a secretary to Elizabeth Blee Frasch. (Chesler, "Interview with Grant Sanger," 35.)

2. Though the Netherlands was a neutral nation, Germany imposed a submarine blockade on the British Isles on February 18, canceling MS's scheduled sailing to England. (Arthur Marwick, *The Deluge: British Society and the First World War* [Boston, 1965], 52.)

3. The Dutch Nieuw-Malthusiaansche Bond (Dutch Neo-Malthusian League), founded in 1881, was the first league to provide contraceptive information directly to the poor through pamphlets and after 1892 via clinics staffed by midwives, doctors, and lay nurses. Johannes (Jan) Rutgers (1851–1924), a Dutch physician, socialist, and secretary of the Dutch Neo-Malthusian League (1899–1917), was the key force behind these birth control centers. MS probably met with Rutgers on February 9 and 10, though she later claimed she attended daily training sessions with him for several weeks. (MS, *My Fight*, 109–10; MS Diary, Feb. 10, 1915 [LCM 1:19]; Ledbetter, *Malthusian League*, 173–81, 260.)

4. MS went to Delft and Haarlem sometime between February 14 and 21. The Frans Hals Museum, dedicated to the work of the Dutch portrait painter (ca. 1580–1666), opened to the public in 1913.

5. William Sanger was arrested on January 19, but MS was probably referring to his January 21 letter describing the arrest. His case was set for trial on March 15.

6. This was probably a reference to the federal penitentiary there.

7. With a letter of introduction from her Montreal friends, the Bains, MS wrote to Carpenter requesting a meeting shortly after her arrival in London. On January 29,

Carpenter responded, asking her to call; they met in the British Museum on January 30. (MS, *Autobiography,* 121, 130–31; Carpenter to MS, Jan. 29, 1915, and MS to Carpenter, Apr. 13, 1918 [*MSM* S1:406, C1:264].)

8. Frederik Willem Van Eeden (1860–1932), a physician, psychiatrist, and socialist journalist, probably met MS in Amsterdam. (Albert Verwey, *Frederik van Eeden* [Santpoort, Netherlands, 1939].)

9. Olive Schreiner (1855–1920), a South African novelist feminist writer, was one of Havelock Ellis's former lovers. MS read and admired *Women and Labour,* Schreiner's 1911 tract on women's political, economic, and sexual equality. She met Schreiner, probably in January 1915, through Ellis. (*Dictionary of South African Biography* [Johannesburg, 1968].)

10. MS left Amsterdam on a cargo boat on February 28. (MS Diary, Mar. 11, 1915 [LCM 1:21].)

53. *To the Editor of* Mother Earth[1]

[*London, England*]
[*February ?, 1915*][2]

Dear Comrade—

In the November number of your publication, I have read with pleasure an article by Harry Breckenridge[3] on my case. Through your columns I wish to thank Comrade Breckenridge for his article and also the other comrades of the Ferrer School who, I understand, have also attempted to get up some agitation on the case.[4]

It may not be known to the readers of Mother Earth that there are three federal indictments against me, based on the March, May and July issues of *The Woman Rebel.*[5] It may be supposed that though I might get away with these three indictments based solely on an opinion of obscenity, there remains the August, September and October issues, which were suppressed, and contain material for further forthcoming indictments. So that if I were to fool about defending myself in the courts, I would be forced to spend half the winter dallying about at the beck and call of a few officials.[6]

When the case first came up in August before Judge Hazel, I was not placed under bail, but allowed to go on my own recognizance. When the case was called in October before Judge Foster, I had no objection to the case going on the day it was fixed on the calender, and said that I was ready to proceed. When, however, day after day dragged on, and I was supposed to sit at the end of a telephone awaiting the call of the District Attorney, I objected.

I asked for postponement in order to do many things I had to do. The Judge refused a postponement. Thrice he refused it, and the only natural thing for me to do was to take it myself, which I did.

There is other work more important to me than fussing over an opinion of obscenity, which is all the case against me was based on. There was no information concerning the prevention of conception given in the columns of my papers; consequently the only things the case was based on were the questions or articles in those three issues which advocated the prevention of conception—articles considered "obscene" "filthy" and "vile."

So far as the freedom of the press is concerned, it is a most important issue, and one which concerns everybody in the United States. Especially does it concern us in the revolutionary movement, for it is here that we need the freedom of expressing our ideas and our thoughts, because they are in direct opposition to the prevailing and stagnant ideas of the day.

But I began a fight for the right of giving out information on the prevention of conception. That is my present and immediate work; and I am not to have that work sidetracked by an opinion on "obscenity"—even though it involves Free Speech, I shall do this first. When I have said all that I have to say and all others have said on this subject, I shall turn to take up the fight of the suppression and confiscation of the five issues of *The Woman Rebel,* and fight for its continuation.

We who have lost faith in the justice of the Courts of law are bound to work out a different method to achieve our purposes than those who still fall into the trap of its ponderous machinery. So that if the way I work may not be along the lines that other comrades have followed, I can only ask your patience and faith in my sincerity in doing what I consider the best and quickest way to accomplish my object. There are always various opinions on these questions and all that we can ask is that each comrade do that which out of his or her years of experience and reflection seems the cleanest and most direct from the revolutionary standpoint.

Again, some of the comrades have sighed and criticized me for mixing the issues, as they say—declaring that had I not published the article on the defence of assassination by Herbert H. Thorpe, that all the rest would have been easy.[7] I take this opportunity to state that I have no apology to make for publishing that article. There would have been no objection to an article against assassination, and if free speech and free press mean anything in the United States, certainly that article, reasoning and scientific, has a right to be published and read and discussed. That one may or may not agree with the material in the article is not the point. The point is that Mr. Thorpe had opinion on a question which at that time was the cause of throwing all of Europe into a state of war. And he has the right to express his opinion.

The work I am at present engaged in[8] will take at least several weeks longer, I shall then continue the trial.

There is one fact which naturally assuages my conscience, and that is that the Federal authorities will always be there to receive me at any time I decide to turn up. I think I can safely say that they will still be "on the job" to gather me into their "fold."

I will frankly say that I was keenly disappointed at the silence of MOTHER EARTH in regard to this outrageous tyrannical attitude of the Post Office authorities toward *The Woman Rebel.* I expect very little publicity on the "delicate subject" from the capitalist press, but naturally I look for an attitude of solidarity and comradeship from the radical press.

But as the indictments were returned in August and there were three suppressions since March—and not a word in any paper until November,[9] it makes one feel quite alone in a fight that so concerns the workers and all of us. However I wish to express my thanks to those comrades who have written me encouraging and sympathizing letters, and to those who are furthering and spreading the propaganda. Gather together all those interested in its spreading influence and together we will fight for the open and free discussion of this subject which so vitally concerns every working man and woman. Fraternally,

MARGARET H. SANGER.

The financial burden of the *Woman Rebel* and all this propaganda has been carried on almost alone.[10] I can not continue it much longer unless some financial help comes along. If the propaganda has been worth a little to you, let me know.

M. H. S.

Mother Earth, Apr. 1915, 75–78 (*MSM* S1:420–22). The original letter was not found. An editorial note by Goldman was added below the letter, asserting that though MS failed to inform *Mother Earth* about her case until August, during that time "we pushed *The Woman Rebel* and discussed its editor's case before thousands of people throughout the country. Under the circumstances it seems very unfair on the part of our comrade to accuse MOTHER EARTH of indifference. But then it is human to feel neglected when one faces one's first great battle with the powers that be, in behalf of an unpopular cause."

1. Emma Goldman was then editing *Mother Earth* with Alexander Berkman.
2. Though published in April, this letter was probably drafted early in February.
3. "The Persecution of Margaret Sanger," written by Alexander Berkman under the pseudonym Harry Breckenridge, attacked the capitalist government for its efforts to censor birth control information and called on working men and women to support MS.
4. A short article published in the *Modern School Magazine* lamented the fact that MS's case had drawn little notice and called on friends of the Ferrer Association to assist her. Leonard Abbott and other Ferrer associates helped raise funds for MS and held meetings in support of her case. (Stewart Kerr, "The Woman Rebel," *Modern School,* Nov. 1914, 6–7.)
5. For these indictments, dated August 25, 1914, see *MSM* C15:29.
6. The combined September–October issue, the last one printed, included a discussion of the August indictments and articles on neo-Malthusianism, questions and answers about birth control, and quotes from prominent European medical authorities

on contraception. Though no suppression letter was found, this issue was likely censored for its articles advocating birth control. (See "Birth and the War Machine," "Government," "Another Opinion to Be Suppressed," and "A Little Lesson," *Woman Rebel*, Sept.–Oct. 1914, 49–53.)

7. There is little evidence to support MS's claim that her socialist comrades deserted her for publishing Thorpe's article, though the *New York Call* did assert that Thorpe's piece "will serve to complicate the case." Harold Hersey, one of MS's biographers, was told that Goldman considered the article too dangerous to print in *Mother Earth*. (*New York Call*, Oct. 20, 1914; Hersey, "Margaret Sanger," 122; Chesler, *Woman of Valor*, 126.)

8. She was probably working on the *Methods* pamphlets.

9. Brief mentions of MS's pending legal battle appeared in the *Masses* in May 1914 and the *New York Call* on August 26 and October 20, 1914. However, several notable leftist publications were silent about her ordeal, among them *Mother Earth*, the *National Rip-Saw*, the *Nation*, *Solidarity*, and the *New Republic*.

10. No Goldman-Sanger correspondence was found between June 1914 and April 1915, but Goldman sold the *Woman Rebel*, gathering contributions for MS during her 1914–15 lecture tours. (Wexler, *Emma Goldman*, 211.)

54. To Anna E. Higgins

Sanger went to Paris on March 11, where she was joined by Portet on March 15. They left for a brief tour of the south of France on March 19 and then joined Portet's wife and children in Barcelona. Sanger stayed several weeks there and spent much of her time writing a series of essays on Spain. (MS Diary [LCM 1:22 and 130:398B]; MS, draft of "Modern Schools in Spain" [LCM 130:126].)

Barcelona Spain
[*March 25 or 26?, 1915*]

Dearest Nanny—

The world does move some these days & some of us do moves with it—I came down here a few ~~weeks~~ ↑days↓ ago on the invitation of Mr & Mrs Portet who's home are here part of the time & in Liverpool the other part. There has been one of the strongest movements here in my work among the working people & practical—very practical. I thot I should not miss this opportunity of coming down here especially as I was invited & to have some one here to speak for me is a rare treat. I have not heard from N.Y. since I left London but I intend to leave for Canada in April or May early & perhaps spend the hot months there with the children if Bill will send them on to me there.

That seems the best way for me to do, as far as I can see for the hot city is no place for them in July & Aug.

The weather is glorious here of course & the ease & contempt for time the people show in their living delights me.

They lounge about & eat & drink & talk—no hurry no rush—& they get there just the same.

Your nice letter reached me on my return from Holland & I did not have much time in London before I came to Paris & then on down to the South of France where I spent a few weeks & then here.

My health & spirits began to glow in the new climate but London is terrible on the lungs & throat.[1]

Did you receive the new pamphlet on "English Methods of Birth Control"? by me. I sent you one but am not sure if it had been posted as many of them are kept for a time to see if those sent get to the persons they were sent to.

Do you see the children. I do hope you will discourage Bills allowing anything to be done about Peggy's foot until I get there—[2]

The poor dears—they are having a rough time of it these days—

Bill had to get mixed up in my work after all & of course make it harder for me & and all of us!

The tea room was only for a few months to tie me over with room rent,[3] I hate it myself & will try something else in Canada—[4] Im holding fast to my return fare— Thank you dear for your kind offer of help I trust not have to accept it, my love [*written along right margin*] to you & kiss my Peggy & Grant for me. Tell me of Stuart, address me same in London. lovingly

Peg.

ALS MSP, DLC (LCM 5:1215–17).

1. MS's tubercular glands affected her neck and throat, and she frequently complained of breathing difficulties in cool, wet climates. She may have also been suffering from tonsillitis. (Havelock Ellis to MS, Aug. 25, 1915 [LCM 4:104].)

2. Peggy Sanger burned her foot on a radiator in February 1914. According to her brother Grant, she apparently contracted polio in the summer of 1910 and thereafter wore a brace on one leg, which may have complicated the foot injury. MS never discussed Peggy's polio or the fact that she wore a leg brace in any of her autobiographical writings or interviews. (William Sanger to Peggy Sanger, Feb. 5, 1914; Chesler, "Interview with Grant Sanger," 15.)

3. MS had little income during her exile and probably took on temporary work to tide her over. No other references to this waitressing job were found.

4. Fearful of returning to the United States, MS planned a trip to Canada but kept putting it off pending the outcome of William Sanger's trial.

55. *To Stuart Sanger*[1]

Barcelona, Spain
March 29—[*1915*]

My darling Stuart

I have not heard from you for a long time. Did you ever get the dollar bill I sent you in a letter from England?[2]

The nice box of writing paper you sent me for Christmas I want to thank you for it dearest Sunny Jim.

Last Sunday I saw a bull fight. Ill send you a picture of one of them. They have them here in Spain every Sunday. The people go to Church in the morning & to the bull fight in the afternoon. Six bulls are killed during the spectacle one after the other and usually three horses to every bull. The men are not hurt at all—but you would not like it because it is not only cruel but it is not a good sport even. The men do not fight the bull at all only tire it out with banners until it is nearly exhausted, then kill it with a sword.

The people here always put off everything until later on. They are easy going in their living, but hot tempered & quick to love & hate.

They are very very polite even more than the French but if you will take your Geography you will see that the French are their nearest neighbors & naturally people live more like their neighbors do.

I have not been to the South of Spain & can not go this time but I hope the next time I come you will be able to come too & we will go South nearer to Africa. The Ferrer Schools are here & Francisco Ferrer lived here & began his schools here & was imprisoned here in a prison which stands high on a mountain fortress—the mountains & prison are called Monjuick. It is there where the Catholic Church has tortured the people of Spain—tortured them to death because they would not belong to the Catholic Church—& so with Ferrer he wanted to educate the children of Spain & teach them to believe in science & think for themselves & because of this he was shot.[3] I went to his grave & tho't of you & was proud that my Stuart had attended the first Ferrer School in America.[4]

There are so many beggars here & so many blind people here that it half spoils the beauty of the place.

Well my darling Lutey,[5] tell me all that you are doing—

Ill give you my address in London & you can write to me directly.

This is Easter week—next Sunday being Easter. The people here make little trees of palms & hang colored balls & trinkets on the palm trees as we do on Christmas trees.

I expect to leave England for Canada or U.SA. next month & shall hope that father can arrange for you Grant Peggy & I to camp near some Lake or river in Canada—we will have a nice summer.

Give my love to Mrs Winn & tell her I am going answer her nice & kind letter very soon.[6] I am busy as can be. My love to you Sweetheart & a thousand kisses on the "nosey posey." As ever

Mother

ALS MSP, MN-SSC (*MSM* S1:407–10).

1. Stuart, age eleven, was still attending the Winnwood School.
2. The letter was not found.
3. Francisco Ferrer y Guardia (1859–1909) was an educational reformer and Spanish revolutionist who founded the Escuela Moderna (Modern School) in Barcelona in 1901, a libertarian school movement that advocated freedom from institutional, governmental, and religious restraints. It also served as a center for propaganda and revolutionary training. The Spanish government shut down the forty-eight Ferrer schools in Spain in 1906 and implicated Ferrer in a plot to assassinate the king. He was executed in 1909 by a firing squad at Montjuich, a fortress prison in Barcelona, which became infamous in 1896 after hundreds of Spanish anarchists were arrested, imprisoned, and tortured there. (Avrich, *Modern School Movement*, 3–6, 23–26, 31–32; Paul Avrich, *An American Anarchist: The Life of Voltairine de Cleyre* [Princeton, N.J., 1978], 112–13; MS, "Portet and Ferrer.")
4. Emma Goldman and Alexander Berkman founded New York City's Ferrer Association in 1910 to honor the martyred educator. In 1911, they opened the Ferrer Center on St. Mark's Place in New York City, which offered small adult classes and lectures on social issues, attracting a cross-section of radical writers, artists, journalists, educators, and activists. It was moved to a larger space on East Twelfth Street, where in January 1912 a day school was opened that emphasized free thought, independence, and self-development in an unstructured environment and exposed students to issues related to sexuality, evolution, and other topics public schools generally avoided. Among the students enrolled in the first year was Stuart Sanger. (Avrich, *Modern School Movement*, 35–45, 69–96.)
5. The derivation of this nickname was not found.
6. Elizabeth R. Winn was the founder and director of the Winnwood School. The letter was not found.

56. *To* William Sanger

Margaret Sanger left Barcelona for London (via Paris) in early May.

[*London, England*]
May 31st 1915

Bill dear:—

Your two letters of the 20 & 21st came this afternoon and I have cabled you to the effect that I shall remain here until I hear the results of your trial.[1] I trust that you will cable me the results, exactly, if postponed, or not, if granted a jury trial, or if you are to let it go until October. It is so long between our letters that your plans & mine conflict, almost constantly. That is why I decided after your letters today to cut out Canada. You seem to think I was going there for a lovely time. Instead I was trying to go there to releive you of the children & of course to be with them myself for even th'o you have given the impression I have deserted my children & have turned people against me, I can wait until these storms in life pass, & my love for them will be proven in the future. Until then I must wait.

You say Miss Marot & Miss Pratt think you should have no consideration for me & that they do not like me— Do they know me? & what consideration do they think I am getting. Allow me Bill once & for all time to releive you of any duty toward me which you might have at one time performed and on the receipt of this letter you may feel privilidged to send the three children to me on the first boat & consider your duties to them & to me ended for all time.

Your stay in Paris was one sacrifice to me, & one attempt to hide from you the fact that it was a sacrifice— I have no regrets, unless it be that my sacrifices were made for one too childish & unworthy to appreciate the depth of their sincerity. I am resolved on the receipt of your two letters today to remain where I am. You may go on with birth control propoganda. I notice that th'o ↑(highbrows)↓ they are out for it, every one assumes the legal aspect of the subject. All that they any of them will dare to do will be done legally[2] & when you ask me, or suggest, without any responsibility, (I recognize the Sanger in you there) to come & give myself up to the United States government, I wish to reserve a decision until I see what they do with you before I do so.

The court closes in July & opens in October, people go to their sea resorts & mountain homes in luxury & comfort during these trying months & no doubt would object to be troubled about me or you during these months. Ill not test their sincerity again. I tried it before I began this work & found them all cowards.[3]

This is Peggy's birthday, I wrote Miss Marot & enclosed a letter for the darling, both Helen Marot & Caroline Pratt are splendid women what I know of them, & certainly I owe them a debt of gratitude to have to take my obligations toward my little ones.[4]

I regret that I am not inclined to send you my power of attorney your letters to me are of the kind which tells me plainly your attitude & feelings toward me. If I must earn my living & that of my children's, then at least we are on an equal footing & can begin at once.

I told you I borrowed that amount on the Hastings place & it is already mortgaged.[5] You will please send me any money sent to me either thr'u Maisel[6] or any other people who contribute to the propoganda.

And if you can find your "considerations" it would be interesting to see them. At least don't trouble too much over them. I do not desire them, nor have I recived any that I have recognized. Send the children on to me any time you are tired of them. No doubt the same charity exists in Europe as you have solicited in America. If you can't write to me in a spirit of comradeship—you will save yourself & me much unhappiness by not writing at all. I can feel the poison of that fossolized Gus Myers[7] in every letter. It is death to know him. Good Night

Margaret.

ALS MSP, MN-SSC (*MSM* S1:425–32).

1. There are no surviving letters from William Sanger to MS between January 22 and September 3, 1915. William Sanger's March 15 trial date was rescheduled for April 15 and postponed to May 10 and again to June 18.

2. This was possibly a reference to the NBCL, which, according to MS, refused to support the *Woman Rebel* on the grounds "that a law-abiding organization, formed primarily to change the laws, could not logically support a person who had broken those laws." (MS, *My Fight,* 125.)

3. She might have been referring to her difficulty in raising funds in 1912 for the IWW organizers Ettor and Giovannetti, who were arrested for murder during the Lawrence strike. (See MS to Nancy Brush Pearmain, Nov. 4, 1912, note 2, herein.)

4. Peggy Sanger was then five years old. She and Grant, who had been staying with Pratt and Marot, entered the newly opened Stelton School in New Jersey (formerly the Modern School, which had moved from New York City) on May 16. Located within a new Ferrer colony, Stelton consisted of an old farmhouse that lacked modern conveniences, a barn, and a sparsely furnished dormitory. The Sanger children joined twenty-seven others as boarders, their tuition covered in part by the school and through donations from friends and sympathizers, including Gertrude Pinchot. The letters to Marot and Peggy Sanger were not found. (Avrich, *Modern School Movement,* 219–22; Abbott to Schroeder, July 2, 1915 [TSP]; William Sanger to MS, Sept. 21, 1915 [*MSM* S1:462].)

5. MS borrowed money against the Hastings house and worked out a separate mortgage agreement with William Fishel, who completed mortgage payments in 1914. (William Sanger to MS, Jan. 11, 1914 [*MSM* S1:71]; Gray, *Margaret Sanger,* 36, 48.)

6. She was referring to the bookseller Max Maisel.

7. Gustavus Myers (1872–1942), a muckraking journalist who exposed municipal corruption, joined the Socialist Party in 1907 and published *The History of American Fortunes* (1909–10), a notable exposé of the evils of unfettered capitalism. Myers grew disillusioned with socialism over what he charged was its growing materialism and abandoned the party in 1912. (*DAB*)

57. FROM LEONARD D. ABBOTT

New York [*N.Y.*]
June 1, 1915

Dear Mrs. Sanger,

Your letter received, with copy of new Memorandum concerning your case, issued by the Neo-Malthusian Bureau.[1] I had already seen copies of the Memorandum, and will send for a bundle. I am glad that you wrote at this particular time. I was just on the point of writing you. I know that Bill Sanger keeps you posted; and doubtless he has written you that he and I are in almost daily touch. At the same time, I am glad to have another word with you direct.[2]

I feel very different from when I wrote you last.[3] There have been many important developments. The whole atmosphere, so far as the subject of "birth control" is concerned, is changing for the better. The meeting at the Academy of Medicine last week has led to widespread discussion in almost all the papers.[4] I presume that Bill has sent you clippings. I am saving everything that appears ↑regarding your case & regarding birth control↓ in daily papers, weekly papers or magazines; and when you get here, you can look them all over.

When I wrote you last, I hesitated about advising you to return. Now, I unhesitatingly advise you to return. Your "background" is big enough to ensure success and publicity: By "success" I mean that you will now be able to "get over," through the newspapers and through other channels, what you stand for. Your arrest and imprisonment (if you are imprisoned) will not go by in the dark. Everybody in the country will know what is happening.

I have heard from hundreds of people in response to the appeal sent out in your ~~be~~ and William Sanger's behalf last March.[5] Among the ~~people~~ writers are distinguished men like Robert Herrick, the novelist, and Prof. Charles Zueblin,[6] as well as scores of the "rank and file." I am keeping all these letters for you.[7]

Money has come in in amounts ranging from $25 to 25 cents. Gilbert E. Roe has had $350 from me so far. He has succeeded in keeping Bill out of jail until now.[8] There may be another postponement over the summer. Roe tells me that he thinks that the authorities may drop Bill's case if you return. They are after <u>you</u>, not him.

Bill has had about $90 from me so far, for himself and for the children.[9] I hope to be able to send you, through him, $50 or $100 this week. Sincerely,

Leonard D. Abbott [*signed*]

TLS MSP, DLC (LCM 7:645–46). Letterhead of the Free Speech League of New York.

1. He was referring to the International Bureau of Correspondence and Defense, formed at the Third International Neo-Malthusian Conference in 1910 to coordinate efforts to defend those prosecuted for publishing or distributing neo-Malthusian materials. For a copy of the "Memorandum concerning the Prosecution of Mrs. Margaret Sanger," see *MSM* C15:163. The letter to Abbott was not found. (Ledbetter, *Malthusian League*, 194.)

2. In a July 2, 1915, letter to Theodore Schroeder, Abbott noted that William Sanger and MS were both "nervous wrecks as a result of what they have been through." (TSP)

3. In a May 1, 1915, letter to MS, Abbott reported growing interest in birth control and in both Sanger cases, noting "a great deal of propaganda can undoubtedly be made out of your return." But he also told her she would still likely face a long prison term. (LCM 7:643.)

4. The New York Academy of Medicine sponsored a May 26 meeting to discuss an amendment to the state Comstock law that would exempt physicians from the ban on providing contraceptive information or devices, which generated a flurry of publicity. The academy, however, failed to approve the resolution, calling instead for further investigation. (*Harper's Weekly* and *New York Tribune*, May 22, 1915; *New York Herald*, May 21, 1915; *New York Sun* and *New York Times*, May 27, 1915.)

5. A version of Abbott's appeal appeared in his article "The Status of the Sanger Case," *Mother Earth*, Mar. 1915, 451–52. See also Free Speech League to Friends, 1915 (*MSM* C15:90); and Abbott to Friends, Feb. 11, 1915 (TSP).

6. Robert Herrick (1868–1938) was an English professor and novelist whose writing focused on urban life, domesticity, and feminism; Charles Zueblin (1866–1924) was a sociologist and writer who supported the NBCL. (*ANB; New York Times*, Sept. 16, 1924.)

7. Specific support letters were not found. Abbott did tell Theodore Schroeder that he had received many letters asking for copies of *Family Limitation*. (Abbott to Schroeder, Apr. 29, 1915 [*MSM* C15:67]).

8. The Free Speech League retained Gilbert E. Roe to defend William Sanger, raised his bail, and covered other expenses. (Rabban, *Free Speech*, 56–57; Abbott to Schroeder, Apr. 29, 1915 [*MSM* C15:67]; Abbott, "Conviction of William Sanger," 268–69.)

9. Even without legal expenses, William Sanger was barely able to support himself and their children on his meager income. Ethel Byrne assisted by paying Stuart's tuition at Winnwood and cooking and caring for Grant and Peggy at his apartment. (Van Voris, "Olive Byrne Richard Interview," 4–5; Chesler, *Woman of Valor*, 132; Abbott to Schroeder, July 2, 1915 [TSP].)

58. *From Caroline Nelson*[1]

San Francisco, Cal.
June 12, 1915.

Dear Margaret,

Received your letter and the bundle of letters.[2] I am now engaged in copying the addresses. But I don't know when we shall get the paper started.[3] Some of those most interested think that we don't need any paper. And my own money that I intended to use for it is tied up for one more year. However, things are coming our ↑way↓. I suppose that you know that we have now a Birth Control League in Portland and here in Frisco. The League in Portland seems to be more active than any other. They meet up there in the public library.[4]

It seems strange, but it is almost impossible to interest the workers in this. Of course, it is because they are ignorant. I have been trying since I came back to talk this matter up among the workers, while they want to get the information in secret, they cannot discuss it in public without giggling and blushing and this holds good to our very learned radical men, or at least some of them. So that our League here consist mostly of professional people. We have a woman lawyer, secretary of the Game and Fish Commission, a contractor, a labor leaders wife, but no real working people, and only one or two working women besides myself.[5] This outfit will simply keep it as a semi-fashionable League. They are people who don't need the information and never did, and how we are going to get it to the workers is the problem that I constantly harp on. "They wouldn't know how to use it." is the answer that I constantly get. They have no bath-rooms, they are too tired after a day's work to get up and douche, they ↑[*are*]↓ too timid to ask for the material in the drug-store, etc. I myself think that if the Leagues are ever to amount to anything, they must send trained nurses into the workers districts, who speaks the language of the district, whatever that maybe. Or send reliable women who is paid for that work, by the professional people who are interested.

Some people are of the opinion that you will go free when you return, because of the stir now made for birth control all over. I hope that is so, but I would be careful. On the other hand, they might take you and make an example of you. One can never tell what the foxy government is up to. I gave most of the pamphlet away that you sent me,[6] and most of those I gave them to sold them for from ten cents to twenty-five cents. But they ↑are↓ mostly poor devils who sold them to working prudes, so we should worry.

By the way, Mrs. Lavroff from Tacoma writes me that she has sent you five dollars to Emma Goldman and a friend of hers also sent some. So just ask Emma if she hasn't some money for you, if she has not sent it.[7] We hope to get up a benefit for you before very long. We have formed a Woman's Defense League here to defend you and other women that may get into trouble.[8] But it consist mostly of Jewish women, who think that the information is so easily gotten hold of that there really was no necessity for you to publish the pamphlet. And we certainly have hard times now. Never in the history of San Francisco have so many people been out of work and wages so low, and it all has an effect on the workers. There seem to be no get up among them anymore.[9]

Did you see the last Mother Earth where Berkman tells you that he was Comrade Brickenridge and attempts to laugh you down over your letter? I think that the laugh is on him, since he as an editor hides behind a fictitious name, which shows that he was a coward in that case. Several people tell me that they have sent money to you, I wonder if they have. A Mrs. Bain.

I suppose that you know that Comstock lost his job?[10] He got his foot in it when he got hold of you and your husband. I wonder what the Defense League is doing in New York?[11] Lincoln Steffen was here resently. He is said to have joined the Birth Control League in New York, but he never said a word about it in any of his speeches here, and the crowd he associates with here are dead against it, or pretend to be.[12] A fashionable woman wanted me to visit her in her country home, but when I told her that I might be run in any day for distributing obscene literature in the form of this information I havn't heard from her since. It is wonderful how cowardly people are. I don't mind being run in, as I am pretty nearly worn out, and I have no children to cry over me, and some of my supposed friends would enjoy it, and besides it would give the case much more airing, but the lawyers wouldn't get any money out of me, for good reasons.

Our Leagues will do some good however, when you come back they can protect you and bill you through the country. I had a letter from Tacoma where Mrs. Lavroff said that she would take up the matter to start one, and I also got in touch with Georgia Kotsch in Los Angeles, who said that she would try to get a League going there.[13] So you see, a ring is growing up that may look formidable to Uncle Sam. This is no longer a free love busines that can be swooped down on by the help of mother Grundy.[14] Here in the United States the whole question has taken on a moral side. I must say with great shame to our labor editors that the capitalist editors in many instances have been much more liberal and sensible on this question than they have, which shows that our class is not yet out of the woods of gullibility with its sewage minds, and sewage minds are not clear instruments for thinking.

I think that we will let the paper proposition rest until you come back and you yourself continue it, if you escape prison. I got an article in a labor paper here regarding your case, but I think that the editor got his for publishing it, as I havn't been able to get a smell in since, but every little bit helps.[15] The best member we have I got through that.

Dr. Robinson don't believe in Birth Control Leagues, although he will let them form, he says. He thinks that he can do much more alone, according to his statement in the Critic and Guide. He rather deplores that the argument for it he has held out for twenty years and that they are borrowed from his writing without any thanks. Dear Doctor you can't be exclusive any longer and have a little hobby to ride alone as a little light of hope. It is too bad. Looking at the East Side close to where the doctor have worked alone so long, one should think that he would be tickled to death to have some help in disseminating the information, which to all appearances he never got out among those who needed it the most. Maybe his income will suffer, or something.[16]

I think that you will get some help from Portland. I am sending your address up there and telling them that you must have help now. I am also going to suggest to them that they hold some kind of benefit for you. It is no more than fair that some of those well-fed mortals do something. They are going to re-print you pamphlet up there, they say. They published a little pamphlet of their declaration of principles and reference notes,[17] which they paid an outrageous sum for. So they must have money up there, and I will see if I can't get them to "divy" up a little bit with your kids. Great Scot! you must be lonesome. But you would have been much more lonesome in prison and perhaps not so healthy. I wondered how Katherine Davis would have reformed you?[18] The worst thing about those places are the diseases and bad foods and bad companions that surrounds one. I wrote to the Masses, asking them to give me the names of their subscribers here on the coast to get some members for the birth control Leagues, but nothing doing. They were awfully sorry, but someone had written before me in another territory and they had had a conference and decided not to give the names out, that constituted a precedense which could not be violated, except by the sanction of Max Eastman himself who is travelling in Europe.[19] Sometime I wonder how far a group's sincerety goes. I wrote under the authority of secretary to Woman's International Defense League. So the request ought not to have made such an awfull fuss.

I wonder why you couldn't edit the paper in Canada? I should think that it would be just the thing, provided you could get the funds to do it. And I still hold that it would be beneficial to change the name. You ↑know↓ the workers are so afraid of being suspected of immorality, and [*they*] love the word—Moral with an effection worthy of something better than it stands for today. That is why I cling to the name of—New Moral. After all, what we must do is to catch the worker's wife and daughter. I went out to the medical Library the other day and read all the information both in German and English. The librarian was a young girl who didn't even know was against the law, another young girl was with me, who is a librarian in Portland, who says that they have Havelock Ellis' books up there, but that they had removed the important one to the city hall to keep it out of reach of the unworthy ones.[20] I tried to convince her that they were just the people that ought to have the information. I don't know if she goes back and advices the librarians of that fact. But what impressed me most, was that here were those young girls looking up the information and seeing the pictures of the preventatives as unconcernedly as though it was the most ordinary thing in the world. Now, why in the world can't our working girls get to the same point of view. Those girls were strictly conventional and church-members, yet, we have radical people who hold that young girls should not know, and we have such a state of affairs that it cannot be talked about in labor circles. Here we have a terrible pioneer work that you and I must do or see that it is done. Deletante Birth Control Leagues may help as the workers take their morals from the upper class, but they will not go very far.[21] They will not reach down to the bottom, anymore than they have ever reached down to the bottom in England and other countries. I am amused at the long string of titles after the names of the League in England,[22] and then I think of the slums there where children swarm like rats, and mothers give birth to children without a stitch of clothes to put on them. Then I know that ordinary people will have to roll up their sleeves and take the information to them and give them the material free of charge. Yes, dear Margaret, this is the mere beginning of us working women to do our work. The working men have gone around in a vicious circle, until today they are engaged in the very lawful occupation of killing each other, and where they are not killing each other they are running around begging for a job to feed their starved families. All this, after seventy-five years of revolutionary propaganda and scientific economy and academic discussion that the working woman had interest in, chiefly because they were not practical, and did not touch her life, and the radical woman is chiefly an echo of the radical man, even in the sex question. Let us see what we can do now? I hope that we will soon have you back among us, even across the borderline is better than away over in Europe now, where so little can be done now among the war crazy people. with much love,

Caroline [*signed*]

TLS MSP, DLC (LCM 9:887–89).

1. Caroline Nelson (Rave) (1868–1952) was a Danish-born socialist and IWW member who contributed regularly to socialist and radical journals. A birth control advocate who first met MS in New York City in 1912, Nelson contributed the article "Sacred Motherhood" to the June 1914 issue of the *Woman Rebel.* (CA Death Index; Nelson to Dennett, Aug. 27, 1930 [*MWDPM* 19:229]; Katz, "Dual Commitments," 661–62*n*1.)

2. These were possibly requests for birth control advice; the letters were not found.

3. Nelson may have planned a radical birth control journal along the lines of the *Woman Rebel,* but there is no evidence that she ever published one.

4. The Portland Birth Control League, founded in March 1915 by H. C. Uthoff (who changed his name to Dekker in 1917) and the IWW member Louise Olivereau (1884–1963), reprinted and distributed *Family Limitation* and held educational meetings, but it went out of existence during World War I. (Vreeland, "Process of Reform," 410–11.)

5. The San Francisco Birth Control League, founded by Nelson and others in February 1915 to aid working-class women, distributed birth control information for a few months (in violation of the law). By December 1916, an influx of middle-class club women voted in a new board that repudiated law-breaking practices. Though Nelson

retook control in 1917 and kept the league in the public eye through lectures and educational efforts, it dissolved sometime in 1919 or 1920. (Vreeland, "Process of Reform," 369–70; Caroline Nelson, "San Francisco," *BCR*, Apr.–May 1917, 15; Katz, "Dual Commitments," 652–54.)

6. She was referring to *Family Limitation.*

7. Jennie Amour Lavroff (1880–1955) was a birth control supporter. Goldman was on a western tour, heading to San Francisco. When Goldman lectured on birth control, she distributed both *Family Limitation* and *How and Why the Poor Should Not Have Many Children,* a four-page pamphlet she and Ben Reitman had drafted; she also collected funds for MS's defense. (CA Death Index; Falk, Cole, and Thomas, eds., *Emma Goldman: A Guide,* 72; Wexler, *Emma Goldman,* 211.)

8. No information was found on the Woman's Defense League. The San Francisco International Worker's Defense League sponsored a Margaret Sanger protest meeting on April 18; it is possible Nelson was referring to a woman's branch. (*Oakland World,* Apr. 17, 1915.)

9. The 1915 Panama Pacific International Exposition put San Francisco into a serious economic slump. Rising food prices and a glut of seasonal workers made efforts to organize labor there difficult. (Michael Kazin, *Barons of Labor: The San Francisco Building Trades and Union Power in the Progressive Era* [Urbana, Ill., 1987], 15.)

10. Rumors were circulating that Comstock, who had made many enemies, was going to lose his commission as special agent of the post office for overzealousness and fanaticism; he was formally removed from his position at the end of June. (*New York Times,* Sept. 22, 1915.)

11. She was referring to the Free Speech League's Sanger Defense Committee, organized to raise money for William Sanger.

12. Lincoln Steffens (1866–1936), a muckraking journalist known for his 1904 exposé of municipal corruption, *The Shame of the Cities,* became a socialist and supported such groups as the Free Speech League. He was one of the founders of the NBCL. (*ANB; Survey,* Apr. 3, 1915, 5.)

13. Georgia Taylor Kotsch (1863–1953), a feminist, socialist organizer, and writer, was active in the Woman's Socialist Union. In January 1916, at Nelson's suggestion, Kotsch, Frances Noel, and other socialist women organized the Los Angeles Birth Control League, with Kotsch as secretary. At its first meeting, it quickly adopted a resolution protesting MS's prosecution. (CA Death Index; Buhle, *Women and American Socialism,* 276, 287; Katz, "Dual Commitments," 108–9, 655–56.)

14. Mrs. Grundy, a fictional character depicted as the arbiter of proper social behavior in Thomas Morton's 1798 play, *Speed the Plough,* came to personify prudishness and strict propriety.

15. Nelson's "Neo-Malthusianism in America" urged the working classes to subscribe to the *Woman Rebel* and discussed the tendency of the government to prosecute the poor for violating the Comstock laws more harshly than the rich. Originally published in the *International Socialist Review* in November 1914, it was republished on December 12, 1914, in *Organized Labor,* an Oakland, California, paper edited by the Norwegian-born labor leader Olaf Anders Tveitmoe (1865–1923). (*ANB*)

16. William J. Robinson (1869–1936), a Russian-born physician, socialist, and publisher who wrote popular articles on health, birth control, and sex education, helped arrange

the New York Academy of Medicine's birth control meeting. He was also the author of *Birth Control; or, The Limitation of Offspring* (New York, 1916) and editor of *The Medical Critic and Guide,* a popular journal. In a brief May 1915 column entitled "Birth Control Leagues," Robinson admitted such leagues were beneficial, but he refused to join them, claiming he could do better work through his journal. Concerned about not getting enough credit, Robinson contended some birth control advocates were "presenting the matter as if it were something entirely new and novel." (*New York Times,* Jan. 7, 1936; William J. Robinson, "Birth Control Leagues," *Medical Critic and Guide,* May 1915, 167–68.)

17. The only surviving Portland version of *Family Limitation* is a revised third edition, ca. 1917; the first edition was probably published in 1915. Other Portland Birth Control League pamphlets have not been found. (*MSM* C16:771.)

18. Katharine Bement Davis (1860–1935), a social worker and prison reformer who headed the Bedford Reformatory for women (1901–14), became New York City's first woman commissioner of corrections (1914–15). As commissioner, she abolished many prisoner privileges and eliminated racially segregated prison wards. MS had been highly critical of Davis, calling her a "fossilized reactionary female" who attempted to coerce prisoners into "snitching on their comrades." (*NAW;* MS, "Cantankerous Katherine," "Yes?" and "Another Woman," *Woman Rebel,* July 1914, 35, Apr. 1914, 11, and Aug. 1914, 43.

19. The *Masses* (1911–17), a libertarian socialist monthly founded by Piet Vlag in 1911 and after 1912 edited by Max Eastman (1883–1969), focused on art, culture, and politics. Always controversial, the magazine championed a range of radical causes and issues, from anarchism to free love. Eastman emerged as a leading figure among Greenwich Village intellectual radicals. He was touring France and other war-torn European nations in June and July of 1915. (Max Eastman, *Understanding Germany* [New York, 1916], 144; William O'Neill, ed., *Echoes of Revolt:* The Masses, *1911–1917* [Chicago, 1966], 5, 18–23.)

20. She was probably referring to *Sex in Relation to Society* (volume 6 of Ellis's *Studies in the Psychology of Sex*), which dealt with sex education, the value of sexual love, and other related topics. Ellis considered it the most important volume in the series. (Brome, *Havelock Ellis,* 147.)

21. Nelson misspelled *dilettante,* referring to organizations run not by working-class reformers but by wealthy or middle-class reformers without a personal commitment to the cause.

22. Nelson was referring to the Malthusian League's practice of appending titles and degrees to its officers' names.

59. *Fabian Hall Speech*[1]

The following speech was given at the Fabian Society Hall, 25 Tothill Street, Westminster, in London. The British Fabian socialists focused on education and social research and were less committed to the kind of political activism that American socialists promoted. Sanger later recalled that her audience, "representatives of nearly every social and civic organiza-

tion in London," was very different from the socialist women she had addressed in the United States because they "had the rationalist attitude and preferred to listen to principles and theories." (MS, Autobiography, *170.)*

[*London, England*]
[*July 5, 1915*]

By the title of the subject to be discussed tonight, I would not have you think that I have originated a special [*propoganda*] of which I have a special [*monopoly*] nor would I have you think I have cornered the market as Americans Say but I simply wish to show that there is a special side of our present day propoganda which should recive more of our attention as propogandists and there is always room in a field like the Socialist or Anarchist [*philosophies*] for some of us to lay special stress on & concentrate our work on special parts of the whole— My work on the nursing field in U.SA. gave me my first introduction to the ~~physical~~ ignorance of the working women [*concerning*] the physical care of their own bodies or its physiological function.

Tho I was rocked in the cradle of Socialism—for my father was one of the early pioneers of Socialist thot in USA[2] yet with my nursing experience among women—I could see the [*great*] undermining & weakening of that class both physically & mentally [*through*] ignorance of the care of their own bodies & especially the physiological functioning of the ~~sex~~ ↑generative↓ organs.

In USA. you are all aware of our world famous Puritanism which has made any mention of sex a prison offense & always reminds me of that Story of which you are no doubt familiar but which bears repeating here. The story of the Queen of Spain travelling through the rural districts to one of the provinces had need to pass through a manufacturing town made famous for its excellent production of hosiery & gloves. The inhabitants of the town being simple & loving people desired to please the lady & show honor to her by presenting to her some of their best & choicest productions. The magistrate of the town assembled the people together to receive the queen & presented her with the gifts. The Escort bowed low & graciously over the gloves & thanked the people for the gift, but declined to accept the stockings by saying "never forget that a queen of Spain has no legs". This is quite on a par with our Puritanism in America & it is this barrier that must be broken down around the American working girl before you can proceed a step in reaching her—

As you already know there has been throughout the world within the last ten years a tremendous awakening in all civilized countries among women. Every where women have shown tendencies to overthrow some of the old regulations of society & throw off some of the [*fetters*] which have held them down so long—

This awakening has definitely shown itself in two forms—or groups, one the most universal the desire for political freedom & recognition or the votes for women groups.

The other & more advanced & more recent is perhaps more psychological in its effects but have likewise formed themselves into the Feminist groups.

I shall not go into detail about the votes for women—woman—for she concerns me little & fortunately the working girl has not been greatly enthused in this propoganda.[3] But sufficient is it to say that as far as I have been able to gather their vision of life goes as high as obtaining political positions for women now today & aspiring to the lofty attitude of police women, detectives, police [*commiss*] etc. The women of Chicago have been able to elect some of their sex as police and when the great cloke makers Strike was in progress—the working girls found to their great surprise that the policewoman club hurt just as much swung from the fair hands of her own sex, as it did from that of the policemans—[4] Again—in N.Y. we have C. B. D.[5] the Police [*Comissn*]—for years Police Matron in the Bedford Home for girls. If one could describe the hope which sprang into the hearts of the women of the underworld when they knew that at last a woman was to be over the Institution wherein they suffered so bitterly and what a keen dissappointment awaited them— She went at her work for public [*applause*]—Prison was prison and was no joy house—& accordingly she went to her job to make prison sentence so hard & cruel that no one would return. She refused to allow the inmates to recive outside meals until they were weak & ill & unless there was someone outside to help them they were usually fit for a hospital—this & a few such cruelties K. B. D. brought into the Prison—& today there is little hope for the hands of a woman—

In ~~San~~ California it is the same a letter from a friend tells me at the last election that the women had gone mad on prohibition that they were going to tie the state up so dry, that a working man would have to pay five shillings for a perscription to keep a pint of cider vinegar in the house.[6]

So much for votes for women. Its not that I deplore votes for women for certainly if votes are good for men they are good for women too, but the vision of these women is too narrow & ~~voting~~ women as police~~man~~ matrons etc are the same tools in the system as the men are so long as this system [*remains.?*] The other group of awakened women are the feminists—the basis of which is one of the first steps towards womans emancipation & future development—the ownership & control over her own body—

This movement like all other big vital thots, has been cut up & narrowed down to such a degree that it is scarcely recognized as Feminism—for instance last year in N.Y.C. there was the Feminist Movement launched upon the unsuspectg Puritans—but it was Feminism in name only—& ignoring the basis of the whole movement, lest it should shock the morals of the people, it began to treat of superficial results of its development. For instance—these women—wanted the right to work: the right to ignore fashions: the right to keep her own name, & such poor longings of a bougeous class suffering from loss of vitality. I issued a working womans paper called the Woman Rebel which viewed feminism from the working womans point of view & demanded not the right to work, but the right to be lazy, & guaranteed to find seven millions of women—laundresses, cloak makers, suit makers, cap—kimona makers scrubwomen, domestics, telephone girls, shop workers, etc etc who would gladly change places with these women who wanted the right to work.[7]

The working girl had never troubled herself about ignoring fashions— It was compulsory on her part.— She had to—

The right to keep her own name was a most revolutionary demand for these women to make. Instead of Mrs ~~Ma~~ Frank Brown, she wanted the right to be Mrs Mary Brown— Why she must loose her identity in Brown when her own name was Jones—was a step too far for them to explain—& why she should tag herself with "Mrs" or a wedding ring was too shocking for these blue stocking prudes to think of & when I suggested that the basis of feminism was a womans right to be an unmarried mother—a stony silence surrounded them & they drew aside their skirts less they be difiled by such tho'ts.[8]

So much for the feminists whose program had no place for the working womans development, or no thot of her emancipation but fundamentally has a basis for her to use of which I shall refer later on.

If the votes for women & Feminist movements as well as nearly all other movements I know of have ignored the working women there have ↑has↓ been one kind & ever loving friend who has grasped the opportunity to assist her this friend is the master class or the boss—who has subtly & silently instituted in most all the large shops & stores where many women work—a Welfare Society, which so far has been a wonderful tool in the hands of the boss to blind the workers ~~to~~ ↑of↓ their slavery.[9] Heres how it works—two thousand women pay into a welfare fund $10 weekly out of their wages—for this they receive medical attention when they are ill etc. this amount[10] makes $200 a week or 50£. out of which they pay 5£. for one nurse & less than that to another nurse a week, who binds up hurt fingers etc at once, so they do not loose time & get back to work again quickly— She also tells them that they need milk eggs etc, but does not tell the boss that to see that they get an increase in wages so as to get them oh no, One nurse attends to the hospital while the other one dresses up poorly like the girls themselves & goes among them—she dances, with them plays the piano in the lunch room, gets them to confide in her, walks home with them, and as one of them said to me ~~feels~~ keeps her fingers on the pulse of the shop to see there will be no strikes. This is not all. This same Welfare League aims to [*educate*] these girls & authorizes

& pays ~~well~~ good prices women to come twice a week to lecture to them.— The lectures consist of all kinds of subjects but the tone of all these lectures the key note of all is to inject into these girls a slave morality which is the most detrimental teaching of today & is not being combatted sufficiently to offset the treachery of it.

Here is some of it—"obedience"—"courtesy" "punctuality" "loyalty"—"honesty" "duty" etc. Implisid obedience—ask no questions but obey when you are told. "Courtesy" rise & bow to your master & show deference to his authority over you—"punctuality" to always be on time—not a minute after 8, but better a minute before so as to give the full days labor for the pay you recive "loyalty"—stand up for the man who gives your daily bread—"honesty" to come & tell when you spoil your work, & not accept full pay for poor work, making these girls a tame, lifeless spiritless mass, without personality or life—and as Nitzsche says a gently—grunting domestic animal—[11] My propoganda to offset this was the working girl agrees only to sell her <u>labor</u> to the boss—not her morality— Its none of his business if she's courteous, loyal, honest dutiful obedient. She's never to forget that there is a war constantly going on—between her class & the boss class—& its up to her to get the largest wage for the least amount of toil & to keep in mind a blow at his profits is a useful weapon to her class.

Just as the working woman must fight for this right to retain her own morality & psychology—so must she fight for the right to own & control her own body, for the ownership of her own body to do with it as she desires—& its no ones business what those desires may be.

This right naturally involves a high standard of idealism as well as a knowledge of the prevention of disease & conception. It is none of Societies business what a woman shall do with her body unless she shall inflict upon Society the consequences of her acts, like venereal diseases or offspring—then Society is concerned & it is its right to be concerned, this then involves knowledge on these [*subjects*] both are important, but I wish to dwell upon only one the knowledge of the means to prevent conception for the working woman (both sexes).

With this she should be concerned not only as an individual but also as a member of that class, who produce all the ↑wage↓ slaves of the world.

1st because the wages of the average man are scarcely sufficient to keep more than one child as it is.

2nd That the cost of living is constantly increasing while wages are practically at a stand still.

3. No matter what increase a strike will bring—one baby added to the family will more than [*reduce the*] increase even in its first year—which is the year it needs the least expenditure.

[*4*]th The uncertainty of employment & [*the*] far reaching effect of abortions [*when*] resorted to.

[5]th The terrible loss of infant mortality [*among?*] the working people to-day—Something like 85,000 death of infants under one year old in one state alone.[12] A little army slaughtered by the carelessness of an indifferent Society.

6th [*while*] child labor exists she should not add a child slave to its perpetuation.

7th that it is 9 out of ten girls living the life of the underworld who come from parents who had large families & whose fathers belonged to the unskilled & unorganized laborers.[13]

8th Societies attitude toward the workers off spring is entirely an alleviation of present day misery & ignorance. Rather than go to the root of the question & [*it can?*] refuse to have more children while Society is in this chaotic condition & here is the means to prevent it. It ~~allows~~ forces them to remain in ignorance & institutes out of their sentimental minds better baby funds, Little Mother leagues, milk Stations for babies, child nurseries for the children while the mother slaves in factories.[14] ~~&~~ As these are almost all charitable affairs—~~it goes to~~ it is usually the factory owners money which supports the child nurseries while the mother heaps up profits for him. These & hundreds of other reasons why the working woman should have this knowledge & use it. In England you have the Mothers Pensions & I should think it would be a slap in the face to a self respecting woman to have offered to her the small miserable sum to keep her child the few weeks after it is born. These are growing popular is USA too, & no doubt they will soon be an established thing there soon too,[15] & I have no doubt but that the working class will rise & bow, with hat in hand with a 'thank you sir' attitude & accept another crumb for the table & be content still a little longer.

Out of this agitation in the Woman Rebel (which issue as it came out was succisively confiscated by the P.O. & our moral guardian Anthony Comstock), came the organization of the Birth Control Leagues throughout the U.S. So far there are five reaching from coast to coast[16] & promise an agitation among the workers on this subject which should have marked results in the next four or five years. The propoganda is not a one-sided Neo Malthusian doctrine—it is one rounded out with the workers economic moral & psychological attitude. It is full of vitality & intense with indignation anger & contempt. The object is to inject into the working woman a class independence which says to the masters produce your own slaves—keep your religion your ethics & your morality for your selves— Ill have none of it & we refuse to be longer enslaved by it for we are creating our own & are building up a new Society through the process of which we are creating our own morality & individuality.

ADf MSP, DLC (LCM 129:167–75). The words "England" "Fabian Hall," and "Jl 5, 1915" were added to the top of the first page by an unidentified author. Ink blots on first two pages; pages torn. The final version was not found.

1. No formal title for this speech was found.

2. Though a vocal advocate of progressive social causes and the rights of labor, Michael Higgins was unknown outside of Corning, New York.

3. MS was echoing the arguments of many American socialist women who criticized the woman suffrage movement as a middle-class, conservative attempt to claim women's "sex rights," while ignoring their "class rights." Suffrage did become a major issue for organized working women, particularly after 1914. (Buhle, *Women and American Socialism*, 214–23; Ellen Carol DuBois, *Woman Suffrage and Women's Rights* [New York, 1998], 176–209.)

4. She was referring to the 1910–11 strike of forty thousand Chicago garment workers (mostly young women), marked by police violence against the strikers. Although women were not appointed to the Chicago police force until 1913, a few police station matrons supervised women in custody. (Raphael W. Marrow and Harriet I. Carter, *In Pursuit of Crime: The Police of Chicago, Chronicle of a Hundred Years* [Sunbury, Ohio, 1996], 128–29, 348–49, 397; N. Sue Weiler, "The Uprising in Chicago," in *A Needle, a Bobbin, a Strike*, ed. Joan M. Jensen and Sue Davidson [Philadelphia, 1984], 114–45; Women's Trade Union League of Chicago, *Official Report of the Strike Committee, Chicago Garment Workers' Strike, Oct. 29* [Chicago, 1911], 3, 9–10, 30–31.)

5. This was a reference to Katharine Bement Davis.

6. The letter was not found. California women attained the right to vote in November 1911, and it was popularly believed that women's votes carried a state temperance measure passed the same year. (Gilman Ostrander, *The Prohibition Movement in California, 1848–1933* [Berkeley, Calif., 1957], 116–20.)

7. She was referring to the "Feminist Mass Meeting," sponsored by members of Heterodoxy, a feminist circle founded in 1912, and the Feminist Alliance, a 1914 outgrowth of Heterodoxy, held on February 17 and 20, 1914, at New York City's Cooper Union, at which the speakers focused on self-development and, in Nancy Cott's words, "individual psychic freedom." MS later claimed when she told the audience she planned to publish the *Woman Rebel*, "I struck no responsive chord." (MS, "New Feminists"; Schwartz, *Radical Feminists*, 126; Nancy Cott, *The Grounding of American Feminism* [New Haven, Conn., 1987], 13, 37–40 [quote on 39]; MS, *Autobiography*, 108–9 [quote on 108].)

8. MS included the right to be an unmarried mother in a list claimed by "Rebel Women" in her editorial "On Picket Duty," *Woman Rebel* (Mar. 1914), 3 (*MSM* C16:517).

9. This was a reference to mutual assistance associations, educational programs, employee assistance programs, and other forms of "welfare capitalism" designed to counter unionization efforts. (Alice Kessler-Harris, *Out to Work: A History of Wage-Earning Women in the United States* [New York, 1982], 162–64.)

10. Written in left margin: "2000
.10
$200.00"

11. This was a loose paraphrase of Nietzsche's claim that European society ruled by Christianity had degenerated, "until at last a dwarfed, almost ludicrous species has been produced, a gregarious animal, something obliging, sickly, mediocre, the European of the present day." In a draft of a speech she planned to give on his philosophy, MS wrote,

"Nietzsche sees the world becoming peopled with a ludicrous species—a tame, obliging, sickly, mediocre kind of gently-grunting domestic animal." (Friedrich Wilhelm Nietzsche, *Beyond Good and Evil* (1886; trans. Helen Zimmern, Buffalo, 1989), 84; for MS draft, see LCM 130:360B.)

12. Her infant death figure appears to have been grossly inflated. New York had the nation's highest recorded totals, but the number of deaths among children under one year was closer to 25,000–27,000. (Walter Wilcox, *A Special Report on Vital Statistics* [Albany, N.Y., 1910].)

13. Although few studies on prostitution dealt with family size, Katharine Bement Davis's work on Bedford Reformatory inmates claimed that 85 percent of prostitutes there came from families with fewer than six children. ("A Study of Prostitutes Committed from New York City to the State Reformatory for Women at Bedford Hills," in George J. Kneeland, *Commercialized Prostitution in New York City* [New York, 1913], 217.)

14. These Progressive Era child welfare efforts aimed at reducing infant mortality by improving maternal and child health and hygiene culminated in the 1912 creation of the Children's Bureau, which coordinated the activities of disparate and largely volunteer organizations. MS echoed many leftist radicals who criticized Progressive reformers for treating the symptoms, not the causes, of the problem and for imposing their own middle-class values on the poor while remaining indifferent to the realities of their lives. (Meckel, *Save the Babies,* 113–24; see also MS, "Notes on Address When Contemplating Trial re Woman Rebel," Jan. 1916 [LCM 130:342].)

15. The 1911 British National Health Insurance Act, successfully promoted by the Women's Cooperative Guild, provided a 30 shilling benefit for the wives and widows of working men to cover medical costs and lost wages. A majority of U.S. states passed similar welfare measures for widows, deserted wives, and single mothers who maintained "suitable" homes for their children, but the funds were generally too small to support a family, forcing the women to take additional work to survive. (Jane Lewis, *The Politics of Motherhood: Child and Maternal Welfare in England, 1900–1939* [London, 1980], 167; Meckel, *Save the Babies,* 188; Linda Gordon, *Pitied but Not Entitled: Single Mothers and the History of American Welfare* [New York, 1994], 41–50.)

16. In addition to the NBCL, birth control leagues were established in Portland, San Francisco, Los Angeles, and Seattle.

60. To Marie C. Stopes[1]

[*London, England*]
[*July 6 or 7, 1915*]

My dear Mrs Stopes:

It was a jolly talk,[2] and I felt that there was afterall a real human being in England—

I shall be most pleased to join you for dinner on Wednesday evening and it will be no end of pleasure to meet Mr. Maud.[3]

Im sending you the naughty pamphlet tomorrow when I return to my Torrington Sq room where the books & pamphlets are.[4]

Yes, if only the war were over— a lot could be done on both sides of the Atlantic so much needed—

All for now until Wednesday. Thanks

Margaret Sanger

ALS Stopes, UK-BL (*MSM* C1:48–50). The year was added to the top of the first page by an unidentified author.

1. Marie Carmichael Stopes (1880–1958) was a Scottish-born paleobotanist and suffragist who, following the 1914 collapse of her marriage, turned to the study of sex. She was at this time revising *Married Love,* a sex education guide that countered the Victorian construction of "passionless women." (Rose, *Marie Stopes,* 71–78.)

2. Stopes first met MS after her July 5 Fabian Hall speech and invited her to tea the next day.

3. The dinner was on July 14. Aylmer Maude (1858–1938), a Tolstoy biographer and translator, had known Stopes and her husband for several years. He lived with them briefly in 1913 and become her confidant, hastening the dissolution of her marriage. (*London Times,* Aug. 26, 1938; Rose, *Marie Stopes,* 73–75.)

4. She was referring to *Family Limitation.* MS's first London residence was a small room on the top floor of 67 Torrington Square, just behind the British Museum. Sometime in late May or June 1915, she moved to a room in the London suburb of Hampstead Gardens, next door to the Malthusian League president Alice Vickery. (MS, *My Fight,* 101–3.)

61. *To Edith How-Martyn*[1]

[*London, England*]
[*July 17, 1915*]

Dear Mrs How Martin.

At dinner with Dr Stopes a few nights ago Mr Elmer Maud suggested to draft a sort of protest letter addressed to President Wilson[2] and signed by prominent Scientific people here on my case. They were both highly interested and offer to do all they can to make things known.

I have written Miss Doty[3] & trust I may hear from her later.

I have been feeling so down & depressed I have decided to get out of London very soon & go north for a quite ten days or two weeks where I can draft out my trial before I leave for U.S.A.[4]

I just dread going back & placing myself in their merciless hands. Yet each mail brings letters that it is the only thing to do to save the propoganda & to push on the Cause, which has rested down again. I feel like one feels when you <u>first</u> dive from a high board into the Ocean. About the little gathering you suggested, of friends who might wish to say good-bye.[5] As my sailing or the date of it, is still so uncertain I wonder if it will be advisable to do it.

America is still so uncertain and all friends agree that I should remain here if there is war, and yet I want to get away where I can get in good trim before I sail—

It would be so splendid & such a victory if only I were able to proove to a jury that I had helped to form & conduct a clinic in England and the people were still as virtuous & not more immoral (perhaps less) than in USA. Days & weeks drag on and one could be really doing something in the meantime. But at any rate I feel I had best get away from London (not to visit) & rest & get in fighting trim for two weeks & see what that time may bring.

If U.S.A. goes to war Ill return & talk clinics.

What do you think, with regards to you—all—

Margaret Sanger

ALS EHMP (*MSM* C1:57–64). Return address: "67 Torrington Sq." The date was written at the top of the first page by Edith How-Martyn.

1. Edith How-Martyn (1875–1954) was a British feminist, social reformer, and lecturer in mathematics. A member of the Women's Social and Political Union (WSPU), How-Martyn was arrested and imprisoned in 1906 for trying to make a speech in the House of Commons. Critical of the Pankhursts' leadership of the WSPU, she and several other women left in 1907 and formed the Women's Freedom League. One of the earliest suffragettes to advocate birth control, How-Martyn joined the Malthusian League in 1910 and met MS in June 1915 when MS addressed a group of British feminists at the home of Alice Vickery. (Banks, *Biographical Dictionary of British Feminists,* 105–6; MS, *My Fight,* 103.)
2. She was referring to Woodrow Wilson (1856–1924), U.S. president from 1913 to 1921.
3. The letter was not found. Madeleine Zabriskie Doty (Baldwin) (1879–1963) was a lawyer, suffragist, and peace worker who met MS through her association with the Greenwich Village Liberal Club. (*New York Times,* Oct. 16, 1963.)
4. MS left for Brighton on July 25, 1915, and probably returned to London on July 31. (MS to How-Martyn, July 25, 1915 [*MSM* C1:71]; How-Martyn to MS, July 27, 1915 [LCM 14:215].)
5. No information was found on whether this gathering took place. (See How-Martyn to MS, July 19, 1915 [LCM 14:213].)

62. *To Comrades and Friends*

This letter was included at the end of Sanger's third pamphlet, Magnetation Methods of Birth Control.

London, [*England*]

AUGUST 1, 1915.

COMRADES AND FRIENDS,—

In closing this series of pamphlets on "Methods of Birth Control," I wish to express my thanks to all those who have written me letters of encouragement and appreciation during the past several months, and also to those who have come to the aid of Mr. Sanger in the defence against his outrageous arrest by Anthony Comstock.

In the first issue of the *Woman Rebel* I promised to give to my subscribers the information to prevent conception.[1] Even though seven issues out of nine were suppressed and confiscated,[2] and three indictments returned against me, I have succeeded in doing what I was determined to do, and what I was convinced was my duty to do if I was to call myself a *woman.*

I lay no claim to pioneering in the Birth Control movement in America. The industrial and economic conditions had done all the pioneering which was done in America, and especially among the working people; but as soon as I was convinced that the information to prevent conception was a necessity for woman's as well as man's emancipation, I set to work at once to do my part in giving it.

When any one man or woman knows the evils which the lack of this knowledge causes to society, and, knowing it, fails to give it because a criminal law forbids it, to me such a person is a coward, and should be branded as such. But as a real fact even doctors and nurses have known no other methods of prevention than the condom and withdrawal.[3] The question has had very little discussion in medical circles. In my past year in America I have had many doctors confess their ignorance of other methods.

That the Academy of Medicine in New York City came out for Birth Control[4] a few months ago gives hope for discussion on the subject, and perhaps for newer and better methods of Birth Control than are at present known in other countries. At least we know that an interest has been aroused in the subject, and if anything I have done has in any way contributed in arousing this great interest, I can only say that sacrifices, sufferings, worry, and misunderstandings of the past year recede into the background at the joy this thought gives me.

The question now comes to me as I finish this work, shall I return to America to take up the fight with the Government, or shall I remain in England and continue my work unmolested here? It has been difficult to decide, but the feeling within me is that my work is not done until I have the liberty of conducting a Birth Control clinic in New York City, just as free from Government interference as I can conduct one in London. This feeling has prompted me to return. I hope to establish a free clinic in the Lower East Side in New York, where poor women can come for advice and instruction concerning Birth Control.

Of course, this cannot be done until the indictments now pending against me are dismissed.

I call upon you all to help in this fight, *one of the most important for woman's freedom ever waged.* Mr. Sanger has been refused a jury trial, and his case comes up before three judges, who will in a few days decide his case.[5]

One word more in closing. After the suspension of the *Woman Rebel,* all money orders which I received for subscriptions after December 1, 1914, were returned to sender. Kindly look into the matter if you have not received it, and let me know.

Again accept my thanks, and join hands with me in this fight for a free and intelligent humanity. Fraternally,

MARGARET H. SANGER.

Address:—Free Speech League, 241 East 201st Street, New York City.

TFL MSP, DLC (LCM 129:4A).

1. See MS, "Aim"; and MS, "The Prevention of Conception," Mar. 1914, herein.
2. Seven issues, not nine, of the *Woman Rebel* were published, and the post office interdicted all but the April and June issues.
3. While some members of the medical profession may not have known about the full range of birth control devices or methods, clearly many did, for they condemned their use as immoral or unsafe. Advertisements for contraceptives, often disguised as feminine hygiene products, suggest that the general public also knew about these contraceptive methods. (Brodie, *Contraception and Abortion,* 212–18.)
4. In November 1915 and again in December 1916, the academy rejected the proposed resolution supporting birth control legislation. (See Abbott to MS, June 1, 1915, note 4, herein; and *New York Times,* Nov. 19 and Dec. 27, 1916.)
5. William Sanger's attempt to get a jury trial was denied on July 9. His case was scheduled for September 3. (*Reports of Cases Heard and Determined in the Appellate Division of the Supreme Court of New York* [Albany, N.Y., 1915], 835–36.)

63. *From Leonard D. Abbott*

[*New York, N.Y.*]
Aug. 28/15

Dear Margaret,

Your letter of last month[1] is received & greatly appreciated. Rose thanks you for your kind words. She & the baby are both doing fine.[2]

I also received the third pamphlet,[3] & admire, more than I can say here, your courage & perseverance in carrying through the series, despite all the difficulties.

Now I have the registered letter of 13th, with the first of three articles on "Modern Schools in Spain" for The "Modern School" magazine.[4]

Four letters from you I have sent or given to Bill. Four or five letters that have come to me for you, I have sent on to you, care of Dr. Drysdale.[5]

I am sorry that I have not been able to send you more money, but the fund collected is almost exhausted, & I am personally hard up, at the moment.

I shall probably issue another appeal soon, & get some more money.[6]

Bill's trial is now definitely set for next Friday, September 3rd, so, by the time this letter is in your hands, his case will have been settled, one way or the other. I am in favor of taking advantage of every technicality of the law, & of appealing the case, if we lose.

You will surely wait, now, I suppose, until you hear the result of Bill's trial.

We had no assurance that Bill would be released if you returned prior to his trial; hence I did not advise you to return earlier.

Mr. Roe thinks that you will be granted bail, if you return & are re-arrested; but he also thinks that it will be heavy, on account of your escape last summer.

I have read your article with interest & sympathy, & shall print it, probably, in the September issue of "The Modern School." I thought you would write a brief article. I am more than pleased to receive the initial instalment of what promises to be so complete & conscientious a piece of writing. Sincerely,

Leonard D. Abbott.

ALS MSP, DLC (LCM 7:647–48). Letterhead of the Free Speech League of New York.

1. The letter was not found.

2. Abbott, who had lived with Rose Yuster (1890–1930), an anarchist and Ferrer Center regular since 1913, married her in April 1915. Their first child, Voltairine (after the anarchist Voltairine De Cleyre), had died shortly after birth in 1914. Their second child, William Morris, was born on May 30, 1915. (Ellis Island Passenger Ship Database; Avrich, *Modern School Movement,* 168, 171, 278, 338–39.)

3. He was referring to *Magnetation Methods.*

4. The registered letter was not found. MS's three articles were published in the *Modern School,* which Abbott edited in 1915–16, as "Modern Schools in Spain," May and June 1916, 5–9; "Schools and Education in Spain," September 1916, 88–90; and "Schools and Teachers," October/November 1916, 114–18. (For draft versions, see LCM 130:560.)

5. The letters possibly included her letter to William Sanger on May 31, 1915 (*MSM* S1:425); the other letters were not found.

6. The Free Speech League's Sanger Defense Committee raised over $500 by June 1915. Most of the money was used for William Sanger's legal costs, though he and MS received

$150 for living expenses. Some money was also sent specifically to assist her. (Abbott to Schroeder, July 2, 1915 [TSP]; Abbott to MS, May 1, 1915 [LCM 7:643]; Abbott to MS, June 1, 1915, herein; see also Free Speech League, "The Latest Comstock Case—The Arrest of William Sanger," 1915 [*MSM* C15:15].)

64. *From Elizabeth Gurley Flynn*

N.Y. City. [*N.Y.*]
[*August ?, 1915*]

Dear Margaret:—

I have wanted to write to you for a long time but had no idea how to reach you until I happened to meet Bill the other day and secure your address.[1] I was sorry to hear from him that English weather does not agree with you and hope it does not seriously impair your health. He also told me that you do not receive much financially from your pamphlets and I was certainly surprised, because I know many people have sold them. This must be very discouraging to you, Margaret, and make you feel that your work is not appreciated and perhaps forgotten. So I want to tell you a few impressions I received during a four months' trip I have just completed. I went to the Pacific Coast and back, speaking in all the larger cities, occasionally on the Small Family question. Everywhere there was the greatest possible interest in your work, your plans etc. But my trip was a hurried one, usually one day in each city and I was not able to do anything special in connection with your case. I am convinced however, that Defense Committees could be organized, particularly among women. I spoke in Spokane to the Socialist women and in Portland to a woman's club about it and the best result in arousing public interest and financial support, would be ↑accomplished↓ ~~for~~ by you to take a nation-wide lecture trip yourself. I am sure the I.W.W. locals would gladly arrange meetings wherever they exist and supplemented by anarchist groups, woman's clubs etc. a splendid trip is possibly. Never mind if you don't like speaking, Margaret, one talk on the general purposes of your work, would be sufficient.[2] I'm afraid if something of this sort isn't done, to gather together the forces really interested, there will not be much force behind you when you go to trial and other things will come up and supersede your case in their minds. I am enclosing a booklet published by a Portland "conservative" group which is certainly a reaction from your efforts.[3] In Chicago 5000 short extracts of your booklet were published and one girl told me the women in the Stockyard district kissed her hands, when she distributed them.[4]

I don't know whether you have decided to return, but if you have wouldn't it be possible to arrange for bail and take the trip before the trial? Or come in some other port than N.Y.—Florida (via Italy) or New Orleans and start from the Coast eastwards? With a strong chain of defense organizations behind you, which means a public opinion created on the subject, the trial will probably take on a more favorable aspect.

I would be glad to hear from you and put you in touch with all the people I think will help you, if you consider the plan feasible.

Carlo and I think of you often and hope you will soon be with us enjoying some spagetti and vino.[5]

With love from both of us and all good wishes, I remain, Affectionately yours,

Elizabeth.

ALS MSP, DLC (LCM 8:679–83).

1. She was referring to William Sanger.
2. MS often mentioned her nervousness about public speaking. She later recalled trying to conquer her anxiety by practicing her speeches on the roof. (MS, *Autobiography*, 192, 263.)
3. The booklet was not found.
4. She was referring to *Family Limitation.*
5. Flynn married Archibald Jones in 1908 and had one son. She met Carlo Tresca during the 1912 Lawrence strike and lived with him until 1925. (*NAW*)

65. To Edith How-Martyn

[*Paris, France*]
Sept 6 1915

Dear Mrs How-Martin—

Yours of Sept first just camc to me.[1] I have been intending each day since my arrival[2] to write you but you know how a day passes & how difficult it is to do what we desire most. I tried to get a few days in London after the main part of my work was done to remain & see many who had been so kind to me but I slept so badly at night & ached so by day that in desperation I fled to Paris even before I had completed my work in London.[3]

Two friends a Doctor & lawyer are both helping me get an outline of my trial. They are both most advanced women & expect to be in New York later in the winter.[4]

I am being announced in USA for lectures etc even now so at present I am doing more to building up my shattered nerves than any thing else in preparation for the ordeal which no doubt is mine.

I am doubtful about returning to England. If you knew what torture it is to enter or leave that little [*page(s) missing*]
attended the meeting that day. Of course I could not promise as I intended to leave. They were all requests to address either committees or Societies in Sept.

Nov. Dec & Jan. & all suggesting dates. It shows how many must be interested in the subject and how necessary it is to get it to them. I am feeling so much better since I came here even this short time. Someone said you were out in the country & had not been well.

Mrs Drysdale gave me a jar of "Nerve Food"[5] which really helped me so quickly that Im almost ashamed to tell any one. It looks ↑so↓ like "Christian Science" but if you sleep badly & are shakey try it do.

I trust you are going to be well & not let munitions work[6] you too hard.

All that you said in your last nice letter was true every word—& yet so many women, girls & men are being arrested each day throughout USA for my pamphlet that it seems I simply must return & fight it out.[7] The famous anarchist woman Emma Goldman & her manager were both arrested in San Francisco for giving out "Family Limitation" & were each fined $100,[8] another working girl in Chicago, a boy in Phila & several others all over all in conflict & know so little of the subject they do not feel able to enter the courts to fight it out so they pay a fine—you can readily see how it makes it necessary that some one must fight & I surely seem to be that someone. I am feeling stronger & as my physical health increases my nerve & spirit do too so I hope for a good fight & victory. Ill write you again when I know definitely of my sailing Mr Sangers trial was to be yesterday am waiting for a cable.[9]

Regards to Miss Thompson[10] & your own good self. Sincerely as ever

Margaret H Sanger

ALS EHMP (*MSM* C1:83–90). Letterhead of the American Express Co. Reverse side bleeding through.

1. The letter was not found.

2. MS arrived in Paris on August 28.

3. MS was suffering from a severe cough. She had worked for weeks to get her *Methods* pamphlets printed and shipped. According to her *Autobiography,* two thousand of them were lost when the HMS *Arabic* was sunk by a German submarine on August 15, 1915, forcing her to prepare another shipment. She was also working on an article (never published) on Ralph Waldo Emerson, Henry David Thoreau, John Humphrey Noyes, and the Oneida community. (MS, *Autobiography,* 173–75; Havelock Ellis to MS, Sept. 6, 1915 [LCM 4:110]; Stella Browne to MS, Sept. 7, 1915 [*MSM* S1:437].)

4. The friends were not identified. For the trial outline, see MS, "Notes for the *Woman Rebel,*" Jan. 1916 (LCM 130:342).

5. Nerve Food was a quack medicine that promised to cure nervousness and insomnia. Examples of these popular nostrums were Dr. Hartman's Brain and Nerve Food, made of dried eggs, milk, gum, potato starch, and water; and Sanatogen, simply cottage cheese, salt, and glycerin. Other such products contained alcohol and, in some instances, narcotics. (American Medical Association, *Nostrums and Quackery,* vol. 1, 2d ed. [Chicago, 1912], 470–77.)

6. Because of the massive shortage of skilled workers in the early days of war, Britain

passed the Munitions of War Act in 1915 to allow industries to employ both unskilled and female workers. How-Martyn was evidently working in one of these factories. (Haste, *Keep the Home Fires Burning,* 63, 157.)

7. MS enclosed a letter (not found) she received from Floyd Dell that warned her against returning to the United States if she wanted to avoid a stiff prison sentence. How-Martyn agreed with Dell, reminding MS that British suffragists had "wasted much of our human material in laying too much stress on going to prison." She added that because the United States would probably soon be drawn into the war, MS's return would be even more dangerous. (MS to How-Martyn, July 25 [*MSM* C1:71); How-Martyn to MS, July 27, 1915 [LCM 14:215].)

8. Ben Reitman (1879–1942), a hobo, social reformer, and physician who treated prostitutes for venereal diseases, was Emma Goldman's former lover and manager and accompanied her on a cross-country lecture tour. They were actually arrested on August 6, 1915, in Portland, not San Francisco, for distributing birth control literature. Both were convicted and fined a hundred dollars; the cases were dismissed on appeal. (Louise Bryant, "A New Adventure in Arcadia," and Ben Reitman, "The Tour," *Mother Earth,* Sept. 1915, 235–38, 246.)

9. William Sanger's trial was set for September 3, not September 5.

10. Louise M. Thompson was a British suffragist who worked closely with How-Martyn. (MS, *My Fight,* 103.)

66. From William Sanger

After another postponement, William Sanger's case was finally heard on September 10. Recognizing there was no hope for an acquittal, Sanger dispensed with his attorney, Gilbert E. Roe, just prior to the trial. He was convicted and jailed from September 10 to October 9, 1915.

The Tombs[1]—"The Dormitory" [*New York, N.Y.*]
Sept 12, 1915

Peg my sweetheart

Here I am—a guest of the City for 30 days after the most exciting time—I've had in quite some time. I have experienced some intense moments of my life—but this holds its own with any—

I prepared a "statement"—to be read in "court"[2]—but half of it came to grief— I was advised before hand that McInerney—had already expressed opinion on the case was an ardent bigoted Catholic—the other two were equally bigoted but not so inquisitorial.[3]

I came to the stand—stated the actual facts of my case— I started to read the other part first interruption "we don't want to hear all that" "You don't" I replied the upper Courts have deprived me of my constitutional guarantee—you want to finish it by denying me the right to make a statement in my own behalf. "You sit down"—"I don't intend to You cant intimidate me"—

At my own leisure I went to the inside of the railing—& for the first time face the 3 black robed-hounds. [~~He~~] ↑Mc↓Inerney started to chirp out "Your crime not only violates the laws of the state but the Law of God." I got away with a little slice & finally let them have it. The storm broke—the court room it fairly raised the roof. I paused for a minute before I allowed the—guard to lead me out. The three black robed ginks[4] just were pale— The radicals yelled to heaven got on their seats [*waved*] their hats hissed the judges[5]—it was a solid-phalanx of enraged humanity— It was inspiring. I knew I was going to get it. There was no hope of an acquittal this I knew—I felt—I was not deceived—

If I detained a lawyer I had no guarantee—that I would get free with my feelings—intact—an acquittal with a lawyer—only meant an anti-climax— It would all be an legal affair—not much publicity either. Then the overpowering feeling dominated me that I hated the courts . They are to my mind the "succession of the Kings" they are the real despots. An adultered symbols of authority more subtle, cunning & remorseless than the industrial Despotism they have as a background—

Here was a chance to strike at Authority—I may have done it feebly—after the smoke is cleared but I did my best considering I was up a steep wall— & Catholicism in particular. I could not very well eliminate Birth control— from the my case— If anything I think [*we?*] have broken the silences of the Press.—[6]

Many people have told me in fact all agree that your case is much improved, as I only got 30 days and I defied the court—

Enclosed you will find Clipping.[7] If I have failed—to make your ~~rocky~~ road—an less rocky one to an ultimate acquittal I shall be grieved—and keenly disappointed—

The Associated press with the world Journal, Tribune & Times came to jail & got the ↑permission of the↓ warden to Interview me—one asked me if I thought I was doing any good by taking 30 days rather than pay a fine of $150— Yes. I replied.[8] I am already repaid—because the despotic action of the courts are helping to make Birth Control—a household term—

John Waldo Fawcett[9]—a big Western Editor [*writes*] me that the trial created a situation which has rarely been equalled for spontaneous intensity in the history of the N.Y. Courts. It makes a decided departure in such matters and I doubt will find it as efficacious as you have. He is going to help on your case as a valuable addition to the newspaper we can rely on. Stuart is off— safe—with the Winns. Peggy & Grant are happy I hear have all they desire—[10] I am sad not to see them the little dears. I shall never have them from me after this. What will you do. As I am sending this—I wonder whether you have really started or are going to remain—

All the papers have asked me if you intend to return—I replied that you would—after publicity—you know—you can disregard it—& stay. Its hard to advise you to return—but the air seems to be charged with expectancy of your early return. When you see the clipping Judge for yourself,—

Heres to my only love— Who ever thought I should pass your birthday in jail—but its in the "last analysis"—for you. So here goes—with a big long kiss—as of old

Bill

ALS MSP, MN-SSC (*MSM* S1:447–52).

1. The Tombs was a common name for the notorious Manhattan House of Detention on Centre Street.

2. For the complete text, see Fawcett, *Jailed for Birth Control.*

3. The presiding judge, James J. McInerney (1875–1941), was a devout Catholic and the father of six children. The other two judges were Henry W. Herbert (1871–1937) and Arthur C. Salmon (1853–1931). (*New York Times,* Aug. 7, 1941, Dec. 25, 1937, and May 16, 1931.)

4. "Ginks" was a pejorative for "fellows." (*OED*)

5. About a hundred supporters, characterized as anarchists and socialists, were present, including Berkman, Flynn, Abbott, Tresca, and Robert Minor. After his sentence was imposed, they cried and hooted in protest. (*New York Times,* Sept. 11, 1915; Abbott, "Conviction of William Sanger," 268–71.)

6. Sanger vacillated between trying to stay out of jail and fighting for the principle of First Amendment rights. As Leonard Abbott noted, "He has worked, from the first, to take the second attitude, but he has not been strong enough." (Abbott to Theodore Schroeder, Sept. 3, 1915 [TSP].)

7. Specific clippings were not found, but the trial was covered in the *New York Times, New York Call, New York Tribune,* and *New York World.*

8. A brief report of this interview was published in the *the New York Times* on September 2, 1915.

9. James Waldo Fawcett (1893–1968), a journalist, writer, and public relations consultant, was working as an editor and reporter for the *Pittsburgh Dispatch.* (Robert D. Christie, "James Waldo Fawcett," *Western Pennsylvania Historical Magazine* 52 [Jan. 1969]: 101–2.)

10. After summer camp, Stuart returned to Winnwood, while Grant and Peggy continued boarding at the Stelton School. (Stuart Sanger to MS, Apr. 29, 1915 [*MSM* S1:462].)

67. To Marie C. Stopes

Paris, France
Sept 15—1915.

Dear Marie Stopes—

For weeks & weeks I have been going to write you— but each week brought nothing but indefinite plans, so I continued to postpone. Nevertheless you have been so very very often in my thots. I can only wish I have one tenth of your thots in the same way.

I am at last decided to return to U.S.A. no matter the results I expect to leave the 18th from Bordeaux & am all ready to go, & await a cable of the result of Mr Sanger's trial today.[1]

I went to Brighton after I saw you & there found two American women friends, one a Doctor & the other an Attorney who insisted on my remaining with them there & be taken care of. So I did. I began to feel splendid & strong & ready to attack a lion to say nothing of that miserable Comstock who by the way has fought his way back into the Gov't position.[2] Then I went back to London for two weeks & got all set back & decided to come to Paris & sail from France.[3]

Someone said you were out of London at the time I was there & as I was having sleepless nights & was not very cheerful I decided to keep close to my bed & not to see any one.

I have been wondering how you are & how you are progressing with the book—the new one[4] & if you are well & strong & happy.

It seems quite definite that U.S.A. can not come into the war owing to the very large German population, the Irish who dislike England & and the Jewish people who dislike Russia, So all have banded together for neutrality tho the Gov't & the Conservative Press are strong Pro-Ally.[5]

Then too the manufacturers of munitions are anxious because France & England owe them over one hundred millions of dollars payable in gold & should Germany win—she can claim indemnity from U.S.A. for violations of neutrality. All of which agitates the nation to say nothing of Mexico waiting for U.S.A. to become occupied so they can cast into the fire all Belgian French, British & Russian bonds & shares in Mexican oil & rubber wealth.[6]

Its truly a wonderful th'o terrible epoch the like of which was never before— American homes are more broken & divided & wretched than the Belgians and yet they continue to send into Belgium each month over four millions of dollars worth of food & clothing since the war began.[7]

The feeling in London was very bitter against Americans in public places and reports here at the Embassy are that Americans are openly insulted in Paris too. The passport difficulties show the feeling against Americans more strongly than any place I have met. How it shall end is the question.[8]

I have been working on my trial but have not the satisfaction I hope to get later.

I shall write you at once on my arrival & cable you if anything <u>real</u> occurs.

I am certain the plan of signatures you suggested would have great weight.[9] If I am out on bail Im going to organize the whole intellectual & Scientific country in my case—if possible. <u>I just can't fail!</u> & <u>I won't</u>.

My very tenderest thoughts go out to you & my thanks for your kindness & help. Cordially as always & with love

Margaret H. Sanger

Address

M. H. S. 241 East 201 St. N.Y.C. c/o Free Speech League until later

---

ALS Stopes, UK-BL (*MSM* C1:91–97).

1. The cable was not found.

2. Comstock had been appointed to represent the United States at the International Purity Congress in San Francisco. (Heywood Broun and Margaret Leech, *Anthony Comstock: Roundsman of the Lord* [New York, 1927], 258.)

3. MS spent the first two weeks of August in London and left for Paris on August 28, where she stayed until at least September 20. She sailed from Bordeaux on September 25, 1915. (Havelock Ellis to MS, Aug. 27, Sept. 1, and Sept. 20, 1915 [LCM 4:106, 108, and 122].)

4. Stopes had worked on her book *Married Love* since 1910, but she destroyed the first manuscript. She sent a new draft to publishers in 1915. (Rose, *Marie Stopes*, 75–76, 88.)

5. Americans in 1915 were equally divided over both the inevitability and desirability of U.S. entry into the European war. However, by September, the Wilson administration had moved from strict neutrality to an increasingly anti-German stance following several German submarine attacks against U.S. vessels and the sinking of two British ships, the HMS *Lusitania* and the HMS *Arabic*, both of which carried American passengers. Privately a pacifist, MS defended U.S. neutrality, but Harold Hersey reported that upon seeing him in uniform in 1917, she said, "I'm against all war, just as my father is—just as all my friends and associates are—but if I take a stand against it, become an active pacifist, the Birth Control movement will suffer." (MS, *Autobiography*, 132; Hersey, "Margaret Sanger," 106.)

6. The debt owed to U.S. businesses and financiers by Britain and France was probably much higher, and there was growing concern over possible German claims for indemnity from the United States. MS's presumption that profiteering by munitions makers propelled the United States toward war was typical of many involved in the peace and antipreparedness movements. Her concerns about Mexico reflected views similar to those held by such groups as the Anti-Preparedness Committee (later the American Union against Militarism), which campaigned against American imperialism in Latin America. (Blanche Wiesen Cook, ed., *Crystal Eastman on Women and Revolution* [New York, 1978], 11–12; articles from April through Sept. 1915 in the *New Republic*, the *Masses*, the *Nation*, and the *New York Call*, especially Robert Minor's cartoon "The Forgotten Hyphen—Munitions-American," Aug. 28, 1915, and "Business as Usual," Aug. 22, 1915.)

7. Belgium's attempts to resist German occupation aroused admiration and sympathy in Britain and the United States, particularly after the Allies exploited stories of German atrocities. The Commission for Relief in Belgium, a private organization founded in October 1914 by Herbert Hoover, contributed over $1 billion in food and clothing between 1914 and 1919.

8. With the passage of the 1914 and 1915 Defense of the Realm Acts, England effectively restricted travel in and out of the country by requiring passports consisting of a photo, a physical description of the bearer, and an occupation. U.S. citizens seeking to leave

England were increasingly subjected to displays of anti-Americanism by British citizens angry over U.S. neutrality. MS published an article on the problem, noting, "To be an American today in England is almost as unfortunate as to be a German, but to have a passport in the bargain brings upon you all the cunning trickery of which the official English mind is capable." (Paul Fussell, *Abroad: British Literary Traveling between the Wars* [New York, 1982], 9, 28–29; "The Danger of Carrying an American Passport," *New York Sunday Call,* Oct. 24, 1915, 3 [LCM 128:676]; for a draft version, see LCM 130:417.)

9. When Stopes had met MS in July, she had suggested presenting a petition to President Wilson, signed by British dignitaries, to help strengthen MS's case. The signatories were Percy Ames (1853–1919), a poet and literary scholar; William Archer (1856–1924), a drama critic and champion of Henrik Ibsen; Lena Ashwell (1872–1957), an actress and women's rights supporter; Arnold Bennett (1867–1931), a playwright and author; Gilbert Murray (1866–1957), a classical scholar; as well as Edward Carpenter, Aylmer Maude, H. G. Wells, and Stopes. (*WWW England; DNB;* for the petition, see Sept. 1915 [*MSM* C15:75].)

68. *From William Sanger*

Margaret Sanger returned to New York City on October 6, 1915, a few days before William Sanger was due to be released from prison. She did not visit him but instead spent time with her children. She waited a week before announcing her return to the authorities and in the meantime contacted Mary Ware Dennett and William Robinson to see if the NBCL and the New York Academy of Medicine's birth control committee would support her. (MS, My Fight, *123–26.)*

The Tombs [*New York, N.Y.*]
Oct 6—[*1915*]

Peg Dear Soul

Today the glorious news reached me thru Abbott that you had at last come back. When I read the news a thousand emotions seized me. A whole year of pressing events seem to have crowded themselves in the space of a single moment Certainly I have experienced some dramatic situations and this morning was another.

My memories recede back to the good old days of White Plains & Dusenberry hill ever memorable in my mind, when I consider that it may have been <u>all different</u>—& that I may never have seen you again—all past differences & understandings—recede to nothing—in the thought that I shall behold your dear presence once again.

I hope the impression you receive for this near incident to my trial will be a favorable one— I shall be sad indeed if you [*should*] conclude that my thirty days in jail shall have cast a cloud over your ultimate acquittal.

I come out Oct 9th Saturday 9am after attending a few things I will come out to Stelton—

You beat me now to see the Kids first to get that first smack—I was looking forward to the time when they would recognize you.—& [*give*] you that first kiss in a year! but some things are denied—me—I shall be curious to hear how Peggy took it all when she beheld you. Did she know you I wonder—& Granty little soul—he is a Joy!

Now sleep long & well—& eatwell—if on receipt of this letter you need anything write me to 277 W. 11th[1] mail it ("hold until called for")—& Ill arrange to bring over what you wish—

Your Call article—on the passport question arrived Oct 4 th[2] sent it over the same day I cant understand why it has not been published as yet.

Kiss the kiddies for me! Love as of [*old love?*]

Bill

ALS MSP, MN-SSC (*MSM* S1:482–83).

1. William Sanger's apartment was at 217 West Twelfth Street; no information was found on who was living at 277 West Eleventh Street.
2. See MS to Marie Stopes, Sept. 15, 1915, note 8, herein.

69. To Marie C. Stopes

New York City, [*N.Y.*]
October Eleventh. [*1915*]

Dear Marie Stopes:

What a wonderful woman you are! Your dear letter of Sept 20th & the registered one with enclosures came & were most welcome.[1] Yes indeed you have a splendid list of names I see you have Carpenter's name.[2] Did you ask Ellis?[3] There is no doubt that this statement with such signatures will have a splendid effect in America, and your letter too. I regret however that you have laid so much stress on the sentence about abortion.[4] No one in America views it in the same way. No one doubts of my views on the subject. Mainly because I have so strenuously attacked the abortionists & the Government for creating them.

With the pamphlets on Family Limitation was sent a letter written by me calling attention to the outrageous slaughter of women each year thr'u abortion. It was printed in February in the Malthusian[5] perhaps you would care to read it.

Then too the general impression here is that there are just as many "attempts" at abortion in England thr'u drugs which have a worse effect on the child.[6]

Not one voice here has been raised against that part of the pamphlet, and so I regret you have raised that objection to it, for always people are looking for an objection to climb on. However I think what you said in the letter was magnificent. I have today informed the U.S. Dist Atty that I am here and now I expect proceedings to begin.[7] Shall let you know. I should be pleased indeed to place the MSS. for you if you will send it on to me. I also hope to see Norman Hapgoode in a few days & find out about the articles.[8]

Mr Sanger came out of his 30 days sentence yesterday.[9] Anthony Comstock died ten days after Mr S.'s trial. There was a terrific demonstration in Court which made the three judges turn pale & gave Comstock a shock from which he never recovered.[10]

My children are well and lovely and except for my London-cough I am well too, th'o I was very ill in Paris—

All for now. A letter in a few days again. Thank you dear lady again & again Ill find out about news agency and let you know. With love <u>ever</u> affectionately

Margaret H. Sanger

[*Written above letterhead*]: Address hotel Rutledge (M. H. S.)

ALS Stopes, UK-BL (*MSM* C1:100–105). Letterhead of the Hotel Martha Washington.

1. Stopes to MS, Sept. 20, 1915 (*MSM* S1:459); the registered letter (not found) was probably a copy of Stopes's September 1915 letter to President Wilson, with the petition enclosed (*MSM* C15:72).

2. She was referring to Edward Carpenter.

3. Havelock Ellis never signed the petition. He explained that Stopes never asked him to sign it, apparently because she thought "his opinion might be taken for granted." (Ellis to MS, Nov. 8, 1915 [LCM 4:148].)

4. In her letter to President Wilson, Stopes argued, "The fact that Mrs. Sanger has even apparently condoned abortion may be seized upon as a justification for her condemnation. But, if this is truly & impartially considered, it will be seen to be on the contrary a condemnation of the system which she is so valiantly fighting—a system under which it is possible for secret abortionists to have large practices, so flourishing that queues of poor women stand outside their doors as if waiting for a popular theatre to open. Yet these tortured women who <u>dare not</u> let the unwanted child develop within their sacrificial bodies, are deprived by the prurient ignorance of Comstockery of clean, scientific, & healthful methods of preventing conception." MS, who did condone abortion at that time, though she conceded that women were driven to it because contraceptives were not available, wrote in an early version of *Family Limitation,* "Abortions will become unnecessary when means to prevent conception are better understood." (*MSM* S76:844.)

5. See her letter to "Comrades and Friends," October 28, 1914, which followed the article "Neo-Malthusianism in the United States," *Malthusian,* Jan. 15, 1915, 3–4.

6. The June 1914 issue of the *Malthusian* estimated that 100,000 women per year attempted abortion through drugs. A wide variety of home remedies and commercially

available mixtures was used, many containing lead-based compounds or such traditional emmenagogues as savin, tansy, quinine, or ergot. The growing practice was decried in British medical journals as immoral and dangerous to women's health. In 1920, MS expanded on this, arguing, "There are no statistics, . . . by which we may compute the amount of suffering to mother and child from the use of such drugs, but we know. . . . that the woman's own system feels the strain of these drugs and that the embryo is usually poisoned by them. The child is likely to be rickety, have heart trouble, kidney disorder, or to be generally weak in its powers of resistance." (McLaren, *Birth Control*, 241–42; MS, *Woman and the New Race*, 126–27.)

7. Her letter to Assistant U.S. Attorney Harold Content was not found.

8. Stopes was having difficulty getting *Married Love* published in England, and MS had offered to see if she could get an American publisher. Norman Hapgood (1868–1937), an author, editor, and brother of the writer Hutchins Hapgood, was editing *Harper's Weekly*, and MS had written him (letter not found) suggesting that *Harper's* publish an article or series by Stopes on birth control. (Rose, *Marie Stopes*, 88; *New York Times*, Apr. 30, 1937; MS to Stopes, July 20, 1915 [*MSM* C1:66].)

9. William Sanger was released on October 9, not October 10.

10. On September 10, Comstock had heatedly spoken out during the trial without the court's permission. Following the demonstration by William Sanger's supporters, when Sanger had been allowed to address the court formally, Comstock had shouted that he had been threatened with being shot if he did not drop his prosecution of this case. He came down with pneumonia the next day and died on September 21. (*New York Times*, Sept. 22, 1915.)

70. From Harold A. Content[1]

New York [*N.Y.*]
October 13, 1915.

My dear Mrs. Sanger:

I have in your favor of the 11th inst.,[2] and in reply thereto beg to state that the three indictments against you in this District are still pending.

I must confess that I was rather annoyed at your disappearance, particularly in view of the fact that I tried at all times to be courteous to you and considerate of your rights. However, it will serve no useful purpose to dwell on this phase of the matter at this time.

You state that after a week or ten days with your children, you thought it might be well to go over the "pros" and "cons" before your case is called for trial, and I think that is a very sensible suggestion. Since I have occupied the position I now hold, I have at all times endeavored to display the utmost fairness; and you may be assured that if you will call upon me, you will be treated with the same fairness that I endeavored to manifest in the past.

Would you be good enough, then, to advise me whether I may expect a call from you some time between this date and October 23, 1915? If so, I should suggest your writing or telephoning to inform me when I may expect you. Respectfully,

Harold A. Content [*signed*]
Assistant U.S. Attorney.

TLS MSP, DLC (LCM 11:202–3). Letterhead of the Department of Justice, U.S. Attorney's Office. Reference number: "HAC/11053." Addressed "c/o Leonard Abbott, 241 East 201st St., New York, N.Y."

1. Harold A.Content (1887–1944) was a lawyer who worked for H. Snowden Marshall's firm (1911–13) before Marshall became the U.S. attorney for New York's Southern District and selected Content to be assistant U.S. district attorney. Until he left office in 1918, Content was well known for his prosecution of radicals. (*New York Times,* Feb. 9, 1944.)
2. The letter was not found.

71. To William Sanger

[*New York, N.Y.*]
Oct 13—1915.

Bill dear:

As we do not seem able to talk things over without each insulting the other I am going to try to write the things I want to say to you.

Let us first not discuss the causes of our feelings towards each other. I recognize that you feel exactly the same toward me that I feel toward you. Just what to call that feeling I do not know for it is a mixture of memories, beautiful, ugly, disappointing, inspiring, happy & sad. It has no name, only its existing means a parting of the ways naturally because it pains & causes pain every time we meet. The fact is we can not forget. You have had a trying winter thr'u which you have blamed me for your sufferings.

I have had a trying winter thr'u which I blamed you for my suffering. No excuses, no intention, now can erase the scars those bitter tho'ts have left in either of us. There is only this difference now in us. I knew my feelings toward you would be this way before I came here. I could have told you the same things in February, but after your arrest I wanted to help you and I did not want you to blame my letters to you for any failure you might meet. But I find it was a foolish way to do, for no matter how one tries to protect your feelings—they are blamed. I give up Bill. Your vindictiveness & the reports & lies you have passed on in either anger or confidence (I do not accuse you of inventing them, you have repeated them, which from you stamped them with the truth) have increased the breach which can never be bridged.

Your insulting remarks & actions last night before the ~~nigger~~[1] porter & hall boy only convinces me that I subject myself to abuse & insult each time we meet.[2] I should like to return your name to you, or drop it, & unless you will come to a sane & agreeable or mutual understanding with me I shall be forced to proceed in a way much against my inclinations. Sincerely & affectionately,

Margaret.

ALS MSP, MN-SSC (*MSM* S1:484–86).

1. The author of the strikeout was not identified.
2. The quarrel probably took place at the Hotel Rutledge on Lexington Avenue, where she was staying.

72. From Leonard D. Abbott

New York City [*N.Y.*]
Monday [*October ?, 1915*]

Dear Margaret,

Your last message is received.[1] I have been thinking much of your problem. I don't know that we want any more conferences. The important thing is to come to a definite conclusion and to stick to it.

Either you should go into court without a lawyer, defy the law, stand outside of it or beyond it (as Bill Sanger tried to do).

Or else you should employ a lawyer in the regular way, using every loophole that the law affords.[2]

My recommendation is that you employ a lawyer, & that you appeal to your people (the ones who have already contributed or shown interest) for the money to pay him.

I think that Harry Weinberger[3] is the best man.

Whitney[4] I know nothing about, and Quinn[5] would probably not go into the case without a retainer of several hundred dollars. Sincerely,

Leonard.

I am not sure Weinberger is the <u>ablest</u> of the lawyers we have been considering. But I like his personality; I like his attitude, in a general way; I like the way his mind works in relation to your problem. He has followed the case closely; he is an idealist, he is deeply interested.

ALS MSP, DLC (LCM 7:655–56).

1. The letter was not found.
2. MS's legal advisers, Abbott and Roe, debated for months over whether she should plead guilty and hope for a light sentence or plead not guilty and challenge the law but risk a conviction and stiffer sentence. (Rabban, *Free Speech,* 69; Bolton Hall to Abbott, Dec. 13, 1915, Roe to Abbott, Dec, 15, 1915, and Goldman to MS, Dec. 16, 1915 [LCM 11:463 and 563, 8:903].)

3. Harry Weinberger (1888–1944) was a pacifist, lawyer, and civil liberties advocate MS consulted through December. (*New York Times,* Mar. 3, 1944; Abbott to Schroeder, Dec. 14, 1915 [TSP].)

4. This was possibly Travis H. Whitney (1875–1934), an attorney who was then secretary of the Public Service Commission. (*New York Times,* Jan. 9, 1934.)

5. This was probably John Quinn (1870–1924), a lawyer and arts patron. Although he specialized in banking law, Quinn's interest in modern art and literature led him to give advice and appear in several notable censorship cases. (*New York Times,* July 29, 1924; Boyer, *Purity in Print,* 47–48.)

73. From Harold A. Content

Peggy Sanger came down with pneumonia toward the end of October while at the Stelton School, where the crude conditions in the unfinished dormitory probably exacerbated her illness. She was transferred to Mount Sinai Hospital, one of New York City's premier medical institutions, where her aunt Ethel Byrne, a staff nurse, could oversee her care. The five-year-old died a week later, on November 6, with her mother at her side.

New York [*N.Y.*]
November 9, 1915.

Dear Mrs. Sanger,—

Mr. Abbott has just informed me of your bereavement, and I hasten to convey to you the personal expression of my most profound sympathy. Faithfully yours,

Harold A. Content

ALS MSP, DLC (LCM 11:206). Letterhead of the Department of Justice, U.S. Attorney's Office.

74. From Bessie Ingham Drysdale

Sanger received sympathy letters from such American friends as Jessie Ashley, Alexander Berkman, James Waldo Fawcett, and Gilbert Roe, as well as from her newfound British friends, including Charles Drysdale, Binnie Dunlop, Edith Ellis, Havelock Ellis, Stella Browne, and Marie Stopes. (See MSM *S1:493–594.)*

[*London, England*]
Friday 26th Nov. [*1915*]

My dear poor friend

Your letter arrived this Tuesday last, and the horror and dismay of your news ~~was~~ staggered us.[1] I had somehow never dreamt of such an awful possibility, tho' one foresaw that the darling would need watchful care in the future. It seemed to us both in our own tragedy[2] that no-one had or could be called on to bear a loss so unique, and that you, our brave little friend should too lose the [*illegible*] dearest possession: I know from what you have told me, how special a place little Peggy held in your affections and ambitions. And so fine and beautiful a child! It seems somehow as tho' these perfect children are in many ways ↑un↓fitted for a hard vulgar world. In our own bitter sorrow, my greatest comfort is that my sweetheart had all the joys of happy childhood, and was not destined to wring my heart with the sight of sorrow and disillusionment in her dear eyes.

It is poor consolation, and a bitter reflection on the world as it is, that, apart from one's own loss and loneliness, one can hug to one's heart the sense of comfort in that their peace and security from life's tragedies. is secured

If only either of us can do anything to help you, dear Margaret, let us know in the name of friendship and sympathy, we beg you. I am grieved to hear that Mr Sanger is not well:[3] the great sacrifice you have all made has I fear been too heavy for his health. Your heroic words at the close of your letter touched us all deeply.

Every kind thought and tenderest sympathy to you and Peggy's father and brothers. Yours lovingly.

Bessie. D.

ALS MSP, MN-SSC (*MSM* S1:523–25).

1. The letter was not found.
2. Bessie and Charles Drysdale's daughter, Eva Marie (1901–1914), died of scarlet fever. (Bessie Drysdale to MS, Nov. 9, 1915 [*MSM* S1:496].)
3. William Sanger was extremely depressed after his daughter's death. (Chesler, "Interview with Grant Sanger," 15.)

75. *To Leonard D. Abbott*

In late November, Abbott was attempting to persuade the government to shift the subject of the prosecution from the Woman Rebel *(which was deemed obscene for advocating birth control) to* Family Limitation *(which provided explicit contraceptive advice). (Abbott to Schroeder, Nov. 26, 1915 [TSP].)*

[*New York, N.Y.*]
[*November 26?, 1915*]

Dear Leonard:

This inclosed statement seems to be all I can say.[1] It is enough I think & they can take it or leave it.

As soon as this is settled Ill send out notices of the results & begin a rousing propoganda on giving out information not discussing it.

You were kind to come down yesterday & I appreciate it much I always feel you understand & like your opinion above all others.

Really it is so immaterial to me which way the thing goes that I am glad to have had energy to decide any thing. It is difficult to get heart for any thing & one could be no more lonely in jail than the world seems at present outside.[2]

Grant & Stuart are together in the Winnwood School & seem happy. Stuart has leaped ahead in his studies & is preparing for Regents which delights me too.[3] I fear Grant will feel the lack of freedom he had at Stelton & of course he may not like it, but poor darling Peggy's nature was so dominating, that her refusal to obey Doctors order only strained her heart & hurried her death. The problem grows deeper everyday. We try to bring them up to rebel against institutions & yet they must enter some kind of institution at every turn of life and are unprepared for them. A long preample this Leonard—forgive me. Sincerely

Margaret

P.S. Its only under the promise that my case is not to come up in open court, that the inclosed is to be issued.

M.

ALS RGP, WHi. Return address: "26 Post Ave c/o Byrne." Reverse side bleeding through.

1. MS may have been referring to a letter she drafted (though probably did not send) to Assistant U.S. Attorney Harold Content, indicating she would plead guilty to the *Woman Rebel* charges, "tho I cannot accept the opinion that there is one word or sentence or article in any of the above mentioned articles which can be called 'Obscene' or in any way conflict with section 211. I feel however, that as my object was to open a discussion on the birth control subject, which was denied me through the post office censorship, it has been gained by other publishers during the past year, and a further pressing of this phase of the subject is useless." (*MSM* C1:110; no final version was found.)

2. In Abbott's November 26 letter to Schroeder, he wrote, "Poor Margaret! She seems to me in a very confused state of mind. She is understandably crushed by her troubles. She wavers between the attitude prompted by her own weaknesses, and her desire to be consistently radical and revolutionary." (TSP)

3. Following Peggy's death, MS pulled Grant from the Stelton School to join Stuart at Winnwood. The "Regents" were a statewide series of required academic examinations.

76. From Samuel Untermyer[1]

New York [*N.Y.*]
December 6th, 1915.

Dear Mrs. Sanger:

Replying to your letter of the 3rd inst.[2] I regret to note that you hesitate about pleading guilty. It seems to me that would let you out of your troubles very fortunately and without loss of principle or dignity. The law may not be what it should be, but you have certainly offended against the law and should feel yourself fortunate at the outcome that has been suggested.

You can gain nothing by trial. You cannot even get publicity in these days when the papers are crowded with international news and the big things of history are happening.

I do not believe that your work in the future would be nullified by adopting the course which all of us agree is in you best interest.[3] Some of the articles you cannot defend. Before the law you can defend none of them. Your plea will not interfere with any efforts you may make to change the law when you are again in normal times.

I read with interest the article in the Malthusian Magazine[4] and thank you for having sent it to me. Sincerely yours

Samuel Untermyer Esq [*signed*]

TLS MSP, DLC (LCM 8:958). Letterhead of Guggenheimer, Untermyer & Marshall. Addressed to "163 Lexington Avenue, New York City."

1. Samuel Untermyer (1858–1940), an attorney who specialized in constitutional law, was popular among liberals for his commitment to antitrust actions and other public interest cases. According to MS, she first consulted Untermyer about her case in 1914 at the suggestion of the *Masses* editor, Max Eastman. (*New York Times,* Mar. 17, 1940; MS, *Autobiography,* 183.)

2. The letter was not found.

3. MS remained uncertain about what to do, particularly after she was offered a plea bargain. She later claimed that Untermyer got Assistant U.S. Attorney Content to agree to drop the charges if she promised in writing not to break the law again, and Theodore Schroeder claimed Content suggested to him that an agreement could be worked out in chambers, where "the whole matter will be disposed of." However, by mid-December, the offer had been withdrawn. (MS, *Autobiography,* 183; Content to Schroeder, Nov. 29, 1915 [*MSM* C1:111]; H. Snowden Marshall to Abbott, Dec. 15, 1915 [LCM 11:207]; see also letters to Abbott from James Warbasse, Dec. 7, Bolton Hall, Dec. 13, and Gilbert Roe, Dec. 15, 1915 [LCM 11:780, 463, and 536].)

4. See MS to "Comrades and Friends," Oct. 28, 1914, herein (published in the *Malthusian,* Jan. 15, 1915, 4).

77. From Emma Goldman

Chicago, Ill.,
12/7/15.

My dear Girl:

The enclosed money order for $40.00 represents the forty dollars collected at my Birth Control Lecture for you. I am sure it will come very handy, as you must be terribly hard pressed at the present time. It is my intention to use all other lecturers on the same subject as a means of raising some money for you. I know that it is not enough to express my affection for you and my devotion to the thing we both love so much, but in our materialistic age, the money question is very pressing indeed.

I really think it is impardonable on your part to blame yourself for the death of Peggy.[1] I am sure that it is due only to your depressed state of mind as I cannot imagine anyone with your intelligence to hold herself responsible for something that could not possibly have been in your power.

No doubt the child would have been given better care in your home, but whether that would have saved her life is a mere speculation, which ought not to take possession of you in the way it evidently has. Please, dear, don't think me heartless. I feel deeply with your loss but I also feel that you owe it to yourself and the work you have before you to collect your strength. After all dear, it is a thing which has passed and cannot be redeemed whereas you need your vitality and unless you will take hold of yourself you will lose whatever little you have and yet not change the inexorable.

The Birth Control question has taken hold of the public as never before. That ought to be a tremendous satisfaction to you. It is this growing interest which will have no little bearing on your case and which in a measure may explain the indifference on the part of the authorities to open up your case.[2] However, I do wish there was some decision one way or another. It would be such a wonderful thing if you could make a trip across the country. It would pull you out of yourself and at the same time give the movement an impetus of great force.

We have had interesting meetings here, but with the exception of the one on the Birth Control not so large as we had hoped. The sale of literature is phenominal. We leave for St. Louis to-night where you can reach me if you answer this by return mail, c/o of the Marquette Hotel. If not, write me general delivery, Indianapolis, Ind. until the 15th.[3]

Hoping that you are feeling better and that the enclosed amount may help to give you some joy, I am devotedly and affectionately,

E. G. [*initialed*]

TLI MSP, DLC (LCM 8:897–98). Letterhead of the L. H. Crall Company.

1. The letter to Goldman was not found.

2. Goldman and Alexander Berkman were alone in encouraging MS to plead not guilty and risk a jail term. (See letters to MS from Goldman, Dec. 6 and 16, 1915, and from Berkman, Dec. 18, 1915 [LCM 8:899 and 903, 11:349]; see also Abbott to Theodore Schroeder, Dec. 14, 1915 [TSP].)

3. Goldman was on a nationwide tour, just completing a series of lectures in Chicago. (Goldman to Jacob Margolies, Dec. 6, 1915 [*EGPM* 9].)

78. To Rockwell Kent[1]

New York City [*N.Y.*]
[*December 29?, 1915*][2]

Dear Rockwell Kent:

Really I was so overjoyed to receive your drawing,[3] that the family think I've quite lost my wits. I hope you will sign it for me the next time you come up. By the way if you and yours are not engaged New Years Eve would you not go with me to <u>the</u> ball of the radicals about eight thirty.[4] It may be a little shocking (?) but I know you will like so many of the people there. I hope you can both come or if not both, you alone.[5]

I have been so depressed & absent minded that I was ready for the hospital.[6] The boys being here are keeping me so busy that I have no time to think which is sometimes good.

I trust you & your little ones[7] had a happy Christmas. I hope I can come out to see you some day soon. I love your version of "truth" in your picture. Its splendid and I thank you much.

Let me know about New Years Eve. Regards & best wishes to you all. Sincerely

Margaret Sanger

ALS RKP, D-ArA. Return address: "26 Post Ave."

1. Rockwell Kent (1882–1971) was an artist, author, and illustrator noted for his woodcut illustrations of literary classics and stark nature and landscape paintings. Kent, an active Socialist Party member, met and befriended the Sangers in New York City around 1911. (*ANB;* Traxel, *American Saga,* 41–57, 71.)

2. The letter was written sometime between December 26 and December 30.

3. The specific drawing was not identified.

4. She was probably referring to a New Year's Eve dance on East Fourteenth Street given by the Twelfth and Fourteenth Assembly District branches of the Socialist Party. (*New York Call,* Dec. 31, 1915.)

5. Kent married Kathleen Whiting (1890–1990?) in 1908. (*ANB;* SSDI)

6. MS was still suffering from severe depression over Peggy's death. On December 30, her personal physician, Morris Kahn, drafted a letter (never used) stating that MS had

experienced a "nervous breakdown from excessive mental and physical strain" and that she would be "unable to attend to any matters of business or society for about two months." (Morris Kahn to "To Whom It May Concern," Dec. 30, 1915 [LCM 8:1253].)

7. Kent had four children at the time, ranging in age from six months to seven years. (Traxel, *American Saga*, 45–91.)

79. From Lorenzo Portet[1]

BARCELONA [*SPAIN*]
DEC 31 [*1915*] JAN 3RD 16
ONE MONTH WITHOUT NEWS. HEARTFELT GREETINGS. LOVINGLY
PORTET

TEL MSP, MN-SSC (*MSM* S1:561). Addressed to "163 LEXINGTON AVE NEW YORK." A note by MS added at the bottom reads, "After loss of my daughter Peggy."

1. Before her return to the United States, MS had planned to settle her legal case, rejoin Portet in France with her children, and work in his Paris publishing house "selecting books to be translated into French & Spanish for women's education." By December, however, she was still grieving over Peggy's death and preoccupied with preparations for an American propaganda campaign. Portet sent her a formal offer of employment on February 10, 1916, possibly to pressure her to join him, but she made no further mention of returning to Europe. (MS to Lawrence Lader, Dec. 12, 1953; Portet to MS, Dec. 8, 1915, and Feb. 10, 1916 [*MSM* S42:301, S1:542 and 604].)

80. To Friends and Comrades

[*New York, N.Y.*]
January 5, 1916.

TO MY FRIENDS AND COMRADES:

I returned to this country on October 6th,—four days before William Sanger was released from Jail. On the sixth of November, my little daughter died from pneumonia.

A few days after my arrival, I informed the United States Attorney of my presence, asking him if the indictments issued against me a year ago were still pending, inasmuch as the issue on which I was indicted—birth control has been so thoroughly discussed during the past year in the various journals and magazines throughout the United States, and also inasmuch as no editors or publishers have been indicted. He replied that the indictments were still pending.[1] The case was called for trial at the end of December, and postponed until January 4th.[2] It is now set for Tuesday, January 18th., and will positively be tried on that date.

The opportunity was offered me to plead guilty, thereby ensuring my release after payment of a small fine. I refused to do this, because the whole issue is not one of a mistake, whereby getting into jail or keeping out of jail is of importance, but the issue involved is to raise the entire question of birth control out of the gutter of obscenity and into the light of human understanding.

The present indictments are based on twelve articles published in "The Woman Rebel", eleven of which discuss birth control. The twelfth is a philosophic defence of assassination. My case differs from William Sanger's in this respect—that these indictments do not (in my opinion) violate the law. No question of distributing information in regard to the prevention of conception is at present involved.

I shall go into court on January 18th. without an attorney, because I cannot find any lawyer whose mental attitude toward this case is right.

I appeal to you to give me your moral and financial support at this time. Write letters to Judge Clayton, of the United States District Court, Post Office Building, New York City, before whom the case is to be tried.[3] Write letters to newspapers. Hold protest meetings and send resolutions to your Congressmen and to the President of the United States. Raise funds for publicity. Address all communications to me at 26 Post Avenue, New York City.

(Signed) MARGARET H. SANGER.

TRcy MSP, DLC (LCM 129:6).

1. See Harold Content to MS, Oct. 13, 1915, herein.

2. MS's trial, scheduled for December 15, was postponed at her request. (Abbott to Schroeder, Dec. 14, 1915 [TSP].)

3. Henry DeLamar Clayton (1857–1929), a Democratic congressman from Alabama and the author of the Clayton Anti-Trust Act, became a federal district judge in 1914. MS claimed that Clayton, who was receiving at least forty letters per day, "piled them in wastebaskets and remarked in a bored tone to Mr. Content 'Take these Sanger letters away.'" (*New York Times*, Aug. 2, 1929; MS, *Autobiography*, 186; for the few surviving letters written on her behalf, see National Archives Department of Justice, Investigative Files [*MSM* C15:94–153] and LCM 11.)

81. From Max Eastman

New York [*N.Y.*]
January 11, 1916.

Dear Margaret Sanger,

Our talk was so brief and unsatisfactory the other night, that I am going to tell you something else I would have said, in a letter.[1]

I think that with eminent counsel and the District attorney agreeing to it, you could accompany your plea of guilty with a statement, both before the

Court and for the press, which would make it a far more signal attack upon the law to whose violation you would be pleading guilty than a plea of not guilty. It would do a thousand times more good. At the same time, it would satisfy your pride, or your feeling that you ought to be brave enough to stand up for what you think, or whatever it is that is making you refuse the advice of counsel, and the wonderful opportunity to make sure of your freedom and go on with your work, that has been offered to you.

I can't help saying that I think you are not facing clearly in your own mind the motive of your action, whatever it is. Although you can write perfectly clear English and think clearly, the crucial sentence in your letter to your friends and comrades (the second sentence paragraph 3) has absolutely no meaning.[2] I think if you would once write a definite and clear statement of the reason why you are risking the wonderful chance to go ahead with your work for human liberty, you would see that it is no reason at all. At least it has to do only with the salvation of your own self and not of the world.

Now I have said all I have to say and probably you will pay no attention to it, but at least I will feel better the next time I ~~will~~ see you. Yours sincerely,

Max Eastman [*signed*]

TLS MSP, DLC (LCM 8:407–8). Letterhead of the *Masses*. Addressed to "26 Post Ave., New York, N.Y."

1. The two may have talked after MS's January 6 appearance at the Fireside Club, where she announced, in her first public statement since her return from Europe, that she would fight the indictments, claiming, "It is not so much Margaret Sanger that goes on trial but rather it is your inherent right to own and control your bodies." (*New York Call*, Jan. 8, 1916; *New York Times*, Jan. 7, 1916.)
2. See MS to Friends and Comrades, Jan. 5, 1916, herein.

82. "HOTEL BREVOORT SPEECH"

On the eve of her scheduled trial, Sanger addressed 150–200 supporters gathered for a dinner organized by the feminist Alice Carpenter to demonstrate solidarity. Other speakers included Mary Ware Dennett, who argued for free distribution of birth control information, and Abraham Jacobi, who called for the legal right of physicians to prescribe contraceptives. The next day, Sanger was accompanied to her hearing by a large group of supporters, including Elizabeth Gurley Flynn, Jessie Ashley, and Fola La Follette, only to have the case postponed to January 24 and then to February 14. (New York Times, Brooklyn Daily Eagle, *and* New York Tribune, *Jan. 18, 1916.)*

[*New York, N.Y.*]

Jan. 17, 19^{16}

It seems to me that this evening and this gathering are significant and important, not only because the idea of birth control has brought together ~~all of~~

~~us~~ workers of such diverse outlook~~s~~ and temperament~~s~~, but especially because of the time chosen for it—the eve of my trial ↑. . . .↓ and because of the dignified and representative intelligence which has supported me in this battle. ~~FOR~~[1]

I realize keenly that many of those who understand and would support ~~the~~ birth control propaganda if it were carried out in a safe and sane manner, cannot sympathize with nor countenance the methods I have followed in my attempt to arouse ~~the~~ working women to the fact that bringing a child into the world is the greatest responsibility.

They tell me that The Woman Rebel was badly written; that it was crude; that it was emotional, ↑and↓ hysterical; that it mixed issues; that is was defiant, and too radical.

WELL, to all of these indictments I plead guilty↑!↓ I know that ~~any, and perhaps~~ all of you are better able to cope with the subject than I am. I know that physicians and scientists have a great technical fund of information—greater than I had on the subject of family limitation.

THERE is nothing new, nothing radical in birth control. Aristotle advocated it; Plato advocated it;[2] all our great ~~and~~ modern thinkers have advocated it!

It is an idea that must appeal to any mature intelligence.

~~But~~ ↑Yet↓ all this scientific and technical discussion has ↑only↓ had the effect of producing more technical and scientific discussion—all very necessary and very stimulating to that very small group of men and women who could understand it.

BUT, all during the long years ~~while~~ this matter ~~was being~~ ↑has been↓ discussed, advocated, refuted, the people themselves—~~the~~ poor people especially—were blindly, desperately practicing family limitation—just as they are practicing it today.

~~BUT~~ To them birth control does not mean what it does to us.

TO THEM it has meant the most barbaric methods. It has meant the killing of babies—infanticide,—abortions,—in one crude way or another.

WOMEN, from time immemorial, have tried to avoid unwanted motherhood.

WE ALL KNOW the tribe of professional abortionists which has sprung up and profited by this terrible misfortune.

WE KNOW, TOO, that when the practice of abortion ~~s~~ was put under the ban by the church, ~~the~~ ↑an↓ alternate evil—the foundling asylum, with its horrifying history—sprang up.

THERE IS NO NEED to go into the terrible facts concerning the recklessness, the misery, the filth, with which children have been and still are being brought into the world.

I merely want to point out the situation I found when I entered the battle.

ON THE ONE HAND, I found the wise men, ~~the~~ sages, ~~the~~ scientists, discussing birth control among themselves.

But their ideas were sterile. They did not influence nor affect the tremendous facts of life among the working classes and the disinherited!

HOW COULD I ~~APPROACH~~ ↑Bridge↓ THIS CHASM?[3] How could I reach these people? How could I awaken public opinion to this tremendous problem?

I MIGHT HAVE TAKEN up ~~the~~ ↑a↓ policy of safety, sanity and conservatism—but would I have got a hearing?

AND AS I BECAME MORE AND MORE CONSCIOUS of the vital importance of this idea, I felt myself in the position of one who has discovered that a house is on fire; and I found that it was up to me to shout out the warning!

THE TONE OF THE VOICE may have been indelicate and unladylike, and was not at all the tone than many of us would rather hear.

BUT THIS VERY GATHERING—this honor you have thrust upon me—is ample proof that intelligent and constructive thought has been aroused.

SOME OF US may only be fit to dramatize a situation—to focus attention upon obsolete laws, like this one I must face tomorrow morning.

THEN, others, more experienced in constructive organization, can gather together all this sympathy and interest which has been aroused, and direct it.

I THANK YOU for your encouragement and support. ~~AND~~ MY REQUEST TO YOU TONIGHT is that all you social workers—so much better fitted to carry on this work than I—that you consider and organize this interest.

THIS IS THE MOST NEXT IMPORTANT STEP AND ONLY IN THIS WAY CAN I BE VINDICATED!!

[*Handwritten*] Let us put U S. of A upon the map of the civilized world!

TDf MSP, DLC (LCM 129:588–91). Handwritten notes, possibly by MS, at the top of the first page read, "Hotel Brevoort" and "Maiden Speech." Handwritten corrections were possibly by MS. A revised version of the speech was included in *My Fight*, 132–34.

1. The previous phrase was not included in the *My Fight* version.

2. Aristotle, in *Historia Animalium,* explained that women could use oils or frankincense to make the womb "smooth" and thus inhospitable to semen. In both *The Republic* (Book V) and *The Laws* (Book V), Plato urged regulating fertility to strengthen the human race, stabilize the community, and limit the dispensation of inherited property. (McLaren, *History of Contraception,* 18, 27.)

3. The abbreviation "l.c.," possibly indicating lower case, was written in left margin.

83. From B. Greenberg[1]

Sanger received copies of many letters sent by Socialist locals, unions, IWW members, Free Speech League members, and numerous individuals writing without affiliation to President Wilson and the judges. She was also sent signed resolutions and petitions on her behalf.

Devils Lake, N.D.,
Feb 10/16

Dear comrad M. Sanger

Enclosed find Reselutions from 2 organisations.[2] If I had the time to go and get the signatures I could have a cople hundred of the socialist local and about [20] of the workmen's circle but I did not have the time. You can copy the signetures on thouse Extra copys and send one to the Judge clayton and one to the presedant and one to the press. Yours

B. Greenberg

ALS MSP, DLC (LCM 8:949). Letterhead of the Auditor's Office, City of Devils Lake.

1. B. Greenberg was a member of the Lake Region Branch of the Workmens Circle No. 452 of Devils Lake, North Dakota (*MSM* C15:151; additional petitions and letters can be found in *MSM* C15.)

2. For the February 1916 resolutions from the Devils Lake Socialist Local and the Lake Region Branch of the Workmens Circle, see *MSM* C15:151. See also *New York Call,* Feb. 13, 1916, for the announcement of support resolution by the Union of Russian Workers.

84. From Walter Roberts[1]

New York City [*N.Y.*]
February 11, 1916

Dear one:

It was a dear, queer letter,[2] and I have read it over I can't tell you how many times. Yes, I, too, have thrilled deliciously since I was last with you—actual physical pangs of sheer joy in thinking of you and imagining you near me, in my arms. They are all the argument I need to convince me that you are wrong, wrong, dear heart, in considering any reasons why we should not love each other important. We do love and should refuse to sacrifice even the smallest fraction of anything so beautiful and sweet. That is what I feel. Do you not feel it, also? Say you do, and let us plan some way of being closer, of living our lives more wholly together.

No doubt you have problems to solve. But I have them, too. We should discuss everything frankly and help each other to arrive at our decisions.

But do not tell me not to love you, or say that you are all wrong in loving me. I feel you close beside me at this moment and breathe the perfume of your hair. I want you. I need you. Already our friendship has been the greatest thing that has ever come into my life. And I believe that it is going to grow more deep, more tender, more understanding.

Walter

ALS MSP, MN-SSC (*MSM* S1:606–7). A note by MS on the back of the letter reads, "How poor one feels before so great & richly gifted individual—Why does not the inner heart of my heart respond?"

1. Walter Adolphe Roberts (1886–1962), a Jamaican-born poet and journalist, was an associate Paris correspondent for the *Brooklyn Daily Eagle* (1914–16). He later worked as a *Birth Control Review* editor (1918–19), periodically drafting and editing articles for MS. They began a love affair in January 1916 that continued, on and off, for the next two or three years. (*New York Times*, Sept. 17, 1962.)
2. The letter was not found.

85. *From Harold A. Content*

New York [*N.Y.*]
February 15, 1916.

Dear Mrs. Sanger:

I have seen the interview apparently given by you to reporters, and inasmuch as there are some inaccurate statements therein contained, I thought it my duty to bring these to your attention in order that you may not be misinformed. I refer particularly to the statement that I assured you that trial would go on on February 21, 1916.[1] Permit me to state now that I never gave you any such assurance. I told you that the Government would not ask for any adjournment, but that it was not certain that the case could be reached on that day.

You told me yesterday—and you apparently told the reporters—that it was disgraceful how the Government was adjourning this matter.[2] You were down to see me but a few days ago, when I explained the situation to you and told you that as soon as Judge Dayton arrived,[3] I would try to set a day for trial and would try to give you a week's notice, in order that you might procure witnesses. You left without any understanding on your part or mine that the case would go to trial on Monday, yesterday; and I must say that I was very much surprised to see you yesterday, as I did not expect you, because I had promised to give you a week's notice of trial.

In view of the fact that you have no attorney who is in this neighborhood and can watch the Calendar, I have endeavored to extend to you every possible courtesy; but I must confess that your remarks to me yesterday were quite exasperating, in view of the fair treatment that I have tried to give you. You seem to forget that the case could have been tried over a year ago, and was on the Calendar for trial, and we were waiting for you to appear, but you left the jurisdiction in violation of the trust that Judge Hazel imposed in you when he released you on your own recognizance. You also forget that within the last three or four months, adjournments have been granted at your request,[4] and you retained attorneys just for the purpose of securing adjournments; but you do not mention these things to the reporters. You seem to think that your case is the only case that this office has to try.

I shall continue to try to extend every possible courtesy to you, and I shall also telephone to you toward the end of the week to let you know what the prospects are for actually trying your case on Monday next; but again I call your attention to the fact that neither I nor any one else can give you any assurance that your case will go to trial on that day. Respectfully,

Harold A. Content [*signed*]
Assistant U.S. Attorney.

TLS MSP, DLC (LCM 11:211–13). Letterhead of the U.S. Attorney's Office. Reference number: "HAC—11053." Addressed to "26 Post Ave."

1. A February 15, 1916, *New York Herald* report included a statement by MS quoting Content as telling her that he would try her case "next Monday, if I live."

2. As early as January 26, MS publicly asserted that her trial would begin on February 14. Content's claim that she knew it would not go forward on that day and that her arrival in court was posturing for the press could not be verified. (See MS to Friends, Jan. 26, 1916 [*MSM* S1:603].)

3. Alston Gordon Dayton (1857–1920), a Republican congressman from West Virginia, was appointed U.S. district judge (West Virginia Northern District) in 1905. He was called to New York City on February 14, 1916, to replace Henry D. Clayton as presiding judge. (Harold Chase, ed., *Biographical Dictionary of the Federal Judiciary* [Detroit, 1976], 69; *New York Times*, Feb. 19, 1916.)

4. Although the early postponements had been at MS's request, by 1916 the additional time was requested by the U.S. attorney.

86. To the Editor of Mother Earth

*In mid-February, U.S. Attorney Harold Content sent a memorandum to Judge Dayton requesting that the charges against Sanger be dropped. According to a press report, Content explained, "We were determined that Mrs. Sanger shouldn't be a martyr if we could help it." The government's case against Sanger was dismissed on February 18. (*New York World, *Feb. 19, 1916.)*

[*New York, N.Y.*]
[*April 1916*]

There seems to be general dissatisfaction among the readers of MOTHER EARTH over the result of my trial.

Many of them have written me that the law remains unchanged. That any man or woman may still be rushed into prison, whose case may not be "dismissed."[1]

True—all too true.

The Socialists have been telling us this for years. They have been telling us that "direct action" does not accomplish anything until the laws are changed.

You have taken an interest in my trial. You have written letters to Judge Dayton, U.S. Dist. Attorney and other officials requesting the dismissal of my case— You have pleaded the Cause of Birth Control thru thousands of letters to these officials—you have been heard—the authorities dismissed the case, as you requested—and now you are disappointed and "mad" at ME because they did it.

I made no requests of the authorities: on the contrary I informed them, before the case was dismissed, that I should continue my work until working women in America should have the same freedom to get Birth Control knowledge as the women of wealth.

I have tried to tell you that going in to jail or staying out of it was of slight importance to me. My work—my Cause, is the cry of anguish which comes to me from the women of the Cotton Belt—the cry of working women tortured with the dread of child bearing and begging for relief from it. I am free and have relieved nearly three hundred of these women in the past four weeks: to continue to do this work—via direct action—is my Cause.[2]

William Sanger went to jail—the law remained the same—I did not go to jail—you say the law remains the same. Then the Socialists must be right. Will Emma Goldman's *trial*[3] change the law, or will it serve as William Sanger's and my case has served—as precedents only? Opinions expressed by several prominent members of the legal profession have been to the effect that the "dismissal" of my case by the Government is of *far greater value* as a precedent than an acquittal by a jury.

Comrades—let's on with our work and stop quibbling.

M. H. S.

Mother Earth, Apr. 1916, 402–3 (*MSM* C1:132). The original letter was not found.

1. *Mother Earth* reported that "as far as the stupid laws are concerned, absolutely nothing was gained" and that the next person, less well-known and with less support, would "have to pay the penalty." *Mother Earth* went on to reprint a February 19 *New York Globe* editorial reiterating the view that the "quashing of the indictment settles nothing." ("Observations and Comments," Mar. 1916, 422.)

2. MS had continued sending *Family Limitation* to those who requested birth control information.

3. Goldman, arrested in New York City on February 11 for lecturing on birth control, was tried and convicted on April 20, 1916. She served fifteen days in the Queens County Penitentiary. (Wexler, *Emma Goldman,* 213–14.)

87. From Marie Equi[1]

Denied the platform of a trial when the Woman Rebel *charges were abruptly dismissed, Sanger set off on a national tour to bring her message directly to the public. She delivered several versions of her speech in some twenty cities. After a June 19 speech at the Helig Theater in Portland, Oregon, three union men were arrested for selling copies of* Family Limitation. *On June 23, in response to protests against the mayor and police for these arrests, the Portland City Council passed an emergency ordinance declaring the pamphlet obscene and prohibiting its sale or distribution in the city. At a June 29 meeting at the Baker Theater, Sanger spoke in support of the arrested men and challenged the city ordinance by selling a copy of Portland physician Marie Equi's revised* Family Limitation. *She, too, was arrested, along with Equi and two Englishwomen, Mrs. F. A. Greatwood and Maude Bonner, setting off a large demonstration. Sanger, Equi, and Bonner refused to go free on bail and spent the night in jail. All seven of those arrested were tried on July 1, found guilty, and fined ten dollars. The arrests generated tremendous publicity, greatly increasing the demand for copies of Sanger's notorious pamphlet.* (Portland Morning Oregonian, *June 20, 24, and 30, July 1–2, and July 8, 1916; MS,* My Fight, *148.)*

Portland, Oregon
Saturday [*July ?, 1916*]

My beloved Margaret:

The wisdom in love is the only wisdom which avails in the bitter agony of life. Your love reaches out to me this morning when all the bitterness of my first jail experience[2] swept thru me—engulfing me—leaving me barren and waste. Your love has enfolded me these days and nights with you—taken from out my bruised soul the scar and anguish.

At that time it was a spiritual death—and afterwards a burning out of the old rebellious attitude to many things—and the awakening of a higher stronger remote spiritualized self. Tho my body moved and lived—it was as if my higher senses had become inanimate.

You have brought back into being the very essence of life itself for me in a measure—and I know I can find in the future a larger and fuller conception of the sweetness that is for me—thru the strength and sureness of your beautiful love and friendship for me. If I could tell you all—all that I feel will result from your tenderness to me—that it will give me balance and help me overcome this intolerance which I have been forced to assume as a protection of all that I could protect ~~of~~ my inner self from utter despair—you have given me a revisioning—a passionate instinct for the creating of a new life out of the ashes of the old. Last night when you leaned over me—held me within the shelter of your arms —the very warmth and beauty of your nature became embodied within my heart and brain.

It was as if my [*mortal*] love could discern—could compass no more of the deeper consciousness of the joy—the anguish of love within love—that you gave me. The remembrance of you will live as a delicate visualized you—high courage strength—ideals that you have bravery to put into being.

My Sweet, sweet girl I love you with an ecstasy—an understanding of Spirit that you alone have imparted to me thru the very brightness and flame of your intellect.

My arms are around you. I kiss your sweet mouth in absolute surrender. Ever thy own

Marie

ALS MSP, MN-SSC (*MSM* S1:631–37). Letterhead of the Hotel Oregon.

1. Marie Equi (1872–1952) was a lesbian-feminist, radical labor activist, and birth control activist who had herself performed illegal abortions. She first met MS during this trip and may have fallen in love with her. Though MS did not reciprocate, she later wrote of Equi, "Her reputation is Lesbian but to me she was like a crushed falcon which had braved the storm and winds of time and needed tenderness and love. I liked Marie always." (*Portland Scribe,* June 30–July 6, 1973, 8–9; for MS's description of Equi, see *MSM* S83:623; see also Equi to MS, Nov. 2, 1916 [*MSM* S1:650].)

2. Equi had been jailed in 1913 for protesting efforts to restrict the rights of free speech and assembly of striking workers of the Oregon Packing Company. (*Portland Scribe,* June 30–July 6, 1973, 8.)

88. To Charles and Bessie Drysdale[1]

In the various versions of the stump speech she used during her cross-country tour, Sanger incorporated the more polished rhetoric and rationale she had acquired abroad. She also began to employ a sentimentalized autobiographical style that highlighted her nursing experience. It was in these speeches that Sanger first told the "Sadie Sachs" story (though she did not yet use the name) as the catalyst for her crusade for birth control. The story involved a young immigrant woman who had been warned by her doctor to avoid another pregnancy, but she was unable to get him to give her contraceptive information and died from blood poisoning after a self-induced abortion. Never confirmed, the story was likely a composite of several cases that Sanger packaged together for dramatic effect. It served as a simple allegory of good and evil on which she could build and then leave pathetically unresolved. As she claimed in her speech, "I threw my nursing bag in the corner and announced to my family that I would never take it up again, that I would never take another case until I had made it possible for working women in America to have the knowledge to control birth." Sanger then detailed her efforts to secure birth control, both within and outside the law, arguing that the United States should look to Europe and Great Britain for more advanced ways of handling the problem and should work for the establishment of birth control leagues and clinics. Sanger reported on the impact of her tour in the following letter, most likely written for publication in the Malthusian. *(For one example of the stump speech, see "Birth Control," ca. Apr. 1916 [LCM 129:12].)*

New York, [*N.Y.*]
Aug. 9th, 1916.

I have been promising myself each day since my return from the West that I would write to tell you of the wonderful trip I had, and also of the great enthusiasm shown everywhere in this country on the subject of Birth Control.

I left New York on April 16th and delivered a trial lecture in New Rochelle before starting.[2] I spoke in Washington, Pittsburgh, Cleveland, Chicago, Detroit, Racine, Milwaukee, Wisconsin, St. Paul and Minneapolis. Then I turned back a little and went down to Indianapolis to speak at the National Convention of Charities. I will tell you of it later. The next stop was in St. Louis, then Denver, Los Angeles and San Francisco. After two weeks in that glorious State, I went up to Portland (Oregon), by boat; spoke also in Seattle and Spokane (Washington), and thus ended my first and maiden tour in U.S.A.

The first two meetings in Pittsburgh and Washington were mild in numbers and enthusiasm compared with all the other meetings I had.[3] In Cleveland I spoke in the Unitarian Church in the afternoon, under the auspices of some social workers, while in the evening there was an overflow meeting arranged by a radical group.[4] Both meetings were splendid. Since then a strong Birth Control League has been formed in Cleveland of over four hundred members, and I enclose the little paper they have just issued—the first[5] wee voice of Birth Control in the U.S.A.

In Akron, near Cleveland, I was not permitted by the authorities to speak at all.[6] In Chicago, a young Jewish girl who has been for the last two years spreading the information to the women of the stock-yards in her own language, got up three large public meetings for me there. There were also several private meetings.[7] There is the promise of a debate there this fall between a prominent woman physician and myself, which promises a good piece of propaganda if it can be arranged.

In Racine, the organizer of my meeting was the wife of a working man and the mother of seven children; nevertheless she was socially ostracised for having anything to do with "that woman" as I was called.[8]

In Milwaukee I had an amusing experience. The women who arranged the meeting for me were very "respectable," and were allied with other lines of social work which they did not want to compromise by coming out too strong for anything which might be "obscene." They whispered to me that it was a most conservative city, and they hoped I'd put the soft pedal on too radical ideas, etc. (Milwaukee is the one city in the States which has had a Socialist Mayor!) At any rate I had no choice, for before the meeting the city physician with four detectives came up to me and demanded to be given a synopsis of the lecture before I was allowed to proceed. I would have made a fight for free speech then and there, but the friends interested preferred to let it go that way.[9]

In Detroit over nine hundred pledges to form a League were given, and a very enthusiastic meeting was held. Several women doctors there expressed a wish for clinics to be formed, and it is to be looked for soon. The nurses in St. Paul were greatly interested. I addressed one of the nurses' societies, and a clinic is on its way there also. Minneapolis, as well as St. Paul, have two strong Leagues carrying on educational work on Birth Control.[10]

The Ramsey County Medical Society of St. Paul refused to allow me to speak before them, though several members of the Society had requested me to do so; but in Indianapolis the interest was tremendous—all social workers—and all had been feeling the terrible need for this work for years. Nevertheless, the Catholic element was strong in the meeting, and when one woman rose to ask me "What about the order from the Divine book?—'suffer little children to come unto Me,'" the house went into a rage with her. They—the social workers, always on the fence in any really vital issue—actually hissed the woman down, and also every other opponent who dared to raise his head against birth control that day. It was thrilling. Then after the conference the women living in the city formed a League there, and a very representative group was interested.[11]

St. Louis was the best of all. Another Russian girl, a social settlement worker, arranged the meeting for me and engaged a theatre. When we arrived, however, the doors of the theatre were closed, and the manager said he was compelled to do it, as the Catholics in St. Louis had threatened to boycott him if he allowed me to speak there. They had offered to pay any loss he might be put to if I sued him for breach of contract. They also issued the same orders to all other managers of theatres and halls, and for two days friends hunted all over that city for a place to speak in. Two private meetings had been arranged, however, one at the City Club, where the business men dine each week, the other at a Women's Dinner Club. Both were filled to their utmost capacity, and it was said that neither Taft nor Roosevelt had had such a big attendance. Forty Catholic members of the men's club resigned that day. I am going back this winter to fight it out with St. Louis.[12]

At Denver I had the pleasure of having Judge Lindsey act as chairman of the meeting. The women there were splendid, and took a very active interest in establishing a clinic at once.[13]

At Los Angeles a league had been formed at the time of my trial. It was doing fairly good work, but needed a bit of a push. Five hundred women signed their willingness to join the league at one meeting. We had two public meetings, both overcrowded, and two private meetings at women's clubs. They are getting "Family Limitation" translated into Japanese and Mexican.[14]

In San Francisco I had a collapse, and was three days in bed under medical care, but recovered sufficiently to hold six meetings.[15] Two prominent medical men are at the head of the league there, and it is hoped there will soon be a clinic formed.

In Portland a Birth Control League has been established since the publication of "Family Limitation," and has been doing very splendid work. They reprinted the pamphlet, and have given away thousands of them. They have also held educational meetings each month, at which Mr. Uthoff and his wife conducted. They asked very specially about you, and are deeply interested in the subject from the theoretical point of view, and, I think, would like to carry on that side of the work rather than the actual giving of information.[16] When I arrived there one of the men in the labour movement asked me if he could sell the revised pamphlet at my meeting. I said I had no objection, providing it did not interfere with the rules of the league. To make a long story short, it was sold, and three of the men were arrested. They were allowed out on bail, and a postponement of the trial was permitted so that I could deliver my lectures in Seattle and Spokane and return to be called as a special witness for them. On my return, I found that the City Council (the Mayor a Puritan) had met in secret and passed an ordinance against that special pamphlet. This action on the part of five men enraged all the women in Portland, and they issued leaflets, saying: "Shall five men legislate in secret against ten thousand women?" Then one of the women doctors revised the pamphlet on "Family Limitation,"[17] and at the protest meeting on the night before the men's trial, I asked for women volunteers to sell the pamphlet. Ten women came forward, and four of us were arrested—the doctor, myself, and two English women living there. We spent the night in jail, all of us refusing to accept bail, saying: "Let those who put us in take us out."[18]

The next day the trial of the seven of us took place, and I want to say that it was simply magnificent. Two lawyers came and offered their services, and took the case without anyone's consent. They were both men of the old democratic type, trying to keep a few of the old principles of democracy alive. We had nothing to say about consulting a lawyer: they just went ahead and were splendid. It would be impossible for me to give you the details of that trial, but one of the significant things was that no one took an oath. We all refused to swear, and by the afternoon session the officers in charge did not even ask us to. Both pamphlets were on trial, the first and the second. I enclose them both. Both were considered "obscene." We were all found "guilty" and the men fined ten dollars, which the judge said they need not pay, and the women were not fined at all. The interest was intense, the room packed. On the day before we had fifteen men with ten transparencies walking up and down the streets with such sentences as "Poverty and large families go hand in hand," "Poor women are denied what the rich possess." I don't remember them all, but each was good and to the point. It took the judge a week to decide the case, and in the meantime letters were pouring into the press, and thousands of requests for the pamphlets came to all of us.[19]

In Seattle also a league had been formed since a year ago, and had been doing educational as well as practical work. The two lectures there were good in every way. In Spokane the lecture was given in the Unitarian Church, which was crowded, and a league was formed the next day.[20]

I distributed over twenty thousand pamphlets on my trip, and had over one thousand letters from St. Louis alone.[21] Women came to me in the hotels with babies in their arms; men ready for work, carrying their lunch baskets, came early to get a little private advice before I left. The farm women way down in Texas and Arizona who never got out to a lecture or meeting of any kind were the ones whom I cared most to reach; their letters were most touching and tragic.

On my way back, the Cleveland League gave a banquet for me, and the interest in the work was very earnest.[22]

On my arrival in New York[23] I found to my dismay another meeting before me. A young man named Van Kleick Allison, of Boston Mass., had been arrested and just received a three year sentence in the House of Correction for giving a detective a leaflet on Birth Control.[24] I wired him to have the case appealed. He did so. Then they had a protest meeting in one of the theatres there, and I went to offer up my wee voice in that. It was one of the greatest meetings I ever attended. They now have a good Defence League, and I trust they will make things hum there in Boston. The Judge who sentenced Allison was a Roman Catholic, as was also the District Attorney and all those who were on the prosecution![25]

So this is a brief summary of the trip and the meetings. I consider we have a big movement started from coast to coast, and I hope to open a free clinic here in New York City in September, and also get out a regular monthly paper dealing with Birth Control from all points of view. I trust you are all well. There is a great interest in you both here, and when I mentioned to several Leaguers that we might get you both here this winter, or early in the spring, there was great enthusiasm. I am certain splendid meetings could be arranged for you as soon as the Leagues get into shape. I am anxious for the people here to get your ideas of population straight from you. There are three arrests here in New York pending trial in the fall.[26] So it looks as though we should have another winter of fighting the ignorance which keeps every great movement backward.

The pamphlet "Family Limitation" has been pirated by many, and is being sold from house to house, as well as from shop to shop in the small towns, in factory and mill. Heaven only knows what the Churches will do in another generation if this keeps up!

Malthusian, Sept. 1916, 83–84. For a partially transcribed version, see *MSM* S1:638–40; the original letter was not found.

1. During the war, Charles Drysdale left his position as joint secretary of the Malthusian League and entered government service. (Ledbetter, *Malthusian League,* 63–64.)

2. She delivered her trial lecture, "Birth Control," on April 15. (McClearey, "Noonday Devil," 4/1.)

3. MS spoke in Washington, D.C., on or about April 18 and gave a lecture entitled "Poverty and Family" in Pittsburgh on April 20 under the sponsorship of the philanthropist Bertha Floersheim Rauh. (MS, *Autobiography,* 196.)

4. Her Cleveland lectures took place on April 23. (Vreeland, "Process of Reform," 401.)

5. A footnote was added here by Binnie Dunlop, who replaced Drysdale as editor of the *Malthusian,* identifying the paper as the *Birth Control News.* Made up of both radicals and more conservative society women, the Ohio Birth Control League, formed in Cleveland in June 1916, sponsored talks by such radicals as Emma Goldman, Ben Reitman, and Becky Edelsohn, but it disbanded during World War I. (For the single issue of the paper, see MdBe; Meyer, "Birth Control Policy," 60–64; Vreeland, "Process of Reform," 401–4.)

6. Seven days before her scheduled April 22 speech, pressure from the Woman's Council of Akron led to the cancellation of the lecture. Unable to block the action or locate another site, MS instead gave a newspaper interview on April 21. (McClearey, "Noonday Devil," 4/3–5.)

7. With the organizational help of Fania Mindell (1891–?), a Russian-Jewish immigrant who had moved from New York City to promote birth control among union workers, MS delivered versions of her "Birth Control" speech in Chicago on April 25 and 30 and on May 7, and she participated in discussions about opening a Chicago clinic. She had hoped to address the Chicago Woman's Club, but it rejected her request. (*New York Call,* Feb. 3, 1917; Lader, *Margaret Sanger Story,* 108; MS, *Autobiography,* 196–98; McClearey, "Noonday Devil," 4/7–9.)

8. On May 4, MS lectured to a small audience in Racine under the sponsorship of the United Woman's Club; the organizer was not identified. (McClearey, "Noonday Devil," 4/11.)

9. The Socialist mayor was Daniel Webster Hoan (1881–1961), who served from 1916 to 1940. The women organizers were not identified. MS delivered her address, sponsored by the Mother's Circle of the Milwaukee Maternity Hospital Association, on April 27. (*ANB;* McClearey, "Noonday Devil," 4/9.)

10. MS spoke in Detroit on May 2, in St. Paul on May 8 and 12, and in Minneapolis on May 11. The Detroit Birth Control League remained an informal association until 1922. The Minnesota Birth Control League was formed in St. Paul in May 1916 by Sylvie Thygeson and Alice Bacon, who later opened an informal and illegal birth control clinic, staffed by two male physicians. A Minneapolis Birth Control League was also formed in May, and the two merged in December 1916. Neither league survived after 1918. (McClearey, "Noonday Devil," 4/10–12; "List of Birth Control Centers," *BCR,* Feb. 1917, 1; *St. Paul Dispatch,* May 12, 1916; Sherna Gluck, ed., *From Parlor to Prison: Five American Suffragettes Talk about Their Lives* [New York, 1976], 49–50; Helen C. Thomsen, "What the Birth Control Leagues Are Doing," *BCR,* Apr.–May, 1917, 14–15.)

11. The St. Paul–based Medical Society was founded in 1870 to foster professional ties among physicians. On May 15, MS spoke before delegates to the National Conference

of Charities and Correction in Indianapolis, an unofficial appearance hastily arranged by Frederick Blossom, the director of Cleveland's Associated Charities. MS organized the Indianapolis Birth Control League at a meeting of social workers on May 16, which led to plans to open a birth control clinic, but there is no evidence that the league ever did so or that it remained active after 1916. MS gave her final address in Indianapolis on May 17. (MS, *Autobiography,* 198–99; McClearey, "Noonday Devil," 4/14–16; *Indianapolis Daily Star,* May 17, 1916.)

12. Clara Taylor, a nursing instructor at Washington University, had reserved the Victoria Theater in St. Louis for MS on May 22, but its manager, W. C. Markham, closed the theater just hours before her scheduled appearance. Recognizing that the audience would not hear of the cancellation in time, MS went to the theater and dramatically shook the locked doors, shouting to reporters that she would sue the theater for five thousand dollars. She briefly addressed the collected crowd of approximately two thousand, creating a spectacle that generated enormous press coverage and support. She finally gave her speech at the Hippodrome Playhouse on May 24. She delivered a luncheon speech at the Men's City Club and a dinner speech at the Women's Town Club on May 23, but there is no evidence that any Catholic members of the Men's Club resigned in protest. (Vreeland, "Process of Reform," 387; MS, *Autobiography,* 200–201; *St. Louis Globe-Democrat,* May 23, 1916; McClearey, "Noonday Devil," 4/18.)

13. Benjamin Barr Lindsey (1869–1943) was a Denver-based juvenile and family court judge who focused on reforming marriage and juvenile offenders' laws. A birth control advocate, he also supported such controversial issues as trial marriage and companionate marriage. After meeting MS in 1916, he and his wife, Henrietta Brevoort Lindsey, became frequent correspondents. MS's Denver appearance was on May 26, 1916, but despite the enthusiastic response she received, Denver women did not open a clinic until 1926. (*DAB*)

14. The Los Angeles meetings were held on June 2, 4, and 5. MS's appearances helped the Los Angeles Birth Control League attract support from women described by Georgia Kotsch as "high and mighty ladies who would not have touched the B.C.L. with a pair of asbestos tipped tongs prior to the coming of Margaret Sanger." In 1917, the league began a legislative campaign and was unique among early leagues in winning the endorsement of the Los Angeles Obstetrical Society. However, after its legislative work failed, the league disbanded sometime in 1919–20. (Katz, "Dual Commitments," 655–59 [quote on 656]; McClearey, "Noonday Devil," 2/3.)

15. Caroline Nelson arranged many of MS's West Coast speaking engagements on this tour. The Birth Control League of San Francisco (BCLSF) sponsored her appearances there on June 6, 9, and 11. An additional lecture, to be cosponsored by the BCLSF and the International Radical Club, was canceled when the sponsors became critical of MS's luxurious hotel accommodations and the twenty-five cent admission fee she routinely charged for her lectures. But she gave an additional lecture in San Francisco on June 13 and in Oakland on June 10 and 14. She later recalled that "by this stage of the trip I was seemingly always tired. The dead grind went on and on, an endless succession of getting off trains, introductions, talking to committees, pouring yourself out—and nothing happened. Physically and psychically it was one of the lowest periods of my life." (McClearey, "Noonday Devil," 4/25–26; MS, *Autobiography,* 203 [quote].)

16. The Portland Birth Control League was formed by radical leftists influenced by British neo-Malthusian theory. After MS's 1916 appearances in Portland, Meta M. Dekker, H. C. Uthoff's wife, reported on her efforts to visit women and provide them with practical contraceptive advice. (Meta Dekker, "Birth Control in Oregon," *BCR*, Dec. 1917, 10; Vreeland, "Process of Reform," 410.)

17. Marie Equi revised *Family Limitation*, changing the order of some of the text and providing several additional remedies for "suppressed menses," including hot douches, enemas, sitz baths, and osteopathic and vibratory treatments. She also added a forward describing the "stupid persecution" by Portland authorities and a closing in which she argued that physicians, bound by superstition and prejudice, would rather tend diseased women through dangerous pregnancies than allow abortions. (Portland edition of *Family Limitation*, 1916 [*MSM* C16:771].)

18. The three union men arrested were Carl Rave (1877–1950), an iron worker who later married Caroline Nelson; E. L. Jenkins, a steamboat worker; and Ralph Chervin, a chauffeur. It was Rave, with the assistance of an unknown "lady friend," possibly Marie Equi, who reprinted *Family Limitation* for distribution at the June meeting. Portland's mayor was Harry Russell Albee (1867–1950). The leaflets were not found. (CA Death Index; *Portland Morning Oregonian*, June 24 and July 1, 1916; Katz, "Dual Commitments," 661*n*1; see also Marie Equi to MS, July ?, 1916, headnote, herein.)

19. The enclosure was not found. The two lawyers were Isaac Swett (1873–1921), later a municipal judge and civic leader known for philanthropic activities; and Charles Erskine Scott Wood (1852–1944), an army officer, anarchist, civil rights crusader, and acclaimed author of fiction and poetry. Arthur Langguth (1869–1959) was a shipbuilding executive, state senator, and municipal judge. The pamphlets she mentioned were *Family Limitation* and the Portland version of it. (*Portland Morning Oregonian*, June 30, 1916, Sept. 20, 1921, Aug. 27, 1959; *DAB*.)

20. The Seattle Birth Control League, probably formed in 1914, focused on distributing *Family Limitation* in mining camps near Seattle. It sponsored MS's June 20 and 21 speeches. The Spokane lecture was on June 23. The Spokane league was not very active. (Vreeland, "Process of Reform," 419; *Spokane Spokesman-Review*, June 24, 1916.)

21. The letters were not found.

22. Some 130 people attended the July 14 banquet, held at Cleveland's Statler Hotel. ("The Fight from Coast to Coast," *BCR*, Apr. 1918, 10.)

23. She arrived home on or about July 16.

24. Binnie Dunlop added a lengthy footnote reporting on the Boston case and referred readers to a letter by William Robinson also published in that issue.

25. Van Kleek Allison (ca. 1894–?) was a scion of a wealthy New York family and an editor of the *Flame*, a radical Boston paper. He was arrested and convicted in July 1916 for distributing Emma Goldman's birth control pamphlet. Allison was prosecuted by Joseph G. Pelletier, an officer of the Knights of Columbus, who quoted the papal encyclical condemning birth control at the trial. On July 26, Judge Michael J. Murray proclaimed during sentencing that Allison was guilty of defying both divine law and state law, and he meted out a stiff three-year sentence. Supporters formed the Allison Defense League, and the protest meeting was held on July 31 at the Majestic Theater. (Ames, "Margaret Sanger's Influence," 3–4; Vreeland, "Process of Reform," 78, 389; "A Telegram," *Masses*, Sept. 1916, 15; MS, *Autobiography*, 207–8.)

26. She was referring to the pending trials of Bolton Hall, Ida Rauh Eastman, and Jessie Ashley, arrested on June 5, 1916, for distributing birth control material at a May 20 Union Square rally protesting Ben Reitman's conviction for the same crime. (*New York Times,* May 21, June 6, Oct. 7, and Oct. 31, 1916; "The Birth Control Fight," *Blast,* July 1, 1916, 5.)

FIVE

The Birth of the Birth Control Movement

THE SUCCESS OF SANGER'S cross-country tour emboldened her to continue law-defying tactics. Four months of almost daily speaking appearances, newspaper interviews, protests, and encounters with police proved her flair for propaganda and increased her media savvy. Sanger's crusade charged the air in 1916 as radicals held rallies culminating in a series of arrests that focused on the free speech and moral ramifications of birth control. But Sanger stood alone among radicals in dedicating herself to this single cause and planning a strategy to push the fight beyond First Amendment challenges.

She had announced a plan to open a free clinic in New York's Lower East Side as early as August 1915, and during her lecture tour she repeated her intent to establish a network of clinics modeled after those she had seen in Holland. Upon returning to New York in the summer of 1916, she made it her immediate goal to open a clinic, bring about her own arrest, and make her argument in court. According to Sanger, after meeting with a group of Brooklyn mothers seeking contraceptive advice, she chose Brownsville, a squalid tenement neighborhood of mostly poor Jewish and Italian immigrants, as the ideal site for a clinic. She later noted that "as long as I had to violate the law anyhow, I concluded I might as well violate it on a grand scale by including poverty as a reason for giving contraceptive information."[1]

Sanger opened the two-room clinic on October 16, 1916, with her sister Ethel Byrne, a registered nurse, and Fania Mindell, a Jewish immigrant fluent in Yiddish who served as interpreter and receptionist. To ensure that the opening of her "secret" clinic would not go unnoticed, she contacted the press and informed the Brooklyn district attorney, though he never responded. From its first day, the clinic was a success; hundreds of women lined up, patiently waiting their turn. For a ten-cent registration fee, they met with Sanger or Byrne, who showed them how to use a pessary and told them where to obtain one. Some may also have received recipes for suppositories and douches and one or more of Sanger's pamphlets. Pessaries and condoms were probably offered for sale at the clinic, though Sanger later denied this. Over four hundred women visited the clinic before police shut it down ten days later, on October 26, arresting the three women.[2]

Sanger and Byrne were convicted and jailed in early 1917. The trials and imprisonments resulted in tremendous national publicity for the fledgling birth control movement, spreading the debate over the legalization of contraception to households, club meetings, and union halls. The media attention gave Sanger a decisive leadership advantage over the lesser-known NBCL. It also drew a socially prominent group of supporters to Sanger's side, who quickly organized the Committee of 100 to raise defense money and sponsor mass meetings to promote birth control.

The final outcome of the Brownsville trials gave Sanger much of what she wanted. A 1918 New York State court of appeals decision broadened the interpretation of the law by enabling physicians to prescribe contraception to women for general health reasons rather than exclusively to prevent venereal disease. In effect, Sanger's illegal action led New York State to provide legal protection for doctor-staffed birth control clinics.

To provide a public forum for birth control, Sanger also started a new monthly, the *Birth Control Review* (*BCR*). Under the direction of Frederick Blossom, a socialist social worker, the *BCR* was launched in February 1917 with an article by Sanger justifying her tactics. "No law is too sacred to break," she wrote, boldly setting her actions alongside those of such other notable lawbreakers as Moses, Christ, Joan of Arc, George Washington, and John Brown.[3] The *BCR* quickly became the chief source of information for birth control supporters; subsequent issues contained articles by Sanger and other prominent figures in the movement, political cartoons, poetry, book reviews, and letters.

The journal nearly folded in the summer of 1917 when Sanger accused Blossom of embezzlement and mismanagement. The disagreement between them erupted into an angry battle, with Blossom's socialist supporters denouncing Sanger for airing dirty laundry. The conflict reflected the growing chasm between Sanger and the radical organizations she had been so closely tied to in earlier years. Though she did not abandon her radical friends or leftist causes, she dropped many of her formal ties to political organizations. As she pressed for the acceptance of birth control by the medical establishment, she also distanced herself, at least publicly, from her former anticapitalist arguments.

By 1917, the socialist and anarchist supporters who had helped Sanger orchestrate her *Woman Rebel* defense were a negligible factor in the movement. Radicals had serious problems to contend with in these years: government intimidation of leftist radical organizations and suppression of antiwar sentiment. With the passage of the 1917 Espionage Act and the 1918 Sedition Act, criticizing the U.S. government in any form became a federal crime. Ostensibly passed to protect the military, the government used these laws and the 1918 Immigration Act not only to restrict antiwar expression but also to suppress almost any form of radical dissent in the years after the war. Imprisonments and scare tactics crushed the IWW and sent many labor leaders, socialists, and anarchists to prison, including Sanger's friends Eugene Debs, Marie Equi, and Bill Haywood.

Sanger, an observer of the war from both sides of the Atlantic, spoke out forcibly against the draft in a June 1917 *BCR* article. Urging American women to defy the government, she wrote, "You will make it necessary for this democracy, which has set out to conscript your men for foreign warfare, to take them over the dead bodies of the protesting womanhood of the United States."[4] Over the next two years, she defended her comrades on trial or imprisoned for their antiwar sentiment, even becoming an advisory board member of the League for Amnesty of Political Prisoners. She used the *BCR* to publish antiwar cartoons and editorials criticizing the government's assault on the Left.[5] Though the government pressured Sanger for Comstock law violations, periodically confiscating issues of the *BCR* and hounding and finally imprisoning its militant street hawker, Kitty Marion, it ignored Sanger's political dissent even as other prominent radicals were prosecuted for similar kinds of speech. Though she was kept under surveillance,[6] government authorities may have backed off because of her expanding network of politically powerful New York friends or out of concern that Sanger would turn a federal prosecution under the Espionage Act into another platform to discuss birth control. Sanger herself may have passed through the repressive wartime atmosphere unscathed, but the official intolerance took its toll on grass-roots birth control groups around the country, many of which suspended their work or disbanded altogether.

Sanger's most fulfilling work during this time was running her "little room," an informal birth control consultation clinic funded by a new friend, Juliet Rublee, a wealthy and politically well-positioned eccentric, who would help fund nearly every aspect of Sanger's campaign and become her closest confident for the next forty years.

Apart from the *BCR* and her little clinic, Sanger had no clear agenda and no organization to coalesce support. Stung by the wartime breakup of past alliances and indifferent to the NBCL and its moderate legislative focus, she was, by 1918, unsure how to proceed. Nor was she secure in her personal life. Though she had romantic liaisons with such stimulating writers and poets as Billy Williams, Harold Hersey, and Walter Roberts, who all worked periodically at the *BCR*, she was not interested in serious affairs. Her life was further complicated by a flare-up of her tubercular lymph nodes and bouts of severe exhaustion. She finally resigned herself to a period of recovery and contemplation.

With funds provided by friends, Sanger went to California in the winter of 1918–19 to rest and write. There she developed the theoretical underpinnings of her crusade in *Woman and the New Race,* a book in which she merged her radical politics and feminism with science-based inducements for smaller families. But the trip did little to improve her health. As the decade ended, Sanger was forced to stop everything and retreat for a month to regain her strength.

NOTES

1. MS, *Autobiography,* 213–14; MS, "Why I Went to Jail," *Together,* Feb. 1960, 20 (quote) (*MSM* S72:1017). On the clinic, see *New York Times,* July 22 and Sept. 12, 1916.
2. MS, *Autobiography,* 215–19.
3. MS, "Shall We Break This Law? *BCR,* Feb. 1917, 4 (*MSM* S70:769).
4. MS, "Woman and War."
5. For a Robert Minor cartoon, see *BCR,* June 1917, 5.
6. Margaret Sanger, FBI File 36-1301, obtained under the Freedom of Information Act from U.S. Department of Justice, Federal Bureau of Investigation. Requested as "Margaret Sanger, FBI file," Sept. 1994; received Feb. 1998.

89. From William J. Robinson

Providing contraception was illegal under Section 1142 of the New York State Criminal Code. The only exception to that law was covered in Section 1145, which enabled physicians to prescribe contraceptives for the cure and prevention of disease—commonly understood to mean the provision of condoms to men to prevent venereal disease. Sanger hoped her clinic would fall under Section 1145, and, as she later recalled, "I began to think of doctors that I knew. Several who had previously promised now refused. I wrote, telephoned, asked friends to ask other friends to help me find a woman doctor to help me demonstrate the need of a birth control clinic in New York. None could be found. No one wanted to go to jail. No one cared to test the law. Perhaps it would have to be done without a doctor. But it had to be done; that I knew." No letters survive documenting Sanger's efforts to seek a physician for her clinic, but she solicited advice from William J. Robinson, one of the few American Medical Association members who supported birth control, on the probable reaction of the medical community, which was hostile both to the idea of free clinics and to medical services provided by laywomen. (MS, My Fight, *152–53; Meckel,* Save the Babies, *126–27.)*

New York [*N.Y.*]
September 13, 1916.

Dear Margaret:

I have your note.[1] The American Medical Association[2] cannot and will not in any way interfere with you—it is outside of its domain. The only Society that could have something to say would be the New York County Medical Society, but I am quite certain that you need fear nothing at their hands, because their province is only to interfere with illegal practitioners, with people who treat disease. As you will not deal with treatment, only with hygienic advice, they can have nothing to say to you.[3] Of that, I repeat, I am quite certain. Neither can Federal authorities have anything to say in the matter. The only people you have to be afraid of are the State authorities, or the Vice Society.[4] If you conduct the thing properly I believe you will have no trouble.

And the first and most important thing for you to do is to have every woman who applies for advice sign a slip that she is a married woman and that she wants the information for her personal use, as for either hygienic, hereditary or economic reasons she feels herself unable to have any more children. Of course you cannot demand of the women to bring their marriage certificates, but the fact alone that they sign such a statement would absolve you from any blame and from any possible accusations of fostering "immorality." If you should publicly declare yourself willing to give that information to unmarried women you would have the law down on you at once.[5]

If you do it as I say and if you don't charge the people anything for advice, which I know you won't, they would have great difficulty in doing anything to you, and this Birth Control Clinic might become the germ of thousands of similar clinics.

The whole thing is to conduct it in such a way as to avoid all unnecessary antagonism. You will have enough unavoidable antagonism but with this we have to count.

As to the photo play, let Mr. M. call me up and I will give him an appointment.[6] I will certainly be glad to read it, and if it meets with my approval I shall certainly give it all our moral support. Most sincerely yours,

Wm. J Robinson [*signed*]

P.S. Again I say, go slowly and carefully in the matter of the Birth Clinic. It is a splendid opportunity, and it would be a pity to spoil it.

TLS MSP, DLC (LCM 10:4–5).

1. The letter was not found.
2. The American Medical Association was founded in 1847 to create medical standards, improve education, and organize physicians. MS was, in her words, frustrated by the "stol-

id indifference and ignorance of the medical profession on the entire subject. The man who was an expert in performing gynecological operations seemed quite unaware of the importance of preventing conception." She was particularly angry that "abortion laws were broad enough to allow in such cases a 'duly licensed physician' to perform an abortion in order to save the life of either the woman or the child. It all seemed such a chaotic state to me—that it was perfectly legal to go thru the sufferings of abortion, but illegal to prevent conception." (MS, Letter to the Editor, *Medical World,* Nov. 1917, 402–4.)

3. Though MS claimed she provided only verbal advice to women and did not sell or otherwise furnish contraception, she did not make as sharp a distinction between "advice" and "treatment." One of the arresting police officers claimed to have heard her say, "A doctor or midwife may fit this for you, or if you bring it to me, why I shall adjust it myself." (*New York v. Sanger,* 222 New York 192, 118 N.E. 637 [*MSM* C15:298].)

4. He was referring to the New York Society for the Suppression of Vice, then headed by John S. Sumner.

5. When a woman arrived at the Brownsville Clinic, her history was taken, including questions about her husband's trade and wages. MS later admitted asking the women if they were married but not whether she gave them birth control information if they were not. (MS, "Clinics, Courts and Jails," 3–4.)

6. This was probably an early version of *Birth Control,* a silent film that dramatized MS's early work on the Lower East Side through the fortunes of a struggling mother too poor to purchase contraceptives and a middle-class woman with a small, healthy family. MS wrote the screenplay, possibly with the help of Frederick Blossom. "Mr. M." was B. S. Moss (1878–1951), a theater syndicate founder who produced the film in 1917 through his Message Feature Film Company. (Message Photoplay Press Sheet [MSP, DLC unfilmed scrapbooks]; Brownlow, *Behind the Mask,* 48–50; *New York Times,* Dec. 13, 1951.)

90. Newspaper Interview: "Police Can't Stop Me"

*On October 16, 1916, Sanger opened the doors of the nation's first birth control clinic, a small storefront at 46 Amboy Street in Brooklyn. A donation of fifty dollars from Kate Crane Gartz, a philanthropist Sanger had met in Los Angeles during her 1916 tour, paid the first month's rent. Sanger and Fania Mindell, who had returned from Chicago to help with the clinic, circulated flyers proclaiming, "Mothers, Do not kill, do not take life, but prevent" by obtaining "safe, harmless information" from "trained nurses" in English, Yiddish, and Italian. Several papers ran stories on the operation of the clinic and her goals. The following newspaper interview was given by Sanger six days after the clinic opened. (Brownsville Clinic flyer, Oct. 1916 [*MSM *S62:835]; MS,* Autobiography, *214–16. For other articles on the clinic during its first two weeks of operation, see* New York Call, *Oct. 20, 1916;* New York Tribune, *Oct. 24, 1916; and* Brooklyn Daily Eagle, *Oct. 22 and 24, 1916.)*

[*New York, N.Y.*]
[*October 22, 1916*]

"The poor, century-behind-the-times public officials of this country might just as well forget their moss-grown statutes and accept birth control as an established fact. My new national plan makes it as inevitable as night and day."

Mrs. George[1] Sanger, short and smiling, with a tinge of red in her hair and more than that in her eye, sat in her little two by four hotel bedroom and said that here today. Within the last forty-eight hours she has established semi-secretly in this city the first out-and-out birth control clinic in the United States—the law, a Federal indictment and numerous arrests all over the country to the contrary notwithstanding.

Law Can't Reach Her.

"The police are hunting my clinic today," she went on. "They can't find it. If they should, they can't hurt it. It is an oral clinic, and the law says nothing about not spreading birth control information orally.[2] If they do try to interfere, I am legally prepared to carry a hard and bitter fight to the highest tribunal in the land, with the best legal talent there is.

Four more secret clinics will be running in New York within a week. In less than a year there will be clinics in Washington, Cleveland, Detroit, St. Paul, Minneapolis, Milwaukee, Denver, St. Louis, Los Angeles, San Francisco, San Diego, Portland, Seattle, Spokane and Butte. They are every one organized and ready to open the minute I say the word. The Washington clinic will open within a few days.[3]

Women are Eager.

Do the women like it? Say, you ought to go down in the neighborhood we have canvassed with secret circulars the last forty-eight hours. The women have been coming in by the dozens. You can hear them calling from house to house in the congested district, 'Oh, Mrs. Rosenbaum, you ought to see this; this is something fine!'

Within two years every man and woman in this country will know how many children they can afford to have. And, when they know that, I predict that two generations of birth control will wipe out all the slums, eliminate the birth of mental defectives, minimize the number of humans in our insane asylums and automatically put a stop to child labor and prostitution.

I say it will wipe out child labor because statistics show that 97 per cent of our child labor is recruited from families that are too large to be cared for by the parents.[4]

I say it will wipe out the worst of prostitution because statistics prove that 95 per cent of the girls taken from lives of prostitutes and placed in industrial homes come from poor parents, with nine or more children.[5]

Lack of Attention.

Poverty doesn't force these girls into prostitution, but the lack of attention they get, with so many children at home, and the general sordid tone of their lives naturally leads them to such a life.

My friends and myself are going to bring the people of this country to realize that a man making only $15 a week cannot afford to marry, much less have children.[6] And they'll learn that the average workingman's family should not exceed two children, even under the most favorable physical conditions.

This is the work the law and public officials are trying to stop. The poor, blind officials really are not to blame, they simply live in their law books; They don't live along in everyday life; and, as the law is a century behind the times, so are the officials."

New York Call, Oct. 22, 1916, 8. The article by George Martin ran under the title "'Police Can't Stop Me,' Says Margaret Sanger," with the subheading "Birth Control Clinic Secret and Oral, She Declares—More to Be Opened Soon."

1. This was an incorrect reference to Mrs. William Sanger.

2. While the federal Comstock Act was limited to the use of the postal service, Section 1142 of the New York State Penal Code made it a misdemeanor to sell, lend, exhibit, or advertise contraceptive materials and held criminally responsible anyone who "gives information orally, stating when, where, how, of whom, or by what means" one could get contraceptives. (William McKinney, ed., *The Consolidated Laws of New York, Annotated,* vol. 39 [Northport, N.Y., 1917], 417–18.)

3. MS had rented rooms for a Manhattan clinic on Avenue A, but she focused on the Brownsville site first. She abandoned the Manhattan rooms after her second arrest. Apart from Brownsville, the only clinic that opened in 1916 was a short-lived informal clinic in St. Paul, Minnesota. (*New York Times,* Sept. 12, 1916; *New York Call,* Oct. 20, 1916; *New York Tribune,* Oct. 24, 1916; MS, "Clinics, Courts and Jails," 3.

4. She probably based her assertions on a 1915 article that inferred from investigations by the National Child Labor Committee from 1912–15 that large families produced most of the child workers. (Mary Alden Hopkins, "Large Families and Child Labor," *Harper's Weekly,* Aug. 7, 1915, 135–36.)

5. The source for MS's figures was not found, though studies indicated that prostitutes were more likely to come from overcrowded, poverty-stricken homes. (New York Committee of Fourteen, *The Social Evil in New York City* [New York, 1910], 197–200; A. Maude Royden, *Downward Paths* [London, 1916], 21.)

6. In 1914, the average weekly pay for a production worker was $12.68; by 1920, this had increased to $29.39. (U.S. Bureau of the Census, *Historical Statistics of the United States* [New York, 1976], 172.)

91. *Newspaper Interview: "Mrs. Sanger to Reopen Clinic"*

The police monitored the Brownsville Clinic from its opening and sent a female undercover agent to purchase contraceptive supplies. On October 26, they shut down the clinic, arresting first Sanger and Mindell and then Byrne later that night. During the raid, the police confiscated twenty-nine Mizpah pessaries, an assortment of condoms, tablets, supposito-

ries, and medical equipment, as well as twenty "books on young women," most likely What Every Girl Should Know. *Sanger and Mindell spent the night in the Raymond Street Jail, Byrne at the Liberty Avenue Station in Brooklyn. All were released the next day on five hundred dollars bail. Following several postponements, all three were arraigned at Brooklyn's Adams Street court on November 6 and scheduled for trial in the court of special sessions. What follows is an interview with Sanger conducted a week after her arraignment, part of a longer article on her arrest.* (New York Call, *Oct. 27, 1916; Magistrates Docket, 10th District Brooklyn, Oct. 26, 1916 [MSM C15:171]. For documents relating to the trials and appeals, see* New York v. Margaret Sanger *(Brownsville trial) [*MSM *C15:176–298 and S69:17–172]; for the complete list of confiscated items, see* MSM *C15:173.)*

[*New York, N.Y.*]
[*November 13, 1916*]

"I consider it my duty to reopen my clinic," said Mrs. Sanger yesterday at her office, 104 Fifth avenue, where she is preparing the first number of her magazine, The Birth Control Review, that will appear December 1.[1] "The success of the clinic during the ten days before the raid by the police showed that it is a wonderful boon to the poor women of that congested section of Brooklyn where all the people are poor and have no knowledge of the means to limit the size of their families. Hundreds of women of all nationalities came to the clinic for information.[2]

"The news of the opening of the clinic, which was the first in the United States, reached to all parts of the country, and women have journeyed from distant points on Long Island, from Massachusetts and Maine to get the information we alone would give them. A woman came from Maine and brought her children with her because there was no one to leave them with at home. After all the long journey she found the doors of the clinic locked. The neighbors told her where she could find me so her trip was not in vain.

"I will make the fight in Brownsville alone this time and will keep the clinic open until it is closed again by a police raid[3] or until it is going so successfully that I can leave it in the charge of a nurse. Then I will open another clinic in Manhattan. I have all the material for the Manhattan clinic but will not undertake that until the Brooklyn fight is settled.

"I do not understand why the police and the district attorney keep on hounding me. The most conservative agree that a clinic is the best method for the spreading of information about family limitation to poor women to whom every child means a tremendous burden. The district attorney of New York County promised women interested in birth control agitation that he would not interfere with them as long as their propaganda was conducted 'decently.' They gave out some leaflets at Union Square and now are awaiting trial, having been arrested despite the district attorney's promises."[4]

"Mrs. Sanger to Reopen Clinic," *New York Call,* Nov. 13, 1916, 5.

1. The first issue of the *BCR* did not appear until February 1917. Her first editorial was "Shall We Break This Law?" 4 (*MSM* S70:769).

2. MS estimated that she saw between 480 and 500 women prior to the police shutdown of the clinic. (*People of New York v. Sanger,* 222 New York 102 [1918]; MS, "Clinics, Courts and Jails," 3–4.)

3. MS reopened the clinic on November 13 and was arrested a second time on November 14, on charges of maintaining a public nuisance. Police were then stationed at the clinic to see that it remained closed. Indicted by the Kings County Grand Jury in December or January, she pleaded not guilty and was released on another five hundred dollars bail. This indictment, moved from the court of special sessions to the county court for jury trial, was later dismissed. (*New York Times,* Nov. 16, 1916, and Jan. 26, 1917.)

4. She was referring to the prosecutions of Jessie Ashley, Bolton Hall, and Ida Rauh Eastman, who were convicted and fined despite District Attorney Edward Swann's (1862–1945) promise not to interfere with the distribution of birth control pamphlets. (See MS to Charles and Bessie Drysdale, Aug. 9, 1916, note 26, herein; and *New York Times,* Sept. 21, 1945.)

92. *To James J. McInerney*

James J. McInerney, one of three judges assigned to hear the Brownsville *case, had presided over the trials of Jessie Ashley and William Sanger, at whose trial he said, "Too many persons have the idea that it is wrong to have children. Some women are so selfish that they do not want to be bothered with them. If some persons would go around and urge Christian women to bear children, instead of wasting their time on woman suffrage, this city and society would be better off." At Ashley's October 1916 trial, McInerney dissented from the majority ruling that let her off with a fine, saying that he would have sentenced her to thirty days in jail. Sanger released a press statement (not found) in which she accused McInerney of being "judicially unfit" to try her case and characterized him as "steeped in the grossest bigotry and religious prejudice." (McInerney quoted in Abbott, "Conviction of William Sanger," 270;* New York Times, *Oct. 31, 1916;* New York Tribune, *Nov. 27, 1916; and* New York Call, *Nov. 27, 1916.)*

New York City, [*N.Y.*]
Nov. 26th 1916.

An Open Letter to Judge J. J. McInerney:
Sir:

As a man, as a citizen of a democracy, as an American pledged to the principles and spirit on which this republic was founded, as a judge obligated by oath to fair and impartial judgment, do you in your deepest conscience consider yourself qualified to try my case?

In those Birth Control cases at which you have presided you have shown to all thinking men and women an unfailing prejudice and exposed a mind steeped in the bigotry and intolerance of the Inquisition.

To come before you implies conviction.

Now, in all fairness, do you want a case of this character brought forcibly before you when the defendent feels and believes that you are prejudiced against her?[1]

Margaret H. Sanger.

TRcy MSP, DLC (LCM 11:216). Return address: "104 Fifth ave." Handwritten notes by an unidentified author read, at the top, "An Appeal to a Judge's Sense of Justice," and at the bottom, "NOTE—Two days later req to be relieved from sitting on this case [*illegible*]."

1. MS declared she would not attend her November 27 trial if McInerney presided, and she requested a jury trial. McInerney then released a statement denying that he was prejudiced but agreed to recuse himself. MS's request for a jury trial was denied, and her case was heard by a three-judge tribunal. (*New York Call*, Nov. 28, 1916.)

93. *Prison Diary*

The Brownsville trials began with Ethel Byrne's on January 4, 1917, before the court of special sessions. In a courtroom filled with socially prominent women, the defense attorney Jonah J. Goldstein argued that Section 1142 of the State Penal Code (under which all three defendants were charged) was unconstitutional. But the court refused to hear the defense's main witnesses (including Sanger's physician Morris Kahn, whose birth control study for New York City's Department of Health concluded that two-thirds of patients knew nothing about the prevention of conception) and limited Goldstein's argument to fifteen minutes. Byrne was convicted on January 22 and sentenced to thirty days in the Blackwell's Island workhouse. She promptly went on a hunger strike. Sanger's trial began on January 29 before Justices John J. Freschi, Moses Herrman, and George G. O'Keefe in a courtroom overflowing with socialites, reporters, and about fifty Brownsville Clinic clients, many of them subpoenaed by the prosecution to testify. The clients unwittingly incriminated Sanger by testifying that she had provided birth control information and contraceptives, but their tragic stories of multiple miscarriages, infant deaths, incessant childbirth, poverty, and disease substantiated her socioeconomic arguments. Sanger was found guilty on February 2. In the wake of Ethel Byrne's hunger strike, the justices tried to avoid making Sanger a martyr by offering her a suspended sentence if she would promise to abide by the law. Sanger, who challenged not her guilt but the law itself, replied, "I can't respect the law as it exists today." She chose a thirty-day prison sentence over a fine and was taken into custody on February 5 and processed at Blackwell's Island (currently Roosevelt Island) before being transferred to the less infamous Queens County Penitentiary. Sanger kept the following diary of her imprisonment. She later included a transcribed version in My Fight for Birth Control, *179–81. The changes and insertions in her transcription, save for minor adjustments in grammar and punctuation, are indicated in endnotes. (*Corning Leader, *Feb. 2, 1917; MS,* Autobiography, *229–37 [quote on 237]; Jonah J. Goldstein, "The Birth Control Clinic Cases,"* BCR, *Feb. 1917, 8;* New York Times, *Jan. 26–29 and Feb. 2–5, 1917.)*

Queens Co Penitentiary [*Long Island City, N.Y.*]
[*February 6, 1917*]

First Day,

Only a few minutes after the reporters left me at the workhouse— I was taken into the Hospital or Doctors room to be examined & finger printed I refused both.[1]

Then taken back to Mother Slatterys[2] room & all my possessions returned to me— I was passed over to a woman & man placed into a wagon & driven some length down the Island in front of the Penitentiary. We then got on the boat & came to N.Y.C. 57 St I think not a word as to where I was being taken—Alice in Wonderland I truly was. After various changes on cars—came to Long Island City to Queens County Penitentiary. Warden—a nice youthful chap—met me asked me about lunch & hoped I was not going on a hunger strike which I said no—not unless I was forced on one from bad food. ~~Sen~~ Introduced a very motherly matronly woman to me & sent up some lunch.[3] Put me into cell 210, where Josephine Blank is also near by in same corridor.

Josephine is a very interesting type—a half wild nature[4] irritated by chains & bars. Naturally intuitive—high tempered & quick—outspoken to an unpleasant degree at times—

Has no use for men or men women—but drinks a "bit" once in a while. A kind big hearted woman considered off, but I think very intelligent—[5]

Afternoon drags slowly—& supper bread & molasses & tea seemed tasteless—locked in at 6PM—lights out 9 oclock. Other women in corridor work for warden & only come in at 7 oclock. So days alone with Josephine.[6]

Wednesday [*February 7, 1917*]

Cells open at 7, but bells ring at 6 oclock—breakfast oatmeal & salt & milk & coffee—two slices bread [*untouched?*][7] clean cells—a walk in air—talked with little colored girl "Liza" who knew of Mrs Sanger & called out "Youse eats don't you"?[8]

Dinner of stew & bread— Afternoon four letters—called to Wardens room to be finger printed—told him I objected to being classed as a criminal[9] supper of—tea bread stewed peaches.

Women like Warden McCann & Matron— Atmosphere here very different from Workhouse or Raymond St. Jail—[10] Women are not treated as well as men though—not allowed papers—or to send out for anything[11] which men are allowed—no visitors only two a month. All letters read going & coming which is an outrage.

Thursday— [*February 8, 1917*]

Hominy & coffee (no sugar ever) walk—talked to semi negress woman[12]—dope fiend—indefinite sentence. Horrible liberties a State takes with human lives—for a "crime" of drink—or dope which should be considered diseases—a court has a right to sentence her for 1 day to 3 years. Women[13] look pathetically around the ground to see if the men prisoners have left stubs of cigarettes around—tragic—to see human beings forced to so a low a level—[14] Some lovely looking girls here—dope mainly dinner meat potatoes corn, meal pudding—no knives or forks only one large spoon—

Letters today & telegrams again question of finger prints—Warden very decent about it all—no visitors.

AD MSP, DLC (LCM 1:32–36). Incorrect date of "Feb. 8th" was added later by MS at the top of the first page.

1. MS refused on the grounds that she was a political prisoner, not a criminal. After struggling with two deputies who attempted to force the fingerprinting the night before her release, she reported, "Yes, they seized me and didn't handle me very gently either. . . . They did their best, but I did my best too, and they couldn't make me do it." Warden Joseph A. McCann (1885–1937) tried again to convince her to comply on the following morning. She resisted once more, proudly proclaiming, "I've won. My finger prints are untaken." (*New York Times,* Jan. 18, 1937; *Brooklyn Daily Eagle,* Mar. 6, 1917 [quotes]; *New York Herald, Brooklyn Standard Union,* and *New York Call,* Mar. 7, 1917.)
2. Margaret A. Slattery was the head matron at the Blackwell's Island workhouse, whose office served as an admitting room. (*New York Times,* Jan. 24, 1917.)
3. This was Matron Whittaker, whom MS characterized as a "kindly and humane person." (*New York Times,* Mar. 7, 1917.)
4. In the *My Fight* version, she replaced "nature" with "creature" (180).
5. In *My Fight,* she inserted "Has been arrested over seventy times" (180).
6. In *My Fight,* she edited this sentence to read, "So my days are spent alone with erratic Josephine" (180).
7. In *My Fight,* she omitted this word and added "(salt peter said to make it taste so queer)" (180).
8. In *My Fight,* she added "referring to Mrs. Byrne's hunger strike" to the end of this sentence (180).
9. In *My Fight,* she added "and would not submit" (180).
10. She was referring to the Blackwell's Island workhouse and Brooklyn's Raymond Street Jail, where MS was held on October 26, 1916, after her first arrest, and on February 5, 1917, following her conviction. The jail had a reputation for being dirty and unsafe. (MS, *Autobiography,* 221, 329; *New York Times,* Feb. 6, 1917.)
11. In *My Fight,* she added "like food, papers or cigarettes" (180–81).
12. In *My Fight,* she replaced "semi negress" with "mulatto" (181).
13. In *My Fight,* she added "out in yard" (181).
14. In *My Fight,* she added "digging in the frozen ground with fingers for stubs" (181).

94. To Ethel Higgins Byrne[1]

[Queens County Penitentiary, Long Island City, N.Y.]
[February 14, 1917]

Dearest Eth:

Your welcome letter[2] came today— Comm Kelley made a call today & the girls here made known their various wishes while the iron was hot.

Little things like crackers & cakes & candies they have not been able to receive— I hope they get them. I am glad oh so glad to hear you are well enough to go out to New Rochelle[3]—rest up in the air a while. Someone said you looked "darling" with your hair bobbed!! No doubt you do too. It's a good idea glad you did it. Yes I was ushered into the work house just long enough for them to take a look at your sister. They have some respect for you over there for your fight— Every prisoner seems to have been awakened to the interest of b.c. thr'u your hunger strike—naturally so for it was their life & interest & world that you had entered.

I too count the days "fore & aft" am thankful in many ways to be hear instead of the workhouse mainly because I can sleep nights. The beds do allow a good sleep & I know that would not be allowed at the workhouse— On the other hand I feel the latter place needs a house cleaning which several of us together can do if we get at it once.

Am glad too that you are out & made the finest fight ever made by any woman in U.S.A.

Did you write to Mary?[4] I hope Nan does not find it too cold down there. It will give her no time or rest to think & meditate.[5]

I have been looking for such a treat myself for the past year—just to be alone—but somehow it never comes to me. Lillian[6] near drove me out of my mind with her kindness & attention until I swore by all the Saints I should never have another visitor beyond <u>one</u> night or 24 hours stay. As dear & lovely as she is—I am thankful she has gone. Nan will not like it there & she is foolish to remain cold & miserable. Waldo[7] could easily look after the place in the day time & it could be closed at night. However—let it go if she likes it.

I want you to have twenty-five dollars for yourself to get what you want as tonic—eggs etc. I thot you might go to Atlantic City—but New Rochelle will be just as good—anywhere to get the air—

J. J.[8] sent me a basket of fruit yesterday—so I shall revel in luxury for a week at least. Yes the whole law business makes me convinced how foolish one is to put any hopes in it— But we have given it a trial—So.

What would you think of speaking now & then?

You can do it you know if you want to. R. A. P.[9] could help to word & phrase your thoughts, the rest would be your own personality. Think it over. It is true that the fashionable seem far removed from the cause & its necessity—but we can not doubt that they & they alone dominate when they get an interest in a thing. So little can be done without them—yet a while— But the time will come.

Your other case comes up the 23rd.[10] I am wondering what will happen— My other will come up too but a jury trial will at least be of interest.

Bill[11] seems to be greatly impressed by your wit & humor so does Fania—! They are only getting acquainted with you.

All for the present.

Let me hear from you & don't rush yourself—for you are far from strong & need time to mend. With love ever & always

Margaret

ALS MSP, DLC (LCM 7:1263–66).

1. Following the example of the British suffragettes, Byrne went on a five-day hunger strike while she was in prison and finally had to be force-fed. The publicity tactic succeeded as newspapers ran daily reports on Byrne's deteriorating condition, until MS negotiated Byrne's early release with New York's Governor Charles Whitman.

2. Recovering at home, Byrne wrote about her improving health, remarking on the support she had received from MS's new wealthy friends. (Byrne to MS, Feb. ?, 1917 [*MSM* S1:665].)

3. New Rochelle was a popular recreation area and waterfront resort on Long Island Sound, located in Westchester County, New York.

4. Mary Higgins still worked as a live-in domestic worker for the Abbotts.

5. Anna Higgins had moved into an apartment below Byrne's.

6. Lillian Griffs Fassett (1885–1974), a Washington State socialite and secretary of the Spokane Birth Control League, came to New York City to support MS. (SSDI; *Brooklyn Daily Eagle,* Jan. 4, 1917.)

7. She was probably referring to James Waldo Fawcett, who had grown close to the Sangers and was serving as her secretary/assistant.

8. J. J. was Jonah J. Goldstein (1886–1967), a Canadian-born lawyer who offered his pro bono services to MS in the Brownsville trial and appeals. Goldstein probably became her lover at about this time. Madeline Gray, one of MS's biographers, asserted that he paid the rent on her West Fourteenth Street apartment. (*New York Times,* July 23, 1967; Gray, *Margaret Sanger,* 204; MS, *Autobiography,* 224–25.)

9. R. A. P. was the writer and editor Robert Parker, who was still living with Byrne.

10. This was a reference to a second charge against Byrne for aiding Fania Mindell in selling *What Every Girl Should Know.*

11. This was probably William Sanger.

95. To Ethel Higgins Byrne

[*Queens County Penitentiary, Long Island City, N.Y.*]
Feb 21—[*1917*]

Dearest Ethel:

Someone said Rob was ill[1]—I hope it is not serious & I also hope you will get Lizzie or someone to help you & not over do in nursing him—

Enclosed find Newtons letter (Lillians husband).[2] It may interest you the personal feeling he has for us—destroy it after reading. I am wondering which is the harder to stand the slow starvation for 30 days or to make a neat clean job of it. For the past two days I have been starved. It's a new sensation for me because I don't usually care a rap about food.

However it wont hurt me a bit & the regular life & early to bed makes a restful life at least.

B. S. wrote me he had been down to see the boys[3] & that they are well as usual. He seems not to have much liking for J. J.[4] again as usual but I don't feel there is any kick coming certainly I never expected to be acquitted nor did you I guess. Fania—perhaps[5]—but when once we realize that the whole force of the Church was out against us—why we get some idea of the forces behind. Editorials of all C. Papers called upon the Judges to give those "lovely intellectual women" a good dose of jail.[6] Its absurd to call J. J. names now & to expect that he should have saved us— To me he did everything in his power to clear the issue & to keep it clean— He at least kept the commercial taint out of it—& that is what the enemy tried hardest to put in—

But then B. S. was always a chronic kicker so whats the use—

J. J. wrote me that your case of the 23rd may be dismissed—[7] I hope so— I wish mine would be too except that a jury trial will be of interest.

Write me of your visit to [*Mae*] & of Robs illness—& of how you feel.

Women from the workhouse keep coming here & ask for you. love always.

Margaret

ALS MSP, MN-SCC (*MSM* S1:654–59). The author of the marginal notes was not identified; notes at the top of the first page read, "In prison—" and "1916↑7?↓"

1. Robert Parker was a polio victim, but he was probably suffering from influenza.

2. Newton C. Fassett (1882–1931) was a German-born millionaire businessman from Spokane, Washington; his letter was not found. (*New York Times,* Nov. 20, 1931.)

3. The letter from William Sanger was not found. At the time, he was working as a draftsman in New York City; Grant and Stuart were still at the Winnwood School.

4. J. J. was Jonah Goldstein.

5. Unlike MS and Byrne, Fania Mindell was charged only with distributing obscene literature. Convicted on January 29, she was fined fifty dollars on February 2, 1917. Her conviction was reversed on appeal in November. (*People of State of New York v. Fannie Mindell, Brief for Respondents, before Court of Appeals, State of New York, 1917,* 3–5 [*MSM* C15:631].)

6. The "C. papers" may have been some dailies that MS believed had a Catholic slant.

7. Byrne's other charge was dismissed in November 1917. ("Status of Birth Control Cases," *BCR*, Dec. 1917, 5.)

96. To Herbert Sturges[1]

Queens Co. Penitentiary Long Island City [*N.Y.*]
[*February 23, 1917*]

Dear Herbert:

You surely received my thoughts for only a few days ago I was thinking of you in Paris & our walks & talks & it all brought you very close & near to me. I can never think of you without thinking of Peggy too someway. I don't know why she seems to be associated with you in memory I feel that there are no pains left on earth for me again—jails bread & water, hunger nothing can give me pain again compared to the torture of the realization of my loss.

I in fact have never really faced it—I keep putting it away & away, or I could not go on.

I am sending your article over to the office[2]—it is a very interesting view-point to take and not a new one—Dr Sprague in Heredity[3] this month also argues in favor of large families among the rich— But I am strong on the "Single Eye"[4] I am not especially concerned with the rich—they are not our problem. Their children are not in the ranks of the Prostitutes, paupers, jails or insane asylums and neither would the poor mans children fill them so abundantly if there were less of them.

I'm strong on keeping the issue clear—cutting the birth rate among the poor—& leaving it to individual women to have as many as they desire & no more. My thanks to you dear friend for your kind letter[5] love to your wifey[6] from Bill the boys & myself. Ever cordially

Margaret Sanger

ALS FRP, MN-SSC (*MSM* S1:660–64).

1. Herbert Arthur Sturges (1882–1958) was a mathematician and statistician who had met the Sangers in Paris in 1913, had loaned William Sanger small sums of money, and had helped MS obtain material on European contraceptives. (*Arizona Daily Star,* Apr. 12, 1958; William Sanger to MS, Feb. 3, Feb. 5, and Mar. 3, 1914 [*MSM* S1:132, 138, and 187].)

2. The article was not found.

3. Robert J. Sprague (1868–1929) was an economics professor who wrote "Constructive Aspect of Birth Control," which argued for birth control for the lower classes and "birth release" for the upper classes to "preserve the vitality of America." (*Journal of Heredity* 8 [Feb. 1917]: 58–62.)

4. See Matthew 6:22: "The light of the body is the eye: if therefore thine eye be single, thy whole body shall be full of light."

5. The letter was not found.
6. His wife was Lila Sturges (1891–1972). (SSDI)

97. *From Eugene V. Debs*[1]

Terre Haute, Ind.
February 25th., 1917.

My dear Comrade Sanger:-

I have been down with the grip or this acknowledgment of your very appreciative letter would have been sooner made.[2] You are a brave and noble comrade and when I think of you caged like a beast all my blood boils with bitter indignation. It seems impossible that such a great soul as you should be locked up in a community called civilized as if you were an all-devouring beast.

But I know that you are shedding no tears on your own account. You are too great to think of yourself for even a moment for you are fighting for a principle, a cause and you can take what comes without flinching and without regret. Think of the beasts at large who are responsible for your being in a loathsome steel cage and you will have sufficient reason to congratulate yourself upon being where you are. But every hour you are in jail strikes a month or more from the lease of the brutal system of which you are the victim. They may jail you but they can't arrest the march of the liberating forces you have let loose upon the world.

I almost weep as I think of the cruel fate of those poor "dope fiends" of whom you write.[3] I wish I could wrap them all up in my arms and love them back to life again. But the same beastly system which ruined them will pursue them implacably to the morgue and the pottersfield. Your heart bleeds for them and so does mine but alas, how less than little we are able to do for them. All we can do as we look upon these suffering creatures is to swear that by all the gods we will fight all the harder to destroy the damnable system and institutions that are responsible for inflicting such suffering upon human beings.

Most earnestly do I wish success for the Birth Control Review and I shall gladly do all I can to help it along.[4] You have already done a work greater far than you know and your capitalist persecutors and would-be tormentors and even murderers are now fitting you in their own peculiar way for the infinitely greater work which lies ahead and which you are destined to do in the great cause of emancipation.

My love goes to you in your prison cell, dear comrade, and to your husband and children and I am always, Loyally your comrade,

Eugene V. Debs [*signed*]

TLS MSP, DLC (LCM 8:148–49). Letterhead of the Office of Theodore Debs.

1. Debs, then editing the *National Rip-Saw,* turned down the Socialist Party's 1916 presidential nomination to run (unsuccessfully) for Congress on an antiwar platform. In 1917, he embarked on an antipreparedness speaking tour. (Bernard Brommel, *Eugene Debs: Spokesman for Labor and Socialism* [Chicago, 1978], 147–48.)

2. Debs had written a February 14, 1917, letter to MS praising the *BCR,* published in the April–May 1917 issue. Her response was not found.

3. See her "Prison Diary," February 8, 1917, entry, herein, for another reference to "dope fiends" in prison.

4. Debs's "Freedom Is the Goal" was published in the *BCR,* May 1918, 7.

98. To William Sanger

Margaret Sanger was released from prison on March 7, 1917.

[*New York, N.Y.*]
March 21, 1917.

Will you kindly inform me at your earliest convenience what you propose to do, or what you will do in co-operation with me, to secure a legal separation for us both?[1]

I have always hoped that one with your pretended ideas of woman's freedom, and independence of State interference where two adult individuals are concerned, would respect my personal and private liberty without the aid of a policeman's club.

But from your insulting attack upon my character last Friday night[2] I realize at last that I must protect myself as well as my friends and <u>even business acquaintances</u> from your filthy, vile mouth and slanderous onslaught by the only power left for a woman in my position to use:—the State.

I hereby request you to state in what way you will co-operate with me to obtain a complete divorce with as little unnecessary gossip and discussion as possible that both your work and mine may be free from all injury.

I want to return your name to you in the same condition as I obtained or accepted it, and I call your attention to the fact that in fourteen years of public life that name was not assaulted until your assailed it last Friday night.

I will appreciate it if you will name your part in the support of the children. And also to name any articles or property of yours in my possession. I today returned all your pictures and will be glad to send you any more of yours that I find.

I wish to wipe from my memory all thought of connection with you and shall appreciate any effort on your part to further that end.[3] Very truly yours,

---

TLcy MSP, MN-SSC (*MSM* S1:675). Return address: "104 Fifth Avenue."

1. The Sangers had separated at the end of 1913, and MS had requested a legal separation or divorce as early as December 1914.

2. The confrontational meeting on March 16 probably occurred following the New York Birth Control League's testimonial dinner for Margaret Sanger and Ethel Byrne. (Invitation, Mar. 16, 1917 [*MSM* C12:1082].)

3. Though his letters to his wife from this period were not found, William Sanger sent MS flowers and a note of apology, to which she replied, "My work is piling up and it is impossible to do justice to it or to give the thought and attention it requires while I am in this unsettled state of mind. Won't you please help me? Won't you put yourself aside? Won't you . . . let me have the freedom and a future happiness which I think is my right? . . . If the affection which you feel for me is deeper in your being than your love for yourself and the pity that you have for your own loneliness, you will either grant me a separation at once or go away where we will not be tormented by the presence of each other. There is nothing I have to give you in love, there is nothing to be repaired, there is no way that we can go on together." William Sanger continued to hold out hope for a reconciliation and left for Spain in June 1917 without a separation agreement. (MS to William Sanger, Mar. 24, 1917 [*MSM* S1:676].)

99. *To Gertrude Minturn Pinchot*[1]

Many of the members of the Committee of 100, a group of prominent women who pledged to support the Brownsville Clinic defendants, came from the NBCL, which did not attempt a major campaign until 1917, when it lobbied to repeal New York State's Comstock law. NBCL leaders opposed Sanger's law-defying tactics as well as her association with radicals and militant propagandists, and they were reluctant to endorse her formally or lend financial support to the BCR. *For her part, Sanger refused to join the NBCL and challenged it by creating the New York Birth Control League (NYBCL) in 1916, which served as her defense fund. (Dennett to Friend, Dec. 16, 1918 [*MWDPM *13:746–47];* New York World, *Feb. 12, 1917; Chen,* Sex Side of Life, *181–84, 205–8.)*

[*New York, N.Y.*]
April 16th 1917.

My dear Mrs. Pinchot:

I have just read your note received this morning.[2] I will pass the check for twenty five dollars you enclosed to the secretary of the Mothers' League of Brownsville,[3] and tell Mrs. Stone of the transaction. The League will be very glad to have this money, and it will help to defray some of the expenses they have had.

I am enclosing a clipping from yesterday's New York Call which has just been shown me. You will note that it states that I have just opened new offices at 21 East 46th street. This, as we all know, is quite untrue, and distresses me considerably because it only tends to confuse the people who are interested in what I personally am trying to do.[4]

My only headquarters for the public are at 104 Fifth avenue, where, thanks to the courtesy of Dr. Blossom,[5] I have had desk room for the past eight months. All my correspondence has been handled from that address.

I feel especially distressed because of the personal obligation that I feel toward Dr. Blossom for what he has done and sacrificed that I may have this headquarters in New York City.[6] You and many of the women who have come into the movement more recently may not realize the tremendous odds and difficulties which surrounded me during the early period of this work, and although the National League had finances and influential supporters never was there any assistance from to me personally nor to the work which I was carrying on until you formed the Committee of One Hundred.[7] Many people have told me that they have sent me letters in care of the League, and sent them monies for my work: never have I heard from these nor had the acknowledgment from the League that such was the case.

You can readily understand that I have been far more interested in the movement as a whole than in any factional parts, and consequently have never challenged this action or made any comments about it. But I do feel now that as Dr. Blossom has spent all that he has on the maintenance of this place for my convenience, and has almost no support, that it is not fair to him that contributions for the movement should go elsewhere if intended for me and the work I am trying to do.

I feel certain that you understand this, and the regret is that there is not harmony between all groups in New York so that there could be one office, one staff, one bill to be presented to the Legislature, one aim and one ideal to be fought for.

I wanted to speak about this when talking with you on over the 'phone but now that this clipping has been shown me I feel that it is imperative to bring it to your attention that you may co-operate with me in arranging a working basis which will not be so confusing to the public.

Always my good wishes and sincere regard, Cordially,

MS [*initialed*]

TRcyI MSP, DLC (LCM 9:1135). Return address: "104 Fifth Avenue."

1. Gertrude Minturn Pinchot (1872–1939) was a suffragist, a philanthropist, an NBCL member, and the wife of the prominent lawyer Amos Pinchot. She had supported MS during the *Woman Rebel* trial, attended William Sanger's *Family Limitation* trial, and arranged for her sister, Grace Cram, to support Grant's and Peggy's board at the Stelton School during William Sanger's imprisonment. Pinchot attended the Brownsville trials and accompanied MS to Albany to plead for Byrne's pardon. (William Sanger to MS, Sept. 14 and 21, 1915 [*MSM* S1:456 and 462]; *New York Times*, Jan. 18, 1916, and May 17, 1939; *New York Call*, Jan. 5, Jan. 31, and Feb. 2, 1917; *New York Tribune*, Jan. 18, 1916, and Jan. 5, 1917.)

2. The letter was not found.

3. The Mothers' League, or Mothers' Club, was formed at the Brownsville site by MS, Helen Todd, and Fania Mindell to protest the clinic's closing. (*New York Herald,* Mar. 4, 1917.)

4. It was the NBCL that had opened offices at that address, in space provided by Amos Pinchot, with Gertrude Pinchot presiding. (*New York Call,* Apr. 15, 1917; *MWDPM* 13:713.)

5. Frederick Augustus Blossom (1878–1974), an author, librarian, and socialist activist, met MS in Cleveland during her 1916 tour. He moved to New York City in September to help establish the NYBCL, assist MS with her legal battles, and lobby for state birth control laws. Blossom was the president of the NYBCL and the managing editor of the *BCR.* (Reed, *Birth Control Movement and American Society,* 109; Blossom to Sirs, Nov. 16, 1931 [FBP].)

6. Blossom probably donated his own money to cover the fledgling movement's expenses. Between November 1916 and March 1917, he worked diligently to publicize MS's trial, organized lecture series, and gave speeches on birth control. (Blossom to Rose Pastor Stokes, Nov. 11, 1916 [RPSP]; Blossom to Sirs, Nov. 16, 1931 [FBP]; *New York Call,* Dec. 13, 1916.)

7. Pinchot organized the Committee of 100 at her home on November 28, 1916. MS described the committee as "one hundred women who . . . will take turns operating the clinic, and as soon as one is arrested another will take up her work," but in actuality committee members served more to provide high-profile support at the trials. (Minutes of the Committee of 100, Jan. 21, 1917 [*MSM* C12:1084]; *New York Tribune,* Nov. 27, 1916 [quote].)

100. To Gertrude Minturn Pinchot

[*New York, N.Y.*]
May 6th 1917.

My dear Mrs. Pinchot:

I returned from Albany last evening. The hearing was a failure, we were discriminated against shamefully.[1] I do so wish that Mrs. Rublee and yourself could have been with me; in that case we might at least have received more polite consideration.[2]

Another discouraging matter awaited my return this morning. Commissioner George Bell has refused to permit the motion picture to be shown in public, charging that it is obscene, indecent and immoral.[3] The theatre was to have opened to-night. We want to have the film shown privately this evening to a representative group of friends and would have liked to have had you present. We will try to-morrow to get out an injunction against the Commissioner, restraining him from further interference. Anything you feel you can do to aid our efforts will be of great value.

To further complicate matters, my attorney tells me that our appeal (on my conviction) must be ready within thirty days.[4] This means several weeks of solid writing and editing of all the material we have gathered during the last two months for this purpose. I shall be obliged to shut myself up for at least ten days for this work, and simply refuse to consider anything else.

But as soon as I possibly can I will search out the letters, etc., on which was based my thought that persons had confused the National League work with my own and supported the League while meaning only to support what I was trying to do.[5] This will take several days, too, for the letters received at that period are not very well organized. In the meantime I trust we will not let this matter too greatly interfere with matters which are more properly due for first attention. I think it should be especially borne in mind that any indiscriminate discussion of the subject will injure our cause, and give rise to a useless and painful controversy.

I want to thank you for the check you sent, $5 of which I am turning over to the Brownsville mothers work as you direct. Ever, Yours cordially,

---

TLcy MSP, DLC (LCM 9:1139).

1. After Albany's commissioner of public safety refused to permit her to lecture there on April 10, 1917, MS sought his removal. Mayor J. W. Stevens refused to replace him. (*New York Times,* May 5, 1917.)

2. Like Pinchot, Juliet Barrett Rublee, a member of the NBCL and the Committee of 100, had influential social connections.

3. MS rewrote her five-reel silent feature, *Birth Control,* to include a fictionalized version of her Brownsville Clinic arrest and conviction. Produced in 1917, with MS starring as herself, it ended with a shot of her in prison over the subtitle "No Matter what happens the work must go on." It was scheduled to premiere on March 7, but George Bell, the New York City commissioner of licenses, declared the film indecent and closed the theater. The producer, Message Photo-Play Company, won an injunction against Bell in the New York State Supreme Court, but the decision was overturned on appeal. No copies of the film were found. (Brownlow, *Behind the Mask,* 6; *New York Times,* Mar. 28, May 7, May 10, and June 7, 1917; "A Decision for Liberty," *BCR,* June 1917, 2; *Message Photo-Play v. Bell,* 179 App. Div. 13; 166 New York Supp. [*MSM* C15:481 and 486].)

4. After her Brownsville conviction was affirmed by the state appellate division, MS filed an appeal with the New York State court of appeals on August 18, 1917. (*New York v. Sanger,* 222 New York 192, 118 N.E. 637 [Court of Appeals 1917]; for court records, see SCR [*MSM* C15:298].)

5. Pinchot believed MS had accused the NBCL of misappropriating funds. There was no evidence that MS ever provided documentation for her charges. (Pinchot to MS, Apr. 17 [LCM 9:1140].)

101. From Havelock Ellis[1]

[*London, England*]
19 May/17.

Dear Margaret,

I am delighted to receive your long letter of 30 April, enclosing also portrait & pamphlet of Sanger trial.— I am still grieved to have lost that long letter which you wrote in the enjoyment of leisure & which went astray.[2] Now you seem to be in a whirl of affairs, but I trust keeping well & not worried. And I hope you are getting some good warm weather at last. How about Cape Cod?[3]

It must be very trying to lecture when it makes you feel so ill beforehand. But I am sure you must be a good lecturer, for all good speakers have that feeling beforehand.

I am sure you are perfectly right in maintaining that instruction in birth control should be given by qualified people—doctors, nurses, & midwives. Even if I didn't agree it ought to be recognized that your opinion, ~~carries~~ being based on knowledge & experience, carries great weight. But I feel sure you are right. So don't worry if silly people do call you "reactionary." They don't know you! "Do not hurry: have faith!" as Ed. Carpenter says[4] (& as Edith[5] was always saying to herself). I hear, by the way, that Carpenter has been ill, much upset by the death of an old friend; he has aged considerably since you left & will not, I fear, live long.[6]

American contingents & war ships are being greeted in these parts of the world with much enthusiasm—as you well know. The end of the War seems to begin to be in sight. Both American participation & the Russian Revolution have also given a powerful stimulus to discussion of larger ideas of harmonious re-construction after the war.[7] It is a good sign that members of the Government are now taking a chief public part in such discussions.— I shall soon begin to look forward to your visit to Europe! I often think how delightful it will be to see you in this room again—where nearly everything remains pretty much as you left it (at the moment a Dutch jar happens to be on the table with wallflowers in it)—even still including those two wan [*vistas*] you once mysteriously left behind! Yours always [*lovingly*]

Havelock Ellis.

I hope the article on Marriage has safely reached you.[8]—I have heard nothing further of the "B.C. Review", since the first number.

ALS MSP, DLC (LCM 4:358–60).

1. In the two years following MS's 1915 return to the United States, she and Ellis corresponded frequently, though few of her letters were found. (For Ellis to MS, see LCM: 4 and 5.)

2. The letters were not found; the pamphlet was James Waldo Fawcett's *Jailed for Birth Control.*

3. In March 1917, MS bought the journalist John Reed's cottage in Truro, Massachusetts, which she had seen when he purchased it in 1913, describing it as "a little house on a hill, one of the most ancient in the village. . . . The kitchen was bright and warm, and seemed as though many cookies and pies had been baked in it." Reed, leaving for Russia, sold the house and its furnishings to MS for $2,045 (to be paid by 1921 in five installments). The Truro house provided MS and her sons "with three carefree months every summer in what still seems to me one of the most beautiful spots in the world." (MS, *Autobiography,* 264–65; Memorandum of Agreement between MS and Reed, Mar. 27, 1917 [*MSM:* C17:535].)

4. The quote is from "Have Faith," included in Carpenter's *Towards Democracy* (1883).

5. Edith Mary Oldham Lees Ellis (1861–1916), a psychologist, lecturer, and writer, was on a U.S. lecture tour when MS arrived in England in 1914 and began her affair with Havelock Ellis. He wrote his wife about the relationship, and though Edith was a lesbian, a fact her husband knew and accepted, she felt jealous and abandoned. On her return, Edith had a mental and physical breakdown and was institutionalized in March 1916. After a suicide attempt and a move to another institution, she checked herself out, but her health deteriorated. Edith Ellis came down with pneumonia and died on September 14, 1916. (Grosskurth, *Havelock Ellis,* 214–63; Ellis, *My Life,* 432–579.)

6. Carpenter's former lover, the socialist George Hukin, had died on March 22, 1917. (Chuschichi Tsuzuki, *Edward Carpenter, 1844–1929* [Cambridge, 1980], 70–72, 184–85.)

7. The United States declared war on Germany on April 6, 1917. Though the American forces did not land in France until June 24, the arrival of six U.S. destroyers off the coast of Ireland in early May marked the beginning of an American presence in Europe. New hopes for peace and a realigned, reconstructed Europe were aided by the start of tentative peace talks and the overthrow of the Russian Romanov dynasty in February 1917.

8. He was referring to "The Objects of Marriage," which had actually been published in the *BCR* the previous month (Apr. 1917, 3–4, 8). Ellis wrote little else in the months of Edith's illness and death, save for *Essays in War-Time* (London, 1917).

102. To Juliet Barrett Rublee[1]

Truro, Mass
July Thirteenth [*1917*]

Dear Julieet:

Your letter with check for Havelock Ellis enclosed was forwarded to me & reached me yesterday.[2]

I sat right down & sent the check to Havelock for I know he will be glad to have it. He received the other one & said he felt guilty to take so much for so short an article, but as needs were pressing just now he would take it & hope to make up to us in some other way later.[3]

Im so glad that has gone & off the boards. Now for my book "The Case for B.C." It is all ready at the printers & I am short three hundred dollars before it can be released.[4]

Orders are coming in for them & will be able to pay for themselves.

I wrote Mrs Straight[5] & shall send her a copy as soon as I receive them & your two copies will be sent also. Have you any suggestions as to how to go about it to get even a loan so these books can be out. I wanted the N.B.C League to advance the amt but Mrs Pinchot said it was too late to get the Ex. Com together. I hoped Mr Maisel would advance the amount but he has not been selling any girl books & says I am far ahead now of my royalties.[6]

I think there will be thousands of them sold when once they get out, but oh me or mi—when they do. Have you ever seen any thing have such barriers in its way as birth control? Here that moving picture should be moving before a public & make the cause almost independent of small financial difficulties. Instead of which I may soon have to take up my bag & return to private practice again ~~soon~~. You will be amused to hear of Dr B. He has been so petty that I am ashamed of the masculine. However it is all over—he shares the office until Oct or until I make other arrangements. But he is out as far as representing me is concerned.[7] I do wish a big convention could be called in Chicago in October or November. I also wish the Chicago League would take charge of it. You might talk it over with Prof Field when you go out again.[8]

I have wondered how your mother is getting on & I trust very nicely.[9]

Your place, with its lovely quiet & charm has made me lonely for the mountains & trees.[10] We have the Ocean here & the dunes & the river but no forests or Mountains. I am sorry I was not in the city to see you. The Blossom affair greatly upset & depressed me for days & days, so I just ran away here. I just cant deal with "fish-wife minds" & must let them alone. I think you have been simply splendid about the Ellis money & the article really should be yours or what ever use you wish to make of it.

Let me hear from you do, & any suggestion you might give concerning the Book will be gladly received. Ever my best wishes & my love

Margaret Sanger

ALS JRP, MN-SSC (*MSM* C1:181–92). Return address: "Box 78."

1. Juliet Barrett Rublee (1875–1966) may have met MS in 1914 at Mabel Dodge's salon. After the Brownsville trial, she became one of MS's closest friends. An heir to the Barrett Company fortune (a Chicago roofing supply and tar manufacturer) and a dancer when she married the attorney George Rublee in 1899, she served on the first NBCL executive committee in 1915 and helped form the Committee of 100 in 1916. She also organized financial support for the *BCR*, funded many of MS's other endeavors, and drew influential social and political figures into the birth control movement. MS later

wrote of Rublee, "More than to any other single individual credit is due to her for making the idea of birth control acceptable in professional and conservative circles." (Paul Marashio, "A Feminist Voice in New Hampshire," 1982 manuscript [NhD]; Marashio, "Interview with Horace Rublee"; MS, *My Fight,* 231 [quote].)

2. The letter was not found.

3. Ellis faced a huge burden of debt, much of it incurred by Edith Ellis's excessive spending and the costs of supporting his younger sisters. The checks were for Ellis's two *BCR* articles: "Birth Control in Relation to Morality" in February 1917 and "The Objects of Marriage" in April 1917. The letters were not found. (Grosskurth, *Havelock Ellis,* 273–74.)

4. *The Case for Birth Control: A Supplementary Brief and Statement of Facts* (1917) was a 251-page compilation of statistics, historical data, and writings by MS, Ellis, and several health experts, as well as material from the Children's Bureau and other government sources. Designed to buttress her legal appeal by presenting "the social and racial value of knowledge to prevent conception," the book offered medical and eugenic rationales for birth control and muted overt feminist and socialist concerns. MS recycled the data collected in the book frequently in her later writings. She borrowed the three hundred dollars to pay the printer from two of her sisters, probably Mary and Anna. (MS to Rublee, Aug. 9, 1917 [*MSM* C1:200].)

5. Dorothy Payne Whitney Straight (1887–1968), a philanthropist, publisher, and educator, was married to Willard Straight, a diplomat and financier. She helped launch and publish Herbert Croly's *New Republic* (1914–32) and campaigned for woman suffrage and a variety of other reforms. She also contributed a hundred dollars to help MS publish *The Case for Birth Control.* (*ANB;* MS to Straight, June 13, 1917 [LCM 10:672].)

6. Max N. Maisel published *What Every Girl Should Know* and *What Every Mother Should Know* from 1916 to 1920.

7. After a major argument sometime in April 1917, Blossom resigned as managing editor of the *BCR* (though he remained the NYBCL's treasurer). MS claimed the dispute was over Blossom's support for U.S. entry into the war, while Blossom charged that it stemmed from his accusation that MS was profiting from the movement. The breach deepened as they disagreed over the disposition of *BCR* funds and their shared office and furnishings. On July 2, MS wrote Blossom requesting a full financial accounting. (MS, *Autobiography,* 253; Blossom to Sirs, Nov. 16, 1931 [FBP]; MS to Blossom, July 2, 1917 [LCM 7:1002].)

8. The Illinois Birth Control League (IBCL), organized in Chicago in 1917, was fairly inactive until 1923. James Alfred Field (1880–1927), an economics professor at the University of Chicago and the author of several books on economics, population, and eugenics, was president. (IBCL, *Annual Report* [Chicago, 1937–38]; *New York Times,* July 17, 1927.)

9. Alice Delia Brush Barrett (1843–1924) was the daughter of Charles Francis Brush, a Cleveland inventor and industrialist, and the wife of Samuel Eddy Barrett (1834–1912). (CBP Finding Aid; John W. Leonard, *The Book of Chicagoans* [Chicago, 1905], 44.)

10. MS was referring to Crossways, Rublee's Cornish, New Hampshire, home. The Rublees were a part of the Cornish Colony, a group of artists, writers, and politicians that included George De Forest Brush, Augustus Saint-Gaudens, Maxfield Parish, the American novelist Winston Churchill, and Judge Learned Hand. (Virginia R. Colby and

James B. Atkinson, *Footprints of the Past: Images of Cornish, New Hampshire, and the Cornish Colony* [Concord, N.H., 1996].)

103. To Carl Zigrosser[1]

Truro, Mass.
Aug [*7?, 1917*]

Dear Comrade:

Thank you for your letter of Aug 3rd.[2] There is not much for me to write on Sex. I have the sad news of the death of my beloved friend & comrade Lorenzo Portet in Paris. I'll write a brief [*memoir*] of him & send it to you as soon as I collect my mind over the shock—[3]

To me he was the biggest mind in Europe. Ferrer knew his man when he choose Portet successor & the King rejoiced over his going I know.[4] My regards to [*Miss*] King.[5] Ever fraternally

Margaret Sanger

ALS CZP, PU (*MSM* C1:197–99).

1. Carl Zigrosser (1891–1975), an art historian and curator, was an instructor at the Ferrer School and the editor of the Ferrer Association's *Modern School* from 1917 to 1919. Under Zigrosser, the journal attracted contributions from such notable artists and writers as Man Ray, Rockwell Kent, and Mike Gold. (Avrich, *Modern School Movement,* 106, 161–62, 331.)

2. Zigrosser's letter asked MS for additional articles on her Spanish travels or other aspects of libertarian education or nursing, acknowledging, "I suppose you have more or less had your say on sex education." (*MSM* C1:196.)

3. Lorenzo Portet died of tuberculosis in a Paris nursing home on May 10, 1917. There is no evidence that MS wrote a Portet memorial. (Charles Malato to MS, July 19, 1917 [*MSM* S1:689].)

4. As successor to Francisco Ferrer, Portet was also considered an enemy of the state. (See MS Diary Entry, Dec. 13, 1914, note 6, herein.)

5. Florence King (1880–1945), a social worker and executive secretary for the Equal Suffrage Society, married Carl Zigrosser in 1915. (U.S. Bureau of the Census, *Fourteenth Census of the United States, 1920;* Carl Zigrosser, *My Own Shall Come to Me: A Personal Memoir and Picture Chronicle* [Philadelphia, 1971], 94, 97.)

104. To Juliet Barrett Rublee

[*New York, N.Y.*]
August twenty-third. [*1917*]

Dear Mrs Rublee;

Thank you so so much for the book "Spirit Intercourse"[1] which I just received today on my return from Monticello, where we held a lecture.

We had the usual difficulties with "Authority" who attempted to stop the meeting, but we took a wild ride at midnight down to Kingston to see Judge Hasbrooke who protected our "rights" by giving us an injunction. He's a most interesting man by the way, especially advanced and keen sighted concerning women. We discussed Vance Thompson's "Woman" and my mind kept running off in imagining what a nice wife he must have, no man can know so much of women unless he has a wonderful companion and perhaps vast experience.[2]

It was dear of you to send the book to me. I shall take it back to Truro and absorb every word of it, for from its contents and the hurried glance I had of its pages, it must be thrilling.

My baby brother is off today to Harvard to practice bomb-throwing and bayonet drilling and expects to leave for France early in Sept.[3] I am sick and distressed to see him go and I can not help wondering what there is in "Democracy" that it should demand so great a sacrifice. When do you plan to return to Town? I am going out to Truro the end of this week, and shall stop off at Boston over Sunday. I expect to remain ~~there~~ ↑at Truro↓ until Sept Fifteenth when the boys must return to school again.[4] I think so often of your charming home and more often still of your charming self and wonder when I shall see you again.

I am sending to you under separate cover two books 'The Case for Birth Control' and wonder if you could in some tactful way get one of them to Judge Hand[5] and the other give to Mr Dowe[6] without their knowing I sent them. Im afraid they would both think I am trying to prejudice the Courts and the Colleges. I am too, but they should not know it. And will you let me give you one from me?

Everything is slow here but I hope in the fall all will begin actively again. My love to you dear lady and my sincerest thanks,

Margaret Sanger [*signed*]

TLS JRP, MN-SSC (*MSM* C1:205–6). Return address: "104 Fifth Avenue."

1. MS was referring to James Hewat McKenzie's *Spirit Intercourse, Its Theory and Practice* (London, 1916).

2. MS spoke at the Lyceum Theater in Monticello, New York, on August 21, 1917. Gilbert D. B. Hasbrouck (1860–1942) was a New York State Supreme Court judge (1904–30). Married to Julia Mary Munn (?–1926), he had three daughters. *Woman,* a 1917 novel by Vance Thompson (1863–1925), dealt with the burgeoning feminist movement. (Courtesy of Jack Conway, Sullivan County, New York, historian; *New York Times,* June 6, 1942, and June 8, 1925; *NatCAB.*)

3. Robert Arlington Higgins (1893–1969), MS's youngest sibling, was a first lieutenant in the U.S. Army infantry. (Robert A. Higgins to Mary Higgins, ?, 1917 [MS Unfilmed, MN-SSC].)

4. MS and her sons stayed at Cape Cod from August 25 until the boys returned to the Winnwood School.

5. Learned Hand (1872–1969), Rublee's Cornish neighbor, was a lawyer and judge who served on the U.S. District Court for the Southern District of New York (1909–22), where he heard several free speech cases, including a 1919 case against the *Masses;* Hand's opinion enjoined the postmaster from banning it. (Gerald Gunther, *Learned Hand: The Man and the Judge* [New York, 1994], 151–52.)

6. Louis H. Dow (1872–1944), another Rublee neighbor, was a professor of French at Dartmouth College. (*New York Times,* Mar. 9, 1944.)

105. From William Sanger[1]

Santiago de Compostela [*Spain*]
Aug 25/17

Peg

Let this be the last you shall hear from me. It is best that you go your way and I go mine. It is impossible for me to live with you— I have thought it all over and I have decided that I shall live my life alone—

Bill

ALS MSP, MN-SSC (*MSM* S1:703).

1. William Sanger remained in Spain from June 1917 until 1919, mostly in Santiago de Compostela and Madrid. He finally agreed to a legal separation in December 1917. (William Sanger to MS, Dec. 12, 1917 [*MSM* S1:712].)

106. To Frederick A. Blossom

Sanger and Blossom continued to spar over the BCR's *financial records. On October 18, after Sanger again demanded the accounts she had been requesting since July 2, Blossom wrote, "I might add that it will be quite out of the question to give you all the minute details you demand. You know perfectly well under what circumstances we worked last winter. While you were taking things easy at home and going out to dinner parties and to the theatre, your admirers were slaving day and night. . . ." (Blossom-MS letters, Oct. 11, 15, and 18, 1917 [LCM 7:1009–12].)*

[*New York, N.Y.*]
October 22, 1917.

Dear Fred:-

I regret that in your letter of Oct. 18th. you again inject personalities where they do not belong. Our different "philosophies of life" are not now ↑the↓ subject of our correspondence and I fail to understand what possible bearing they can have of your giving a financial statement as manager of the

Review.[1] It will be time to discuss such things after you have rendered your financial statement.

I shall do as you suggest and count the number of subscribers on file and send for the printing bills. This is not, however, "all the necessary information." It is the least of the information necessary. Fortunately, you left me the list of subscribers, but it would have been just as simple to leave the list of contributions and other books.

Will you, by return mail, send me the book in which you kept the detailed account of receipts and contributions of moneys received from sales of the Review and literature? Also send me the bank book, check book and vouchers of the Review account and I will prepare a statement which I will submit to you for correction before taking it to the committee of friends who are willing to help me.[2]

It seems to me that it would take you less time to furnish a statement than to write lengthy excuses concerning it. Your neglect to furnish it has stood and still stands in the way of obtaining support to carry out obligations assumed to friends and subscribers. Your constant hedging justifies one in thinking what I do not want to believe. Your interest in the Socialist movement, particularly on the finance committee should prompt rather than delay, your giving this matter your prompt attention.[3] If you are too busy to send these books, I will be glad to send for them. Sincerely yours,

---

TLcy MSP, DLC (LCM 7:1013).

1. Blossom had written, "Your sentimental appeal to me to get up this report at once on the ground that I 'owe it to the movement and to myself' leaves me unmoved. For you to maintain that I owe anything to your movement is amusing. As to what I owe to myself, I think I am the best judge. My social philosophy emphasizes much less than yours does what we owe to ourselves as compared to what we owe to humanity." (Blossom to MS, Oct. 18, 1917 [LCM 7:1012].)

2. She was probably referring to the group of wealthy women who were subsidizing the *BCR*.

3. Blossom claimed he was too busy working on the mayoral campaign of Morris Hillquit (1869–1933). (*ANB;* Blossom to MS, Oct. 18, 1917 [LCM 7:1012]; and Eugene Schoen to Friends, Oct. 1917 [MHP].)

107. To Juliet Barrett Rublee

New York [*N.Y.*]
Dec 4 [*1917*]

Juliet Rublee—dear, <u>dear</u> lady—

What a blessed woman you are to always think & remember— The little room is the joy of my life—women coming from all over.[1] I'm feeling like a mother to the world these days—all kinds of questions, problems to be solved and men & women seem to think by coming & looking at me—all will be right.

An Italian coal dealer whose little wife has come for advise just came to ask me to write a letter to the papers for the small dealers who can not get coal for the poor & wants me to explain why the small dealer does more for the Country than the big coal men etc etc etc. Then the enclosed letters will touch your heart I know[2]—what can be done for this woman I wonder—think of giving up your baby!! I went to Phil'a last week spoke at Mrs Horatio G. Lloyds home on B.C. had a fine meeting.[3]

The National have upset me a good deal on their decision not to help the Review—[4] It seemed such an opportunity for them to do a very important thing— Certainly the B.C. Magazine has a <u>future</u> and the burden of <u>all</u> the movement should not fall upon <u>so few</u> to carry. Were it not for your friendly spirit I'm afraid I should have run away, this week, to some cave and spent the rest of my life in laughing at the world. The task before me seems so colosal to undertake alone— And that is what it means since the N.B.C.L. decided not to help. Fortunately Jessie Ashley[5] wants to help—and Mrs Pinchot personally gave a hundred dollars for the December issue of the Review which clears me of debt for that issue and gives me a start for the January issue. Jessie Ashley was just here and is anxious that we get <u>ten</u> women who will back up the Review. Take stock perhaps or any other interest necessary— It would ~~require~~ be necessary to have <u>some</u> of these able to write & help with the work— I just met Hutchins Hapgood who says Mr Dow is ill.[6] I hope not seriously—

So much has been doing with Mr Blossom that I just <u>had</u>, to give over his letter to Mr Goldstein to attend to for me.[7] The Slanders & insinuations were to too beneath me to notice—"going over to the rich" etc etc. He is doing himself (only) much harm.

It's impossible dear lady to express to you how deeply I feel and what gratitude for your help with this office.

I have had to take the other one too as Blossom wanted me to move in or move <u>out</u>. So I moved in— He has rendered a partial statement only—[8]

More later on but now my thanks & my love—as always

Margaret Sanger

[*Written along right margin of last page*] This is <u>not</u> an answer to your letter. I'll do that tomorrow.[9]

[*Written on verso of last page*] Forgot to enclose these letters.[10] Will send the one from Camden tomorrow. Goodnight lovely lady Margaret.

ALS JRP, MN-SCC (*MSM* C1:229–33). Return address: "104 Fifth Avenue." The year was added by an unidentified author.

1. MS was referring to her suite at 104 Fifth Avenue, which served as the *BCR* office and where she provided birth control advice on a casual, unadvertised basis to women, who probably found the address in *Family Limitation.* No patient records were found. (*MSM* S76:900.)

2. The letters were not found.

3. Mary Helen Wingate Lloyd (1873–1934) was the wife of a prominent Haverford, Pennsylvania, banker. No information was found on the November meeting. (U.S. Bureau of the Census, *Fourteenth Census of the United States, 1920; New York Times,* Jan. 22, 1937.)

4. The NBCL rejected MS's appeal for *BCR* funds in October 1917, though some members donated money. By the following April, the NBCL was providing support in return for publicity. By July, each *BCR* issue included an NBCL page devoted to the details of its work. (MS to Rublee, Oct. 10, 1917 [*MSM* C1:217]; Gertrude Pinchot to MS, Apr. 17, 1917 [LCM 9:1140]; Virginia Heidelberg to NBCL Members, Mar. 1, 1918 [*MWDPM* 13:727]; "The Fight from Coast to Coast," *BCR,* Apr. 1918, 5.)

5. Jessie Ashley (1861–1919) was a lawyer and wealthy socialist-feminist known for her pro bono work on behalf of the radical labor movement. Ashley probably met MS at Socialist Party meetings in 1911 and worked with her on the Paterson strike. An NBCL founder, she served on the Committee of 100 and the *BCR* editorial board. (*New York Times,* Jan. 22, 1919.)

6. The writer Hutchins Hapgood knew Louis Dow from their student days at Harvard University. (Hutchins Hapgood, *A Victorian in the Modern World* [New York, 1939], 421.)

7. On November 20, after Blossom indicated he needed yet another week to prepare the financial records, MS turned the negotiations over to the attorney Jonah J. Goldstein, an NYBCL member, who pressed for the financial statements and raised the possibility of filing criminal charges against Blossom. (Blossom to MS, Nov. 20, 1917, and subsequent correspondence between Blossom, Goldstein, and Henry Fruchter, LCM 7:1020 and 1025–52.)

8. MS and Blossom shared an office at 104 Fifth Avenue, each paying half the rent and phone charges. After learning that she had leased an adjacent office, Blossom asked to take over the shared room or have MS take both as of November 1. (See Blossom to MS, July 31 and Nov. 13, 1917, and MS to Blossom, Nov. 16, 1917 [LCM 7:1003, 1016, and 1020].)

9. MS's promised December 5 letter was not found, nor have any of Rublee's letters prior to 1919.

10. The enclosed letters were not found.

108. To Juliet Barrett Rublee

With the Blossom dispute still unresolved, Sanger struggled to keep the BCR *running through its first year with revenues from street sales, subscriptions, and donations from wealthy benefactors, including Rublee.*

New York City [*N.Y.*]
Dec 29 [*1917*]

Dear dear Lady—

I'm in the middle of the book—captivated—enchanted, a more interesting book on the other side I have not known. Thank you dear lovely one for sending it to me. How very dear of you to think of me. I know your little gift did not reach you on time, because my son Stuart registered it before I found the street address, I wrote at once to the P.O. & asked them to deliver it to your home: It was nothing any way only I did want you to know my thots were with you that day.

The Review is out again the January issue is very good I think & I have material for the February issue but my deposit for this week was only fourteen dollars.!!! Kitty Marion[1] sold a thousand copies of the Dec. issue but there are many expenses to its up keep. Do you think we can get <u>ten</u> women who will contribute <u>each</u> month enough for the printing. Jessie Ashley will be one but like your self she is always doing things & I wish we could interest new people.

There should be a big place in the U.S.A. for such a magazine. Dr Robinson will take this one over & run it big if I wish it. I never have liked the way he treats the subject & of course feel that women must be found who believe enough in this cause to carry this magazine without making it a <u>trade</u> journal.[2] Yet unless women can be found who are ready to do this for a year at least. I may have to pass it over to him.

Helen Todd[3] came in a few hours the other evening.

My boys are home for the vacation. Stuart has out grown his school & I am sending him to Peddie Institute at Heightstown N.J. a preparatory for Princeton.[4] Of course I could not do it were it not that he can earn some himself & reduce the tuition fees. The room 2004 is at last free a lock was put on the door & just on time for the gentleman tried to get in after hours for the file etc. He took all the furniture and oh such a desolate looking place.[5] I went out to the second hand furniture place & bought some things to sit on—<u>no statement yet</u>.

Havelock Ellis is going to write another article for the Review—<u>free</u>— He said because of the beautiful treatment his last article received.[6]

I sent you some copies of the marriage article bound did you get them? Do you want more?

Would there be interest in a meeting (private) in Washington on B.C. Or perhaps war is too much in their veins for other interests. My brother goes to France next week, one is there is now—and the other is in the Navy & has been going back & forth ever since U.S.A. entered, so we have much of it on all sides—[7] Thank you dear lady ever & always

Margaret Sanger

[*Written at top of first page*] May the New Year bring you into realms of peace and joy [*illegible*]. Understanding life as you do & living it as you do ↑1918↓ should bring you great happiness. May it be so, truly.

ALS JRP, MN-SSC (*MSM* C1:240–43). Return address: "246 West 14th Street."

1. Kitty Marion (1873–1944), a German-born actress, immigrated to England and became a suffragette before moving to New York City. By 1917, she had become a daily fixture on Thirty-fourth Street, in front of Macy's, hawking the *BCR* despite frequent verbal abuse and police interference. (*New York Times,* Oct. 10, 1944; *New Yorker,* July 4, 1936, 22–24.)

2. William Robinson aggressively publicized his own work and role in the birth control and sex education movements in the *Medical Critic and Guide.* MS was aware of Robinson's egotism but acknowledged he was "business man enough to make everything pay that he touches." Her fear of "trade journals" may have reflected her concern that Robinson's focus was on medical professionals and that he saw little role for laywomen in the movement. (MS to Stopes, Dec. 20, 1917 [*MSM* C1:236]; Reed, *Birth Control Movement and American Society,* 46.)

3. Helen Todd (ca. 1870–1953), a suffragist, social worker with the International Child Welfare League, and member of the Committee of 100 and the boards of the NYBCL and *BCR,* probably came to the office to assist MS in getting out the January *BCR.* (*New York Times,* Aug. 16, 1953.)

4. Stuart started at the Peddie School in Hightstown, New Jersey, his uncle Robert Higgins's alma mater, in January 1918. Grant was still attending Winnwood.

5. Blossom probably removed the furnishings and equipment between November 20 and early December.

6. Ellis wrote, "I feel that I owe an article (for nothing) after the generous treatment of my last article." (Ellis to MS, Nov. 18, 1917 [LCM 4:413].)

7. In 1918, Robert Higgins became a senior instructor in the Musketry and Bayonet Section of the Third Army Corps School based outside of Paris; Richard P. Higgins (1888–1966), serving in the Railway Artillery, Replacement Battalion of the American Expeditionary Force, was stationed in France in 1917; and Clio Lawrence Higgins, generally called Lawrence (1886–1939), who was in the navy, was stationed near Paris on and off in 1917–18. (Robert Higgins to Mary Higgins, ?, 1917, and Dec. 11, 1918, and Anna Higgins to Michael Higgins, Nov. 6, 1918 [MS Unfilmed]; Hersey, "Margaret Sanger," 28.)

109. To Juliet Barrett Rublee

For several weeks, Sanger had been working on a plan to finance the BCR *by selling shares in a company that would oversee the journal. The idea was formalized with the incorporation of the New York Women's Publishing Company (NYWPC) in February 1918. Run by a board of directors that included Sanger, Mary Ware Dennett, Rublee, Jessie Ashley, and eleven other women, most of whom were members of the Committee of 100, the NYWPC issued a thousand shares of stock at ten dollars per share and published the* BCR *until May 1923. (For NYWPC minutes and reports, see* MSM *S62:640–759.)*

[*New York, N.Y.*]
January twenty-second [*1918*]

Dearest Juliet:

Only too well I know how very difficult it is to write. I too have been trying to write to you but always something interrupts.

First I wanted to know if the package had been delivered to you for by the enclosed you will see there was no trace of it.[1] Am so glad it got to you—and glad too you liked it.

The N.B.C.L. are planning an upstate tour. I am to meet with them tomorrow to see if there are any suggestions I can offer. Will let you know what comes of it. Mrs Mary Ware Dennett is to go as organizer.[2]

Then Helen Todd has a plan to help me with the Review. She is holding a meeting next Friday at the City Club.[3] The idea is to have a luncheon as I told you about and offer the Review for sale in shares— Say 1000 shares at ten dollars each would place the Review on its feet & keep it going for two years & perhaps for three. By that time the movement should be victorious. If the war is over. The idea is to ask people not only to take shares but to get other people to take some— Every share holder to have a part in the magazine. The Federated Charities are now doing this & it is over subscribed.[4] Its so much easier for people to give small amounts than large. And people give so much more freely & gladly if they know it is to last for a special length of time. If this can be done—I can then employ a good secretary or a managing editor to do much of the grind work I am now doing. I could then write, lecture, & attend to <u>moving</u> the <u>movement</u> again.

You will smile to hear Dr Blossom has left the Rand School & is teaching French & Spanish at a cooperative School in Brooklyn.[5] Perhaps he's looking for something higher. Who knows—

Thank you for the check you know dear lady you need not pay for anything you want here. Those pamphlets were sent to you to send to friends.[6]

Ill write H. E. to write about the subject we discussed. Will let you know his answer.[7] Am sending you some Reviews today. The January issue is considered the best one yet. After I see what the National are trying to do, I'll make plans for Washington. As you say we can have a parlor meeting at least & out of that may come a big meeting later on.[8]

The case before the Court of Appeals at Albany was affirmed—but with ~~it~~ ↑the↓ decision came an opinion by Judge Crane in which he stated that under <u>1145</u> Physicians can & may give information to women in order to <u>prevent</u> disease or to <u>cure</u> disease.[9] This is considered by the Judges & Lawyers here as a victory for us! We can no longer say that the Doctors can not give this information to [*tuberculour*] women & those suffering with other ailments. Now we must ~~make~~ ↑let↓ the Doctors know this decision, & get the women to ask them for it. My brother [*from*] U.S.S. Pueblo expects to visit me in a day or two.[10] He has been across dozens of times taking troops etc over. Another young chap from Camp Upton visited me Sunday— It seems such a shame that all his training of years can not be put to service now. He is an expert in Insurance matters. Has worked night & day to become an expert and now as a private there is no use made of his ability. Do you happen to know of anyone who might speak a word for him & put him in the work he can do well? He is such a nice chap—only twenty-seven or eight ambition to serve well.

Of course you may not, and if not, don't trouble about it. It is so cold here, no heat in office. When will it be over!! I am quite sure too that the German people will not revolt—there is a possibility of every <u>other</u> country doing this first.[11] But it's the old story of the slaves kissing the chains that bind them. But militaritism must go—the world is sick of it and will not allow even Germany to have it—[12] My best love to you dear lovely lady. As always

Margaret.

ALS JRP, MN-SCC (*MSM* C1:249–54). Return address: "104 Fifth Avenue." The year was added by an unidentified author.

1. The enclosure was not found. The "package" was a Christmas gift. (MS to Rublee, Dec. 29, 1917, herein.)

2. Mary Ware Dennett (1872–1947), a suffragist, antiwar activist, and sex education advocate, was the NBCL's executive secretary. Her interest in birth control emerged after a series of life-threatening pregnancies led doctors to advise her to avoid another. Ignorant of contraception, she relied on abstinence, which, Dennett believed, destroyed her marriage (she was divorced in 1913). A censorship opponent, Dennett sought to remove contraception from the list of obscene materials banned by the federal and state Comstock laws, but she eschewed MS's sensational law-breaking tactics, preferring to work quietly behind the scenes. During the ten-day tour in the spring of 1918, she organized NBCL committees in six upstate New York cities. (*NAW;* Chen, *Sex Side of Life,* 49–57, 162–65; Minutes of the Eastern Conference on Birth Control, May 10–11, 1918 [*MSM* C14:918].)

3. No information was found on this meeting.

4. MS probably heard of the Federated Charities stock plan through Frederick Blossom, who had been business manager and financial secretary for the Baltimore-based organization. (FBP Guide)

5. The Rand School of Social Science, founded in New York City in 1906 by a group of socialists, including Morris Hillquit and Charles Beard, educated working men and

women in such subjects as economics, history, literature, and socialist theory. In 1918, Blossom worked briefly at the Downtown Brooklyn Cooperative School. (Statement of D. N. Ditchek, Oct 27, 1922 [*MSM* S69:311].)

6. MS was referring to reprints of Ellis's "Objects of Marriage." (MS to Rublee, Dec. 29, 1917, herein.)

7. MS solicited an article on women's sexuality from Ellis, who submitted "The Erotic Rights of Women," which was written "with the new pattern you [*sent*] from Mrs. Rublee." MS renamed it "Love Rights of Women" because, she explained, it "seemed to mean just that as I read it, love rather than erotic. . . . In U.S.A. the word Erotic is more Scientific but also less used in a love sense." (MS's letters to Ellis not found; Ellis to MS, Feb. 28, 1918 [LCM, 4:432]; see also letters of Mar. 10 and Apr. 6, 1918 [LCM 4: 434 and 448]; and MS to Rublee, June 12, 1918 [*MSM* C1:268].)

8. MS was probably referring to one of the "home meetings" hosted by wealthy women to encourage support for birth control and the formation of local leagues. No information was found on a Washington meeting. (Vreeland, "Process of Reform," 264.)

9. Judge Frederick Evan Crane (1869–1947) upheld MS's conviction in a January 8, 1918, decision, but noted, "This exception [to section 1142 of the Penal Law] . . . is broad enough to protect the physician, who in good faith gives such help or advice to a married person to cure or prevent disease. 'Disease' by *Webster's International Dictionary*, is defined to be, 'an alteration in the state of the body, or of some of its organs, interrupting or disturbing the performance of the vital functions, and causing or threatening pain and sickness; illness; sickness; disorder.' The protection thus afforded the physician would also extend to the druggist, or vendor, acting upon the physician's prescription or order." (*New York Times*, Nov. 22, 1947; *Opinion of Justice Crane*, Jan. 8, 1918 [*MSM* C15:264].)

10. This was her brother Clio Lawrence Higgins.

11. Strikes that broke out in Germany and Austria in mid-January 1918, paired with reports of food shortages and severe rationing, inflated rumors of a revolt among the German people. In January 1918, both the English and American press speculated that Germany falsely paraded stories of internal strife and conflict with its allies to draw more favorable treatment in peace negotiations. (*New York Times*, Jan. 24, 1918.)

12. For MS's antimilitarism, see her "Woman and War," as well as antiwar pieces by Olive Schreiner ("Breeding Men for Battle," *BCR*, April–May 1917, 5); the British Malthusian League ("Fourteen Reasons against War Babies," *BCR*, Jan. 1918, 8); and Theodore Schroeder ("Birth Control and the Great War," *BCR*, Mar. 1919, 8).

110. From Stuart Sanger[1]

[*Hightstown, NJ*]
[*February ?, 1918*]

Dear Mother

I received bouth your letters this morning and also the magizines.[2] Thank you very much for send them I enjoy them very much. I am glad I can come home and get fat, I am very thin and a little pale. It will be a change and I will have something to dream about and look forward to. I receved the check, and the stamps and thank you for them. I have been sick almost two weeks, two weeks on the next [*Friday*]. One side has gone down all and the other about half way. The doctor [*said*] maby I could get out on Friday or Saturday. I feel much better but my one jaw pains.

Don't forget to write every day, as I look forward to your letter that [*is*] the only thing I do~~o~~.

I will close now. Love to Aunt [*Mary*][3] and yourself

Stuart

ALS MSP, MN-SSC (*MSM* S1:737–39).

1. Stuart, who was in the school infirmary recovering from the mumps, wrote his mother several letters asking if he could come home to recuperate. (See Stuart Sanger to MS, Feb. 16 and Feb. ?, 1918 [*MSM* S1:727 731].)
2. The letters were not found.
3. Mary Higgins may have been visiting MS.

111. To Juliet Barrett Rublee[1]

[*Truro, MA*]
August tenth. [*1918*]

Dearest Juliet:

Your very nice long letter of July seventh came to me yesterday forwarded to me here.[2] Thank you dear Lady for your check. It comes in good time and really that little room is a blessing to womankind. We have all our Board meetings there and during the past six months It ha~~ve~~↑s↓ has averaged twenty-five women a week, coming there for advice.

Some days ten or fifteen come. Its really a clinic only there is no noise about it and the quiet work goes on. Im keeping a record of them.[3] You will be interested in the work your donation has done I know.

What an interesting time you have had!!

How sick at heart you must be to see such slaughter & distress & human waste. The feeling here has changed tremendously during the last winter. Three of my brothers are over there and every one I know lives from day to day in anxiety.

The Casualty list is the first thing we all look for these days— Yet the news now is hopeful and the drive back is thrilling.[4]

Now for news. The August issue of the B.C. Review has been held up by the P.O. because of a very good <u>review</u> of Marie Stopes book "Married Love". The book is considered unmailable and any reference to it is likely to take away one's mailing privilege—[5] So you see dear Lady after this war is over we will need you to help us wage a big fight here in U.S.A. for womans liberty—

The magazine is going nicely. The stock idea is placing it on a firm financial bases. That is what is needed. A great sensation ↑was↓ caused about a month ago when the newspapers flared out the news that "Mrs Sanger was ousted from Birth Control League." It came out that F. A. B. had a reporter at the N.Y.L. meeting on a re-election of officers and "condemned" me for my sanctioning the act of issuing Charges against him in the Dist atty's office—[6]

The fact that Hiram Myers J. J. Goldstein were at the meeting and accepted offices was because they wanted to get the League away from the influence of B—

They succeeded at one meeting. Helen Todd was chairman & helped a lot.[7] Then at the next meeting (held in his private apartment with cakes & sandwiches on the table) every one not on his side was refused admittance so they found out later on. The issue was hot boiling hot. Blossom had refused to give over statement or any financial report of Leagues activities— So Hiram Meyers went to Dist atty's office & ordered an inquiry. Blossom went wild. Ran all over the Rand School and said I had done it, and put himself up as a Martyr being persecuted etc etc. It was too pitiful for words—really. Finally Myers & Goldstein withdrew charges for D.A.'s office on the promise that a Committee of three—(Dr Anna Konikow of Boston who was present & was indignant that any one should go to DAs office.) be delegated to go over accounts & render a report.[8]

Blossom got the committee under his thumb "eating out of his hand" they never came to check up finances with my office staff or files but whitewashed a report that everything was O.K.[9]

That was the meeting when B— had the reporter. Of course I had never belonged to the League so could not very well have been ousted.[10]

The "National" made a very good statement but it was made late & had very little effect.[11]

That was some weeks ago and B— is reaping what "he has sown," people are wondering if he is honest or not—and are looking upon him with distrust.

So far so good— I brought out a Statement in the August issue about it—[12] In case your number was held up I am sending you the Statement under separate cover so it will reach you. ~~For~~ I want very much for you to see it.

Now I am ordered away for three months!!! So I came here with the boys & will remain as long as I possibly can.[13] Of course three months will be utterly impossible— I had an old T.B. fight some years ago— Lately about two weeks ago symptoms of it began—temperature, loss of weight—a lump on my neck—etc. So I fled to a surgeon who claims it is not T.B. but caused by Suppressed nervous Fatigue. They claim the aviators have the same ailment and a few months rest cures them without an operation.

So here I am hoping against hope a rest will do it. Sometimes I feel the fight has just begun— But any way there is every evidence that the B.C. message has reached far & wide in this country. I have women working, circulating the pamphlets in mines, shops and mills—in all languages.[14] One Italian woman in Pittsburg arrested & sentenced to nine months last month for giving it to miner's wives! She is a mother of six children—

I am sick over her case but hope to get her pardoned.

Dearest girl I could write volumes to you and then not say all I have to tell you—but dear accept my thanks and the gratitude of every weary soul who comes into that room— You are the only one who has contributed toward it's upkeep. Mrs. Pinchot has helped with the Polish and Lithuanian pamphlets ten thousand of each. Every one seems interested in the Stock and I feel so glad for that. I have not the heart to mention the other needs to the few who never refuse our appeals—

There are several groups organized to "save the baby", since the war, I am confident the future step will be b.c. as soon as they realize the baby can not be saved while there are so many coming so fast.[15]

Have you met Marguerite Tracy?[16] Mr Dow must be the one who brought your lovely necklace to me. Im so proud of it. Everyone who sees it asks about it. I hear quite often from Havelock Ellis— Isn't he a darling? I knew he would like you— He does [*immensely*][17]

I am going to see Mrs Lattmer as soon as I go back to N.Y. She was most interested in you. Told me about herself a little & her experiences. I have had a great deal of it myself since I saw you (writing I mean). She claims we can all do it—I think we can if we will give the time to it.

Try to see Mr Rawson or to hear him lecture in London. They say he has done wonders for the soldiers in guiding them in warfare.[18]

Marie Stopes book is greatly liked here by the few who have read it— But of course the P.O. censorship prevents many from reading it now.

Its such a crime to have it suppressed— They held up ↑the↓ Ellis article in the Review—but finally let it pass.[19]

Well dear Lady I must be off to bed. So here is wishing you good health & joy in your work and accept my thanks for the check. Ever my love to you as always lovingly

Margaret.

ALS JRP, NhD (*MSM* C1:281–93).

1. Juliet Rublee accompanied her husband, George, a delegate to the Allied Maritime Transport Council, to Paris and London in the spring of 1918, where she met several of MS's friends, including Ellis. She returned to Paris in June, volunteering as a Red Cross mobile hospital nurse through the summer and fall. (*New York Times,* Feb. 18, 1919, and Apr. 27, 1957; Ellis to MS, Apr. 26, 1918 [LCM 4:457].)

2. The letter was not found.

3. The NYWPC board met at 104 Fifth Avenue, in the same room MS used to provide birth control information.

4. This was probably a reference to the July 1918 Allied offensive during the Second Battle of the Marne, which marked the beginning of the German retreat.

5. MS was referring to Bianca Van Beuren's review of *Married Love* (1918), which had become a best-seller in England. MS secured William Robinson's Critic and Guide Publishing Company to publish an American version in August 1918. Despite Robinson's heavy editing to get it past the Comstock law, the book was declared obscene. (Bianca Van Beuren, "Married Love—A Review," *BCR,* Aug. 1918, 6; for her efforts to secure a publisher, see MS to Stopes, 1916–17 [*MSM* C1 and S1; LCM 14]; "The Forbidden Book," *Medical Critic and Guide,* May 1919, 202–3; see also "How About This, Mr. Burleson?" *BCR,* Nov. 1918, 14.)

6. MS finally received Blossom's financial statements, which indicated that she owed him $221.34. After comparing his report with bank statements, MS charged that Blossom actually owed her $369.25. As relations between the two rapidly deteriorated, factions formed within the NYBCL, until a majority turned against MS and expelled her on July 6. Blossom angered many NYBCL members by inviting a reporter to that meeting. (Blossom financial statement, ca. May 1918, and Bank of Manhattan to MS, Apr. 12, 1918 [LCM 7:968 and 1031]; *New York Sun,* July 8, 1918; statements of Henry Fruchter, Nov. 11, 1922, and Antoinette Konikow, n.d. [*MSM* S69:295 and 301].)

7. At the May 11 meeting (possibly the one chaired by Helen Todd), Hiram Myers (1891–1986), a civil servant for the New York Bureau of Family Rehabilitation and Relief, was elected NYBCL president, and Jonah Goldstein was elected treasurer. (MS, "Statement of Facts.")

8. The effort of Myers and Goldstein to initiate a criminal investigation of Blossom and MS's willingness to allow it infuriated many NYBCL members, who pressured her to drop the formal inquiry and allow the NYBCL to investigate. In addition to the Russian-born physician and socialist Antoinette Konikow (1869–1946), the committee was composed of Blossom's friends, including the labor organizer and NYBCL secretary Henry Fruchter and Ben Esecover. Goldstein was probably removed as treasurer at the May 25 meeting that barred pro-Sanger members. He wrote, "I was then convinced more than ever that Mr. Blossom wanted a 'Blossom Benevolent League' and not a Birth Control League." (Buhle, Buhle, and Georgakas, *Encyclopedia of the American Left,* 415–20; Goldstein to Fruchter, May 27, 1918, and Louis Greene to Goldstein, June 11, 1918 [LCM 7:1035 and 1052].)

9. The NYBCL committee exonerated Blossom at the July 6 meeting, though Konikow and Fruchter later admitted their chief concern was to salvage the NYBCL's reputation and punish MS, not to examine financial records. They acknowledged that Blossom controlled NYBCL meetings and attempted to bribe members and the league's accountant. The committee's 1918 report was not found. (Ben Esecover to Blossom, July

25, 1918, and statements of D. N. Ditchek, Oct. 27, 1922, Henry Fruchter, Nov. 11, 1922, and Antoinette Konikow, n.d. [*MSM* S69:297].)

10. No NYBCL membership list was found, but league members clearly believed MS was a member when they ousted her.

11. On July 16, Dennett issued a statement: "To correct any misleading inferences from recently published statements calculated to discredit Margaret Sanger's relation with the organized birth control movement, the National Birth Control league wishes to state that there are now, and always have been, cordially cooperative relations between the league and Mrs. Sanger. The league is the only national organization for birth control. There are a number of local leagues affiliated with it, but the New York league which took action against Mrs. Sanger is not one of these." (*New York Call*, July 16, 1918.)

12. For MS's version, see MS, "Statement of Facts."

13. The family stayed in Truro until September. (MS to Juliet Rublee, Sept. ?, 1918, herein.)

14. MS reached out to immigrant women by distributing copies of *Family Limitation* in Italian, Hebrew, Polish, Yiddish, and Lithuanian. (See MS to Rublee, Oct. 10, 1917, [*MSM* C1:217]; for foreign language versions, see LCM 129.)

15. A national baby-saving campaign, coordinated by the U.S. Children's Bureau in 1916, reached its peak during and immediately after World War I. The bureau worked with local women's clubs and parent-teacher associations to organize health clinics and education drives aimed to reduce infant mortality. By 1920, such efforts had led to the formation of permanent child health bureaus in thirty-five states. (Molly Ladd-Taylor, *Mother-Work: Women, Child Welfare, and the State, 1890–1930* [Urbana, Ill., 1994], 82–91.)

16. Marguerite Tracy (1875–?), an American expatriate journalist and writer who helped publicize Twilight Sleep, a form of painless childbirth, met Ellis in February 1916 and soon became one of his many close female friends. (Grosskurth, *Havelock Ellis*, 288, 294; Judith Walzer Leavitt, *Brought to Bed: Childbearing in America, 1750 to 1950* [New York, 1986], 130, 136.)

17. See Ellis to MS, Mar. 15–July 1, 1918 (LCM 1:436–81).

18. Frederick Lawrence Rawson was a British theosophist who claimed he could allay "the suffering of the wounded, the perils of the missing, and the pangs of the starving prisoners in Germany." (*London Times*, Jan. 17 [quote] and 29, 1917.)

19. Ellis's "Love Rights of Women" also appeared in the suppressed issue.

112. *From Billy Williams*[1]

[*Truro, MA?*]
Sunday Evew. [*August ?, 1918?*]

Heart of My Heart:—

I have just come a long swim, all by myself. Started at Snow's landing, lured by the fastest tide by far that I've ever seen here—simply speeding until you could hardly stand up in it,—and swam down even to the second church, or nearly to Postoffice Bridge. I could have made it clear there without effort, but the last decent landing that I knew of looked too good to pass up for a chance to wade a hundred yards barefooted and barelegged through eel grass. I guess that section of the swim was about a mile and a quarter, linear measure. I got into the water again at that dory South of your house, at the foot of the sand hill and it was a pretty fight to swim back to your house against that tide.

Now I'm warming up in my courduroys and sweater. And do you know what I want—I want to be lying at your feet, with your fingers in my hair (of course you wouldn't—I know it! But all the same—) listening to you talk for hours— I want you to go right on about the Lawrence children, and the hearing before Congress—and right on with that story which I love and which so fascinates me. I want to look up and see the lights play in your face. Were tears in your eyes the other morning when you told me about the children singing the Internationale?[2] They were so heavy in mine that I could not see yours. You told it so simply, so beautifully, and it's [*one*] of my soft spots—one of my bitter spots, soft for the children and their enthusiasms, bitter for what we do to them. Oh I wanted to hold you close just then, but I suppose my embarrassment at the tears cloaked every thing else. Damn these walls of selfconsciousness that come up between us.

I want you to talk to me hours and hours this evening and tonight about those things.

I wonder if it would be possible sometime to follow up the B.C. lists that you have accumulated with something for the freedom of children—a mother's revolt for the child, to follow her revolt for herself? I think it's worth keeping in mind—a more [*concrete*] idea, or someone with the time and the idea might come along sometime, or someone who could be given a hunch in this direction.

It's exceedingly boyish, I know, but I nearly have a fit when I think of that old thief of a friend of mine who was willing to raise, and could raise so much money for a damned prostitute newspaper.[3] What could we not do with that half million or more? Why, your million pamphlets wouldn't make a real good sized dent in it, and it could be done NOW!

Don't wonder that I am persistently and unreasonably presumptuous in the matter of love, Golden Girl—about all we have in this movement is an inability-to-quit. And the great work you have done is about the best example of that situation that I know of. Christ, the words of that old man come back to me sometimes, and now particularly, with this FAB thing on,[4] in awful mockery. Damn them, we've one advantage of them, anyhow. They love their hides and property to the point of enslavement, and with us, those go into the cauldron along with the rest. So we are freer than they, though we haven't so many tools to work with. But that wad of money—the price of prostitution from men who wouldn't stake a dollar on my life itself for any permanent human betterment.

My hearts is yours, Golden Girl—and that means, you must know, yours to do with just what you need and wish to do with it—nothing else. I am sending you always wishes of love, not only from me but from everyone, and joy. The love that I bear you grows astoundingly deeper each day. Oh I love you so, I love you so.

TL MSP, MN-SSC (*MSM* S1:769–70).

1. William E. Williams (1882–1920), a Kansas City reporter and writer (who sometimes used the pen name Cleveland Edwards), worked as a publicist for the Rand School and the People's Council and became a fund-raiser and uncredited *BCR* editor (1917–20). Williams and MS became brief lovers in 1918; he stayed at her Truro house in the summer of 1918. (David Karsner, "John Reed and Billy Williams: Two Portraits," *New York Call Magazine,* Sunday supplement, Oct. 24, 1920, 1–3.)

2. He was referring to the February 1912 Lawrence strike and children's evacuation. As the children were marched through Grand Central Station, the waiting crowd sang the "Marseillaise" and the "Internationale." (See MS, "Testimony on the Strike at Lawrence, Mass.," Mar. 5, 1912, herein; "Children of a Strike," 1791.)

3. He might have been referring to the *Masses* editor Max Eastman, who often published pieces justifying prostitution as a social necessity, an outcome of the sexual double standard and economic oppression. Williams was possibly still angry that Eastman, who published his controversial poem "The Ballad," satirizing the Immaculate Conception in the *Masses* (January 1916), also published pieces glorifying Christ. (Watson, *Strange Bedfellows,* 161; Fishbein, *Rebels in Bohemia,* 119, 153–54.)

4. He was referring to the Blossom controversy.

113. To Juliet Barrett Rublee

Both vigilante groups and government officials harassed and intimidated the IWW amid antiradical and nativist hysteria. When the IWW further antagonized its opponents by refusing to honor a wartime no-strike policy adopted by the American Federation of Labor, the federal government stepped up its efforts to suppress the organization. After passage of the 1917 Espionage Act, the Justice Department moved in. In September 1917, federal agents raided IWW offices throughout the country, arresting and indicting 166 leaders on charges of conspiracy to obstruct the conduct of the war. The press and much of the public stigmatized the largely working-class and foreign-born IWW membership as treasonous even before its leaders were tried. Though the government's evidence was flimsy, the trial against the indicted IWW leaders began in April 1918. Sanger published an article in August calling for a fair trial and honest assessment of the IWW's contribution to the working classes, risking government suppression for referring to it as "a distinctly American institution" whose members "have given up home, comfort and necessities—have risked liberty and life itself to bring an end to those evils which society itself is constantly struggling to eradicate." The trial ended on August 31, with most defendants sentenced to between five and twenty years. (MS, "Let's Have the Truth," BCR, *Aug. 1918, 8* (MSM *S70:797.)*

[*New York, N.Y.*]
[*September ?, 1918*]

Juliet dearest:

Am back again. Sent you the Review which contains the I.W.W. article calling for truth & fair play.

The only one objection ever sent into the office came from Mrs D— While many [*ministers*] & liberals wrote us of it favorably.[1]

The only reason I did it was because nearly all the boys in jail helped me distribute pamphlets back in 1914—and translated the family Limitation pamphlet in all languages taking them courageously into the lumber camps & mines. Tell me if you think it is too bad etc. Ever lovingly

Margaret

ALS JRP, MN-SSC (*MSM* C1:398).

1. The letters were not found. Though Dennett was a member of the Woman's Peace Party and the American Union against Militarism, she refused to support illegal forms of activism. She later argued that aligning the movement with such law-breaking organizations as the IWW had associated birth control with an "atmosphere of violence" that hampered efforts to legalize it. (Chen, *Sex Side of Life*, 189–202; Dennett, *Birth Control Laws*, 168–74.)

114. From Havelock Ellis

London S.W. [*England*]
10 Nov./18

It is lovely to find your letter, Margaret Dear, on returning from a few days at Tunbridge Wells where I have been staying at my sisters'. Your letter is dated 16 Oct. & you say it is "two whole weeks" since you wrote. But the last that reached me is dated your birthday, & that is four whole weeks.[1] But I feel quite reconciled to having waited so long, now that your beautiful letter has at last come, for it is somehow so full of yourself that I feel you very very close to me as I read it. Still, I am sad to hear of your trouble with the gland, & trust that by the time this reaches you it is over.[2] No use trying so many remedies, better to stick to one, if it's a good one. And I feel sure that what you need is rest & care & freedom from worry, which you would perhaps be most likely to find in a change over here. So come along as soon as you can! This place is much as you left it, & will be glad to see you back again, and remember that I have been told that I am "better than a desert island"! I won't say "better than Ireland," but that we can talk about when you come. Today the news has come of the Kaiser's abdication, & tomorrow we may hear that the war is over.[3] So the way is being made clear for all sorts of things.

I hope you have escaped the Spanish flu,[4] as I have so far, though many I know have had it badly, & my French friend Françoise[5] has been in bed for a fortnight. The weather just now is fair dry & bright, though coldish, & suits me fairly well so that I keep well & busy, but my [*bad*] time is no doubt shortly coming. I have just finished a little paper on D^{r}. Stopes's "fundamental pulse" theory, which I am going to send to M^{r}. Robinson for the "Medical Review of Reviews".—[6] With your letter I found one at last from M^{rs}. Rublee just back from France, and staying at the Ritz, where I expect to go & see her in a few days. She mentioned she was meeting D^{r}. Stopes yesterday & was going to talk over plans of circulating her book in America. ↑She also asked after you.↓ Your article on D^{r}. Millard is good, though he may think you have over done his celebrity.[7] He is a good man in a good position, but hardly "famous".— It is sad about [*written in left margin*] M^{r}. S.'s attitude.[8] Disappointed love is so apt to turn to something very like hate. I trust a settlement will be found that is satisfactory. But I wouldn't worry about the next incarnation till it comes. Remember what Thoreau said: "one world at a time, if you please, one world at a time."—[9] Goodbye, dear sweet woman

Havelock

ALS MSP, DLC (LCM 4:512–13).

1. The letters of September 14 and October 16 were not found. Ellis often visited two of his four younger sisters, Laura and Mary, in Tunbridge Wells, southeast of London. (Grosskurth, *Havelock Ellis*, 275.)

2. In mid-November, MS had her tubercular lymph nodes—thought to be the cause of her frequent illness—removed at New York City's Rockefeller Institute. (MS to Mary Higgins, Nov. ?, 1918 [*MSM* S1:765]; MS to Juliet Rublee, Dec. 18, 1918 [*MSM* C1:301].)

3. Kaiser Friedrich Wilhelm Viktor Albert (1859–1941) abdicated on November 9; an armistice was signed on November 11, 1918.

4. In 1918–19, an unusually virulent strain of influenza grew into a pandemic, striking one-fifth of the world's population in 1918. Global mortality estimates range from 20 to 100 million. (Gina Kolata, *Flu: The Story of the Great Influenza Pandemic of 1918 and the Search for the Virus That Caused It* [New York, 1999], 7–11.)

5. Françoise Lafitte (Cyon) (1886–1974), a French-born socialist and writer, had worked for Edith Ellis in 1916 but was never paid. Separated from her husband, Serge Cyon, and rearing two sons, she contacted Havelock Ellis in 1917 for reimbursement. Describing her to MS as "a dear little French woman (one quarter German, with two small boys, and a Social Revolutionary (not Bolshevik) Russian husband," Ellis was soon smitten. MS apparently responded, perhaps only partially joking, that she was angry that a French woman was driving an Irish woman out of his heart. He assured her "there is no danger of that Irishwoman you speak of being driven out of my heart by any Frenchwoman, & much as I like to be reminded of her, there is no need to be reminded of her, for I always love to think of her, & it always thrills me to think, as I often do, of her first kiss."

By the summer of 1918, however, Lafitte and Ellis had become lovers. (*London Times;* the letter from MS to Ellis was not found; Ellis to MS, Apr. 6 [first quote] and May 19 [second quote], 1918 [LCM 4:448 and 465]; Grosskurth, *Havelock Ellis,* 276–84.)

6. In chapter 4 of *Married Love,* Stopes diagrammed a specific menstrual curve of sexual desire in women. Ellis, who had earlier argued that women's sexual drive increased just prior to and after the menstrual period but had not mapped the cycle, tested and confirmed her theory. In his review, he asserted that Stopes had made "a notable advance." Victor Robinson (1886–1947), a Russian-born urologist, medical historian, and son of the medical publisher William Robinson, edited the journal. (Havelock Ellis, "The Menstrual Curve of Sexual Impulse in Women," *Medical Review of Reviews* 25 [Feb. 1919]: 77; *New York Times,* Jan. 9, 1947.)

7. Charles Killick Millard (1870–1952) was the medical officer of health for Leicester. MS had praised Millard's call for worldwide birth control as the only means to prevent another world war. (MS, "Birth Control—The Cure for War," *BCR,* Nov. 1918, 12; for coverage of Millard's statement, see *BCR,* Oct. 1918, 8–9.)

8. Ellis was referring to William Sanger's refusal to give MS a divorce.

9. The quote was attributed to Henry Thoreau on his deathbed by Parker Pillsbury, who asked him, "You seem so near the brink of the dark river, that I almost wonder how the opposite shore may appear to you." Thoreau responded, "One world at a time." (Quoted in Frederick Benjamin Sanborn, *The Personality of Thoreau* [Boston, 1901], 68–69.)

115. From Grant Sanger

Lake Grove, N.Y.
Nov. 17, 1918.

Dear Mother,

I received the marshmellows. Thank you very much.

Mother will you come down on Thanksgiving Day?[1] Now you put down in your engagment book, "Nov. 28 Go down to see Grant." Ans. soon. Lots of love

Grant.

"over."[2]

ALS MSP, MN-SSC (*MSM* S1:761). Letterhead of the Winnwood Home School.

1. MS did not visit Grant, then age ten, on Thanksgiving. (Grant Sanger to MS, Nov. 28, 1918 [*MSM* S1:762].)

2. On the reverse is a letter from Grant's school friend Oliver (Nov. 17, 1918 [*MSM* S1:760].)

116. "When Should a Woman Avoid Having Children?"

Sanger first employed the list format used in the article below in English Methods *(1915) and continued it, in various versions, through the 1930s. (See MS, "Chicago Address to Women," 1916; "The Case for Birth Control," Feb. 23, 1924; and "What Birth Control Can Do for India," Nov. 20, 1935 [*MSM *S70:759, C16:212 and 384].)*

[*November 1918*]

IF ONE JUDGES by the letters and personal inquiries that come to an advocate of Birth Control the one thing that women wish to know more than any other, is how to escape the burden of too frequent child bearing. Next to that they are interested in the question of when a woman should avoid having children.

One who has examined the books bearing upon the latter subject is quickly brought to the conclusion that there has been a great amount of disagreement among so-called authorities in regard to this matter. Once it seemed that every one who discussed it, whether it was from the standpoint of medicine, morals, social welfare or individual rights disagreed with everybody else who had attempted to give an answer.

Within the past few years, however, medical and social science have made such strides in this direction that it is now comparatively easy to separate the worthwhile conclusions from those which are of doubtful value or plainly worthless. Those who have made a careful, scientific study of Birth Control are pretty well united upon the points which I shall set forth in this article.[1] I do not give them as my own opinions so much as the result of investigation by others, which I have proved correct by my own studies.

THERE ARE MANY circumstances to be considered before one attempts to advise a woman who asks when she should avoid having children. When all is said and done, the answer is never the same in any two cases. There are certain things which the mother or prospective mother should know. Then she must decide for herself.

(1) *Generally speaking, no woman should bear a child before she is twenty-two years old. It is better that she should wait until she is at least twenty-five.* Not only is it desirable from the mother's viewpoint to postpone child bearing until she has attained a ripe physical and mental development, but it is all-important to the child. The best authorities agree that a child born when a woman is twenty-five or older has the best chance of a good physical and mental equipment, provided, of course, that the health of the mother is good.[2]

(2) *Child bearing should be avoided within two or three years after the birth of the last child.* Common sense and science unite in pointing out that the mother requires at least this much time to regain her normal strength in or-

der to give a new baby proper nourishment both before and after its birth. For the mother's sake it is sufficient to point out, as does Findley in "Diseases of Women" that "frequent child bearing . . . almost certainly results in some sort of pelvic ailment."[3]

(3) *By all means there should be no children when mother (or father) suffers from such diseases as tuberculosis, gonorrhea, syphilis, cancer, epilepsy, insanity, drunkenness or mental disorders. In the case of the mother, heart disease, kidney trouble and pelvic deformities are also a serious bar to pregnancy.*[4]

Thousands of volumes have been written by physicians upon the danger to mothers and offspring of having children when one or both parents are suffering from the diseases mentioned above. As authorities have pointed out in all these books, the jails, hospitals for the insane, poorhouses and houses of prostitution are filled with the children born of such parents, while an astounding number of their children are either still born or die in infancy.

These facts are now so well known that they would need little discussion here, even if space permitted. Miscarriages, which are particularly frequent in cases of syphilis and pelvic deformities, are a great source of danger to the health and even to the life of the mother. Where either parent suffers from gonorrhea, the child is likely to be born blind. Tuberculosis in the parent leaves the child's system in such condition that it is likely to suffer from the disease. Childbearing is also a grave danger to the tubercular mother. A tendency to insanity, if not insanity itself, may be transmitted to the child, or it may be feeble-minded if one of the parents is insane or suffers from any mental disorder. Drunkenness in the parent or parents has been found to be the cause of feeble-mindedness in the offspring and to leave the child with a constitution too weak to resist disease as it should.

(4) *No more children should be born when the parents, though healthy themselves, find that their children are physically or mentally defective.* No matter how much they desire children, no man and woman have a right to bring into the world those who are sure to suffer from mental or physical affliction. It condemns the child to a life of misery and places upon the community the burden of caring for them, probably of their defective descendants for many generations.

(5) *There should be no more children whenever the conditions of life and the uncertainty of livelihood make it improbable that the children can be given proper care, both as to their physical and mental needs.*

AT LEAST ONE CHILD in every seven that dies in the United States perishes from malnutrition or some disease due to poverty.[5] It is neither just to the baby, to the mother nor to the father, to bring into the world a child that is likely to lack for proper food, medical attention and healthful home surroundings. The want of these things inevitably bring disease and disaster to the child and a crushing burden to the parents, to say nothing of the burden to society at large. If there is not accorded to the infant the mercy of an early death, the jail, the poorhouse, and the house of prostitution have a great chance of claiming it. This is another point upon which medical and social authorities are now well agreed.

This, then, is the answer of science for all women generally. But I want to impress upon the mind of the reader who belongs to the toiling masses that women who labor, who do useful things in the world, have a special and exceedingly deep interest in Birth Control. Society, for ages past has been and still is indifferent to the needs of the worker's children. Every now and then some new law is passed which attempts or pretends to give the child of the worker some protection. Usually the protection amounts to so little that we might as well have been spared the mockery of it.

So I have no hesitancy in putting down the following answers to the question:

WHEN SHOULD A woman avoid having children?

If she is a working woman she should have no more children while society remains indifferent to the needs of her offspring and forces them to toil in mills and factories.

"Industrial diseases" due to accident, overwork, lack of fresh air and lack of play, stunt both the mental and physical development of the child, which through the pressure of poverty at home, has been driven to coin its childhood into dollars.

The working woman should have no more children while the profit system exists, for it dictates where you shall live, and what you and your children shall eat and wear.

In the case of the majority of workers it dictates too little food, adulterated food, food of inferior quality, shocking living quarters, exposure to disease and inadequate medical attention.

While there is a struggle between the forces of Poverty and Plenty the working woman should have no more children. Every child is likely to have to go into the mill or the factory and compete with its father and mother for its daily bread.

THE WORKERS WILL win their fight for better conditions, only when they cease to produce cheap labor for the labor market, and use birth control as the most immediate weapon for their emancipation.

The mothers of workers have made human life cheap with battalions of unwanted babies. As long as life is held thus cheap, society will continue to waste life prodigally in under paid toil. It will not place a higher value upon the life and the health of the worker until the women of the working class make babies scarce.

Do not be deceived. Your children are commodities—they are bought and sold in industry. And the price of infants like the price of everything else, goes up when the commodity grows scarce.

The war has brought women into industry as never before. Poverty has driven them into the factory and the mill beside their fathers and brothers. It has taken their children with them.

All of the creative energy of womanhood, the maternal energy that is looked to for the renewal of the world, goes into a sordid, dead, unfeeling machine. That is society's decision in the matter, and from it there is no appeal. But until Society permits woman to give to the bearing and rearing of children the maternal energy given her by Nature for that purpose, and *so long* as she must give it to a factory machine, she must for her own sake, for the sake of other workers, for the sake of the child, avoid bearing children.

BCR, Nov. 1918, 6–7 (*MSM* S70:807–8). For a handwritten version, see *MSM* S70:805. Portions of this article appeared in chapter 7 of her 1920 book, *Woman and the New Race.*

1. By the 1910s, sexologists, eugenicists, and authors of medical texts generally agreed that women should avoid childbearing if they suffered from health conditions that posed a risk to either mother or child or if there was a family history of congenital disease, but there was very little consensus about what other factors should influence childbearing decisions. The growing consensus to which MS refers was the World War I acceptance of eugenics theories and race betterment arguments, evident in both medical texts and popular health books, as well as in public preoccupation with epidemics of venereal disease and tuberculosis. (See chapters 4 and 5 in MS, *Case for Birth Control;* Stopes, *Married Love,* 102–29; William J. Robinson, *Practical Eugenics* [New York, 1912], 17–26; Walter J. Hadden, Charles H. Robinson, and Mary Ries Melendy, *The Science of Eugenics and Sex Life* [n.p., 1914], 293–304; Bloch, *Sexual Life,* 714–16.)

2. Ellis argued that though women were physiologically able to give birth as early as age fifteen, they should wait until age twenty. Eugenicists, as well as maternal and infant welfare experts, reported lower infant mortality rates among women who gave birth between the ages of twenty and twenty-five, and they found older women more likely to bear children with congenital malformations. In *Woman and the New Race,* MS suggested that women who delayed childbirth until age twenty-two had time to attain "a ripe physical and mental development." (Ellis, *Sex in Relation to Society,* 518–22; Paul Popenoe and Roswell Hill Johnson, *Applied Eugenics* [New York, 1927], 346; U.S. Children's Bureau, *Results of a Field Study,* 122, 142; MS, *Woman and the New Race,* 89.)

3. Palmer Findley (1868–1964) was an obstetrician and author. The full quote read, "Frequent childbearing and miscarriages almost certainly result in some sort of pelvic ailment." (*New York Times,* Nov. 11, 1964; Palmer Findley, *The Diagnosis of Diseases in Women: A Treatise for Students and Practitioners* [New York, 1903], 22.)

4. Physicians who supported these assertions included S. Adolphus Knopf (*The Tuberculosis Problem and Section 1142 of the Penal Code of the State of New York* [1915]) and Heinrich Kisch (*Sexual Life of Woman,* cited in MS, *Case for Birth Control,* 156, 172).

5. In 1918, approximately 225,000 infants, or one in seven, died before their first birthday. The U.S. Children's Bureau, which had been investigating infant mortality since 1915, concluded that economic conditions were critical factors in infant mortality. In response to these reports, the *Delineator,* a women's magazine, initiated a public health campaign,

"Save the Seventh Baby." (U.S. Department of Commerce, *Statistical Abstract of the United States, 1921* [Washington, D.C., 1922], 88; Franz Schneider Jr., "The Seventh Baby Campaign," *American City*, Aug. 1917, 129–32; U.S. Children's Bureau, *Results of a Field Study.*)

117. From William Haywood

*Haywood, the IWW secretary-treasurer from 1914, was among those arrested in the 1917 sweep of IWW leaders. Tried and convicted in September 1918, he received the maximum sentence of twenty years and was imprisoned at Leavenworth Federal Penitentiary. (*ANB; *Preston,* Aliens and Dissenters, *123; Haywood,* Bill Haywood's Book, *303–13.)*

Leavenworth, Kansas,
Feb 1st 1919

My dear Margaret

Your letter post marked Jan 27th is just received.[1] I first saw the account of the death of Jessie Ashley[2] in the papers. I at once ↑wrote↓ to Anita,[3] realizing how deeply grieved she would be, Jessie was much like a mother to her, wish it were possible for me to see Anita and offer the condolence and sympathy that is in my heart, words on paper are cheerless, cold and lack feeling an expression or touch of sympathy will convey more than a ream. I could never tell how much I will miss Jessie though I never wrote to her often, I communed with her frequently in my thoughts, I knew where she was, occassionally heard what she was doing, could imagine what she was thinking Jessie was the one best woman friend I ever had, a greater tribute I cannot pay her. I only hope I was as much to her life and being as she was to mine. A real friendship is a much more wonderful thing than passing love— Please telephone to Max Eastman find out if my letter to Anita was received at the Liberator office and if it has been delivered to her.[4]

My present address is above. My health is good, spirit super fine, I am employed here in the Departure Department "dressing out" the prisoners that are leaving in civilian clothing. This pententiary is located at Leavenworth Kansas. If you make a trip West be sure and come to see me. Can have a short but I am sure an interesting visit. You remember what I said at the subway station one evening about "it coming" Margaret all my dreams are coming ↑true↓ my work is being fulfilled, Millions of workers are seeing the light, Russia Poland, Germany France Great Britain, Australia South America, we have lived to see the breaking of the glorious Red Dawn.[5] While you and I and others were doing a little in this country other men and women were doing much in other countries. The world revolution is born, the change is here, we will of course not to live to see it in its perfection. But it is good to have been living at this period.

92 came here with me as a result of the Chicago trial, last Saturday 38 more members of the I.W.W. in all over 200 of us here now,—[6]

If you see Jack Reed tell him to send me copy of his book "10 Days that Shocked the World".[7]

Give my love to Anita when you see her, and remember me kindly to any friends you meet. Come when you can. With love

Bill

ALS MSP, MN-SCC (*MSM* S1:831–32).

1. The letter was not found.

2. Ashley, who was Haywood's lover in 1913 and helped him recover from the Paterson debacle by taking him to Provincetown and Paris, had temporarily replaced MS as *BCR* editor in December 1918. She died of pneumonia on January 20, 1919, at age fifty-seven. (*New York Times,* Jan. 22, 1919; Carlson, *Roughneck,* 221–23.)

3. Anita C. Ashley (1863–1924?), Jessie Ashley's sister, was a painter who became close to William Sanger in Paris in 1914. She was a Committee of 100 member, corresponding secretary for the *BCR,* and NBCL executive committee member. (*New York Times,* Dec. 25, 1924; Chris Petteys, ed., *Dictionary of Women Artists* [Boston, 1985], 27; MS to Max Ehrmann, Dec. 28, 1918 [*MSM* C1:307].)

4. After Eastman's journal, the *Masses,* had been shut down in November 1917 for publishing antiwar cartoons and articles, he launched a new monthly in 1918, the *Liberator,* with his sister, Crystal Eastman, and Floyd Dell. (Fishbein, *Rebels in Bohemia,* 24–25.)

5. He was referring to the Russian Revolution and the general strikes and worker revolts erupting in postwar Europe.

6. Haywood was among ninety-one other convicted IWW members at Leavenworth. After government raids on IWW offices in Fresno, Wichita, and Omaha, additional members were tried and convicted. (Dubofsky, *We Shall Be All,* 433–41.)

7. John Reed (1887–1920), a journalist and revolutionary socialist/communist, reported for several leftist and socialist journals, including the *Masses* and *Metropolitan Magazine.* He probably met MS during the 1913 Paterson strike and pageant and became a loyal supporter of her work. He drafted a letter to the *New York Times* in January 1916 in which he argued: "The whole purpose of Mrs. Sanger's work is to tell the great mass of poor women, in language understood by everybody, how to keep unwelcome children from coming into this world. . . ." The piece was not published because, he asserted, the paper would not "dare use the words 'prevention of conception.'" Reed went to Russia to cover the revolution in 1917 and, upon his return in 1918, wrote his famous journalistic account, *Ten Days That Shook the World* (1919). (*ANB;* Reed to MS, Jan. 12, 1916 [LCM 9:1218]; for the draft of Reed's *New York Times* article, see LCM 9:1219.)

118. Excerpt from California Diary

In her second autobiography, Sanger recalled her feelings of loneliness during the winter of 1918–19 and her need to "get acquainted with my son," whom she only saw during school vacations. In early February 1919, she pulled Grant out of school (her older son, Stuart, was still adjusting to the Peddie Institute) and headed for Coronado, California, where she planned to rest, regain her health, and draft her book Woman and the New Race, *in which she linked overpopulation and uncontrolled childbearing to the problems of war, poverty, unemployment, and a variety of social ills. They left New York on February 8 and arrived in California on February 12, 1919. What follows are diary entries for selected days during this trip. (MS,* Autobiography, *266; MS Diary [LCM 1:48–49].)*

[*Coronado, CA*]
[*February 15, 1919*]

Telegram from J. J. usual business man's way nevertheless it was good to get a word from "back home."[1]

Sailors are everywhere—here & airplanes flying always. Left the San Diego Hotel for Coronoda—find agent most accommodating really a treat—so courteous & interested—Mr Parker his name.

Grant made acquaintence at once with neighbors boys but I am in the grip of despondency. Changes have this effect on me so often. It may be the change of climate but any way it is a most awful anguish one suffers. Peggy—Portet—everything—seems to loom up before one like a nightmare—[2]

Birds are singing & goodness knows one should be happy.

To bed after a visit to the Hotel.

[*February 17, 1919*]

Grant went to Public School today—seems to like it.

Maid Catherine came for four hours to get lunch & prepare meals—two dear telegrams from J. J. that means no letters has been written—two letters from Billy—ever faithful one—they almost brought tears of gratitude such a fight against the "blues" I have not had since my days in London.[3]

I wonder why I remain when I am so lonely. Can't seem to get at work at all. Neck a bit troublesome again—but it is good to rest & sleep and to be with Grant so closely. He seems very happy and glad to be here.

Ramona[4] is so fascinating. Why not an opera of this story I wonder? It would be worthy of the effort.

[*February 18, 1919*]

Another day of depression. It must be the change of climate— The Ocean Boulevard is very wonderful at night—the golden sun set is most alluring. Press down here the same as in New York read just what is meant that we shall read. Pres. Wilson who has been in Europe for Peace Conference is returning home. Senators here object to League of Nations.[5] No one seems to know any thing definite about it all or what it all means.

The war is over and that seems to fill their hearts with gladness & no one cares what responsibilities are in the future.

Its almost like a dead nation so lacking in public interest are the people everywhere

[*February 19, 1919*]

Days much the same things are most depressing the I.W.W. boys are being deported but I should think they would prefer any country on earth to this one today where every vestige of liberty of speech & press is dead. Poor Thomas Pain how his spirit must grieve for the beloved land of his dreams—this land which was to be an asylum for liberty seekers!![6]

Perhaps this war has given or shall prove to give liberty to some of the worlds nations in Europe—but certainly it has deprived us here of all the treasured hopes upon which this country was founded. Grant & I read in bed at night— He is getting strength & more lovely each day. No letters from anyone!!

[*February 20, 1919*]

At last I feel like ↑doing↓ a bit of work. Got off a chapter on Voluntary Motherhood today & sent it off to be polished by Billy.[7]

Its most facinating to work here on this sunny porch. Report of Clemenseau French Premier shot today—the "Tiger" seems to have nine lives so there is strong hope of his recovery.[8] It's a wonder there have been so few assassinations in all the countries at war. So much hatred & bitterness everywhere—and so much <u>Fear</u>.

[*February 21, 1919*]

The Irish landlady took me for a drive around this lovely island—

She is fat & fair—a remarkable business ability & sense of value— Runs her own car a feat which I envy every woman who does it well. Another telegram from J. J. today my pen is going on strike from now on—[9]

Another chapter off today. But am tired easily & can not rest enough—

Louise Bryant & Jack Reed are reported to be on trial in Washington for Bolshevike utterance.[10] Report that Scott Nearing has been freed—[11] He like Debs must be freed—[12] These two men belong to a different sphere than most agitators— Berger & other Socialists sentenced to 20 years in Chicago by Judge Landis.[13]

[*February 23, 1919*]

Another day of sunshine. Went over to the Isis Theatre to San Diego to hear Mrs Tingley speak.

She is a famous Theosophist in charge of organization at Point Loma.[14]

Found her not especially to my liking. The kind of woman with will-power whose personality spells Success. There was a coldness about the place not to my idea of a great truth.

Grant & I took a long walk on beach. Hes growing very handsome these days. Telegram from J J. saying Daisy is better.[15] A fine & a nice evening.

[*February 24, 1919*]

Lots of mail today am feeling better in every sense. Getting out chapter of book on labor today. Sent it off & working on war now.[16] This atmosphere in Coronado is typical of wealthy communities cold, hot.

[*February 27, 1919*]

Went over to hear Max Eastman speak on "Hands off Russia." San Diego turned out fairly well for this meeting.[17]

Met some vegetarian comrades & missed last car had to remain over night.

[*February 28, 1919*]

How much even the hotels are like Spain— Was ill in the night & could not sleep well. Met the same vegetarian group for breakfast & then left for Coronado meatless, eggless hamless women—but lots of courage nevertheless.

AD MSP, DLC (LCM 1:50–55). For the complete diary, covering January 1 through October 5, 1919, see LCM 1:40–110.

1. The telegrams from Jonah J. Goldstein were not found. He may still have been courting MS. (Gray, *Margaret Sanger,* 153–56.)

2. Lorenzo Portet was the only one of her lovers for whom MS expressed both passion and a strong sense of allegiance.

3. The telegrams from Goldstein and letters from Billy Williams were not found. Memories of Peggy and Portet, the persistent entreaties of Williams and Goldstein, along with her health problems, appear to have induced MS's depression. (MS, *Autobiography,* 133.)

4. Helen Maria Hunt Jackson's 1884 romantic novel was about the experiences of a fictitious half–Native American, half-white heroine against the background of the passing of Spanish patriarchal life in California. MS was reading it to Grant.

5. At the Paris Peace Conference (January 18–June 28), President Wilson insisted on including a provision for the establishment of the League of Nations in the Treaty of Versailles. But he met strong Republican opposition to the league when he returned home, and the Senate refused to ratify the treaty.

6. Wartime nativism and antiradicalism resulted in the passage of two laws specifically designed to quash the IWW: the Immigration Act of 1917 called for the deportation of any alien advocating the destruction of property, anarchy, or the overthrow of the government, and the 1918 Immigration Act added membership in or support of radical organizations as deportable offenses. Over 150 IWW members were arrested under these acts. Some 54 radical aliens were being held for deportation at Ellis Island at this time; 27 were deported in 1919. These laws, designed to suppress radical dissent, ran counter to the call for freedom of thought and action by Thomas Paine (1737–1809), who envisioned a new nation that would serve as a haven for the oppressed. (Preston, *Aliens and Dissenters,* 72–117, 182–83, 206; *New York Times,* Feb. 19, 1919; *ANB.*)

7. In 1919, MS was calling her manuscript "Voluntary Motherhood." She changed the

title to "The Door to Woman's Freedom," then "The Modern Woman," before finally settling on *Woman and the New Race.* Billy Williams edited the manuscript for her. (MS to Rublee, Aug. 28, 1919 [*MSM* C1:347]; Chesler, *Woman of Valor,* 192.)

8. Georges Clemenceau (1841–1929), premier of France (1907–20) who was nicknamed the Tiger for his bold and ruthless wartime administration, was shot by an anarchist on February 20, 1919, though his injuries were not serious. (*New York Times,* Feb 20, 1919.)

9. The telegram was not found.

10. John Reed and his wife, the journalist Louise Bryant (1885–1936), were not on trial; rather, they were voluntarily testifying before the Senate Judiciary Subcommittee, which was investigating Bolshevik propaganda in the United States because they believed the Communist position had been distorted by an array of anti-Soviet witnesses. Bryant was called on February 20, 1919, and Reed the next day. Later that year, Reed was charged with treason and fled to the Soviet Union, where he died of typhus at age thirty-three. (*ANB; New York Times,* Feb. 21, 1919; Robert A. Rosenstone, *Romantic Revolutionary: A Biography of John Reed* [Cambridge, 1990], 343–45.)

11. Scott Nearing (1883–1983), a radical socialist, antiwar activist, and author, was indicted for treason under the Espionage Act for publishing an antiwar pamphlet, *The Great Madness: A Victory for American Plutocracy.* He was acquitted on February 19. (Buhle, Buhle, and Georgakas, *Encyclopedia of the American Left,* 541–42.)

12. Debs was serving a ten-year sentence at the Atlanta Federal Penitentiary for violating the Espionage Act during a June 18 antiwar speech. He was pardoned by President Warren G. Harding in 1921. (*ANB*)

13. Victor L. Berger (1860–1929), a founder of the Socialist Party of America and a congressman-elect from Milwaukee, Wisconsin, was convicted of sedition and disloyalty on January 8, 1919, at a trial presided over by Judge Kenesaw Mountain Landis (1866–1944). He and four others were sentenced on February 20 to twenty years at Leavenworth. The U.S. Supreme Court overturned all five convictions on January 31, 1921. (Buhle, Buhle, and Georgakas, *Encyclopedia of the American Left,* 83; *ANB; New York Times,* Jan. 9 and Feb. 21, 1919.)

14. Theosophy, a spiritual mix of Western occultism, informed by Kabbala, Gnosticism, and Hinduism, was founded in 1875 and promoted worldwide by Annie Besant (1847–1933), a social reformer and birth control advocate. Katherine Augusta Tingley (1847–1929) was a spiritual medium, who in 1897 founded the Theosophical Society's international headquarters at Point Loma, an expansive campus that included the Theosophical University, a home for orphans, and a Greek theater. (*DAB;* Emmett A. Greenwalt, *The Point Loma Community in California, 1897–1942* [Berkeley, Calif., 1955], 16–22.)

15. Daisy Mitchell (1883?–1959) was a domestic worker employed first by Jonah Goldstein and, starting about 1918, by MS. She worked for MS for approximately thirty years as caretaker, maid, and cook, and she formed especially close bonds with Grant and Stuart. (Grant Sanger to MS, Oct. 23, 1959 [*MSM* S55:1052].)

16. This was chapter 12, "Will Birth Control Help the Cause of Labor?" of *Woman and the New Race,* in which MS asserted that worker servitude sprang from competition due to the oversupply of workers and that by failing to support birth control, unions could not resolve the problem. In chapter 13, "Battalions of Unwanted Babies the Cause of War," she argued that reactionary and militaristic nations encouraged high birthrates and

called on women to "see past the call of pretended patriotism" and refuse "to produce the human food upon which the monster feeds." (MS, *Woman and the New Race,* 163, 166.)

17. Eastman was on a cross-country tour, speaking in support of Lenin, Trotsky, and the Bolshevik Revolution. (Eastman, *Love and Revolution,* 144.)

119. "Birth Control and Racial Betterment"

After the court of appeals ruling in the Brownsville *case, Sanger made a strategic decision to win support from eugenicists by strengthening her biological arguments for birth control. She was especially keen on attracting support from well-known scientists, hoping their approval would help counter religious opposition, increase the likelihood of passing favorable birth control legislation, and draw money to the movement. Associating birth control with scientifically respectable eugenics also offered an opportunity to obscure the radical feminist and anarchist roots of the movement, which, in the suppressive, antiradical atmosphere of the postwar era, had become a dangerous liability. However, most eugenicists opposed birth control, arguing that it fostered licentiousness and would lead to a further decline in the birthrates of the white middle and upper classes by enabling women to shirk their biological duty. In the article that follows, as well as several others written in this period, Sanger sought to capitalize on the popularity of eugenics by emphasizing the shared goals of the two movements.*

[*February 1919*]

Before eugenists and others who are laboring for racial betterment can succeed, they must first clear the way for Birth Control. Like the advocates of Birth Control, the eugenists, for instance, are seeking to assist the race toward the elimination of the unfit. Both are seeking a single end but they lay emphasis upon different methods.

Eugenists emphasize the mating of healthy couples for the conscious purpose of producing healthy children, the sterilization of the unfit to prevent their populating the world with their kind and they may, perhaps, agree with us that contraception is a necessary measure among the masses of the workers, where wages do not keep pace with the growth of the family and its necessities in the way of food, clothing, housing, medical attention, education and the like.

We who advocate Birth Control, on the other hand, lay all our emphasis upon stopping not only the reproduction of the unfit but upon stopping all reproduction when there is not economic means of providing proper care for those who are born in health. The eugenist also believes that a woman should bear as many healthy children as possible as a duty to the state. We hold that the world is already over-populated. Eugenists imply or insist that a woman's first duty is to the state; we contend that her duty to herself is her first duty to the state.

We maintain that a woman possessing an adequate knowledge of her reproductive functions is the best judge of the time and conditions under which her child should be brought into the world. We further maintain that it is her right, regardless of all other considerations, to determine whether she shall bear children or not, and how many children she shall bear if she chooses to become a mother. To this end we insist that information in regard to scientific contraceptives be made open to all. We believe that if such information is placed within the reach of all, we will have made it possible to take the first, greatest step toward racial betterment and that this step, assisted in no small measure by the educational propaganda of eugenists and members of similar schools, will be taken.

One fundamental fact alone, however, indicates the necessity of Birth Control if eugenics is to accomplish its purpose. Unless contraceptives are used, a child is likely to be born within a year of the last one. Even when the mother is exceptionally robust this frequent child-bearing is a heavy drain upon her system and nine times in ten, it is drain upon the offspring. The mother's system has not had time to replenish itself with those elements which have been so radically diminished in bringing the child to birth, and of course it has not had time to establish that reserve stock of these same elements which are necessary to the strength and well-being of the next child. The mother's health is more than likely to be wrecked and the later children are almost sure to fall short of that nervous and muscular health which might otherwise have been theirs. Thus we hold that the fruits of the most perfect eugenic marriage are likely to be bad health in the mother and in the later children, if Birth Control is not utilized for the purpose of properly spacing the progeny.

This principle asserts itself in all of the economic layers of society but its effects may be modified to a considerable extent by those women who have the means to provide adequate care of themselves during the ante-natal period and adequate care of the child after it is born. With the great masses of the people, however, such care is either exceedingly difficult or impossible. Among the majority of wage-workers, the frequent arrival of children means not only the wrecking of the mother's health and the physical handicapping of the child, but often the disheartening and demoralization of the father, the stunting of the children through bad living conditions and early toil, and in that generation or the next, the contributing of morons, feeble-minded, insane and various criminal types to the already tremendous social burden constituted by these unfit.

While I personally believe in the sterilization of the feeble-minded, the insane and the syphiletic,[1] I have not been able to discover that these measures are more than superficial deterrents when applied to the constantly growing stream of the unfit. They are excellent means of meeting a certain phase of the situation, but I believe in regard to these, as in regard to other eugenic means, that they do not go to the bottom of the matter. Neither the mating of healthy couples nor the sterilization of certain recognized types of the unfit touches the great problem of unlimited reproduction of those whose housing, clothing, and food are all inadequate to physical and mental health. These measures do not touch those great masses, who through economic pressure populate the slums and there produce in their helplessness other helpless, diseased and incompetent masses, who overwhelm all that eugenics can do among those whose economic condition is better.

Birth Control, on the other hand, not only opens the way to the eugenist, but it preserves his work. Furthermore, it not only prepares the ground in a natural fashion for the development of a higher standard of motherhood and of family life, but enables the child to be better born, better cared for in infancy and better educated.

Birth Control of itself, by freeing the reproductive instinct from its present chains, will make a better race. A family subsisting upon a certain wage will naturally give better care to one or two children upon that wage than it would to four or six or eight or ten, and the two children are much less likely to have to go into child labor factories and sweat-shops than are the eight or ten. The situation is too plain for argument.

Concrete examples of the eugenic effects of Birth Control are the most convincing evidence. In Holland, where Birth Control is taught in clinics conducted by nurses specially trained for that purpose, military statistics show that the average stature of men has increased four inches in thirty years.[2] Ninety per cent. of the men were fit for army service, while in the United States, less than 50 per cent. were.[3]

The fighting qualities of the French poilu, his endurance, and his fitness have been the amazement of military authorities in the Great War. The present generation of Frenchmen, as everyone knows who remembers the horror with which "anti-race suicidists" greeted the French tendency to Birth Control, is the product largely of Birth Control methods.[4]

Eugenics without Birth Control seems to us a house builded upon the sands. It is at the mercy of the rising stream of the unfit. It cannot stand against the furious winds of economic pressure which have buffeted into partial or total helplessness a tremendous proportion of the human race. Only upon a free, self-determining motherhood can rest any unshakable structure of racial betterment.

BCR, Feb. 1919, 11–12 (*MSM* S70:813–14).

1. The term *feeble-minded* was popularized by the psychologist Henry Herbert Goddard (1866–1957), who divided the mentally deficient into "morons," "imbeciles," and

"idiots" at the bottom level. Convinced that "feeble-mindedness" was inherited, psychologists and eugenicists, such as Goddard and Ellis, argued that these individuals, lacking a moral sense, were more fecund and must be prevented from reproducing. The prevailing solution was to segregate these "mental defectives" in state institutions, separated by gender. With the emergence of safer, less invasive surgical techniques, however, MS and others became convinced that sterilization was a more effective and humane solution. (*ANB;* Kevles, *In the Name of Eugenics,* 78; Ellis, extracts from *Race Regeneration,* 1911 pamphlet, in MS, *Case for Birth Control,* 26–36; Larson, *Sex, Race, and Science,* 8, 23–26.)

2. Her figure was probably from Soren Hansen's report to the 1912 Eugenics Congress, though Hansen demonstrated that men's height had increased during the previous fifty years, not thirty. (Charles Vickery Drysdale, "The Progress of Holland: Wages and the Cost of Living," in MS, *Case for Birth Control,* 246.)

3. She was comparing two different systems of evaluating fitness for service. During World War I, the Dutch army accepted nearly all men without major physical disabilities. The American figures come from a widely reported government study of draft records, which found 557 physical defects (in 468 men rejected for service) per 1,000 men. However, more than 20 percent of what the U.S. military defined as "defects" were simply such things as common foot problems and short stature. (Henrik Van Loon, "The Citizen Army of Holland," *National Geographic* 29 [June 1916]: 609–22; Albert G. Love and Charles B. Davenport, *Defects Found in Drafted Men* [Washington, D.C., 1920], 28–30, 53–55.)

4. MS's interpretation of the impact of the French birthrate was not widely shared except among the most ardent Malthusians. Even before the war, pronatalists warned that France's reduced birthrate had weakened its military strength. When the French army failed to defend its borders and the nation lost 2 million people between 1914 and 1918, the government sought to raise the birthrate through pronatalist incentives, which culminated in July 1920 with the criminalization of both abortion and birth control propaganda. (Richard Tomlinson, "The 'Disappearance' of France, 1896–1940: French Politics and the Birth Rate," *Historical Journal* 28, no. 2 [1985]: 405–10.)

120. *Excerpt from California Diary*

Sanger spent much of March in San Diego and Los Angeles visiting with friends, including her old Claverack classmates Gola Beagle and Esther Farquharson. In early April, she spent approximately ten days in Fresno. (MS Diary [LCM 1:56–70].)

[*Fresno, CA*]
[*April 5–15, 1919*][1]

A good meeting at Fresno— Dr Whittaker[2] asked me to speak. I did, a great deal of opposition on the part of two Socialists (at a Socialist meeting) aroused the audience. The same old question that women can have all the children they want under Socialism—

The fact that they can today never dawns upon them but the fact that women shall not desire to be breeders under a Socialist Republic no more than she wants to be today is difficult for them to see.

There is harder work to do among the "dyed in the wool" radical than with the average person. He has Marxian blinders on his eyes & will not see.

Left after meeting for San Francisco. Arrived in morning at [*illegible*] and found brother there too on furlough.[3] Much mail awaited me and one letter in particular which made a new outlook of the future imperative.[4]

The day was a nightmare. The following also— It did not seem to me one could suffer so intensely inside when judgment, & reason ruled so strongly against it. The lecture the following night was a fair success dear old Doc Equi[5] in the audience she & Kathaleen O'Brennan[6] from Ireland were here speaking on tour; Catherine Schmidt was also here and I had a nice visit with her. My heart is so heavy th'o it seems difficult to go on at all—yet one does— I sent a telegram to J. J. saying things are O.K. and one to Anna giving address she wanted.[7]

AD MSP, DLC (LCM 1:67–72).

1. MS's entries did not always correspond to the printed date in her diary book. The range of dates presented here has been constructed from events mentioned in the entries.

2. The Reverend Robert Whitaker (1863–1944), a British-born radical clergyman and author, addressed an IWW meeting on April 13, at which he asked MS to speak and answer questions. "Nearly a dozen mothers came with their babies to hear the address," according to the local paper, but "apparently the theories of Mrs. Sanger did not meet with their approval." (*WWW America; Fresno Morning Republican,* Apr. 14, 1919.)

3. This was probably Clio Lawrence Higgins.

4. Her biographer Madeline Gray claimed that MS received a letter from Goldstein demanding she marry him or he would marry someone else, but no such letter was found. (Gray, *Margaret Sanger,* 153–56.)

5. A copy of the lecture was not found. Equi, an antiwar activist and member of the American Union against Militarism, had been convicted under the Sedition Act for a June 27, 1918, speech in which she declared that American workers should not be forced to kill fellow workers and that the IWW should emulate the Irish in fighting an oppressive government. Sentenced to three years, Equi was free on appeal. She served ten months beginning in October 1919 before her sentence was commuted in 1920. (*Portland Scribe,* June 30–July 6, 1973; Kreiger, "Queen of the Bolsheviks," 60–68.)

6. Kathleen M. O'Brennan, an Irish journalist and nationalist who was raising money for the Irish Republicans and Sinn Fein, was Equi's lover and headed her defense committee. (Kreiger, "Queen of the Bolsheviks," 66, 68; Elizabeth Gurley Flynn, *Rebel Girl: An Autobiography,* new rev. ed. [New York, 1955], 269–70.)

7. The telegrams were not found. Anna Lifshiz (also spelled Lifschitz) was MS's first full-time office worker. Her responsibilities included secretly distributing copies of *Fam-*

ily Limitation and other birth control material. To ensure that the materials did not go to undercover police, Lifshiz regularly deposited them in scattered post boxes, making it difficult to trace the sender. ("Anna Lifshiz Remembers," in "Our Margaret Sanger," ed. Erma Brown, Dorothy Brush, Mesako Ledward, and Ellen Watumull, 1959 manuscript, 162–69 [*MSM* S77:946]; Gray, *Margaret Sanger,* 143.)

121. Diary Entry

[*On train from San Francisco to New York*]
[*April 27–May 3, 1919*]

The second lecture not so successful as far as numbers go[1]—but the women are interested and eager to know— The boys who managed lectures very greatly disliked here—[2]

Still Im glad Im homeward bound. Grant & I leave for home.

Its so depressing to feel in ill health have been taking hypos of iron but I grow thinner in spite of consuming quantities of food. Had hoped to stop off to see Emma Goldman & Kate O Hare[3] but Big Bill was to have been in Chicago and one stop was all I could take. Bill was not out on bail yet,[4] so I did not stop anywhere— Regret this state of health which makes every desire an effort. Arrived home at last—[5] Nan gone to country, father & Tom to Truro—[6] Billy Williams met us at train & we went to dinner together.

Dear old Billy! One can be proud of such a loyal friend as he.

Often I think we women scarcely deserve that men be fair to us—when men so big & generous & devoted offer their all—their strength labor, energy talents love at our feet and tho its appreciated & valued yet these very essential qualities of & in themselves do not seem to bring out of us that love they should again I am inclined to feel "chemical love" has a big part to do in our affairs of life—[7]

Met Harold Hersey in the street who sent me the next day a poem "So you have come back like the spring." The old ache has been present but determined it must be delt with as it should.[8]

J. J. called up—8am Daisy came and we wept together. Three days of anxiety and determination of the future.[9] Book is going well. Billy & I working hard on revising it & getting it into shape.

Am still far from well neck somewhat troublesome again—

Everyone so dear— Meetings of Board O.K.[10] J. J sent some strawberries—very delicious ones too. Went to dinner with him and talked of movement etc. A queer lad—facinating at times—but does not try to be—or is not conscious of it. A good friend and th'o quite undeveloped emotionally and in some things intellectually & artistically—yet his human intellect is very keen—"mortal mind" Nan says he knows.

Old Jewish re-actions are strong with in his make up—but his good sense does away with much which otherwise would enslave him generous to the extreme and [*while torn*] between these impulses his lot may not be so easy as it seems.

Going to Texas to invest his interests he will see some thing outside of N.Y. Saw Mary Halton and decided to go into hospital again to rest & perhaps lump in neck will go.[11]

AD MSP, DLC (LCM 1:78–86).

1. MS spoke to a group of San Francisco working women on April 26. (MS, "Western Women Demand Information," *BCR*, June 1919, 5.)

2. Caroline Nelson reported that an anarchist named Belinsky organized the lecture, but MS, complaining that he was "shabby," initially refused to speak. (Nelson to Dennett, Apr. 1, 1930 [*MWDPM* 19:203–5].)

3. Both were serving time at the Missouri State Penitentiary in Jefferson City. Goldman, who (along with Alexander Berkman) had been convicted for publishing articles in the June 1917 issue of *Mother Earth* encouraging men to resist the draft, had already served fourteen months of her two-year sentence. She was deported on December 21, 1919. Kate Richards O'Hare (1876–1948), a journalist and Socialist Party official, was convicted in 1919 for delivering an antiwar speech in North Dakota in July 1917 and served one year before her sentence was commuted in May 1920. (*NAW;* Richard Drinnon, *Rebel in Paradise: A Biography of Emma Goldman* [Chicago, 1961], 188–201; *ANB.*)

4. Haywood was scheduled to be released in April, but prosecutors stalled, and he remained in prison until July 28. It is possible MS never saw him again, for Haywood fled to the Soviet Union in 1921 after being charged with conspiracy to overthrow the government. Disillusioned with the Bolshevik experiment but unable to return to the United States, he died in Moscow. (Melvyn Dubofsky, *'Big Bill' Haywood* [Manchester, England, 1987], 128–40; Carlson, *Roughneck,* 294–325.)

5. MS and Grant reached New York City on May 3.

6. MS was referring to her sister Anna Higgins; her father, Michael Higgins; and her brother Thomas Higgins (1877–1923), who worked at the Corning Glassworks. (Chesler, *Woman of Valor,* 27, 45.)

7. In another diary entry, MS wrote, "A nice letter from J. J. today—these chemically facinating men must needs be dismissed from our consciousness. I often wonder if love is not based on chemistry & if that is why married people grow so indifferent as age advances—" (MS Diary [LCM 1:59].)

8. Hersey, discharged from the army in 1918, edited and published several journals, including the *Quill,* and wrote books of poetry. The poem, published in the *BCR* in April 1921 read in part, "So, you've come back like the spring / Our dream went out like the day / To be lost in a chorus of stars / Our dream went out like a candle / Snuffed by restrained bitterness / . . . I shall whisper to my heart and remember. / I shall wonder and be satisfied / I have learned to covet / Then to know the pleasure of coveting what I cannot desire" (12). MS was probably referring to the end of their affair in 1915 or 1916. (*NatCAB*)

9. MS may have told Daisy Mitchell about the possible marriage ultimatum from Goldstein.

10. She was referring to the NYWPC board meetings. (Minutes, May 13, 1919 [*MSM* S62:694].)

11. Mary Halton (1879?–1948), MS's physician, was a Committee of 100 member and sat on the NYWPC board. She told MS, who spent two weeks in mid-May resting and receiving X-ray treatments in a New York City hospital, that it would take at least two years to regain her health. (*New York Times,* Jan. 27, 1948; MS Diary [LCM 1:87]; MS to Rublee, July 16, 1919 [*MSM* C1:327].)

122. From Juliet Barrett Rublee[1]

In Studio Cornish—[*NH*]
Aug 6th [*1919*]

My darling child—

I think the book is simply wonderful—I can hardly wait to have it published.[2] I would hardly change a word—or take out a thought. Just one or two little notes I have made— The words "breeding machine"—& "urge" are used very often. I don't like the latter word—but you may be specially fond of it!— There are so many people I want to send this book to, that I don't see how I can keep quiet until September! Can it not be advertised at once—as "Soon to appear—Margaret Sanger's Call to the World for the Freedom of Women." "A new theory—more basic than the League of Nations to stop all war." etc. etc. Some bully advertisements could be concocted—if you could get the right news paper men interested. If rightly advertised & you can keep the price down—I think it will sell by the hundred thousand.

You see you are speaking for the hearts of women, all over the world— The book will help to free them—inside—to make them think for themselves, to give them courage to trust & to follow their own feelings, instead of accepting the stupid decrees of men & the church & a false tradition.

It occurs to me that because you tell the truth about the church, many newspapers & magazines may be threatened by the church, with the loss of Catholic advertisements if they advertise your book— Do you think this is possible? Surely the Catholics themselves must see the unanswerable truth of what you say— There must be many fine & able & open, fair minded men among them. Don't you think so? If not, I think it would be well to offset their activity, by having this thought about them, suggested in the preface— or in a letter written to you by some distinguished & well known person, that you could publish. We have got to get around them somehow—& sell this book by the million! What do you think of Scribner as a publisher?[3] He is so respectable, & I see he is advertising Galsworthy's "Saint's Progress"[4] better than any other book I have noticed. Well—do let me know what you decide—and above all make them hasten— But don't rush yourself too much. My dear—there is immense work ahead of you—you must get well & strong—you are too frail just now—I feel it—not robust enough— Please eat a great deal & drink oceans of milk— It will give you a reserve from which to draw— It was such a joy to have you here—[5] Endless love—as always—

Juliet

ALS MSP, MN-SSC (*MSM* S1:843–45).

1. Rublee, one of three American delegates on the Interallied Women's Council, which met in Paris during the Paris Peace Conference, returned from Europe in the summer of 1919. She continued to generously fund the *BCR*. (*New York Times*, Feb. 18, 1919; MS to Rublee, June ? and Oct. 4, 1919 [*MSM* C1:323 and 359].)

2. Though several publishers had expressed interest in *Woman and the New Race*, most found the subject matter too controversial, and MS was still without a contract. (MS to Rublee, Aug. 13 and Dec. 13, 1919 [*MSM* C1:342 and 389].)

3. Charles Scribner II (1854–1930) headed a prestigious New York publishing firm established in 1846. (*ANB*)

4. Rublee was referring to a 1919 novel by John Galsworthy (1867–1933) in which an English clergyman grapples with love, religious faith, and loneliness.

5. MS had visited Rublee from July 30 to August 4, when she went on to Boston and then Truro. (MS Diary [LCM 1:102–4].)

123. To Edward Mylius[1]

*Sanger's persistent health problems apparently led her to fear an early death and may have prompted a series of farewell letters to some of the men of her past. This letter and a similar one addressed to Walter Roberts on the same date were probably not sent but were retained in her files until her death. She would write a similar but more extensive letter to William Sanger a few weeks later. (MS to Walter Roberts, Sept. 24, 1919 [*MSM *S1:869]; MS to William Sanger, Dec. 1, 1919, herein; on her health, see MS to Juliet Rublee, Aug. 28, 1919 [*MSM *C1:347].)*

[*New York, N.Y.*]
Sept 24—1919

Ned dearest friend—

These letters are so full of the great loving expression of your dear self—I want you to have them when I pass on to the Great Unknown.[2] It was you dear with your great true love of a cause, with your high understanding of the cosmic urge within me finding its expression it was you who helped this urge to flow and to you I owe more joy & happiness because of this than to any other man or woman who [*even*]. Always there has been the bond of love

& understanding between us. It shall ever be. Adieu dear Ned of the understanding heart. Adieu

Margaret Sanger

ALS MSP, MN-SSC (*MSM* S1:865–88).

1. Mylius was working as a bookkeeper and advertising manager for Max Eastman's *Liberator,* until he was fired for stealing money in 1921. (Eastman, *Love and Revolution,* 262–63.)

2. For surviving letters, see Mylius to MS, Feb. 24, 1914, May 17 and 19, 1915, Nov. ?, 1915, and Nov. 1, 1916 (*MSM* S1:181, 245, 247, 526, and 644).

124. From Secretary of Narcissa Cox Vanderlip[1]

Many opponents of birth control, as well as those supporters primarily interested in limiting undesirable segments of the population, bombarded Sanger with their fears of "race suicide," the result of increased use of birth control among middle- and upper-class white women. As World War I reignited fears of Anglo-Saxon demise and intensified calls for increased fertility among the "better classes," Sanger continued to be confronted with these arguments.

Scarborough-on-Hudson, [*N.Y.*]
November 5th, 1919.

My dear Mrs. Sanger,

Mrs. Vanderlip has asked me to reply to your letter of the 30th.[2] She says she would be far more enthusiastic about the Birth Control Movement, if with this propaganda went a counter one to the well-to-do urging them to have more children. At present, Mrs. Vanderlip feels that this class is allowing the Anglo-Saxon race to die out while they indulge in motors, instead of babies.[3] Sincerely yours,

G. M. Affleck[4]—[*signed*]
Secretary to Mrs. Frank A. Vanderlip.

TLS MSP, DLC (LCM 10:909).

1. Narcissa Cox Vanderlip (1880–1966), a philanthropist, a suffragist, and the first president of the New York League of Women Voters (1919–23), was married to the president of the National City Bank in New York City and had six children. (Angela Zophy, ed., *Handbook of American Women's History* [New York, 1990], 634.)

2. MS had written to Vanderlip (letter not found) requesting funds for birth control speakers and had received a twenty-five-dollar check. (Affleck/Vanderlip to MS, Nov. 14, 1919, and MS to Vanderlip, Nov. ?, 1919 [LCM 10:910].)

3. MS responded to race suicide arguments, popularized by Theodore Roosevelt in 1911, indirectly on several occasions and at length in a December 1917 article in which she noted, "The trouble with nearly all writers who oppose birth control is that they consider only proximate instead of ultimate effects. They want large numbers of high quality citizens. Therefore, they contend, let the existing high quality citizens have more children. . . . In other words, they expect quality to take care of itself. We advocates of birth control know that one cannot make quality by insisting on quantity. One cannot make better people simply by having more people." (Roosevelt, "Race Decadence"; MS, "Birth Control: Margaret Sanger's Reply to Theodore Roosevelt," *Metropolitan Magazine*, Dec. 1917, 66–67, a rebuttal to Roosevelt's "Birth Control—From the Positive Side," *Metropolitan Magazine*, Oct. 1917, 67–70. MS's article was reprinted in the Dec. 1917 *BCR* as "An Answer to Mr. Roosevelt," 13–14 [*MSM* C16:108].)

4. This was Grace Morris Affleck (1889–1972). (SSDI)

125. "Breaking into the South—A Contrast"

On November 2, 1919, following a meeting in New York with a North Carolina newspaper editor, Sanger gave a talk entitled "Woman's Place in the Twentieth Century" to an Elizabeth City, North Carolina, audience of about eight hundred. The lecture was advertised as containing nothing that would be construed as "vulgar or suggestive" and was, according to the Elizabeth City Independent, *"the first public meeting for the discussion of birth control ever held in the south." Sanger met with approximately two hundred white and African American women after the lecture to explain how to obtain literature on birth control. Since North Carolina had no laws against the verbal dissemination of contraceptive information, neither police nor local officials interrupted the meeting. Sanger addressed a smaller audience of African Americans that evening at a local church. In the following article, she summarized her trip to the South, contrasting it with earlier New York City meetings. (*Independent, *Oct. 24, Oct. 31, and Nov. 7, 1919.)*

[*November 1919*]

The first public lecture on birth control in the South developed into a series of addresses within twenty-four hours, and was in every way a gratifying surprise to me. I had the feeling that it would be hard to break the ice for the birth control movement in a city in which not even a suffragist had delivered a public lecture. To my delight, however, I found that people, both white and black, in Elizabeth City, N.C., were so eager to know about birth control that every possible moment of my time was given to speaking.[1]

The first lecture, which was the only one I expected to deliver in Elizabeth City, was arranged by Mr. W. O. Saunders, editor of *The Independent*.[2] It was delivered in a theatre Sunday afternoon, November 2nd. Women in the audience requested an address for women only, and this was given immediately following the general lecture. These meetings were attended by white women of all classes and conditions, some of them being farmer's wives—mothers of five, six or more children—some of whom drove fifteen or sixteen miles to hear about birth control.

After the lecture, a number of elderly women lingered to ask further questions and to express their appreciation of the movement. They were singularly unanimous in their expressions. "The message comes too late for me," was the tenor of their words, "but thank God it comes in time to save my daughters from what I have undergone."

A committee of negro women urged a public address for negroes in a negro church for the same evening.[3] This was delivered and was followed the next day by a short talk on "Education" at the negro normal school, and in the afternoon a lecture for negro women only on methods of birth control.

Meanwhile, women who came from near and far were gathering at the hotel where I stopped. Among these were a number of social workers and public-spirited citizens, who asked help in establishing a clinic for the mill workers. A temporary committee was formed, and is going ahead with the work of bringing fundamental, practical help to those women who work in the mills.

All this happened between noon on Sunday and three o'clock Monday afternoon.

Never have I met with more sympathy, more serious attention, more complete understanding than in my addresses to the white and black people of this Southern mill town. Each element in the audience seemed to look at the question from its own standpoint. All in all, these audiences were a striking demonstration of birth control's universal message of freedom and betterment.

Among the white people, the argument which appealed most strongly was that of family betterment and increased happiness in the home, where the size of the family can be kept down to a point in which the father's earnings and the mother's attention are adequate for the care of children. That birth control results in longer life among women and decreases the mortality among infants and children of tender years appealed to representatives of insurance companies, who made it plain that they had got the point. Even a mill-owner, who is perhaps the most powerful citizen of Elizabeth City, was open-minded enough to recognize that birth control, in bettering the condition of the workers in his mills, would tend to increased efficiency.[4]

That the wives of farmers and of other workers recognized the liberty, the mental, physical and spiritual advantages that come with birth control was made plain by their attention, by their questions, and by their expressions of appreciation. They need it most, and doubtless it was they who best understood.

If Elizabeth City is an index of the South, it is ready, waiting, crying for the message of birth control.

It is with somewhat similar pleasure I look back upon a lecture given October 28th before members of the League for Women Voters in New York City. It was an interesting audience. These were workers—active business women, some in clerical positions, some of them professional women, some of them housewives. They were mostly women who have grappled with practical problems and who have been tasting the first fruits of an expanding freedom. Their attitude was one of intelligent reasoning—they wanted the message; they wished to weigh it and decide for themselves whether to apply it. There was in this audience but one objector—a mother of four children, who said she wished she had four more. The rest of the audience joined in the hope that since she desired them, she might have them.[5]

In unhappy contrast to these meetings was the Conference of Social Hygiene, a division of The League for Women Voters, at which I was one of the speakers. This was held at the Park Avenue Hotel, New York, October 20th. At once one could feel hostility in this audience, composed almost entirely of women physicians. One wondered whence such antagonism could come, but when the lecture was over and questions and discussion began, one was not left long in the dark. The antagonism was among the women physicians themselves—the people whom one would least expect to have that attitude. Yet there it was.[6]

One physician rejected birth control because she believed I claimed too much for it. She did not believe that it can accomplish as much for women as I believe it can—therefore she dismissed the whole subject!

Another objected to birth control, saying that when a woman's children are arriving so rapidly as to make her lot unendurable, she should leave her husband. Asked what a woman living in the slums, and having four or five children barely supported by her own earnings and those of her husband should do with the children, this physician blandly dismissed the whole matter by saying she *should take them with her!* This from a woman physician whose practice is, presumably, largely among the poor!

A third woman physician objected to any discussion of the subject, saying that it was "nasty." It is hardly to be supposed, however, that this physician refuses either to give her services or accept fees in maternity cases. Dr. Mary Halton quickly settled this point by her positive assertion of the beauty and cleanliness of all that relates to the sex life. Her defense of birth control was clear, strong, and illuminating.[7]

But let us not deceive ourselves as to the general attitude of either women or men who are attached strongly to institutions—whether these institutions be professional organizations or something else similar in spirit. Usually their egos have become attached to these institutions—they have built up the old organizations—upon those organizations they depend largely for their standing and personal success. Subconsciously these well-meaning people know that their institutions are going to tumble into disuse before the vigorous, fundamental remedies which we propose to apply. The women physicians who follow the old manner of thinking subconsciously know and fear the effect of birth control, which will largely dispense with their services as they are now rendered. These will never take the initiative in freeing the world from its chains. They love their institutions, their prejudices, their own chains, better than they love humanity and the truth.

BCR, Dec. 1919, 7–8 (*MSM* S70:829–30).

1. Elizabeth City, North Carolina, was a shipping center for the Albermarle Sound region, also known for its lumber and cotton manufacturing. African Americans made up approximately 37 percent of the population. (Federal Writers' Project, *North Carolina: The WPA Guide to the Old North State* [Columbia, S.C., 1939, 1988], 191.)

2. William Oscar Saunders (1884–1940), the editor of the progressive weekly from 1908 to 1937, was a politician known for his agnosticism, outspoken opposition to racism and anti-Semitism, and support for birth control. (William S. Powell, ed., *Dictionary of North Carolina Biography* [Chapel Hill, N.C., 1994]; see also "Making People Think," *BCR,* Dec. 1919, 3–4.)

3. MS, who spoke at the Corner Stone Baptist Church, suggested to audience members that they devalued their labor by having too many children. "You make anything cheap," she told them, "by making it plentiful." (*Independent,* Nov. 7, 1919.)

4. The textile industry, notorious for low wages, long hours, and few child-labor restrictions, was the major employer of white women and children in the South. Elizabeth City housed several cotton and hosiery mills. Though barred from working in the mills, African American women played an integral economic role as low-paid domestics for the white mill workers. (Victoria Byerly, *Hard Times Cotton Mill Girls* [Ithaca, N.Y., 1986], 11–13, 44–45, 125.)

5. MS had spoken to about a hundred League of Women Voters (LWV) members at their New York City headquarters. Launched in 1920, the LWV was made up of former woman suffrage activists, social workers, and progressive reformers. Though some members favored birth control, the LWV, fearing the association with sexual promiscuity and immorality, was slow to endorse it. (Young, *In the Public Interest,* 33–37; Björkman, "Light Ahead," 9–10.)

6. The conference of the LWV Sub-Committee on Social Hygiene, at which Gertrude Pinchot also spoke, included the heads of various state social hygiene committees and many female doctors who were in New York City to attend the International Conference of Women Physicians. MS's opponents at this meeting were probably American physicians, who were more likely to share the hostility of male physicians to birth control than were European doctors. One observer contradicted her, claiming, "The discussion brought out no serious comment that was not entirely favorable." The subcommittee did not adopt birth control as one of its official aims but acknowledged that individual members might work quietly for contraception, "until public feeling had been brought to a point where a definite stand could be openly taken." (Björkman, "Light Ahead," 10 [quotes]; Young, *In the Public Interest,* 35–36.)

7. At the time, Mary Halton headed a NYWPC committee to test the *Crane* decision. She sent two women—one suffering from tuberculosis, the other from syphilis and kidney disease—to New York City hospitals to ask for birth control advice. The hospitals refused to provide contraceptives but were willing to provide abortions to such women. Other physicians who spoke out in support of birth control were Edith Hale Swift, Rachel Yarros, and Mabel Ulrich. (Mary Halton, "The Investigation of Hospitals," *BCR*, Dec. 1919, 5; MS, *My Fight*, 206, 357–58; Björkman, "Light Ahead," 10.)

126. To Juliet Barrett Rublee

Again ill, Sanger spent four weeks (from early November to early December 1919) resting at a retreat in the Dongan Hills section of Staten Island, New York. Her stay was paid for by Juliet Rublee. This letter was probably written during the week of November 17. (See MS to Rublee, Nov. 25, Nov. 30, and Dec. 1, 3, and 5, 1919. (MSM C1:368, 372, 374, 380, 394.)

Dongan Hills, S.I. [*N.Y.*]
[*November ?, 1919*]

Juliet dearest:

How perfectly dear of your mother!![1] Will you tell her how pleased & happy this is making me and I am really very greatful.

How did you come to get pink paper? When did you purchase it? I never used this color before but last week I saw this & liked the color. It is a color of health & vitality so it is said.

Here is what I do—first I sleep with all windows open top & bottom. I awaken usually from habit about 8:30 I spend that time in breathing from the Solar Plexus & filling the lungs with fresh air and concentrating on <u>power</u> while I do this breathing—I do this until breakfast comes which is about 9 oclock. The windows are closed and I have breakfast & read the paper—then I sink back again into a dreamy state—trying to reach the sub conscious & also trying to commune with my inner Self.

I talk to it—as to a personality I dream on this way for an hour perhaps then I get up if I am not sleepy & while the bath is running I open a window with the sunshine pouring in and I breathe again from the Solar Plexus holding the thought of the Sun as a Power & I as a power radiating love & warmth & joy & Power & wealth etc etc. This I do for fifteen minutes absolutely naked. Then I take my bath and it is then eleven often twelve oclock I go down on the veranda & read until luncheon. Then I eat soup—meat two or three vegetables desert—tea—at one oclock. I have gained five pounds since I came here. The afternoons vary. I usually go back & rest & meditate & breathe again—I want to develop the capacity of my lungs for I could see on Dr Hirsh's face that day a look that meant my lungs were O.K. but were not in a condition to resist in case trouble came.[2] I decided to breathe & expand them

& develop their capacity in this air—then the little book named "The Solar Plexus" just how to Wake it came into my hands & I decided this was for me.

It is written by Elizabeth Towne & published in Holyoke, Mass.[3]

So this helps me to breathe correctly and I feel a new sense in directing ones breath into Power etc. The afternoon means a walk & letter writing & sleeping again until time to dress for 7:30 dinner which is very late. I get into my room again by nine oclock & read until ten sometimes—breathe again after the lights are out & windows opened & again Concentrate. So you see dear lady all my time seems taken with the inner persons development.

Dinners are elaborate soup—fish—meat—three vegetables—salad—deserts & coffee fruit etc.

All very well combined which are better than they sound. I do not take milk because I know it would interfere with meals & I would rather eat at the table the things which are so nicely prepared as breakfast is light I send for a special bottle of cream <u>every other</u> day which is a luxury truly, but it makes the breakfast better coffee & cereal especially. I wish you could take those morning hours Juliet dear to sink or submerge yourself into the subconscious. I just learned the trick while out here—and it rests one so quickly—then when you do this & commune with your Inner Self—you get up all aglow & rosy. I never had this before. Its fascinating & you get so you like to be alone as if you found a new person whom you loved & who knew you perfectly.

I do not know the Long book Juliet it sounds splendid. Perhaps you will bring it with you when you come to town.

I am really childish with joy over having you say Mrs Churchill[4] liked the things— Isnt she dear to <u>know</u>. I really believe that little man has the best & purest creams & soaps in N.Y. He makes a special study of skins. Do let me send you some dear lady. He was so pleased when I sent them to Mrs Churchill he will be delighted again & have another thrill. He has an office or parlor at 11 East 41st St having moved from an upstairs shop a few months ago. If you are in town this winter & want scalp or facial treatments that is the only scientific place in New York. Ill send to him & ask to send you the soap cream and other things—then just watch us <u>bloom</u>!!! His name is Frey, Charles Frey and is a simple little lame man who adores his wife. She has a radiant complexion and is the expert on facial work but is not there at present—tired out.[5] The first thing to do is to heat a wash cloth ↑in↓ hot water—lay it gently over the face until it cools—then take a dab of the complexion soap & rub it all over the face & neck with the fingers or a soft brush is advised then wash it off with hot water & the cloth. Then rub the skin food into the pores—gently all over the face & neck until it is absorbed—as much as the skin will take—wash it off with hot wash cloth & cold water then a piece of ice rubbed over the face & neck when muscles are weak or wrinkles getting under way—wipe dry & that is all.

It sounds a lot to do but I do it every night or two when I have ice & you can avoid double chins & some wrinkles by this treatment—of course when it is done there at the shop—the vibrator does the work & the violet rays & manipulating the skin all stimulate it & keep it in a good condition the hands too need skin food.

This little man says half the cold cream has zinc in it & ruins the skin & the powders have lead & take the life out of it too— He makes all the things necessary for the care of skin & scalp.

How lovely it would be if we could send a message— Let us try it, either the morning before noon would suit me any hour—or at noon itself is a good time as many Societies use noon for concentration of thousands of their members—which charges the currents with vitality.[6]

Just to start off I'll send you a message each day at noon—Ill write it down each day & send them all to you at the end of a week—

I will also write down all thoughts I get in connection with you—as I am alone these days I can do it easily—

They may have no connection with what you recall—but Ill do it— I'm positive we could do it had we both the time— Do Juliet try that submerging effect turn your head into the pillow & sink all your thoughts & outer self down into your inside self—thats the only way I can explain it. Let me know if you get it. All will be black, but don't care—just like the blackness & even think about it joyously. Don't expect anything to happen yet—just get the enjoyment from the communion—later we must get more— All love to you darling girl— Isnt it joyous to have time!! devotedly

Margaret.

ALS JRP, MN-SSC (*MSM* C1:399–418).

1. It is not clear what Alice Brush Barrett's gift was.

2. She was probably referring to Isaac Seth Hirsch (1880–1942), a physician and director of Bellevue Hospital's X-ray department. MS may have undergone X-ray treatments to reduce her swollen neck glands. (*New York Times,* Mar. 25, 1942; MS to Rublee, July 16, 1919 [*MSM* C1:327].)

3. The eighteen-page pamphlet *Just How to Wake the Solar Plexus,* by Elizabeth Jones Towne (1865–1961), argued that deep breathing techniques could stave off illness and provide spiritual health. (W. J. Burke and Will D. Howe, *American Authors and Books, 1640 to the Present Day,* 3d ed. [New York, 1972].)

4. Mabel Hall Churchill (1874–1945), a Rublee neighbor in Cornish, was the wife of the American novelist Winston Churchill. (*WWW America*)

5. She was writing about the cosmetician Charles Frey and his wife, Ruth. (MS to Ruth Frey, Aug. 31, 1942 [*MSM* S21:528].)

6. MS and Rublee, who shared an interest in the parapsychological and spiritual

worlds, were at this time experimenting with thought transference. (MS to Rublee, Dec. 4, 1919 [*MSM* C1:376].)

127. To William Sanger

This letter was held among Margaret Sanger's papers with her handwritten note on the outer envelope reading, "Stuart or Grant give enclosed to William Sanger to be delivered after my death."

[*Staten Island, N.Y.*]
December first 1919.

Bill dear:

After I went to see your exhibition of Spanish paintings[1] I came over here for a brief rest—and have had time to review many things & acts which the busy activities of life in New York ever prevent. I wish I could tell you what emotions & memories surged through me when I went into those rooms where your paintings were. How they danced & swirled about me—how they hugged & carressed me each stroke of your brush seemed to stand out as a word to me which only you & I understand. I was thrilled and grieved—two emotions interwining themselves into every shade of color you used to express what you saw in Spain. I was thrilled because you had achieved what I knew when I used to sit beside you & watch you paint, you would achieve and I was grieved because I knew of the suffering you have endured in the achievement.

That I have had a part in the latter role I fully realize—that you have suffered because of me I know—but I know too that just as some have achieved a certain kind of success on the wings of love—that no great Soul has ever won ↑lasting↓ fame but ~~through the~~ upon the ladder of grief & pain. Tragic?—of course it is—and tragedy is expressed by you in nearly everything you do.

My life seems to have been in the hands of forces I could not control. My early days at the hospital seemed so hard & cruel at the time, but today I see how necessary they were for the accomplishment of the work I am doing today.

My marriage to you and our love and the coming of the children, the saving for a home—the building of the house—the seeking, shifting, changing, interesting life all today have meaning & full value to me in this cause of humanity to which my life is dedicated.

Often I have felt your lonliness & sorrow—often I would like to seek you & fling my arms about you & hold your aching head to my heart to tell you of my tenderness for you and my love—but—— Forces stronger than physical desire—stronger than personal love held me to my task to the work I have undertaken to do. But I want you to know this—for I have told it to many—that you are to me the lover of all the world— Your love for me beautified my life and made possible the outlook on love & passion & sex—which has given me the courage & strength to go forth to do.

For this I owe you much and though my love for you is big & broad & tender it is the same today as when first we decided to go the path of life together. It has never changed. Sometimes I think it was not to be that I should love too intensly.

This letter will be given to you only when I am out into the Great Beyond—when ever that is to be but I could not let life pass by without telling you that your great love has meant much to the world—and to womankind as well as to me. I miss you in the big decisions of my life and always regret that your nature is so intense that you could not accept my friendship & comradeship when it was out of my power to give you the love you desired—But it is well. Au-revoir dear one ever lovingly

Margaret

ALS MSP, MN-SSC (MSM S1:877–82). Additional handwritten notes by MS on the top of the envelope read, "letter 1919," "June 22/42," and "March 13 52."

1. William Sanger had returned to New York City from Spain and was living in a Greenwich Village studio. His paintings were exhibited at Touchstone Galleries in New York City in November. (For a review, see "Spanish Scenes," *New York Times,* Nov. 9, 1919.)

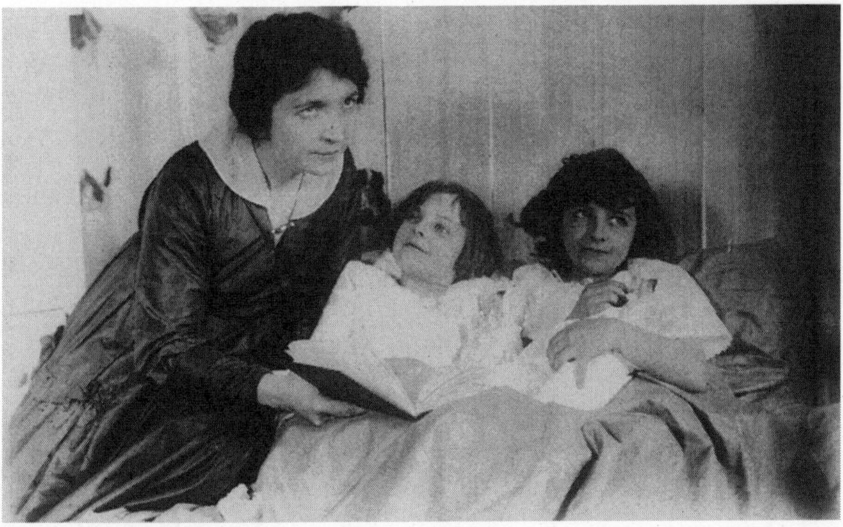

Still from *Birth Control,* the silent film written by and starring Margaret Sanger, 1917 (Library of Congress, Manuscripts Division [LCMS-38919-2]).

Margaret Sanger (*second from left*) with sisters Anna Higgins, Ethel Byrne, Mary Higgins, and their father, Michael, August 1919 at Truro, Massachusetts (Margaret Sanger Papers, Sophia Smith Collection, Smith College).

J. Noah H. Slee, ca. 1920s (Margaret Sanger Papers, Sophia Smith Collection, Smith College).

Margaret Sanger, 1922 (photograph by Underwood and Underwood, Margaret Sanger Papers, Sophia Smith Collection, Smith College).

BIRTH CONTROL REVIEW

Edited by Margaret Sanger

TWENTY CENTS A COPY NOVEMBER, 1923 TWO DOLLARS A YEAR

Official Organ of

THE AMERICAN BIRTH CONTROL LEAGUE, INC., 104 FIFTH AVENUE, NEW YORK CITY

Cover of the *Birth Control Review,* November 1923 (Margaret Sanger Papers, Sophia Smith Collection, Smith College).

Secretarial staff of the ABCL, ca. 1924–25. *Seated left to right:* Elizabeth Grew Bacon, Margaret Sanger, and Fanny Jacobs; *standing left to right:* Dixie Travis, Edith Husted, Bertha Potter Smith, Anna Lifshiz, Anne Kennedy, Rose Newman London, Kitty Marion, Hazel Ryland, Sara Levine, and Evelyn Burg (Library of Congress, LC-USZ62-105460).

Interior of the Clinical Research Bureau, ca. 1925. Standing behind the desk are Hannah Mayer Stone and James F. Cooper (Planned Parenthood of New York City).

Michael Higgins, flanked by Grant and Stuart, in Truro, 1925 (Margaret Sanger Papers, Sophia Smith Collection, Smith College).

Hugh de Selincourt, 1927 (photograph by Martin and Callnow, Margaret Sanger Papers, Sophia Smith Collection, Smith College).

Margaret Sanger ice skating in St. Moritz, 1927 (Margaret Sanger Papers, Sophia Smith Collection, Smith College).

Sanger and Slee in Potsdam, 1927 (Margaret Sanger Papers, Sophia Smith Collection, Smith College).

Marie Stopes, 1921 (Library of Congress, LC-USZ62-118338).

Mary Ware Dennett, ca. 1930 (Schlesinger Library, Radcliffe Institute, Harvard University).

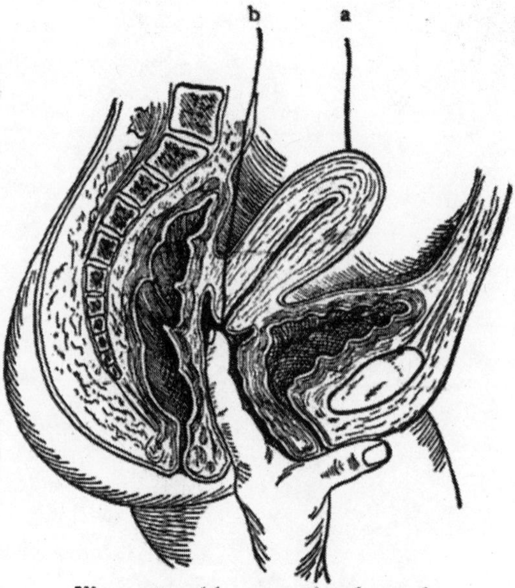

Illustration from *Family Limitation,* revised 10th edition (1920).

ABCL board of directors and Charles V. Drysdale at the Sixth International Neo-Malthusian and Birth Control Conference in New York City, March 23, 1925. *From left to right:* Annie Goodrich Porritt, May Billings, Katharine Beach Day, Charles Drysdale, Juliet Barrett Rublee, Margaret Sanger, Charlotte Delafield, Eleanor Dwight Jones, Anne Kennedy, Frances Ackermann, and Mabel Blagden (© Corbis/Bettmann).

SIX

Organization and Professionalization

As the decade of the 1920s began, Sanger continued to feel desperate about her health—the tubercular glands in her neck kept her febrile and fatigued. Yet in the months after her rest cure, Sanger threw herself into keeping the *BCR* going, with, in her words, "never sufficient finances to see a month ahead, with more meetings to attend than I could physically stand, with my own personal health and resources depleted."[1] Sanger felt besieged, exhausted, and alone. As she would often do in the years to come when she needed an escape, she retreated to Europe, traveling to England in the spring of 1920 to deliver a series of lectures and gauge postwar interest in birth control.

When she returned to England, Sanger, buoyed like many Americans abroad by the postwar ascendancy of the United States, was afforded new respect. Many in Britain had followed press accounts of Sanger's law-defying exploits in the cause of birth control, and this time she arrived in England not as a fugitive but as a figure of some prominence, sought after for her expertise, engaged for her notability, and given access to people of power and prestige.

Though no longer the alluring young exile whom Ellis affectionately called "rebel woman,"[2] as if she alone had manifested the sexual intensity of the American bohemians, Sanger still drew men to her side. In England, she enjoyed a sensual-sexual feast without the regret or self-consciousness that marred the free love experiments of prewar Greenwich Village. Mature, discreet, and reveling in pleasures of mind and body, Sanger began love affairs with H. G. Wells and Hugh de Selincourt, two writers of divergent talents who, like Sanger, shrugged off traditional domestic unions and made sexual expression and exploration a sacred part of life. She spent a number of days at de Selincourt's country estate, once owned by the poet Shelley's family, where Hugh; his wife, Janet; and her live-in lover, the critic and librettist Harold Child, invoked the hedonism of the Shelley circle. She had rendezvous with H. G. Wells, describing the renowned literary figure as a "naughty boy man."[3] And she spent time with Ellis in London, where she was also charmed and pursued by several other prominent men, including the writer and free speech attorney E. S. P. Haynes and the Asian expert J. O. P. Bland. Energized by the exuberance of postwar England, Sanger refused to let her poor health become the tether it had been the previous year. As she wrote to de Selincourt in June, "It's a nice world afterall."[4]

Sanger went to Europe again in 1921 to work on another book, secure a prominent keynote speaker for a major birth control conference, and attend the International Congress on Contraceptives in Holland. When her tuberculosis once more flared up, she sought medical treatments in London and the therapeutic air of the Swiss Alps. She also found time to regard the advances of a new suitor, J. Noah Slee ("Mr. S" in her letters), the wealthy South African–born founder and president of the Three-In-One Oil Company, who always managed to be in Sanger's vicinity since the two met in New York earlier that year.

She returned to New York in the fall of 1921 to finalize plans for the First American Birth Control Conference, held on November 10–12. The conference, which Sanger designed, inaugurated her more broad-based, accommodating approach to the movement, one that addressed the economic, biologic, genetic, and public health implications of birth control and offered new assessments of contraceptive techniques and methods. Sanger intended to focus public debate over birth control on its importance as a remedy for the major social ills of the world: war, crime, poverty, famine, and disease.

The chief aim of the conference was to launch the American Birth Control League (ABCL), a national organization with an ambitious agenda of legislative reform, education, and research. Though she generally found social reform organizations inhibiting and full of "rule-and-rote minds," Sanger needed a vehicle for pushing the movement into the mainstream, drawing in "the club women" to "use their power and money" to "obtain freedom and knowledge for the women of the poor."[5] While the ABCL's goals were broad, the league's enterprising spirit and overstuffed agenda contrasted favorably with the limited program set up by Mary Ware Dennett's Voluntary Parenthood League (VPL).[6]

The ABCL initially drew its officers and sponsors from the NYWPC board and the Committee of 100, women who were converted to the cause by the force of Sanger's personality. One observer described her staff as devoted hero-worshipers.[7] For clients, supporters, opponents, and the press, Sanger had become synonymous with birth control, and most of the league's day-to-day work revolved around her activities.

As the driving force of the ABCL, Sanger directed every facet of the birth control movement and remained its most visible leader. She was protective of this position, which she felt she had earned by having outwitted and outworked her opponents and through tremendous personal sacrifice and suffering—exile, imprisonment, the death of her daughter, and the condemnation of a conservative society. And she was quick to denounce other movement leaders who challenged her judgment or diminished her achievements. While many disagreements with Mary Ware Dennett or Marie Stopes were policy-driven, Sanger was charged with displaying an irrational distrust of rivals or potential rivals, even within the ABCL. As one of her more disgruntled coworkers later charged, Margaret Sanger "was number one, and there was no number two; she would let no one approach her that closely."[8] But Sanger's opponents often exhibited jealousy and outright vitriol; after watching Sanger speak, Dennett, for example, wrote of her, "She was a charming vision in a reddish gown—and she surely is a genuine spell-binder. But oh, her English, and her facts that aren't facts, and her logic that isn't logic, and her amazing faculty for being the whole 'moomunt'!"[9]

Many of Sanger's policy decisions centered on distinguishing the ABCL's legislative mission from that of the VPL. Dennett argued that birth control should be readily available to everyone and pushed for a "clean repeal" or "open bill" that would remove the words "prevention of conception" from all state and federal Comstock laws. Sanger, however, convinced that doctor-fitted diaphragms were the most effective method of contraception and concerned over the potentially dangerous methods promoted by medical quacks and a shady women's hygiene industry, countered with a "doctors-only" bill that did not challenge the entire ban on contraception but exempted physicians and nurses from the prohibition. She centered her legislative reform proposals on the need for medical supervision of contraceptive delivery. While this strategy represented a calculated reversal of her earlier free speech arguments, Sanger defended it as the only way to ensure that contraception would be both safe and reliable. But her decision to cast her lot with physicians was also based on her intuitive understanding that to persuade legislators to repeal the Comstock Act required the active support of the medical community—a perception Dennett lacked.

Sanger's educational and lobbying campaigns extended the ABCL's influence and succeeded in cultivating new support among not only middle- and upper-class women but also physicians, scientists, academics, and the rapidly growing ranks of eugenicists. Sanger crafted and broadcast her message specifically to appeal to these influential groups she believed were critical to her efforts to make birth control respectable. She needed activist women to organize state and local birth control leagues and clinics and to agitate for legal reform;

physicians to confirm that contraceptives were both medically sound and critical to women and children's health; and eugenicists to reinforce her economic and social rationale for contraception and to make birth control acceptable to conservative, old-stock Americans.

Sanger sought to capitalize on the popularity of eugenics by delineating its connection to birth control. Eugenicists, who assumed that all mental and physical traits were rooted in heredity, argued that scientific breeding could prevent physical and mental defects from being transmitted to future generations. They also claimed that the mentally deficient were more prone to procreate, resulting in entire nations and races that were biologically inferior. Some went further, seeking to limit the fertility of the poor, nonwhites, and recent immigrants who, they believed, were more likely to pass on such inferior character traits as shiftlessness, intemperance, sexual immorality, criminality, and mental retardation. By promising to resolve social problems and relieve society of the burden of supporting the poor, the insane, the criminal element, and the "feebleminded," eugenics attracted progressives and reactionaries, socialists and National Socialists, all convinced, at least for a time, of the importance of building a better society through scientific breeding.

For Sanger, eugenics was mostly diagnostic; birth control was remedial. She embraced many eugenic assumptions about the economic and social burdens imposed on society by the "unfit;" accepted the apparent science-based links between physical or mental health and character, supported the sterilization of the mentally diseased or deficient, and made public statements supporting immigration restriction (this, the most pragmatic and least ideological of her eugenics positions). Sanger did not accept economic or race-based assessments of those defined as "unfit" to reproduce, and in *Woman and the New Race,* she dismissed characterizations of recent immigrants as biologically "unfit," arguing that they came from "countries where the iron hand of economic and political tyrannies had crushed great populations into ignorance and want" and proclaiming that "the cell plasms of these peoples are freighted with the potentialities of the best in Old World civilization. They come from lands rich in the traditions of courage, of art, music, letters, science and philosophy. . . . The immigrant brings the possibilities of all these things to our shores. . . ." She also rejected all attempts to promote fertility among the "best stock." Sanger's focus remained on making birth control the foundation for the betterment of the entire human race.[10]

If Sanger failed to question or fully explore the science or social policy implications behind widely accepted eugenic theories, she was not alone—there were few vocal critics of the eugenics movement prior to the rise of Nazi Germany in the 1930s. Any reservations she had about the objectivity and biases of prominent eugenic scientists were muted by the approval of many eugenic premises by prominent writers, philosophers, scientists, and reformers, including the three Englishmen she so admired—Havelock Ellis, H. G. Wells, and George Bernard Shaw.

By the end of 1922, Sanger's increased prominence extended beyond Europe. Few reformers or social commentators held a postwar passport that rivaled Sanger's; in the four years following the armistice, Sanger visited throughout Europe, including Germany, and completed a world tour of Asia and the Middle East. Her international profile solidified her leadership of the U.S. movement and provided a platform for her postwar predictions of the social disorder and decay that would ensue in a world without access to birth control.

NOTES

1. MS, *My Fight,* 206.
2. See, for example, Havelock Ellis to MS, Dec. 26, 1914, herein.
3. MS Diary, July 26, 1920 (LCM 1:406).
4. MS to Hugh de Selincourt, June 26, 1920 (LCM 3:401).
5. MS, *Autobiography,* 300 (first quote); MS, *My Fight,* 191 (second quote).
6. ABCL Annual Meeting Minutes, Jan. 12, 1922 (*MSM* S61:46).
7. Vreeland, "Process of Reform," 147; Mary Knoblauch quoted in Hersey, "Margaret Sanger," 270.
8. Elizabeth Grew Bacon quoted in Gray, *Margaret Sanger,* 145–46.
9. Mary Ware Dennett, "Congressional Report," Dec. 16, 1920, 4 (*MWDPM* 12:501).
10. MS, *Woman and the New Race,* 32 (first quote), 36 (second quote); see also MS, *Pivot of Civilization,* 23–27.

128. To Juliet Barrett Rublee[1]

Sanger sailed for England on the SS Adriatic *on April 24, 1920, landing on May 5.*

Birmingham, [*England*]
May 18—[*1920*]

Juliet dearest:

I am here on a weeks visit to my brother who came over & married an English girl & remained here.[2]

The old cold I got on the boat has just begun to leave me & I have been quite ill with that deep painful cough & no Juliet to drive it away.

Someway I missed meeting Lord [*Queenborough*]. His secretary sent me a letter but I had left so it followed me here too late to let him know. Enclosed find his letter nice & cordial, rather.[3]

I'll meet him later I hope 'th'o he's quite unknown to the average person here. He is no doubt a person of influence.[4]

There are many calls for me to lecture everywhere. The Daily Sketch had an interview also Lloyds Weekly a very good one[5] & the News wants one when I return. The big meeting at Caxton Hall was ↑~~ful~~ [*composed*] of↓ the usual convinced persons.[6] I had been in bed all day & my voice (American anyway) was not up to its usual strength. Mrs How Martyn a councilwoman from Essex was in the chair,[7] many American women came to see the good points in the antis arguments. But Juliet darling I'm dying for a word from you. Havelock & I are planning picnics & glorious days together as soon as I get one or two off.[8]

I am asked to speak in Belfast, Ireland & Glasgow Scotland in July. I still want to go to Germany.[9] Havelock thinks I can do as well by writing, but I do not agree with him. I want to do some work at the Museum and I don't know how I am to do all I want to do to make this trip worth while & get back on time to get the boys off to school.[10] You don't know how good it is to feel so rich.[11] Things are quite as expensive here as in U.S.A. clothing [*shoe*] etc. [*not?*] rent, perhaps food a little less but very little difference. They gave me a very royal welcome at both meetings, but it is a most difficult situation here.

The Drysdales are very anti-labor people as is Marie Stopes. They ↑are the↓ only people who have touched upon the subject.[12] ~~That~~ This has placed a mark on the subject as anti labor—and I'll have a hard job getting the message where it belongs—in labor & working people circles. Of course were I to live here or to remain a year or two I'd go at it hard. The labor people are very nice to me & are asking me to speak, but I'll have to take sides quite definitely—they ask you to place your self on record as one or the other. Its quite a good thing too 'th'o awkward for visitors and also for some of us who are able. I want to get in touch with some mediums here or rather in London. Can you give me the names of one or two. Dearest girl I think of you constantly and love you dearly. Ever devotedly

Margaret

ALS JRP, NhD (*MSM* C1:454–61).

1. Rublee took over numerous duties in MS's absence, chairing NYWPC board of directors' meetings, interviewing prospective board members, and soliciting *BCR* articles. (NYWPC, Board of Directors, Minutes, Apr. 27–June 8, 1920 [*MSM* S62:719].)

2. She was referring to Richard Higgins and his wife, Mabel Pullen Higgins (1892–1956), who had a two-year-old daughter, Mabelle. (CA Death Index)

3. Almeric Hugh Paget, the first baron of Queenborough (1861–1949), was a wealthy businessman and former Conservative M.P. The secretary's letter was not found; for the enclosure, see Queenborough to MS, May 15, 1920 (*MSM* C1:450). (*New York Times*, Sept. 23, 1949.)

4. MS met with Lord Queenborough on May 28 to interest him in birth control. She found his "simplicity and ease . . . a treat. His manner is more like the American man I think. . . . I sent him some material on B.C. He asked me where my wedding ring was!!! And if I being an advocate of B.C. had any children." (MS to Rublee, May 29, 1920 [*MSM* C1:478].)

5. The *Daily Sketch* interview was not found. In the *Lloyd's Weekly* interview, MS contended that "the time is ripe to make birth control a national issue" and urged England's strong labor movement to adopt a birth control program. ("Women Enslaved by Maternity," *Lloyd's Sunday News,* May 16, 1920.)

6. MS lectured there on May 12 under the auspices of the Malthusian League. (MS Diary [LCM 1:395]; "Our Public Meeting for Mrs. Sanger," *Malthusian,* June 15, 1920, 42.)

7. Edith How-Martyn, who unsuccessfully ran for Parliament in 1918, was elected in February 1919 as the first woman member for the Middlesex County Council, serving three years. She arranged MS's Caxton Hall lecture. (*London Times,* June 7, Nov. 26, and Nov. 30, 1918, and Feb. 7, 1919; MS, "London Birth Control Meetings," 7.)

8. MS and Ellis had corresponded regularly since 1915, even after his increasing intimacy with Françoise Lafitte, but this was their first meeting in five years.

9. MS spoke in Glasgow in July but did not go to Belfast. Her interest in going to Germany was to investigate a new chemical contraceptive. (For a list of her Glasgow meetings and lectures, see 1920 Calendar, May 9–2 [LCM 1:403–4].)

10. This was a reference to the British Museum Library. The boys had probably spent the summer in Truro before returning to school. It is unclear how MS paid for their tuition, but her sister Anna Higgins may have contributed.

11. MS may have received an advance on *Woman and New Race* from Brentano's, which agreed to publish it that spring. But her money concerns soon returned, and she was worried enough to return to the United States in October, noting, "I have spent so much more than I ever dreamed things could cost." (MS to Rublee, Oct. 11, 1920 [*MSM* C1:575]; see also MS to Rublee, June 7, 1920, herein.)

12. In one 1920 editorial, Charles Drysdale called trade unions "enemies of society," accusing them of war profiteering and retarding postwar economic recovery. Stopes had, by this time, emerged as one of England's leading authorities on sex and birth control and similarly opposed socialism and trade unionism. (Charles Drysdale, "Trade Unions," *Malthusian,* May 15, 1920, 37–38; Hall, *Passionate Crusader,* 152; Marie Stopes, *Babies and Unrest* [New York, 1920].)

129. To Juliet Barrett Rublee

London. [*England*]
May 27—[*1920*]

Juliet darling—

Goodness but it is good to have a letter from you—[1] The one on the train was so full of news— Fancy your having snakes thrown about & people! I think the Russian a very wise seer perhaps—especially of the past.[2] Did you get in touch with Martins the food man. The day I was leaving I sent you a brief article of his,[3] hoping you would write him & get in touch with him if you cared to. I may go to Belfast and do send me the names of people there of interest to us. I am quite out of that line of thought here—[4] Everyone I know quite materialistic but idealistic nevertheless Juliet—for your private ear—& secret!!! at the Cambridge meeting the suggestion came that I start a clinic here in England[5]—they, who know conditions think M—S— not capable to deal in physiological questions—and fear her methods would fail & harm the movement.[6] They seemed to think my experience of great value & want me to remain long enough to do this. I wrote Marie Stopes of the suggestion telling her they started a fund of sixty pounds right off—and she wired me to come to see her & spend the day tomorrow.[7] I feel she does not like me to do it. It will be interesting.

The Caxton Hall meeting was fairly good—but I was ill in bed all day & could not lift the audiance—anyway Juliet the thought here is masculine—& difficult to raise. I don't know what success I'll have. I do know I'll be glad to see you—dearest girl—

Margaret

ALS JRP, NhD (*MSM* C1:474–77).

1. The letter was not found.
2. Rublee may have written to MS about a dream or occult activity.
3. The article was not found.
4. MS was referring to her interest in finding spiritualists. (See MS to Rublee, July 7, 1920, herein; and David Gow to MS, July 7, 1920 [*MSM* C1:518–19].)
5. MS spoke before a small group on May 21 at the home of the Malthusian League member Noel Porter, after which the attendees suggested she open a clinic in England and collected nearly three hundred dollars. (MS, "Clinics the Solution," *BCR*, July 1920, 6–8 [*MSM* S70:843].)
6. The reference was to Marie Stopes, who had generated criticism from many quarters, including the Malthusian League, for her egotism and lack of medical training. In addition, many opposed Stopes's promotion of small cervical caps rather than the larger occlusive pessaries. (Soloway, *Birth Control*, 223–24; Marie Stopes, *Wise Parenthood* [London, 1919], 29, 54–55.)
7. See MS to Marie Stopes, May 25, 1920. Stopes's telegram to MS was not found, but her letter to MS on May 26, 1920, also called for a meeting. (*MSM* C1:469 and 473.)

130. *To Juliet Barrett Rublee*

[*London, England*]
June 7 1920

Juliet darling:

Your dear letter of May 24th with card & clippings just came.[1] Thanks so much. I shall go to "Light" office[2] soon & get in touch with that circle if possible—

No dearest Lady Astor[3] did not come to the Caxton Hall meeting as far as I know—though many people of influence were there and no one knows just how they heard of the meeting. It is a most difficult matter to "break into" circles here because of the prudery & influence the Church people hold over all circles.

But the best work I am doing is lecturing nearly every day to the Women of the Co-Operative Guild.[4] These are the best & most advanced women of the working class. They are so splendid and are so anxious to have all knowledge to make the love they have a finer thing.

They go among the poorer & less advanced women in their districts and take the message there. Then last Saturday night I had a splendid meeting in a most godforsaken district where Socialists & trade unionists were present.[5] These men have not believed in B.C. here and it was a splendid opportunity to show them in fact what conditions have arisen from their own breeding. The women were splendid & fought them back. They want me to speak to the garment workers (women) and I am booked up day after day & sometimes night & day until July 15.[6]

Now dearest my cough is really better. I have moved out to the Garden Suburbs[7] where I am in the garden all day & have sunshine & air & good food. I am living with two charming women— I'm the only other person so Its nice & private. Do give me an idea just a hint why I must return in Sept. It seems everything conspires to keep me here. And yet I was told I could never undo the harm done were I not in U.S.A. to avoid the harm.[8] I wonder what it is. If it is personal—I should not care—but if it touches the movement then Ill fly back of course. Am so glad you went to see Mrs Moskowitz. She is the "Power behind the throne" but she is such a politician I doubt that she would be honest.[9]

I spoke to Marie Stopes about the names on this side— She is delighted. Putnams publish it here—but Robinson did not give her back the copyright—not for three years—the wretch!

I am arranging about a statement with good names & will send it to you to give it the right publicity. I told Putnams here about the idea & they said they would get in touch with you.[10]

No Marie Stopes will not return with me. She is not well—had a terrible time in ↑child↓ birth.[11]

I do not hear much of the affairs of the movement. Did that Federal bill get passed?[12]

You have no idea how I miss Portet. His spirit is everywhere—I have not missed him in U.S.A. so much. Am to see Wells—he wrote me such a nice letter.[13] I am to spend Sunday with Hugh de Selincourt a friend of H.E's. a writer read "Soldier of Life"[14] am to see Olive Schriener Wednesday[15]—and everyday the most interesting people.

I only saw M. Tracy once. I am quite certain H. E. is not in love with her.[16] He & I spend the day tomorrow at Kew.[17] He is very nice & younger than he was five years ago. I shall go to Paris later on when I shall get over lecturing. Its just as hard & busy as in New York.

I honestly wonder what I should have done had I attempted to live on my original two hundred dollars— It went in no time or rather I should be returning to U.S.A. if that had been my limit. Things are far more expensive than at first seems to be the case.

Well darling I will indeed write you every week. I know how hard it is to write letters in New York— All love & power to you ever lovliest of women. devotedly

Margaret

ALS JRP, NhD (*MSM* C1:486–96). Letterhead of the American Express Co.

1. The letter was not found.

2. *Light* was a weekly journal founded in 1881 and published by the London Spiritualist Alliance. (Janet Oppenheim, *Spiritualism and Psychic Research in England, 1850–1914* [Cambridge, 1985], 46.)

3. Nancy Langhorne Astor (1879–1964) was an American-born feminist and the first woman elected to Parliament (Conservative Party, Plymouth, 1919–44). Married to Waldorf Astor, a British peer, she was a controversial and outspoken figure devoted to the causes of women and children, temperance, and education. (*New York Times,* May 3, 1964; Leathard, *Fight for Family Planning,* 51.)

4. Founded by working-class housewives in 1883, the Women's Co-operative Guild, under the leadership of the socialist Margaret Llewelyn Davies, allied itself with the local Labour Party and trade unions; supported equal political rights for women, protective labor legislation, divorce law reform, and maternity benefits; and sponsored at least ten of MS's speeches on this trip. (Gillian Scott, *Feminism and the Politics of Working Women* [Bristol, Pa., 1998], 4–6, 21–22, 169–72; MS Diary [LCM 1:398–402].)

5. On June 22, MS spoke to more than a hundred men and women in the dockyards of Rotherhithe, London. (MS Diary [LCM 1:401]; MS, "London Birth Control Meetings," 7.)

6. According to her diary, MS saved June 26 for the "garment workers," though no information was found on the event. Before leaving London on July 3, she gave approximately thirty lectures for the Co-operative Guild, the feminist Emily Davidson Club, the Lyceum Club, the National Council of Public Morals, the Workers Educational Association, and the Infant Welfare Conference. (MS Diary [LCM 1:401].)

7. Hampstead Garden Suburb was a planned residential community, seven miles northwest of London, where MS had briefly lived during her 1915 exile. (See MS to Stopes, July 6 or 7, 1915, herein.)

8. This was probably a reference to the problems with Mary Ware Dennett, who was competing with MS's *BCR* circle for endorsements by women's clubs. Rublee may have wanted MS to return for the New York State Federation of Women's Clubs convention. (MS to Rublee, July 29, 1920 [*MSM* C1:528]; Chen, *Sex Side of Life,* 221.)

9. Belle Israels Moscowitz (1877–1933) was a social worker, political adviser, and a former Republican Progressive active in the campaigns of several leading New York State politicians. She switched to the Democratic Party in 1918 and became New York governor Alfred E. Smith's primary political adviser. (*NAW.*)

10. In 1920, G. P. Putnam's Sons took over the publication of Stopes's *Married Love,*

including its American distribution. William Robinson most likely retained U.S. publication rights until 1921. MS promoted both *Married Love* and *Woman and the New Race* by circulating statements in England and the United States. In December 1920, she had gathered signatures from such British dignitaries as H. G. Wells, Havelock Ellis, Dean W. R. Inge, W. Arbuthnot Lane, and Eden Phillpots. MS met with Stopes on May 29 and again in December. (MS Diary [LCM 1:397]; Rose, *Marie Stopes*, 135; for form letters and responses, see LCM 14:259–76.)

11. In July 1919, Stopes gave birth to a stillborn child and spent many months grieving and recuperating. (Hall, *Passionate Crusader*, 152.)

12. This was a reference to the VPL's efforts to get an "open bill" passed. In March 1920, Delaware's Senator H. Heisler Ball, a former physician, had agreed to introduce the federal bill but then reneged. As Dennett said, "The sponsor has been found, but also found wanting." (Quoted in Chen, *Sex Side of Life*, 226.)

13. H. G. Wells, who had signed the 1915 petition in support of MS's *Woman Rebel* case, met MS for the first time in London on June 9. They were quickly taken with one another, and, at his invitation, she met him again in his London flat the following day. The letter was not found. (MS Diary [LCM 1:399].)

14. Hugh de Selincourt (1878–1959), a novelist and drama and literary critic, was best known in England for his chronicles of village cricket matches. His novel *Soldier of Life* (1916) told the story of a crippled soldier who grappled with the conflict between life-affirming love and the destructive forces of war. De Selincourt met MS on June 11. (*London Times*, Jan. 22, 1951; de Selincourt to MS, June 2, 1920, and MS Diary [LCM 3:373 and 1:399].)

15. MS first met Schreiner, Ellis's friend and former lover, in London in 1915. Schreiner was an outspoken opponent of racism and colonialism and an ardent pacifist active in the Union for Democratic Control. She had married the lawyer Samuel Cronwright in 1894 and had a daughter. MS greatly admired Schreiner, later recalling, "Olive, in her commonly dark mood, was encouraged more by the work being done for women in birth control than by anything else. She herself, who had but one child, which had died, realized its significance." A few weeks after her June 9 meeting with MS, Schreiner returned to South Africa. (Ruth First and Ann Scott, *Olive Schreiner* [London, 1980], 298–320; MS, *Autobiography*, 138–40 [quote on 140]; MS Diary [LCM 1:399].)

16. It is unclear when MS met Marguerite Tracy, but she apparently did not like her, referring to Tracy, perhaps only partly in jest, as an "Impertinent huzzy!" (See Ellis to MS, Jan. 18, 1921 [LCM 4:633].)

17. On June 8, MS accompanied Ellis to the 300-acre Royal Botanic Gardens on the banks of the Thames. (MS Diary [LCM 1:395–439].)

131. To Hugh de Selincourt[1]

[*London, England*]
[*June 15, 1920*]

It was such a treat to be with you these lovely days[2] dear man and this is the very first morning, for weeks, that I have felt rested enough to want to get up when I was called.

Havelock thought I looked much better. I told on you too and asked him if he ever would say I "looked sixty" he replied politely as a proper gentleman should, that he would not even think of saying such a harsh thing. So— I hope he scolds you when he sees you.

He was delighted with the flowers and that I had such a happy time. He read some of Mr Childs poems[3] to me after I told him how nice a man he was to tell me I had beautiful hands!!! I liked the swing & run of the first two very much and wish your lovely Janet would put it or them to music. I don't mean the words, you know. If I were a painter I'd do it in colour such were the emotions it stirred in me. I hope to spend Thursday evening with your Lady and am looking forward to it.[4]

I missed the birds this morning and your own smiling eyes. I think yours is the house of childhood for I felt young & happy & did such a lot of talking about my children. When you come to London won't you let me know and let me have an hour or two with you while here.

Am reading the mss[5] and shall take it Thursday unless word comes before, directing a different delivery. I am happy & greatful to know you a thousand thanks & a kiss to Bridget.[6]

Margaret Sanger

ALS MSP, DLC (LCM 3:398–400). Return address: "52 Rotherwick Rd Garden Suburb, N.W.4."

1. De Selincourt, who was married to the pianist Janet Wheeler de Selincourt, became MS's lover shortly after they met and continued the affair through the 1920s whenever she was in England. He also became one of her closest confidants and most frequent correspondents.

2. MS spent the weekend of June 11–13 with the de Selincourts at Wantley, their country estate in Storrington, Sussex.

3. Harold Hannyngton Child (1869–1945) was a British writer, poet, drama critic for the *Observer* (1912–20), and coeditor and frequent contributor to the *Times Literary Supplement.* Though Child, a widower, was Janet de Selincourt's lover, the de Selincourts' open marriage enabled him to live at Wantley. (*DNB*)

4. MS and Janet de Selincourt spent the evening of June 17 together in London. (MS Diary [LCM 1:400].)

5. This was probably a draft of *One Little Boy,* de Selincourt's controversial book dealing with adolescent sexuality, including masturbation. (De Selincourt to MS, June 2, 1920 [LCM 3:373].)

6. Bridget de Selincourt (1912?–?) was the only child of Hugh and Janet de Selincourt.

132. *To Hugh de Selincourt*

[*London, England*]
Saturday [*June 26, 1920*]

Yes, I hope you will let me be your friend even the Irish part of me.[1] But oh Hugh de Selincourt you just must write a book on birth control. Yesterday there was a meeting. I was the speaker. Those in the audiance were Social Workers and ↑(or)↓ "uplifters."[2] I wanted to uplift them all with dynamite. You can do it— They are fiends really. They are in the road. They are barriers to truth. They hate beauty. They believe that the act of creation is loathsome & vile.

They said so. Two of them did. Many more said "here here". A woman Physician said right out in meeting. "To say there is elevation or a spiritual side of sex is purely an American idea". Again she said "That idea will never go in England".

She had not heard of our king my white Giant Havelock.[3]

But there she is. And she represents power and influence.

Wont you move all of those women out of these ideas? You can really do it. I dreamed you could.

And oh yes—I went to a luncheon—I was guest of honor (?) Dean Inge was there. And several other Tories. ↑Is that a "y" or an "i"?↓ My dear hostess had a hard time keeping my conversation in form.[4]

I wore a black bow tie an emblem of anarchy.[5] That must have caused the difficulty I had in getting any one to agree with any idea I ever heard of before.

It's a nice world afterall.

Your little boy story[6] is the most beautiful thing in world—no one else has done it so well.

I am off to Glasgow in a few days—Ireland too perhaps— All letters sent to American Express 6 Haymarket will always follow me. When am I to see Wantley again?

Margaret Sanger

ALS MSP, DLC (LCM 3:401–3).

1. This was probably a response to his last letter (not found). Their last meeting was on June 13.

2. No information was found on the lecture. (MS Diary [LCM 1:401].)

3. In one of his first letters to MS, de Selincourt called Ellis "a king among men." Thereafter, he and MS regularly referred to Ellis as the "King." (De Selincourt to MS, June 2 and 14 [quote], 1920 [LCM 3:373 and 374].)

4. This was a reference to a June 24 luncheon that included G. P. Putnam's editor Charles Huntington; the *Edinburgh Review* editor Harold Cox; and the Reverend William Ralph Inge (1860–1954), dean of St. Paul's Cathedral (1911–34), who was a conser-

vative on such issues as socialism and divorce but an ardent supporter of birth control. The hostess was not identified. (*DNB;* MS Diary [LCM 1:401].)

5. According to the historian Paul Avrich, the black tie was a well-known anarchist symbol, worn since the nineteenth century, but the effect it had on MS's audience is difficult to confirm.

6. She was referring to *One Little Boy.*

133. *To Juliet Barrett Rublee*

Glasgow. [*Scotland*]
July 7—[*1920*]

Juliet darling—

Oh I am busy & tired. Just one meeting after another.[1] Am waiting to hear from David Gow concerning Belfast.[2] I went to Light office but only a very silly girl was there who knew nothing— I wrote Mr Gow & am waiting to hear. I will go to Belfast Tuesday next if I hear before that time.

I will also get in touch with the medium when I return. There is much doing here along same lines only these people I am with are dead against it all. So you are in touch with Bryant![3] Am so glad. Lord Q.[4] does of course know Lady Astor but she is out of favor just now. I am to see him when I can he is waiting for me to tell him when it is convenient—but there is little he can really do just yet.

I have not met Lady A— As people are shy of her now. She told a member of Parliament "to be quiet" and that is an offense not to be forgiven. The women can not forgive her attitude on divorce— So no one wants me to meet her.[5]

Marie Stopes is quite sweet about the clinic only she wants to be the <u>first</u> to open one here.[6] Im dying to know more about the Belfast Clinic & group[7]—and if necessary will come back again later on to investigate.

I am to spend several days with Mr & Mrs Chance at their Seaside home—[8] He is a man of wealth in Birmingham—a well known County Council man— Is to retire & devote all his wealth & time on Birth Control. It is the only cause he believes in doing anything for—I met his wife & wonder if you or Mr Rublee[9] met her brother Mr Whyte who was sent to U.S.A. on the League of Nations. He lectured at Cambridge on "Seeing America thr'u European Eyes".[10] If Mr Chance will support the clinic for a year—so I can feel it is worth while I shall engage a nurse & a clerical worker—get rooms & supplies & start it as soon as I return from Holland & Germany if I go.[11] Then I also spend the week end of July 25th at H. G. Wells home[12] that should be very jolly. I do like him— Then E. S. P. Haynes is very charming to me <u>very!</u> a friend of H. G.'s.[13] Then darling Havelock wants me to go away for a quiet rest & visit with him. We thot of Ireland—but the strike etc makes that impossible—[14] Then Hugh de Selincourt is also charming & oh darling to me. Writes me nearly every day— So I have a lot of personal interests as you see—but I long for you— I wonder if man will ever interest me again! They did not know of the book The Road to the Stars[15] at Light office. Yes I am trying to get time to get up a proper Statement for Marie Stopes book. Mr Huntington[16] asked me to do that and I will as soon as I can get to it.

Meetings here overcrowded oh Juliet never was there such a cause— Poor pale faced wretched wives—men beat them they cringe before their blows but pick up the baby—dirty, & illkempt & return to serve him. "It's the biby I'm thinking of" She says to explain why she has to endure his blows—

I want to talk for a week to you. The cough comes & goes—when I'm tired it comes on—when rested it goes away— I am quite well otherwise dearest girl—really. More later. lovingly

Margaret

"Gallons of milk and a cow" kept me laughing a week—

ALS Lader (*MSM* C1:520–25).

1. MS began her Glasgow lecture series on Sunday, July 4, at a noon meeting on the Glasgow Green. "Nearly two thousand shipyard workers," she wrote, "in caps and baggy corduroys stood close together listening in utter, dead stillness without cough or whisper." That evening she spoke at a socialist hall and the following night at a meeting for women only. She gave nine lectures before she left Glasgow on July 13. (MS, *Autobiography,* 274 [quote]; MS Diary [LCM 1:403–4].)

2. MS had asked David Gow (1865–1939), a Scottish journalist, a poet, and the editor of the *Light,* to put her in touch with a lecturer at Queen's University in Belfast. (Leslie Shepard, ed., *Encyclopedia of Occultism and Parapsychology,* 3d ed. [Detroit, 1991], 682, 962–63; Gow to MS, July 7, 1920 [*MSM* C1:518].)

3. This was probably one of the spirit mediums from whom Rublee sometimes sought counsel. (See MS to Rublee, June 22, 1921 [*MSM* C1:711].)

4. She was referring to Lord Queenborough.

5. According to her biographer, Lady Astor's "respect for the rules of parliamentary debate was markedly absent." Calling herself a widow before marrying Waldorf Astor, she opposed a law making it easier to obtain a divorce in England. When it was revealed that her first marriage to Robert Shaw had ended in divorce, many in England viewed her as a liar and a hypocrite. (Sykes, *Nancy,* 212–18 [quote on 212].)

6. When MS talked of the invitation to open a clinic, Stopes immediately responded, "Mr. Roe and I have long been planning to found the first Birth Control Clinic in England as a memorial to our marriage" and were just looking for suitable quarters. After she and MS discussed the issue at Stopes's home, MS did not pursue further plans to open a British clinic. (MS to Stopes, May 25, and Stopes to MS, May 26, 1920 [quote] [*MSM* C1:469, 473, and 564]; Rublee to MS, May 27, 1920, herein.)

7. She might have been referring to those planning to open a gynecological clinic at

Royal Maternity Hospital. An informal clinic opened there in 1924. Marie Stopes opened the first actual clinic in Belfast in 1934. (Dickinson, "Contraception"; Mary G. Adams and Denise I. Fulton, "Family Planning: A Survey of Clinic Patients," *Ulster Medical Journal* 32 [June 1963]: 49–60.)

8. Clinton Franklin Chance (?–1953) was a wealthy investment consultant and a Malthusian League and Eugenics Society member, and Janet Whyte Chance (1885–1953) was a feminist and the founder of a sex education center for working-class women. The Chances, who lived in Dorset, offered funds for MS's birth control projects. (MS, *Autobiography,* 359; Clinton and Janet Chance to MS, July 19, 1920, and Nov. ?, 1922 [LCM 14:230 and 354]; Obituary, *Eugenics Review* 45 [Apr. 1953–Jan. 1954]: 174–76; Banks, *Biographical Dictionary of British Feminists,* 42–45; MS, "Clinton Chance," Sept. 1953 [*MSM* S72:859].)

9. Juliet's husband, George Rublee (1868–1957), Woodrow Wilson's legal adviser on economic and trade issues, lent his name to many birth control initiatives and helped his wife recruit many of his associates in Washington and New York City to the cause. (*New York Times,* Apr. 27, 1957; Harold Nicholson, *Dwight Morrow* [New York, 1935], 322, 337–38.)

10. G. Aird Whyte (1888–1967), a British Eugenics Society member, worked in the investment business with his brother-in-law Clinton Chance. MS had attended a lecture by Whyte entitled "Seeing America thru European Eyes" in Cambridge on May 21. (Obituary, *Eugenics Review* 59 [Sept. 1967]: 153–54; MS Diary [LCM 1:396].)

11. Traveling with her socialist friend Rose Witcop, MS left London for Holland on August 18 and moved on to Germany on August 22 to tour clinics and speak before socialist and communist groups. She returned to London on September 25. (MS, *Autobiography,* 280–90; MS Diary [LCM 1:409–14]; MS, "Women in Germany," *BCR,* Dec. 1920, 8–9 [*MSM* S70:846].)

12. MS stayed at Easton Glebe, Wells's estate in Dunmow, July 24–26. Wells was aware that she also spent time with Ellis and de Selincourt in those months, just as he continued his adulterous relationship with Rebecca West (with whom MS lunched on July 30). He dealt with the issues of romance, sexual desire, and jealousy in his novel *Secret Places of the Heart,* in which he portrayed MS (in the character of Miss Grammont) as a charming American woman "with a real firmness of character to back up her free and independent judgements." Sir Richmond Hardy, the protagonist, was attracted to her not just because of her sexuality but also because he "could talk with her as if he talked with a man like himself—but with a zest no man could give him." (Smith, *H. G. Wells,* 403–4; MS Diary [LCM 1:405 and 419]; for detailed description of her visit, see MS, *Autobiography,* 269; H. G. Wells, *Secret Places of the Heart* [New York, 1922], 181, 149.)

13. MS saw Haynes, who was also Wells's attorney, almost as frequently as she saw Ellis. (MS Diary [LCM 1:373–400]; Haynes to MS, Oct. 20, 1920 [*MSM* S1:983].)

14. Rail travel in Ireland was crippled because of a national strike that had begun in May and the ongoing military struggles between the British army and the Irish Republican army. (Lydon, *Making of Ireland,* 350; Oliver MacDonagh, *Ireland: The Union and the Aftermath* [London, 1977], 93–94.)

15. *The Road to the Stars and Other Essays* (London, 1919) was "by an officer of the Grand Fleet."

16. Charles Huntington, Stopes's editor. (Hall, *Passionate Crusader,* 161, 200.)

134. To Juliet Barrett Rublee

Sanger and Ellis vacationed in Ireland starting on August 4, stopping in Dublin, Glengariff, and Killarney. The couple returned to London on August 11. Sanger was probably feeling ill, for she later apologized for being "nervous impatient & horrid." Unhappy that she could not spend much time with him after their return, Ellis consoled himself with recalling the trip, "which will always be a delicious memory to me." (MS Diary [LCM 1:407]; MS quoted in Ellis to MS, Aug. 13, 1920 [LCM: 4:581]; Ellis to MS, Aug. 17, 1920 [LCM: 4:583]; Grosskurth, Havelock Ellis, *298; Chesler,* Woman of Valor, *182.)*

[*Killarney, Ireland*]
August 8. [*1920*]

Juliet dearest:

This is a most heavenly spot. Have you ever been here?

H & I have toured across the County Cork and now in Kerry not because we can afford it, but the railroads are in the hands of the military authorities and no one goes on them.[1]

Poor Ireland!

We stop here over the week end & then if I can find Scotas glen we will go to see my grave you remember that my quabal said I was Queen Scotia. Well there was such a person the daughter of Pharoa supposed to be long before history began.[2]

I am getting lonely to see you—& oh darling girl I went to a medium suggested by the Light people. She is young and I think if I see much of her she may teach me how.

She described Jessie Ashley so perfectly that it was surprising then she said a little girl is here—and Peggy came & talked—and Juliet without any questions from me. Peggy said—"Mother I could not talk to you on that trumpet my voice was not strong enough—but I did try to."[3]

Was that not surprising. Then she said "Uncle Tom is here". Then the medium said "did this man have a stroke—?" I said "I did not know he had passed over" and then acute pain took her back of the neck & she could not say more. But I do not know if my brother Tom is ill or not.[4] I am telling you this before I hear from home and it will be an interesting experience to see.

This is all for today. I wish you & I were going over these places. I see old women who look like witches & I know they could tell us lots we want to know.

So glad to know Kitty Marion is safe[5]—I was nearly ill over it. lovingly—ever

Margaret.

ALS JRP, MN-SSC (*MSM* C1:538–45). Letterhead of the International Hotel.

1. British troops took over the railroads, but Irish nationalists regularly attacked the trains throughout the summer of 1920. (Lydon, *Making of Ireland,* 350.)

2. Kabbalah or cabala is a form of mysticism that focuses on finding the secrets and mysteries contained in the Hebrew scriptures. Irish mythology holds that Queen Scotia or Scota invaded Ireland from Spain around 350 B.C., defeating the indigenous Tuatha De Dannan. Scotia, the supposed daughter of Pharaoh Nectanebus, died in the assault, and a marker (made at a later date) is located three miles south of Tralee, in County Kerry. (Seamus MacManus, *The Story of the Irish Race* [New York, 1974], 9–10.)

3. MS repeatedly tried to communicate with her deceased daughter through mediums and other psychic channels. (See "Horoscopes and Psychic Writings," n.d. [*MSM* S83:827].)

4. Thomas Higgins, who suffered from a heart condition, died in 1923. (Hersey, "Margaret Sanger," 30.)

5. After nine arrests for selling the *BCR* on street corners, Kitty Marion had vanished on July 14, leaving a suicide letter in which she accused the police of persecuting her. She was found in Monticello, New York, on July 27, living in a tent in the woods. (*New York Times,* July 26 and 28, 1920; MS to Rublee, July 29, 1920 [*MSM* C1:527].)

135. From H. G. Wells

Easton Glebe, Dunmow [*Essex, England*]
Saturday [*October 23?, 1920*]

Dear Margaret Sanger

I do want to see you extremely. Our little [*connection?*] was so jolly that I want to snatch just a little more before you sail.[1] But I'm tied here because I told Northcliffe I'd be at home here to lunch on Monday or Tuesday. [*It was*] rather urgent he should be put right about Russia.[2] But why not send a wire on Monday—may I come & stay night ↑coming anyhow by the |2.30 4.50 6.30| train.↓ I come down by the afternoon train & stay until you must go on Tuesday. DO. There are trains as [*motor cabs?*] from Liverpool Street. And I really want to see you I am rather inclined to bite thru chains because you are not coming to day. Please

H. G.

[*Written at top left*] Cut any Monday evening engagements. They can't be as important as me.

ALI MSP, DLC (LCM 11:91).

1. Wells, who had returned in mid-October from a month-long tour of Russia, had probably not seen MS since the weekend she spent at his estate in late July. It is not known whether he saw her before she sailed for the United States on October 27. (MS Diary [LCM 1:406 and 419].)

2. Alfred Charles William Harmsworth, Viscount Northcliffe (1865–1922), was a journalist and the publisher of the *Daily Mail* and the *London Times*, whose editorial comment on foreign affairs attracted wide attention. (*DNB*)

136. To Juliet Barrett Rublee

[*SSOlympic*]
Nov 2. 1920

Juliet darling:

Here I am nearly home again— Are you in New York I am wondering? If so Anna has told you that she received a cable from me that I am sailing.[1] I am longing to see you—simply dying for a sight of you! There will be so much to tell you & so much to hear—

I am terribly grieved over Mr Williams—[2] I cant tell you how I shall miss him— He meant so much to me and I leaned on him & depended upon his time & good nature & generosity far more than I realized. Im simply <u>sick</u> over his going! We may help him though, you & I, dearest, and I do know if any human being <u>can</u> come back to me in spirit—he <u>will</u>!

We land tomorrow morning & I shall fly off to see you if you are in New York & are free to see me—unless my boys[3] come to meet me of course then I will have to spend the day with them—but I'll call you up & it will be lovely to hear your voice anyway. Ever my love dearest of women—

Margaret.

<u>What</u> <u>is</u> your city number? heavens!

ALS JRP, NhD (*MSM* C1:591–93).

1. She was referring to Anna Lifshiz; the telegram was not found.
2. Billy Williams had contracted Bright's Disease or nephritis, which led to kidney failure. By late September, he had slipped into semiconsciousness and died in New York City on October 17. MS received a telegram notifying her of his death while in London. Ironically, John Reed, another of her old friends, died the same day. (Williams to MS, Sept. 4, Sept. 29–30, and Oct. 15, 1920, Mary Halton to MS, Sept. 30?, 1920, MS to Williams, Oct. 16, 1920, and St. Luke's Hospital to MS, Oct. 18, 1920 [*MSM* S1:927, 930, 949, 954, and 951–52].)
3. Stuart and Grant met her when her ship docked in New York City on November 3. (MS Diary [LCM 1:420].)

137. From Carrie Chapman Catt[1]

R.M.S. "IMPERATOR".
Nov. 24, 1920

My dear Mrs Sanger & Mrs Rublee:—

I have read both your letters and I have read the little book which Mrs Rublee sent from cover to cover.[2] It is well written, [*delicately?*] and clearly stated and I am glad to have read it.

I have not been unaware of Mrs. Sanger's heroic defence of her cause and [*all*] reformers recognize and respect the spirit which urges other reformers on. Nor am I unacquainted with the Neo-Malthusian movement in Europe where I know fairly well several of its most conspicuous advocates.[3] I am however not ready to give you my name as Mrs Rublee suggests.

Civilization is not produced by a single movement. It is rather a fabric woven of many threads, each of which is necessary to its perfection. I do not feel that I want to pull on every thread. What little time is left of my working life I must give to those causes which most strongly appeal to my especial trend. I liked especially Mrs Sanger's comparison of the bull fight.[4] It is a fact that apponents brainless, thinkless prejudiced, are waving flags in the face of every proposed change ~~the~~ ↑in↓ the great mass of flag waving, it is difficult for the average mind to see the ideals that are slowly pressing forward.

So my dear Mrs Sanger, please be assured that I am no apponent, even though I do not stand by your side.[5] The truth is I hold some contrary views, but these I do not bring forward to combat yours. I've had many a tilt with my dear friend Dr. Jacobs,[6] and neither of us makes a [*dent*] in the others views.

I may say however, that in my judgment you claim too much ~~for~~ ↑as↓ the result of one thing. Most reformers do that. Your reform is too narrow to appeal to me and too sordid. When the advocacy of contraceptives is combined with as strong a propaganda for continence, (not to prevent conception) but in the interest of common decency, it will find me a more willing sponsor. That is, a million years of male control over the sustenance of women has ↑made↓ them sex slaves, which has produced two results: an over sexualizing of women and an over sexualizing of men. No animal is so uncontrolled as is the mass of men. Now, merely to make indulgence safe doesn't do enough. This very briefly are my views. They won't intirest you but I want you to know why I cannot join your group. There will come some gains even from the program you advocate—and some increase in immorality through safety. The gains will slightly overtop the losses however, so I am no enemy of you and yours.

I shall hope someday to have the pleasure of meeting Mrs. Sanger whom I have not seen. Most Cordeally,

Carrie Chapman Catt

ALS MSP, DLC (LCM 8:20–24). Inkblot on the first page.

1. Carrie Chapman Catt (1859–1947) was the president of the National American Woman Suffrage Association (1915–20) and the founder and honorary president of the League of Women Voters. Catt worked for peace and international disarmament, founding the National Committee on the Cause and Cure of War. She was en route to London for a board meeting of the International Woman Suffrage Alliance. (*ANB;* Mary Gray Peck, *Carrie Chapman Catt: A Biography* [New York, 1944], 352.)

2. The letters were not found. In the fall of 1920, Rublee had sent copies of *Woman and the New Race* to a number of prominent individuals, along with a request for a sympathetic press statement. (MS to Rublee, Oct. 11, 1920 [*MSM* 1:575].)

3. Among Catt's friends were the Dutch physician Aletta Jacobs and the Drysdales, who had been involved in the woman suffrage movement for more than a decade. (Jacqueline Van Voris, *Carrie Chapman Catt: A Public Life* [New York, 1987], 85, 237*n*5; Benn, *Predicaments of Love,* 191–94.)

4. In chapter 7, "Will Birth Control Help the Cause of Labor?" MS described Spanish bull fights, claiming, "As bull after bull went down, his magnificent, defeated strength bleeding away through wounds inflicted by his weak but skillful assailant, I thought of the world of workers and their oppressors. . . . As each bull was sent into the arena, he was confronted by one assailant and twenty *confusers.* . . . No sooner was his real antagonist in danger, than one of the confusers fluttered a flag before his anger-maddened eyes. With one toss of his horns he could have ripped the life from the toreador, but his confusers were always there with the flags. . . . Finally, utterly bewildered and exhausted, too spiritless to meet the attack, he falls under the sword thrust of the toreador. . . . It is the drama of labor." (MS, *Woman and the New Race,* 148–49.)

5. Most nineteenth- and early-twentieth-century women's rights advocates and suffragists supported "voluntary motherhood," or periodic abstinence, rather than birth control, fearing that artificial contraception would inhibit women's power to refuse sexual relations with their husbands, promote extramarital sex, and weaken family bonds. Moreover, few suffragists or feminists would risk undermining their claims of moral superiority over men by associating themselves with discussions of sex or women's sexuality. (Gordon, *Woman's Body,* 95–110; McCann, *Birth Control Politics,* 26.)

6. Aletta Jacobs (1854–1929), a Dutch physician, feminist, and suffragist, ran the first free birth control clinic in Amsterdam (1882–93) and then retired from medical practice to concentrate on feminist and peace activities. In 1915, Jacobs had refused to see MS because she believed only physicians should dispense contraceptives. Jacobs and Catt met through their work with the International Woman Suffrage Alliance. (Aletta Jacobs, *Memories,* ed. Harriet Jacobs [New York, 1996], 124; Ledbetter, *Malthusian League,* 177–80.)

138. To Hugh de Selincourt

In the weeks following Sanger's return to New York in November 1920, she attended NYWPC meetings and delivered a series of lectures, including several in Harlem, on such topics as "Sex Problems of the Unmarried" and "Preparation for Parenthood." In December, she engaged in a well-publicized debate on birth control with the lawyer and Catholic convert John Winter Russell. At the start of 1921, her focus was on lobbying for a New York State birth control bill. (MS Diary [LCM 1:419–32]; "Mrs. Sanger's Lectures," BCR, *Feb. 1921, 16;* Debate on Birth Control, *Dec. 12, 1920 [*MSM *S76:923].)*

[*New York, N.Y.*]
February 24— [*1921*]

Your letter of Feb 10—[1] finds me in bed—a splendid place for me to be & next to lying on the lawn at Wantley I like it best.

I wrote you a few days ago Hugh in pencil I am sure.[2] Havelock allows me to do that. He also allows me to write all over the letter and likes it, even, So.

Now in answer—to No 5—"Soon" means right away.[3] Did you receive my letter asking you to write something on Olive Schreiner—[4]

Then here is a Standing order always—all my life—I want to make February (Havelocks birthday month) the best & most important month in the year— I wanted to devote all the Review to him, but was not free to do it. But next year & forever after you will—(won't you blessed,) send me the lovliest thing in the magazine of him— An appreciation or something.[5]

Mr Hersey wrote a bit to him & gave it to me on his birthday I print it in the March issue.[6] I will go ahead & get out your "vice" booklet.[7] I'll love doing it. What joy it will be Hugh to be back in England again. I think I won't leave it again for a long long time.

Your Realms of Day[8] I read—I think that was the first thing of yours I ever read. I remember how anxious that dear King[9] was for me to read everything of yours before I was to meet you. I must tell you of that sometime it was so like him & so loyal to you. What a boy you are—that I must have a warm summer evening or the fragrance of anything to read your book— No Hugh, you & what you think & feel are more to me than—well I just don't have to have a setting to follow your every thought, to love your horridst characters or to "get you" as the Americans say when they mean enter into the spirit with you.

I know your book will go.[10] The magic wand hovers near you now. Did not Harold "come back like the Spring" to you and is he not there now with you?[11] oh, I want to be there too. I am having queer times these days— I feel like Jean Valjean[12]—thats queer is it not. But oh Hugh dear, we in this new land have so much to learn. Here where one gives up home, a loving husband, children, reputation, friends, love money all the things most people live for, to work for an ideal, For this you ~~do~~ get insolent toleration. Your name is whispered and the ideal for which you work is mentioned in tones lower still. Yet on top of this conduct comes ministers of the Governments of Japan, & Mexico, telling you that your ideal & your message is changing the thought of the people of these countries more surely than Darwin changed the thoughts of the centuries.[13]

[*I*] am invited to go to Mexico. I am requested to write a series of articles of ten thousand words for a magazine in Tokio Japan[14] with the possibility of an invitation with expenses paid of course to go there to help those interested to learn more of the subject that it this ideal, may be put into realization. So there you are—Hugh. How can one tell the road to go? We are pushing a bill in the Legislature and oh the ↑number of↓ stupid minds ruling this country is unbelievable.[15] All these ideas Japan Mexico etc sound as if England will be far away. But these are only in the air—while England is in my heart. And heart things always win with me. I loved ~~hea~~ reading about the little Austrian girl & Bridget—

And I love very much reading about the big tall laughing eyed boy. All that you do interests me. All that you feel & say I like. But please don't like that horrid fat looking picture of me in the Review.[16] I never looked like that <u>honestly</u> I didn't—

Love to all of you—bunches of it to Hugh and then some. Good night dear

Margaret.

ALS MSP, DLC (LCM 3:770–77).

1. De Selincourt to MS, Feb. 10, 1921 (*MSM* S1:985).
2. MS to de Selincourt, Feb. 16, 1921 (LCM 3:425).
3. "No 5" refers to de Selincourt's February 10 question, "Thank you for the promised delight of doing more work for you. (What does '<u>soon</u>' mean in America?)"
4. De Selincourt claimed he never received MS's February 16 letter in which she asked him for a memorial to Olive Schreiner, who died on December 11, 1920. (See de Selincourt to MS, Mar. 7, 1921 [LCM 3:369]; *New York Times,* Dec. 13, 1920; for de Selincourt's article, see "Visions of Olive Schreiner," *BCR,* Feb. 1921, 8.)
5. In 1919 and then again from 1922 to 1929, MS printed birthday tributes and articles on Ellis each February in the *BCR.*
6. See Hersey, "Vision."
7. De Selincourt's manuscript, "Knowledge Leads to Vice: A Study of the Comstock Attitude Being Variations on a Moral Theme," was apparently never published. (MS Unfilmed.)
8. His 1915 novel, *Realms of Day,* dealt with commitment, jealousy, and the convention of marriage, featuring a free-spirited, freethinking older woman who passes her wisdom and ideals on to her grandson.
9. She was referring to Havelock Ellis.
10. This was probably the book de Selincourt described as "an old man's life and letters of a woman he adored," published as *Evening Light* (1936). (De Selincourt to MS, Feb. 10, 1921 [*MSM* S1:985].)
11. This was a reference to Harold Child, who was still at Wantley with the de Selincourts, and the poem Harold Hersey wrote for her. (See MS Diary Entry, Apr. 27, 1919.)
12. Jean Valjean was the fugitive hero of Victor Hugo's novel *Les Misérables* (1862), who was unjustly sentenced to penal servitude and, after years of suffering, tried to build a new life.

13. After a Japanese journalist published a 1920 interview with her, MS's ideas quickly spread in Japan. No letters from Mexican or Japanese government officials were found. (MS, *Autobiography,* 296; Ishimoto, *Facing Two Ways,* 183, 231.)

14. *Kaizo* (Reconstruction), a liberal Tokyo magazine, published several of her articles by the end of 1921. In addition, she evidently wrote an introduction to a Havelock Ellis article, also published in *Kaizo.* (For her *Kaizo* articles, see "Birth Control—Past, Present and Future," June 1921, 140, reprinted in three parts in the *BCR,* June 1921, 5–6, 11–13, July 1921, 5–6, 15, and Aug. 1921, 19–20, and "Woman's Power and Birth Control," Apr. 1922, 15 [*MSM* S70:901, 908, and 950, C16:161]; MS, *My Fight,* 238; Ellis to MS, Oct. 28 and Dec. 2, 1921 [LCM 4:689 and 703].)

15. Samuel McCune Lindsay (1869–1960), a Columbia University sociology professor and child labor reformer, had drafted a birth control bill to amend Article 106, Section 1145, of the New York State Penal Code by allowing physicians and registered nurses to supply birth control information for the cure and prevention of disease. In January 1921, MS had begun seeking a sponsor for the "Lindsay bill." (*NatCAB;* MS, "How Shall We Change This Law," *BCR,* July 1919, 8–9; "Outline of Legislative Work at Albany.")

16. This was probably a reference to a photo taken for a *Woman and the New Race* advertisement. (See *BCR,* Nov. 1920, 2.)

139. *To Mary Ware Dennett*[1]

In 1918, Mary Ware Dennett, a founding member of the NYWPC, irritated Sanger by trying to use the BCR *to publicize her own birth control work. In 1919, Dennett left the NBCL and essentially re-formed it into the Voluntary Parenthood League (VPL). As executive director, Dennett aimed to pass a federal "open bill" to remove contraception from the Comstock law. In 1921, as Sanger focused her efforts on lobbying for the Lindsay bill, Dennett, angered by Sanger's encroachment into legislative reform, attacked her for being too radical. After Sanger called for a five-year moratorium on childbirth for all women, Dennett resigned from the NYWPC, claiming her legislative work would be "seriously menaced by injecting into the situation a militantly feminist policy." In a March 1921 editorial in the* BCR, *Sanger criticized the "clean repeal" approach, noting, for example, that to "offer a pamphlet to a woman who cannot read or is too tired or weary to understand its directions, is like offering a printed bill-of-fare to a starving man." The editorial prompted Dennett to dispute Sanger's claims in a letter to the BCR editorial board. What follows is Sanger's rejoinder. (VPL Annual Report, May 1, 1921–May 1, 1992, and Dennett to NYWPC, Jan. 20, 1920 [*MWDPM, *12:953, 14:331]; MS, "A Birth Strike to Avert World Famine,"* BCR, *Jan. 1920, 3; Dennett to the* BCR *Board, Mar. 12, 1921 [*MSM *C1:631]; MS, "Editorial," Mar. 1921, 3–4.)*

[*New York, N.Y.*]
March 19, 1921

Dear Mrs. Dennett,—

In reply to your communication of the 12th inst. addressed to the editor of the Birth Control Review, I beg to call your attention to a certain misunderstanding on your part of the editorial in the Review, due no doubt to my lack of lucidity in expressing our aims.[2]

The intention was not to start a controversy concerning the relative merits of the state or federal legislative agitation, but was rather to explain, for our active workers, the intention of the various phases of our work, and to show why each person and each group must be left to decide the next best immediate step.

To publish your communication in its present form would be the inauguration of a controversy concerning tactics and methods which, it seems to me, could hardly interest our readers, upon whom it is always the aim of the editors of the Birth Control Review to impress the larger aspects of Birth Control as an immediate world-problem.

I write thus because our next number is already in the press. If you desire to clarify your stand we would publish in our May issue a letter covering two points, one which especially interests me; you say: "But in the thirty states by the passage of the federal measure the legal status of contraceptive knowledge will automatically be changed." This is a very important point, and one upon which we have had the best legal advice obtainable. If you, however, have legal opinion which bears out your statement, I will be delighted to publish such statement over the signature of such legal authority any time it is presented to me.

I also wish to call your attention to a statement which you make in reference to the proposed New York State Bill—the Lindsay draft, (a copy of which I enclose), in which you say that this bill "provides no advance over the statute of 1881 except to empower nurses as well as doctors to give information to prevent or cure disease." If you will read the proposed New York State Bill, which we are pushing in this session of the Legislature, you will note that this does not mention the word disease.[3] I simply call this to your attention, for no doubt, you have overlooked the wording of the new draft. Sincerely yours,

Margaret Sanger [*signed*]

TLS MWDP, MH-S (*MSM* C1:649–50). Letterhead of the *BCR*.

1. A divorced mother of two, Dennett needed a salary, and many of her difficulties with the NBCL stemmed from the organization's inability to raise sufficient funds to pay her. When her New York State legislative campaign failed, the NBCL cut back her work and relied more on volunteers. With her salary in arrears for two months, Dennett resigned. When she founded the VPL in 1919, she took most of the NBCL's members with her, and the older league collapsed shortly thereafter. (Chen, *Sex Side of Life*, 212; Marie Stopes to Dennett, Aug. 22, 1921, *MWDPM* 14:489–90.)

2. In her editorial, MS outlined three great tasks confronting the birth control movement: agitation and education; political and legislative action; and practical scientific teaching.

3. The 1921 draft of Lindsay's bill, revised in consultation with Brooklyn's Represen-

tative Walter F. Clayton, read, "An article or instrument used or applied by physicians lawfully practicing, or by their direction or prescription, for the cure [*or*] prevention of disease, is not an article of indecent or immoral nature or use, within this article. The supplying of such articles to such physicians or by their direction or prescription is not an offense under this article. The giving by a physician licensed to practice, to any person applying to him or her, of any article or medicine for the prevention of conception, is not a violation of any provision of this article." Neither the 1919 nor the 1921 revision omitted the phrase "for the cure or prevention of disease," though subsequent drafts left out the original exemption for registered nurses. Despite Clayton's work on the draft, he refused to sponsor it, fearing it would, in his words, "do me an injury that I could not overcome for some time," and the ABCL soon dropped its legislative efforts. MS concluded that "it will be many years to come before this sort of legislative work will be pushed through and in the meantime, agitation and publicity and education is the big part that we should play." (Quoted in "Outline of Legislative Work in Albany," 11 [first quote]; for the enclosed Lindsay bill, see *MWDPM* 19:595; MS to Ida Trachtenberg, Mar. 18, 1921 [second quote] [*MSM* 1:648].)

140. From Client

Thousands of women continued to ask Sanger for help, finding her through her publications, doctors, or sympathetic friends. She claimed to have received hundreds of such letters a week at times—71,841, for instance, in 1923 alone. Though most were destroyed, several hundred have been preserved, many of them edited for publication in the BCR, *or in Sanger's 1928 compilation of letters,* Motherhood in Bondage. *The following letter was edited and prepared but not published. (ABCL, Reports, 1923 [*MSM, *61:172].)*

Tindall, Idaho.
May 31 1921

My dear friend:

How I wish I could help the cause in a financial way but I can not at present.

But how I have thanked you a million times in my thoughts when ever I think how you have brought to my knowledge some thing that will help me.

We live 100 miles from the rail road but my mother obtained "Family Limitation" and sent it to me.

My husband is afraid however that I will use some thing which will injure me but I tell him I'd rather be dead than have a wee-one (no matter how I love them) every year.

Then this last one a seven month baby came when I was all alone with just my other babies. So when I think what I went thro that terrible night I feel that I can never have another.

We have been married six years this June and I really havent had breathing spells between "Lambings" as we call it out west. But oh! how I love them when once I get them in my arms but I am so tired out I can hardly appreciate them.

Hoping you the greatest success and wishing that it was in my power to help more I am yours sincerely

[*Name omitted*]

ALS MSP, MN-SSC (*MSM* S1:1007–8). In the interest of privacy, the editors have omitted the author's name.

141. *To Juliet Barrett Rublee*[1]

Sanger returned to England in May 1921 to seek a prominent British speaker to headline the First American Birth Control Conference and to consult with British physicians about her deteriorating health. The trip also promised undisturbed time to write, regain her strength, revisit her playful romance with Hugh de Selincourt, and, as always, spend time with Havelock Ellis. Sanger remained in England through the middle of July before traveling to Paris and Switzerland.

[*Plymouth, England*]
June 12—[*1921*]

Juliet dearest.

It seems ages since I have had a word from you, but I keep your dear letter to reread so I feel close to you in spite of silence.[2] I am here for the week end, it was so cold in London & the Doctor wanted me to get into the sunshine.[3] But it is just as cold down here. I return tonight or tomorrow to work on the revised edition of my book, which is to be ready for publication [*illegible*] in July.[4] This holds me to work but it must be done.

I am anxious that the book be brought out in England. Marie Stopes has sold over a quarter of a million of hers. She has the clinic going nicely, but oh she is killing herself with her ego. Her husband presented her with a house for her clinic so she is safe from the Police & landlords objection forever more.[5] I have not seen her personally, though I did attend her very fine meeting at Queens Hall.[6] I paid for a ticket in the gallery & went alone. I got out of bed to do it & knew I could get back into bed again providing no one knew I was about. Then it was a nice rest to attend a meeting & judge as one of the audiance. Not to be called upon to speak was a treat. It was the finest & biggest & most respectably represented meeting ever held in England on this subject.

All lectures & meetings for me have been cancelled. The X Ray Specialist will not treat me if I do one meeting before two months.[7] There was one set for July 4th at Caxton Hall but I had to give it up too.

From the letters I get it seems that all goes well at the office. H. H. was not expected to return before June 15th. Poor darling but he is young & vital & conceited loves H. H. better than anyone in the world.[8] That helps. I spent last week end at Wantley, Hugh is such a darling—another one full of self satisfaction though. I like Harold Child very much.[9]

Ellis wants to go away to the seaside—he has been so ill.[10] I doubt he has fully recovered. I may spend next week end near him— But all these adorable friends take ones time away from my work. I will never get the book revised if I accept all the invitations pouring in to me.

I am going to settle down hard to work at it tomorrow. So I will not write to anyone for a few weeks.

Ellis & I went to see the Russian Ballet.[11] Wonderful! Spanish dancing marvellous. Are you better dearest?[12] Interesting about Wiggs. Did you find Bryant? Month of May————? How can one tell what is good for one.

Much to tell you about Wantley. Ever devotedly & lovingly dearest of dears.

Margaret.

ALS Lader (*MSM* C1:695–700).

1. Rublee, president of the NYWPC board of directors, again took charge of the *BCR* in MS's absence. She continued to lobby for the Lindsay bill and began work on *Appeals from American Mothers,* a booklet of "mothers" letters published by the NYWPC in 1921. (MS to Ida Trachtenberg, Mar. 18, 1921, and MS to Rublee, June 17 and July 14, 1921 [*MSM* C1:648, 708, and 730].)

2. The letter was not found; no 1921 Rublee to MS letters were found, probably because, as MS promised, "I destroy all your darling letters. It's always best to do so." (MS to Rublee, Aug. 27, 1921 [*MSM* C1:810].)

3. MS spent June 12–13 with her old socialist friend Stella Browne in the seaport city of Plymouth, where they met some friends arriving from the United States. (MS to Eleanor Beach, June 12, 1921 [*MSM* C1:690].)

4. The London firm of Jonathan Cape published the British edition of *Woman and the New Race* in 1922 under the title *The New Motherhood,* with an introduction by Harold Cox added to the original one by Ellis. It omitted chapter 3 of the American version, "The Material of the New Race," which dealt with the negative consequences of immigration, and included two new chapters, "Wasting Our Human Resources" and "The Tragedy of the Accidental Child." (MS to Rublee, July 29, 1920 [*MSM* C1:529]; for a copy of the British contract, see "Memorandum of Agreement," June 17, 1921 [LCM 14:282].)

5. The reference was to Stopes's *Married Love.* On March 17, 1921, Stopes had opened the Mothers' Clinic in London, operated by a nurse-midwife. Stopes hoped that as the first birth control clinic in England to legally distribute contraceptive information, it would demonstrate the positive effects of birth control and pressure the government to

expand its public health service to include contraception. However, many believed the success rates she claimed for the clinic were exaggerated. Stopes's egotism was remarked on by many. Ellis wrote that "there is something quite childlike, simple, ingenious, about her even in her self-conceit." (Soloway, *Birth Control,* 215; Ellis to de Selincourt, Apr. 21, 1921 [LCM 5:714].)

6. On May 31, 1921, two thousand had gathered to hear Stopes and other prominent British birth control advocates. Within three months, Stopes founded the Society for Constructive Birth Control and Racial Progress, which soon rivaled the Malthusian League. (Soloway, *Birth Control,* 214–16; Hall, *Passionate Crusader,* 192.)

7. MS had started X-ray treatments in London in early June on her tubercular right tonsil with a Dr. Knox, who advised her to go to the Alps for at least a month and then undergo a tonsillectomy. (MS to Rublee, May 24 and June 4, 1921 [*MSM* C1:676 and 680]; Lader, *Margaret Sanger Story,* 168.)

8. Harold Hersey, who was appointed an associate editor of the *BCR,* had sailed from London for the United States on June 4.

9. MS saw Child at de Selincourt's home on June 4–8. (MS to Rublee, June 4, 1921 [*MSM* C1:680].)

10. Ellis had had a serious ulcer attack in March 1920 while visiting his sisters at Tunbridge Wells. (Grosskurth, *Havelock Ellis,* 298–301.)

11. *The Cuadro Flamenco* was performed by Serge Diaghilev's Ballets Russes at the Princes Theatre in London. (*London Times,* June 1, 1921.)

12. Rublee, who battled sleeplessness and exhaustion throughout her life, had experienced some personal financial losses, leading to bouts of depression. (MS to Rublee, May 24, 1921 [*MSM* C1:676].)

142. To Juliet Barrett Rublee

British Museum [*London, England*]
[*June 22, 1921*]

Darling Juliet:

How glad I am to get your letter of June 5 in which you say you at last received a word from me.[1]

How thrilling to have you closely in touch with those marvelous psychics. I wish I had some time to give to the study. I feel certain we could advance tremendously through it all.

But I seem doomed to continue this work— Every day the problem grows keener & the necessity for us with vision & love of the cause to continue.

I had a very nice letter from Mr S— who is at the Hague.[2] He says the hotel he is in is costing more than his income & expects to go back to Paris where he joins friends. (a widow)

He asks if I am to be in Paris and if not he will fly over to London to spend the day. That is the fashion now to fly over & back in a day.

I went to Margate for the week end with Havelock but he is so devitalized that his company at a long stretch is not good for me.[3] So I came back earlier than I had expected. There are few people whose vitality is not waning. They all want to be with women who stimulate & give them pep & energy.

Don't you worry your blessed dear head a minute about me & Mr S— darling girl— He has not money enough to pay the price— He could not inspire me to love— So as I wrote you before—it would be for love or money enough to put the b.c. movement on the map. He has not the means to do either. But besides that and all joking aside dearest, I am <u>not</u> inclined to marriage. Freedom is too lovely & I want to enjoy it for a time. I spend next week end with Mrs Chance—yes they are helping me again.[4] They are very lovely friends & have plenty & like to feel they are helping me to get well—which they are— I am working on my book and will try to get away into the mountains of Switzerland in July or August.[5] Dr & Mrs Drysdale[6] are going to Switzerland too. Then Havelock & Marguerite Tracy, Francoise & I are to meet at Paris & spend a week together at Marguerite's home. These plans all if I am finished with the book & am well.[7]

I went to Plymouth with Stella Browne for a week end— She goes down there for two weeks & I may join her for a few days next week.

All the love in the world dear. Glad you like little sister Nan.[8] She is dear & dainty.

Thinking of you constantly as if we were bound together by bonds of love eoens & centuries strong. devotedly

Margaret

ALS Lader (*MSM* C1:711–14).

1. The letter was not found.

2. J. Noah H. Slee (1860–1943) was a South African–born businessman who immigrated to the United States in 1873 and founded the Three-In-One Oil Company in 1894. Slee, separated from Mary Roosevelt West, probably first met MS at a party given by Rublee in New York City in the spring of 1921. Immediately smitten, he began to court her tirelessly. He was at the time vacationing in Europe with friends. The letter was not found. (*New York Times*, June 23, 1943; Chesler, *Woman of Valor*, 243.)

3. MS visited Ellis, recuperating from his ulcer attack in the seaside town of Margate at the home of his friend and former lover Mneme Smith Kirkland and her husband, on June 18–19. (Grosskurth, *Havelock Ellis*, 301.)

4. Janet and Clinton Chance donated funds for her personal expenses, as well as organizational costs.

5. This was probably a reference to *The New Motherhood*, though she was also drafting *The Pivot of Civilization*.

6. She was referring to Charles Vickery Drysdale, who had assumed the presidency of the Malthusian League from his mother, Alice Vickery, on February 21, 1921, and Bessie Drysdale. (Benn, *Predicaments of Love*, 209.)

7. MS had met Ellis's lover Françoise Lafitte in London in 1920. MS's health prevented her from joining the group in Paris for this trip. (Grosskurth, *Havelock Ellis,* 302–3; Brome, *Havelock Ellis,* 198–199.)

8. This was a reference to her sister Anna Higgins.

143. *To Juliet Barrett Rublee*

Sanger left London for a Swiss Alps rest cure in mid-July. She spent a brief time in Paris, reached Chamonix on July 14, and then moved on to Zermatt.

[*Zermatt, Switzerland*]
July 20 [*1921*]

Juliet darling:

It is simply wonderful here—alt 5000 ft. I expect to go up even higher & remain until the middle of August. Then I'll get back to London & undergo the operation (I wrote you about the decision of the gland specialist.)[1] This must be done early if I am to speak or do any work at the conference.

It is a trouble to go thru, but perhaps it will end my gland troubles for ever. Yes I understand M. W. D. is trying in every way to short stop the effect of our conference. I am quite decided that I have been too Christian like with her—I have continued giving & advertising her work while she does not reccomend either my book or the Review. I have decided to ignore absolutely her or her meetings in the future.[2] I wrote you about Stopes— Surely you will be building a very bad & sentimental foundation to help her get a foot hold with M. W. D. in America.[3] I have cabled Mrs Kennedy today to ignore the meeting as far as the Review is concerned.[4]

I have talked to many people in England they are afraid to associate with Stopes. Best people advise against boosting her— Say she is brainless as far as real thinking goes—& wins favor only thru sentimental unscientific material. People who stood by with Married Love say Radient Motherhood neutralizes etc etc etc.[5] At any rate I have decided that the Review & the movement that has been built up by work & effort is not going to be used for the personal vanity or utility of either D or S—[6] This is very important to understand Juliet. You will see it when I can speak more freely. All now—wish I were with you dearest one—ever devotedly

Margaret

ALS JRP, MN-SSC (*MSM* C1:745–47). Letterhead of the Hotel Victoria et D'Angleterre.

1. See MS to Rublee, May 24 and June 4, 1921 (*MSM* C1:676 and 680).

2. The reference was to Dennett, who opposed MS's plans to form a national orga-

nization that would compete with the VPL. (See Dennett to MS, July 29, 1921, herein.)

3. Rublee had been circulating a statement to lift the U.S. postal ban on Stopes's *Married Love* and apparently had not viewed the VPL's support of Stopes as a problem, but MS warned her that Stopes "is getting up a League all by herself & like Mrs D— only wants the peoples names. . . . She gives the impression the whole B.C. idea is her own discovery." (MS to Rublee, July 14, 1921 [quote], July 29 and Oct. 11, 1920 [*MSM* C1:730, 528, and 572]; Mary Watson Comly to Rublee, Dec. 16, 1920 [LCM 11:544].)

4. The telegram was not found. Anne Kennedy (1885–1966?), a divorced club woman from California, had begun managing MS's lectures and speaking arrangements in November 1920 and by February 1921 was an associate editor of the *BCR*. Kennedy was also organizing the upcoming First American Birth Control Conference in November 1921. MS was referring to an October 27 VPL meeting at which Dennett invited Stopes to speak. (MS, *Autobiography*, 261, 292.)

5. In addition to two practical birth control guides, *Wise Parenthood* and "A Letter to Working Mothers on How to Have Healthy Children and Avoid Weakening Pregnancies," Stopes published *Radiant Motherhood* (1920), on prenatal care, eugenics, and sex education for children. Though the book was generally well received, some reviewers complained that her advice reflected a middle-class bias, while others charged her medical opinions were not well founded. MS, however, had described the book as "challenging and stimulating" and maintained that it would encourage "suggestions for new lines of thought and scientific investigation." (Soloway, *Birth Control*, 224; Hall, *Passionate Crusader*, 173; MS, "A Review by Margaret Sanger," *BCR*, Apr. 1921, 13.)

6. These references were to Dennett and Stopes.

144. From Mary Ware Dennett

New York City, [*N.Y.*]
July 29, 1921

Dear Margaret:

I was mighty sorry to hear that you had again been seriously ill, and I trust you are now making a quick recovery, and one "for keeps".

Despite the terrific heat, things are moving here. Plans are under way at last for that long anticipated New York Clinic for diseased parents, and Dr. Stopes is to come over in October specially for a V.P.L. public meeting to describe to Americans her London Clinic and all that it means.[1]

I hear that the plans for your November Conference are also developing fast. It ought surely to be a great service and impetus to the movement.

Last Monday, July 18th, Mrs. Lane[2] and I had a talk with Mrs. Kennedy, as the executive of the Committee in charge of the preparations for the Conference, and the result of our talk was the enclosed letter to that Committee. It explains itself. Since then, word has come from Mrs. Kennedy that no decision on the three points in the letter can be made without consulting you.[3] Therefore, as she does not seem to know the exact time of your return, and says it will probably be sometime next month, I am sending you the letter now, that no precious time may be lost. And I ask you to express your opinion to the Committee and to the V.P.L. as soon as you possibly can.

I realize, of course, from your March editorial in the Birth Control Review and from many other indications, that you have found it hard to recognize the V.P.L. as a useful factor in the Birth Control movement.[4] But now, will you not, along with us, realize that the time has come when all of us should do our very utmost to stand for and work for those activities which will advance the movement the fastest.

Ever since I knew you in the first year of your work for birth control, your major emphasis has been Clinics and personal help. You have many times alluded to legislation and organization as minor matters. Your interest in clinics and your appeals for them have been your sustained effort. Your activities and your policies as to legislation and organization have fluctuated. Now, however, with the plans for the Conference, which announce in advance the organization of a new league,[5] you evince interest in organization, and the work of your Committee with the New York State Legislature last spring indicated a revival of legislative interest.[6]

We, on the other hand, while just as interested as you in clinics, have during these years put our emphasis on getting the laws changed, as the greatest stroke in developing public support for the giving of contraceptive knowledge, in all the existing clinics, hospitals, dispensaries etc., in other words as the quickest way to make clinical service possible everywhere. Within the last few months, however, we have become convinced of the worthwhileness of establishing some special ↑independent↓ demonstration clinics in a few big cities, by way of showing all the hospitals that this instruction should be added to their already existing service. We are now preparing a pamphlet on this subject and have sent out newspaper publicity relative to it.[7]

There seems to be every reason for hoping that the time is ripe now, for a careful survey of the field and a great joining of forces instead of further splitting them by forming still another organization.

There will surely be greater strength in every phase of this work if all resources are pooled instead of dissipating the energies of the movement by the formation of another national league.

We ask you to join whole heartedly as we are ready to do in the sincere effort to conserve every valuable part of the B.C. movement up to date, to discard all prejudice and to eliminate every move which does not mean taking the longest and the quickest steps ahead. What do you say?

We shall await your answer with deep interest. With all good wishes to you personally, Yours in faith to the Cause,

Mary Ware Dennett [*signed*]
Director.

TLS PPFAR, MN-SSC (*MSM* S2:17–18).

1. Dennett wanted to open demonstration clinics in New York City to attract support from doctors and public health officials for her federal bill. On October 26, 1921, she organized the New York Parenthood Clinic Committee, which included many VPL members, and despite her promise that unlike MS's efforts, "Our function is to promote clinics, not to run them," the committee did neither. (Mary Dennett, "Confidential Report to the VPL Council, #20," Nov. 30, 1921 [quote], and VPL Annual Report, May 1, 1921–May 1, 1922 [*MWDPM* 12:935 and 953].)

2. Vera Perin Lane (ca. 1879–?) was the assistant director of the VPL.

3. Dennett enclosed a letter to the *BCR* board of directors, protesting the creation of a new organization at the First American Birth Control Conference. She proposed that the VPL be given time at the conference to present its agenda and recommendations regarding a new national organization and that MS cease advertising the formation of a new organization before the conference delegates determined one was needed. (For enclosed letter, see Dennett to *BCR* Board, July 25, 1921 [LCM 10:1017]; for more on wrangling between MS and Dennett about the conference, see MS to Dennett, Sept. 23 and Oct. 10, 1921, and Dennett to MS, Oct. 13, 1921 [*MSM* C1:831, 847, and 850]; Dennett to Kennedy, Oct. 24, 1921 [*MWDPM* 14:359].)

4. MS, "Editorial," Mar. 1921, 3–4.

5. For letters announcing plans for the formation of the ABCL, see First American Birth Control Conference, Form Letters, *MSM* S67:740–43.

6. Though MS convinced the Health Board of the New York Academy of Medicine to endorse the Lindsay amendment and persuaded doctors, judges, economists, and others to sign petitions in support of it, she was unable to get a state assembly member to sponsor it before the legislative session closed. ("Outline of Legislative Work in Albany.")

7. The VPL pamphlet *Birth Control Clinics in the United States Why? When? How?* was released in September 1921.

145. *To Marie C. Stopes*

Zermatt [*Switzerland*]
July 29 [*1921*]

Dear Marie Stopes:

Here I am far away in the Alps regaining my health & strength yet preparing to undergo an operation as soon as I return to London. How are you?

Mrs Chance said you were tired out too. It is a strenuous life yours as well as mine in U.S.A.

I have not seen you at all since my arrival owing to the conditions of my health & of course your being out of town. I trust I may see you upon my return for Mrs Rublee writes me today & seemed greatly upset over the rumor that you are to be in New York under the auspecies of the Voluntary P. League.[1] Mrs Rublee & several other very fine women have been working quietly but steadily on getting your book released from the Post Office ban— They have succeeded in doing a great deal, but you may not be aware of the fact that the League in question has been entirely repudiated by the medical profession as well as by the most influential people who formerly gave it their support.[2]

Your being in America under such auspecies would not only undo the work of many of your staunch supporters but would necessitate the abandon of their names in correction with your work.

I trust you will consider this in confidence. Only at the request of Mrs Rublee would I consider it my place to tell you, as I personally consider Mrs D— outside the pale of honesty & decency. I will be in London Sept 1.[3] 6 Haymarket. Trust to see you then & hope all goes well with you as ever

Margaret Sanger

ALS Stopes, UK-BL (*MSM* C1:758–61) Letterhead of the Seilers Hotel Riffelalp.

1. The letter was not found.
2. In 1920, Dennett had tried to gain backing from the New York Academy of Medicine for her legislative program, but she was rejected by both the academy's Birth Control Sub-Committee and its Public Health Committee. (Dennett to VPL National Council, Jan. 3, 1921, and Subcommittee on Birth Control to the Public Health Committee, New York Academy of Medicine, Nov. 15, 1920 [*MWDPM* 12:1–13 and 85].)
3. MS actually arrived on August 31.

146. To Juliet Barrett Rublee

Zermatt, [*Switzerland*]
July 30 [*1921*]

Adorable Juliet:

Yes I do realize what a chance I have.[1] I am taking it against all other attractions like Paris with Havelock. Sea shore sailing etc with Mrs Chance, London operation on tonsils, Italy & battle fields with Mr S— and all kinds of facinating invitations (even Germany) are pouring in—but here I am & here I stay[2] until I leave for the B.C. conference in Holland[3] Aug 28th & London Sept 1— If my money holds out. I am borrowed to the hilt, but what difference does it make! I feel like an object of charity any way but my book will be out in Sept & I get an advance on that.[4] I am resting dear—open air since July 1st night & day—in bed two days just because.

Pain all gone from neck, tissues softened & really I feel like my old self before you knew me. You blessed woman—why will you worry Juliet. I will never die doing the work I love. Always remember that. But this winter my religion is to be health & work, nothing else.

I am going to take Saturday & Sunday out of the city—"sink or swim, live or die survive or perish" no lectures until after the Conference at all.

I am laying down a programme to follow giving me the greatest amount of time to myself & [*allowing*] the greatest amount of work to be accomplished. It's a trial of course. But we will see.

Darling don't worry over conference— Please—and do not put so much faith in personalities. Let us put it into the Spirit of Universal Progress— Let it guide & direct & choose our speakers for us—

I am going to be guided in the future by this as I was in the early days—Making Principle work out our problems for us. I always get a truer vision of things when I get away alone. Then strength & decision comes back strong.

I went to see Dr Stopes clinic—her little nurse told me all she knew & taught the women she learned from Margaret Sanger lectures. It was a year after that she met Dr Stopes and then through the B.C.R.[5] Laughable isnt it?

For Stopes to open a clinic in America is positively humorous! She is not a M.D. nor a nurse—[6] She learned all she knows on B.C. from "Family Limitation." She has a lot to learn yet.

She is not being invited to the International Conference at the Hague (Aug 27 & 28) to discuss methods of B.C. Because she is not considered an authority. So it is amusing to have her called to America to open a clinic—

She may not go. I believe she wants money & unless D— gets it more easily than in the past.[7] It will not come off. [*page(s) possibly missing*] you thought she should be told.

Of course she is such a climber she believes all that Mrs D— tells her—[8]

The clinic idea was of course not surprising. Dr. Halton has been trying to get support all the winter.[9] I would not care to go with her she is a darling but is as uncertain as Mrs Knob is—[10] If they can work up a clinic let them do it— But our movement is not going to be used as a tail for their kite.

I do not want Mrs. K—[11] back on the Review. I can not work with her—and if she & Mrs D— can work together I am glad let them be—

Let us keep on our own work, but it is all we can do without keeping them to do theirs. I have learned a lesson in England. They would have exposed Mrs D— as Blossom was exposed. It is the only way to do. This is all I am going to say about it. Do not let us loose our heads or get excited over her coming or their work— If it is good it will live if it is not it will die of its own stagnation. We have kept D— alive by our agitation & education & silence about her duplicity. She accepts all our principles after she fights them a while & finds people are with our ideas. Do you notice that. Clinics for instance? Doctors & dispensaries? Instead of the open road as she tried to advise—

I shall not go to Paris— I am just adoring this high quiet wild place and were it not for the conference I'd remain here until October.

If I have to have my tonsils out Ill have to get it done & over early. I expect to return to N.Y. about the 20th of Sept to get the boys back to school.[12] Ill come up to you the middle of October if you are in Cornish so we can be fresh for the conference.

Poor Mrs Kennedy I do wish she would rest too. This movement kills anyone who loves it. Your friend Mrs Corbett Ashby wrote me[13] I hope to see her when I return.

What dreadful conditions in U.S.A. It is almost equal to the Russians prediction isnt it? What can we do about you darling?[14] Please don't send that thirty for the room— I left my royalty money to be drawn upon for Ruth's salary, Miss [*Dastre's?*][15] & rent might as well be included. You have been so dear & generous—heavens it makes me gulp down tears when I think of how adorable you are.

I never had greater confidence in the work than now. It is absolutely the only issue which is alive which is fundamental & which can save civilization from the wreck which charities & other weak & sentimental agencies have made of society. My new book is going well. I am calling it "The Pivot of Civilization".[16]

The contents are:—

I Introduction—The world today.
II The Waste of Motherhood.
III The over-production & [*undervaluation*] of children
IV The Fertility of the Feebleminded
V Charity—a Symptom
VI The Gospel of Marx—Its failure
VII The Limitations of Eugenics
VIII The Educational Value of B.C.
IX The Ethical Necessity for B.C.
X Science & Birth Control
IX Conclusion—our vision.[17]

I am dictating a few hours a day on my veranda— I may be able to finish it before I return. I want to. This much is done only. I have to polish it & tone it up. Etc etc. It's a little high brow & not the woman urge of the other books. But its for Social workers & people like that.

Tell me what you think. Ever my love & devotion blessed woman—

Keep cool & well & don't worry—you can live with me—I can cook you know.

We must treat for those conditions.

Juliet dearest I love you <u>always</u> <u>always</u> and ever devotedly

Margaret

Can hear the roaring of a falling avalanche— Its gloriously cool, crisp & bracing yes lets live in England. It's the place for our Spiritual developt

---

ALS Lader (*MSM* C18:12–28). MS wrote at the top of the first page, "Riffel Alps Matterhorn in front of me" and "(over 7000 feet high)."

1. The Rublee letter was not found, but this was probably a reference to having time to recuperate.

2. The references were to Janet Chance and her husband, Clinton, an avid yachtsman, and to J. Noah Slee. When doctors advised her to stay in the mountains at least a month, MS remained in Zermatt, before moving to St. Moritz (August 8–15) and then Lucerne. (See MS to Rublee, June 12, 1921, note 7, and June 22, 1921, herein; and MS to Rublee, June 4, Aug. 8, and Aug. 15, 1921 [*MSM* C1:680, 787, and 796].)

3. The International Congress on Contraceptives in Amsterdam, August 29–30, 1921, attended by doctors and birth control representatives from Europe and the United States, included discussions and demonstrations of birth control devices and techniques. ("International Neo-Malthusian Bureau of Correspondence and Defense," *Malthusian,* Sept. 15, 1921, 74–75.)

4. *The New Motherhood* was not published until February or March 1922. (A. M. Heath & Co. to MS, Jan. 12, 1922 [LCM 14:336].)

5. Despite Stopes's boasts of its spectacular success, the clinic, located on Marlborough Road in the impoverished Holloway area of North London, saw only about three people per day in its first year. Maud F. Hebbes, a nurse/midwife, suffragist, and Malthusian League member, ran the clinic. MS had published a letter from Hebbes in the February 1921 *BCR,* which may have brought her to Stopes's attention. (Rose, *Marie Stopes,* 144–45.)

6. Stopes, who held a bachelor of science in botany from London University, a doctor of philosophy from the Botanical Institute of the University of Munich, and a doctor of science from the University of London, always referred to herself as "Dr. Stopes." (Rose, *Marie Stopes,* 262.)

7. Unlike MS, Dennett was not an effective fund-raiser, and both the NBCL and the VPL were chronically short of money. (Mary Dennett, "Confidential Report," May 17, June 23, and July 29, 1921 [*MWDPM* 12:916–17].)

8. In an August 6 letter to MS, Stopes asked why she should not accept the VPL's invitation to speak in New York City and challenged MS's intimations that the U.S. publication of *Married Love* would be threatened by her association with Dennett, particularly among physicians. MS told Stopes, "If you are associated with the V.P.L. they will not give their names nor have anything to do with anyone or any thing associated with it. This has been told us by the best known Physician on another [*matter*] and right or

wrong there it is." (Stopes to MS, Aug. 6, 1921, and MS to Stopes, Aug. 8, 1921 [*MSM* C1:785 and 819].)

9. No information was found on Mary Halton's fund-raising efforts.

10. Mary Bookstaver Knoblauch (1875–1950), a suffragist, a NYWPC board member, and the wife of the successful businessman Charles Knoblauch, was acting *BCR* editor from February 1919. MS probably distrusted Knoblauch because as an NBCL member, she was on better terms with Dennett than were many of MS's other associates. (MS to Rublee, June ?, 1919 [*MSM* 1:323]; Cornell University Press Release, July 31, 1952 [Bryn Mawr Archives]; *New York Times,* Oct. 12, 1934, and Nov. 29, 1950.)

11. "Knoblach" was interlined, possibly by Juliet Rublee.

12. Grant, age thirteen, joined Stuart, age seventeen, at the Peddie School.

13. Margery Corbett Ashby (1882–1981) was a British suffragist who had met Rublee at the Paris Peace Conference. The letter was not found. (Michael Ashby, ed., *Memoirs of Dame Margery Corbett Ashby* [West Sussex, England, 1997], 104.)

14. With the postwar recession in the United States, Rublee's investment income may have decreased.

15. Ruth Albert was a *BCR* office worker (1921–24), and Jessie A. Dastre was a secretary or nurse who worked in MS's "little room" at 104 Fifth Avenue. (ABCL Annual Meeting Minutes, Jan. 13, 1923 [*MSM* S61:87]; see also "Birth Control Organizations," *BCR,* May 1921, 2.)

16. In *The Pivot of Civilization,* published by Brentanos in 1922, MS argued that "civilization, in any true sense of the word, is based upon the control and guidance of the great natural instinct of Sex. Mastery of this force is possible only through the instrument of Birth Control" (1), adding, "As a social program, Birth Control is not merely concerned with population questions. . . . It looks for the liberation of the spirit of woman and through woman of the child" (16).

17. With the exception of chapter 4, "The Fertility of the Feeble-Minded," none of these draft titles was used.

147. To Juliet Barrett Rublee

Lucerne [*Switzerland*]
Aug 25, [*1921*]

Juliet darling:

Leaving tonight for Amsterdam to attend Conference on B.C. Methods.[1] I do not know who or how many will be there, but Dr Drysdale & Dr Rutgers & Dr Haire & someone from Japan will be there any way.[2] I am so glad to tell you dearest that at last I have secured Harold Cox for our conference. Heaven only knows where the money is to be got to pay his expenses. But it has always come when I have gone ahead before So I continue to trust the Universal Provider in this too. Its a big card to get him. He is a man of brains & Intellect. His standing is on top in the English mind & press.[3] He's almost better than Dean Inge[4] for <u>our</u> purpose. Any way I am delighted that he will come & I am hurrying home now as quickly as I can get a boat.

If only we had money enough to secure Dr Haire too as an expert in Methods. We could hold our own with any group of Medicos or Scientists in the world ever since Plato. I am to see Dr Haire in Amsterdam tomorrow & Ill hear him speak & then if he makes the impression I want I'm likely to ask him to come—no matter the cost.[5]

This conference is to be the turning point in U.SA's psychology—yes dearest?

I'm so much better Juliet. Really very much better. Only here is what I have decided to do. When I get to London I think it would be very wise for me to have that special operation performed. I have found the only Surgeon in the world who has discovered the cause of glandular troubles. He examined my throat & found the pocket beneath tonsils & my tonsils are the horrid type.[6]

If I do not have this done now I will only have another winter of troubles and the next time it will not be so easy to recover as it was this time.

I hate to take ether. I hate to think of it all—but there is no use playing at curing when the cause has been established. Portet died with T.b. of the throat & there is reason to think that deadly germ can play havoc with my throat if it continues. So hear goes darling Juliet. It will all be over when you get this letter. I will have been out into the astral & I wish I may be able to remember some of the things I see there.

I'll sail about Sept 13th arrive N.Y Sept 20th latest get the boys off to school[7] & come up to see you at once, they are gone if you are at Windsor & are free to have me for a few days.

All the love of my heart dearest of women. Ever devotedly

Margaret

Someone sent me $150 via pouch Bankers Trust Co N.Y, Who? Do you think it could be Mrs Tuttle for Geneva?[8] Saw Mr [*Sweetser*] at St Moritz.[9] [*Written along right margin of last page*] more when I get to Holland.

ALS JRP, NhD (*MSM* C1:804–9). Letterhead of the Grand Hotel National, Lucerne.

1. MS arrived in Amsterdam for the International Congress on Contraceptives on August 26. (For additional information, see MS, "Impressions of the Amsterdam Conference," *BCR*, Nov. 1921, 11 [*MSM* S70:922].)

2. Norman Haire (1892–1952), an Australian-born gynecologist and Malthusian League member, organized the Amsterdam conference with Charles Drysdale to discuss birth control clinics with other neo-Malthusians. The Malthusian League's Walworth Women's Welfare Centre was opened in November 1921, with Haire as medical director. Dr. Johannes Rutgers, who had resigned as the league's honorary secretary in 1917, was unable to attend the conference, but several of his students gave demonstrations. The Japanese delegate was not identified. (*London Times*, Sept. 13, 1952; Benn, *Predica-*

ments of Love, 212–13; "Conference on Contraceptives at Amsterdam, August 29th and 30th," *Malthusian,* Sept. 15, 1921, 74; Ledbetter, *Malthusian League,* 16.)

3. Harold Cox (1859–1936) was an economist, journalist, Conservative member of Parliament (1906–9), London City Council alderman (1910–12), and editor of the *Edinburgh Review* (1912–29). He also chaired the Walworth Women's Welfare Centre's fund-raising committee. Cox had met MS in 1915 and saw her again in 1920 and 1921. (*DNB;* MS, *Autobiography,* 172, 296; MS to de Selincourt, June 26, 1920, herein; for letters between Cox and MS from Mar. 2 to Aug. 1921, see LCM 14:278–88 and *MSM* C1:727.)

4. The Reverend William Ralph Inge, the cochair of the National Birth-Rate Commission and a Eugenics Society member, was far more conservative than Cox. (*New York Times,* Feb. 27, 1954; Soloway, *Demography and Degeneration,* 9, 83.)

5. MS was considering Haire for the First American Birth Control Conference. Haire did not attend but furnished a letter included in the conference proceedings on the question of birth control and morality. His lecture at the Amsterdam conference was not identified. (*Birth Control—What It Is.*)

6. George Ernest Waugh (?–1940), a member of London University's medical faculty, an authority on children's diseases, and a pioneer of a new operation for the complete enucleation of the tonsils, performed MS's tonsillectomy on September 1. (*London Times,* Apr. 6, 11, 1940; MS to Hugh de Selincourt, Sept. 3, 1921 [LCM 3:1090].)

7. She sailed from Plymouth, England, on September 8, arriving in New York City on September 17. (MS to Dennett, Sept. 23, 1921 [*MSM* C2:24].)

8. Florence Guertin Tuttle (1869–1951), a suffragist, pacifist, and *Brooklyn Daily Eagle* reporter, was a *BCR* contributor and had became an associate editor in April 1921. (*New York Times,* Apr. 17, 1951.)

9. Arthur W. Sweetser (1888–1968) was a journalist who served as an "unofficial" American ambassador to the League of Nations. (*New York Times,* Jan. 21, 1968; Mary Breed to MS, Dec. 19, 1927 [LCM 122:530].)

148. From Hugh de Selincourt

Wantley. Storrington. [*England*]
14th September. [*1921*]

The king of dearness wrote to me about the journey to Plymouth which was a great comfort.[1] It was unpleasant to hear the awful hurricane three nights ago and to think of your poor darling throat and of you in such sore need of rest and quietness.[2] Dear lovely Margaret after long longing to be with you, close and peaceful and really together, it was rather terrible to see you for those snatched moments, in the hustle of departure, for which you were utterly unfit. But bless you, you wonderful darling, it is a joy to see you at all under any circumstances, and though I should like best of all to write for you, that does not make it less delightful to be allowed to do messages or lick envelopes: any more than to take off you darling shoes (AND pull the stockings down from the toes!) makes me want less to hold you in my arms. Forgive my being fearfully explicit about this. I hate misunderstanding. It's my insatiable ego wants to see its name in your paper—ten times more than Harold Hersey![3]—and it's my insatiable ego thinks my stuff would help the cause. Your insatiable ego picks me out to use me; I believe your instinct is right. Your lovers will serve you more usefully than your useful acquaintances, however practical or named or successful these latter may be.

How are you, beautiful Margaret? Oh you did look lovely, lying on that bed, darling, amid all that dreariness, that indescribable dreariness, that unspeakable blatant bed-room. Such a picture of you I hold in my mind. How you dare risk your health for any blasted conference! Oh well, I suppose you may do anything. But I am bitterly disappointed that I could not see you properly. How can I help it? The only thing that does make me help it is the thought of you lying there ill, looking so unutterably lovely in that awful bedroom, because that memory of beauty, my dear, is a possession for ever which burns up disappointment very quickly. Some time we shall be together.

I enclose a paragraph which ought to be in the Review I think as Keynes is an important man,[4] and now I find that silly old Frank has cut it out of the Sunday Times and sent it away;[5] so it will have to come later. Probably Harold Cox who writes in the S.T has sent it to you already.[6]

I am longing to hear how you bore the journey; and how you are; and the prospects of the conference, which I shall see probably in the B.C.R. My love to you always and always, adored and adorable Margaret.

Hugh

ALS MSP, MN-SSC (*MSM* S2:21–23).

1. Havelock Ellis accompanied MS to Plymouth before she sailed for the United States. (Ellis to MS, Sept. 13, 1921 [LCM 4:665].)

2. MS complained of a sore, diphtheritic throat following her tonsillectomy. (MS to Dennett, Sept. 23, 1921 [*MSM* S2:24].)

3. Hersey's literary contributions to the *BCR* included two poems, a book review, a song, and a play. MS was by this time losing interest in Hersey both personally and professionally. (MS to Rublee, June 12 and Aug. 27, 1921 [*MSM* C1:810]; for Hersey's *BCR* contributions, see "Vision"; "So You've Come Back," Apr. 1921, 12; "Song," Aug. 1921, 12; and "The Hidden Queen," July 1921, 9–13, 15.)

4. John Maynard Keynes (1883–1946), a notable economist, was a Malthusian League member and a vice-president of Marie Stopes's Society for Constructive Birth Control. The clipping was not found, but it referred to the fourth article in Keynes's *London Times* series entitled "Europe's Economic Outlook." De Selincourt probably highlighted the paragraph in which Keynes argued that one path to social improvement is "by a reduction and control of the birth-rate." (*DNB;* "The Earnings of Labour," *London Sunday Times,* Sept. 11, 1921.)

5. Frank T. Carter (1853–1934) was a landscape painter who lived with the de Selincourts. (Grosskurth, *Havelock Ellis,* 307.)

6. Cox contributed monthly essays to the *London Times* on such topics as unemployment, railways, population, and taxation.

149. From Heman A. Harding[1]

Barnstable, Mass.,
October 4, 1921.

Dear Madam:-

I have the pleasure to enclose you herewith the Decree Absolute of Divorce,[2] Margaret H. Sanger vs. William Sanger, for desertion, with custody of minor children to the Libellant. This completes your matter and you would be at the liberty to remarry just as though you had never been married. Yours truly,

Heman A. Harding [*signed*]

TLS MSP, SCC (*MSM* S2:32). Legal letterhead.

1. Heman A. Harding (1871–1936), a former state representative and state senator, practiced law in Barnstable. (*Boston Evening Transcript,* Aug. 4, 1936.)
2. MS first filed for divorce on September 17, 1918, in Provincetown, Massachusetts. The notice appeared in the *Provincetown Advocate,* but her registered letter notifying William Sanger was apparently returned in November 1918. MS did not file a new request until the spring of 1920. (See Harding to MS, Feb. 10, 1920; for enclosed decree see Oct. 4, 1921 [*MSM* S1:902 and S83:732].)

150. *To Charles B. Davenport*[1]

*Sanger sent out numerous invitations to the First American Birth Control Conference, like the one that follows, between June and October 1921, seeking delegates, financial contributions, and speakers. (For general form letters, see June 28, 1921 [*MSM *C14:692] and Sept. 28, 1921 [*MSM *S67:740].)*

New York City, N.Y.
Oct. 4, 1921.

My dear Dr. Davenport:

Many prominent economists, doctors and social workers, as well as individuals, have urged me to arrange for a wider investigation of the subject of Birth Control in the United States. This request has become so insistent that I have decided to call a Conference in New York City, Nov. 11th, 12th and 13th.

The members of the American Public Health Association meeting in New York the following week, have been invited to attend this Conference. Already more than one hundred members of this Association, representing twenty-six states, have replied that they will attend.[2]

As the subject of the findings of the Eugenics Record Office with which you are connected at Cold Springs Harbor, on the heredity of disease tendencies, is really fundamental to a fair consideration of Birth Control, I am going to ask you if you would give a paper on that subject, irrespective of whether you care to speak as an advocate of Birth Control or not.[3]

Harold Cox, M.P., Editor of the Edinburgh Review, one of the most noted economists of England, is coming to America to speak at our conference on population and war.[4] I am desirous that Mr. Cox shall be well backed up by the scientists and economists of America. Birth Control must, we feel, be judged solely upon its scientific merits, and it is to such men as you that we must look for a thorough presentation of the public aspects of the question.

There is also a possibility that Mr. J. O. P. Bland will address the conference for a few minutes at least, on the Asiatic question.[5] Altogether, it promises to be an interesting programme.

Will you not be one of those to help us enlighten public opinion and direct public thought along these lines in the future?

I shall wait anxiously to hear from you. Sincerely,

Margaret Sanger [*signed*]

TLS CBDP, PPAmP (*MSM* C1:839–40). Letterhead of the First American Birth Control Conference. Similar letters were also sent to National Health Association members Henry P. Osborn and Anita McCormick Blaine and probably to Edward Allsworth Ross and Lillian Wald. (For invitations and responses, see *MSM* C1:842, 844, 854, and 866.)

1. Charles Davenport (1866–1944), a biologist, geneticist, and influential eugenicist, was the director of the Station for Experimental Evolution, the Biological Laboratory, and the Eugenic Record Office in Cold Spring Harbor, New York, which opened in 1910 to investigate the inheritance of human personality and mental traits. (*ANB*)

2. MS planned to have the conference coincide with the association's fiftieth anniversary meeting, scheduled for November 14–18, 1921. In preparation, the *BCR* published the results of a survey of association members' support for birth control. (MS, *Autobiography,* 298; *New York Times,* Nov. 15, 1921; "Opinions of the Conference by Members of the American Public Health Association," *BCR,* Oct. 1921, 10.)

3. Davenport argued that behavior was determined largely by race and that the nation's "protoplasm" was threatened by the genetically defective as well as by the poor, the nonwhite, and the nonnative born. He opposed birth control, believing that it had a dysgenic effect among the better "human stocks" and led to sexual immorality. (Kevles, *In the Name of Eugenics,* 45–53.)

4. Cox's lecture, "The Relation of Population to War," was scheduled to open the session entitled "The Morality of Birth Control." (*New York Times,* Dec. 16, 1921; for Conference Program, see *MSM* C14:696 and 703.)

5. John Otway Percy Bland (1863–1945) was a British diplomat, journalist, and author of several books and articles, including *China, Japan and Korea* (1921). He was primarily concerned with overpopulation. His paper was entitled "The Population Question as

Illustrated by Asia." (*DNB;* First American Birth Control Conference Program [*MSM* C14:703]; John Bland, "After Washington: The Future of the Pacific Problem," *Atlantic Monthly,* Dec. 1922, 843–44.)

151. From Charles B. Davenport

[*Cold Spring Harbor, N.Y.*]
October 10, 1921

My dear Mrs. Sanger:

Your kind invitation to participate in The First American Birth Control Conference has been received.

There are two reasons why I am unable to accept your kind invitation. One is that on account of the Eugenics Congress,[1] I am somewhat worn out and away behind in my work. Also, the business of the Congress is far from being completed. Another reason is that it is important that in the public mind eugenics and birth control should not be confused as the same thing.

Because of my special interest in eugenics ↑seems to be rather widely known↓ this idea would become strengthened were I to take an active part in the birth control conference. Very sincerely,

Chas. B. Davenport.
Director.

TLcy CBDP, PPAmP (*MSM* C1:846). Handwritten insertions.

1. Davenport chaired the Committee on Publication for the Second International Congress of Eugenics, held in New York City, September 22–28, 1921, and gave a paper, "Research in Genetics." (*Eugenics, Genetics and the Family,* vol. 1, *Scientific Papers of the Second International Congress of Eugenics* [Baltimore, 1923], 21–28.)

152. From Marie C. Stopes

*Stopes arrived in New York City on October 25, attended a VPL meeting on October 26, and gave a speech at Town Hall on October 27 to a crowd of over a thousand people. Dennett invited Sanger to be guest of honor at Stopes's lecture, but she declined, claiming insufficient notice. (Dennett, "Confidential Report to the VPL Council, #20," Nov. 30, 1921, and Minutes of Conference of Council and Near-By Contributors, Dec. 8, 1921 [*MWDPM, *12:935 and 940]; MS to Dennett, Oct. 26, 1921 [*MSM *C1:868].)*

New York [*N.Y.*]
October 28, 1921.

My dear Margaret Sanger:

I am extremely sorry that you should not have found time to see me.[1]

Frankly, I should have thought no business more important than that we should meet.

Have you forgotten and wiped out 1915 in England and all that followed? I never change, I never cease to admire, respect and love truth and courage and self-sacrifice, and I will always support with my whole heart all who have the untarnished record for these things.

I understand that in the intricacies of your American life, which I confess I do not fully understand, the fact that I have very definitely supported Mrs. Dennett's movement is held to imply that I am "committed to her", and that "committal" is also held, by some foolish people, to imply opposition to you. Nothing could be more mistaken. Anyone who claims that I am committed to one or the other political organization will lose my support. I will never be made the plaything of parties—my work is statesmanship—I am committed only and entirely to the Truth and to the best interests of humanity.[2]

Privately you have deeply wounded me, and I had hoped that we could have had this thing out into the open together and put it right.

It was sweet of you to send me the flowers but a heart to heart talk in the searching light of truth would have been better. You have a great opportunity in your Congress.

Believe me, Yours sincerely,

Marie C. Stopes. [*signed*]

TLS MSP, DLC (LCM 14:307).

1. MS had agreed to meet Stopes on October 28. (Sophia R. Durlauf to Marie Stopes, Oct. 26, 1921 [*MSM* C1:867].)

2. Stopes was aware of the impact of her decision to speak for the VPL. She wrote to Dennett on August 22 that it had gotten her in "hot water" and that MS and others were writing her "indignant protests." (*MWDPM* 14:489.)

153. *To Marie C. Stopes*

New York City [*N.Y.*]
October 29, 1921.

Dear Marie Stopes,

Your letter of October 28th received this morning, and while I regret not being able to have seen you before this, I feel that the National Conference and the thousand duties its successful launching imposes upon my strength and time, is and must be my first consideration.

No, I have not forgotten, my dear Marie, either the years of 1915 or 1920. Both of these years stand out in my memory as beautiful opportunities which you and I had for personal friendship, seldom accorded me since that time.

You state in you letter that you respect and love truth and courage and self-sacrifice and will support with all you heart all who have untarnish record for such things, and yet you did not respect the disinterested advice nor the confidence of one whose record in the past may claim a small part of the above.

I gave you, while I was in Switzerland, my opinion of a group and person under whose auspices you were about to come to America. I gave you this in strict confidence. You promptly violated that confidence by writing my opinion expressed to you, to the parties concerned, who, in turn, used and circulated this for disintegrating purposes to the Birth Control Movement.[1] Surely, Marie, such an lovely act of violation on your part is not in harmony with your early advice "to be as wise as a serpent and harmless as a dove."[2] I, too, am deeply wounded by your conduct.

I wonder if you have ever recognized the fact that for more than a year I bore the brunt of insults from publishers, because I tried to get your book "Married Love" published in America?[3] The very publishers who now rejoice to receive you, were among those who returned your manuscript at that time, stating that it was unworthy of their consideration.

Undaunted by discouragement, my co-workers and my staff jeopardized our freedom and violated the postal laws for the past few years, in order to have the book of Marie Stopes circulated, and her message reach the people in America.

I know of no groups who have done more than we have done to show my appreciation of your message and of your personal help.

I mention this only in a spirit of informing you of facts, and to assure you that I have ever appreciated your help that you gave me in the early days of 1915.

Your public declaration last Thursday evening in support of the Voluntary Parenthood League's activities, places you in my estimation, for all time, outside of the scope of disinterested international adherents to the cause of Birth Control.[4]

You were here but a few days—you were fully aware that controversies existed, yet, you rushed into a partisan support of a group who have constantly denied the use of the very words "birth control" and have done a great deal in bringing about controversies and disintegration to the cause.

You have taken your stand—and it is good to know that you have done so. We are no longer working in the dark. You will always have my admiration for your courage and my best wishes that you may be guided by the vision and wisdom which so marked your works in the earlier years of your activities. Sincerely,

Margaret Sanger [*signed*]

TLS Stopes, UK-BL (*MSM* C1:870–71). For TLcy, see LCM 14:308. Return address: "104 Fifth Avenue."

1. In August, MS had told Stopes that Dennett's VPL had been rejected by the New York County Medical Association, probably referring to Dennett's unsuccessful effort in 1920 to gain the backing of the New York Academy of Medicine for the VPL's legislative program. In the process, Dennett had aroused the ire of the chairman of the academy's Public Health Committee by misquoting him as supporting the legislation in the letter she wrote to his committee. The result, according to Dennett, was an academy blacklist of the VPL. On August 22, Stopes had asked Dennett about this claim. (MS to Stopes, Aug. 8–12, 1921 ([MSM C1:819]; Stopes to Dennett, Aug. 22, 1921, Dennett to VPL National Council, Jan. 3, 1921, and Subcommittee on Birth Control to the Public Health Committee, New York Academy of Medicine, Nov. 15, 1920 [*MWDPM* 14:490–91 and 12:1–13, 85].)

2. From Matthew 10:16: "Behold, I send you forth as sheep in the midst of wolves: be ye therefore wise as serpents, and harmless as doves."

3. On discussions of MS's efforts to get Stopes's book published, see MS-Stopes correspondence, Oct. 1917–Oct. 1918.

4. The main focus of Stopes's speech was her Mother's Clinic, but she also urged complete repeal of the federal Comstock Act. Dennett used Stopes's speech to promote her own clinic drive, as well as to publicize the VPL's lobbying for the federal bill. (*New York Call*, Oct. 28, 1921.)

154. From Mary Ware Dennett

New York City [*N.Y.*]
Oct. 31, 1921

Dear Margaret Sanger:

It is well for you to know that Dr. Stopes read to me the salient portions of the two letters you wrote to her in London, in which you advised her against coming to America under the auspices of the V.P.L., and in which you cast utterly unsubstantiated aspersions on the standing of the League and upon my personal character.[1]

Do you realize that these letters might subject you to action for libel and slander?

I ask you to write at once both to Dr. Stopes and to me, and either retract or else give proof to back the statements you made to Dr. Stopes, namely, that the V.P.L. "has not any medical backing"; "that I severed my connection from the N.B.C.L. in a way which could not be mentioned"; and that you consider me "beyond the bounds of honor or decency".[2]

Not only your letters to Dr. Stopes, but some of your official letters and actions have, I think, greatly dishonored you. I am deeply interested, for the sake of the great cause to which we are both committed, to see you "come back" to the generous-hearted, disinterested service which characterized your earlier work. I do earnestly hope you will put forth your truest effort in the matter. Yours sincerely,

Mary Ware Dennett [*signed*]

TLcyS MWDP, MH-S (*MSM* C1:872). Dennett's note at the top reads, "Return to M. W. D."; her note at the bottom reads, "The above was never answered."

1. In her October 29 letter, Stopes had included several quotes from MS's July 29 and August 12 letters, which Dennett later sent to her supporters. She also met with Dennett before sailing for England and read her the two MS letters. (Stopes to Dennett, Oct. 29, 1921, and Dennett to Augusta Rosenwald, Dec. 4, 1921 [*MWDPM* 14:494 and 393].)

2. For the first two quotes, see MS to Stopes, Aug. 8–12, 1921 (*MSM* C1:819). On the third quote, MS had actually written that she considered Dennett "outside the pale of honesty & decency." (MS to Stopes, July 29, 1921, herein.)

155. "The Eugenic Value of Birth Control Propaganda"

The expanding discourse on eugenics, sparked by the war, the introduction of intelligence testing, and studies holding that "Alpine and Mediterranean races" were "intellectually inferior to the representatives of the Nordic race," fueled concern over deteriorating national intelligence and declining birthrates among the "better classes." The movement grew in popularity in the United States, where eugenics courses were offered in some 350 colleges and universities, state fairs sponsored "Better Baby" contests, and exhibits encouraged "Fitter Families." Sanger argued that encouraging the white middle and upper classes to reproduce and discouraging the "unfit" from doing so, were not "feasible remedies," unless paired with the use of birth control. What follows is one of Sanger's many efforts to convert the still reluctant eugenics community to the cause of birth control. (Quote from Carl Campbell Brigham in Kevles, In the Name of Eugenics, *58, 82–83 [quote], 84–89; Larson,* Sex, Race, and Science, *20–23;* New York Times, *Feb. 16, 2001; MS,* Pivot of Civilization, *178.)*

[*October 1921*]

Seemingly every new approach to the great problem of the human race must manifest its vitality by running the gauntlet of prejudice, ridicule and misinterpretation. Eugenists may remember that not many years ago this program for race regeneration[1] was subjected to the cruel ridicule of stupidity and ignorance. Today Eugenics is suggested by the most diverse minds as the most adequate and thorough avenue to the solution of racial, political and social problems. The most intransigent and daring teachers and scientists have lent their support to this great biological interpretation of the human race. The war has emphasized its necessity.[2]

The doctrine of Birth Control is now passing through the stage of ridicule, prejudice and misunderstanding. A few years ago this new weapon of civilization and freedom was condemned as immoral, destructive, obscene. Gradually the criticisms are lessening—understanding is taking the place of misunderstanding. The eugenic and civilizational value of Birth Control is becoming apparent to the enlightened and the intelligent.

In the limited space of the present paper, I have time only to touch upon some of the fundamental convictions that form the basis of our Birth Control propaganda, and which, as I think you must agree, indicate that the campaign for Birth Control is not merely of eugenic value, but is practically identical in ideal with the final aims of Eugenics.

First: we are convinced that racial regeneration, like individual regeneration, must come "from within." That is, it must be autonomous, self-directive, and not imposed from without. In other words, every potential parent, and especially every potential mother, must be brought to an acute realization of the primary and central responsibility of bringing children into this world.

Secondly: Not until the parents of the world are thus given control over their reproductive faculties will it ever be possible not alone to improve the quality of the generations of the future, but even to maintain civilization even at its present level. Only by self-control of this type, only by intelligent mastery of the procreative powers can the great mass of humanity be awakened to the great responsibility of parenthood.

Thirdly: We have come to the conclusion, based on widespread investigation and experience, that this education for parenthood must be based upon the needs and demands of the people themselves. An idealistic code of sexual ethics, imposed from above, a set of rules devised by high-minded theorists who fail to take into account the living conditions and desires of the submerged masses, can never be of the slightest value in effecting any changes in the *mores* of the people. Such systems have in the past revealed their woeful inability to prevent the sexual and racial chaos into which the world has today drifted.

The almost universal demand for practical education in Birth Control is one of the most hopeful signs that the masses themselves today possess the divine spark of regeneration. It remains for the courageous and the enlightened to answer this demand, to kindle the spark, to direct a thorough education in Eugenics based upon this intense interest.

Birth Control propaganda is thus the entering wedge for the Eugenic educator. In answering the needs of these thousands upon thousands of submerged mothers, it is possible to use this interest as the foundation for education in prophylaxis, sexual hygiene, and infant welfare. The potential mother is to be shown that maternity need not be slavery but the most effective avenue toward self-development and self-realization. Upon this basis only may we improve the quality of the race.

As an advocate of Birth Control, I wish to take advantage of the present opportunity to point out that the unbalance between the birth rate of the "unfit" and the "fit," admittedly the greatest present menace to civilization, can never be rectified by the inauguration of a cradle competition between these two classes. In this matter, the example of the inferior classes, the fertility of the feeble-minded, the mentally defective, the poverty-stricken classes, should not be held up for emulation to the mentally and physically fit though less fertile parents of the educated and well-to-do classes. On the contrary, the most urgent problem today is how to limit and discourage the overfertility of the mentally and physically defective.[3]

Birth Control is not advanced as a panacea by which past and present evils of dysgenic breeding can be magically eliminated. Possibly drastic and Spartan methods may be forced upon society if it continues complacently to encourage the chance and chaotic breeding that has resulted from our stupidly cruel sentimentalism.

But to prevent the repetition, to effect the salvation of the generations of the future—nay of the generations of today—our greatest need is first of all the ability to face the situation without flinching, and to cooperate in the formation of a code of sexual ethics based upon a thorough biological and psychological understanding of human nature; and then to answer the questions and the needs of the people with all the intelligence and honesty at our command. If we can summon the bravery to do this, we shall best be serving the true interests of Eugenics, because our work will then have a practical and pragmatic value.

BCR, Oct. 1921, 5 (*MSM* S70:913).

1. The term *race regeneration* was often used interchangeably with eugenics and was popularized by Havelock Ellis, who wrote, "Our sense of social responsibility is becoming a sense of racial responsibility. It is that enlarged sense of responsibility which renders possible what we call the regeneration of the race. . . . It is we who are, more immediately, the creators of men. We generate the race; we alone can regenerate the race." Ellis was critical of such eugenic pioneers as Francis Galton, who failed to offer practical applications for eugenic theories and suggested that people with hereditary defects would voluntarily refrain from marriage for the good of the race. (Havelock Ellis, *The Problem of Race-Regeneration* [London, 1911], 50–51 [quotes]; Havelock Ellis, "Birth Control and Eugenics," *Eugenics Review* 9 [Apr. 1917]: 35–37; Kevles, *In the Name of Eugenics,* 85–88.)

2. MS argued that the war killed off "not the weak and the helpless, but the strong and the fit." (MS, *Woman and the New Race,* 161.)

3. MS derived her views from various British eugenicists, including the biologist J. Arthur Thompson, William Inge, George Bernard Shaw, H. G. Wells, and, most prominent, Ellis. She also relied on the findings of Henry Herbert Goddard and Charles Davenport and statistics from the U.S. Public Health Service to validate what she called "the notorious fecundity of the feeble-minded." MS, like Ellis, defined as "unfit" to reproduce those thought to have genetically transmittable mental diseases and physical disabilities. (MS, *Pivot of Civilization,* 80–104 [quote on 86].)

156. From H. G. Wells[1]

Arlington Hotel Washington [*D.C.*]

Tuesday [*November 8, 1921*]

My very dear Margaret Sanger.

I'm not coming to your meeting. I just can't. I'm dog-tired with talk & today I can't ↑think or↓ write. People gnaw me to pieces in America; there's no quiet of the mind in the continent. If I don't sleep more I get off the everlasting sage talking that ↑goes on↓. I shan't get my articles done. I wish you were here in a secret room with a tea kettle & I'd come & sleep friendly in your best arm chair & then go out & do—everything. I've written a letter ↑for you↓ to sort of use if you want to.[2] But I can't even write a letter today. You wont think I've failed you, will you? Yours

H. G.

ALS MSP, DLC (LCM 11:90).

1. Wells was covering the Washington Conference on the Limitation of Armaments, which began on November 12, for several British newspapers.

2. Wells's statement to the First American Birth Control Conference, read, "I am very sorry indeed that I cannot be at your meeting. I am convinced that Birth Control is a fundamental necessity if mankind is to go on to any better social or international order; and that your propaganda has been and is of primary importance among progressive movements." (Wells to MS, Nov. ?, 1921 [*MSM* S2:63].)

157. The Use of the Pessary

*The First American Birth Control Conference, held in New York City on November 11–13, brought together leading scientists, physicians, economists, social workers, and other movement supporters and activists to undertake a "wider investigation of the subject of birth control." Sessions were offered on health, social problems, population, and war, as well as the legal aspects of birth control in the United States. At the conference, Sanger launched the American Birth Control League (ABCL) and announced plans for the opening of a clinic. The following is an extract from an invitation-only roundtable meeting for members of the medical profession on contraceptive methods. Prior to Sanger's comments, Lydia Allen DeVilbiss, the chair, introduced the session and the four topics under discussion: surgical methods; sterilization; mechanical and chemical contraceptives; and miscellaneous methods. Discussants included Drs. Edward W. Lee, William F. Martin, S. Adolphus Knopf, Alice Butler, and Isabelle McMillan. Corrections of mistranscriptions by Sanger's staff have been supplied by the editors. (MS to Friends, Sept. 28, 1921 [*MSM *S67:740]; First American Birth Control Conference Program, Nov. 11–13, 1921 [*MSM *S67:794].)*

[*New York, N.Y.*]
[*November 11, 1921*]

MRS. MARGARET SANGER: Madam chairman, and friends. In Holland the particular method that is recommended there is the [*occlusive*] pessary. More than thirty five years ago at the medical congress of Amsterdam, the physicians decided that this subject of birth control was one that must be [*taught*] to their people if they would remain within their borders.[1] At once the medical profession began to test out the use of a pessary. They have from that time on used and recommended what is called the [*Mensinga*] pessary, which has, I believe, seven sizes. It is a little different from the one used in England and also the one used in the United States. This is made of different material and different sizes. Altogether I have seen as many as fourteen different pessaries devised and effected in Holland. Now, the physicians soon came to recognize that it was quite necessary to take their time, to find a way to teach the woman who was normal the use of a pessary, and so Dr. Rutgers, who was most interested in this subject at that time, has instructed the nurses how to fit the pessary upon a normal woman who is not suffering from disease. It is most interesting to see these women come to these clinics and to be there and to witness the instruction. They are first taught to douche. A small syringe is used, and they are taught the use of this syringe. Next this pessary is inserted with soapsuds and is fitted. The nurse does this until she gets the correct size. When this round one does not fit, there is another kind which does fit almost always. You see what that does? It covers the whole wall.[2] It is not like the small American pessary which I will show you later. That is the kind of pessary that is used in Germany, and in Austria, and in Holland.

This small pessary is the one that is used in France and now has been taken on in England.

My personal experience from women whose records I have is that this is the kind of pessary that accidents happen from. This can be pushed aside.[3] It does not seem to have the same skin, and it does not seem to fit so well over the cervix as that other kind which is called here the [“*mizpah*”]. The top comes off and seems to be a more practical kind.[4]

This kind, the little one, the French pessary, has been used in France for many years, and of course there have been no records kept so you cannot tell how many times this has failed.

In England today this is the method being used there in the so-called mother clinics.[5] In America we have the records of the 1250 families who have used methods successfully for at least one year; the pessary, 335 families have used the pessary followed by a douche, of which 265 have used the douche following the use of the pessary; the condom—355 people have used the condom successfully, and 171 of these people have followed the use of it by a douche; next on record is the suppository, 181 families have used suppositories, and 108 have followed it by a douche. The other methods that are here, an antiseptic douche, only 264 people. Most of us know that an antiseptic douche is not a preventative, but is a hygienic measure. Coitus [*interruptus*], 175 families have used that method, 61 have followed by a douche.[6]

This is recent information we have had of people in the United States who have used those methods and have been willing to give us the information.

As far as pessaries are concerned, I think that the kind used in Holland is the best. The records there for five years show that there were only 1% failure, and five years previously 3% were failure.[7] But they claim that if a woman is normal, if her organs are normal, and if she is taught and knows how to insert a pessary, that this practice cannot fail.

Now, they do not advise the woman to leave this in the body only over night. The next day when the husband is gone and the children are out at school, the woman is advised to take a cleansing douche and to wash the pessary and put it away. The reason they like it best is because it is not expensive; the only cost is its first outlay. And before the war they had the right kind of rubber and it was supposed to last from three to five years, and the charges were something like a gilder or a gilder and a half, which meant about sixty cents. Altogether the pessary is considered in Holland and in France the most successful method of birth control. (applause)

THE CHAIRMAN: I have asked Mrs. Sanger if this type of pessary was available in America. And she told me not this kind. In as much as this is the kind we are able to get in America, I would like to ask her if they use an ointment or something like it in connection with this.

MRS. SANGER: The idea is this. A little powder, any antiseptic dry powder in the cup before it is put on doubly secures against pregnancy, particularly if it is well fitted.[8] That is always one reason why I have stood so definitely for the principle of birth control being disseminated by the medical profession. As a nurse myself, I know that all women are not alike, that they are different. That it means individual examination or individual instruction. And with powder placed in the cup before it is inserted, and with the woman taught how to insert it, we have had a great deal of success, and very few failures with the right kind of pessary.

QUESTION. Will you kindly state what kind of powder?

MRS. SANGER: Boric powder, and even bicarbonate of soda.[9]

TRcy MSP, MN-SSC (*MSM* S67:754–57). No published version of this session exists; for the published version of other sessions, see *Birth Control—What Is It, How It Works, What It Will Do.*

1. This was a reference to the Sixth International Medical Congress, held September 7–14, 1879, in Amsterdam. ("The Population Question in Amsterdam," *Malthusian,* Oct. 1879, 66–71.)

2. The German physician Wilhelm Mensinga had designed the occlusive pessary in 1881. First used widely by Johannes Rutgers in his Dutch clinics, it was nicknamed the Dutch pessary or Dutch cap. Because the occlusive pessary covers the entire vaginal wall rather than just the opening to the cervix, many American birth control reformers preferred it to the cervical cap. The Mensinga pessary, made of a flat watch spring covered with black opaque rubber, was produced in many sizes and required accurate fitting. But it had a tendency not to return to its original shape after repeated use. As a result, Americans began using the Ramses, a slightly smaller version of the Mensinga pessary, which used a coiled watch spring to maintain its shape more effectively. Because of the slight possibility that some spermatozoa could pass round the edge of the cap, spermicidal cream or jellies were used to seal this off. (Cooper, *Technique of Contraception,* 135–37; Himes, *Medical History of Contraception,* 318–21.)

3. MS probably displayed a French cervical cap, which just covered the mouth of the cervix. (Cooper, 54–61.)

4. The Mizpah, an American variation of the French cervical cap, was constructed in two parts. In *Family Limitation,* MS cited it as "one of the best" (12), but Marie Stopes attacked it on the mistaken assumption that the user was supposed to leave the rim inside the vagina between uses. (Cooper, *Technique of Contraception,* 57; Stopes, *Contraception,* 166.)

5. Stopes's clinic used the "Pro-Race" cap, a French cervical cap that she modified by adding a higher dome. (Cooper, *Technique of Contraception,* 54–61.)

6. Using the letterhead of the "Margaret Sanger Research Bureau," MS had sent out 31,000 questionnaires earlier that year to her client list asking for information about family size, reasons for using birth control, and contraceptive methods employed. Compilations of the results, as well as transcriptions of nine responses, can be found on LCM 34:60–73.

7. She probably got her figures at the recent International Congress on Contraceptives in Amsterdam.

8. It was commonly held that neither pessaries nor contraceptive ointments by themselves offered the desired level of protection, but in combination women could come close to 100 percent protection. Dr. James Cooper noted that "the pessary prevents a 'direct hit' or ejaculation into the cervical canal, while the acid jelly kills all the sperms much more quickly than would otherwise be possible." (Cooper, *Technique of Contraception,* 145.)

9. Following MS's remarks, more than a dozen doctors joined the discussion, debating the efficacy and safety of the pessary. The discussion then moved on to miscellaneous methods, including the safe period, withdrawal, various suppositories, X-ray sterilization, and the use of iodine drops in Russia. Several doctors interrupted to warn of the potentially harmful effects of chemical and mechanical contraceptives. A few doctors also broached the subject of how sexual positions and technique could improve the effectiveness of coitus interruptus. MS concluded with a statement on the legal aspects of dispensing birth control.

158. To the Editor, New York Times

*The finale of the First American Birth Control Conference was to be a mass meeting at New York City's Town Hall on November 13 on the morality of birth control, with Harold Cox as keynote speaker. But the meeting was canceled minutes before when police captain Thomas Donahue ordered the doors locked. Thirty minutes later, as the doors were unlocked to release the crowd already in the hall, those outside, including Sanger, burst into the auditorium. When Sanger took the podium and began to speak, Donahue ordered her arrested. Other activists then sought the stage, and one of them, Mary Winsor, a member of the ABCL national council, was also arrested. The two, followed by a large crowd of supporters, were brought to the police court and charged with disorderly conduct. (*New York Times, *Nov. 14, 1921.)*

New York, [*N.Y.*]
Nov. 15, [*1921*]

To the Editor of The New York Times:

In your editorial this morning, Nov. 15, you criticise the action of the birth control advocates who were arrested Sunday night at the Town Hall for not obeying the police when they told them to leave the hall. You further state that there is a legal way to adjust these matters, and that one has redress in the courts.[1]

Do you realize in making such statements that they are inconsistent with the facts of the case? Do you realize that the officer who placed me under arrest had absolutely no right or reason to enter that hall and to prohibit my addressing an audience? This was verified by the dismissal of the case before the Judge the following morning.[2]

Had I left the hall in obedience to the deputy command, I would have had nothing upon which to go into the courts for a decision. It was necessary for the deputy to make an arrest in order to get a right interpretation of the law in this case.

I think your criticism of our meeting was very unjust and does not stand at all for the principle of right which is the essential thing that this Government is based upon.

MARGARET SANGER

New York Times, Nov. 19, 1921 (*MSM* S2:60). The original letter was not found.

1. The *New York Times* editorial "Resistance Was Not the Remedy" condemned the protesters defiance of the law: "they should have obeyed, promptly and quietly." The editorial characterized the reaction of MS's supporters as similar to "a crowd of anarchists" and claimed they gave the police justification for the arrests instead of relying on the power of the courts to punish police misconduct. (*New York Times,* Nov. 15, 1921.)

2. Judge Joseph E. Corrigan dismissed the charges against both women, citing insufficient evidence of wrongdoing. (*New York Call,* Nov. 15, 1921.)

159. To Archbishop Patrick Joseph Hayes[1]

One of the most powerful opponents Sanger faced in these years was the Roman Catholic church, which condemned not only abortion but also all "unnatural" means of birth control. Even liberal clergymen, such as the Catholic University sociologist Monsignor John A. Ryan, argued that contraceptive devices "are debasing to those who employ them, inasmuch as they lead inevitably to loss of reverence for the marital relation, loss of respect for the conjugal partner, and loss of faith in the sacredness of the nuptial bond." He defended the church's position with "race suicide" arguments, and, while he acknowledged the economic benefits of smaller families, he countered, "The end does not justify the intrinsically immoral means. . . ." Unafraid to take on church leaders, Sanger invited New York's archbishop to attend the November 13 Town Hall meeting. She and others charged that Hayes used his representative, Monsignor Joseph P. Dineen, to pressure the police to stop the meeting. When the meeting was rescheduled, Sanger sent the following to the archbishop. (John A. Ryan, "Family Limitation," Ecclesiastical Review, *June 1916, 684–86;* New York Times, *Nov. 15, 1921.)*

[*New York, N.Y.*]
November 15th 1921

Dear Sir:

It would give me great pleasure to have you attend a meeting at the Park Theatre Friday evening and to express your opinion upon the subject of "Birth Control—Is it Moral?"

In view of the fact that the Catholic Church expresses its opposition to the cause of Birth Control on moral grounds, I think it is only just and fair that such opinion as you might wish to express be done at this time.[2]

Mr. Harold Cox,[3] a distinguished Englishman, is here and is willing to express his opinion on this subject at this meeting. I will await your answer with interest and anticipation. Sincerely,

(signed) Margaret Sanger
Chairman

TRcy MSP, MN-SSC (*MSM* S2:59).

1. Patrick Joseph Hayes (1867–1938), the archbishop of New York, was renowned for his social welfare concerns, involvement in temperance and the Catholic Worker movement, and support for Irish independence. In 1920, he founded Catholic Charities, the coordinating agency for hundreds of welfare agencies in the New York archdiocese. (*ANB*)

2. Hayes did not respond to the invitation, but the Reverend William Chase, an Episcopal minister, did present an opposition statement to the audience. (*New York Tribune*, Nov. 19, 1921; *New York Times*, Nov. 20, 1921.)

3. For Cox's speech, see *MSM* S67:888.

160. First American Birth Control Conference: Closing Remarks

The closing conference session, finally held on November 18 at the Park Theater, included speeches by Harold Cox, who used biblical passages to refute religious convictions against birth control, followed by a discussion among birth control opponents—Robert Thomas, Leo Docker, Theodore Jacobs, and the Reverend William Sheafe Chase—and advocates—Joseph Lewis, Mrs. F. L. Simonsohn, and Helen Todd. Sanger then closed the meeting with the following remarks.

[*New York, N.Y.*]
[*November 18, 1921*]

Friends. I feel that it is much more difficult to answer the questions of those who are neither with us nor against us, much harder than it is to have to answer the question of a thorough going opponent. None of those who have spoken tonight have been entirely against us. Most of them have agreed, or both of them have agreed with us on principle, but have disagreed with us on methods. If only we could have more discussion along this line, we would get somewhere.

Now, the assumption of both the last speakers[1] has been that there is some other method of birth control than the mechanical use of contraceptives. They infer that it would be higher and better to perhaps remain continent or to use what is some times termed self control, although those words were not used I presume that that is what they were trying to get at. Now, we want to say that we have no objection to any individuals using self control. (applause) We leave that entirely to your individual freedom. But what we do contend is this. That in the first place, the laws of these various states are so construed that unless a woman gives of herself to her husband, she does not have his support.[2] (applause) A woman cannot attain to any kind of freedom when she is forced into pregnancy every year or year and a half. Women must have leisure. Leisure to think. She must have control over her own body. She must have time to evolve and to develop her own soul development. So must man. And certainly a man who finds that he is the father of a child every year or two soon finds that this home is not the home of his honeymoon dreams, and we find them running out to secure their entertainment in the evening elsewhere than by the fireside.

Now, if we do believe in self-control, what do you mean by that? Do you mean absolute continence in marriage? Then why marry? If you believe in the marriage relationship only for the procreation of children, then that would mean such a union and relationship but once or twice perhaps in a life time.

Now, I contend that that argument is perfectly absurd because it places man upon the same level as animals. In other words, you use the procreative act only for procreation, and I contend that there is another side, and another use of this relationship. (applause) I contend that it is just as sacred and just as beautiful for two people to express their love when they have no intention whatsoever of being parents. (applause) And I contend that they can go into that relationship with the same beauty and the same holiness with which they go into music or to prayer. I believe that it is the right understanding of our sexual power and of its creative energy that gives us spiritual illumination. I say that there is more than one use to make of it, and that is the higher use, the development of our soul development and soul growth.

I find that there is practically no argument against birth control. I have gone far across this country, and almost around the world, and I have never yet met a real argument against birth control. (applause) And why? Because it is the one need of the people, because this subject belongs mainly to women. It is the first step that woman must take to have her real emancipation. It is the first step that we must take to free our children. It is the first, last and final step that we all are to take to have real human emancipation. (applause)[3]

TRcy MSP, MN-SSC (*MSM* S67:916–18).

1. She was referring to the Reverend William Chase and Theodore Jacobs.

2. Because at this time the only legal grounds for divorce in some states, including New York, was adultery, couples often sought annulments, which required the plaintiff to prove that a fraud so severe it would have prevented the marriage had been perpetrated. Wives who refused to engage in sexual intercourse with their husbands (whether out of fear of pregnancy or not) exposed themselves to charges of fraud for entering into marriage without intending to consummate the union. (Nelson Manfred Blake, *The Road to Reno: A History of Divorce in the United States* [New York, 1962], 189, 196–97; *New York Consolidated Laws Service,* vol. 8A, *Domestic Relations Law* [Rochester, 1990], 40.)

3. Following MS's remarks, C. L. Cook, a member of the audience, stated his belief that poor women were incapable of being taught how to properly use contraception. The session was then formally adjourned.

161. To Hugh de Selincourt

Truro, Mass.
Nov. 27—21.

Hugh—

It is over—the Conference and a very great success. Its amazing how well everything went until the last evening when we assembled at the Town Hall to discuss the "moral" aspect of birth control and found two thousand people locked out by the Police and eighteen hundred locked in the hall.

Ill send you all the clippings about it.[1] You will be amused perhaps indignant, like a good Britisher always is when he or anyone is denied the right to speak.

Mr Cox made a splendid impression here, he is so clear & direct in his English not like Oliver Lodge[2] or other noted speakers who ramble all over the world before getting to the point. Sometimes the rambling is very beautiful too. I'd like to be able to do it. Hugh dear—darling—how are you? Where are you? Have you seen the King—[3] He sent me the most marvellous tea for my birthday and cigarettes, the kind I adore & you hate & laugh at you bad darling. The King likes my weaknesses and aids & abets me in them one & all. I'll never forget him the day he came down to Plymouth with me. He's so watchful of your every move so considerate of one— He really unfolds like a golden day the more one sees of him.

There is so much to tell you of my doings here, but why should I dare to think you would care to hear about them.

The most amazing thing was the very bad impression Marie Stopes made here not by her ~~self~~ ↑personality↓ but because she took an open Stand against me and for the Voluntary Parenthood League—a dying organization—[4] People who have lived here have not taken sides, while she was here only four days & advised people in America to support that League instead of other Organizations. She came to open the first American B.C. Clinic !!!

Poor Marie—her egotism will be her downfall. She looked very pretty and has a certain charm but conceit runs like the babbling brook—on forever—

Now what do you think? I am perfectly well—really I am. Even getting fat!! horrors I can hear you say.

I came up here to the cottage to spend Thanksgiving day (Nov 25) with father and to rest & think for the next battle. I have to go back on the "Stand" next Friday, Hugh, to be battered about & questioned by a low down Irish Police Commissioner concerning my objections to being barred from speaking at Town Hall.[5] The Catholic [*last page(s) missing*]

AL MSP, DLC (LCM 3:454–57).

1. The arrests dominated press coverage of the First American Birth Control Conference. All of New York City's dailies and several magazines expressed outrage over police efforts to restrict free speech and criticized Archbishop Hayes for provoking the raid. (See *New York Evening Post,* Nov. 14, 1921; *New York Times,* Nov. 15, 1921; *New Republic,* Nov. 30, 1921; and *Nation,* Nov. 30, 1921.)

2. Sir Oliver Joseph Lodge (1851–1940), a British physicist and one-time president of the Society for Psychical Research who conducted some pioneer experiments on famous spiritual mediums, had toured the United States in January 1920. (*DNB; New York Times,* Jan. 16, 1920.)

3. The reference was to Havelock Ellis.

4. MS's characterization of the VPL as "a dying organization" was, at this point, wishful thinking on her part.

5. Her lawyer Robert Marsh, the American Civil Liberties Union, and several distin-

guished New York City citizens had lodged a formal complaint on November 15 that initiated a police investigation into the Town Hall raid. Chief Inspector William J. Lahey interviewed MS and others on November 22 and December 2. (*New York Call,* Nov. 15, 1921; *New York World,* Nov. 23, 1921; *New York Times,* Dec. 4, 1921; for copy of complaint, see *MSM* S69:320.)

162. To Henry John Gibbons[1]

*When Sanger was arrested, Dennett went to the police station to offer support. As she attempted to speak to a reporter who had just interviewed Sanger, Dennett claimed that Juliet Rublee, who was "standing directly in front of me, turned and struck me, with a backward swing of her arm, saying 'This is our affair, we don't want you in it.' Her blow was so vigorous, that I would have fallen, but for the dense crowd." Sanger wrote the following in response to a VPL member's anger at her treatment of Dennett. (Dennett Note, Nov. 13, 1921 [*MWDPM *14:382].)*

[*New York, N.Y.*]
December 7th, 1921

Dear Mr. Gibbons:

Owing to the police hearing, Mrs. Rublee's arrest[2] and our moving from the twentieth floor to the nineteenth, I have been delayed in answering your two kind letters of the 14th.[3]

It is very difficult to know what is best to do in regard to the police. The Civil Liberties Bureau called for the hearings from the Police Department in order to place the responsibility of those who had stopped the meeting at the Town Hall. As you doubtless have read, the hearing turned out to be an inquisition, which ended with a slap in the face for our pains, by arresting Mrs. Rublee.[4]

There is no use in trying to bring civil protests against the police, so we have decided upon the advice of our attorneys, Mr. Paul D. Cravath and Mr. Robert Mc. C. Marsh[5] to take the case to the Mayor and ask for a public hearing. From him we will go to the Governor of the State and from there to the United States Courts. It seems that we have a right to do this in as much as Miss Winsor is a resident of Pennsylvania,[6] Mrs. Rublee of New Hampshire, while I am a resident of New York. What the results will be, heaven only knows.

I was informed privately last night that twelve detectives have been detailed to get me.[7] Some of their evidence comes from a letter signed by Mrs. Dennett in which she states that I have been sending an illegal pamphlet out to people.[8] Our attorneys recognize that it is up to the police to whitewash themselves by showing me and my co-workers up and by proving that we are doing something illegal.

In regard to your first letter, it is impossible to go into detail concerning the various subjects that you mention. If you are free sometime in the future and could drop along my way about lunch hour, I will be glad to talk things over with you personally.

I note that you suggest that I write a note of apology. It always interests me that even fair-minded persons like yourself jump to a conclusion that one side is right, without even finding out for yourself what the other side has to say. I am not afraid to apologize, Mr. Gibbon, and if you can prove to me that I have been unfair or have not been truthful in anything I have said, I would deem it a duty to apologize to all concerned, but the more I see the acts of the person in question, the more I am inclined to believe that a sanitarium is the proper place for her.

I thank you for your interest and your suggestions. I would like to know you personally and I hope you will give me the pleasure of talking this thing over with you sometime in the near future. Sincerely yours,

(SIGNED) MARGARET SANGER.

TRcy MWDP, MH-S (*MSM* C1:897). A typed note at the top of the first page, probably added by VPL staff, reads, "Copy of a letter written by Mrs. Sanger to a V.P.L. member, who had urged her to apologize to the V.P.L. Director. Various V.P.L. members have reported hearing from Mrs. Sanger to the effect that Mrs. Dennett was insane."

1. Henry Johns Gibbons (1878–1949) was a Philadelphia lawyer who had romantically pursued Dennett in the summer of 1921. Gibbons was under a doctor's care for mental instability at this time and spent several months in a rest home in 1922. In 1923, he was arrested for financial crimes but resisted efforts to be committed to a mental institution. (*Philadelphia Inquirer,* Feb. 27, 1949; for Dennett-Gibbons correspondence, see *MWDPM* 4:854–976; *New York Tribune,* Nov. 28, 1923.)

2. Rublee, a vice-chair of the First American Birth Control Conference, had witnessed the raid and accompanied MS and Mary Winsor to court. Called to testify before Inspector Lahey on December 2, Rublee stated she disagreed with the law prohibiting the dissemination of contraception and was immediately arrested. After four hours in custody, she was discharged for lack of evidence. Rublee's arrest prompted ten prominent New Yorkers, including the attorneys Paul Cravath and Lewis Delafield, the financier Paul Warburg, and the banker/diplomat Henry Morgenthau, to write a letter to Mayor John F. Hylan requesting an investigation. (*New York World,* Dec. 3, 1921; MS, *Autobiography,* 310–13; see also *New York Times,* Dec. 3, 1921, and Apr. 1, 1925.)

3. The letters were not found.

4. In a letter to the mayor, Albert De Silver, the associate director of the American Civil Liberties Union, publicly criticized the manner in which MS and Rublee were questioned, calling for the dismissal of any police officer who "exceeded his lawful authority." (Lucille B. Milner to MS, Nov. 17, 1921 [*MSM* 2:61]; *New York Call,* Nov. 25, 1921; *New York Globe,* Dec. 2, 1921; quoted in *New York Times,* Dec. 4, 1921.)

5. Paul D. Cravath (1861–1940), a prominent corporate lawyer, was married to Agnes

Huntington Cravath, who along with the wives of several of Paul Cravath's clients, including Addie (Mrs. Otto) Kahn and Juliet Rublee, helped finance the *BCR* and the ABCL. Robert McCurdy Marsh (1878–1958), a former associate in Cravath's law firm and the son-in-law of the ABCL board member Charlotte Delafield, witnessed the Town Hall raid. (*ANB; New York Call,* Nov. 15, 1921, and Jan. 24, 1922; *New York Times,* Sept. 10, 1958; for Marsh petition, see *MSM* S69:320.)

6. Mary Winsor (1869–1956), a suffragist, was one of the 1919 White House picketers arrested and sentenced to the workhouse. (*New York Times,* Sept. 11, 1956.)

7. No evidence was found to support this charge.

8. The illegal pamphlet was *Family Limitation;* for the Dennett letter, see "Special Message to the Council, Contributors and Friends of the VPL," Nov. 18, 1921 (*MWDPM* 14:438).

163. From Havelock Ellis

Cornwall. [*England*]
19 Dec/21

So delighted to receive your letter, Dear Sweet President, & delighted to hear that all was going well.[1] I trust that the subsequent proceedings have not proved disturbing, & I look forward to your next letter. Am also hoping to hear about Japan news.[2]

I am settled, most comfortably, here at Cadegwith near the Lizard,[3] & likely to remain till end of January (but better write Brixton as usual). The climate is just now too damp—too much rain coming over from New York!—but beautifully soft & beautiful, & I am very well & cheerful.

I am shocked to hear of Lothrop Stoddard's disrespectful methods of trying to boss you. Just before your letter came I was correcting proof of my review of his book, & if I had known I might have felt sorry the review was so amiable.[4] However, if he is setting out to boss you, he has all his work cut out, poor man.

Please remember (it is my patent idea!) that the birth control does <u>not</u> mean that the later members of the family are cut off; more accurately, it is the intermediate ones that fail to appear, & you can never tell which; therefore, from that point of view, there is never any need to worry over the possible losses by birth control. Archbishop Hayes is appalled to think that America might have lost Benjamin Franklin[5] (I am not sure whether B. F. would have returned the compliment). But if Mrs F. Senior, had refrained from having the intermediate thirteen children, B. F. would have been, <u>not</u> the <u>fifteenth</u>, but the <u>second</u> child, & in that case, by the gain of vitality to his mother, he might never have been the dry old stick that he turned out to be.— Please remember this whenever that silly old argument about the immense value of the twenty fifth child is brought forward. It is an argument only worthy of people who ar themselves twenty fifth children. With my loving thoughts & wishes Dear Woman,

Havelock

[*Written in left margin of last page*] Article of mine in January "Forum."[6]

ALS MSP, DLC (LCM 4:711–13).

1. He was referring to her new position as president of the ABCL; the letter was not found.

2. In the summer of 1921, MS had received an invitation from *Kaizo* (Reconstruction) *Magazine* to give birth control lectures in Japan. Aware of liberal and intellectual support for birth control in Japan, she had accepted and planned to depart early in 1922. (MS, *Autobiography,* 316; Malia Sedgewick Johnson, "Margaret Sanger and the Birth Control Movement in Japan, 1921–1955," Ph.D. diss., University of Hawaii, 1987, 51–52.)

3. Cadgwith was a fishing village located along the Lizard Peninsula in Cornwall.

4. Theodore Lothrop Stoddard (1883–1950) was a political philosopher and writer known for popularizing eugenic theories about Anglo-Saxon racial superiority, most notably in *The Rising Tide of Color* (New York, 1920). Stoddard, an ABCL national council member, may have tried to pressure MS into bringing the ABCL's goals closer to his own nativist and racist views on "race regeneration." Ellis, who had reviewed Stoddard's *Rising Tide of Color* for the British *Nation* on July 17, 1920, told MS, "There is much in his book I don't care for, & for my taste he is too hostile toward colored races." He was then reviewing Stoddard's *New World of Islam.* (*ANB;* Ellis's review of *The Rising Tide of Color* was reprinted as "World's Racial Problem," *BCR,* Oct. 1920, 14–16; Havelock Ellis, "The Islamic Reformation," *Nation and Athenaeum,* Dec. 24, 1921, 504–5; Ellis to MS, Oct. 14 and July ? [quote], 1920 [LCM 4:598 and 621].)

5. On November 20, 1921, Archbishop Hayes had issued a statement condemning birth control and defending his role in breaking up the Town Hall meeting in which he noted, "The seventh child has been regarded traditionally with some peoples as the most favored by nature. Benjamin Franklin was the fifteenth child, John Wesley, the eighteenth. . . . It has been suggested that one of the reasons for the lack of genius in our day is that we are not getting the ends of the families." (*New York Times,* Nov. 21, 1921.)

6. He was referring to "A Tribute to Freud," a review of William McDougall's *Outline of Abnormal Psychology* that appeared in the *Forum* in July 1926. Ellis included a short passage on birth control in the review. (Ellis to MS, Jan. 8, 1922 [LCM 4:720].)

164. Reply to Archbishop Patrick Joseph Hayes's Statement

On December 17, 1921, Archbishop Hayes's Christmas pastoral again repudiated birth control. Read at masses in more than three hundred New York City churches, he warned Catholics to "stop your ears to that pagan philosophy" and to keep birth control literature as "far from the sanctuary of your Christian homes as you would an evil spirit." He argued that neither poverty nor deformity was a justification for practicing birth control, claiming that "the Christ-Child did not stay His own entrance into this mortal life because His mother was poor, roofless and without a provision for the morrow" and that though some children, "through the moral, mental or physical deformity of parents, may appear to human eyes hideous, misshapen, a blot on civilized society, we must not lose sight of this Christian thought that under and within such visible malformation there lives an immortal soul to be saved and glorified. . . ." (New York Times, *Dec. 18, 1921.)*

[*New York, N.Y.*]
[*December 19, 1921*]

I am glad to learn from Archbishop Hayes' Christmas pastoral that the church has a clear understanding of Birth Control separating it definitely from taking life after conception has occurred.

Many people have been of the opinion that the church confused the two ideas and denied vigorously that the church opposed prevention of conception as distinct from interfering with life after conception has occurred. From Archbishop Hayes' statement we at last realize that there is a perfect understanding by the church of what the Birth Control Movement stands for. For this I am grateful.

I do not care to answer the Archbishop's theological statement concerning the will of the Almighty.[1] His arguments are purely those based on assumption and he knows no more about the facts of the immortality of the soul than the rest of us human beings. What he believes concerning the soul after life, is based upon theory and he has a perfect right to that belief; but we, who are trying to better humanity fundamentally, believe that a healthy, happy human race is more in keeping with the laws of God than disease, misery and poverty perpetuating itself generation after generation.

There is no objection to the Catholic Church inculculating the theories and doctrines in its own church and to its own people; but when they attempt to make these ideas legislative acts and force their opinions and code of morals upon the Protestant members of this country, then we do consider this an interference with the principles of this Democracy and we have a right to protest.[2]

TDcy PPFAR, MN-SSC (*MSM* S76:1165). Printed in the *New York Times*, Dec. 20, 1921.

1. Hayes had argued, "Children troop down from Heaven because God wills it. He alone has the right to stay their coming, while He blesses at will some homes with many, others with but a few or with none at all. . . . Woe to those who degrade, pervert, or do violence to the law of nature as fixed by the eternal decree of God Himself."

2. Protesting the efforts of birth control reformers, Hayes had asserted, "To take life after its inception is a horrible crime; but to prevent human life that the Creator is about to bring into being is satanic. In the first instance, the body is killed, while the soul lives

on; in the latter, not only a body but an immortal soul is denied existence in time and in eternity. It has been reserved to our day to see advocated shamelessly this legalizing of such a diabolical thing."

165. To Hugh de Selincourt

[*New York, N.Y.*]
Christmas night [*December 25, 1921*]

Hugh—

It was dear to have your letter, and such a nice one too, almost on Christmas day.[1] I promised a long letter. Here it is. There are volumes to say to you but I'll spare you ~~with~~ ↑by↓ an outline of events only.

The boys Stuart (18) Grant (13) are home for the holidays. I have just put Grant to bed and am sitting in bed myself tired out from long weary weeks of work—and really ↓most↑ tired because of the work yet to be done. Hugh, about the <u>Essays</u>, yours, or what ever you call those glorious works of yours, I would bring out Hullerston Major any moment you say the word.[2]

I am waiting only for the possibility of a larger Publisher to take hold of it. But I shall do it gladly Hugh whenever you are ready. Mrs Brandt[3] said Hubsch[4] had it and was keenly interested. They both wondered if you would be willing to put in some "constructive work"—add to its length by more ideas as a helpful guide to mothers who may have darling Hullerstons themselves with the same problems. I asked just what was meant by her word "constructive" and she (Mrs Brandt) cited the wood cutting or [*saving*?] illustration[5] as a good constructive idea & thought a little more ~~of~~ along that line & right in the same place would be invaluable.

I saw her point and I know you will see it too. I doubt that anything else could make the book better. But there is no doubt that other suggestions would be helpful to [*groping*?] mothers, ever in the dark along these lines of thought.

Perhaps the artist in your darling self can not give way to the teacher side of you. It will not make the slightest difference to me. Ill publish it as it is or with any thing you may add or take away.

I'll see Mrs Brandt in about ten days & have her draw up a contract for us—and shoot it off to you for your approval or rejection. I'll be puffed up with pride to be publisher for such a book—and such an author—but I do want it to have a large sale, & shall hope first that one of the big Publishing companies want it as much as I do.[6] So there.

Now—Knowledge leads to "Vice" will come out in a private edition later[7]— Its one of those pearls that must not be thrown to swine— Just at present Hugh even Birth Control has a hard time to survive, and I've got to pound away a little longer yet to get the idea well over in the consciousness of the race—then I can give another lift—another step forward—and prepare for Knowledge.

Japan seems positive—I hate to go until the situation here is better protected. My arrest was nothing at all. The case was dismissed. The Catholic Church is desperate. The Police were insulting to the limit, we take the case now to the mayor, then to the governor—and then into the U.S. courts.[8] We must have those responsible dismissed. But oh Hugh the time it all takes, sometimes I think I'll accept the nicest & richest man I know who wants me, marry him & leave all the miserable people to wallow in their misery & learn to fight for themselves. Its glorious to do constructive work but this negative kind is discouraging. Last night we had a family party. I have the dearest Irish father. He is 80 years old and younger than I am, He adores a good drink of whiskey, Prohibition has been very hard on him, but yesterday we got him a couple of bottles of good stuff—and he was so happy.[9] He is a poet, and the spirit of the grain sure did make him eloquent. He is very fond of Bill Sanger (my ↓ex↑ husband) and always tries to bring us together. Its very funny. Some of the drinks one gets now is most dangerous. I have home brew which is best. You may be interested to know that Mr Wells had tea here at my house with me a few day ago I know you don't like him, but he did come out for B.C at the Armament Conference[10] which was brave of him & very decent.

Mr Cox made a splendid impression here. Everyone loves him & thought him the best mind England has sent over here in years. Marie Stopes was too dreadful. She caused a lot of trouble here between our two birth control organizations—she betrayed a confidence I imposed on her & entrusted to her and altogether made a mess of her visit.

She hopes to call on Havelock to tell him how unworthy I am of his friendship no doubt, and also to tell him that I am a radical and break laws and I love the spot light of publicity and oh a lot of things she has discovered by her trip across the ocean.[11] Already friends have written that she spoke publicly of me and most unkindly.[12] Poor dear! No one can hurt me but myself. I thought she was evolved enough to understand that.

Tell Harold—that I saw George Arliss in the Green Goddess today.[13] All through it I kept thinking of Harold Child, only I wanted to see him with a pipe and I wanted the flowers of Wantley around him— But it was glorious to think of Wantley all the time all the afternoon—[14]

The boys return to school Jan 4. I begin a strenuous life at once. No doubt I shall open a research clinic—very soon.[15] I want to be through with this marking of time & get on with life—

There is to be a debate with a minister on Jan 27[16]—for which I am to receive a thousand dollars—that will help out a pressing need. Yes what a bore to need money ever. I have such a nice comfortable apartment now Hugh. No telephone!! I have golden walls, golden silk curtains, blue rug & blue hangings (Chinese blue) red cushions—vases—books—very simple, restful, easily cared for, warm, bright sunshiney, loads of flowers. Only bedroom, living room & bath, but convenient & comfortable.[17]

Did I send you cuttings from press? I think so. It was fine of Mr Cox, to send word to Harold Child. What a delightful people you English are! You would like Harold Cox I think. I do. Very materialistic in the head, but not in the heart at all—you know—I'm very tired these days—but very well. No neck troubles. That operation was worth two trips over.[18] I'm a rooter for tonsils out with gland troubles now, no more pains night & day— Its fine. Good night—more later. A real letter next time blessed.

Margaret

ALS MSP, DLC (LCM 3:462–69).

1. De Selincourt to MS, Dec. 10, 1921 (LCM 3:458–61).
2. Hullerston Major is the main character of de Selincourt's novel *One Little Boy.*
3. Zelma Corning Brandt (1891–1990) was a publicist and literary agent with the firm of Brandt & Kirkpatrick. A member of the feminist group Heterodoxy and a birth control supporter, Brandt had begun representing MS in 1920, orchestrating her lecture tours and negotiating the translation of *Woman and the New Race* into several languages. (SSDI; Schwartz, *Radical Feminists,* 117; MS to Brandt & Kirkpatrick, June 20, 1922 [*MSM* C2:34]; MS to de Selincourt, Jan. 27, 1922 [LCM 3:474]; for additional correspondence between MS, Zelma Brandt, and Brandt & Kirkpatrick, see LCM 135:81–93.)
4. The American publisher Benjamin W. Huebsch (1876–1964) decided against publishing it. (*ANB;* MS to de Selincourt, Jan. 27, 1922 [LCM 3:474].)
5. It was not identified.
6. De Selincourt's book was finally published in 1924 by A. and C. Boni.
7. See MS to de Selincourt, Feb. 24, 1921, note 7, herein.
8. When nothing came of Lahey's Town Hall investigation, Mayor Hylan ordered another, this one led by David Hirschfield, the commissioner of accounts. It began on January 23 and ended February 20, 1922, with the vindication of MS and the ABCL and blame laid on Police Commissioner Donahue for misinterpreting orders. (*New York World,* Jan. 8, 1922; *New York Times,* Dec. 10, 1921, and Jan. 18 and Feb. 22, 1922; for complainants brief before the commissioner of accounts, see *MSM* S69:323.)
9. Though the 1919 Volstead Act criminalized the sale of liquor in the United States, "bootlegging" and illegal drinking were rampant until the law was repealed in 1933.
10. MS met H. G. Wells several times in New York City between December 12, 1921, and January 7, 1922. In his November 18 news dispatch, Wells noted, "I submit that the troubles arising from excessive fecundity within a country justify not an aggressive imperialism on the part of that country, but a sufficient amount of birth control within its proper limits." (H. G. Wells, *Washington and the Riddle of Peace* [New York, 1922], 110.)
11. Ellis did not like Stopes, who he thought was aggressive and vulgar, but advised MS a few days later that when dealing with rivals to "leave them alone as far as possible. To just go ahead & do your work as beautifully as possible is the best defense. To dis-

pute, even when you are in the right, is never quite satisfactory." To console her, he described an advertisement featuring a portrait of Stopes "in front of her house, on a large piece of cardboard, with a calendar underneath & a piece of ribbon above!! . . . What a pity her husband, poor man, does not instruct her in the things one ought <u>not</u> to do." Ellis also assured MS that he would not write an introduction for *Married Love.* (Grosskurth, *Havelock Ellis,* 373–74; Ellis to MS, Dec. 28, 1921 [LCM 4:714]. For Ellis's views of Stopes, see letters to MS, Jan. 8 and Oct. 6, 1922, and Sept. 15, 1923 [LCM 4:720, 751, and 847].)

12. The letters were not found.

13. William Archer's melodrama *The Green Goddess* had opened in New York City on January 18, 1921, starring the British actor George Arliss (1868–1946). (Burns Mantle, ed., *The Best Plays of 1920–21* [Boston, 1921], 124, 422; *New York Times,* Feb. 6, 1946.)

14. Wantley was de Selincourt's Sussex home.

15. MS planned to open an ABCL clinic at 317 East Tenth Street but was waiting for a dispensary license from the New York State Board of Charities. (Charles Johnson to MS, Nov. 17, 1921 [LCM 33:543].)

16. She was referring to a debate proposed by the Brooklyn Philosophical Association between MS and the Reverend William Chase. It did not take place because MS, on her doctor's orders, was forced to limit her public appearances. (Harry Cooper to Anne Kennedy, Dec, 5, 1921, and Kennedy to Cooper, Dec. 7, 1921 [*MSM* C1:894 and 896].)

17. She had recently moved from 246 West Fourteenth Street (the same building in which her sister Ethel Byrne lived) to 18 Gramercy Park, where J. Noah Slee had an adjoining apartment. (MS Diary [*MSM* S78:488]; Chesler, *Woman of Valor,* 251.)

18. Her September 1921 tonsillectomy had freed her of tuberculosis-related gland problems. (Chesler, "Interview with Grant Sanger," 19.)

166. To Hugh de Selincourt

[*New York, N.Y.*]
January 27. [*1922*]

Hugh dear—

<u>No darling</u> thats what you are to me—ever & ever—<u>amen</u>.[1] Looking over page proofs all evening of Review in which is your splendid article—tribute to Havelock the King.[2] My but that is ripping Hugh— The King will die of joy over it. Its simply too splendid for words I was thrilled to get it— Kept sending you wireless S.O.S. to do it—not to forget, and nearly all February material went to printers—began to get nervous & faint as if some Prince I knew once had not arrived on a white horse at the right moment to rescue me from some horrible fate. Then along came your precious packet & there it was—gold—golden all through—every line. Oh Hugh you are the dearest in the world to remember. That pleases me beyond words—thats all.

Where shall I begin to tell you all the things that are happening? Did you get the long bed letter I wrote you?[3] Here is another bed letter. Saw Mrs Brandt about Hullerston Major. Nothing has happened since I wrote you. It is still with Hubsch— Now it goes to Scott & Seltzer[4] with the promise that I'll guarantee five hundred copies of the first edition. I'd make it a thousand if I were to be here—but I leave for Japan on Feb 21st San Francisco— I do hope Scott takes it. I told Mrs Brandt not to fail to hold it for me for we'll publish it in fall if another publisher does not take it before that time. I know they can give it a better boost than we can & advertise at a better advantage. Things have been moving fast. Police hearings, meetings, Public insults,[5] Episcopal church Bishop also behaving badly—Roman Church pressing upon it for repudiation of B.C. Movement.[6] Along comes Marie Stopes announcement today that God spoke to her in the woods & told her to open a clinic.[7] She saw him too. This brings howls of laughter from the enemy etc etc.

I had to speak today at a performance of "Ghosts". Mary Shaw the famous Ibsenite played & gave a benefit for our cause. The Catholics objected to my speaking & hounded the manager of the theatre & threatened a boycott.[8]

There is to be a farewell meeting to me on Feb 5th at the Lexington Opera House.[9] I leave N.Y the 6th speak in Rochester, Detroit, Chicago, San Francisco.[10] I may take Grant with me,[11] I'd love to take you— It will be such fun to see Japan with him. Oh Hugh—Sometimes I envy you your quiet & beauty & all the peace & harmony you seem to have attained. I was legally divorced some months ago, and for some strange reason two very fine men have been thrust my way. One a millionaire and sixty—terribly American typical type of respectable business man, church going widower—generous—happy, thinks I'm "sensible" likes me for that stupid quality. He could with his wealth make life very comfortable & insure the financial success of my cause— Shall I accept him?[12]

The other a bachelor—about 42—writes on Asiatic population problems—Eugenist—good birth—fairly wealthy—not enough to make cause successful—

But free & believes in womans advancement.[13] You & he & the King would be pals—But I don't like him so well as I like my cause— He's very pressing for marriage. I don't believe in that institution particularly—do we? No. I could have such a beautiful time if that cause were won. I'd buy Wantley[14] for you. I want to live in London near Hill Road. Good Night adorable Hugh—Margaret—Margaret

Margaret

ALS MSP, DLC (LCM 3:474–77).

1. See de Selincourt to MS, Jan. 3, 1922 (LCM 3:472).
2. She was referring to de Selincourt's "Havelock Ellis: A Great Humanist," *BCR*, Feb. 1922, 4–6.

3. See MS to de Selincourt, Dec. 25, 1921, herein.

4. She was referring to the publisher Benjamin Huebsch and a publishing firm established in 1919 by the English writer/editor Temple Scott (1864–1939), whose real name was Isaac Henry Solomon Isaacs, and Thomas Seltzer (1875–1943), an editor at the *Masses*. Seltzer had formed his own publishing company, Thomas Seltzer, Inc., in 1920, though MS continued to use the old name. (*Dictionary of Literary Biography*, vol. 46 [Detroit, 1986], 333–35; *New York Times*, Oct. 29, 1943.)

5. This was a reference to the January 23, 1922, hearing, which abruptly ended in a "furious row" when Commissioner Hirschfield refused to allow Robert Marsh to present MS's case. Marsh was replaced by Emory R. Buckner at subsequent hearings on February 1, 17, and 21. (*New York Times*, Jan. 18 and Feb. 22, 1922; *New York Call*, Jan. 24, 1922 [quote]; *New York Post*, Feb. 2, 1922.)

6. She was referring to Episcopal Bishop William Hall Moreland's Joint Commission on Home and Family Life, which released a July report recommending a ban on birth control. The report endorsed the 1920 Lambeth Conference of Anglican Bishops, which characterized contraception as "involving grave dangers to physical health, as well as moral innocence, and threatening the future of the human race." It was referred to the church's Social Service Department on September 15 but never endorsed. (*New York Times*, July 20 and Sept. 16 [quote], 1922; *Journal of the General Convention of the Episcopal Church* [New York, 1922], 305.)

7. In July 1920, while sitting beneath a yew tree, Stopes claimed to have received a message from God in support of birth control. She "re-dictated" the message as a memorandum to clergymen preparing to meet at the Lambeth Conference and published it in 1922 as *A New Gospel to All Peoples: A Revelation of God Uniting Physiology and the Religions of Man*. (Rose, *Marie Stopes*, 136–37.)

8. MS spoke before an ABCL benefit performance at the Broadhurst Theater of Henrik Ibsen's 1881 drama, in which venereal disease and moral contamination undermine a family. Mary Shaw (1854–1929), a suffragist and actress, best known for bringing *Ghosts* to the American public, was a birth control advocate and member of the ABCL national council (1921–29). (*ANB*; ABCL Report, 1922 [*MSM* S61:159]; *New York Herald*, Jan. 28, 1922.)

9. The proposed meeting was canceled after the newspaper publisher Frank Munsey (1854–1925) declined to serve as chair. The *BCR* blamed the cancellation on MS's hectic schedule and fatigue, promising a mass meeting on her return from Asia. MS instead attended a small farewell dinner at New York City's Cosmopolitan Club on February 5. (Kennedy to Munsey, Jan. 28, 1922, and Titherington to Kennedy, Jan. 31, 1922 [*MSM* 2:24 and 26]; "News Notes," *BCR*, Mar. 1922, 28.)

10. MS addressed a doctors-only meeting on February 7 and met with Rochester women on February 8. In Detroit on February 10, she spoke to twelve hundred at the United Auto Workers Hall, before taking a night train to Chicago, where she stayed February 11–14, visiting friends and meeting with small groups of activists. She arrived in San Francisco on February 17 and spoke before a mass meeting sponsored by the American Women's Independence Committee on February 19. (MS Itinerary, Feb. 6–17, 1922 [*MSM* S78:278].)

11. MS pulled Grant out of Peddie to accompany her, while Stuart, a football team

captain, remained in school to prepare for college entrance exams. (MS, *Autobiography*, 316.)

12. She was referring to J. Noah Slee, who was then divorcing his wife. MS, troubled by Slee's views of her activities, confessed her concerns to Ellis, who responded, "With regard to marrying Mr. 'Satan,' I hope you'll think a long, long time about it first, however nice & kind & generous he is. A sort of 'repentant' millionaire, who felt that you were doing all the things he would on his inside like done, or think right, might possibly work out. But a really committed one who disapproves or dislikes everything that is really <u>you</u> doesn't seem as a husband to work out at all. I'm glad you think there are a hundred million things to consider first." (Divorce Decree, Oct. 4, 1921 [*MSM* S1:902, S83:732]; Ellis to MS, Jan. 15, 1922 [LCM 4:722].)

13. This was probably John Otway Percy Bland, a China expert MS later described as a "dark-haired, witty, amusing North-of-Irishman who had lived much in the Orient. . . . He was one of those who always helped to hold up your right hand." Bland was probably a widower by the time he met MS. (MS, *Autobiography*, 299; see also MS to Slee, Feb. 28, 1927 [*MSM* S3:770].)

14. Poor book sales contributed to his financial woes, which forced de Selincourt to sell Wantley and purchase Sand Pit, a less expensive cottage in Sussex, sometime in 1921. (De Selincourt to MS, Nov. 20, 1921 [LCM 3:1010].)

167. To Stuart Sanger

Sanger was held up for several days in San Francisco, attempting to obtain a travel visa denied her by Japan's Department of the Interior over her plans to lecture on birth control. Accompanied by Grant and J. Noah Slee, she was finally allowed to sail on February 21 with a Chinese visa on the SS Taiyo Maru *docking at Shanghai. But she had to sign an agreement that she would not attempt to disembark during stops in Japanese ports. (MS Diary, [*MSM *S70:26]; MS,* Autobiography, *317; for agreement, see Feb. 18, 1922 [LCM 18:944].)*

[*San Francisco, CA*]
[*February 17–21, 1922*]

Stuart dearest:

Your letter came & I guess Grant has told you the news.[1] I do not want it to be generally known until I return from Europe next August. So just keep it to your self for a while longer.

Dr S—[2] said you could get a very good suit of clothes in Trenton perhaps you can. I left him $100 for your car fare, allowence, clothes books, and office expenses I hope you will make that do for everything until school is over in June. Then you can get some money from Anna,[3] but go light until you need it. I may send you a check in April for your Easter vacation. You might run up to Truro for the week, or stay in the apartment at 18 as you wish.[4]

About your vacation I wish you would settle down to either a summer school or a tutor until my return in August. Then we will all go to Truro together if Uncle Tom is not there. I do not believe either Tom or Aunt Nan[5] will go there again, but in the early part of summer please study hard. If you wanted to get a tutor on two or three weak studies until summer school begins Id do it. Make the best price you can & go to it. Ill pay for it, if you will work & be sure it will pay you to do so. I am anxious to hear about your leg. If you pass your exams for College[6] Ill see to it that you get in, but I do not know how far you are in toward that event. Clark Smyth lives here & spent the day with Grant. We saw Uncle Laurence & the family—Gertrude is lovelier than ever.[7] I stopped at Buffalo & spent the day with Aunt Mary, all are well.[8] Don't harbor up resentment about that week end. It was a case of establishing Authority, as one has to do now & then.[9]

Be sure to get Daisys address & let her know your plans & let her take care of you.[10] I may have some trouble in getting to Japan. The old government wants big families the people do not. So I am getting my ticket for Shanghai, China & write me c/o American Express there. I don't know the street number but Anna will get it for you. Then after April send letter c/o A. Ex to 6 Haymarket London.[11] I won't be able to hear from you only at Shanghai until I know my Japan plans.[12] Do settle down to get in some good hard work like a dear. It will please me no end & will make your own life more fun. Make your brain work for you & life begins to be interesting & facinating.

Grant & J. N. are getting acquainted but Grant is not trained to respect his elders yet.

Take care of your health. Train your body & mind in good habits. Keep both clean & high. Buckle down to regular brain drill each day. Write to me when you can. lovingly ever

Mother.

ALS MSP, MN-SSC (*MSM* S2:119–24). Letterhead of the Hotel St. Francis.

1. The letter was not found. She was probably referring to her official engagement to Slee.
2. Dr. Roger W. Swetland (1861–1934) was the headmaster of the Peddie School (1898–1934).
3. Anna Lifshiz was left in charge of her personal affairs.
4. She meant 18 Gramercy Park.
5. She was referring to Thomas Higgins and Anna Higgins.
6. Stuart failed the French portion of his college entrance examinations in the summer of 1922.
7. MS's brother Clio Lawrence Higgins, a naval officer; his wife, Gertrude McCarthy Higgins; and their daughter, Tillie, lived in San Francisco.
8. She was referring to Mary Higgins and her employers, the Abbotts and Schoellkopfs.
9. This was possibly a reference to MS clamping down on Stuart's spending habits and his penchant for drink and parties.

10. Daisy Mitchell was the housekeeper.

11. MS arrived in Japan on March 10 and then moved on to China, Hong Kong, Singapore, and Ceylon. The party then sailed west, making stops in Yemen and Egypt and reaching Europe in June. They traveled through Italy, Switzerland, and France before reaching London on July 1. (MS World Trip Journal [*MSM* S70:31–203].)

12. Upon her ship's arrival in Tokyo Bay on March 10, Sanger was detained until she promised Japanese officials she would refrain from public speaking and would merely travel in Japan. (MS, *Autobiography*, 320–21.)

168. To Hugh de Selincourt

[*London, England*]
Saturday 8am. [*July 15, 1922*][1]

Hugh dear—

Since my return there has been nothing I have wanted to do more than to see you.

I have not tried to write because I wanted to tell you everything & being Irish I never tell the same thing alike twice. Any way the thing I would have told you had I seen you is that during my illness in Japan & Cairo I had some trouble with my heart. The heat I think. It did act badly going through the voyage and I was certain I was to be thrown to the water animals & eaten up, but here I am, not so bad as that, but just the same old thing has followed me ashore.[2] Yesterday I had two attacks fainting in a most mid Victorian fashion. I got over them & went to attend a promised lecture and got home at one a m.[3] Then the thing began again. A friend was sent for & nursed me through the night. The Doctor is worried not because of my condition, but because of my stubbornness I want to go to Wantley today just the same. He will not allow me to take the journey, but insists I get away to Wales or some place high. We choose the Alps. So off I go to Switzerland instead of going to Wantley.[4] Later.

Your voice was so bored on the 'phone dear Hugh, especially at first. But it was good to hear you—oh what a darling voice it really is— I am feeling very blue & discouraged with Mrs Sanger— She is unable to do the things she loves to do. She is unable to be with the friends she adores—while she finds all her time taken up talking to very horrid disagreeable people she does not like at all.

But Hugh the cause is moving. It will really come to pass. We will see it too. I did want you to know all my dear co workers—Mrs Rublee has heard me talk of you & wants to know you. She is a dear. If you can let her come down to Wantley do it. She is the dearest woman America has produced. I am filled with strychnine & other things.[5] Isnt it immoral to be like this. I had a nice visit with Mrs Laurence, oh what a fine soul she is Hugh— Did you know that she resigned from Marie Stopes board because of her attack on poor little me.[6]

That was for you—dear darling Hugh. She is so fine in her friendship for you that she would be true to your friends. I was terribly & deeply touched by that (nearly wept when I read it.) I want to tell you about Grant. He has not seen or talked to a boy of his own age since last February 3rd.

He has been with adults & babies—until he is lonely for his own kin— He talked a lot about you & then would refer to "his kid girl" very often. He wanted to know if she played tennis rode horse back. If she had a dog was your or Janets[7] "favorite", as if there was a large family—

Then a letter came from his school asking to get him tutored & ready for next years work.[8] It related the doings of the boys at Camp, & hoped he would come on for the August term.

That settled it. I had to get him off. He sent three dolls to Bridget & is taking a bottle of essense of rose to a girl he knows at home. So there you are—

I spent a nice day with the King, but I feel someone has captured his heart.[9] He was dear & lovely to me, oh so dear. Yet I feel a pang of seperateness I never felt before.[10]

Perhaps had I seen him again it would be gone.

The Conference was a success. I am not emotional enough to stir a British audiance. I am afraid of them—these Britishers, who sit so silently & move not.[11]

Where is Harold Child? Two telegrams from him saying the same thing but coming two days apart.[12]

My friends are worried about me. There is such a lot of work to be done during the next two years. I must be well to do it. You are a dear to say you will give us something regularly for the Review.

I wish now I had asked you to come & write up the conference. I could then have offered to pay your expenses & could have seen you at the same time. But I looked pale & tired & worn out and you would have hated the conference & reported it in a bad way.

Oh <u>why</u> did I not ask you to do this?? I am going to take this one month at getting really strong.[13] Then I'm going to let everything go & push with all there is in me to end this work & succeed in getting it over— Come & help me Hugh— Have you read my new book?[14] Is it any good?

Your voice follows me around the room. But you are in Wantley, lovely Wantley and I am here in this barn where wild & crazy people think they live. I shall marry for wealth some day soon & come & live near you—yes? There are things to do—rest—<u>medicine</u> (oh) and I am asked to stop. Please be kind & forgiving to me Hugh— When I am fit & strong Ill come leaping back across the world to you—

Love to Janet & Harold & you you a hundred times to you.

Margaret.

Have you something for the September Review?[15] Send it to me Bankers Trust Co. Paris where it will be forwarded or Ill write & let you know where I am soon. Your new book is it out?[16]

M

[*Handwritten note by MS at top of first page reads*]: "Now that paper & printing is down Im going to tackle the job of publisher Yes?"[17]

ALS MSP, DLC (LCM 3:407–22). Letterhead of the Hotel Russell. A note added later, probably by MS, to the top of the eighth page reads, "Pethick."

1. MS was in London July 1–23. She misdated this letter as 1921. (MS Calendar, 1922 [*MSM* S78:507 and 514.)

2. In March, MS came down with a severe cold. On May 19, suffering from dysentery, she fainted on board the SS *Penang* en route to Ceylon, and a doctor administered a heart stimulant to counter a low pulse. She became faint again in Cairo on June 9 after many hours in the sun, and in mid-June she suffered another dysentery attack. (MS to Rublee, March ?, 1922, World Trip Diary, and 1922 Calendar [*MSM* C2:28, S70:147, S78:505].)

3. MS led the American delegation to the Fifth International Neo-Malthusian and Birth Control Conference held in London on July 11–14. She was probably referring to an afternoon session on propaganda at which her ABCL colleagues Annie Porritt and Clara Louise Rowe spoke and an evening meeting for working men and women in South London. (Conference Program, July 11–14, 1922 [*MSM* S67:18].)

4. She left England for Paris on July 23 and left for Montreaux on July 29. She spent August touring the Alps, staying in Interlaken, Murren, Spiez, Chateau-d'Oex, and other resorts. (MS Diary [*MSM* S78:510–14].)

5. In therapeutic doses, strychnine improved the appetite by stimulating the central nervous system. Often used as a tonic for ill-defined conditions of weakness, it was also prescribed as a heart medication because of its tendency to raise blood pressure. (Arthur R. Cushny, *Pharmacology and Therapeutics* [Philadelphia, 1934], 300–310.)

6. Emmeline Pethick-Lawrence (1867–1954), a wealthy radical suffragette and peace activist, had been arrested numerous times for her militant tactics. In 1915, she had befriended Hugh de Selincourt, whose writing she admired. The attack MS mentions was likely "Unifiers Who Won't Unite" in the *BC News* (July 1922), in which Stopes quoted an exchange between "a public man, of world fame" (probably H. G. Wells) and the VPL, which characterized the ABCL as a new organization that was "not working practically as we have been doing on the *major task* of the birth control movement . . . the repeal of the Federal law, which is the key to the whole situation" (4). Though Pethick-Lawrence offered to resign as a vice-president of Stopes's Society for Constructive Birth Control, she did not. (Emmeline Pethick-Lawrence, *My Part in a Changing World* [London, 1938], 315–19; Pethick-Lawrence to Stopes, Oct. 4, 1922 [Stopes].)

7. She was referring to Hugh's daughter, Bridget, and his wife, Janet.

8. The letter was not found. Grant sailed home on July 18.

9. This was possibly Jane Burr (pseudonym of Rosalind Guggenheim Winslow [1882–1958]), an American feminist writer and journalist, who began a casual affair with Ellis in the summer of 1922. MS saw Ellis on July 3 and again on July 6. (Grosskurth, *Havelock Ellis,* 295–96, 309; Ellis to MS, Dec. 10, 1922, and Sept. 1, 1924 [LCM 4:765 and 916]; MS Diary [*MSM* S78:507].)

10. MS later added "(Interesting)."

11. MS complained the British treated birth control so soberly and scientifically that they limited their ability to gain widespread publicity. In its summary of the conference, the *BCR* referred to British birth control as "a man's movement" and noted that MS alone grasped "all sides of the question, combined with her infinite pity and sympathy for the griefs and difficulties of suffering women." ("Margaret Sanger's Impressions" and "The Fifth International Birth Control Conference," *BCR,* Sept. 1922, 175–76 and 171–74 [quotes on 172].)

12. The telegrams were not found.

13. MS returned to London from the Continent on September 1. She visited Wantley for the last time before the de Selinourts moved, met with Ellis, and on September 18 secretly married J. Noah Slee in London. On September 23, they sailed for New York City on the SS *Aquitania.*

14. This was a reference to *The Pivot of Civilization.*

15. De Selincourt did not publish any *BCR* articles in September.

16. The book was not identified; de Selincourt was working on several writing projects.

17. This was probably another reference to finding a publisher for *One Little Boy.*

SEVEN

A Legal Clinic

MARGARET SANGER returned home from her world tour in the fall of 1922 with a new husband, the millionaire J. Noah Slee, though she kept the union secret for over a year. After numerous welcome-home receptions and meetings, she turned to unfinished business: keeping the ABCL afloat and establishing a birth control clinic. Using as her legal base the 1918 *Crane* decision, which upheld the right of physicians to prescribe contraceptives for the cure and prevention of disease, Sanger planned to open the clinic not only to provide birth control services but also to accumulate statistical evidence on the effectiveness of contraceptive methods. The results, she hoped, would pressure the medical community into accepting the safety, effectiveness, and public health benefits of birth control.[1]

Though she had planned to open the clinic in 1921, the project was delayed when Dr. Lydia DeVilbiss, hired as the medical director, backed out after the ABCL failed to secure a dispensary license. Sanger then decided to operate the clinic as a research bureau and in short order found a doctor, Dorothy Bocker, willing to take on the legal risk. With funds donated by the English manufacturer Clinton Chance and the socialite philanthropists Dorothy Whitney Straight, Katharine Dexter McCormick, and Addie Wolff Kahn, the Clinical Research Bureau (CRB) opened on January 1, 1923, across the hall from the ABCL offices at 104 Fifth Avenue.[2]

From the start, the clinic staff collected personal histories of each patient and tracked success and failure rates for various contraceptive methods. Dissatisfied with available contraceptives and frustrated by the legal ban on importing pessaries (diaphragms), which were not yet manufactured in the United States, Sanger sought cheaper, more readily available, and more effective forms of birth control. She kept apprised of the latest contraceptive research and initiated contacts with contraceptive manufacturers in the United States and Germany, establishing the CRB as a leader and facilitator in the development of modern birth control methods. Sanger also opened the doors of the CRB to physicians interested in learning contraceptive techniques, as well as others seeking to promote birth control, and she sent its medical and administrative staff to speak to hundreds of social work, health, and charitable organizations.

But the CRB was, first and foremost, a birth control clinic, serving some twelve hundred patients in its first thirteen months.[3] Though the clinic adhered technically to New York State law by accepting only married patients seeking contraception for specific health reasons, over the years, clinic staff treated countless patients under a catchall of medical indications, such as "general debility." Sanger also provided contraceptives to women interested in spacing children by calling it a preventive health measure. However, patients seeking abortion were officially turned away. While sympathetic to their plight, Sanger was unwilling to jeopardize her broader efforts by openly providing abortion referrals or by allowing therapeutic abortions at the CRB. She did not interfere if ABCL staff members took it upon themselves to provide unofficial referrals.[4] Energized by the clinic's patients and the thousands of letters she continued to receive from women seeking birth control information, Sanger remained grounded in a woman-centered campaign. Never abandoning the "oppressed mothers," she continued to send out copies of *Family Limitation*, and she focused most of her speeches and articles on the essential right of every woman to decide whether and when to have children.

In January 1923, still persuaded that medical support was critical to the success of the movement, Sanger backed a bill even more physician-focused than in 1921, one that eliminated nurses and midwives from the clause allowing only medical professionals to dispense contraceptives. In 1924, she created a CRB medical advisory board composed of well-known male physicians. Convinced that the medical profession should eventually manage contraceptive services, Sanger negotiated with Robert Latou Dickinson, a prominent obstetrician/gynecologist and contraceptive advocate, to get him to merge his Committee on Maternal Health with the CRB, but it was a rocky and ultimately unsuccessful alliance. In the end, she could not relinquish control of the CRB to physicians.

Sanger continued to court a wider array of medical and scientific professionals by organizing the 1923 Middle Western States Conference on Birth Control, inviting prominent academics, scientists, and physicians to give papers on the impact of birth control on public health, hereditary diseases, and population control. She intensified her efforts to define the eugenical need for birth control in articles and speeches on how birth control could keep the "unfit" from reproducing. In these years, she also cultivated a small group of well-respected scientists and academics, nearly all of them eugenicists but representing a new reform strain; they rejected pure biological determinism and gave weight to nurture as well as nature in the determination of mental traits. She increasingly relied on this group for advice and guidance in grounding the movement in the mainstream.

Birth control continued to draw fire from the Catholic church, which, after the war, supplanted the government as Sanger's most powerful and dogged opponent. Such opposition was often indirect, as when legislators refused to support her bills for fear of offending Catholic constituents. Occasionally interference was more overt, as when Catholic church leaders pressured local officials into banning public discussions of birth control. Sanger excelled at turning these confrontations into personal and public victories, keeping the movement in the media spotlight, controlling the public debate, and thereby building a larger audience for her message. Birth control, as she pointed out in 1924, "has been made to thrive by these ill-advised attempts to extirpate it from the American mind."[5] Under Sanger's leadership, this increasingly popular protest movement had evolved from street theater to a sophisticated public relations enterprise.

With her marriage, Sanger ascended to a new level of society and wealth that dominated her private and public life. When her marriage became public in February 1924, with such headlines as "Mrs. Sanger Admits She Married Rich Oil Magnate," she felt compelled to tell the press, "My private life and my work for the birth control movement are kept separate entirely. . . . He has his business. I have mine."[6] But within a matter of months, Slee was acting as the ABCL's treasurer, and by 1922, he was contributing nearly ten thousand dollars annually to the organization. He also undertook the tricky business of smuggling diaphragms into the United States from Europe.

With access to Slee's wealth, Sanger was freed from personal dependence on the largesse of the society women who had carried her through the tribulations of the previous years, though she still solicited their support for the ABCL. She now lived a life of luxury, splitting her time between a Park Avenue apartment and Willowlake, the grand stone house in Fishkill, New York, that Slee had built as a wedding present. She took winter vacations and indulged herself in fur wraps and extended spa retreats. She could also afford to educate her sons at Ivy League schools: Stuart at Yale; Grant en route to Princeton. Slee's money now allowed Sanger to help her old radical friends, including Carlo Tresca, Alexander Berkman, and Agnes Smedley, whom she never wholly abandoned in spirit. But her new wealth, she knew, would not satisfy all her needs. "We will be happy," Sanger wrote to Slee shortly after their first anniversary, "in spite of your money."[7]

By 1924, Margaret Sanger was the undisputed leader of the birth control movement. Her main rivals had faded away: Mary Ware Dennett struggled to sustain the VPL in the wake of another legislative defeat, while Marie Stopes lacked both Sanger's international stature and the respect of many scientists and reformers even in her own country. No other prominent birth control advocate could compete with Sanger's renown, her skill, her delight in manipulating the press and driving public opinion, or her new access to wealth and power.

NOTES

1. Gordon, *Woman's Body,* 259–60.
2. MS, "Clinical Research Fund," 1923 (LCM 34:179); MS, *Autobiography,* 297–98, 358–61.
3. Dorothy Bocker, *Birth Control Methods* (New York, 1924), 1.
4. For abortion referrals, see Penelope Huse, "Confidential Report to Executive Committee," Dec. 1929 (PPFAR).
5. MS, "War against Birth Control," 235.
6. Quoted in *Buffalo Times,* Feb. 20, 1924.
7. MS to Slee, Nov. 8, 1923, herein.

169. To Dorothy Bocker[1]

To legally operate a clinic under the provisions of the 1918 Crane *decision, Sanger had to obtain a dispensary license from the New York State Board of Charities, which would allow nurses to treat patients under doctor supervision. When the state rejected the ABCL's license application because it was not incorporated as a charity or medical organization, Sanger decided to redefine the clinic as a medical "research bureau," where all subjects would be seen by a licensed physician. (Charles Johnson to MS, Nov. 17, 1921; "Notes on the New York Clinic," n.d.; ABCL Application to the New York State Board of Charities, May 12, 1922; Richard Wallace to Anne Kennedy, May 16, 1922 [LCM 33:543, 551, and 554].)*

[*New York, N.Y.*]
October 17, 1922.

Dear Dr. Bocker:—

Mr. Siddall was kind enough to bring me your letter to him of October 13th.[2] He and I have gone over very thoroughly the idea of opening a clinic.

You remember perhaps that I had the pleasure of meeting you last year for just a brief moment.[3] I have always regretted that it was not longer.

I will not go into detail about the many things that have happened to prevent the opening of our clinic; but the main thing was—we could not find a doctor with courage enough to take a stand. To be brief, the situation is this:

The American Birth Control League has been incorporated under the laws of the State of New York. It is incorporated to change the law. The judge has specifically stated that this League could not open clinics.[4] So far, so good. We never really wanted to, but we did hope to have the medical staff conduct such a venture. This means that we must organize a separate committee to stand behind the doctor who will give information to diseased persons only. We can organize this committee. I believe we can also get the finances and have it in the bank before we start.

You may not wish to take on this work, in view of the fact that the League would not be behind you, but personally I think if you and I take the responsibility of opening this clinic without another soul, we would get on much better than bothering with a committee of either lay people or doctors. This is my personal view, and I will tell you more of this if you decide that you could give the time to come up here about the end of this month, when we could talk matters over.

The next important thing to tell you is—that we would open the clinic on the authority of the Court of Appeals, of the State of New York, who rendered a decision in my case, claiming that "doctors in this state could give information to prevent conception for the cure or prevention of disease." This decision was rendered in 1918. There has been no legislation rendered since in contradiction to this opinion. It does state, however, in this decision that this would be in the capacity of the physician's private practice, which means that if you would do clinical work we would not advertise the opening of a clinic. To all effects and purposes, it would be a birth control clinic and you would keep clinical records upon which other public clinics would be established in the future.

Now, Dr. Bocker, I want to be perfectly frank with you and tell you exactly what I think; for I want you to come into this work with us in the same spirit that we are in it—and that is to give all you have, and to take the consequences for good or for bad. By that I mean, there is a possibility of your going to jail, or at least of your standing trial, also as you state yourself, of losing your New York State license. This is the worst that can happen to you.

On the other hand, for one doctor to stand up and assert her right under this legal opinion, would give tremendous impetus and encouragement to thousands of other doctors throughout the country to do likewise.

Again, I believe if you will do this, we can get a splendid backing of medical men and women all over the country to protest vigorously against your arrest or anything else that will happen to you. If this does happen, I believe you will get such a good boost of publicity, that we can put you on the platform lecturing throughout the country for the next two years.

I am not afraid of the results—no matter which way the cat may jump, but I cannot assure you a peaceful, harmonious, or uneventful year. It is not likely to be this.

After you have considered the subject from the worst possible angle, (We will leave the good angle to kind providence) and if you make up your mind that you will take a stand with us, let me know if you can arrange to come up here, arriving here the 29th or 30th. We have a Welcome Home Meeting, at Carnegie Hall, on the 30th, which I would be glad to have you attend.[5] If you could come here for two or three days to talk over personally with me the possibility of opening the clinic, I will, of course, send you your fare. Let me know frankly what you think of this whole procedure.

We are giving up the lease of our clinic on November 15th.[6] Of course, we can always get other rooms—and perhaps cheaper ones. I would like you to look over this little place before we scrap it.

May I hear from you as soon as you made up your mind, or wire me if necessary.[7]

Here is trusting that our paths may unite harmoniously and happily in the immediate future, I am Sincerely yours,

---

TLcy MSP, DLC (LCM 31:406–7).

1. Dorothy Bocker (1878?–?), a New York–trained physician, served as director of the Georgia State Board of Health's Division of Child Hygiene. MS hired Bocker at six thousand dollars annually (an inflated amount that Bocker demanded to cover her legal risk) for two years. (U.S. Bureau of the Census, *Fourteenth Census of the United States, 1920;* Bocker Resume [LCM 21:415]; Slee to Bocker, Dec. 29, 1922 [LCM 31:413].)

2. Dudley A. Siddall (1891–1934), a newspaper manager, suggested Bocker to MS as a potential CRB medical director. (U.S. Bureau of the Census, *Fourteenth Census of the United States, 1920;* the Oct. 9 letter from Siddall was not found; Bocker to Siddall, Oct. 13, 1922 [LCM 31:405].)

3. No record of this initial meeting was found, but Bocker may have attended the First American Birth Control Conference.

4. The ABCL was formally incorporated in April 1922 to collect and disseminate information on birth control, publish the *BCR,* and secure the "lawful repeal and amendment of State and Federal statutes which deal with the prevention of conception" but not, according to the attorney general of New York State, "to carry on dispensary work." (Anne Kennedy, "Report of ABCL Activities, 1921–1923" [*MSM* C12:458]; ABCL Constitution and Richard W. Wallace to Anne Kennedy, May 16, 1922 [LCM 22:15 and 33:554].)

5. MS was slated to be the guest of honor at the ABCL's October 30 meeting, chaired by the liberal newspaper columnist Heywood Broun. (*New York Times,* Oct. 31, 1922.)

6. MS had rented space for the ABCL clinic at 317 West Tenth Street in November 1921, but without a dispensary license, she did not renew the lease. (ABCL Board of Directors Minutes, May 22 and Nov. 3, 1922 [*MSM* S61:64 and 71]; MS, *Autobiography,* 358.)

7. Bocker signed the contract in November. (Rose G. Kroener to MS, Nov. 24, 1922 [LCM 31:411].)

170. To Hugh de Selincourt

New York. [*N.Y.*]
Nov 5. [*1922*]

Hugh dear.

The big meeting is over and tho' it was not what other meetings have been it was not what I had hoped for.[1] Two or three things to tell you briefly one I am just announcing my marriage to Mr Slee the man I told you of. I am not going to make it public only to my friends & co-workers.[2]

Another experience Hugh to enrich ones life and to help me on to the greatest of all quests to "Know thyself."

I must be happy & am but I tremble for the cause I hold so dear.

I loved every word you wrote me of Joyces book. Hugh—you have never failed me!! You are the Mountain Star.

I read it with the King & almost had to leave the room with nausea.[3] But as the King left instead I wondered— Later we talked & I adoring his opinion above all else, could only excuse my difference of feelings because of my ignorance.

I told Havelock I was not educated up to it. Nor am I. Nor do I wish to be. And now you—you dear faithful ↑essence of↓ beauty in all things—feel as I do. I am happy that I am not wrong. You were also absolutely right in your advice about Mrs. Dennett & her League. They have both gone out of the movement.[4]

Strange things are happening & I need all the love & help I can find to keep the cause afloat these few years.

Again Mrs Brandt has not said what can be done,[5] but I have dinner with her tomorrow night. Another letter then. Ever my love—

Margaret

ALS MSP, DLC (LCM 3:979–82). Return address: "18 Gramercy Pk."

1. MS was referring to the October 30 Carnegie Hall meeting at which she spoke on birth control in China and Japan. Designed to increase ABCL membership and raise money under the slogan "A Million Members for a New Civilization," the meeting drew about two thousand people, including two police stenographers. Though clearly relieved there was no police interference, MS may have been disappointed that the event did not meet its financial goal. (*New York Times,* Oct. 31, 1922; Anne Kennedy to Josephine Bennett, Oct. 27, 1922 [*MSM* S36:38]; "World Aspects of Birth Control," *BCR,* Dec. 1922, 244–45.)

2. The press did not learn of MS's marriage to Slee until February 1924. Though she never explained why she kept the marriage a secret, her statements to the press suggest she feared public presumptions about wanting to enhance her social status and secure the movement's finances. (Marriage Certificate, Sept. 18, 1922 [*MSM* S83:734]; *Buffalo Times,* Feb. 20, 1924.)

3. MS was referring to James Joyce's *Ulysses* (1922), which de Selincourt called a "terrible blasphemy," though Ellis found it an "epoch-making work." (De Selincourt to MS, Oct. 26, 1922 [*MSM* S2:194].)

4. De Selincourt advised MS on how to handle Dennett in a letter written in late 1922, telling her that "your only weapon against her is graciousness; which is queenly disdain of her unfortunate existence." MS again overstated Dennett's failure; though the VPL was plagued by financial problems that had forced it to close briefly in October 1922, Dennett was still actively lobbying Congress. (De Selincourt to MS, 1922 [*MSM* S2:232]; Dennett to Marie Stopes, Oct. 4, 1922 [*MWDPM* 14:511].)

5. The reference was to Zelma Brandt's efforts to get de Selincourt's *One Little Boy* published. A few weeks later, MS reported it was accepted for publication. (MS to de Selincourt, Dec. 10, 1922 [LCM 3:478].)

171. From Client

As one ABCL member noted, "The name of Margaret Sanger seems to be a magnet that attracts suffering humanity. . . ." Her writings continued to elicit appeals for help from all parts of the country, especially Woman and the New Race *whose sales were boosted, in part, by a deceptive advertising campaign that implied the book contained technical birth control advice. A reply form enclosed in each copy encouraged readers to write Sanger for more information. (Bertha Smith, "Report of the Motherhood Department," Jan. 12, 1926 [quote] [*MSM *S61:190]; Chesler,* Woman of Valor, *194; Vreeland, "Process of Reform," 100, 273.)*

Middle Brough Ky
nov 27, 1922

Dear [*mam*]

I order one of your Book the Woman and the new Race to fine out how to ceep from Bringing those Little one into this afel world I am a poor woman and have work so hard all of my Life and I have Ben married 4 years the 25 december and I have all Redy given Birth to 3 childern and all 3 of my childern ar Boys and I am all most Broken down and am only 24 yers old I have got a good working husban But at all that don't ceep me from suffering I all most suffer death Every time yet and my Baby ar 3 months old and mrs sanger I do want you to write me an Return mail what to do to keep from Bring these Little one to this awfel world Please do write and tell me at once and thay want noone no But me and I will kinly thank you and I will pay you fer your truble. I Bought your Book and paid 2.00 for it and has Read it thoug your frend

[*Name omitted*]

my olest Boy ar ded and I only have the to and that ar a nuff of childern for me

ALS MSP, DLC (LCM 9:1214). A note by MS at the top of the first page reads, "sent Dec 1/22." In the interest of privacy, the editors have omitted the author's name.

172. To Hugh de Selincourt

Sanger was the principal speaker at the evening session of the First Ohio State Conference on Birth Control in Cincinnati on November 21, where she discussed birth control in Japan and China. Catholic organizations opposed the conference and petitioned Cincinnati's Mayor George P. Carrel to ban the meeting, but he refused to interfere. The conference resulted in the formation of a Cincinnati branch of the ABCL. (Conference Program [MSM S67:925]; "Birth Control in Ohio"; "News Notes," BCR, *Jan. 1923, 5;* New York Times, *Nov. 22, 1922.)*

[*Cincinnati, OH*]
[*November 24 or 25, 1922*][1]

Hugh dear:

This clipping I send on to you to read after send it to The New generation at 24 Victoria St. they may like to know about the Conference.[2] All kinds of Catholic pressure was used to keep us away & to prevent the Conference. Even the Hotel is boycotted by the Knights of Columbus a Catholic Mens Organization for allowing us to be here.[3] I always quote Havelock & Dean Inge in my work, but H. G.'s name is so well known here that he is always quoted in the press.[4]

I am browsing around had a queer black magic experience with these Catholics. I must tell you when I see you. Shall go to Pittsburg & then to a brothers wedding in West Virginia & then home.[5]

I do hope your books begin to circulate: What a fight it is to get an idea over! Love always

Margaret

ALS MSP, DLC (LCM 3:1079–80). Letterhead of the Hotel Gibson.

1. MS left Cincinnati on November 26.

2. The clipping was not found. In January 1922, the Malthusian League had changed its name to the New Generation League and renamed its journal the *New Generation* in an attempt to broaden its reach. However, with Charles Vickery Drysdale continuing as president and editor until 1923, the league retained its conservative political focus. The *New Generation* did not cover the Cincinnati conference. (Ledbetter, *Malthusian League,* 223–26.)

3. When Mayor Carrel refused to authorize a ban, the Knights of Columbus boycotted the Hotel Gibson, the site of the conference, canceling its upcoming banquet there. ("Birth Control in Ohio"; "News Notes," *BCR,* Jan. 1923, 5.)

4. MS regularly cited Ellis on eugenics, sexual fulfillment, and marriage and quoted Inge on ethics and morality, as well as on economic scarcity as a justification for birth control and positive eugenics. She frequently paraphrased Wells's belief that the world is crammed with meaningless lives and that man's reproductive powers are greater than his intellectual development. (On Ellis, see, for example, *English Methods of Birth Con-*

trol, 1915, 13 [*MSM* S76:883]; "World Aspects of Birth Control," *BCR*, Dec. 1922, 244; and MS, *Pivot of Civilization*, 171, 194; for Inge, see MS, *Pivot of Civilization*, 186–90; for Wells, see MS, "Indianapolis Speech Notes," Nov. 18, 1922, and "Philadelphia Speech Notes," Feb. 4, 1921 [*MSM* S70:943 and 896].)

5. MS was in Pittsburgh November 26–30 to speak at the ABCL's Allegheny County branch. She stayed in Clarksburg, West Virginia, from November 30 to December 1, attending the November 30 wedding of her brother Robert Higgins and Virginia Gaylord (1898–1973). (1922 Calendar [*MSM* S78:519]; "News Notes," *BCR*, Jan. 1923, 5.)

173. To Harold Cox[1]

Guy Aldred and Rose Witcop, communist publishers who befriended Sanger during her 1914–15 exile, published a 1920 version of Family Limitation *through their Bakunin Press. In December 1922, police arrested and charged the couple with violating British obscenity laws, the major charge centering on an illustration demonstrating the insertion of a pessary, as well as a veiled reference to abortion. The New Generation League hired a defense attorney, and Sanger wired fifty pounds to help cover the legal costs. Prominent English birth control advocates, including John Maynard Keynes, Harold Cox, Dora Russell, Bertrand Russell, and Sir Arbuthnot Lane, publicly defended the pamphlet, though Marie Stopes condemned it as prurient, refusing to support the defense effort. Aldred and Witcop were acquitted on January 10, 1923, but the magistrate ordered the pamphlets destroyed because they had been published "indiscriminately" and could fall into the hands of young people. Aldred's appeal was dismissed in 1924. (Aldred,* No Traitor's Gate, *439–42; Soloway,* Birth Control, *230–31;* London Times, *Jan. 11, 1923; Ettie Rout Hornibrook to MS, Mar. 12, 1923 [*MSM *S2:291]; Rose,* Marie Stopes, *162.)*

[*New York, N.Y.*]
January 3, 1923.

Dear Mr. Cox:-

Your letter arrived promptly on New Year's Day. It was in fact the first letter I read in 1923. The clipping that you promised to enclose was not enclosed, so I am at a loss to know just what has happened to one of my books.[2]

The fact that you mentioned Aldred[3] makes me believe that it is something about the little pamphlet "Family Limitation." I gave him a supply to distribute among the workers, back in 1916. I enclose a copy of this pamphlet, which has since been somewhat revised.[4] If you get an opportunity to look over the two, I would be delighted if you could do it. One is never sure if changes were made without my consent—but perhaps not.

So many of the workers in Scotland and in London preferred "Family Limitation" for the workers to the pamphlet gotten out by the Malthusian League and also Marie Stopes' "Letter to Working Women"[5] that I authorized Aldred the use of it. I knew he had the entrance to many unions and will be able to make good use of it among the unemployed.

However, I would not like to have Aldred go to jail for me, and if there is any possibility of this happening, I would be greatly obliged to you or to Mr. Cape to employ an attorney for me to defend this publication, and I will come over in February and try the case myself.[6] I could not come in January, but I could come early in February, if you could get the case postponed until that time.

I believe it is vitally important to the movement that this issue should be fought to the finish, and while my pamphlet is not accompanied by religious sentiments, its information is based upon plain, practical experience and will stand the test of indecency and obscenity.

I have just sent you a cable asking if you could postpone the case for me.[7] I am most anxious that this be done, for if the word comes to U.S.A. that England has put a ban upon this booklet, it will be much harder to do our work over here. As a matter of fact, more than a million of these pamphlets have been circulated in the United States without interference from our government, neither could I say it has been done by their sanction;[8] but as soon as the British Government comes down upon it, they will give the American Government the opportunity and the right to stop its circulation. So it is vitally important for the movement here that this issue be fought, and while it will be a great inconvenience for me to come over in February, I will stop everything else and rush to defend this right, if you think it is advisable.

I am going to depend much upon your judgment and advice. So please advise me what is best to do.

My love to Edith[9] and your dear self. All best wishes for the coming year.

Most cordially,

Dictated but not read.

TLcy MSP, DLC (LCM 14:362–63).

1. Harold Cox, who had declined the nomination for president of the New Generation League in July 1922, remained opposed to the Drysdales' conservative politics but became more active as their control of the league diminished. (Soloway, *Birth Control*, 175, 204; Ledbetter, *Malthusian League*, 159, 225.)

2. Cox, who probably meant to enclose the December 21, 1922, *London Times* report on the Aldred case, wrote that he was "to be called as a member of the general public" to testify that the MS pamphlet "is not obscene." He also reported that both J. O. P. Bland and H. G. Wells had contributed to the defense costs. (Cox to MS, Dec. 28, 1922 [*MSM* S2:217].)

3. Aldred, who published socialist and communist pamphlets, had been imprisoned for antimilitarism and war resistance from 1916 to 1919. It was Aldred who had arranged MS's July 1920 Glasgow lecture tour. (Aldred, *No Traitor's Gate*, 452; Caldwell, *Come Dungeons Dark*, 287; MS, *Autobiography*, 274.)

4. The Bakunin Press edition was based on the ninth American edition, which retained MS's political statements regarding the exploitation of the working class and references to using quinine as an abortifacient (these were removed from the tenth American edition, also published in 1920). The illustration that elicited protests from English authorities was nearly identical to one used in every edition since the first in 1914: a drawing of a hand inserting a pessary into a vagina. In the sixth American edition (1917), this illustration was turned from a horizontal to a vertical rendering, suggesting a woman standing instead of reclining—a less clinical orientation. At the trial, objections were made about the ambiguous ownership of the hand. MS justified the illustration in May 1923, noting, "I find the women that we are trying to help so utterly ignorant of their own bodies that they need such a diagram, and as the picture is supposed to represent a physician's examination, it has served its purpose extremely well with a great majority of ignorant women." MS enclosed the fifth American edition (1916) with this letter. (MS to Ettie Rout Hornibrook, May 23, 1923 [*MSM* S2:326]; *Family Limitation*, 5th ed., 1916, and 10th ed., 1920 [*MSM* S76:901 and 944]; the 9th American edition was not found; for the 1920 Bakunin Press edition, see MSRBR; on the pamphlet's revisions, see Joan M. Jensen, "The Evolution of Margaret Sanger's *Family Limitation* Pamphlet, 1914–1921," *Signs* 6 [Spring 1981]: 548–67.)

5. The Malthusian League's 1913 "Hygienic Methods of Family Limitation" was a one-page summary of contraceptive methods that did not require a physician: withdrawal, douching, and condoms. It was revised and expanded to nineteen pages in 1922 by Norman Haire, with new information about the Malthusian League, moral and medical arguments for birth control, explanations of how conception occurs, and more detailed recommendations for contraceptive methods. Stopes's *Letter to Working Mothers: On How to Have Healthy Children and Avoid Weakening Pregnancies* (1919) was a sixteen-page condensed version of her book *Wise Parenthood.* (Ledbetter, *Malthusian League,* 209–10; Rose, *Marie Stopes,* 125.)

6. Jonathan Cape (1879–1960) was a British publisher whose list included the American authors Sinclair Lewis, Eugene O'Neill, and Ernest Hemingway, as well as the British editions of most of MS's books. She did not go to England in 1923. (*DNB*)

7. MS's cable was not found, but Cox cabled back, "Postponement Impossible." (Cox to MS, Dec. 28, 1922 [*MSM* S2:217].)

8. Her estimate of more than a million cannot be confirmed, though thousands of *Family Limitation* pamphlets had been mailed without major incident, even though it was deemed obscene in several courts. (Gordon, *Woman's Body,* 232.)

9. Edith A. Baines, Cox's secretary, had accompanied him to the First American Birth Control Conference in November 1921. (Baines to MS, Nov. 20, 1921 [LCM 14:321].)

174. To William J. Fielding[1]

The CRB opened on January 1, 1923, and during its first year it received little publicity, relying on referrals from the ABCL. To attract more patients, Sanger sent out letters introducing the clinic to physicians and others sympathetic to the cause. (MS, Autobiography, *358–60.)*

[*New York, N.Y.*]
February 10 1923

My dear Mr. Fielding,

At last I am able to announce to you and a few other devoted friends of the Birth Control Movement, that arrangements have been made to give contraceptive information to those who are entitled to it under the law. This work is being forwarded for the purpose of obtaining scientific data; this is the great need at the present moment and must go hand in hand with the progress of the movement.

I shall be glad to refer such persons as you send to Dr. Dorothy Bocker, who has left the directorship of the Division of Child Hygiene, Georgia State Board of Health, to do this work for me. If it is possible we should like to have you visit us and let us tell you further about the project. Sincerely,

Margaret Sanger [*signed*]

TLS WJFP, NNU-T (*MSM* C2:187). Return address: "104 Fifth Avenue." For a similar letter, see MS to Adolf Meyer and Raymond Pearl, Feb. 10, 1923 (*MSM* C2:187–88).

1. William John Fielding (1886–1973) was the author of popular books on psychology, love, and sexual relations and the publisher of the Little Blue Books series, which included MS's *What Every Girl Should Know.* He frequently reviewed books for the *BCR.* Fielding's response was not found. (*New York Newsday,* Apr. 12, 1966.)

175. Statement on the Rosenman Bill

On February 14, 1923, Assemblyman Samuel I. Rosenman (1896–1973) introduced Assembly Bill 852, an amendment to Section 1145 of the New York State Criminal Code to extend the right of physicians to dispense contraception to all married women, not just those suffering from disease. In April 1923, Sanger traveled to Albany to testify before the Committee on Codes. Following an introduction by Assemblyman William Duke, several supporters and opponents testified, including James Rooney, an Albany physician who claimed that some birth control methods caused abortion and that the medical community opposed the bill; Eleanor Dwight Jones of the Women's City Club of New York, who argued that a law that denied citizens scientific knowledge was "oppressive and un-American"; the Reverend Philip Frick, who discussed the burden unwanted children posed to society; and Rabbi Sidney E. Goldstein, who argued for the benefits of small families. What follows is an extract from Sanger's testimony. (ANB; *Proposed Amendment to Section 1145 of the Penal Code for Physicians* [MSM C15:734]; *"News Notes,"* BCR, *Mar. 1923, 62.*)

[*Albany, N.Y.*]
[*April 10, 1923*]

MRS. MARGARET SANGER: Ladies and Gentlemen: I want to just say that section 1145 that is probably before you is one in which it claims that a person cannot have information to prevent conception, only for the cure of disease.[1] We are trying to amend that law so that a woman will not have to be diseased to child bearing in order to be spared for her children and for her family.

Some time ago we took a young woman, already a mother of several children, who was suffering from tuberculosis, tuberculosis of the glands, the bones of her hands had been removed—we took this woman with two witnesses to 31 hospitals in New York City.[2] Every one of the 31 hospitals refused to give that woman any information how to prevent having more children and how to prevent conception. They did, however, tell her in some cases that if she became pregnant, and under the laws of this State a woman who becomes pregnant and suffers from certain diseases, such as tuberculosis, heart disease, kidney disease, may be aborted, and it was possible for that woman after conception had taken place that if her pregnancy was jeopardizing her health or life, under those conditions she could be aborted, if you please, but to give her simply, scientific information how to prevent becoming pregnant was against the law, and they said, it is not our job to change the laws, you people who see this, go and get the laws changed.

We cannot in our public institutions give such information. So we are here to ask that the women who have children, the women who are already mothers, the women who today perhaps have a remnant of health, we ask that those women be preserved, and we think that it is absolutely unfair that such women are practically conscripted to motherhood under the laws of this State. I say it because it is true, that a woman unless she gives her body to her husband, that the laws of this State do not make that man support her.[3] Then, that really means conscripted motherhood, because there is no way that she can prevent herself from being a mother when she does not want to be.

Now, what is birth control? Birth control is a conscious control of the birth rate by means that prevent conception. It has nothing to do with abortion; it has nothing to do with interfering with or disturbing life after conception has taken place. There has always been some control of the population ever since time began, but we have not liked the methods that have been used to control populations because those have been diseases, famine, pestilence, floods, and wars.

We believe not in controlling the population after life, after individuals are born, but in controlling the birth rate before life begins. That, it seems to us is more scientific, is far more human. Does a woman who has eight or nine children, does she have to wait for death to take one or two of those children out of the family so as to make a husband's income do for them all? And that is what it means today, it means an infant mortality, maternal mortality, disease, famine, hunger—these are the things that are controlling our population and weeding them out and cutting them down.

We say it is absolutely unnecessarily cruel to woman and I tell you if the man who was here a few moments ago,[4] if he could only have eight or nine of the children of some of the women who are here today, and who came here to plead with you men to think of what they are going through—if that man only had to have one child, physically had to have it, I think he would probably have had a different tune to sing. (Applause)

It is easy enough for these gentlemen who are not even married to stand up before you and talk about the laws of God.[5] Why I would like to ask them a few things about the laws of the State of New York—I doubt that he knows them so well. The laws of God and the laws of nature are not cornered by any human being. We all have our ideas about the laws of God and we believe in a fine and very much higher regard of the laws of God, that it is better to use our intelligence than it is to be a master of the laws of nature, as some people are today.

Man after all has freed himself by controlling the laws of nature, and so must woman free herself from incessant child bearing, from the slavery of maternity, because that is what it is. Women who have eight, nine, ten, eleven children, they write me by the thousands and thousands. I brought here with me today ten thousand letters from mothers, and these have come to me within the last six weeks. Through the month of January I had personally directed to me six thousand thirty-three letters from mothers in this country. The month of February I had seven thousand four hundred and seventy of them, and these have just come here from the last six weeks, that I have not counted.[6] You gentlemen are welcome to read some of these letters. If you could just read one or two of them, the things that women ask. What do they ask? They ask for an opportunity to sleep one whole night before they die, just one night through without being disturbed by children, the crying of babies. They ask for a chance to know their husbands a little better. They say they are keeping them away from them because they are afraid, the man goes out of the home and they write me and say how can we get him back again. They write so they may have an opportunity to know their children, develop their mother love, because they do not do that.

Talk about the sanctity of mother love, in many of these women it has not been developed, it has not a chance of being developed, and these women are asking just for a chance, as they say, to have a breathing spell so they are not overworked. They are overworked far more than the cattle of the State, because after all there are laws in the State which will not allow breeders of animals to breed their cattle when they are diseased, but women of this State, women suffering from insanity, women whose husbands are insane, suffering from epilepsy, kidney disease, who to bear a child means practically death, yet they are compelled to bear children.

THE CHAIRMAN:[7] I do not like to interrupt, you, Mrs. Sanger, but those particular people that you speak about, the women who are epileptic, you might say, are women of low mental standards and so on, they are the people that you want to prevent having children. I think that everyone agrees that in some way if that could be accomplished it would be a grand thing, but do you think those are the people who would receive the benefit under this law?

MRS. SANGER: Yes, absolutely. I was just going to go further and say how could ↑this↓ be done. There are three kinds of birth control, three kinds. They are classed: continence is certainly a very good method of birth control; sterilization by both exray and surgical means[8] is another means of birth control, and then there are the chemical and the mechanical means of birth control. Now, either one of those three are really means to control birth or prevent conception.

We are not discussing, nor do we want the responsibility of giving methods, that is why we ask for this law. We ask that this be given to the medical profession, that the medical man may, in his judgment, use his judgment according to the individual, and if she is feeble-minded, ↑if↓ her husband is insane and she is not insane, and she is willing to be sterilized, certainly that belongs to her and ↑is↓ her right, if the physician thinks that is the thing to do, and so we say that this belongs to the medical profession.

The Jewish people and Italian families, who are filling the insane asylums, who are filling the hospitals and filling our feeble-minded institutions, these are the ones the tax payers have to pay for the upkeep of, and they are increasing the budget of the State, the enormous expense of the State is increasing because of the multiplication of the unfit in this country and in the State.[9]

ASSEMBLYMAN ESMOND:[10] Isn't it true that sometimes out of the most unpromising stock there comes a genius that by his brilliancy revolutionizes the whole country for good.

MRS. SANGER: Yes, sir, there are, but there is also the fact that if they did not have to support so many feeble-minded and unfit they would have more money to spend on geniuses that are already here. (Applause)

Gentlemen, I believe that this bill is only just, is only right for the women. Women are the sufferers; they are the ones. I spoke to a woman the other day who came to me who is already a mother of six children, she said to me, "Yes, I am all right, I haven't tuberculosis I haven't heart disease, I haven't kidney disease, but two of my children are not well cared for, my husband he is an operator, it is hard for him to make enough to feed the children and bring them up properly", and she said, "Can't you do something, can't you tell me what to do?" And I said, "It is against the laws of the State to tell you what to do, but," I says, "We are going up to Albany next Tuesday and when we are there we are going to see if we can get this law changed so that you may be given the proper instruction for this." And she looked up at me and said,

"Oh, can I go with you? I will plead with them, I will beg them, I will be on my knees before them and plead with them to change this law. They cannot know what it means." And I have brought ten women with us today, women who are mothers of five and six and eight children, who are living on very small incomes, and as one of the legislators said, if it is necessary for the legislators and doctors and ministers to keep their families small because of economic reasons, how much more is it necessary for the man on a limited wage?[11]

And so I say that the women, there are thousands of them in this state, there are hundreds of thousands of them who are bent, bound, broken on the wheel of maternity, and they ask you to do justice, and we ask you to do justice by those women to have this law passed.[12] (Applause)

TRcy MSP, MN-SSC (*MSM* S69:389–401). From *Proceedings of Hearing, before Assembly Committee on Codes, on Assembly Bill, Print No. 884, Amending Penal Law in Relation to Birth Control.* Handwritten interlineations and strikeouts by an unknown author on an unknown date have not been rendered in this transcription.

1. For Judge Crane's interpretation of Section 1145 in the 1918 appeal of the *Brownsville* case, see MS to Rublee, Jan. 22, 1918, note 9, herein.

2. On the Halton investigation, see "Breaking into the South—A Contrast," Nov. 1919, note 7, herein.

3. See MS, "First American Birth Control Conference: Closing Remarks," Nov. 18, 1921, note 2, herein.

4. Alden A. Steward, a Vermont physician, testified that birth control disturbed "the sanctuary of reproduction and our Christian honor."

5. Louis A. Cuvillier (1871–1935), a Democratic assemblyman from New York City and an opponent of woman suffrage and prohibition, had testified that birth control advocates were "blasphemers" who should be "swept from the face of the earth." He called MS a "fanatic" and referred to the proposed bill as "un-Godly." (*New York Times,* May 19, 1935, and Apr. 11, 1923 [Cuvillier quotes].)

6. See Client to MS, May 31, 1921, herein.

7. The chair was William Duke Jr. (1883–1956), a Republican assemblyman from Allegany County (1915–23). (*New York Times,* July 2, 1956.)

8. Surgical sterilization came to be used in the 1890s but usually was reserved for those with severe and permanent pathological conditions. Methods for men consisted of vasectomy (cutting the vas deferens) and, in rare instances, castration; for women, salpingectomy (cutting or tying of the Fallopian tubes) and hysterectomy. In 1912, Robert Latou Dickinson perfected a female sterilization method in which the uterine openings of the Fallopian tubes were closed by an electric cautery. After 1915, X-ray sterilization (administration of high voltage X-ray to the pelvic area) began to be used primarily to treat fibroids and persistent uterine bleeding and in cases where surgery was too risky. Radium was also sometimes used on both men and women, producing similar atrophic changes to the ovaries or testicles. These irradiation methods entailed risks and were frequently ineffective. (McLaren, *History of Contraception,* 236; Cooper, *Technique of*

Contraception, 123–31; Robert L. Dickinson and Louise Stevens Bryant, *Control of Conception: An Illustrated Medical Manual* [New York, 1931], 133–34, 147–48.)

9. Henry H. Goddard had noted that with approximately a quarter of a million "feeble-minded" Americans and not nearly enough institutions in which to confine them, an "army of feeble-minded people, are propagating . . . at somewhere two to six times as fast as the intelligent people are propagating their kind." In a widely publicized 1922 report to the House of Representatives supporting immigration restriction, Eugenics Record Office superintendent Harry Laughlin (1880–1943) claimed that immigrants from southern and eastern Europe (predominantly Italians and Jews) disproportionately filled America's mental institutions. Though it was unusual for MS to accept racist designations assigned by immigration restrictionists to particular nationality groups (she typically used Malthusian justifications of overpopulation and the spread of disease to justify her support of increased restriction, without referring to a particular nationality or race), she had invited Laughlin to speak on behalf of the Rosenman bill. (Henry H. Goddard, *The Menace of Mental Deficiency from the Standpoint of Heredity* (1915), in MS, *Case for Birth Control,* 206–7; Kevles, *In the Name of Eugenics,* 75, 132; *ANB;* MS, "Wasting Our Human Resources" and "Birth Control—Past, Present and Future," *BCR,* Mar. 1920 and June 1921 [*MSM* S70:837 and 903]; MS, *Woman and the New Race,* 32; James W. Trent, *Inventing the Feeble-Mind* [Berkeley, Calif., 1994], 131–83.)

10. Burton D. Esmond (1871–1944) was a Republican assemblyman from Saratoga County (1922–33). (*New York Times,* Jan. 12, 1944.)

11. Nearly thirty physicians, ABCL officers, and ABCL staff members attended the Albany hearing, including Juliet Rublee, Charlotte Delafield, Anne Kennedy, and Drs. Alfred Kahn, Benjamin Tilton, and Dorothy Bocker. Delegations from Brooklyn, Schenectady, Syracuse, and Ithaca also attended. ("News Notes," *BCR,* May 1923, 109.)

12. For the concluding portion of MS's testimony, see *MSM* S69:401.

176. From J. Noah Slee[1]

Slee and Sanger corresponded frequently when apart. In his letters to his wife, Slee typically recounted his daily activities, including minute details about meals, travels, ailments, and sleep, and affectionately expressed his loneliness. No correspondence between Slee and Sanger prior to 1923 was found, and extant letters and telegrams from the mid-1920s represent only a sampling of the many hundreds they probably exchanged; others (especially telegrams) were probably lost or destroyed. For more of Slee's letters to Sanger, see MSM *S2–4.*

[*New York, N.Y.*]
8 p.m. May 20th [*1923*]

My very adorable wife,[2]

I've had you very much on my mind all afternoon & feel your meeting was most successful & that you made as always a tremendous impression. Its futile for me to write you I am truly lonely without you & miss you terribly, each time you go away it seems more so, I love you so ardently that no one is interesting & I long only for you. I rec'd your wire. I sent you a night letter last night about 11—o'c.[3] Our trip was most successful though tiring, we motored nearly 200 miles, the driver was a pleasant chap & was very careful, going up the East Side through the various towns, the foliage was superb, there was plenty of wisteria in bloom, dogwood in abundance & lilacs. We reached the lake[4] at 1—o'c, had lunch on the hillside, which we all enjoyed hugely. Sarah & Jim and also the girls[5] were enchanted with the beautiful lake & surroundings, the stone work I feel sure will please you, as there are many wide or deep pieces, they have only reached the front door level in masonary & progress to me seems slow, perhaps they will go ahead faster now, since Mr McGill[6] has been up so recently. We left the lake at 3 o'c crossed the ferry at Newburgh went around the [*new*] road of Storm King[7] & through that parkway, & then [*returned*] Bear Mtn at [*Tuxedo*], & crossed the ferry at Nyack where we were held up one hour & forty minutes, as the first boat could not hold all the cars. I had supper at the Vanderbilt. The Steuarts had theirs waiting just to be warmed up, but I preferred to go down town, I was quite tired & sleepy & did not get up until 10 o'c, ate an orange & having a hearty meal last night went to Church without breakfast, & dined with the Steuarts where I remained until 5 o'c went home had a nap & took a good supper here—I will be glad to retire early. I assume you are very much in evidence & I hope the Social workers will be intelligent to sense BC is the root of <u>all</u> their problems. I suppose you took my key to your room,[8] as I did not find it on my dresser. Am going to let the piano removal as per schedule tomorrow, will look in & see if the painters are busy, but think I should wait before deciding to move Thursday,[9] will take up with the moving people the possibility of Thursday. Good night my darling God given adorable wife & sweetheart. Come home soon please I need you to clasp you in my arms always. Love divine always more & more. Ever Your Lover husband

Noah

ALS MSP, MN-SSC (*MSM* S2:318–25). Letterhead of the New York Club. Slee regularly used an "x" to end a sentence, which we standardized as a period.

1. Slee, still running his Three-In-One Oil Company, had become more involved with the ABCL financial management and was named assistant treasurer in April 1924.

2. MS was in Washington, D.C., where on May 20 she addressed the Annual Conference of Social Workers. On May 21, she was honored at a tea by the National Woman's Party. ("The Case for Birth Control: The Social Workers" and "The National Woman's Party," *BCR,* June 1923, 140–41.)

3. The telegrams were not found.

4. Slee was referring to Willowlake, the English manor-style stone house he had begun building for MS in 1922 on 110 acres in Fishkill, sixty miles north of New York City. (MS Unfilmed, "Homes," Box 14.)

5. Slee was accompanied by James Law Steuart (1862–1930), his attorney; J. Sarah

Bartow Steuart (1865–?), his attorney's wife; and their daughters, Elizabeth (1896–?) and Matilda Steuart (Dordet) (1901–93). (*New York City Directory,* 1923–24; *Baltimore Sun,* Dec. 26, 1930; U.S. Bureau of the Census, *Fourteenth Census of the United States, 1920; Who's Who of American Women.*)

6. Henry Joseph McGill, an architect with Murphy, McGill, and Hamlin, was in charge of construction and interior design at Willowlake. (McGill to MS, Jan. 13, 1924 [*MSM* S2:468].)

7. The Storm King Highway runs alongside the west bank of the Hudson River, in Orange County, New York.

8. Slee and MS still had adjoining apartments at 18 Gramercy Park and subsequently maintained separate quarters in each of their homes based on an agreement (not found) made when they married. (Lader, *Margaret Sanger Story,* 205.)

9. The couple moved to 39 Fifth Avenue later that month.

177. To James A. Field

*During the spring and summer of 1923, Sanger worked with Helen Graham Carpenter and Rachelle Yarros of the Illinois Birth Control League (IBCL) on a joint ABCL-IBCL Middle Western States Birth Control Conference, which they hoped would revive the IBCL and establish a clinic in Chicago. The organizers invited public health officials, social workers, and birth control advocates, as well as well-known gynecologists, geneticists, eugenicists, and representatives from social welfare groups, women's clubs, and Protestant and Jewish organizations. IBCL president James A. Field was a conservative birth control reformer who focused on legislative reform, not clinics, and disapproved of Sanger's more sensational propaganda strategies. The collaboration with the IBCL reflected Sanger's desire to assert her vision over that of Dennett's within the larger community of birth control reformers. Gaining access to the IBCL's contacts in Chicago was crucial to organizing the conference. (Middle Western States Birth Control Conference Program, 1923 [*MSM *C14:759].)*

[*New York, N.Y.*]
5 June 1923

My dear Professor Field:

This is the first opportunity I have had to write you since Miss Rowe brought your letter to her to my attention.[1]

You will find enclosed a rough outline of the proposed programme for the Birth Control Conference in October.[2] Prof. E. M. East of Harvard[3] will present the first paper on Tuesday morning. Prof. E. A. Ross of the University of Wisconsin[4] has consented to speak, also Prof. H. A. Miller of Oberlin.[5] Two professors from Johns Hopkins and one more from Harvard[6] have promised to give a definite answer in June.

Mr. Harold Cox has offered personally to ask Sir Arbuthnot Lane to come to this country to take part in this Conference. As you know, Sir Arbuthnot Lane is considered one of the two leading gynecologists of England, and we feel confident that he will consent to come.[7]

With these eminent men on our programme, we will proceed to interest leading professors of the Middle Western universities to take part. In furtherance of our plan, I expect to arrive in Chicago on June 17th, when I will be glad to see you or any members of your Committee. Will go to the Hotel Drake.[8]

In the meantime, I am writing on the question raised in your letter of giving a place on the programme to the Voluntary Parenthood League. For me, this is a difficult problem. As you know, the basic principle of the American Birth Control League is that Birth Control information should be treated on a scientific and medical level and given only through the best possible agencies, which all agree, is the medical profession.

I have come to realize that the more ignorant classes, with whom we are chiefly concerned, are so liable to misunderstand any written instruction, that the Cause of Birth Control would be harmed rather than helped, by spreading abroad unauthoritative literature.[9]

The great majority of the fifteen thousand members and many of the chief supporters have come into the American League because our policy in this respect is differentiated from that of the Voluntary Parenthood League. Moreover, some of the most important members of our Board and Council have discontinued their support of the V.P.L. in favor of the A.B.C.L. when they have learned of the difference of policy.[10]

Plans outlined the beginning of this year allowed that a Bill, carrying out our policy, should be drawn up during the summer and presented to the 68th Congress.[11] I particularly want this Bill ready for the Chicago Conference and hope then to have plans discussed for carrying on the Federal work.

If a place is given to the Voluntary Parenthood League on the programme of this important Conference, would it not be misleading to the people of the Middle West? Would we not appear to sponsor a Bill which is contrary to the chief aim of our League?

Do you not think that the Chicago group would be willing to help with the Conference and leave in abeyance the whole question of Federal legislation until they have time to examine our proposed Bill?

I am answering your letter fully and frankly because I do not want anyone to give his name in support of the Conference without knowing how we stand on the question of Federal legislation.

I shall be in Chicago from the 17th to the 20th of June, excluding the 19th, when I shall be in Madison.[12]

Looking forward to seeing you and other members of your Committee on my arrival. Most cordially yours,

President

TLcy ABCLR, MH-H (*MSM* C2:331–33).

1. Clara Louise Rowe (McGraw) was an ABCL secretary who arranged several conferences and scheduled some of MS's lectures. The letter was not found.

2. For the Middle Western States Birth Control Conference's tentative program, see May 15, 1923, *MSM* C14:759.

3. Edward Murray East (1879–1938), a biologist and geneticist at Harvard University's Bussey Institute for Applied Biology, was one of the few eugenicists who supported birth control. Though he did not attend, he sent a paper, "Civilization at the Crossways," which argued that because population growth exceeded natural checks, places "suitable for Caucasian colonization" would become oversaturated with people. (*ANB;* East to Pauline Daniel, Oct. 19, 1923 [*MSM* C2:832]; for a published version of his paper, see *BCR,* Dec. 1923, 328–32.)

4. Edward Alsworth Ross (1866–1951), a political economist and pioneer of American sociology, was a eugenicist who supported immigration restriction and other nativist and racist strategies aimed at ensuring "race betterment." Ross chaired a panel entitled "Social Aspects of Birth Control" and presented a paper suggesting that U.S. social and economic conditions would decline without immigration restriction, legal reform, and prohibition. (*DAB;* Middle Western States Birth Control Conference Program, 1923 [*MSM* C14:759].)

5. Herbert Adolphus Miller (1875–1951), a sociologist known for his studies on the Americanization of immigrants, presented a paper entitled "Social Control and Birth Control." (*NatCAB*)

6. The references were to the biologists Raymond Pearl and Herbert Spencer Jennings and the physician and Harvard professor of hygiene Roger Irving Lee, none of whom attended. (Middle Western States Birth Control Conference's tentative program, May 15, 1923, and Pearl to Rowe, Aug. 14, 1923 [*MSM* C14:757 and C2:472]; responses from Jennings and Lee were not found.)

7. Sir William Arbuthnot Lane (1856–1943), a British surgeon, gynecologist, and birth control proponent who served on the board of Marie Stopes's Medical Research Committee, did not attend. (*DNB;* Leathard, *Fight for Family Planning,* 14; Lane to Harold Cox, May 23, 1923 [LCM 14:453].)

8. MS held meetings in Chicago June 17–19 but did not see Field. (MS, "Itinerary, June 16–Aug. 2" [*MSM* S78:284]; Field to MS, June 24, 1923 [*MSM* C2:358].)

9. MS argued that the "open" bill would open the mails to contraceptive advice from commercial concerns, quacks, and uneducated and untrained lay people, making it more difficult to discern reliable advice. (Minutes of ABCL Board of Directors Meeting, Nov. 27, 1923 [*MSM* S61:91].)

10. Despite their common interests, the boards and national councils of the ABCL and VPL shared only two members from 1921 to 1923, and there is no evidence that any VPL members defected to the ABCL. MS may have been referring to individuals who rescinded cards they had signed earlier endorsing VPL legislative policy. (Dennett to Annie Porritt, June 13, 1924 [*MWDPM* 14:396].)

11. Though the ABCL had not yet sponsored a federal bill, it defined its "doctor's only" policy while pushing the 1923 New York State Rosenman bill and a series of other legislative efforts in New York, Connecticut, and New Jersey. In 1924, the ABCL board drew up a federal bill but did not begin lobbying until after the January 1925 failure of the VPL's

Cummins-Vaile bill. (Anne Kennedy, "Report of the ABCL Activities," 1921–23, and Minutes of the Annual Meeting of the ABCL, Jan. 10, 1924 [*MSM* C12:458 and S61:92].)

12. No information was found on MS's Madison trip.

178. *To Anne Kennedy*[1]

*Sanger and Slee toured British Columbia, the Yukon, and Alaska for much of July, sailing from Vancouver, Canada, to Skagway on July 4. While the trip was primarily a vacation, Sanger lectured in Canada and Alaska. (Itinerary [*MSM *S78:284–86].)*

S.S. Princess Alice en route from Skagway to Vancouver [*Canada*]
July 22 1923

Dear Anne Kennedy:

We are returning from Alaska & reach Vancouver tomorrow.[2] A glorious trip this! I have sent to you, or rather in your name a package of soiled linen and in side a dozen or so of pessaries for Dr Bocker.[3] I sent them to you so as not to arouse curiosity in the P.O. Dept.

If you can send the soiled things to a laundry Ill be pleased, but Anna could send a card to Daisy[4] to come & get them & keep them for my return. I do hope the Auto has been sold, if not the next thing is to take it out of storage. But I'll probably send it up to Truro later if it is not sold.

They use the National a lot out in Canada.[5]

Tell Mrs Porritt[6] there was a very good meeting for me ↓July 19↑ at the Womens Club of Skagway. I spoke for an hour & a half fine old pioneer women there. Love to all, later letter.

Margaret Sanger

ALS Lader (*MSM* C2:442–43). Letterhead of the Canadian Pacific Railway Company.

1. Kennedy became the ABCL's executive secretary in November 1921, managing the office and MS's lectures and serving as her primary assistant.
2. MS and Slee arrived in Vancouver on July 23.
3. Since the federal Comstock Act prohibited the importation and mailing of contraceptive devices, MS was smuggling them in from Canada for use at the CRB.
4. The references were to Anna Lifshiz and Daisy Mitchell.
5. MS was referring to the Canadian National Railway Company.
6. Annie Goodrich Porritt (1861–1932) was a British-born feminist, suffragist, and ABCL board member. She contributed articles and book reviews to the *BCR*, served as its managing editor (1922–25), and compiled meetings and other events for the "News Notes" column. (Lee, *Biographical Cyclopaedia of American Women*, 124–26; "News Notes," *BCR*, Sept. 1923, 220.)

179. ABCL Newsletter

New York [*N.Y.*]
July—1923.

Confidential to Members[1]
Dear Member:-

It is my plan to send you every six weeks or thereabouts a news letter in short form, telling you of the events that have taken place in the movement and other things that we plan to do. I hope in this way to keep you informed of the American Birth Control League and its activities.[2]

First, I wish to tell you something of what we have done last year. You will then see why the cause has grown so rapidly and what your membership has helped us to accomplish. Below is a brief summary of some of our activities for the year 1922.

6,525	persons called at Headquarters for interviews.
73,300	letters received and replied to.
25,754	new letters since January 1st.
18,250	phone calls received.
25,000	persons attended B.C. meetings.
160,000	copies of "[*Woman*] and the New Race" published.
213,500	free pamphlets and leaflets distributed.
110,000	copies of "Birth Control Review" circulated.
10,300	copies of "Birth Control Review" sold in street.
190	newsdealers in different cities in the United States sell the Review.
32	foreign countries reached thru magazine and League.
81	principal magazines in Japan carried Birth Control articles in one month.
100	special articles in the Chinese press on Birth Control in one month.
1	clinic established in Tokio.
1	" " " Kyoto.
1	" " " Pekin.

Leagues established in Shanghai, Honolulu, Tokio, and Kobe.[3]

Thousands of other books and pamphlets have been circulated.

Hundreds of other activities have taken place which are not mentioned here, including legislative work in two states.

Birth Control conferences in several states, and an International Conference in London, and many other things while of equal importance, we have not space to relate.[4]

Second, I wish to tell you a little about the clinical research work being done by Dr. Dorothy Bocker, at our headquarters. Dr. Bocker is devoting her whole time to collecting data and doing research work for future use. We have a well equipped doctor's office, and under the law in New York State certain men and women suffering from ailments or diseases have a right to receive contraceptive information.

Dr. Bocker sent out a questionnaire to over one hundred doctors and to one hundred hospitals in New York State and asked if they gave birth control information. Only six doctors out of a hundred replied that they would tell their patients how to prevent conception, and then only if the patient is very ill. Only four of the hospitals replied that they would give contraceptive information.[5]

These facts warranted us in arranging a research department and three months ago this clinical research work was begun. I am informing only our friends and members of the League about this work, because we hope to work quietly and secure scientific data of a thousand cases before we make our knowledge public. I will keep you informed from time to time of what we are accomplishing.

The following case represents the average mother who calls to our Research Department for help:

> Mrs. B— age 40, mother of 7 living children, married 18 years; husband's wages $21.00 a week. she has high blood pressure, also kidney trouble, and has much trouble because her womb has fallen. Mrs. B. has been pregnant 11 times. Her 4 last pregnancies resulting in the death of the first child soon after it was born. The second was born dead, and the third and fourth were miscarriages.

Can we continue to call ourselves civilized if we permit such unnecessary human suffering? This clinical research work is the most important advance the Birth Control Movement has made this year.

We need the help of every member of our League to continue this. If you live in New York or nearby tell your neighbors or friends to come to us. If you cannot come yourself, send us money that we may help others who do come. If you cannot send us money, help us to get new members for our League. Write me what you think of this news-letter and if you desire to hear from time to time what we are doing. You may look for another one sometime during the month of July.[6]

With my deep appreciation of your interest and help, I am Faithfully yours,

MARGARET SANGER
President
AMERICAN BIRTH CONTROL LEAGUE.

TFL RLWP, CSt-H (*MSM* C12:539–40). Return address: "104 Fifth Ave." Carbon blot on the first page.

1. The ABCL had 18,000 members by the end of 1923. (Vreeland, "Process of Reform," 157.)

2. For additional ABCL newsletters, see *MSM* C12:546–66.

3. In the wake of MS's 1922 tour of Asia, birth control leagues were established in Osaka, Kyoto, and Tokyo, Japan, and in Beijing and Shanghai, China. (Ishimoto, *Facing Two Ways,* 231; MS to de Selincourt, May 6, 1922 [LCM 3:831].)

4. MS was referring to state conferences in Philadelphia on January 13, 1922; Cleveland on November 21, 1922; Albany on January 23, 1923; and Baltimore on January 25, 1923, and to the Fifth International Neo-Malthusian Conference in London, July 11–14, 1922. (For programs, see *MSM* S67:922–31.)

5. The questionnaire and responses were not found; for Bocker's discussion of the survey, see *New York Times,* Dec. 6, 1923.

6. MS probably meant to refer to the next newsletter, distributed in October.

180. To Juliet Barrett Rublee[1]

*After leaving Vancouver on July 23, Sanger and Slee toured the American West, stopping at Mammoth Hot Springs in Yellowstone Park and the Grand Canyon, arriving in Denver on August 2, and spending most of August at Troutdale, a resort in Evergreen, Colorado. They returned to New York City on August 28. (Itinerary, Aug. 2–28 [*MSM *S78:287–89].)*

[*New York, N.Y.*]
[*September 17, 1923*]

Juliet dearest

Yes my hair has grown wonderfully well & thick all the way down since it was singed & cut. Mr Frey[2] does the singing first & then cuts huge chunks off. It also ceased falling out after that was done. I think you need to have some one help you do it so you get the split ends all cut. If your hair does not grow from the bottom it may be because the ends are dry & split—look.

About the Federal bill the only form of bill Dennett has introduced or tried to was one which simply(?) removed the words prevention of [*conception*] from the entire law.[3]

A fine idea & one I thought out way back in 1913 myself but———the very people who believe in it wont help & those who will help wont have that.[4] It is Section 211 Penal Code.[5] I don't think the argument against quacks is our strong one. Our reason for working by States is for Clinics—because we know women ↑the kind we want to help↓ cant read directions in books or pamphlets & must be personally taught & instructed to get good results. We are not against the Federal Law. It's a question of what we find best to work for to get the results we want and the Federal bill does not answer the problem (solve) for the poor ignorant tired woman.

Do get all the ideas possible & suggestions for the lawyer.

I am sick to think I did not ask you to come here the evening you left for

Cornish. Im writing to Miss Little she did telephone me.[6] Anne comes this a m & we talk conference.[7] love dearest one always adoringly

Margaret

J. N. was touched by the telegram you darling![8]

ALS JRP, MN-SCC (*MSM* C2:575–82). Return Address: "39 Fifth Ave." The date at the top of the first page was added by Juliet Rublee.

1. Rublee had recently returned from Mexico, where she accompanied Anne Kennedy on a birth control speaking tour of Mexican cities. ("News Notes," *BCR*, Sept. 1923, 221.)
2. She was referring to the beautician Charles Frey.
3. On January 10, 1923, Senator Albert B. Cummins (Republican, Iowa) and Representative John Kissel (Republican, Brooklyn, New York) introduced "open" bills (S. 4314 and H.R. 13756) drafted by Dennett's VPL to amend the criminal code by omitting references to "preventing conception" from the category of obscene items prohibited from distribution. Neither legislator was able to bring a vote on the bill. (For the bill, see *MWDPM* 12:961.)
4. This was a reference to free speech activists who initially supported birth control but turned to other concerns during World War I. The new birth control advocates—society women, progressive physicians, academics, and social workers—were less interested in overturning censorship laws and providing unfettered access to contraception than in advocating contraception as a public health program that would also reduce the size of poor, foreign-born families. (Gordon, *Woman's Body*, 250–54; Chesler, *Woman of Valor*, 162–63.)
5. This was the Comstock Act.
6. Hannah Pauline Little (1877?–?), a registered nurse living in Connecticut, may have replaced Clara Louise Rowe after Rowe's resignation in the summer of 1923. (MS to Little, Oct. 3, 1923, and to Rublee, Oct. 5, 1923 [*MSM* C2:723 and 747].)
7. MS was referring to Anne Kennedy and the Middle Western States Birth Control Conference.
8. The telegram was not found.

181. To Ross D. A. Gunn[1]

Because Sanger believed that those with mental limitations could not be taught to use birth control, she was persuaded by Ellis and others that sterilization remained the only safe, reliable, and effective way to prevent such people from reproducing without restricting individual liberty and at less cost to the state. But opposition to sterilization from scientists, doctors, psychiatrists, and religious leaders on ethical grounds was growing, and its eugenic value began to be questioned. By the early 1920s, many states had declared sterilization laws unconstitutional. Sanger wrote the following letter in response to a note written on the reverse of a reservation card for the conference, which asked, "Why do you not spend your time, money and energy, teaching the people and getting suitable laws enacted for the sterilization of all mental and physical defectives, criminals, syphilitics and tuberculars (and may be others)? If the above could be made effective the great majority of defective children will be eliminated and the normal citizen will naturally take care of the 'Birth Control.'" (Larson, Sex, Race, and Science, *8, 23–28; Gunn reservation card, Oct. ?, 1923 [*ABCLR*].)*

[*New York, N.Y.*]
October 8, 1923.

Dear Dr. Gunn:-

I regret that you will not be able to attend the special session of our Conference.[2]

Enclosed you will find the "Principles and Aims" of the American Birth Control League. I beg to call your attention to the sixth paragraph under the title "Aims" which deals with sterilization.[3]

Indeed, it has been a great surprise to me, during the past several years to find, that neither the medical societies throughout the country nor even the Eugenic Society—both with unlimited means for the enactment of such legislation, have failed utterly to encourage sterilization of the unfit or to educate the public that it should be done.[4]

It is unfortunate that you cannot attend the Conference. I think you would be better informed regarding our organization—what we have been doing, and still hope to do. Sincerely yours,

President.

TLcy ABCLR, MH-H (*MSM* C2:765).

1. Ross Delano Aldrich Gunn (1859–1935) was a physician in Oberlin, Ohio. (*Cleveland Plain Dealer,* June 8, 1935.)

2. MS was referring to the "Special Session for the Medical Profession" of the Middle Western States Birth Control Conference on October 30.

3. This was an ABCL pamphlet first drafted in 1921. The paragraph read, "Sterilization of the insane and feeble-minded and the encouragement of this operation upon those afflicted with inherited or transmissible diseases, with the understanding that sterilization does not deprive the individual of his or her sex expression, but merely renders him incapable of producing children." It was deleted from the 1926 version. ("Principles and Aims of the American Birth Control League," Nov. 1921, 1925, and 1926 [*MSM* C12:32 and 52 and S61:17].)

4. The American Eugenics Society recommended more eugenic and less punitive sterilization laws, but it made no public pronouncements on the issue. Although most eugenicists still supported sterilization, some called for a more conclusive scientific consensus on what defined an individual as "unfit," before promoting sterilization. (Kevles, *In the Name of Eugenics,* 93–94, 108–11.)

182. Dream

Sanger had become interested in dream analysis following a series of dreams she had in 1915 that she believed forecast her daughter Peggy's death, and she recorded a dozen or more dreams in her diaries and journals. She also shared them with close friends Havelock Ellis (who wrote numerous essays on the subject) and Juliet Rublee. Many of her dreams involved babies and children, which Sanger interpreted as meaning "there was some kind of troublesome news not far away." (MS, My Fight, *214 [quote]; for additional dreams, see "Dream," Nov. 3, 1923, herein; Excerpt from London Diary, Oct. 16, 1924, herein; MS Diary [LCM 1:127, 2:566–67]; and Dreams Journal [*MSM *S70:509]; see also MS,* Autobiography, *175–76.)*

Chicago, [*Ill.*]
Oct 21—1923

queer dream—

Large rat came out of somewhere—I seemed to be upstairs in small farm house—but ran up only because it was raining & lightening especially—water was pouring down the Stairs as I ascended.

After the rat came out—very bold & large & fearless—it seemed to pull at some clothing on the floor— I had a large iron bar & pushed it toward the rat to kill it— Then I was in some way trying to choak or kill several children all in one bed—one especially that I disliked (the hang over of the rat) but as soon as I took the iron away two children got up very stiff & queer looking & the one I disliked got up too, I was surprised & awoke.

AD JRP, NhD (*MSM* C16:14).

183. Dream

Chicago, [*Ill.*]
Nov 3. [*1923*]

Dream—

I was standing out side of a large building in N.Y. Seemed to be in the rear yard, buildings around were very high & the tops were coming down. I could hear them but did not see any fall. Then suddenly I remembered my little girl (passed away 5 years ago) who seemed to be in the home of a friend, but now that I thot of her it came over me that I had neglected her for years & did not even know where she was.[1] I began to run thru the streets always I was carrying an infant in my arms with a very sweet face it was in white clothes & lay horizonical in my arms, throughout.

I thot of my lost child & wept & cried aloud & pulled my hair. I was grief stricken & awoke.

AD JRP, NhD (MSM C16:15–16).

1. Peggy Sanger had spent most of the last two years of her life with extended family and friends.

184. To J. Noah Slee

[*Chicago, Ill.*]
Thursday, [*November 8, 1923*]

Sweetheart mine:

It was thrilling to hear all about the house in your letter just received and I am dying to get back to see it & to you.[1] I got into Chicago at midnight & your letter to Stuart upset me terribly so I did not sleep until daylight.[2] I worried because words sound so harsh on paper & when a young thing is in a strange place it should not be parent's ways to make conditions harder. Stuart was told by me that I'd allow $200 a year from Sept 1923 to Sept 1924 for his clothing. When he heard he was going to France he cancelled the order for the second suit, the day he was leaving for the boat a telephone came from the New York store that the suit was all finished & had been cut & nearly made when the cancellation came. So we had to take it & the affair was settled.

You would do better dear one to talk these things over with me & find out the details before you jump to conclusions— Well I'm not going to say any more about it, but I'm trying to give the boys a certain independence & experience of using their judgment under our guidance— I am packing for Denver[3]— I love you adorable Noah. I shall never never forget the beauty in your face & the tenderness in your voice when, on my way to the platform that first nervous night you came up to me & touched me & said "God Bless you darling" etc oh that was worth all the agony I was to go through just to have you so close to me then.[4]

You are a darling Noah & I should not be away from you & then we would never have these horrid disagreeable questions coming between us. I'll be home the rest of the year except for one day in Boston[5] & one or another here or there. We will be happy in spite of your money! If only we were living on my earnings I'd make you the happy King of the land. Indeed I would. "The world would be a ruby for your finger ring" as the poet said—[6]

Indeed you are my king & all that one could reverence or adore or worship— A hug—a thousand kisses and my loving embrace

Margy

ALS MSP, MN-SSC (*MSM* S2:399–402). Letterhead of the Drake Hotel.

1. The reference was to construction on the Willowlake estate; the letter was not found.
2. MS arrived in Chicago on or near October 15 to prepare for the Middle Western States Birth Control Conference. She took a brief trip to Madison, where she spoke before the University of Wisconsin's Social Science Club and returned on November 7. The

letter was not found. ("News Notes," *BCR*, Nov 1923, 285; Slee to MS, Oct. 20, 1923 [*MSM* S2:390].)

3. She left on November 9 to address the Denver Professional and Business Women's Club the next day. ("News Notes," *BCR*, Dec. 1923, 324.)

4. This was probably a reference to the first night of the Middle Western State Birth Control Conference, October 29, 1923.

5. MS returned home on November 19 and did not travel again in 1923.

6. The line was from the prefatory poem to the 1901 novel *If I Were King* by the English novelist Justin Huntly McCarthy (1861–1936). The actual lines read, "The stars should be your pearls upon a string / The world a ruby for your finger ring, / And you should have the sun and moon to wear / If I were king."

185. From Client

Fayetteville W. Va
Nov 21, 1923

Mrs. Margaret Sanger:

I am a girl fifteen years old married and have two children my fother left my mother with ten children three sets of twins and I the oldest one had to find some way to make a living I married a poor man and he is a poor provider and I don't want to bring no more children here in poverty. So I ask you to please send me one of your pamphlets. I purchased your book[1] and like it fine. Yours truly

[*Name omitted*]

ALS MSP, MN-SSC (*MSM* S2:428). In the interest of privacy, the editors have omitted the author's name. A note at the top, possibly written by MS reads, "Ch II [*illegible*]." An extract from this letter was published in *Motherhood in Bondage*, chap. 1, letter no. 3.

1. This was probably *Woman and the New Race.*

186. From Havelock Ellis

Hillside, Cadgwith, Ruan Minor, Cornwall [*England*]
8 Dec/23.

Your lovely letter[1] reached me yesterday dear Margaret Woman, & is as ever cheering.[2] But those "Royalties"! It is very sweet of you to send them when I haven't the faintest claim in the world to them.[3] I hope anyhow that shows that the book is still selling, as it ought to.

So glad the Conference was a success.[4] I am not at all surprised that "himself"[5] should say, as I do, that you are "reckless". He is getting to know you! And it is quite natural he should say, as I always do, that you use up at once all the benefits of a vacation. Still there may be something in your question:

"What else is it for?" I very much agree with your aim of "finishing up" with B.C. as soon as you get half a dozen clinics started. Then it will move by itself. I should be so sorry to see you become a mere B.C. fossil, incapable of anything else, & from whom noone in the world dreams of expecting anything else. You ought be able to turn your large & beautiful mind in other directions also, & to be free to give one of the charming touches of your hand in helping forward other great causes now & then. There will still be plenty of people left who are only able to move in one narrow rut!

You don't seem to follow this "New Generation". The Drysdales have retired from it, & it is edited by a man called, I think, Kerr, who has plenty of sprit & aggressiveness, & making it a good & living paper.[6] Stella Browne gets on well with him, so far, writes much for it, & also goes around the country lecturing on B.C. etc.[7]

Yes, I remember Edith much admired Washington, & it must be a wonderfully fine city.[8] Did I tell you that two volumes of her uncollected essays (including that on me) & stories are being hand-printed for a private edition by Joseph Ishill of Berkeley Heights, N.J.[9] He is an enthusiast over her work & is not out for profit. I have lately had a tablet put up in the garden of the Golden Green Crematorium (your old neighborhood), just to say that her ashes were scattered there, & leaving a space to add, when necessary, that mine are also scattered there.[10] It is a peaceful & pleasant spot though I don't suppose you ever went into it.

I was sorry not to be of any help as regards school in France for Stuart. I set some inquiries on foot, but they led to nothing. There seems considerable hardship in school life in France (& worse still for the teachers, according to Françoise), but I am glad to heard that, in spite of that, he likes the experience.[11]

As you expressed no wish last year for the Diary re-fill I did nothing this year. But luckily the Diary number & address is on my Address book here. So I shall be just delighted to be able to get it & send it to you. Much love always

Havelock

Glad to hear the wonderful house is progressing.
[*Written on left margin of last page*] I quite agree about the Man Ray photograph of me.[12]

ALS MSP, DLC (LCM 4:856–59).

1. The letter was found.

2. Sometime in 1922 or early 1923 Ellis's companion, Françoise Lafitte, began an affair with Hugh de Selincourt, though MS was not yet aware of it. Ellis, consumed by jealousy and despair, told Lafitte in 1923 that his friendship with MS was not compara-

ble, describing it as merely slipping "once or twice (very seldom) into little acts of physical intimacy." But he also argued that MS "has never done anything to cause me suffering, & she has never given me joy & inspiration." (Grosskurth, *Havelock Ellis,* 312–33, 326 [quotes].)

3. They were probably for his preface to *Woman and the New Race.*

4. This was a reference to the Middle Western States Birth Control Conference, which MS said "went over big." It received some newspaper coverage, and the *BCR* reported that its sessions were well attended. One attendee was struck by its success in bringing together members of diverse professions to discuss birth control. (MS to de Selincourt, Nov. 8, 1923 [LCM 3:993]; *Chicago Tribune,* Oct. 31 and Nov. 1, 1923; "The World We Live In" and "The Conference," *BCR,* Dec. 1923, 316–23.)

5. He was referring to J. Noah Slee.

6. Charles Drysdale and Bessie Drysdale resigned from the Malthusian League in January 1923, making it more attractive to socialists. Robert Bird Kerr (1867–1951), a Scottish-born attorney, a Fabian socialist, and the league's secretary, took over as editor of the *New Generation.* (Benn, *Predicaments of Love,* 216; Ledbetter, *Malthusian League,* 78–80.)

7. Stella Browne, who had stayed with the league despite her political differences with the conservative Drysdales, welcomed Kerr's arrival. In 1923, she reported on international birth control events and published socialist rationales for birth control in the *New Generation,* and she lectured before women's cooperative guilds and labor organizations. (Soloway, *Birth Control,* 175.)

8. This was a reference to his wife, who had visited there in 1915. (Ellis, *My Life,* 531.)

9. Edith Ellis's *Stories and Essays* were posthumously published in 1924 by Joseph Ishill (1860–1938), whose Free Spirit Press specialized in limited edition literary and philosophical books. (*New York Times,* Mar. 17, 1938.)

10. The crematorium was located on Hoop Lane, just north of the Hampstead neighborhood where MS lived in June 1915. The marker read, "The ashes of Edith the wife and comrade of Havelock Ellis were scattered over this garden on the eighteenth of September 1916." Ellis himself would be cremated there in 1939, followed a month later by Sigmund Freud. (Ellis, *My Life,* 619; Grosskurth, *Havelock Ellis,* 446; see also MS to Marie Stopes, July 6 or 7, 1915, herein.)

11. MS had apparently asked Ellis to suggest a French school for Stuart, who went to the Ecole du Montcel in Jouy-en-Josas, France (near Versailles) from October 1923 to April 1924 to improve his French and pass his college entrance exams. Ellis's lover, Lafitte, was a French teacher at a school in West Ham. (Stuart Sanger to MS, Oct. 9, 1923, and Mar. 27, 1924 [*MSM* S2:378 and 561]; Grosskurth, *Havelock Ellis,* 208.)

12. Ellis had sent MS a photo of himself taken on his August trip to Paris by the surrealist American painter and photographer Man Ray (1890–1976), who, Ellis remarked, "is rather fashionable just now with the younger school of people. But I think his effects are too misty for portraits. . . ." The letter from MS was not found. (*ANB;* Ellis to MS, Sept. 15 [quote], Oct. 9, and Oct. 18, 1923 [LCM 4:842, 822, and 846].)

187. To Client

Sanger sent out form letters through the ABCL, modified for each situation, to address the many requests she received for abortions or abortion referrals. The incoming letter that she responded to below was not found.

New York City, [*N.Y.*]
[*1923?*]

Dear Friend:-

I am sorry that there is nothing I can advise you to do except to consult your doctor who, if your health demands it, may help you.

When you ask me the question "How can I bring myself around; I am pregnant two months", you are asking for abortion.

Please understand that Birth Control, as I understand it, is never abortion. I do not approve of abortion, nor can I give the address of anyone who will perform this operation.[1]

I do not advise the use of drugs to bring about the result you desire, since the effects of such drugs are almost always disastrous to the child, even if the mother seems to escape. The object of this movement is to help women avoid abortion and the dangers attending it. Sincerely yours,

Margaret Sanger [*stamped*]

TFL ABCLR, MH-H (*MSM* C12:582). Return address: "104 Fifth Avenue."

1. While it was against ABCL policy to refer patients to doctors for therapeutic abortion, MS's personal secretary, Anna Lifshiz, was known to make exceptions for "sad cases" who came to the offices. By the 1930s, more evidence exists that the CRB staff made these informal referrals, but it is unlikely that anyone risked giving abortion referrals by mail. (Penelope Huse, "Report to Executive Committee," Dec. 1929 [PPFAR]; Chesler, *Woman of Valor,* 300–302; Marjorie Prevost to MS, Feb. 15, 1932 [*MSM* S6:810]; MS to Prevost, Feb. 17, 1932 [LCM 32:225].)

188. To Charles H. Johnson[1]

Despite the ABCL's use of the term clinic, *without a dispensary license, the CRB could only operate as a research bureau. In January 1924, a New York State Board of Charities inspector visited the CRB and noted the discrepancy, prompting state board secretary Charles Johnson to caution Sanger not to employ terms that might indicate the CRB was a legal dispensary clinic. (Richard Wallace to Anne Kennedy, May 16, 1922 [LCM 33:553].)*

[*New York, N.Y.*]
January 17, 1924

My dear Mr. Johnson:

Your letter of January 15th has been received. I wish to thank you for your courtesy in calling our attention to the usage of the word "clinic" and the fact that it is slightly synonymous with the use of the term "dispensary".[2]

We have no intention of giving the impression that we are conducting a Birth Control Clinic, but we do wish to infer and to state that our research work is conducted by a physician and while making this statement we always insist upon stating that only such persons shall be received whose health or condition comes under the definition of Judge Crane's decision.[3] You can readily understand, no doubt, that the newspapers desirous of making headlines do not hesitate to use the term that suits them best, and while we have been conscientious and as careful as possible, we will in the future lay even greater stress on our research work.[4] Thanking you again, Sincerely,

President.

Dictated but not signed.

TLcy MSP, DLC (LCM 33:566A).

1. Charles Henry Johnson (1870–1948), a social worker, was the New York State commissioner of social welfare (1917–32) and the secretary of the New York State Board of Charities (1917–23). (*NatCAB*)
2. See Johnson to MS, Jan. 15, 1924 (LCM 33:565).
3. This was a reference to the 1918 appeals decision that limited the prescription of contraceptives only "to cure or prevent disease."
4. MS decided against reapplying for a dispensary license in August 1924. (Wallace to MS, Aug. 14, 1924, and MS to Johnson, Aug. 18, 1924 [LCM 33:567A and 568A].)

189. To American Civil Liberties Union

*The New York State Birth Control Conference, scheduled for Syracuse on February 28–29, 1924, and organized by the ABCL and the local city league, became another battleground between birth control advocates and the Catholic church when the Syracuse Common Council passed a February 19 ordinance outlawing public discussion of birth control. As one council member declared, "Birth Control has no business, no right in this country, and there is no room for its advocates." Newspapers, public officials, and Protestant religious leaders speculated that Syracuse's Bishop Daniel J. Curley had exercised improper influence on the council, a charge he vehemently denied. (ABCL form letters, n.d. [*MSM S67:947–49*]; "Late News,"* BCR, *Mar. 1924, 89–90;* Syracuse Post-Standard, *Feb. 26 [quote] and 28, 1924.)*

[*New York, N.Y.*]
FEB 20, 1924

WE NEED YOUR ASSISTANCE PROTESTING AGAINST ACTION COMMON COUNCIL SYRACUSE ORDINANCE PASSED YESTERDAY PROHIBITING ALL DISCUSSION SUBJECT BIRTH CONTROL. LEAGUE MADE ALL ARRANGEMENTS STATE CONFERENCE TO BE HELD SYRACUSE FEBRUARY TWENTY EIGHTH TWENTY NINTH. MAYOR WALRATH[1] HAS NOT SIGNED ORDINANCE YET. IF THIS OCCURS IT ESTABLISHES PRECEDENT YEARS OVERCOME. PLEASE SEND DAY TELEGRAM PROTEST AT MY EXPENSE TO MAYOR AS UNCONSTITUTIONAL UNAMERICAN ACT.[2] GREATLY APPRECIATE THIS HELP.

MARGARET SANGER

TEL, ACLUR, NjP-M (*MSM* C3:79).

1. John H. Walrath (1887–1948), a former Onondaga County district attorney and Syracuse mayor (1922–25), may have had more to do with the ban than he publicly admitted. Dennis Haley, a council member, claimed, "This ordinance originated in the Mayor's cabinet. . . . We took the recommendations . . . we passed the ordinance." (*New York Times,* June 25, 1948; *Syracuse Post-Standard,* Feb. 26, 1924 [quote].)

2. Roger Baldwin, the head of the American Civil Liberties Union (ACLU), telegrammed Mayor Walrath on February 20, urging him to oppose the ban and advised MS to "hold the conference with as many distinguished speakers as you can and let the mayor make arrests if he will." Baldwin promised that "steps will be taken at once to bring it into the courts." (Baldwin to Walworth, Feb. 20, 1924, and to MS, Feb. 21, 1924 [*MSM* C3:84].)

190. To Grant Sanger[1]

[*New York, N.Y.*]
Sunday evening. [*February 24, 1924*]

Grant dear:

It was just the right thing to do to send back the check.[2] I bet five dollars with Pater[3] that you <u>would</u> return it right away & he bet you would not. So I <u>won</u>! He has paid the bet like a good sport & I am sending both the check & cash to the National city bank to <u>your</u> account. Someday when you are out of college you will find this nest egg of great comfort to begin life on. I shall not be home next weekend. I have to go to Syracuse—a fight on there to hold the Conference—& then I go to Utica and Ithica.[4] So I shall not return until the following week. As Easter is so near you had better not attempt to come home until then. Besides your reports are very discouraging Mr McOrmond gave a good report, but he is the only one—[5] They all say you are capable of far better work, only you will not consentrate & apply yourself seriously. Won't you try to do this?

I am banking on you to do the best possible. Love ever & always devotedly

Mother

[*Written at top of first page*] The secret of Pater's & my marriage leaked out all the papers carried it.[6]

ALS MSP, MN-SSC (*MSM* S2:521–23).

1. Grant had entered the private Westminster preparatory school in Simsbury, Connecticut, in September 1923.
2. This was possibly a duplicate check sent to Grant by MS for his expenses.
3. Pater was J. Noah Slee.
4. MS arrived in Syracuse on February 28, leaving for Ithaca on March 3. (1924 Calendar [*MSM* S78:563]; *Syracuse Post-Standard,* Feb. 28, 1924; MS to Slee, Mar. 3, 1924 [*MSM* 2:543].)
5. Raymond Richards McOrmond (1886–1943) was the Westminster headmaster (1923–36). Grant, a good student, had become distracted by his social life and athletics. (*Westminster News,* Jan. 30, 1943.)
6. Newspapers around the country ran a wire report of the Sanger-Slee marriage on February 18, 1924, often accompanied by provocative headlines, such as "Millionaire Married Mrs. Sanger after World-Wide Chase" and "Birth Control Advocate Was Secret Bride." (*New Bedford Standard* and *Syracuse Telegram,* Feb. 18, 1924; see also, for example, the *Poughkeepsie Times,* Feb. 19, 1924, and the *Indianapolis Times,* Mar. 13, 1924.)

191. "The Meaning of Radio Birth Control"

On February 25, after protests by Protestant ministers, university professors, and others, Syracuse's Mayor Walrath vetoed the common council's anti–birth control ordinance. The council could not override the veto, and the conference took place as scheduled on February 28–29. However, the city's commissioner of public safety attended the conference, poised to order arrests if speakers violated the state's obscenity law by actually giving contraceptive information. Birth control and free speech activists packed the sessions, which were "crowded with women anxious to learn all they could about the movement." A large number of pledges were collected, and Syracuse's branch of the ABCL was strengthened and invigorated. Sanger's radio address capped the conference. ("Birth Control in Syracuse," 100–101 [quote on 101]; Syracuse Post-Standard, *Feb. 26 and 28, 1924.)*

Syracuse, [*N.Y.*]
February 29, 1924

Every step forward in our history, from those remote days when our prehistoric ancestors first discovered fire, tilled the soil, and domesticated the animals, has been gained through control over some force of NATURE. One by one these great wild powers, each one of them destructive and overpowering, have been harnessed, directed and mastered by human intelligence and made to serve some constructive purpose. The power of the wind, the power of steam, the power of electricity, all and with increasing rapidity have thus been subjugated.

By each of these successive steps, men have made use of these tremendous forces to free themselves from the slavery of toil. At every step in this long journey they have met the opposition of the prejudiced majority. These opposing groups, which have taken no part in progress, laughed at Columbus when he told them the world was round. They burnt great scientists at the stake. They said that automobiles would be impracticable and dangerous. They scoffed at the very idea of aviation. But in spite of all this opposition, a few have been brave enough, strong enough, courageous enough, to bear aloft and to carry onward the torch of civilization.

In Man's onward march towards civilization, one after another, he has conquered and controlled the forces of Nature. Thereby he has diminished disease, pestilence, and famine. Hygiene, surgery and sanitation have been the outcome of his triumph. In gaining control over these powers of Nature, step by step, mankind has made progress.

Hunger and Love

If you stop to think for yourself, you will agree with me that there are two dominant forces of human nature that drive every one of us onward, day in and day out, to work, to struggle, to achieve; to make homes, to establish families. These are the instincts of Hunger and Love. To satisfy our hunger, men compete in business with their fellow men, they labor to attain a little security in life. And similarly to satisfy our undying need for love, we marry, we make homes, we bring children into the world.

You all know as well as I do that morality means the control of these two instinctive impulses. If we aim to satisfy our hunger by eating too much, by refusing to share our bread with our fellow-man, we become immoral and sink to the level of beasts. We are no less immoral if irresponsibly we bring children into this world without first considering our ability to cherish and protect them; without giving thought to the health and strength of the mother, upon whom the great burden falls. Unless he can assure them health, adequate nourishment, sunlight and care, no man is justified in calling an unlimited number of children into being.

Now, just as Man has freed himself from Nature's bondage through invention and machinery, so must Woman free herself from the crushing slavery of undesired maternity through the instrument of knowledge and science. She must learn to space the years between the births of her children. In this matter, let mothers consider the example of the gardener.

A Garden of Children

Just think for a moment of the meaning of the word kindergarten—a garden of children! To me, that is just what the world ought to be—a garden of children. In this matter we should not do less than follow the example of the professional gardener. Every expert gardener knows that the individual plant must be properly spaced, rooted in a rich nourishing soil, and provided with sufficient air and sunlight. He knows that no plant would have a fair chance of life if it were overcrowded or choked by weeds. To grow into maturity, to bud, to blossom, to produce beautiful sturdy flowers in its own season, each plant must have constant attention, incessant care and tender devotion.

If plants, and live stock as well, require space and air, sunlight and love, children need them even more. The only real wealth of our country lies in the men and women of the next generation. A farmer would rather produce a thousand thoroughbreds than a million runts.

How are we to breed a race of human thoroughbreds unless we follow the same plan? We must make this country into a garden for children instead of a disorderly back lot overrun with human weeds.[1]

In a home where there are too many children in proportion to the living space, the air and sunlight, the children are usually overcrowded and underfed. They are a constant burden on their mother's overtaxed strength and the father's earning capacity. Such homes cannot be gardens in any sense of the word. As each new baby comes, a poor little victim brought unwanted into an already overcrowded home, he has less and less chance to survive in his bitter struggle for life. Statistics prove this fact. In families where there are too many children, there is a high rate of infant deaths. Then the schools are overcrowded. Little tots are driven to work at an age when they should be in fields and playgrounds.

A Miracle of Science

The control of this great overpowering human energy, the instinct of reproduction—is what we mean by Birth Control. We, who are carrying on the battle for the great human right of Birth Control, are fighting for better, healthier children, for a race of strong men and beautiful women here in America. We place quality above quantity. We want each child to have proper food, warmth, sunlight and fresh air, devotion and love.

Birth Control does not mean childlessness. On the contrary, it does mean fewer, finer, stronger babies, happier, healthier mothers, fathers freed from worry, making their way to success and achievement, because they are inspired and strengthened by harmony and love.

You who are listening in tonight, who are taking part in this miracle of science, in this human control over one of the greatest energies of Nature, in this triumph of intelligence over prejudice and ignorance, remember that just listening in is not enough. Let your intelligence likewise be radioactive. Investigate our claims for yourself. Think for yourself. If you do, I am sure every one of you will join in our great movement to broadcast health and the heritage of health to every mother and child in this land.

BCR, Apr. 1924, 110–11 (*MSM* S70:1041–42). Broadcast on radio WFAB Syracuse. MS gave a version of this speech (not found) at the final session of the conference on February 28.

1. MS often used the analogy of society as a garden in which the strong and fecund weeds (the "feeble-minded" or "unfit") are ignored, frequently quoting Luther Burbank, a plant expert and eugenicist. (See MS, "Is Race Suicide Probable?" *Colliers,* Aug. 15, 1925, 24 [*MSM* C16:260]; see also "A Better Race through Birth Control," *Thinker,* Nov. 1923 [*MSM* C16:205]; and "This Business of Bearing Babies," 1925? [*MSM* S71:58].)

192. To J. Noah Slee

[*Syracuse, N.Y.*]
March 1 [*1924*] 8 am.

My adorable Sweetheart—

It was a joy to get your special delivery a few moments ago.[1] How I miss you at night! I awaken a dozen times to see where you are or feel you pull the cover over me—and then lie awake to wonder if you are sleeping—and a secret wish that you too are awake & thinking of me & missing me! Well the conference is over & it has been a great success. Anne Kennedy has done a fine job here and is very tired.[2] Everyone says I look younger than I did two years ago!

Last nights meeting for the Doctors was so cold[3]—oh those stupid men they deserve to be put out of existence by Christian Scientists[4] & other thinking alive groups— I gave my address over the radio at 9 PM. Did you hear me darling? I do hope you did but not until five oclock did I know I was really going to be able to do it. There was censorship on that too. Th'o over a hundred telephone calls came in during the afternoon asking if I was to broadcast at 9.

I am glad you wrote Evans so plain[5]—my heavens—do you mean to say he has kept your check all this time? The man is more than stupid. Mrs Ackerman[6] will be delighted that we have seen his stupidity at last. Mrs Day was here with Mrs Porritt.[7] Dr Vaughan said Clara Louise had her baby so easily that she is out now for big families—[8] Well we have beaten the opposition out of sight— Thank God. I am staying here today & tomorrow trying to get some money. I want to get home to you my love as soon as I can. The meeting at Ithica will also be a big one. Dr Wilcox the most famous ↓~~statisteian~~↑ statistican in this country is to be chairman—[9] I will try to leave that night for New York arriving home Wednesday morning— I do not know about trains yet & Ithica is an out of the way place—but I hope to do this.

Darling sweetheart I love & adore you constantly—day by day, more & more! There is no happiness out of your sweet presence, & I long to be back within your tender arms & loving care—a kiss & hug & a world of love—devotedly,

Margy.

[*Written above date on first page*]: Pay Day!

ALS MSP, MN-SSC (*MSM* S2:537–40). Letterhead of the Onondaga Hotel.

1. See Slee to MS, Feb. 29, 1924 (*MSM* S2:528).
2. Kennedy had compiled invitation lists and assisted the local committee in fighting the Syracuse council's ban. MS wrote of her, "Of course I scold and find fault at every slight thing, but she rises above it & knows I am working with her for perfection in these things." (MS to Rublee, Mar. 1, 1924 [*MSM* C3:107].)
3. Dorothy Bocker, John Vaughan, and James Cooper held a doctors-only meeting on contraceptive techniques. ("Birth Control in Syracuse," 101; for attendees, see *MSM* C14:812.)
4. Christian Science, a religion established in 1879 by Mary Baker Eddy, held that healing could best be accomplished through prayer and meditation rather than traditional medicine.
5. Clarence V. Evans, the ABCL bookkeeper, had been dismissed by Slee for incompetence. (Slee to Evans, Feb. 29, 1924 [MS Unfilmed].)
6. Frances Brooks Ackermann (1875–1935), a suffragist, philanthropist, and clubwoman in Bronxville, New York, was the ABCL treasurer. (*New York Times,* Aug. 11, 1935.)
7. Katharine Beach Day (1853–1942), a suffragist, a social reformer, and the widow of a Hartford, Connecticut, manufacturer, helped MS organize the First American Birth Control Conference in 1921. Both she and Annie Porritt were on the ABCL board of directors. (*Hartford Courant,* Dec. 27, 1942; Lee, *Biographical Cyclopaedia of American Women,* 216–18.)
8. John Colin Vaughan (1875–1940) was a New York City surgeon and member of the ABCL board of directors (1922–28). Clara Louise Rowe McGraw had resigned as the ABCL secretary in the summer of 1923 over MS's charges that she did not have the ability to complete her work. (*New York Times,* Jan. 13, 1940; ABCL Board of Directors Minutes, Oct. 2, 1923 [*MSM* S61:90].)
9. Walter Francis Willcox (1861–1964), a professor of political economy and statistics at Cornell University and an ABCL national council member (1921–34), chaired MS's March 3 meeting at the Unitarian church. MS returned to New York City on March 5. (*NatCAB;* "News Notes," *BCR,* Apr. 1924, 120; MS to Slee, Mar 3, 1924 [*MSM* S2:543].)

193. *To Client*

Sanger rarely answered client letters personally but did so when they presented unusual or complex problems or affected her emotionally. What follows is her response to a twenty-four-

page letter written by a nineteen-year-old single, self-described God-fearing woman who wrote to Sanger because "you are far away and you do not know me. And because I have to have some advice. And I believe you will tell me what to do—And tell me the right thing." The writer chronicled a troubled adolescence, during which she was abused by her father and sent off to full-time work at age fifteen. She fell in love with "Tom" and became pregnant, but an abortion by "a Negro doctor far away" ended the relationship. She met another man who wished to marry her, but she held him off, fearing he could physically detect her past sins. "Can he tell I've ever been touched," she asked. The woman ended by telling Sanger, "You have my life in your hands." (Client to MS, Mar. 3, 1924 [LCM 10:1161].)

[*New York, N.Y.*]
March 7, 1924.

Dear Miss [*Name Omitted*]:-

Your tragic letter was waiting for me upon my return, for I have been absent from the city several days. I am sorry to be delayed in answering it.

I want emphatically to say to you that you must not be discouraged. Your life is ahead of you. Your experience in the past has been terrible—even tragic, I will admit, but just because of this sorrow and such bitter experience greater happiness is going to come to you.

You must not think of yourself or your relations with Tom, whom you have loved, in the wrong light. If you loved him and he loved you, any relations between you were just as holy and as pure in the sight of God as if a marriage certificate had been given you. You must not look upon this relationship as if you were a bad girl. It is love between two people that sanctifies marriage. There are many marriages today that are not so sanctified, because love has flown out of the window.

Now, I come to the important question about the young man you wish to marry and whether you should tell him or not: My advice to you would be—do not do so. Your past life is entirely your own; your future acts after you had met this new man and had become his wife, then become part of his affair; but what happened to you before you met him is certainly not his business and you do not need to tell him anything. He probably could not understand and would misjudge you, and it would cause him a great deal of unhappiness. So as you love him and want to marry him, do so—and remember that you are less selfish in keeping this to yourself than to unburden yourself and cast your confidence upon him and make him unhappy thereby.

As to the other point—he cannot tell whether you had been with anyone before or not, no matter what his medical experience has been. It is impossible for him to tell, especially if you had not had intercourse for a year previous to your marriage. Many women have found that the tissues have grown together in a year's time, and you need not worry on this score; he cannot tell. If you take douches, take an astringent douche before your marriage of salt water and a little alum. This helps to rebuild your tissues.

Keep your head high and your heart light. You must not consider that you are a bad girl; you are not, and do not let yourself be deceived or become oversentimental in telling anyone about your relations with the man you loved. Upon yourself depends your future happiness. I have given the same advice to women and they have kept to it, and they have been far happier in their married lives and in their family than has the poor, silly girl who has told all she knows, because she could not keep it to herself.

Let me hear from you and promise me that you are going to be a sensible girl and profit by the experience you have had and make the man you love happy. I am glad you wrote to me and will be glad to hear from you again. Sincerely yours,

---

TLcy MSP, DLC (LCM 10:1173–74). In the interest of privacy, the editors have omitted the recipient's name. A note written by an unidentified author at the bottom of the last page, probably referring to enclosures sent with MS's reply, reads, "W. Ev. Girl Sh. Know—Letters—[*Y. in Confl*]—Leafl on Sex Enlight."

194. *From Francis E. Fitzgerald*[1]

Omaha, Nebraska
August 8, 1924.

Mesdames:

Your publication "Birth Control Review" is being sent to the Creighton University Library.

The character of this publication and the moral teaching which it advocates is highly offensive to a God-fearing Christian and in behalf of the young men who attend Creighton University I as the Librarian of the institution can not permit it in our reading room. Yours very truly

CREIGHTON UNIVERSITY LIBRARY
Francis E. Fitzgerald [*signed*]
Librarian

TLS MSP, DLC (LCM 75:458A). Letterhead of Creighton University. Addressed to "American Birth Control League, Inc." The word "discontinue" is handwritten across the text.

1. Francis E. Fitzgerald (1901–61) was a pioneer of the Catholic Library Association and a librarian at Creighton, a Jesuit university in Omaha, Nebraska. (Rev. James J. Kortendick, "In Memoriam," *Catholic Library World,* May–June 1961, 476.)

195. To Hugh de Selincourt

[*Willow Lake, Fishkill, N.Y.*][1]
Aug 10. [*1924*]

Dear Hugh:

The book came ↑thank you↓ I am saving it for time to read it continuously.[2] I am next week to be in N.Y. until my staff return from vacation.

I went down last week & was at the office at 8:30 am until 6 pm and th'o the heat was exhausting, I adored being at the desk & getting at the helm of details again. This week promises to be another [*scorcher*] according to the singing of the locusts. Of course you would like horseback. When I come to visit you we will take a ride. The boys[3] & I have been shooting a little mainly target practice ↑on crows↓ I remember how Harold wanted me to go out & shoot a poor little rabbit! I believe he meant it too! Where & how is darling Harold![4] He is a lamb isn't he?

Soon I shall begin to work on our International Conference[5] God help me! Its like pulling together all one has for a final goal. It must be a success! Are you coming over for it? Will you? Suggestions please. Of course you see through Menken. He is just that, but I doubt he practices self abuse he has a very charming mistress while keeping up his home with a mother & brother. Scarcely any need for isolated practices th'o its possible.[6] Any way he has a clear mind & fearless. I don't care how it courses or what direction the fearlessness takes its there. In my article on "the Fight" I meant him & his crowd of "free speechers" when I referred to "bean shooters", yet he was fair enough to publish the article knowing it was a dig.[7] Anyway Hugh I love you & all the things you think. Have you read Olive Schreiner life by her husband[8]—"Ohmygod" it's a husband like that who deserves murder. love & love & love

Margaret

ALS MSP, DLC (LCM 3:503–5).

1. MS and Slee had moved into Willowlake during the spring.

2. The book was de Selincourt's *Cricket Match* (London, 1924).

3. Grant had recently taken his college board exams; Stuart, having completed his studies at the Roxbury School, was preparing to enter Yale University.

4. In response to MS's query about Harold Child, de Selincourt wrote, "Poems are beginning to come out of him again." (De Selincourt to MS, Aug. 26, 1924 [*MSM* S2:630].)

5. The ABCL was to host the Sixth International Neo-Malthusian and Birth Control Conference in the spring of 1925, and invitations had been sent to a large list of scholars and scientists. (MS to ABCL Members, Apr. 28, 1924 [*MSM* 67:83].)

6. Henry Louis Mencken (1880–1956), a journalist and social critic, was known for his witty, irreverent criticism of American and British culture and values. Mencken's mistress was Marion Bloom (1891–1975), a literary agent and nurse. De Selincourt had read

an article by Mencken on women's emancipation and commented that Mencken was "probably dreadfully shy and uncertain and wavering and meek." He wagered that Mencken had "never outgrown the most boyish form of self abuse." (*ANB; Washington Post,* Mar. 10, 1975; H. L. Mencken, "The Sex Uproar," *Nation,* July 23, 1924, 91–93; de Selincourt to MS, July 29, 1924 [*MSM* S2:621].)

7. Dubious about birth control but more offended by censorship, Mencken solicited a birth control article from MS in which she characterized liberals and intellectuals who protested free speech infringements as "school boys armed with bean shooters." (MS, "War against Birth Control," 235.)

8. The biography by Schreiner's husband portrayed her as brilliant but unbalanced and highly neurotic. Described in the *Times* as Cronwright-Schreiner's "pious memorial" to his wife, it muted her feminism, particularly her assertion of women's strong sexual drive. (Samuel C. Cronwright-Schreiner, *The Life of Olive Schreiner* [London, 1924]; *London Times,* Mar. 7, 1924.)

196. To Francis E. Fitzgerald

[*New York, N.Y.*]
August 11, 1924.

Dear Sir:

Your astounding letter of August 8 came to me for my attention.[1]

Surely you, as Librarian, have no right to make yourself censor as to what is good for university students to read.

The Birth Control Review has a circulation of over 15,000, and goes to all the largest libraries in the world.[2] May it not be that it is a great responsibility to set your single opinion up as against the highest authorities of Science.

As the subscription to your Library was paid for by a member of your University, I shall inform him of your conduct, and trust that it will be brought to the attention of the proper authorities. Very truly yours,

(Signed) Margaret Sanger. [*stamped*]
President.

TRcy MSP, DLC (LCM 75:461). Letterhead of the ABCL.

1. See Fitzgerald to MS, Aug. 8, 1924, herein.

2. Combined monthly street and subscription sales of the *BCR* were approximately 18,000 in 1924 ("Report on the *BCR* Year Ended December, 1924" [LCM 20:839]).

197. From Client

The following letter was edited for publication, possibly for inclusion in Sanger's 1926 marriage manual, Happiness in Marriage, *a publication that advanced the feminist view that stable, happy unions required both partners to contribute and be fulfilled. This letter, however, did not appear in the book.*

Logansport, Ind.
August 14, 1924

My dear Margaret Sanger,

To me intercourse[1] is so very, very repulsive. Will you help me? I have been married three years and have two lovely children. A girl, 26 mo. old and a boy 5 mo. old. I have never cared for intercourse as a normal woman should, altho, before my first baby came, I did enjoy it.[2] Six months before the second baby was born I began to grow nervous and irritable. I grew continuously worse, and became so dreadfully nervous when I even thought my husband wanted intercourse.[3] When the penis touches me[4] I felt as if I'd have to scream in spite of all I can do. We practised total abstinence 3 mo. before the baby came thinking that afterwards I would be better, but it is just as bad as ever. I have no more emotion or desire than a child. I have never experienced discharge.[5]

I'm perfectly healthy and certainly no one can withstand pregnancy or have children easier than I.

What do you make of it? I will be anxious for your answer.[6] Yours very truly,

[*Name omitted*]

ALS MSP, MN-SSC (*MSM* S2:623). In the interest of privacy, the editors have omitted the author's name. Handwritten corrections by MS, probably in preparation for publication, are indicated in the endnotes. A note, probably written by one of MS's secretaries, at the top right of the first page reads, "File Lack of desire."

1. The word was struck out and replaced by "married life."
2. The words "enjoy it" were struck out.
3. The word "intercourse" was struck out and replaced by "me."
4. From the start of sentence was struck out.
5. The word "discharge" was struck out and replaced by "that pleasure."
6. The response was not found.

198. To Leon J. Cole[1]

Similar versions of this letter were sent to other physicians and academics, many of them active or interested in eugenics work as well as birth control.

[*New York, N.Y.*]
August 21, 1924.

My dear Prof. Cole:

You of course know that during the past year and a half a few of us have been trying to test out the New York State law by conducting a so-called "clinic" in this City. The object is to try out the decision of the Court of Appeals, rendered by Judge Frederick C. Crane under date of January 8, 1918, which held that any person in New York State may give contraceptive advice "for the cure or prevention of disease."

You also know that Dr. Bocker has had charge of this work. I believe you have received a copy of her report of her first one thousand cases.[2]

What I now desire is to have the benefit of a board or group of men who will help direct this department, and to whom Dr. Bocker shall report her findings. We have been working so far alone, and it does seem that the time has now come to ask for assistance and guidance from friends of the movement whose judgment and opinion would be of value in our efforts.

Dr. Adolf Meyer[3] and Prof. Raymond Pearl[4] have kindly consented to become members of our board. Will you join them in this undertaking?[5] The reports would be sent you each month, or after the completion of each series,—or whenever you considered it wise to have them. We would keep in constant touch with you without being too much of a nuisance or causing you too much trouble.

May I hear from you at your earliest convenience so that this departure may get under way before the work for the International Conference begins.[6]

Sincerely,

Margaret Sanger [*signed*]

TLS LJCP, WU (*MSM* C3:177). Letterhead of the ABCL.

1. Leon Jacob Cole (1877–1948) was a professor of genetics and animal breeding at the University of Wisconsin (1910–47), whom MS first met when planning the Middle Western States Birth Control Conference. (*DSB*)

2. Bocker's thirty-two-page booklet, *Birth Control Methods,* described the results of fourteen contraceptive regimens tested on 1,208 CRB patients between January 1923 and February 1924. It recommended the pessary with contraceptive cream as most effective.

3. Adolf Meyer (1866–1950) was a Swiss-born psychiatrist at the Johns Hopkins School of Medicine and the director of the Henry Phipps Psychiatric Clinic. Meyer, who studied the impact of environment and life events on the development and treatment of

mental disorders, was one of the medical experts MS used to buttress her arguments for the positive psychological effects of contraception. Meyer was also interested in the potential benefits of eugenics. (*ANB;* Adolf Meyer, "Preface" and "The Obligation of Procreative Hygiene," in *Birth Control: Facts and Responsibilities,* ed. Adolf Meyer [Baltimore, 1925], v–xi, 1–10; Adolf Meyer, "Organization of Eugenics Investigation," *Eugenical News* 2 [Sept. 1917]: 66–69.)

4. Raymond Pearl (1879–1940), a biologist and statistician at the Johns Hopkins University, studied world population growth and genetics and was a leading eugenicist. An advocate of sterilization of criminals, he believed that both heredity and environmental factors shaped personality. His research on class-based fertility differentials, which utilized CRB records, supported MS's claim that access to contraception affected birthrates. Pearl was a member of the ABCL's national council (1922–27). (*ANB*)

5. Cole agreed to serve on the CRB's medical advisory council on August 23, 1924, and became a member of the ABCL's national council the same year. In addition to Cole, Pearl, and Meyer, the CRB's medical advisory council included Leslie Clarence Dunn, Edward Murray East, Henry Pratt Fairchild, John Favill, Clarence Cook Little, Stuart Mudd, William Fielding Ogburn, John B. Solley Jr., Benjamin T. Tilton, and Ira Solomon Wile. The acceptance letters from Meyer and Pearl were not found. (Cole to MS, June ?, 1923, and Aug. 23, 1924 [*MSM* C2:373 and C3:178].)

6. For the conference announcement, see March 25, 1925 (*MSM* C14:226).

199. To Dorothy Bocker[1]

[*New York, N.Y.*]
September 15, 1924.

TO Dr. Bocker
FROM Margaret Sanger
Re Specific Information required in report covering work of Clinical Research Department.

I would like the Monthly Report of the Clinical Research Department[2] to include the following information:

1. Number of patients (in total) who call during each month, to be subdivided into—
   (a) new patients
   (b) old patients
2. Kind of advice given new patients, i.e.—
   (a) Ramses)
   (b) Mispah) Pessaries
   (c) Mensinga)
   (d) Kind of Paste given, or suppository.

Note: The above information can be given in totals,—number of patients each month receiving each combination, and what?

3. Old Patients: Information given.

Why, in your estimation, they have failed, or from your questioning, what you ascertain has caused failure?

What advice you are giving to correct these failures.

Note if failure cases were physically examined and properly fitted to pessary, etc, or not.

Several failure cases came to my attention and stated that they were not fitted but only instructed from diagrams by the physician. I believe many failures can be traced to this method of instruction. I trust that this practice has been discontinued.

4. How much material is given away each month?
How much " " sold each month?

TM MSP, DLC (LCM 31:420A).

1. In May 1924, Robert L. Dickinson, whose Committee on Maternal Health had conducted several inspections of the CRB and Bocker's research, read a report of his findings at the American Gynecological Society. Though he claimed that Bocker was "particularly well-informed on contraceptive matters," he was critical of her data-gathering techniques, arguing that "the history forms are full and well balanced but the entries often scant. Medical inspection or supervision or check-up must be trifling or absent. For follow-up they depend on the return of patients for the purchase of supplies. Twenty-one percent fail to return or report." Dickinson charged that all birth control clinics that compiled data were biased toward demonstrating success and lacked the proper scientific reserve. MS may have felt the need to respond to these criticisms to retain the support of physicians and scientists, though she publicly dismissed Dickinson as "tainted with bias." (Dickinson, "Contraception," 600 [first and second quotes]; MS, "Book Reviews," *BCR*, Jan. 1925, 20 [third quote].)

2. Bocker's monthly reports, apart from the June 1924 report, were not found, though summaries of several months survive. In a typed note, possibly a draft of this letter, MS criticized Bocker for not providing information on the CRB's "real work" by including more data on patients who became pregnant. She wrote, "WHY the failure. There should be no 'unexplained' failures in research work." (For Bocker's CRB summaries, see LCM 34:582, 652, 659, and 660A; for MS note, see LCM 34:660B.)

200. *To American Civil Liberties Union*

Sanger was scheduled to speak in Boston in March, but Mayor James M. Curley refused to issue a permit, promising that "Mrs. Sanger, her child murder propaganda, and her allies disguised as free speech defenders, will not appear in any public licensed hall in Boston, if I can prevent it." The ACLU head Roger Baldwin tried to find another venue but as late as January 1926 still had not found any public hall willing "to risk its license during the remaining months of Mayor Curley's term in office." (Curley quoted in Boston Globe, *Feb.*

14, 1925; "Statement by Roger Baldwin," Feb. 16, 1925 [RNBP]; "News Notes," BCR, *Jan. 1926, 30.)*

[*New York, N.Y.*]
September 15, 1924.
Attention Mr. Roger N. Baldwin.[1]

Gentlemen:

Thank you for your letter of September 9.[2]

Mrs. Kennedy has been making a lecture tour of the country and will return to New York about October 1st,[3] at which time your letter will be referred to her, as she will be able to give you more accurate information about the plans we have made for Boston.[4]

Owing to our International Conference being scheduled for March 26–31, 1925, we anticipate a very busy winter.

I ache all over every time I think of Boston,—and the fact that the Mayor was able to keep me out of that city last winter does not set well with me.[5] I want to go back and try it again, but I do not want to fail this time. I do not want a group to undertake it unless we can put it over. The risk and precedent is too great—besides a failure would effect tremendously the International Conference. If you really believe there is a group in Boston, who will not "straddle" the issue, we'll give the Mayor a run for his money. My experience in Boston has shown me that if we achieve a victory we only succeed in starting a fight among the native element. Nobody can match the Irish!

When Mrs. Kennedy returns, she will be able to tell you our available people in Boston for this purpose. Very sincerely yours,

Margaret Sanger [*signed*]
President.

TLS RNBP, NjP-M (*MSM* C3:188). Letterhead of the ABCL.

1. Roger Baldwin (1884–1981) was a civil libertarian whose interest in free speech was sparked when St. Louis police tried to stop MS from speaking there in 1916. An opponent of U.S. entry into World War I and a member of the American Union against Militarism, Baldwin formed the Civil Liberties Union to defend those prosecuted under the 1917 Espionage Act. In 1920, the Civil Liberties Union was transformed into the ACLU, which fought to defend freedoms endangered by government repression, including free speech, the right to strike, criminal justice, and racial equality. (*ANB*)

2. Baldwin to Anne Kennedy, Sept. 9, 1924. (RNBP)

3. Between late July and September 1924, Kennedy met with birth control reformers in fourteen other states en route to California, where she gave over twenty lectures and helped organize five birth control leagues. ("News Notes," *BCR*, Sept. 1924, 266–67, and Oct. 1924, 297.)

4. In October, Kennedy sent Baldwin a list of Boston-area ABCL members, but Bald-

win was unable to organize a public forum for MS. She did speak at several private functions during March 1–4, 1925, including a luncheon at Harvard's Liberal Club and a gathering of the Young Men's Hebrew Association of Roxbury. (Kennedy to Baldwin, Oct. 7, 1924 [RNBP]; "News Notes," *BCR*, Apr. 1925, 122.)

5. James Michael Curley (1874–1958) was the colorful Democratic mayor of Boston who exercised broad power to defend public morality. His censorious actions and regulation of cultural activities popularized the phrase "banned in Boston." (Jack Beatty, *The Rascal King: The Life and Times of James Michael Curley, 1874–1958* [New York, 1992], 172–75.)

201. From Alexander Berkman[1]

Berlin-Wilmersdorf [*Germany*]
Sept. 26, 1924

My dear Peggy:

You will probably be surprised to hear from me, and perhaps even more so at the familiar appellation. But that is the way I think of you, an old habit (do I hear you say "a bad one"?).

The occasion of this writing? Well, since my letters to you—one to London, and later on one to N.Y.—remained unanswered, I stopped writing, of course.[2] But now a letter of yours came to hand.[3] One addressed by you to Leonard Abbott[4] and forwarded to me by Harry Kelly[5] with the marginal note, "I have been carrying this around for months". Somewhat delayed, as you see, for your letter was dated—well, I see there is NO date on it. But it refers to me, and therefore I "take the liberty of writing," as the nurse girl says.

The point is this—I see by your letter that you have not forgotten me, and that pleases my—shall I say vanity? Anyhow, I am pleased to know it, though I have heard that you have proven unfaithful to me and went and got married. The nerve of you! Even without consulting or even telling me! Seriously, is the report true? I am so generous-hearted, as you know, that I should forgive you, even if it were true. And if he is a decent fellow, then you have probably done a very sensible thing. So, there!

But I cannot think of you as anyone's "wife", and I am writing to you as to the Peggy I used to know of old—the one I used to take occasionally dinner ↑with↓ at that Hungarian restaurant in the basement of Second Avenue or spend time together somewhere else in the old environment.[6] I wonder whether you still remember?

Now, then, Peggy, thanks for that letter, for it breathed the old friendship and spirit, and did me good to read it. You mention that you don't know my address and that you therefore got out of touch with me, and that is one of the reasons I am writing. As to my eyes—you seem to have heard that I have had trouble with them—they are much better now. I think it was the strain of writing intensively on my Russian book. Now they are improved, so you need not worry on that account.

That brings me to the very unpleasant subject of the "collection" Harry Kelly and other friends in N.Y. had made in my behalf. They meant well, of course, and I appreciate their motives. But I want you to know—and all those that contributed—that it was done without my knowledge or consent. As soon as I found out about it, recently only, I informed Kelly and Minna Lowensohn[7] that I am VERY SORRY such a thing was done. You will understand that I cannot accept any money of a collection for my personal use, and I have written Harry to that effect. I should like to inform of this EVERY ONE of the friends who contributed, but Harry has declined to send me a list of the people. But I inform you of this, since I see from your letter that you contributed $25.

Meanwhile Kelly sent me $150. of the collection, and Minna brought an additional $50. The $150. I have on hand, subject to the disposition of the contributors. The $50., with Minna's consent, was used for Nestor Makhno,[8] who was at that time arrested in Danzig and in grave danger of being deported to Russia, which would mean death. (I don't know whether you know who Makhno is. Briefly, a modern Stenka Rasin, the leader of the peasant rebels in the Ukraine who had risen against their oppressors, foreign, native, white AND red).[9]

I have suggested to Kelly that, if the money is not to be returned to the donors, it should be used for the fund of my book on Russia. The matter needs some explanation to you, I suppose. Briefly, I have completed a larger work on Russia, called THE BOLSHEVIK MYTH. It deals with Russia during 1920–1922, the most significant years of the Revolution. It is mostly, objective, a psychologic study of the thoughts, emotions and lives of the people, in various walks of life. I think it ought to be published—natural that I should think so. But the publishers politely decline.[10] Most of them have written me very flattering opinions of the MSS., that it is interesting, deserves publication "more than other books written on Russia", etc. But they fear it would not sell, and therefore——

This is the situation at present. Fitzie and Alsberg[11] are trying to get a publisher, but time passes, and I have little hope of finding one. The only thing to do ↑therefore↓ is to pay a publisher to issue the book and put it on the market. That, then, is my plan. We need about a thousand dollars to do that, and I have suggested to Kelly that the $150. he sent me, and the other sum he still has on hands, should be considered as starting a fund for the publication of my MSS. that is, WITH THE CONSENT OF THE DONORS.

So the matter is explained to you now, and I feel easier about it. Wish I could explain it also to all those that contributed to that damned collection.

And now to something pleasanter. How are you, dear Peggy and your work? I received 2 copies of your magazine, a long, long time ago, but it ceased coming after that. So that I could not follow your work. And how is life in general with you and "family"? New members in the latter, I wonder. If you have time and inclination to write, tell me of these things.

There is much to say of many other things, but you are a busy woman, and long private correspondence is an imposition. So 'tis sufficient for today, anyhow. My best greetings to you, and also to any of those you come in contact with and who happen not to have forgotten me.

Should be very happy to hear from you, if you can spare the time to write. As of yore,

S.

TL MSP, MN-SSC (*MSM* S2:650). MS wrote "Sasha" below the initial; at the bottom of the last page, she wrote, "Berkman was a good friend a gentleman & much more sensative than his co worker Emma Goldman whom I could not like. MS"

1. Alexander Berkman (called Sasha by his intimates) was pursued by the government after both the *Blast* and *Mother Earth* were shut down. Prosecuted for his antiwar and anticonscription efforts and convicted under the Draft Act in 1917, he served two years in the Atlanta Federal Penitentiary. Upon his 1919 release, he was deported. Berkman and Emma Goldman went to the U.S.S.R., remaining there until 1922, when they left, disillusioned with the repressive Communist state. (*DAB*)

2. The letters were not found.

3. The letter was not found.

4. Leonard Abbott, who had been active in the No-Conscription League and in 1918 served with MS on the board of the League for Amnesty of Political Prisoners, withdrew from radical activities after 1920 to care for his wife, Rose Yuster, who had contracted multiple sclerosis. (Paul Avrich, *Anarchist Portraits* [Princeton, N.J., 1988], 219; Avrich, *Modern School Movement,* 116, 216, 338–39.)

5. Henry (Harry) May Kelly (1871–1953) was an anarchist and writer, who along with Berkman had been a charter member of the Ferrer Association and helped establish the Stelton School. In 1920, Kelly, Roger Baldwin, and Elizabeth Gurley Flynn formed the League for Mutual Aid to provide interest-free loans to labor activists, political prisoners, and victims of the "Red Scare." Kelly had visited Berkman in Stockholm in 1922. (Avrich, *Modern School Movement,* 173–77, 341–44; Avrich, *Anarchist Voices,* 508.)

6. This was a reference to their early friendship in prewar Greenwich Village.

7. Minna Lowensohn, an anarchist active in the Modern School movement and a close friend of Berkman and Harry Kelly, helped raise funds through the League for Mutual Aid. (Avrich, *Modern School Movement,* 394; Avrich, *Anarchist Voices,* 508.)

8. Nestor Ivanovich Makhno (1889–1934) was a Ukrainian anarchist who fought against both the anti-Soviet (White) army and the Bolshevik Red Army and then went into hiding. Arrested in Poland in 1922, he was seeking safe passage to Berlin. (Max Nomad, *Apostles of Revolution* [Boston, 1939], 302, 310, 319, 338.)

9. Stepan (also known as Sten'ka) Timofeevich Razin (1630?–1671) was a popular Cossack leader and folk hero who led a massive uprising during the rein of Tsar Aleksei Mikhailovich. (Joseph L. Wieczynski, ed., *The Modern Encyclopedia of Russian and Soviet History* [Gulf Breeze, Fla., 1990], 52.)

10. Boni and Liveright published this diary of his Russian years in 1925.

11. These were references to Berkman's former lover Eleanor Fitzgerald, who in 1918 became an executive of the Provincetown Players, and Henry Garfield Alsberg (1881–1970), a journalist who met Berkman in 1920 while touring the Soviet Union as a *New York Call* correspondent. (*New York Times,* Nov. 3, 1970; Falk, Cole, and Thomas, *Emma Goldman: A Guide,* 85.)

202. *Excerpt from London Diary*

Sanger and Rublee traveled to England to find participants and rouse interest for the Sixth International Neo-Malthusian and Birth Control Conference to be held in New York City in the spring of 1925 and arrived in London on October 3. Sanger kept a diary from October 6 through November 1; what follows are entries through October 15.

London [*England*]
Oct 6—1924

Juliet Rublee & I left New York on the Majestic Sept 27—

Arrived Southampton where Janet Chance met us. We did not spend the night with Mrs Chance as Clinton was on a hunting party & they were in the process of moving to London. I thot it wise to postpone our visit.

Loads of letters waiting for me at American Express Co. We went to the Bath Hotel for the night (Dover St.) a queer strange old fashioned place fires going in sitting room furniture muchly "chintzed." Called up Hugh de Selincourt on phone & we both shrieked with laughter just <u>because</u>. The next day Saturday we motored down to Storrington,[1] through Surrey a lovely country rolling hills & darling villages.

Hugh was perfect. He seems to have a new look in his eye, that look which means he has seen through the mist & beyond to the light. He knows.

Bridget is a picture, hair straight to the neck silent but willing not to be. Janet knitting on the hearth was pesant woman & spinx combined primative woman all of her, with a dearness & power to draw men to her forever.[2]

Harold Child the mind man. One who everyone must love. He radiates dearness & takes back love.[3]

Juliet was very silent most of the visit. I was elated & noisy. The new home Sand Pit is charming a memory & fragrance one takes away to last always.

Sunday Evening I got back to see <u>Havelock</u> who came up from Margate on purpose to see me I just had to come back to London when this happened.

Havelock looked fine—well & buoyant, a new painting of him which makes him twenty years older hangs over the bookcase. There was an atmosphere of warmth & comfort in the Brixton flat that was lacking in the past. We had supper—& hock, & some of the rose wine I brot from China to him two years ago. The darling man is never encouraging. It's a queer characteristic for one who has seen so much of life. Perhaps he does not think it good for one. Certainly he has succeeded without much of it. But now it seems as th'o he is really living & loving life. Today Oct 6. I had luncheon with John Maynard Keynes at his apartment in Gordon Square. A lovely face, clear brains & most gracious manner. The Russian dancer was rather silent, but took part in the conversation as she understood.[4]

He is "terrified" of coming to America says he is a writer & must not waste energy on trying to speak. Will help on Conference.

Tea at 6 Raymond Bldgs. with Harold Cox, & Edith a perfect angel of a man always helpful & generous & hospitable.[5]

Dinner with the Drysdales, C. V. & Bessie—[6] She nervous & excitable, talkative. Both fear the revolution as indicated in conduct of employees independence.

'Phone call from H. G. this morning. Asked me to come over for a moment, went to 4 White Hall Court. He looks very well, not unhappy in spite of falling out with Rebecca.[7]

Missed Jennie Baker[8] at luncheon but went to Walworth Center & spent afternoon at clinic.[9]

Mrs Murray & Mrs—↑[*Fuller*]↓ very active & capable women in charge[10] five tables for instruction, one nurse to teach while Physician fits pessary, back to dinner with Juliet and Mary Lawton came in writer, very attractive & amusing American woman.[11] Tonight a talk with H. G. again. Invitation for week end.[12]

This is a nice hotel Stafford Hotel St James Place.

Cable every day from J. N. letter also. Nan in Paris.[13]

Mrs Drysdale went with me to Clinic today. Also Juliet.

Oct 8,

Tonight there is great excitement in press concerning the possibility of Change of government owning to Campbells unfortunate editorial on the workers attitude toward war & strikes. The Ramsey MacDonald government may change now, who can tell.[14] Janet & Clinton Chance were here for dinner tonight. While Clinton was here for luncheon also. I went out to shop for a hat & walked all over Bond St. such ugly hats to be seen all too small for me because my hair is not "bobbed" which has become universal almost.

Rained the longest & hardest today I've ever seen in London. An invitation to lunch with Sir Thomas Horder[15] next week at the Bath Club.

Tomorrow the tea at Harold Coxs John Maynard Keynes wrote me asking for the names of our subscribers for his Nation.[16] I shall send them on. The tea was very successful. Met J. O. P. Bland for a few minutes. He has promised to come over for the conference but says he will come only to "smile" very funny & witty & looks the picture of health, th'o he does not like to be told that. Possibly because he spends so much time at Sanitoriums. At the tea were Lord Gerald Wellsley,[17] Lady Wright.[18] Mrs Graham Murray. Mrs Alec Rea.[19] Lady Asquith & her sister.[20] Lord Gerald is handsome & full of ideas—the lords of this country are far more advanced & independent of tho't than the stupid M.P.'s.

The Government has fallen & an Election takes place Oct 29.[21] In the evening we took Mrs Rae to dinner at Hotel & went to see Storm,[22] after the first act I became violently ill had to return home. The luncheon with Harold Child where paté de fois gras was served may have had something to do with the illness.

The next day Janet & Clinton & I lunched at the Bath Club on Dover St. Sir Thomas Horder called out of town.

In the afternoon Jennie Baker & Miss Daniels[23] (the nurse who was dismissed at Welfare Center for giving mothers birth control [*instruct*]) & Dr Dunlop[24] came in for tea. Jennie Baker is an old labor worker a good head & heart. Mr Kerr[25] called in the morning and told me who's who in B.C. land.

On Sunday Oct 12—1924,

Harold Child & I motored to Oxford. Had luncheon at Mitre Hotel. Went to Brazenose College & also Kings College where Hugh attended. The impression is not ↑as↓ good as Cambridge—tho of course the ↑atmosphere of↓ age is on all around the place Magdalen Bridge & College beautiful.

The drive back was beautiful went through Buckinghamshire where the beeches were turning bronze & russet, a glorious coloring.

Harold is simply one of those men—only one made—to touch is to worship— He is so exquisite in his mind & response that it is beyond description to express the feeling he inspires of course he adores Janet & rightly so.

Monday Oct 13,

Hugh came & spent the day mainly with Juliet.

Havelock came at 5:30 for my M.S.S.[26] & remained for dinner & a talk. We sat up until 12.

The next day Harold Cox, Edith & I went to the Cloth Makers where the old 16th Century Church yard & tower still stands. A few fig trees trying to live. At 4 oclock I ran out to see Rose Witcop & Milly who is here from Berlin.[27]

Then out to Havelocks for dinner, was ill & came home early. Hugh still here.

Oct 15

Kerr of the New Generation came this morning a veritable "boor", but well informed with it all. Janet & Clinton & I lunched together, then Buckmaster (Lord)[28] at tea & finally the big dinner at H.G's.[29] H. G. at head with Mrs Shaw on left & Lady Lane ~~on~~ ↑at↓ right.[30]

Lord Buckmaster, Sir Ray Lancaster,[31] Arnold Bennett,[32] Geo Bernard Shaw, Prof McBride.[33] Mr Salter (League of Nations man.)[34] St. Jn Irving play-write & wife[35] man named Donovan & wife.[36] All told a brilliant gathering.

Shaw was next to Juliet who monopolized him the entire evening. No possible help from that dear gay lady to start anything on b.c. So the best I could do was to arrange to write Buckmaster & give him details.

Nan still in Paris—also A. G. Archibald & Helena.[37]

AD MSP, MN-SSC (*MSM* S70:204–14). We have omitted the underlining of many proper names that appear to have been added later, possibly by a researcher. For the remainder of the diary, see *MSM* S70:215–20.

1. Storrington was the location of de Selincourt's new home.

2. Bridget was de Selincourt's daughter, who was about twelve years old, and Janet was his wife.

3. Though Child continued his casual affair with Janet de Selincourt, MS probably had begun an affair with him in the summer of 1922. (Child to MS, Oct. 13, 1924 [*MSM* S2:734].)

4. Keynes was living with Lydia Lopokova (1892–1981) of the Russian Imperial Ballet, whom he married in 1925. He did not attend the conference but agreed to serve as a foreign vice-president. (*DNB;* Program, Sixth International Neo-Malthusian and Birth Control Conference [*MSM* S67:43].)

5. Edith A. Baines was Cox's secretary.

6. MS was one of the few birth control advocates with whom the Drysdales continued to associate after their retirement. (Benn, *Predicaments of Love,* 216.)

7. Wells had recently ended his ten-year affair with the English critic and novelist Rebecca West (1892–1983).

8. H. Jennie Baker, a British labor leader and a vocal birth control supporter in the Labour Party, had introduced a successful birth control resolution at the National Conference of Labour Women in May 1924. (Soloway, *Birth Control,* 194, 285.)

9. The Walworth Women's Welfare Centre (WWWC) was a medically supervised clinic providing maternal and infant health services and birth control counseling. The Malthusian League opened the center in November 1921 but in 1922 turned it over to a private committee, which named itself the Society for the Provision of Birth Control Clinics (SPBCC) in 1924. (Leathard, *Fight for Family Planning,* 15, 31.)

10. Evelyn Graham Murray was an SPBCC officer and the chair of the WWWC; Evelyn Fuller (?–1937) was the honorary secretary of the WWWC and SPBCC from 1923 to 1936. The last name was possibly inserted later by MS. (Leathard, *Fight for Family Planning,* 31.)

11. The writer Mary Lawton (1870–1945) coauthored the memoirs of Ignace Jan Paderewski in 1939. (*New York Times,* Jan. 23, 1945.)

12. MS spent the weekend of October 18–19 at Wells's Dunmow estate. (1924 Calendar [*MSM* S78:580].)

13. The cables were not found; for Slee's letters to MS, see Sept. 28, Sept. 30, Oct. 1, and Oct. 3, 1924 (*MSM* S2:656–87). Anna Higgins was briefly in Paris to tend the estate of her employer, Elizabeth Blee Frasch, who had died there on September 24. (*New York Times,* Oct. 31, 1924.)

14. Ramsay MacDonald's Labour Party came to power in January 1924 but came under fire for negotiating a trade agreement with the Soviet Union. The party faced more trouble when John Ross Campbell, the acting editor of the Communist *Worker's Weekly,* published a July 25 editorial calling on the military not to shoot their "working-class comrades" during military or industrial warfare. Campbell was indicted for sedition, but when MacDonald's attorney general dropped the government's prosecution, Conservatives became outraged and accused the Labour Party of political interference in the justice system. (T. O. Lloyd, *Empire, Welfare State, Europe: English History, 1906–1992,* 4th ed. [London, 1993], 124–34; Taylor, *English History,* 218–25.)

15. Sir Thomas Horder (1871–1955) was the physician to the British royal family and a clinician at St. Bartholomew's Hospital. A prominent birth control and eugenics advocate, Horder served as president of the National Birth Control Council (1930–31) and the British Eugenics Society (1935–44). (*DNB;* Soloway, *Demography and Degeneration,* 189.)

16. In 1923, Keynes chaired the *Nation and Athenaeum,* a Liberal Party weekly.

17. Lord Gerald Wellesley (1885–1972), the seventh duke of Wellington, was an architect and member of the SPBCC. (*London Times,* Jan. 5, 1972; SPBCC Annual Reports [FPAA].)

18. Jane Georgina Wright (?–1926) was the noted antifeminist Sir Almroth Edward Wright's wife, who a few days later offered MS funds to create a simple birth control leaflet for working-class women. (*London times,* May 29, 1926; Wright to MS, Oct. 10, 1924 [LCM 14:553].)

19. This was probably Marguerite Requa Rea (?–1946), the American-born wife of the British theater manager Alec L. Rea. (*London Times,* Dec. 20, 1946.)

20. Helen Violet Bonham Carter Asquith, Lady Yarnbury (1887–1969), the daughter of the former Liberal Party prime minister Herbert Henry Asquith, was a libertarian who opposed woman suffrage but fought for family allowances and electoral reform. Her half-sister, Elizabeth (1897–1945), married Prince Antoine Bibesco in 1919. (Crawford et al., *Europa Biographical Dictionary of British Women,* 54; Daphne Bennett, *Margot: The Life of Countess of Oxford and Asquith* [London, 1984], 428.)

21. In the aftermath of the Campbell editorial and challenges by both the Conservative and Liberal parties, MacDonald resigned his office on November 1, 1924. In the general elections that followed, Stanley Baldwin's Conservative Party reclaimed the government. (Taylor, *English History,* 216–21; *London Times,* Nov. 1 and 5, 1924.)

22. *Storm; or, The Battle of Tinderly Down* was a play by C. K. Munro. (J. P. Wearing, *The London Stage, 1920–1929: A Calendar of Plays and Playwrights* [Metuchen, N.J., 1984], 522.)

23. Elizabeth S. Daniels was a British nurse dismissed from her public health post for giving patients birth control information. Her 1922 case pushed the Ministry of Health to prohibit state-funded birth control. In 1923, she opened a private birth control clinic, where she trained nurses in contraceptive techniques and distributed contraceptives. (Leathard, *Fight for Family Planning,* 28; *New Generation,* May 1923, 59, and Oct. 1924, 11.)

24. Binnie Dunlop remained active in the New Generation League, serving as treasurer from 1927 to 1946. (Ledbetter, *Malthusian League,* 238.)

25. Robert Bird Kerr was the editor of the *New Generation.*

26. This was possibly an early version of *Happiness in Marriage.*

27. Rose Witcop continued to print and distribute *Family Limitation* and in 1925, with MS's financial help, opened the People's Clinic in London. She and Guy Aldred separated in 1924. Her eldest sister, Milly Witcop-Rocker (1877–1955), a Ukrainian-born anarchist active in British labor issues, married the German anarcho-syndicalist writer Rudolf Rocker (1873–1958). (Witcop to MS, May 12 and July 1, 1925 [LCM 14:619 and 639]; Avrich, *Anarchist Voices,* 7–12, 321–23; Soloway, *Birth Control,* 301; *New York Times,* Sept. 11, 1958.)

28. Stanley Owen Buckmaster (1861–1934), a barrister and Liberal member of Parliament, served as lord chancellor during World War I and then as an appellate judge in the House of Lords. An ardent supporter of free trade, woman suffrage, and divorce reform, he was also an officer of the New Generation League and a founder of the North Kensington Women's Welfare Centre. (*DNB;* Soloway, *Birth Control,* 291.)

29. Wells held a dinner party in London on October 15 to introduce MS to prominent British figures she could invite to the conference. Buckmaster initially agreed to be the main conference speaker, but he pulled out because of a scheduling conflict. (MS to Slee, Oct. 16, 1924 [*MSM* S2:748]; MS, *Autobiography,* 371.)

30. Charlotte Payne-Townsend Shaw (1857–1943), a writer and the wife of George Bernard Shaw, edited collected plays and wrote several tracts for the Fabian Society. Charlotte Briscoe Lane (?–1935) was the wife of Sir Arbuthnot Lane. (Banks, *Biographical Dictionary of British Feminists,* 182; *London Times,* Apr. 29, 1935.)

31. Edwin Ray Lankester (1847–1929) was a zoologist at Oxford University and the director of the British Museum's Natural History Department (1898–1907). (*DSB*)

32. Bennett, a close friend of Wells, and longtime Malthusian League member, had signed Stopes's 1915 petition supporting MS. (Smith, *H. G. Wells,* 157.)

33. Ernest William MacBride (1866–1940) was an eminent biologist and a council member and vice-president of England's Eugenics Education Society, who advocated an alliance between eugenics and birth control. (*New York Times,* Nov. 20, 1940; Soloway, *Demography and Degeneration,* 176, 185.)

34. Sir James Arthur Salter (1881–1975), a British civil servant, economist, and shipping authority, served as director of the League of Nations' Economics and Financial Section (1919–31). (*London Times,* June 30, 1975.)

35. St. John Greer Ervine (1883–1971) was an Irish playwright associated with Dublin's Abbey Theatre, a Fabian Society member, and a lifelong friend of Shaw; his wife was Lenora Mary Davis Ervine (?–1965). (Stanley Weintraub, ed., *Dictionary of Literary Biography,* vol. 10 [Detroit, 1982], 186–88; *London Times,* Jan. 25, 1971.)

36. Francis Desmond Donovan had recently been appointed surgeon dentist to the British royal family. (*London Times,* Oct. 29, 1924.)

37. Adelaide G. Archibald (1879–1946) was a close friend of the Higgins family who over the years supported MS with small donations; Helena (1904–?) was her daughter. (U.S. Bureau of the Census, *Fourteenth Census of the United States, 1920;* MS to Archibald, Jan. 29, 1943, and Aug. 29, 1945 [*MSM* S22:11 and S24:1142].)

203. *From H. G. Wells*

[*London, England*]
[*October 16 1924*][1]

Wonderful!
Unforgettable.

AL MSP, MN-SSC (*MSM* S2:797). An incorrect date of October 8, 1924, was added at the top right, possibly by MS's assistant Florence Rose.

1. This was written following the dinner party Wells gave for MS on October 15 but may refer to the time they spent alone afterward, for the two continued their occasional love affair into the 1930s. (See MS Diary, 1922.)

204. *From Janet de Selincourt*

Sand Pit, Sussex. [*England*]
Oct. 20th [*1924*]

Darling lovely Margaret,

You have got hold of the wrong end of the stick altogether, & if I can't make you feel that you have, I shall curse myself forever for writing that letter.[1] Either there was no need for me to have told you of any pain, as it wasn't you who were causing it in any direct sense, or I should have been much clearer. It was stupid of me not to see how it might strike you. Please sweep away for good any idea of having disturbed my happiness or brought a cloud into my life. I don't want assurance & comfort as you think—I only want you to love me more & more.

There is no hurt to me in the fact of your love for Harold:[2] the pang didn't spring from that; but the sight of his happiness touched up a wound that is very deep in my heart. It wasn't his having found you & your love that hurt, but that I had lost someone else to whom I had gone out in the same way, & it brought it all back & I couldn't enter in straight away!

He will tell you more about it. But the knot in myself came untied in a very short time, & the pain has only brought me a deeper realization of everything: & I know that you by your love for Harold & rousing love in him, have brought a great new wave of life to us all. Bless you! dearest Margaret. It is true. How could I not want you to love him when it means so much to him.

You will give him things I haven't, & what you will receive from him is no crumb or passing interest, or just an overflow from his love for me. Why you adorable lovely person. What man could help falling in love with you.

I shall be coming up tomorrow, & would love to see you, though I feel you shouldn't waste any of your precious spare time when there is nothing to talk over & things are clear with us. I would just adore you to give all the free time you may have to Harold.

But don't don't go on Saturday if you can possibly stay.[3] I'm sure all your dear people in America can do without you a little longer. Hugh is longing to see you quietly & it would be heavenly if you came back on Thursday, but it seems almost too much when the time is short. Let me know.

Janet

ALS MSP, MN-SSC (*MSM* S2:772–74).

1. Janet had confided in the letter that Harold Child's love for MS had caused her great pain and had apologized for her state of jealous "rebelliousness." (Janet de Selincourt to MS, Oct. 17, 1924 [*MSM* S2:762].)

2. MS continued her casual affair with Harold Child during this trip. (Child to MS, Oct. 6–Dec. 10, 1924 [*MSM* S2:695–837]; the MS's letters to Child were not found.)

3. MS sailed for New York City from Southampton on Friday, October 24, arriving on November 1. (MS Diary [*MSM* S70:222].)

205. To J. Noah Slee

[*London, England*]
Oct 23—[*1924*]

Sweetheart Noah:

My darling! what does your letter mean when you say that if I leave you, you will do "something foolish"?[1] That troubles me—profoundly. Surely you could not go with some other woman without love & respect! Is it possible that your love for me is only a satisfying physical passion? To believe that would kill me! I do not believe that. I know the strain on you is great, but with me no other man could satisfy me anyway, my love for you is so wholly & fully all of me, that no other person could meet that urgent demand of my passion as you do. That belongs to you Noah my husband & to you alone. Thats the way I am—are you not the same? When this letter reaches you I shall be in your arms.

Margaret.

ALS MSP, MN-SSC (*MSM* S2:778–79). Letterhead of the Stafford Hotel.

1. In his October 14 letter to MS, Slee had threatened, "You must never leave me again, otherwise I might do something foolish, due to my utter loneliness, more than my poor body can stand." He scribbled in the margin, next to his closing, "I hate BC that takes you." (*MSM* S2:737.)

206. From Harold Child

[*London, England*]
24 October 1924

Margaret,

Do you know what you've done to me, what you mean to me, what you are in me? I could only tell you properly in poetry; & poems are only made with time & agony & joy, & I'm too shaken with feeling to be able to work at what I say. I can only sort of gasp to you—Margaret, my beloved.

Do you know that I'm 55? Beginning to go down the hill, to the time when one can do no more than watch others happy in love. And here you come, you, you, with your beauty & your fire & perfume & the wine of you, & your keen, masterly brain & your wicked, mischievous wit & fun, and your blazing courage, & better than all, your ineffable, indescribable dearness, & pour them all over me, making me young, glad & proud, a very god among men. What can I do, sweet, sweet lover, but fall at your feet & in laughter & tears & adoration tell you the old silly words that mean nothing [*or*] everything—I love you, I love you, I love you. Great lady, great soul, little love, naughty child, Margaret—do you know how every pore of my skin thrills & tingles at your touch, & how the deepest soul of me calls out to you? I love you my queen, my lover, my darling.

H.

ALI JRP, NhD (*MSM* C3:204–5). A handwritten note by MS at the top of the first page reads, "Juliet[1] Please keep this for me. It is too precious to destroy."

1. MS frequently sent Rublee her personal letters to read and then destroy or hold for her.

207. To Leon J. Cole

*Sanger sent the same letter to Adolf Meyer, Raymond Pearl, and probably other members of the CRB advisory committee. (MS to Meyer, Nov. 11, 1924, and Pearl to MS, Nov. 13, 1924 [*MSM *C3:223 and 230].)*

[*New York, N.Y.*]
November 11, 1924.

Dear Prof. Cole:

Enclosed you will find one of the history cards we have been using for our clinical work.[1] Have you any suggestions to make, or changes that would be helpful?

In England the Walworth Centre group confines their questions to health and economics which, of course, lessens the work of the Centre and the embarrassment of the individual.[2]

Do you think it wise to continue the questions on the sexual aspect? We now have about 3000 replies, and I am wondering if the continuation of such questions is not a useless task. It seems to need a tactful and discreet person to get the required information, and so far Dr. Bocker has been doing this, which means that fewer women can get to the clinic in a day, because these questions take time which could be given to instructing at least two more women each hour.

In England I found that a capable nurse instructs the patient in the use and adjustment of the pessary, after the physician fits it and finds the proper size. This is a great saving of time and allows a greater number of patients to get instruction each day. So far, we are able to instruct about 185 women each month,—far too few for the cost involved. Should the cost be a consideration? Also will you kindly give me your opinion on the continuation of each method.

Shall we feel satisfied and discontinue the method after a certain percentage of success? What percentage should we be satisfied with? Shall we try out imitations or duplicates of the same article? By this I mean, the original paste was Leucorrhol[3] imported from Germany in collapsible tubes with glass nozzle. Today there are several imitations of this paste. Dr. Bocker has tried but two of them,—Prekonsol and Mirekahl, both satisfactory.[4] During the time of trying the imitation, the original (Leucorrhol) was dropped, except as those using it sent for it. Any suggestions on this?[5]

I want to give you a brief report each month, and will appreciate your suggestions and help. Cordially yours,

Margaret Sanger [*signed*]

TLS LJCP, WU (*MSM* C3:217). Letterhead of the CRB.

1. The CRB's case history cards contained four sections: social history (nationality, occupation, etc.), sex and reproductive history (number of pregnancies, abortions, frequency of sexual relations), notes on physical examinations, and notes on treatment. (For the enclosed case card, see *MSM* C3:218; for another sample, see LCM 32:57.)

2. The Walworth Women's Welfare Clinic did not collect such detailed and personal information, fearing it would impede its ability to attract patients, and did not follow up on nonreturning patients. (Evelyn Fuller, "A Note on the Work of the Society for Provision of Birth Control Clinics," in *Practice of Contraception,* ed. Margaret Sanger and Hannah M. Stone [Baltimore, 1931], 212.)

3. Leucorrhol was a German-made contraceptive jelly that combined boric, acetic, and tartaric acids with chinosol as a spermicide. (Voge, *Chemistry and Physics of Contraceptives,* 180–81.)

4. Both Preconsol and Mir-E-Kahl were brand names of contraceptive jellies also based

on boric acid and chinosol compound. (Voge, *Chemistry and Physics of Contraceptives*, 180–81.)

5. Cole responded that though he was not familiar with birth control work, trials of similar materials could be abandoned, noting, "The problem before the clinic is [*whether it is*] . . . better to continue the use of the best known remedy in all cases or is it advisable to find by experiment a more effective remedy even though in doing so things may be tried which are not as good as the old method?" (Cole to MS, Nov. 26, 1924 [*MSM* C3:255].)

208. From George Bernard Shaw

[*London, England*]
[*December ?, 1924*]

Dear Mrs. Sanger:

I cannot attend the Conference in March next;[1] and if I could I doubt if I could say anything else that I have not already said. But two things have happened here lately that may interest you. The judicial committee of the House of Lords, in finally deciding against Dr. Marie Stopes, has taken the old ground of simple tapu.[2] Dr. Stopes won on every other point, in spite of the attempt of the judge who tried the first hearing of her case to interpret the jury's verdict in her favor as a verdict for the defendant. Four Lords, three of them over eighty: that is, men who would have been superannuated many years ago if they had been ordinary civil servants, have boldly decided that all references to the reproductive organs are obscene.[3] This takes us back to the eighteen-seventies, when Huxley produced what was ranked as the modern classic text book of physiology without mentioning the forbidden subject of reproduction.[4]

By this the Lords have fortified their position impregnably. There is no arguing with tapu. If people regard reproduction as an obscene subject, or a funny subject (and they are usually the same people), there is nothing more to be said: nothing remains but to live them down, and to be particularly careful meanwhile not to waste time, life, and money in appeals to the law, which is always fifty years out of date. Probably these same ancient Lords, if somebody had accused Dr. Stopes of indecent exposure because she wears a modern dress which leaves her ankles visible, would have found her guilty without a moment's hesitation. I am now an old man myself: and I assure you I never knew that women, as distinguished from little girls, had ankles until I was taken to the pantomime and found that the fairy queen had not only ankles but knees. The shock I received at about six years old, when, without any warning, I went into our drawing room and saw a woman without a crinoline, probably produced a complex which psychoanalysts may be able to trace in my works to this day.

The second notable occurrence is the discovery that there is not room in London for all the people who want to be there. The streets which used to be merely crowded are now choked. This has a certain bearing on birth control. As you know, I have always treated with contempt the notion that the earth is on the curve of diminishing return in the matter of food. That capitalist explanation of poverty ought not to impose on a rabbit, fertile as rabbits are. The fact that productive labor is being crushed by the burden of parasitic labor (to say nothing of parasitic idleness) has no bearing on the food question. The question of room is far more important. We could feed ourselves if we were as crowded as gannets on the Bass Rock;[5] but life would be intolerable under such conditions. All cities are now frightfully overcrowded; and the dispersal of their population over a reasonable acreage might possibly produce a population question. Some day we shall have to ask ourselves, not how many people it is possible to have under Bass Rock conditions, but how many people it is comfortable to have. If uncontrolled fertility does not keep within this limit we shall have to fall back on controlled fertility.

However, that is a speculation as to what might or might not happen after Socialism had effected the redistribution of income which is the most pressing necessity of today. Meanwhile, birth control should be advocated for its own sake, on the general ground that the difference between voluntary, rational, controlled activity and any sort of involuntary, irrational, uncontrolled activity is the difference between an amoeba and a man; and if we really believe that the more highly evolved creature is the better we may as well act accordingly. As the amoeba does not understand birth control, it cannot abuse it, and therefore its state may be the more gracious; but it is also true that as the amoeba cannot write it cannot commit forgery: yet we teach everybody to write unhesitatingly, knowing that if we refuse to teach anything that could be abused we should never teach anything at all. Faithfully,

G. Bernard Shaw.

"Two Notable Occurrences," *BCR,* Jan. 1925, 5 (*MSM* C3:339). The original letter was not found.

1. A written invitation was not found; MS probably invited Shaw when she saw him on October 15, 1924. Shaw did send a brief message to be read at the conference. (See Excerpt from London Diary, Oct. 6–16, 1924, herein; for Shaw's message, see Mar. 1925 [*MSM* S67:380].)

2. This was either an alternate spelling of *taboo* or *tabu,* possibly to highlight its Polynesian origins, or a mistranscription.

3. Halliday G. Sutherland (1882–1960), a British Catholic physician and writer, claimed in his 1922 *Birth Control: A Statement of Christian Doctrine against the Neo-Malthusians* that Stopes experimented on the poor with a harmful method of birth control. Stopes sued him for libel and defamation of character in a highly publicized 1923 trial that aired medical and moral arguments for and against birth control. The jury, in a muddled

verdict, decided that even though the charges were true, they were defamatory and unfair, and it awarded Stopes £100 in damages. Sutherland appealed to the House of Lords, which in November 1924 overturned Stopes's victory, forcing her to repay the original damages and approximately £12,000 in legal costs. (Hall, *Passionate Crusader,* 240; see also Muriel Box, ed., *Birth Control and Libel: The Trial of Marie Stopes* [New York, 1967].)

4. This was Thomas H. Huxley's *Physiography* (1877).

5. This was a reference to an island in southeast Scotland at the mouth of the Firth of Forth where large groups of seabirds congregate.

209. DIARY ENTRY

Shortly before the expiration of Dorothy Bocker's contract as the CRB's medical director on December 31, 1924, Sanger considered the possibility of having Bocker take over full responsibility for running the CRB. However, as negotiations continued, Sanger became increasingly critical of Bocker's job performance, particularly her failure to properly follow up on patients and her use of too many types of contraceptives in her research. On December 20, Sanger dismissed Bocker, telling her that she would oversee the clinic herself. On December 30–31, Bocker returned to the CRB and cut the names from the patient history cards. The following entry was drawn from a diary Sanger kept sporadically through January 1946. (MS-Bocker letters, Nov. and Dec. 1924 [LCM 31:421–38]; Reed, Birth Control Movement and American Society, *115; for the complete diary, see* MSM *S70:223–53.)*

[*New York, N.Y.*]
New Year— Jan 1—1925.

Yesterday Dr Bocker came to the office—it was her last day. The two year agreement for clinical research is over. It was a sorrowful ending to a great venture. The records!! The names taken by her, make the records useless. The betrayal of trust of faith is the hardest thing of all. She seems to be under a spell would talk only very little, but defiant. Sneaked into the office Sunday & took the cards & names.[1]

Must begin all over again.
Regain faith in human beings.
Use greater discretion; trust them less perhaps is the remedy.[2]

AD MSP, MN-SSC (*MSM* S70:223).

1. MS claimed removing the names rendered the cards "absolutely and utterly worthless" because it prevented the CRB from conducting follow-ups. Bocker defended herself by arguing that their research value lay in the aggregate, not in the individual records. (MS to Israel Thurman, Dec. 31, 1924, and Bocker to David Lowenthal, Oct. 31, 1925 [LCM 34:132 and 145].)

2. In March 1925, Bocker sent letters to CRB patients, encouraging them to visit her private practice, an action that infuriated MS. Both hired lawyers. In August 1925, an arbitrator, George W. Kirchwey of Columbia University's law school, was set to hear the

case, but Bocker delayed the proceedings, charging that Kirchwey was a friend of MS and not impartial. The arbitration failed, and the records were never returned. (Bocker to Lowenthal, Oct. 31, 1925, MS to Kirchwey, Dec. 8, 1925, and Florence Rose note, Sept. 26, 1942 [LCM 34:145, 155, and 157].)

210. To Agnes Smedley[1]

[*New York, N.Y.*]
January 8, 1925.

Dear Agnes:

I wonder if you would do something for me.

We have been trying to get some German pessaries for our clinical research work, and have written several times to the firm whose address I give you below, but have received no reply.[2] Would you please go and see them and find out what is the matter.

I know these goods cannot be shipped directly into the U.S., but they can ship any amount to Canada to the address which we have given them. I am enclosing copy of a letter we wrote them which gives the Canadian address.[3] I would be greatly obliged to you if you could make a personal call on this firm and find out what the trouble is and why they have not made any shipments.[4] We want very much to get these pessaries into Canada, and we can take care of them from that point.

My other letter will probably be received by you before this comes to hand. Love always.

Address is:
Hechtel & Le Noir, Zimmerstrasse 77, Berlin SW, 68,

TLcy MSP, DLC (LCM 10:293).

1. Agnes Smedley (1892–1950), a journalist and novelist who managed the *BCR* in MS's absence in 1918–19, was promoting birth control in Berlin. A radical socialist and supporter of Indian nationalism, Smedley had been detained under the 1918 Espionage Act, though the charges were dismissed. In 1924, MS sent Smedley funds to help pay for psychiatric treatment after a nervous breakdown. (*NAW;* on her 1918 arrest, see Smedley to MS, Nov. 1, 1918, and May 9, 1924 [LCM 10:266 and 287].)

2. Slee imported Ramses pessaries through the import-export firm of Hechtel & Ie Noir and the Murray Agency in Montreal. They were transferred to his Montreal Three-in-One Oil Company and smuggled into the United States in oil barrels. (Slee to Hechtel & Ie Noir and the Murray Agency, Oct. 16, 1924, and Slee to Hechtel, Nov. 10, 1924 [LCM 11:579 and 582].)

3. Slee to Hechtel & Ie Noir, Oct. 16, 1924.

4. Smedley found that the package left Berlin on April 21 and verified that while their exportation from Germany was legal, authorities in Canada, which prohibited the dis-

tribution of contraceptive information and devices except in the public good, may have confiscated them. (Hechtel & Ie Noir to Lamke & Stemme, Inc., Receipt for 500 Ramses pessaries, Mar. 3, 1923; Slee to Hechtel & Ie Noir, Oct. 16, 1924, and Smedley to Slee, May 27, 1925 [LCM 11:577 and 580, 10:306].)

211. *To Grace Abbott*[1]

The passage of the woman suffrage amendment in 1920 gave American women the hope that their votes could pressure the government to provide maternal and health services through the U.S. Children's Bureau, established in 1912. Under its first head, Julia Lathrop, the bureau gathered statistics on infant mortality and successfully lobbied for the 1921 passage of the Sheppard-Towner Act, which provided federal funding for state infant and maternal care programs. Approached by Sanger to include birth control in the program, Lathrop and her successor, Grace Abbott, refused, fearing it would risk congressional support for the act. Despite Abbott's personal lack of opposition to birth control, she believed it politically damning and refused to allow the Children's Bureau to provide any advice in response to the many letters it received asking for birth control or even to forward the letters to the ABCL. Though Sanger characterized the Children's Bureau and other government agencies as "more generally opposed to the doctrine of Birth Control than biased in favor of it," she continued seeking support from the bureau. (McCann, Birth Control Politics, *52; MS,* Pivot of Civilization, *30 [quote]; Molly Ladd-Taylor,* Raising a Baby the Government Way *[New Brunswick, N.J., 1986], 180.)*

[*New York, N.Y.*]
February 5, 1925.

My dear Miss Abbott:

Mrs. Robertson-Jones informs me that from your remarks she thinks you disapprove of the principle of Birth Control.[2] Needless to say we are amazed at this news.

If it is not asking too much, could I ask you to dictate to your stenographer exactly how you do stand on this subject.

After years of experience, I have learned to ask the individual for his or her views directly and then there is no danger of misquoting.

I cannot believe that anyone in your position, working as magnificently as you have for children and their welfare, could be opposed to the control of births as a principle. There no doubt may be objections to methods and to other features of the movement.[3]

I would be very glad to know your position in this matter. Very sincerely yours,

Margaret Sanger [*signed by secretary*]
President.

TL RCB, DNA (*MSM* C3:346). Letterhead of the Sixth International Neo-Malthusian and Birth Control Conference.

1. Grace Abbott (1878–1939), a social reformer and public administrator, headed the U.S. Department of Labor's Children's Bureau from 1921 to 1934. A former Hull-House resident, she worked for child labor laws and the passage of the 1921 Sheppard-Towner Act. (*New York Times,* June 20, 1939; McCann, *Birth Control Politics,* 52.)

2. Eleanor Dwight Jones (1880–1965), a suffragist, a civic activist, and the wife of the insurance expert and college professor Frederick Robertson Jones, joined the ABCL board of directors in 1924. She focused on lobbying League of Women Voters' chapters to endorse birth control. (*Radcliffe College Class of 1902: Secretary's Fifth Report* [Watertown, Mass., 1927], 59; *New York Times,* July 31, 1965; "News Notes," *BCR,* Mar. 1925, 90.)

3. Abbott responded the same day, writing, "If Mrs. Robertson-Jones is the woman who spoke to me at the University Women's Club—I did not express my opinion either for or against the principle of Birth Control. I did point out what I thought were some fallacies in the arguments she made in support of it." (Abbott to MS, Feb. 5, 1925 [*MSM* C3:344].)

212. From Client

Oelwein, Ia.
Feb 12, 1925

Dear Mrs. Sanger:

I have bought your book[1] and I have read all through. And Mrs. Sanger I have read where you said that there is a safe way of not having any more children. And you could not tell it in your book or you could not publish it. Now I make it bold to write and ask you how? Oh how I will thank you if you will answer that question. I was 18 years old when I got married I have been married two years and have two children now a girl and a boy the oldest is 18 months old and the baby is 6 months old. And now I am so afraid now to think that I might get in that condition again. Do you blame me for writing to you. One day I asked my doctor to help me & to tell me how I could be free from having any children for a while. And he made just an awful face. And told me that I was an Italian and that all my nationality married young and had babies after babies so why should I keep from having any more. I am nearly wild because I do not want any more. Oh please tell me the way. Thanking ~~th~~ you in advance

Mrs. [*Name omitted*]

ALS MSP, MN-SSC (*MSM* S2:898). In the interest of privacy, the editors have omitted the author's name.

1. She was referring to *Woman and the New Race.*

213. *Diary Entry*

[*New York, N.Y.*]
Sunday Evening: March [*8*]—1925[1]

For the past hour the same old nervousness has been upon me. That same gripping in the pit of the stomach (Solar plexus) that I used to experience in the past.

I expected I would get over it, but it seems to be with me yet.

I am going to speak at John Haynes Holmes Community Church 34th & Park (Forum).[2]

later—

This feeling did not leave me all evening. I did not inspire my audiance—I felt a load, a difficulty in getting my words to fit the ideas. Never a harder lecture. Church packed to the doors & hundred & fifty turned away.

AD MSP, MN-SSC (*MSM* S70:224).

1. MS incorrectly rendered the date as March 7.

2. MS spoke on March 8 to an audience of fifteen hundred on "The Need for Birth Control in America," followed by a two-hour discussion. John Haynes Holmes (1879–1964), a Unitarian minister who was the pastor of the Community Church, was associated with such progressive social and political causes as peace, civil liberties, and racial equality. ("News Notes," *BCR*, Apr. 1925, 121; *ANB*.)

214. *From Carlo Tresca*

From 1919 to 1923, Carlo Tresca organized defense campaigns for Italian victims of the "Red Scare," including Nicola Sacco and Bartolomeo Vanzetti, and promoted radical labor agitation and antifascism through his paper, Il Martello *(The Hammer), vehemently castigating Mussolini. When the Italian government pressured the United States to silence him, Tresca was arrested for running a birth control advertisement in the September 8, 1923, issue of* Il Martello. *After a brief trial, at which he was defended by Sanger's old* Woman Rebel *prosecutor, Harold Content, Tresca was convicted and sentenced to one year and one day in federal prison. Sanger orchestrated a letter-writing campaign for clemency, claiming, "I know Mr. Tresca personally. While his political views may be advanced, he has always confined his activities to his native country. He is a very fine man and I feel his conviction is unjust." (*ANB; *Dorothy Gallagher,* All the Right Enemies: The Life and Murder of Carlo Tresca *[New Brunswick, N.J., 1988], 104–6; MS to Slee, Dec. 10, 1924 [LCM 10:804].)*

Atlanta, Ga
March. 17, 1925

My dear Margherita,

49 days more and I will be free man again. The reduction of the sentence has taken away from me the necessity to spend the summer in this burning

hell of Atlanta.[1] And I how to you a great deal for this. You remember, Margherita, watt I said to you when I get from your office, that preciouse list of sentence on birth control case?[2] I said: this is the best help I could have get for my hopes in the commutation of the sentence. In fact the President based is action in the fact that my sentence was a exorbitant one.[3] So my debts of gratitute to you is incresed immensely. I will repaid it witt a devotion to you and to the cause for wich you so valiantely devoted all your life.

Your visit to me was the must cheerishing thing: it was a day of sunshine in the darkened days of imprisonent.[4] I am feeling well: my mind and my body and my soul are in the best. The jail life just bugan to get a little grip, a little old [*for*] me— At first my mind was very busy in taking notice of everthing and everybody and the days when by [*fastly?*]. But [*now*] come the monotony of the same life days after days, without changes, without opportunity of any exitement. Just live. And among "numbers". It is spring time here with all it forcefull appeal of the Youth, the [*illegible*] Joy and the color of mother eart. How do you feel Margherita? I thinks of you very often and I wish so much I could give to you all the power of my life. Let me know, please, how you are getting along. I read in the Nation the interesting program for the Conference on Birth Controll.[5] Plenty work for you, dear one. My best wish for a great success. I am one of your Cabenet now: I am getting all sort of letters from unknow people about birth controll and some time I get afraid I may take away some plume of glory from your feather of glory for watt you have done and are doing for this [*resteless*] humanity, of wich we are a living part. Excuse me for not writing to you before. It was not negleting a best friend of mine but a cruel impossibility to do watt my heart desire to do. Please send me a word. With love I remain yours affectionate and devote friend

Carlo Tresca, 19149

ALS MSP, DLC (LCM 10:826). Stamp obscuring several characters. A note by MS at the top of page reads, "Anna historical file."

1. On January 6, 1925, Tresca began serving his year-long sentence in the Atlanta Federal Penitentiary. On February 16, after lobbying by the ACLU, Congressman Fiorello La Guardia, MS and others, who claimed that Tresca's conviction was the result of political pressure from the Italian government and that his sentence was unusually harsh, President Calvin Coolidge commuted his sentence to four months. He was released on May 6, 1925. (Roger Baldwin to Thomas M. Woodward, Jan. 6, 1925 [RNBP]; *ANB;* Tresca to MS, Jan. ?, 1925 [LCM 10:825]; *New York Times,* Jan. 10, Feb. 17, and May 7, 1925; Appeal for Executive Clemency—Carlo Tresca, Nov. 17, 1924 [RNBP].)

2. MS had signed a petition for clemency and provided a list of sentences received by other convicted birth control advocates to support the argument that Tresca's sentence

was unusually severe. (For the petition, see Appeal for Executive Clemency—Carlo Tresca, Nov. 17, 1924 [RNBP]; for the list, see *MSM* C3:293.)

3. Department of Justice officials finally admitted that Tresca's sentence was too harsh when compared with other sentences for similar offenses. (*New York Times,* Feb. 17, 1925.)

4. MS had visited Tresca in New York City at Christmas time (December 25–27, 1924), before he was transported to Atlanta. (MS Diary [*MSM* S78:585]; see also Tresca to MS, Jan. ?, 1925, and MS to Tresca, Jan. 7, 1925 [LCM 10:824–25].)

5. This was a reference to the program of the Sixth International Neo-Malthusian and Birth Control Conference, printed in the *Nation* on March 11, 1925.

EIGHT

Beyond the American Birth Control League

ON MARCH 25–31, 1925, Sanger hosted the International Neo-Malthusian and Birth Control Conference in New York City. Approximately 150 international scientists, medical professionals, demographers, and economists, drawn from sixteen countries, gathered together under the auspices of the ABCL to discuss birth control. With extensive press coverage, both in the United States and abroad, the conference signaled a power shift in the leadership of the birth control movement from Europe to the United States and marked Sanger as its leading international proponent.

Having demonstrated her ability to gather a diverse group of experts, Sanger quickly began planning an even more prestigious meeting in Europe. "The scientific flavor of our work," she wrote, "will perhaps help make the idea more acceptable to statesmen."[1] Sanger's immersion into this male-dominated community of scientists, culminating with the 1927 World Population Conference in Geneva, accelerated her efforts to globalize the birth control movement and provide it with an academic pedigree. By reaching into universities, medical societies, and research laboratories to recast the movement and deliver her message in geopolitical terms, Sanger helped erase the taint of radicalism that some believed impeded widespread acceptance of birth control and discouraged medical custodianship of clinics.

As an international figure increasingly operating as a free agent, Sanger no longer required the ABCL to serve as her organizational base, nor, since her marriage, did she depend solely on donations to fund her work. By 1925, J. Noah Slee had become the principal benefactor of the league,[2] while Sanger secured several large grants from John D. Rockefeller Jr., in one of the more remarkable turnarounds in the history of American radicalism; just ten years earlier in the *Woman Rebel* she had called him a murderer, compared him to Caligula, and applauded an attempt to assassinate him.[3]

With this new influx of cash, Sanger hired the British-born physician James M. Cooper as the ABCL's medical director and funded his 1925–26 national tour, during which he spoke before seven hundred medical societies and women's groups to secure support for doctor-run clinics. In the CRB, Dr. Hannah Mayer Stone took over as director early in 1925. Unlike her predecessor, Stone compiled detailed patient records and skillfully managed the growing staff of women doctors. With the dependable Stone at the helm of the CRB and an executive committee in place to run the ABCL, Sanger was free from administrative details and was able to spend many months abroad between 1926 and 1928.

Sanger returned to Europe late in 1926 and traveled extensively through England, the French Riviera, Paris, and the Swiss Alps for four and a half months. Healthy for the first time in years, she reveled in her new leisure, sightseeing and taking ice skating lessons between planning the World Population Conference. She also visited her English friends, initiated new connections with prominent scientists, and socialized with such elite figures as Lady Nancy Astor.

Sanger preferred to spend much of her time away from Slee. She kept her own quarters at Willowlake, and through regular speaking tours and spa retreats, she ensured that their cohabitation remained sporadic. Though they communicated almost daily through letters or cables, Slee grew bitter over the length and frequency of their separations. The couple had difficulty reconciling the different expectations that each brought to the marriage, particularly as Sanger fought to maintain her autonomy. Adding to this tension was her role as a buffer between her husband, who was notoriously exacting, especially when it came to money, and her sons, who resented their stepfather's rigid and frugal ways.

The World Population Conference in Geneva occupied most of Sanger's time from 1926 to early 1928, as she oversaw every facet of the event, including the publication of the proceedings. When she returned to New York City in March 1928, she confronted a major organizational crisis at the ABCL. In her absence, the league had divided into two factions. One, led by the often imperious acting president, Eleanor Dwight Jones, worked to create a more professional organization modeled on the League of Women Voters. Jones and many of the newer board members sought a more centralized organization, supported by contributions from state and local leagues, which would reach out to women's clubs and related social groups for endorsements while continuing to emphasize legislative work. As their agenda shifted power to the board and away from the president, Jones and her clique alienated several of Sanger's loyal, longtime supporters, notably Juliet Rublee, Frances Ackermann, and Anne Kennedy. These women formed a competing faction that fought Jones's tightly structured approach and contested her centralization efforts. Rublee, in particular, harbored resentment over the board's November 1927 dismissal of Anne Kennedy, the executive secretary, because she believed it directly challenged Sanger's authority.

While abroad, Sanger seemed uninterested in these ABCL conflicts and was reluctant to be pulled into the fray. Even when pressured by her supporters to retake command of the league, she remained oddly aloof from the struggle. Faced with an increasingly inflexible organization that seemed to want to check her authority and hamper her leadership style, Sanger chose to sidestep the disputes. Psychologically and physically removed from the league's internecine struggles, Sanger felt liberated and free to focus on those facets of the birth control movement that still engaged her—the CRB, the push for federal birth control legislation, and the growing international movement.

By the end of the 1920s, Sanger had largely succeeded in uniting the birth control movement under her ideals. Activists and financial supporters generally agreed that doctor-controlled access to contraceptives led to better health care for women and wider acceptance for the movement; that race betterment and population control were essential to preserving stability in the world; that birth control was a socioeconomic issue, not a moral one; and that it was a public health problem, not simply a woman's concern. In the space of just fourteen years, Margaret Sanger and the birth control movement had become respectable in a way that few would have predicted in 1914, when she helped coin the term *birth control* in the pages of the *Woman Rebel.*

NOTES

1. MS to Edith How-Martyn, July 4, 1926 (*MSM* C4:177).

2. On Slee's financial support, see MS to Frances Ackermann, Aug. 1, 1928 (LCM 11:634).

3. MS, "Tragedy" and "Civilization," *Woman Rebel,* July 1914, 1, and May 1914, 4.

215. *To J. Noah Slee*[1]

[*New York, N.Y.*]
Friday Evening [*April 17, 1925*]

Dearest Noah:

I have been trying to get the desk cleared up today but too many interrupt so I shall try to do it tonight.

Stuart[2] had a lot on his mind & I think he feels you do not like him. He says you act as if you don't want him around & he thinks you have influenced me, so that I am less sympathetic than I was before I married you. He says all our conversation is what everything costs & both he & Grant[3] are as uncomfortable as they can be, since I've married you. He says they had a home before, where they were welcomed & made to feel they were wanted around. That I went places with them, while now any suggestion of doing anything together meets your opposition & criticism. Well darling I felt perfectly terrible & am hurt to the core to have those boys feel they are not wanted around. I tried to reason with Stuart. He says you gave him just the barest amount to get into Yale $1000 which has scarcely paid his board & tuition,[4] he seems "brooding" about something.

Please don't write to him about it. He will get over it I am sure. I am going to bed now (9:15) very tired & blue. I hope you are enjoying the trip & will have a happy time, lovingly & devotedly wifey—

Margy.

ALS MSP, MN-SSC (*MSM* S3:29–30). Return address: "39—5 Ave."

1. Slee had left for a vacation with the Reverend Karl Reiland in Hot Springs, Virginia, the day before.

2. Stuart Sanger and Slee often clashed over money, discipline, and Slee's old-fashioned approach to molding a young man through harsh criticism. In another letter to Slee written earlier that same day, MS related details about a growth in Stuart's throat that might need surgery, and her sister Ethel's opinion that MS was being too strict with him. MS wrote, "I am trying to be very firm with Stuart but not hard." (*MSM* S3:24–28.)

3. Grant, still boarding at the Westminster School, also periodically rebelled against Slee's strict control over his spending, though he did not appear to resent Slee as much as Stuart did.

4. Yale tuition was $300 per year in 1925; room and board cost $8.50 per week. (George Wilson Pierson, *A Yale Book of Numbers: Historical Statistics of the College and University, 1701–1976* [New Haven, Conn., 1983], 589.)

216. "Editorial"

On March 31, the Sixth International Neo-Malthusian and Birth Control Conference heard a resolution designed to "place the conference on record as favoring the general eugenic idea." Introduced by the Eugenics Society member Roswell H. Johnson, the resolution, which passed despite some criticism, encouraged larger families among those deemed "fit." In a press release, Sanger, who consistently opposed such eugenics policies, responded vaguely that the ABCL was ready and willing to unite with the eugenics movement once they had "a definite line of action." But by May 13, Sanger had drafted a clarification of the ABCL's stand on the issue and sent it to the eugenicists Raymond Pearl, Clarence Cook Little, and Edward

Murray East, asking them if it was "too strong for the eugenic group," because she did not want to "offend or antagonize any of our friends whose backing we desire." Little and Pearl approved of the draft, though East found it "a little stronger in condemnation than is necessary." Their comments and other revisions were incorporated into a revised editorial published in the June BCR.

Because of the collaborative nature of the published version, we have selected Sanger's initial draft as the copy text. Corrections and additions made to this draft by an unidentified member of Sanger's staff have not been included but are described in the endnotes. Major differences between the initial draft and the published version are indicated in the source note and endnotes. (ABCL Press Release, Mar. 31, 1925 [first and second quotes] [MSM *C14:231]; MS to Little, May 13, 1925 [third quote]* [MSM *C3:492]; Little to MS, May ?, 1925 [LCM 122:404A]; Pearl to MS, May 15, 1925* [MSM *C3:499]; East to MS, May 15, 1925 [fourth quote]* [MSM *C3:498]; MS, "Editorial," June 1925, 163–64.)*

[*May 13, 1925*]

So much confusion has been created in the public mind by so-called "eugenic" resolution, passed at the final session of the Sixth International Neo-Malthusian and Birth Control Conference, that an explanation of its origin and nature now becomes imperative.

The conference had been practically adjourned; a final meeting was necessary to adjust certain minor details. The courtesy of the floor was extended to Dr. Roswell H. Johnson, as a member of the national council of the League.[1] Dr. Johnson introduced this resolution: "Resolved: that this conference believes that persons whose progeny give promise of being of decided value to the community should be encouraged to bear as large families, properly spaced, as they feel they feasibly can."

This resolution[2] was passed; and it was immediately seized upon for editorial comment and criticism. "Who are the superior parents?" asked the editors and critics, echoing the question that had been asked by opponents of the resolution at that final session of the conference.[3]

Study and analysis of Dr. Johnson's resolution reveals its weakness and vagueness.[4] But in addition to these faults, it must strike all who have studied the program of Birth Control as irrelevant and meaningless. Even granting that it were possible to pre-determine those parents "whose progeny give promise of being of decided value to the community", it is not within the province of our program to offer gratuitous advice to intelligent mothers and fathers as to the number of children they should or should not bring into this world. That is a matter they must decide for themselves, and provided they are fully aware of the responsibility of parenthood it is not only presumptuous but impertinent for any outsider or group of outsiders to criticize the small size of any intelligently created family.

Our program would be lamentably weakened if we undertook to encourage larger families among the so-called "fit" instead of concentrating our efforts upon the task of liberating those vast sections of the human family who have not yet been educated in the practice of that beneficient instrument contraception. As advocates of Birth Control, in other words, we propose Birth Control as an instrument of liberation for overburdened, conscript mothers. When the obstructions which today prevent the dissemination of Birth Control education shall have been removed, we shall find that the progeny of all parents will give unsuspected "promise of being of decided value to the community"; that automatically all children will be "properly spaced," and that all parents and parents-to-be- will be enabled to decide for themselves the "feasibility" of bringing children into the world.[5]

Dr. Johnson's resolution is characterized by that lack of precision and rigorous thinking that has in the past rendered orthodox Eugenics so sterile and lifeless a doctrine.[6] The immediate and lively criticism it has evoked, not only in the press of America, but of England as well, and the vigorous refutations it has stimulated, are of value to our movement, and indicate a decided progress in public opinion in favor of the more concrete and realistic doctrine of Birth Control, as opposed to vague, impractical, "idealistic eugenics."[7]

But I regret profoundly that this resolution, passed by our conference, may have promulgated the erroneous idea that our program countenanced the inauguration of a cradle competition between the parents of "promising" children and the irresponsible and reckless breeders of the defective and delinquent.

The central aim of Birth Control is more constructive. We claim that all children who are brought into this world <u>must</u> give promise of being of value to the community, and that if there is any doubt or indication to the contrary, in the traits or heredity, such possible parents must refrain from exercising the function of parenthood. It is not our business to offer gratuitous and impertinent advice to those already educated in Birth Control. Our main task is to clear obstructions which now prevent diseased and poverty stricken mothers from educating themselves in the practice of contraception.[8]

In the final analysis the Johnson resolution is harmless. Translated into our terms it reads something like this; "Resolved that persons who practice Birth Control should be encouraged to bear as large families as they choose, by controlling the births of their children." Nevertheless, the unfortunate results of the hurried and thoughtless acceptance of this resolution should be a lesson to all of us who advocate Birth Control of the menace of loose and unrealistic thinking and expression. It should teach us to avoid all vagueness, all irrelevance, all loose thinking which sounds well but means little.

For we must never forget that Birth Control cannot be relegated to the background of human thought as a mere secondary aspect of Eugenics, or described as "negative" Eugenics.[9] Birth Control, on the contrary, is a constructive, creative, program, proffering to suffering humanity an instrument of release, a weapon of liberation. It is not primarily concerned with those classes which by the benefits of contraception have already risen. They are quite able to look for themselves and their children. Primarily our program aims for the release from the hidden reservoir of human potentiality all that vast untouched treasure of talent and genius that lies hidden in the common masses of the race. Birth Control is the instrument by which these latent traits may be bred into glorious, radiant realities.[10]

MARGARET SANGER.

TDf RPP, PPAmP (*MSM* C16:794–97). In the published version, MS added a two-paragraph introduction asserting that one of the basic tenets of the ABCL "includes the racial perpetuation of health, intelligence, talent and all human traits and values of benefit to the community. As I have pointed out elsewhere and repeated many times, the key-word of our program is control. If our critics would take the trouble of looking up the definition of control in any standard dictionary, it would become evident to them that this word means intelligence, mastery and guidance of an activity. Therefore the control of the procreative faculty means, fundamentally, the application of intelligent direction and guidance of this function, with complete consideration of the factors and the lives involved." (MS, "Editorial," June 1925, 163. For another copy of the draft, with identical corrections added by a different, unidentified hand, see LCM 122:402.)

1. Roswell Hill Johnson (1877–1967) was a biologist, psychologist, avid eugenicist, and coauthor of *Applied Eugenics* (1918), who advocated segregation and sterilization for "the feeble minded and other anti-social individuals." Johnson was an ABCL national council member and later the president of the American Eugenics Society. Pearl cautioned MS against giving "too much advertising to Johnson and the eugenics group," and in the *BCR* version, MS deleted all but the first reference to Johnson by name. (*Los Angeles Times,* Jan. 19, 1967; Larson, *Sex, Race, and Science,* 23 [first quote]; Pearl to MS, May 15, 1925 [second quote] [*MSM* C3:499].)

2. The following was added by hand: "under the rules of the Conference the resolution was out of order and if it had been introduced at the fully attended eugenics session. It is very doubtful if it would have passed." This change appears in the *BCR* version.

3. This was a reference to the *New York Times* editorial critical of the resolution for promoting a "new aristocracy" in which "those who are permitted, and rendered financially able," would "enjoy the privilege of giving birth." The *New York Times* reported the question that Aletta Jacobs asked at the session, "How are we to determine what stock is of decided value to the community? . . . Is a committee in each country to decide this point of proper parentage, or are the parents to do so themselves?" (*New York Times,* Apr. 2, 1925; ABCL Press Release [*MSM* C14:231].)

4. Edward East objected to MS's use of the word *weakness* and recommended revising the editorial "considerably if you wish to retain the sympathies of a lot of people whose names have at least some value." (East to MS, May 15, 1925 [*MSM* C3:498].)

5. Both Pearl and East objected to MS's contention that if birth control were legalized, "the progeny of all parents" might hold promise. East argued, "Certainly there will be many children of no value whatever to the community no matter what laws are passed and no matter what educational propaganda is put forth. Individual egotism is too high." In the final version, MS rewrote this sentence to read, "We assume that potentially at

least all normal children who are brought into the world give promise of being of value to the community; that if the potential child promises to be the contrary, a burden, a menace to the community and the race, its coming must be prevented; that the promise of the promising child is often over-balanced and destroyed by the preponderance of unwanted children; and that our fundamental and central task is to clear away those obstructions which now prohibit diseased, overburdened and poverty-stricken mothers from the control of the procreative function." (East to MS, May 15, 1925 [*MSM* C3:498]; MS, "Editorial," June 1925, 164.)

6. East suggested that MS temper this by saying the resolution "is characterized by somewhat of that lack of precision and rigorous thinking that has rendered many of the orthodox Eugenics proposals so sterile and lifeless." In the *BCR* version, she wrote that the resolution "is open to the same refutation that have been evoked by many of the orthodox proposals of the Eugenics school—their tendency to place too much faith in external direction and quasi-paternal direction of breeding, combined with a bland indifference to the importance of liberated self-direction." Continuing with more detailed criticism, she added, "In the first place, it would seem impossible to predetermine those 'superior' persons whose progeny would for certain give such promise, or to deny the possibility of such promise to many who might from all external standards be deemed 'inferior.' In the next place we doubt seriously that those qualities desirable for racial perpetuation can be effectively transmitted from generation to generation by the simple expedient of merely increasing the size of the family, an increase 'encouraged' by the passing of resolutions directed toward prospective parents quite able to make their own decisions and to manage their own affairs." (East to MS, May 15, 1925 [*MSM* C3:498]; MS, "Editorial," June 1925, 164.)

7. MS may have exaggerated press attention to the resolution, though it was mentioned in the British *Eugenics Review* and in the U.S.-based *Eugenical News.* The *New Republic* disapproved of the resolution, arguing that those who chose to have children were "self-indulgent" and that the position was "ill-advised." (Charles V. Drysdale, "Sixth International Neo-Malthusian and Birth Control Conference," *Eugenics Review* 13 [Apr. 1925–Jan. 1926]: 5119–20; "Birth Control and Eugenics," *Eugenical News* 10 [Jan. 1925]: 58; John Langdon-Davies, "Race Suicide No Murder," *New Republic,* Apr. 15, 1925, 210–11.)

8. In the *BCR* version, MS was more forceful in her claim that positive eugenics was not the ABCL's goal: "If we sought as an organization to increase and extend our pro gram to encourage larger families among the biologically superior classes, instead of concentrating upon the more important task of educating those vast sections of the human family to which the beneficent instrument of contraception has been denied, our efforts would be lamentably scattered and weakened."

9. East rejected MS's focus on the relationship between birth control and eugenics, writing, "No matter what you say Birth Control is only a part of a eugenical program. It is a secondary aspect of a larger whole, but it is the key. The mere fact that so many eugenicists have not been able to think straight does not make the abstract subject itself any less valid." She deleted this line in the *BCR* version. (East to MS, May 15, 1925 [*MSM* C3:498].)

10. The *BCR* version ended with an additional paragraph in which she referred to "the militarists and the reactionaries . . . incessantly urging the procreation of larger and

larger families upon the fit and the unfit alike," and she warned of "the danger of confusing our own program with that of our opponents. We have sufficient faith in the fit to look out for themselves and their children." "Our program" she declared, aimed "first and last for the release, from the vast deep reservoir of human potentiality, of the hidden treasure of talent and beauty and genius that lies untouched and unminted in the unprobed depths of the common race. Birth control,—this is our undaunted challenge—is the instrument by which these latent traits may be bred into radiant reality."

217. To Juliet Barrett Rublee[1]

[*Fishkill Village, N.Y.*]
Monday [*July 13, 1925*]

Juliet dearest:

Its doubtful that I can leave Tuesday without such a "fuss" that my visit would be spoiled.[2] When I said I was going J. N. said "That will be nice what train shall we take"? I did not want to "start anything" as there were guests in the house. But there it is Juliet. Are all the material things of this world worth one years bondage of the Soul? Perhaps—just so one can free ~~themselves~~ ↑oneself↓ from material desires & want soul freedom so desperately that it must be had at all costs & Sacrifice.

From that point of view it is interesting to watch myself as Gurdjieff[3] (spelled wrong) would have us do I suppose. Any way should Something come up to make it possible to go Ill leave Tuesday night (not in the afternoon). Ill telegraph either way, but my going is doubtful.

Dr Cooper comes out here today.[4] Im so longing for London & a year over in England that I wonder that I can live without it.

You must not die! Good Lord the world would be drab for me I'd go in a convent & learn How to Commune with you.

Darling you do understand don't you? Shall I throw away everything & act? I doubt that I'm ready for that, lovingly

Margaret

ALS JRP, NhD (*MSM* C3:561–63).

1. After helping MS with the Sixth International Neo-Malthusian and Birth Control Conference in March, Rublee invested in an Italian expedition to search for underwater treasures using a deep-sea diving cylinder and automatic camera invented by Hans Hartman. ("Preliminary Announcement," *BCR*, Mar. 1925, 80; Rublee to MS, Oct. 4 and 5, 1925 [*MSM* S3:250]; Rublee to Charles F. Brush, May 12 and June 12, 1925 [CBP].)

2. MS, who spent most of July at Willowlake, making several trips to New York City, probably hoped to go to New Hampshire before Rublee left on various trips. (Rublee to MS, Aug. 19, 1925 [*MSM* S3:158].)

3. George Ivanovitch Gurdjieff (c. 1872–1949) was a Greek-Armenian mystic and the founder of the Institute for the Harmonious Development of Man in France, whose

teaching of the "Fourth Way" held that humans existed in a "sleep" state, manipulated by outside forces. To "awaken," individuals must establish contact with higher forces and energies that surround them. MS spelled his name correctly. (J. Gordon Melton, ed., *Biographical Dictionary of American Cult and Sect Leaders* [New York, 1986], 103–4.)

4. Dr. James Freyer Cooper (1880–1931) was an English-born physician and medical missionary to China, who specialized in obstetrics and gynecology at Boston University. He became the ABCL's medical director in January 1925 and was probably reporting on the first leg of his national tour. (*New York Times*, Mar. 28, 1931; for Cooper's Jan.–July 1925 reports, see *MSM* C12:56–82.)

218. From Juliet Barrett Rublee

S.S. Conti Verde, [*at sea*]
Sept 11, [*1925*]

Darling—

Have you read Mrs Bertie Russell's little book "Hypatia"? It is magnificent—chapter III is epoch-making! It contains so many of the things I intended to put in my little book—& shall—some day— I am on Chapter IV now which keeps up the pace superbly[1]—but I cannot wait to finish it all before urging you to read it. Darling—we must hurry—hurry—hurry—to pass B-C- on to others so that we can work for this other, deeper, bigger thing—which will make men & women into Gods & Goddesses— B-C- was a necessary step—but useless unless we can also create finer human beings spiritually & mentally—as witness Holland!— The desire & will to Freedom & free imagination & aspiration— Realization of all the Beauties & joys they have dreamed of, must be stirred & awakened in women just as you have succeeded in stirring & awakening them to a desire to control their own bodies— That being achieved they must be helped & inspired to know that they can become Goddesses—forever young & beautiful & kind & true & noble.

Do you know Mrs Russell & if so could you give me a line of introduction to her? Do you like her? does she come up to her book?[2]

Of course "they" never do!—but anyway she must be worth talking to— Ask [*Lovejoy*][3] what he thinks of her book—& let me know.

Also—darling—read the Leadbeatter book & tell me what Ray you belong to—[4] I know immediately my Ray & my "master" on reading it.

Four days more—and then Naples![5] I have been trying in vain so far to get rid of a sore throat—& cough— Stayed in bed all day yesterday—& all of every morning—but it still persists— Have had a great deal of time to think & am clearing up certain things in my mind. It is well I think to be frank with ourselves about our mistakes & admit them. It must help us to be prepared to act differently when the same problem comes around again under a different guise & dress—as it so often does— [*last page(s) missing.*]

AL MSP, MN-SSC (*MSM* S3:183–85).

1. Dora Winifred Black Russell (1894–1986), a British feminist writer, International Labour Party member, and advocate of sexual freedom, married the philosopher Bertrand Russell in 1921. She founded the Workers' Birth Control Group in 1924 and in 1927 opened Beacon Hill, an experimental school, with her husband. Her 1925 book, *Hypatia; or, Women and Knowledge,* was a brief survey of feminism. In chapter 3, "Apasia: The Younger Feminists," Russell asserted that women needed to reclaim their share of enjoyment and pleasure in sex. In chapter 4, "Hecuba: Feminist Mothers," she discussed reasons for having or not having children. Rublee herself never wrote a book. (Sheila Rowbotham, *A Century of Women* [New York, 1997], 612; Dora Russell, *The Tamarisk Tree* [New York, 1975], 168–80.)

2. MS probably met Dora Russell in England in October 1924.

3. This was probably Owen Reed Lovejoy (1866–1961), a child welfare reformer and the general secretary of the National Child Labor Committee. An ABCL national council member, Lovejoy frequently reviewed books for the *BCR.* (*ANB; New York Times,* June 30, 1961.)

4. This was probably a reference to *Masters and the Path* (1925) by Charles Webster Leadbeater (1854–1934), a British occultist and renegade Anglican clergyman who wrote on occult chemistry and psychic teachings, frequently collaborating with Annie Besant. A "Ray" is one of seven streams of energy that, in esoteric science and occultism, define and infuse all objects and beings. The Seven Rays are manifest in corresponding character traits, evolutionary cycles, planets, and so forth. (Gregory Tillett, *The Elder Brother: A Biography of Charles Webster Leadbeater* [London, 1982], 1–10, 268, 278–79.)

5. In September, Rublee joined the journalist and archeologist Alma M. Reed and the inventor Hans Hartman in Naples to begin their underwater treasure hunt, but the adventure quickly fell into disarray as the women feuded over money and responsibilities and grew frustrated by the interference of Italian authorities. Rublee finally went down in the diving cylinder in late November, but the expedition abruptly ended when, according to her nephew, she was kidnaped by the Italian crew of the rented boat and held for ransom. (Rublee to MS, Aug. 19, Sept. 24, Sept. 26, and Dec. 5, 1925, and MS to Rublee, Sept. 10, 1925 [*MSM* S3:158, 210, 232, and 339, C3:628]; Marashio, "Interview with Horace Rublee," 9.)

219. From Katharine Bement Davis[1]

*John D. Rockefeller Jr. donated five thousand dollars to the ABCL in June 1924 and again in April 1925 to cover expenses of the Sixth International Neo-Malthusian and Birth Control Conference. The gifts were made anonymously through the Bureau of Social Hygiene, which Rockefeller established in 1911 to undertake research and program development aimed at ending vice and prostitution. Under Katharine Bement Davis's influence, the bureau extended its work to support research into human sexuality, social hygiene, and population control. In September 1925, Sanger requested funds to support the CRB and to cover a portion of the costs of printing the proceedings of the Sixth International Neo-Malthusian and Birth Control Conference. (MS to Katharine Davis, May 11 and Sept. 24, 1925, and ABCL Budget [*MSM *C3:480 and 632–34]; Charles O. Heydt to Davis, Oct. 13, 1925, and Memorandum to Files, Dec. 2 and 9, 1926 [Rockefeller].)*

New York City, [*N.Y.*]
October 7, 1925

My dear Mrs. Sanger:

I am very glad to inform you that my friend[2] will contribute $10,000.[3] to the work of the clinic in the way we discussed yesterday. He prefers not to be known by name, for a variety of reasons, which you can undoubtedly understand. The check for the amount will be forwarded to you very shortly and I trust will help you to accomplish what you have in mind for the coming year.

With best wishes for your success, Sincerely yours,

Katharine Bement Davis [*signed*]
Katharine Bement Davis
General Secretary

TLS MSP, DLC (LCM 22:3B). Letterhead of the Bureau of Social Hygiene.

1. After leaving the New York City Corrections Office in 1915, Davis chaired the New York City Parole Board until 1917, when she became general secretary of the Bureau of Social Hygiene. Davis's recommendations, along with Raymond Fosdick's, were critical in winning Rockefeller's support of MS's work. (*NAW;* Chesler, *Woman of Valor,* 277.)
2. John D. Rockefeller Jr. (1874–1960) was the philanthropist son of the famous oil magnate. (*DAB*)
3. See MS to Davis, Sept. 24, 1925, and to Fosdick, Oct. 19, 1925 (*MSM* C3:480 and 675).

220. *From Mary B. Higgins*[1]

[*Buffalo, N.Y.*]
Dec 1st [*1925*]

Dearest Margaret.

Could you not spare one day of your busy life to come up to see a rather sick sister? It would give me much comfort and relief. If you feel you can't do it don't send anyone else as the point would be lost. Bronchitis having attached it self make the nights and days long and tiresome but the operations is a great success. Lovingly

Mary

ALS MSP, MN-SSC (*MSM* S3:331–32). Letterhead of the Buffalo General Hospital. A handwritten note by MS on the reverse reads, "Darling Sister Mary died shortly after. Of course I left for Buffalo at once cancelling lectures.[2] She talked of her will & left me sole executator. She was greatly loved—& a genius born MS."

1. Mary Higgins, at age fifty-five, most likely suffered fatal complications (possibly a lung infection) following an appendectomy. (Chesler, "Interview with Grant Sanger," 35; Olive Schoellkopf to MS, Dec. 21, 1925 [*MSM* S3:352].)

2. MS visited Mary on December 4–5, 1925, canceling a lecture at the Theatre Guild and a tea at the CRB. (1925 Calendar [LCM 2:542].)

221. *Diary Entry*

[*New York, N.Y.*]
Jan 11, 1926

To night Nan, Ethel & I leave for Buffalo.[1] Mary died after midnight today.[2] Mr Schoellkopf telegraphed me this morning.[3] It was a shock, for th'o she has been ill a long time, I thot she would recover. Father has had a stroke about Dec 20th, but has pulled through.

Mary was very depressed. An operation for hernea resulted in lung absess after ether. I went to Buffalo to see her & found her depressed. She knew she was going to die. I have had two very queer dreams. One that I saw a false plate of teeth, with one decayed tooth hanging by the roots, which would not fall out.

The other was one of myself walking on the street—hundreds of people were coming the opposite direction. I saw among the crowd Dr C. C. Little[4] & a woman and as they approached I smelled mice, just as tho I was among hundreds of mice. Dr Little works among mice. It was queer. Two nights later Mary died. This is the second dream I have ever had where I smelled a smell & death resulted in a few days.

Ethel dreamed of Mother (dead over twenty-five years)[5] the night before last.

It is a shock to have Mary pass on. She was the stable sympathetic member of a large family—her passing loosens up the foundation.

Much loved by everyone.

She remembered every person at Christmas & birthdays with whom she came in contact.

A dear & loving person—a universal mother. Peace to Her.!

AD MSP, MN-SSC (*MSM* S70:227–29).

1. Anna Higgins was in Truro, caring for their father Michael Higgins, now an invalid. Ethel Byrne was still a nurse in New York City.

2. Mary Higgins died on January 11.

3. Mary's employers were the industrialist Jacob Frederick Schoellkopf Jr. (1883–1952) and his wife, Olive Abbott Schoellkopf (1887–1958), daughter of her former employers, George Abbott and Nellie Abbott. The telegraph was not found. (*New York Times*, Dec. 17, 1952; *Buffalo Courier-Express*, Apr. 19, 1958.)

4. Clarence Cook Little (1888–1971) was a zoologist and eugenicist at the Carnegie Institution's Station for Experimental Evolution at Cold Spring Harbor, who specialized in breeding mice to select out genetic factors contributing to disease, notably can-

cer. He became president of the University of Maine in 1922. Little was a member of the ABCL board and the CRB advisory board. (*ANB*)

5. MS's mother, Anne Purcell Higgins, died in 1899. (Alexander Sanger, "Family Genealogy" [MN-SSC].)

222. To Lawrence D. Tyson[1]

In December 1925, the ABCL opened a Washington, D.C., office and established a congressional committee, chaired by Ida Timme, to secure congressional sponsors and support to pass a "doctors-only" bill that would allow physicians to mail contraceptive information to other physicians, to their "bonafide" patients, or to printers and publishers. The proposed "doctors-only" bill would also permit contraceptives to be sent to importers, manufacturers, distributors, and retail dealers but released to the public only on a physician's prescription. The committee interviewed thirty-one senators and ten representatives but found only a lukewarm response. After interviewing Senator Lawrence Tyson on February 10, Anne Kennedy considered him a good prospect as a sponsor because he said the birth control bill was "the most important legislation before the country today." He agreed to consider sponsoring it, though he made no promises. What follows is Sanger's follow-up letter. ("A Proposed Federal Amendment," 1926 [first quote] [MSM C12:42]; Anne Kennedy, "Congressional Report," Feb. 10, 1926 [second quote] [LCM 27:609].)

[*New York, N.Y.*]
February 20, 1926.

My dear Senator:

Our representative, Mrs. Kennedy,[2] called on you several days ago in regard to our proposed amendment to the Penal Code, Section 211.

You very kindly expressed your interest in Birth Control and your belief that as there was a general interest in the breeding of fine live stock, it was only reasonable to apply the same principle to the human family. You also expressed interest in my book, so that I feel you may in some way realize how great a responsibility I feel to all these poor women throughout the country who are needing help.[3]

The present law is working a great hardship to them. I received over 59,000 letters last year from these over-burdened mothers. Nearly one-third of the women who have received advice in the New York Clinic are Roman Catholics. This speaks for itself.

Our bill is conservative in that it only asks that the mails may be used by the scientific and medical professions. The amendment of this law will give physicians the right to receive supplies and data that are now available from our New York Clinic.[4]

I sincerely wish that you would introduce this bill. There is much support for it in the Senate, and a wide approval of it in every class of society in the United States.

I shall be in Washington on March 12th and hope you will grant me an interview.[5] Meanwhile, will you not give my request your sincere consideration, and I hope that your reply will be favorable.[6] Cordially yours,

AMERICAN BIRTH CONTROL LEAGUE, Inc.
Director

TLcy FRP, MN-SSC (*MSM* S3:439).

1. Lawrence D. Tyson (1861–1929), a Democratic senator from Tennessee (1925–29), favored immigration restriction and prohibition and actively sought women's votes. (*New York Times,* Aug. 25, 1929.)

2. Kennedy, now the ABCL's legislative secretary, did most of the congressional committee's work, splitting her time between New York City and Washington, D.C. ("News Notes," *BCR,* Jan. 1926, 29, and Feb. 1926, 65.)

3. The book was probably *The Pivot of Civilization* (1922).

4. This probably referred to data gathered by the CRB on the reliability of specific contraceptive methods, lists of contraceptive manufacturers and distributors, annual reports on patient treatment, as well as the diaphragms, jellies, and other contraceptive products the CRB was illegally bringing in and distributing to patients.

5. MS spoke to the Women's University Club in Washington on March 12, but no evidence was found suggesting she met with Tyson. (LCM 134:736.)

6. In his February 23 response, Tyson declined to introduce the bill and suggested, "I think you should get some Republican to do that or Senator Copeland, . . . as he is a doctor himself." MS had already approached New York's Senator Royal Copeland, who refused to sponsor the bill. (Tyson to MS, Feb. 23, 1926 [*MSM* S3:444]; for reports of meetings with Copeland and other Congressmen, see Dec. 15–Feb. 23, 1926 [LCM 27:602–10].)

223. *From Robert Latou Dickinson*[1]

In her quest for medical approval for the CRB, Sanger approached Dr. Robert L. Dickinson, a leading physician proponent of contraception and founder of the Committee on Maternal Health (CMH), which conducted contraceptive research in hospital-based clinics. But Dickinson's clinics had failed to attract enough patients to make his research base viable, and he was anxious to access the far larger CRB patient base. In 1925, he entered into negotiations with Sanger to have the CMH supervise the CRB. Both believed such medical management would enable the CRB to secure a dispensary license, a prerequisite for gaining medical acceptance, new channels of funding, and validation of its research findings. However, Dickinson required that the CRB cleanse itself of lay propaganda, including the BCR, and divorce itself from the ABCL. Sanger agreed, and in June 1925, a group of male physicians drawn from the CRB's advisory council and the CMH formed the Maternity Research Council (MRC) to secure the dispensary license and oversee the CRB. Although association with the MRC resulted in a ten thousand dollar gift to the CRB from John D. Rockefeller Jr., the New York State Board of Charities continued to withhold a dispensary license. Since the MRC would not agree to supervise the clinic without a license and

*Sanger would not agree to surrender control over the CRB to Dickinson, the merger foundered. (MRC Minutes, Nov. 12, 1925 [*MSM *C13:787]; MS-Dickinson correspondence, Oct. 1925–Apr. 1926 [*MSM *C3 and LCM 32; MRC Minutes, May 15, 1925–Jan. 18, 1926 [*MSM *C12:780–96]; McCann,* Birth Control Politics, *80–86.)*

New York City [*N.Y.*]
19 March 1926.

Dear Mrs. Sanger:

I had a talk with the executive of the State Board of Charities, Mr. Ford, on Monday. I pressed for an answer to our letters. We have twice ~~asked~~ ↑written↓ the Board to ask for their reasons in declaring, at their January meeting, that the granting of a license was "inexpedient".[2]

The answer is enclosed.[3] In conversation, Mr. Ford said that the clinic did not hang out a sign claiming that it was a dispensary. Also that it was not a dispensary because no treatment was given. I informed him that treatment was given by a physician to the poor, and the use of medical appliances taught to guard against conception, and supplies furnished where the law countenanced this procedure when required "to cure or prevent disease." Therefore it was a dispensary.[4] [*Handwritten*] We shall push this point.

Mr. Ford again raised the question of adequate advice being given by existing institutions. I referred to the evidence, given by Dr. Haven Emerson at the hearing that the Committee on Maternal Health had been earnestly seeking for three years to secure records and reasonable service, with scant results.[5] Dr. James B. Murphy, one of the Commissioners, had recently suggested the Cornell Clinic, and this had been taken up at once. This clinic declined.[6]

Mr. Ford, seeing Dr. Tilton's name on the list of incorporators,[7] said his Board had just approved of the building of a new St. Marks, and suggested that St. Marks might be willing to run the clinic.[8] This idea is in the end of Mr. Johnson's letter, enclosed. I should expect that the Hospital would decline to take an independent group in to do a special piece of work and the incorporators of the Maternity Research Council would decline to hand over to the directors of the out patient department this clinical research. Please let us know how you feel about this.[9]

At the last hearing it was openly stated by members of the Committee that the real objection was that of certain religious bodies, and it was suggested that waivers be secured from these. The opposition of the Roman Catholic Church was specifically mentioned and discussed but ~~their~~ this statement is elided from the minutes of the hearing as furnished to us.[10]

This letter shifts the ground. At the same time, I think it would be expedient to take the matter up with St. Marks Hospital in the way of asking whether the Trustees would be willing to place a birth control clinic in their out patient department that would care for 1500 to 2000 patients a year. If ↑we↓ refused, we should [*not*] be in the position of declining to try a suggestion of the Board. Very truly yours,

Robt L. Dickinson [*signed*]
Secretary.

[*Handwritten postscript*] I shall submit the letter to the M.R.C. incorporators, suggesting and urging continuance of pressure on the Board.[11] I. This is a dispensary according to the law. II. The existing clinics are not and at present cannot meet the need. The Academy of Medicine says so.[12] As you are in Chicago I have not been able to talk this over with you.[13]

TLS MSP, DLC (LCM 32:96). For TLcy, see *MSM* C4:81–82. Letterhead of the Committee on Maternal Health. The handwritten corrections were made by Robert Dickinson.

1. Robert Latou Dickinson (1861–1950) had been a Brooklyn Hospital gynecologist and obstetrician, who had left in 1924 to focus on sexual reform and contraceptive research. His CMH, founded in 1923, conducted clinical research on contraception, sterility, and abortion using the outpatient services of several New York City hospitals. (*ANB;* Reed, *Birth Control Movement and American Society,* 170–72.)

2. Clarence E. Ford (1879–1961) was superintendent of the Division of Medical Charities. Dickinson testified on behalf of the MRC's application on January 15, but on January 19 the Board of Charities tabled the license request, explaining that it was "inexpedient from the standpoint of public policy." (*New York Times,* Apr. 10, 1961; *Sixteenth Annual Report of the State Board of Charities* [Albany, N.Y., 1926]; New York State Board of Charities, *Minutes of the Meetings of the State Board of Charities,* Jan. 19, 1925 [Albany, N.Y., 1926], 6 [quote]; Dickinson to Charles Johnson, Feb. 1 and Mar. 9, 1926 [LCM 32:86 and 94].)

3. In the enclosure, Charles Johnson, secretary of the Board of Charities, wrote that "the Board is not yet satisfied that the investigations and research which the Council proposes to undertake constitute a dispensary as defined by law." (Johnson to Dickinson, Mar. 17, 1926 [LCM 32:95A].)

4. Ford attempted to backtrack from the board's "inexpedient" argument by questioning the CRB's purpose and function. Under Section 290 of the licensing law, a dispensary was any individual or institution that furnished "medical or surgical advice or treatment, medicine or apparatus." ("The Law Relating to the Licensing and Regulation of Dispensaries by the State Board of Charities," in *Laws of 1909, Constituting Chapter 55 of the Consolidated Laws* [Albany, N.Y., 1920], 1 [LCM 33:542].)

5. Haven Emerson (1874–1957) was a physician, a New York City health commissioner, and the head of Columbia University's School of Public Health (1921–40), who testified on the CMH clinics at the January 15 Board of Charities' hearing. Intent upon adhering to "scientific methods" and retaining medical control of contraception, the CMH prohibited members with ties to the birth control movement, but it could not obtain sufficient diaphragms to attract patients. (*New York Times,* May 22, 1957; Dick-

inson to MRC Incorporators, Mar. 22, 1926 [LCM 32:97]; McCann, *Birth Control Politics,* 80–81.)

6. James Bumgardner Murphy (1884–1950) was an experimental pathologist and immunologist at the Rockefeller Institute. The Cornell University Medical College Clinic, founded in 1921, did not offer free medical services, making it a less than ideal choice to sponsor the CRB. (*ANB; The Cornell Clinic, 1921–1924* [New York, 1925], 2, 7.)

7. Benjamin Trowbridge Tilton (1868–1945), president of New York City's St. Mark's Hospital (1910–23) and thereafter chief of its surgical service, was an advocate of medical services for the poor. Other MRC incorporators, drawn from the advisory boards of the CMH and CRB, were Timothy Newell Pfeiffer, Frederick C. Holden, John O. Polak, John C. Vaughan, C. F. Jellinghaus, Adolf Meyer, William A. Pusey, Edward East, and Raymond Pearl. (*New York Times,* Sept. 24, 1945; MRC Statement, Nov. 4, 1925 [*MSM* 13:785].)

8. St. Mark's Hospital, established in 1890 to care for the poor and "'in-betweens,' the clerk, the shop girl, the parents of large families—people who are opposed to receiving charity, but who must have help when sickness comes," began constructing a new wing in February 1926. (*New York Times,* Jan. 25, 1925, and Feb. 6, 1926 [quote].)

9. There is no evidence that MS ever approached St. Mark's.

10. At the January 15 hearing, Board of Charities chairman Lee K. Frankel noted that "there would be opposition to this from many sources, religious bodies and others," and he suggested that the MRC meet with representatives of the "three largest religious denominations." He concluded, "When we get the opinion of other members of the committee along religious lines we will be able to decide." Dickinson attempted to secure statements from various religious groups and protested the decision. ("Stenographer's Minutes," Dickinson to Johnson, Feb. 1, 1926, and Dickinson to MRC, Feb. 26, 1926 [LCM 32:86, 90, and 99].)

11. Dickinson asked for a vote by MRC members on whether to contest the board's decision. (Dickinson to MRC, Mar. 22, 1926 [LCM 32:97].)

12. The academy's Public Health Committee reported that New York City hospitals and individual physicians were not meeting the need for birth control, and in March 1925 it called for a properly supervised nonhospital clinic. (Public Health Committee Report, Mar. 12, 1925 [NCMHR].)

13. MS was lecturing at the Abraham Lincoln Center in Chicago on March 19. (MS Lecture Schedule and 1926 Calendar [LCM 134:739, 2:591].)

224. ABCL Newsletter

New York City [*N.Y.*]
MARCH 1926.

Dear League Member, Subscriber and Friend:

There is so much to tell you concerning the work we are doing in the Birth Control Movement, that only a few of the most important facts can be given you in this newsletter. It is encouraging to report that everywhere there is a general acceptance of the idea except in religious circles (Roman Catholics in particular) which seemingly have closed their minds to reason.

The work in Washington[1] is going so well that the opposition has had to come out in the open to fight us. The National Catholic Welfare Council have a special committee organized to block and defeat our legislative plans not only in Congress but throughout the various States as well.[2] They aim to get non-Catholic organizations to help them defeat us. They frankly state that they intend to legislate for non-Catholics according to the dictates of the church.[3] This means that you, as a member of the American Birth Control League should help us and stand beside us in carrying on our work to the end.

Already several thousand doctors are helping, advising and instructing women in the means of spacing out their babies.[4] Six clinics are already operating in various cities of the U.S.A.[5] Our Doctor James F. Cooper has traveled over the country lecturing to medical societies and informing his profession concerning the best methods of contraception.[6] All this is constructive work. We have not only the foundation but the structure well started toward building a new world for Womanhood.

The Congressional Committee was formed to help change the Federal law. Mrs. Walter Timme is chairman of the Committee.[7] Mrs. Anne Kennedy is legislative secretary and spends all her time in Washington. She has interviewed over forty Senators and twenty Congressmen. It is too lengthy a report to give here the result of those interviews. They can be had from me for the asking.

We want more people to join the Congressional Committee. We need five thousand dollars to cover the field. Only ten dollars from five hundred members would bring us this amount. This letter goes to fifty thousand men and women who have joined our Organization.

We need your help for the next three months before Congress adjourns.

Have you written to or seen your Senator or Congressman? Will you do so? Ask him to give us a hearing. Will you be one of the 500 and send $10.00? It will pay compound interest by decreasing the misery, agony and worry of motherhood.

All together for a final effort to get a hearing. Sincerely yours,

AMERICAN BIRTH CONTROL LEAGUE, Inc.
Margaret Sanger [*stamped signature*]
President.

TFL NCWCR, DCU (*MSM* C12:564). A tear-off contribution form for federal work follows her signature.

1. Anne Kennedy, unable to find a sponsor among legislators who feared that association with a birth control bill would harm them politically, reported that hearings on

the VPL's Cummins-Vaile bill had been "the laughing-stock of the cloakroom for several days." In May 1926, the ABCL committee ceased work, recommending that additional educational work was needed before another legislative push. (Kennedy to MS, Mar. 27, 1926, and Congressional Report, Jan. 1–May 1, 1926 [LCM 27:622 and 638.)

2. The National Catholic Welfare Conference (NCWC) was established by Catholic bishops in 1919 to coordinate educational, missionary, and press activities for the Catholic Church of America. Though the NCWC did not create a "special committee," the suppression of birth control was clearly a chief goal of its general secretary, Father John J. Burke. His Executive Department carried out this work along with, to a lesser extent, the Social Action Department, headed by Monsignor John A. Ryan. The NCWC successfully marshaled Catholic and fraternal non-Catholic groups to oppose the ABCL's legislative lobbying. (NCWCR Collection Description; Douglas J. Slawson, *The Foundation and First Decade of the National Catholic Welfare Council* [Washington, D.C., 1992], 68–77; Dienes, *Law, Politics, and Birth Control,* 106.)

3. Anne Kennedy met with Father P. J. Ward on March 2, 1926, and reported that he told her the Catholic church was "responsible for the morals of the whole human race" and that it was the church's duty "to interfere and block all legislation that will affect the morals of Catholics and non-Catholics." Burke repudiated the report, asserting that Ward was not authorized to speak for the NCWC, but MS dismissed his objections. (Anne Kennedy, "Report of an Interview with P. J. Ward," [*MSM* C12:508]; MS-Burke letters in *MSM* C4 and C12 and in LCM 27.)

4. In 1925, the ABCL gave the work of answering client letters to its newly created Motherhood Department, which in its first year responded to over twenty-eight thousand letters. The department referred the writers to clinics if possible or to physicians willing to prescribe contraceptives (it maintained a referral list of over six thousand physicians) and sometimes contacted a client's physician. (Bertha Smith, "Report of the Motherhood Department," Jan. 12, 1926 [*MSM* S61:190].)

5. By the end of 1925, the CRB operated two clinics, one in Manhattan and one in Brooklyn; the Illinois Birth Control League operated three Chicago-based clinics; and the Los Angeles Mothers Clinic Association operated one. In addition, the CMH sponsored eight hospital clinics. By the end of 1926, some twenty-one birth control clinics operated nationally. (Cooper, *Technique of Contraception,* 205–25.)

6. Cooper continued his national tour and by 1928 had attended 248 medical meetings. (For Jan. 1925–Mar. 1926 reports, see *MSM* C12:56–246; "Summary of Dr. Cooper's Lectures, 1928 [LCM 31:656].)

7. Ida Haar Timme (1875–1940), a suffragist and birth control advocate, was married to Walter Timme, a Columbia University professor and expert on nervous and mental diseases. Timme, a recent addition to the ABCL, was described by MS as a woman who "could harangue audiences in the strong, convincing, and forceful fashion of the early suffrage, soapbox days—nothing delicate or fragile." MS also appreciated her connections, noting, "More than once our bank account would have faded to a mere wraith had it not been for Ida Timme's money-raising talents." (*New York Herald Tribune,* Feb. 9, 1940; MS, *Autobiography,* 417.)

225. To Charles G. Norris[1]

[*New York, N.Y.*]
April 9, 1926.

Dear Mr. Norris:

It is very nice to know that you are contemplating writing a novel on the problem presented by Birth Control.[2]

It would give me great pleasure to meet you and, if possible, take you to our Clinical Research Department where perhaps you might interview some of the mothers who come seeking advice on Birth Control. In this way you will be able to get the facts from the mothers themselves. I would also be pleased to show you some of our records and the histories collected during the past two years.

At any rate, I just want to tell you that I am most interested in the possibility of such a book. I have always hoped that someone would write a second "Uncle Tom's Cabin" and perhaps arouse the country to the shameless waste of motherhood of the world.[3] Sincerely yours,

AMERICAN BIRTH CONTROL LEAGUE, Inc.
Margaret Sanger [*signed*]
President.

TLS NFP, CU-B (*MSM* C4:127). Letterhead of the ABCL.

1. Charles Gilman Norris (1881–1945) was a novelist whose books dealt with controversial subjects of the day, including modern marriage (*Brass*, 1921) and working women (*Bread*, 1923). He was the brother of the writer Frank Norris. (*New York Times*, July 26, 1945.)

2. The letter was not found. His planned book, published as *Seed, a Novel of Birth Control* (1930), detailed the misfortunes of a young novelist and his wife under the burden of too many children.

3. This was the popular 1852 antislavery novel by Harriet Beecher Stowe (1811–96).

226. From Rockwell Kent

This letter was written in response to a letter Sanger wrote after Kent tried to phone her. (MS to Kent, Apr. 9, 1926 [LCM 8:1319].)

Lake Lila, Ne-Ha-Sa-Ne Park, N.Y.
April 11th 1926.

Dear Margaret:—

One always feels a bit embarassed when after a neglet of the courtesies of friendship one needs to look up a friend again. It is no excuse for me that I am habitually careless about keeping up friendships; even, toward you, I am [*even*] less to be pardoned in that so often in hearing of you and of your work I have not obeyed the impulse of writing to you and cheering you on.

Just now, on the occasion of marrying again, I wanted desperately to see you to ask you how best we might avoid that reckless overpopulation of the world to which I am so prone. With five children of my own and another acquired by marriage it does seems that even the most ardent Rooseveltian might have a heart for me![1]

I have heard rumors of a new and better way to control the thing. Wont you tell me about it; or, if you have instructions in printed form, send them to me?[2] Then I can send to New York for what is needful.

There is a chance that we'll return to New York for a few days before going to Europe this spring I would much like to see you then—but its uncertain. We're sailing on the 29th for Ireland where I'm going to work hard at painting.

You have now won too great a recognition for your courage and ideals to ever let one mention them; but you are so fine a person that I do want to see you and keep on knowing you. Faithfully

Rockwell Kent.

ALS MSP, MN-SSC (*MSM* S3:460–61).

1. Kent, by this time a prominent illustrator and painter, had recently divorced his first wife, Katherine Whiting. His phone call to MS coincided with his second marriage, on April 5, 1926, to Frances Lee, a divorced mother of one child. Their marriage, which was childless, also ended in a divorce in 1940. (Traxell, *American Saga*, 151–52.)
2. MS's response was not found.

227. *Dream*

[*New York, N.Y.*]
Morning of May 1st 1926

Last night I dreamed I was in a house with very open sides & windows the house seemed to be placed on the side of a wooded hill. My little daughter Peggy with her golden hair about four or five years old was running through the woods [*above*] beside the house—she would fall but pick herself up again & go on.

She was laughing & not looking behind at me though I knew she was conscious that I wanted her.

I was in the house looking out— Then I saw her stumble into ~~a~~ ↑the↓ stone base of a statue I could not see the statue, but I could see the flat stonework of it. She got up & ran down the pathway of very nice green grass— Then suddenly there was moonlight on her & the whole pathway was flooded with light. It was such a lovely sight to see her playing, laughing in the moonlight woods but she was nevertheless still going away from me.

I awoke with the feeling of delight for the beauty of the scene & sadness that I could not hold her in my arms or at least get closer to her.

AD MSP, DLC (LCM 1:127–29). Written on reverse of an ABCL form letter.

228. To Hannah Mayer Stone[1]

[*Fishkill, N.Y.*]
June 11, 1926.

Dear Dr. Stone:

In case I cannot get over to see you, I want to make a few suggestions.

1. It would be best to consult with Mr. Slee concerning all orders hereafter.[2] He was very much upset over the order of the Ramses from Mr. Reese,[3] because of the fact that he has a thousand Mensingas coming in from Canada and he knows how rubber deteriorates.[4] He does not think that we should order any articles without consulting him as he has had charge of ordering these for me and will continue to do so for the next year.

2. I think that you have made sufficient test of L.A.J.[5] I think now it would be a good plan to change your series and to take Leucorrhol[6] alone without the pessary. A doctor in Fishkill is having splendid results from this without the pessary and finds it does not work so satisfactorily with other preparations. I know of two failures of LAJ without the pessary while there are numerous successes with Leucorrhol without the pessary. I know that Dr. Cooper believes that LAJ is just as good as Leucorrhol, but experience in a small way has not proven this to be true and I believe that it is worth while trying out and get actual facts instead of just an opinion.[7]

I wish you could begin at once and start on about a hundred cases that are good risks. I would not take everyone as they come in but pick your cases and let us get a hundred cases of Leucorrhol alone. I would try other cases with Leucorrhol and the pessary and let us give Leucorrhol as good a test as we have given LAJ.

I do not know how long you have been trying LAJ but I think we should give each of the other chemicals a fair test, too. There is some criticism of our advertising LAJ as if we had some interest in its manufacture. If we can show an equal interest in other preparations we will avoid this criticism. It is a thing that we must constantly watch out, because it is easy for any of us to become partial. Dr. Bocker, for instance, purchased ten times more Mirekahl that any other preparation. It was unfortunate for our research reports.[8]

3. I would like to have all of the sheets to give to Dr. Pearl when he comes

up on the 18th.[9] I want to get out a report of your last year's work. I had hoped that you would give me a summary so that I could ask for money for next year, but I am unable to secure any support until I give a report of our results.[10]

Dr. Pearl will be here on the 18th and I would like all of the sheets of your 1600 cases at that time so he can at least look over the material and give us the benefit of his experience.[11] This will simplify matters considerably. I know you have not had much time to get out a report, but I think the Medical Committee should sign it and one of them—like Pearl or East[12] should look over the material first before a report is issued. Please let Anna[13] know at your earlier convenience if this is possible. I know that you have been working on these sheets and I hope that you will be through with it by the 18th.

I spoke with Dr. Hediger yesterday and she understands that the organization does not give vacations to one connected with us so short a time. She understands that perfectly and will make arrangements to release you.[14]

I would also like a copy of her report each month and I think if you send hers together with your own to me each month I will continue sending them to the members of the Committee.[15] I think it is unfortunate that we have not reported to the Committee last year and the best way I can do is to relieve you of this by having you make out your monthly report to me and letting me take it up with each member regularly.

Dr. Vaughan said he was down to the clinic Thursday afternoon but you were gone. He promised to come in this morning and will through the summer give a morning each week.[16]

4. All complaints concerning material should be made direct to Mr. Slee by the Clinical Director.

5. All goods coming into the Clinic should be examined immediately and complaints made within twenty-four hours directly to Mr. Slee. If possible to order at least one week in advance, which would make Mr. Slee's work less difficult.

I do not anticipate coming into town for sometime, but I will be glad to come in for a clinical meeting if you have anything that is important for me to come over.

I must have a report each month or else I will not be able to get money to support the work. You [*do not*] know how difficult it is to get money unless we give continued proof of what we are doing to hold the interest of those who might be asked to support us.

Dr. Mudd was very complimentary about your address.[17] I was sorry he could not come to see you yesterday but he is taking a dozen of your report to circulate among the physicians in Pennsylvania.

Please let me know about your new assistant. Is she satisfactory? If not, do not hesitate to let me know and do not keep people in our employ over a week or two at least if you do not feel that they are going to worth while. Sincerely yours,

---

TLcy MSP, MN-SSC (*MSM* S3:511–13).

1. Hannah Mayer Stone (1893–1941) was a gynecologist connected with New York City's Lying-In Hospital and St. Mark's Hospital before becoming the CRB's medical director in 1925. Under Stone's direction, the CRB quickly gathered extensive and detailed case records requested by MS in her effort to prove that contraceptives were safe and effective. Stone rapidly gained the regard and confidence of MS, who wrote, "Her gaze was clear and straight, her hair was black, her mouth gentle and sweet. She had a sympathetic response to mothers in distress, and a broad attitude towards life's many problems." (*NatCAB;* MS to Leon Cole, July 1, 1925 [*MSM* C3:570]; MS, *Autobiography,* 360 [quote].)

2. Slee's largely self-defined clinic duties included securing contraceptive supplies. (Slee's Statement to the ABCL, Nov. 25, 1925 [LCM 11:584].)

3. This was probably H. W. Reese of Continental Laboratories. The Ramses pessary, an American modification of the Mensinga, was the diaphragm most often used at the CRB. (Dorothy Bocker to MS, Sept. 10, 1924 [LCM 31:419]; Cooper, *Technique of Contraception,* 133.)

4. This was a reference to Slee's diaphragm smuggling operation.

5. The CRB had been testing the effectiveness of various contraceptive jellies on its patients since 1924. Lactic acid jelly (LAJ) was a spermicide made from a combination of lactic and boric acid. Naturally occurring in the vagina, lactic acid acts as an acidic cleanser, but during coitus it dissipates, allowing sperm to survive. By artificially replacing the lactic acid, LAJ was thought to be more natural and less irritating. It could be used either alone (dispensed through a tube) or in combination with a diaphragm. (Norman Haire, *The Comparative Value of Current Contraceptive Methods* [London, 1928], 6; Cooper, *Technique of Contraception,* 174–76, 185–86.)

6. See MS to Leon Cole, Nov. 11, 1924, note 5, herein.

7. In his *Technique of Contraception,* Cooper claimed that LAJ was generally superior to chinosol-based jellies, such as Leucorrhol, which he claimed had resulted in several cases of vaginitis. Hannah Stone described 109 cases where LAJ was used alone, reporting 4 failures (3.6 percent). After testing the jellies without diaphragms, CRB research studies supported MS's suspicions; it found chinosol-based jellies 98 percent effective in contrast to LAJ at 87 percent. (Cooper, *Technique of Contraception,* 90–91, 187; Hannah Stone, "Therapeutic Contraception," *Medical Journal and Record* 127 [Mar. 28, 1928]: 13–14.)

8. Bocker did use more Mirekahl (Mir-E-Kahl), another chinosol-based contraceptive jelly, than other chemical contraceptives, though other types were also used. ("Brief Summary of Work Done in Birth Control Clinical Research for 1924" [LCM 31:434].)

9. Raymond Pearl requested access to Bocker's patient survey. He was specifically interested in the sexual aspect of birth control and planned to analyze the records "by modern biometric technique." Delighted that Pearl was interested, MS had case reports sent to him each month. Pearl was coming to New York City for a program committee

meeting for the World Population Conference. (Pearl to MS, Nov. 13, 1924, and MS to Pearl, Nov. 18, 1924 [*MSM* C3:230 and 244]; for Bocker's summary of 1,000 patients' responses to the "coitus" portion of the case card, see LCM 31:417.)

10. Stone's report discussed the procedures at the clinic and provided a breakdown by religion, social, and economic status for the 1,655 new cases seen. (Hannah Stone, "Report of the Clinical Research Department," 1925 [*MSM* S65:161].)

11. While none of the CRB patient files survives, summaries of the case files were published in studies by Marie Kopp, *Birth Control in Practice* (New York, 1934), and Regine K. Stix and Frank Notestein, *Controlled Fertility* (Baltimore, 1940), and in more abbreviated form in Cooper's *Technique of Contraception*, 161–204, and Hannah Stone's *Contraceptive Methods: A Clinical Survey* (New York, 1925).

12. She was referring to Edward Murray East.

13. She was referring to Anna Lifshiz.

14. Ella Maria Hediger (Gangwish) (1900–1983), a surgeon and anesthesiologist, supervised the short-lived Brooklyn office of the CRB and was a staff doctor at its main clinic (1926–28). MS was referring to Stone's letter on covering patients during staff vacations. (*Who's Who of American Women;* Stone to MS, May 20, 1926 [*MSM* S3:489].)

15. Monthly CRB reports included income raised from ABCL memberships, literature sales, and clinic fees, as well as the number of new and returning patients, the number treated free of charge, and the contraceptive materials dispensed. Summaries of these reports were sent to members of the CRB advisory council. (See, for example, the monthly report for June 1926 [LCM 34:586].)

16. John C. Vaughan joined the CRB's medical advisory board in 1925.

17. Stuart Mudd (1893–1975) was a physician interested in eugenics and overpopulation and a microbiologist at the University of Pennsylvania's Henry Phipps Institute. He met MS and Stone while he was an associate at the Rockefeller Institute in New York City. Mudd helped organize the first birth control clinic in Philadelphia in 1927 and became an ABCL board member the same year. No information was found on Stone's speech. (*NatCAB;* Reed, *Birth Control Movement and American Society,* 231–34.)

229. Excerpt from "Racial Betterment"

No complete version of the following radio address Sanger gave to the Vassar College Institute of Euthenics has been located.[1] *Several newspapers did include excerpts of the speech, and this version has been taken from the most complete newspaper report. We have included additional text reported in other newspapers in the endnotes.*

[*Poughkeepsie, N.Y.*]
[*August 5, 1926*]

There are two problems now confronting civilization.[2] The pressure of population on the food supply of the world, and the reconciliation of humanitarian practices with race betterment.

I do not intend to treat of the former problem today as it is one which does not concern this present generation as pertinently as it concerns the people of other countries with less arable territory more thickly populated. But the question of race betterment is one of immediate concern, and I am glad to say that the United States Government has already taken certain steps to control the quality of our population through its drastic immigration laws, whereby our gates are closed to those whom she considers undesirables.

There is a quota restriction where only so many people from each country are allowed to enter our shores each month. It is the [*latest*] method adopted by our Government to solve the population problem. Most people are convinced that this policy is right, and agree that we should slow down on the number of immigrants coming here as well as to taking a stand on the kind of people they should be.[3]

But while we close our gates to the so called "undesirables" from other countries, we make no attempt to discourage or cut down on the rapid multiplication of the unfit and undesirable at home.

In fact through our archaic and inhuman laws against birth control information the breeding of defectives, idiots, insane and feeble-minded becomes a necessity.

These types are being multiplied with the breakneck rapidity and increasing far out of proportion to the normal and intelligent classes.[4] In 1923 over nine billions of dollars were spent[5] on State and Federal charities for the care and maintenance and perpetuation of these undesirables.[6] Year by year their numbers are mounting. Year by year their cost is increasing. Huge sums, yes vast fortunes are expended on these, while the normal parents and their children are compelled to shift for themselves and compete with each other for their existence.

The American public is taxed, heavily taxed, to maintain an increasing race of morons, which threatens the very foundations of our civilization.

Over one quarter of the total income of the state of New York is spent on the maintenance of asylums, prisons, and other institutions for the care of the defective and diseased.[7] It must not be assumed that all the undesirable breeders are segregated in institutions. There is only a very small proportion of the feebleminded given over to institutions, the vast majority are living their lives among us, propagating their kind and providing abundant opportunity for the continuation of charities and various pauperizing institutions for generations to come.

When we view the political situation, and realize that a moron's vote is as good as an intelligent, educated, [*thinking*] citizen, we well pause and ask ourselves: "Is America really safe for Democracy?"[8]

In England a few weeks ago the House of Lords passed a resolution[9] sanctioning the giving of contraceptive instruction in all the maternity centers supported by the government.[10]

It now remains for the United States Government to set a sensible example to the world by offering a bonus or a yearly pension to all obviously unfit parents who become sterilized by harmless and scientific means would be unable to pass on their unhappy condition to posterity. It would compel them to refrain from further child bearing, thereby decreasing the numbers of feebleminded, and lessening enormously the burdens of the fit.

Such a bonus would be a wise and profitable investment for the Nation. It would be the salvation of American civilization. It would enable thousands of parents to get a firm footing on the path of life and enable them to give some care to those children they have already borne.

It would mean facing our debts today, here and now, instead of passing them on and piling them up for future generations to pay.[11]

Our statistics tell us that the birth rate of the college men and women is lower than it should be. This applies to all the professional classes, doctors, clergymen, lawyers and skilled workers.[12] There are some who deplore this condition and would remedy it by abusive epithets hurled at this conscientious group of decent and responsible citizens, who would rather have only the number of children they can decently rear, than to enter a cradle competition with the less responsible.

There is only one reply to a request for a higher birth rate among the intelligent, and that is to ask the government to FIRST take off the burdens of the insane and feebleminded from your backs. Sterilization for these is the remedy.[13]

Poughkeepsie Evening Star, Aug. 5, 1926. For a shorter, edited version, see "The Function of Sterilization," *BCR* (Oct. 1926), 299 (*MSM* C16:282).

1. Euthenics, defined in the *Oxford English Dictionary* as the "science and art of improving the well-being of man by the betterment of the conditions of life," was developed by the chemist Ellen Richards (1842–1911), author of books on applying science to the problems of daily life. Vassar's first annual Institute of Euthenics featured lectures by public health specialists and experts in "scientific housekeeping." (*Vassar College Bulletin, Institute of Euthenics* 15, no. 4 [1926].)

2. According to the *Poughkeepsie Eagle News,* August 5, 1926, MS discussed the ABCL at this point, summarizing its aims of trying to "make a new world, a conscious civilization, with women free, and with children free, conceived in love and given a heritage of a sound body and a sound mind."

3. Congress passed a series of restrictive immigration bills in the 1920s, culminating with the 1924 Reed-Johnson National Origins Act, which established an annual quota for new immigrants. With separate quotas for each nation, this act severely limited immigration from southern and eastern Europe and barred all immigration from Asia.

4. In the *Eagle News* report, MS is quoted as saying that the 20 million Americans classed as intelligent had a birthrate of 32 per thousand, compared with the 116 per thousand of the 85 million classed as "mediocre to imbecile." She noted, "The group with the lowest birth rate has the lowest maternal mortality, the lowest infant mortality; it

brings children to full maturity, and they go to high school and its universities. In the other group there is misery, ignorance, poverty, and the perpetuation of their numbers, creating every social problem confronting us today,—the slums, overcrowding, high mortality. We are doing the worst thing about it. We deplore it, and we hope legislation might do away with it. We are moved by generosity, humanitarian feelings; we try to alleviate and ameliorate conditions."

5. MS probably meant 900 million. According to one report, in 1925–26, $936 million in state and federal funds (approximately 14 percent of total spending) was expended on charitable relief for the poor and infirm, workmen's compensation, government employees and mothers pensions, as well as sanitation and health provisions. Another $725 million was spent on police, fire, and war departments as well as correctional and penal institutions. (National Industrial Conference Board, *Cost of Government in the United States, 1925–1926* [New York, 1927], 19, 100.)

6. In the *Eagle News* report, the sentence read, "In 1923, 9 billion dollars were spent for the four D's—disease, defect, delinquency, and dependency. I have no fault to find with charities, but they are unjustly keeping alive undesirable groups; it is unjust both to society today, and to the future of the race." MS also discussed the reduction of infant deaths by 200,000 in the United States but pointed out that the parents of these children "are in utter ignorance as to how to prevent the coming of 200,000 children into poverty next year. There are milk stations and nurses, but how to prevent conception, that's the immediate thing."

7. In 1919, New York State estimated that it spent 25 percent of the state's annual appropriation on maintaining hospitals for the mentally ill and delinquents, charitable institutions, and prisons. By 1927, that figure had dropped to 15 percent. (David M. Schneider and Albert Deutsch, *The History of Public Welfare in New York* [Chicago, 1941], 270–71; "The Direct Cost of the Socially Inadequate to New York State," *Eugenical News* 12 [Sept. 1927]: 121–22.)

8. MS was paraphrasing Woodrow Wilson's April 2, 1917, war message that "the world must be made safe for democracy."

9. This was a reference to the April 28, 1926, House of Lords decision that overturned the Ministry of Health's 1924 prohibition on allowing government-funded maternity and infant welfare centers to provide birth control. (Leathard, *Fight for Family Planning,* 29–35.)

10. In the *Eagle News* version, MS apparently added that though Italy, Japan, and England also faced population problems, "I believe that the United States has a greater problem because of its mixed race, because it has not yet a unity of purpose."

11. In the *Eagle News* version, she added, "We could take a breath and go forward, the light and torch of civilization."

12. A growing number of studies documented the declining size of families in Western nations in the late nineteenth century and early twentieth, especially among the educated classes. This led to predictions of the decline of civilization. (See John C. Phillips, "A Study of the Birth Rate in Harvard and Yale Graduates" and "Further Studies of the Harvard Birth-Rate—Classes 1891–1900," *Harvard Graduates Magazine,* Sept. 1916, 25–34, and Mar. 1926, 385–94; and Raymond Pearl, "Differential Fertility," *Quarterly Review of Biology* 2 [Mar. 1927]: 102–18, which provides a bibliography of relevant studies.)

13. In the *Eagle News* version, MS enumerated the three ways of controlling births: continence, sterilization, and chemical and mechanical devices. She pointed out that great strides had been made in sterilization procedures: "It is no longer the abhorrent thing it once was. The operation for sterilization is going to play an important part in the future." Chemical and mechanical devices, she said, should be controlled by doctors, adding, "We are trying to work to have the laws changed so that physicians may give instruction. The giving of such knowledge is denied to physicians and social agencies. But in farm, stock breeding, and even manufacturing of pins such knowledge is freely given." She also recommended that some women should not have children at all, that families be limited to one child that could be taken care of, that parents should not have another child if the first is "subnormal"; that there should be two or three years between children; that motherhood be delayed until after women reach age twenty-three; and that young couples take at least two years after marriage before having children. (See MS, "When Should a Woman Avoid Having Children?" Nov. 1918, herein.)

230. From Eleanor Dwight Jones

In June 1926, Jones agreed to head the ABCL executive committee, covering Sanger's prolonged absence through the spring of 1928 while she organized the World Population Conference in Europe. Just two months later, Sanger was questioning Jones's proposed fund-raising efforts, writing, "I am much distressed at . . . your reference to the financial status of the League and your inability to take financial responsibility. . . . I had understood that you would not be able to give financial assistance to the organization, but I had supposed that as chairman of the Executive Committee you would take the same responsibility, financial and otherwise, that I had taken. In fact, I had felt that you were taking my place as head of the organization. . . ." In her criticism, Sanger did not hide her aversion to Jones's management style and personality and, later, her anger over Jones's ability to win over members of the board. (MS to Jones, Aug. 27, 1926 [LCM 24:54].)

Lakeville, Connecticut.
September 3, 1926.

Dear Mrs. Sanger,

Thank you for your letter of August 27th, which arrived while I was away, or I should have answered it sooner. I am so very sorry to hear of your loss,[1] and send you much sympathy.

I will try to get advice from the librarian of some college as to the best method of soliciting orders for the Proceedings.[2] Possibly I might get permission from Professor Giddings to use his name in recommending them to professors of economics and of sociology whom he knows.[3]

At the September 10th meeting[4] I will find out whether our directors can interest any members of the Foundation boards in our work, and can get appointments for you to tell them about it. I will ask Mrs. Kennedy[5] to bring lists of the Boards, so that we can go over the names one by one.

I shall of course be glad to do everything in my power towards getting the

League financed, but I cannot raise anywhere near as much money as you can. As you have led the birth-control movement from the beginning, you are acquainted with almost everyone interested in the movement, and they are acquainted with you; you know how best ~~how~~ to appeal to each one of them, and they will respond to a personal appeal from you as they will not to one from a person unknown to them, as I am. Furthermore, I cannot give nearly as much time to League work as you, because my daughters and housekeeping for a family of five on a moderate income take a great deal of my time.[6]

Knowing that I could not raise nearly enough money to support the League as it is now organized, I said when you asked me to accept the chairmanship of the Executive Committee that I could do so only on the understanding that I take no financial responsibility, by which I meant, responsibility for raising the money to support the League. Then at the meeting of the Executive Committee at Mrs. Rublee's[7] the first week in June we understood you to say that you had arranged matters so that the regular expenses of the League were provided for during the next year, and that we should not have to raise any money unless we undertook some special, extra work.

I could not take any responsibility for getting the League financed unless I had authority to reorganize it, cutting the regular expenses (salaries, rent, telephone, etc.) to the amount of the annual dues and the contributions pledged annually in advance by our directors and other persons and by organizations such as the Foundations, increasing these expenses only as we increased the income from such sources; and making special appeals for special undertakings. However, as you will be able to take charge of the League again so soon and to re-assume responsibility for financing it, such a reorganization would be neither practicable nor desirable unless you approved of it.

What, then, shall be done? As you say, we certainly can not go on letting the organization pile up debts as at present, but the directors cannot decide such a fundamental matter without you. Could you possibly attend the meeting September 10th? And if so, could you come at 12.30, so that you and Mrs. Delafield[8] and I may have a little talk before the meeting? If you cannot come to the meeting, will you write me a letter which I may read to the committee?[9] With kindest regards to both you and Mr. Slee, I am very sincerely yours,

Eleanor Dwight Jones [*signed*]

TLS MSP, DLC (LCM 24:58B).

1. MS's father, Michael Higgins, had died of a cerebral hemorrhage on August 7, 1926. She left for Truro, Massachusetts, that day, traveling to Corning on August 8 to attend his funeral. (MS Diary [LCM 2:601].)

2. This was the four-volume *Proceedings of the Sixth International Neo-Malthusian and Birth Control Conference* (ABCL, 1925–26), edited by MS.

3. Franklin Henry Giddings (1855–1931) was a Columbia University sociologist, whose

work focused on social evolution and human nature. A proponent of population control and eugenics, he was an ABCL national council member and participated in the Sixth International Neo-Malthusian and Birth Control Conference. (*ANB*)

4. Fearing the ABCL was running a deficit, the board of directors met on September 10, 1926. When a quorum could not be raised (MS and several others did not attend), Jones called an executive committee meeting for September 22, 1926.

5. With the cessation of the congressional committee's work in May 1926, Kennedy had been assigned to organize James Cooper's national lecture tour and encourage local birth control leagues. (Kennedy-MS correspondence, Mar. 1926 [LCM 27:619–25]; James Cooper correspondence, 1926 [ABCLR].)

6. Jones had two daughters, aged seventeen and twenty; the fifth family member was not identified. (Durward Howes, ed., *American Women, 1935–1940* [Detroit, 1981].)

7. Minutes of the June 1926 meeting were not found.

8. Charlotte Wyeth Delafield (1865–1947), the wife of the prominent New York City lawyer Lewis L. Delafield, had met MS during the Brownsville Clinic trial. She served on the Committee of 100, the First American Birth Control Conference Committee, and the ABCL national council and was an ABCL vice-president (1922–39). Eleanor Jones had appointed her chair of the ABCL finance committee. (*New York Times*, Apr. 25, 1947; see also MS, *Autobiography*, 230.)

9. MS wrote a letter to Jones on September 9, which Jones read at the September 22 executive committee meeting (which MS did not attend). In the letter, MS criticized Jones's inability to keep the league fiscally sound: "What we want and must have is enthusiasm to get money to meet necessary expenses. We must have someone who can do that or shut up shop." In response, Jones offered to resign, but the executive committee refused to accept. Though MS did not oppose Jones's offer to step down, no other board member expressed an interest in taking Jones's place. Many even sided with her, prompting MS to write Rublee two days later: "You seemed to be so completely won over to the side of Mrs Jones, that I was sick all night." The friction between Jones and MS increased over the next few weeks, with Jones accusing MS of harboring personal resentment toward her and MS dismissing such charges as unprofessional: "I keep wondering why personalities creep in to impersonal matters." By November, with her sights set on the World Population Conference, MS reluctantly decided to give Jones and the board "the freehand desired for the year & see results." (MS to Jones, Sept. 9, 1926, and Delafield to MS, Sept. 22, 1926 [LCM 24:55B, 22:354–56]; MS to Rublee, Sept. 24 and Nov. 19, 1926 [*MSM* C4:210 and 261].)

231. To J. Noah Slee

*In preparation for the World Population Conference, Sanger went to London on December 4, 1926, and made several trips to Paris and Geneva to meet with conference participants. Slee followed Sanger to Europe in December, renting Villa Bachlyk in Cap d'Ail on the French Riviera, where he and Sanger entertained Hugh de Selincourt and other guests. Sanger retreated to the villa several times in the winter and spring of 1927. She returned to London at the end of January. (1926–27 Calendar [LCM 2:609–46]; MS to Slee, Dec. 15, 1926 [*MSM *S3:674]; MS to Raymond Pearl, Jan. 30, 1927 [*MSM *C4:290].)*

[*London, England*]
Tuesday [*February 1, 1927*]

Treasure of my Heart—Noah.

Your cable came saying you will leave Palma Thursday arriving at the Villa Saturday.[1]

I have been deeply depressed today & yesterday over the affairs here.[2] I know that were I free to work & keep on the job I could put over a conference that would astound the world— But—Here I am, interests divided & diverted and I can not know what to do.

The movement now needs one dominating force to drive it to Success— The interest is alive—the time is ripe but I shall need to give time to it if it is to succeed. No one else can do it, so it seems— It will Crown my past efforts & repay my sacrifices to see this Conference a Success. Will you help me? Not by money darling one, but by seeing this thing Eye to Eye with me & giving me the time I need to work it up properly. I know how hard it is for you to let me be away from you & I shall try to arrange it so there shall be few seperations, but there must be some and unless you say you can help me, I will not go on—[3]

You have done so much to help me make it the success it has become, that I believe you will help me again—for ever. I can never believe that you have come into my life to hold me back, you who are so vigorous & glorious in your love & splendid in your ideals & generosity! You have helped others to attain their lifes work. You have given support & inspiration to others you love less—and I believe with all my heart with all my faith that you will help me to victory & success.

A very splendid interest is alive here—if I can organize it properly & direct it all will be well.

Dearest love—I will let you know in a day or two what my plans are.

I had tea with Haldane & his wife[4]—the man K. R.[5] admires so much.

Love—darling always my heart is sad, but yours

Margy

ALS MSP, MN-SSC (*MSM* S3:707–12). Letterhead of the Stafford Hotel.

1. The telegram was not found. Slee had toured Palma and the Riviera with Anna Higgins and was en route to Barcelona. (1926–27 Calendar [LCM 2:609–46]; MS to Slee, Feb. 2, 1927 [*MSM* S3:713].)

2. This was a reference to the British biologist, eugenicist, and demographer Sir Alexander Carr-Saunders, who in December 1926 had agreed to serve as honorary secretary of the World Population Conference but suddenly backed out. (Carr-Saunders to MS, Jan. 19 and 26, 1927 [LCM 122:652b and 651]; MS to Raymond Pearl, Jan. 30, 1927 [*MSM* C4:290].)

3. Slee most likely assumed MS was going to spend more time at their Cap d'Ail villa before taking extended trips to London and Paris for organizational work.

4. John Burden Sanderson Haldane (1892–1964) was a Cambridge University geneticist and biochemist who revived Darwinian theories of natural selection by linking them to Mendelian genetics. He authored several controversial popular science books and regular articles for the *Daily Worker* and was on the general council of the World Population Conference. Charlotte Franken Burghes (1894–1969), a journalist and writer, divorced her husband and married Haldane in 1926 after their adulterous affair became public. (*DNB;* see also Ellis to MS, Feb. 1, 1927 [LCM 4:1190].)

5. This was Slee's friend and pastor the Reverend Karl Reiland (1871–1964). (*New York Times,* Sept. 13, 1964.)

232. From Grant Sanger[1]

Princeton, New Jersey
Feb 24, 1927.

Dear Mother,

After writing you three letters to your one, I resolved I'd write when you wrote.[2] And for the 89nth & last time I had a nice time in Clarksburg.[3] I swear I don't know where all my mail goes to.

I take it youre not intending to be back until May at least. Well anyway, if you don't I will pass the vacation somewhere outside New York. Its all according to the amount of money your going to allow. Let this be an understanding. Fifty dollars a week won't be enough. Remember I'm not visiting anybody, and I don't care to but the money you gave for Xmas was generous, it wouldn't have been enough if we hadn't gone to Clarksburg. So at least be broadminded when you figure out the expense money, and remember its awfully hard to arrange anything with three thousand miles of water between us, isn't it. I don't think I'd go to Bermuda, it takes too long, and I don't like ocean trips if it's a rough one. As you know, I always get seasick if anybody does. I think I'll go to some place like White Sulfur Springs,[4] Thats as good a place as I know of.

I was I was planning on seeing you Easter about the clothes allowance, well judge for yourself. I'd like to get a spring suit and a few other things like some shirts and a few ties. Can I go to Lord & Taylor's[5] and get the shirts & ties? And the suit if you agree and are feeling flush, why include that in the money that is to come if you're not ↑to be↓ in the country at Easter time. As I suspected you wouldnt. Probably Stu[6] & I will go together, althou I don't know as yet.

Hereafter, I wouldn't if I were you sign my letters to my sons as "Margaret Sanger Slee", its rather forgetful & exceedingly bad taste.[7] Give my best to Pater & Virginia.[8]

"Please do write & tell me what you did in Clarksburg" "Did they like the presents" etc. Thats a bit of the end of every letter I've received from you in the past three months. Loads of love,

Grant.

ALS MSP, MN-SSC (*MSM* S3:761–62). Letterhead of the Hun School of Princeton.

1. Grant, age eighteen, had graduated from the Westminster School in June 1926 and had entered the Hun preparatory school of Princeton in September.
2. The letters were not found.
3. Grant spent the Christmas holidays with his aunt and uncle, Robert and Virginia Higgins, in Clarksburg, West Virginia. (Grant Sanger to MS, Jan. 28, 1927 [*MSM* S3:693].)
4. This was a resort in the Allegheny Mountains of West Virginia.
5. Lord and Taylor's was a luxury clothing store in New York City.
6. Stuart was then a junior at Yale.
7. The letter signed this way was not found.
8. This was a reference to Slee and to Karl Reiland's daughter, Virginia Field Reiland (Cobb Watson) (1903–91), a Vassar student who stayed with them at Villa Bachlyk over the Christmas holidays. (Vassar College Alumnae Association Records; MS to Slee, Dec. 16, 1926, and Slee to MS, Sept. 22, 1927 [*MSM* S3:677 and 889].)

233. To J. Noah Slee[1]

[*London, England*]
Wednesday 9 PM. [*March 30, 1927*]

Darling Noah:

Just came in from the dinner & meeting where Lord Dawson was Chairman[2] I was so nervous for two days that I lost two pounds. I simply could not eat.

Then I am heart sick over the fact that Mary Dennett's book is out & Marie Stopes is boosting it here to hurt me.

The book calls me all kinds of names in a cleaver way. Quoting from things I said in the early days & things I did not say etc etc. It is supposed to be a bomb shell to the B.C. Movement.[3]

The poor sick woman has failed in her work[4] & in order to explain her failure, she throws the blame on me & my work & early views. Most of them very good but <u>radical</u>.

Anyway I am only anxious that those dear good friends who have loved me like Juliet & Mrs Delafield will be troubled & hurt knowing the things she says if believed will hurt the cause.[5]

They also know I will never bend to reply to her accusations or attacks.

Well this troubled me today but we had a good meeting at Col Leighs home a large drawing room holding two hundred people.[6]

Your cable came at 12 PM. last night[7] they awakened me to deliver it. I was glad to have it & to know you are enjoying the trip & missing me a little. I will not cable to you until I leave for Paris—Monday.[8] I can't get away much before that day. A tea for me tomorrow afternoon[9] & work each day keeps me busy until night.

I had dinner with Anne Smith. She was at the meeting today with her sister. Also the old flame[10] was there & took me to dinner & was very kind.

My heart is lonely for you dear. You are the only love of my heart. For ever. Devotedly

Margaret

ALS MSP, MN-SSC (*MSM* S3:777–81). Letterhead of the Stafford.

1. Slee, probably in Nice, closed up Villa Bachlyk in early April. (Slee to MS, Mar. 27, 1927 [*MSM* S3:784].)

2. This was the March 30 meeting of the Society for the Provision of Birth Control Clinics, at which both MS and Harold Cox spoke. The host, Lord Bertrand Edward Dawson of Penn (1864–1945), a physician to the British royal family, held many other government and hospital appointments. Dawson created controversy in 1921 when he lectured on sexual relationships and birth control to an Anglican church congress. (*London Times,* Mar. 8, 1945; "News Notes," *BCR,* May 1927, 153.)

3. Dennett's 1926 *Birth Control Laws: Shall We Keep Them, Abolish Them, or Change Them?* blamed MS and her radical strategies for congressional reluctance to pass birth control legislation and criticized MS's doctors-only bill as a betrayal of her earlier efforts to get contraceptives to as many women as possible. Dennett also called MS a hypocrite, claiming the ABCL regularly sent birth control information through the mail, noting, "If the very people who advocate 'doctor's only' information are not willing to live up to it, who else could be expected to do so?" Stopes, who advertised Dennett's book in her *Birth Control News,* wrote Dennett that she attended the March 30 meeting and, after hearing MS's discussion of the American legal situation, rose up, waved Dennett's book, and informed the audience of its excellence. "You can imagine Mrs. Sanger's sour face," Stopes gleefully reported. (Dennett, *Birth Control Laws,* 167–73, 201 [first quote], 208; Stopes to Dennett, Apr. 4, 1927 [second quote] [*MWDPM* 14:537].)

4. Dennett and VPL president Myra Gallert were loathe to officially disband the organization and leave legislative work to the ABCL, but by 1925 the VPL's financial problems rendered it largely inactive. (Gallert to Dennett, Feb. 14, 1928 [*MWDPM* 13:187].)

5. Rublee and Charlotte Delafield were among those ABCL board members who remained loyal to MS.

6. Lieutenant-Colonel John Cecil Gerard Leigh (1889–1965) was a member of the London County Council. (*WWW England*)

7. The telegram was not found.

8. MS flew to Paris to join Slee on April 4 and stayed until April 16, taking an excursion to Versailles, indulging herself at the Elizabeth Arden Salon, and meeting with the demographer Warren Simpson Thompson, cofounder in 1922 of the Scripps Foundation for Research in Population Problems. (1927 Calendar [LCM 2:643].)

9. MS had tea with Harold Cox on March 31. (1927 Calendar [LCM 2:645].)
10. This was probably J. O. P. Bland.

234. *To Robert Latou Dickinson*

Additional efforts by Dickinson and the Maternity Research Council to secure a dispensary license for the CRB failed. Without the license, the Maternity Research Council would not move forward with the merger.

[*New York, N.Y.*]
June 4, 1927.

Dear Dr. Dickinson:

Your kind letter of May 27th was awaiting me upon my return to the office from a six-months' trip abroad.[1]

I hope by this time the Committee on Maternal Health has received an invitation from the Advisory Council to send a delegate to the World Population Conference.[2]

Through the advice of Lord Dawson, we were urged not to have a medical session, but to invite physicians from all countries to come and attend the biological, sociological and economic sessions, and to discuss the medical aspect later, if possible.[3] I hope that your Committee might find it possible to send you to represent them. Already there is tremendous interest in the various countries in this question. The Economic Conference which I have just attended in Geneva failed to discuss the population question and it caused a great deal of comment and much criticism.[4]

Now as to your letter, I should be very glad to have the opportunity to talk with you, and if you will call up my secretary and let her know if it will be possible to see you next Tuesday or Wednesday when I am in town, she will try to arrange a time that will be convenient to us both.

I am not inclined to accept the recommendations of the State Board of Charities that the Clinic be affiliated with any hospital at the present time. I hope the time will come when all hospitals will include contraceptive instruction in their regular duties, but in the meantime I feel strongly that a separate clinic, such as we have, is necessary and is useful for those physicians who are not gynecologists and yet desire contraceptive instruction given to their patients.[5]

The Clinic such as we have, standing aloof from the hospitals, takes in patients from all over the city, in fact, from all over the state. Our work this year is proving [*this*]. We have had our Clinic open on full time, and our [*calendar*] is well filled a week and ten days in advance, which shows its popularity and its need.

I think there is nothing at present to prevent any of the hospitals from organizing and establishing such a clinic, while it is quite a good precedent that a clinic as ours should serve as a public utility to the people of the city of New York. I should, however, be pleased to see you and to talk over the progress of the work with you.

Congratulations on what you are doing with the [*American*] Medical Association as well as the Gynecological Society.[6] The cause moves forward steadily and surely. Very sincerely yours,
Dictated but not read

TLcy MSP, DLC (LCM 32:110–11). Carbon smears.

1. In his May 27 letter, Dickinson had informed MS that, on the advice of the State Board of Charities, he had made preliminary arrangements to affiliate the CRB with a New York City hospital but that he would not take additional steps until he had heard from her. MS had gotten back to New York City on May 24. (Dickinson to MS, May 27, 1927 [LCM 32:1088].)

2. Dickinson neither attended nor participated; the invitation was not found.

3. MS and Edith How-Martyn put together a World Population Conference advisory committee of U.S. and European biologists, geneticists, sociologists, and economists. The Europeans suggested that to keep the conference "solely scientific," birth control should not be discussed. (MS, *Autobiography*, 382; MS, *Proceedings of the World Population Conference;* "Notes of Conference between C. C. Little, Margaret Sanger & C. F. Chance," June 9, 1926 [quote] [*MSM* C14:416]; see also Juliet Rublee, "World Population Conference Report," Mar. 13, 1927 [*MSM* C14:422].)

4. The World Economic Conference in Geneva (May 4–23, 1927) brought together delegates from thirty-seven countries to discuss economic problems and conditions resulting from the war, economic policies, taxation, and trade and labor issues. A *New York Times* review by Alfred Pearce Dennis charged that "highly controversial subjects were discretely ignored," and he argued that future conferences ought to feature a "general leavening of the huge world population lump." (*New York Times,* June 5, 1927.)

5. Dickinson's notes from a subsequent meeting with MS indicate that she thought the idea "of continuing a separate clinic, but having it under the auspices of a regular hospital an excellent one." (MRC Report, June 30, 1927 [*MSM* C13:798].)

6. Dickinson described efforts at the American Medical Association (AMA) and the American Gynecological Society (AGS) to pass resolutions supporting the removal of restrictions on birth control information in standard medical books and journals. The AMA's obstetric section passed the resolution in 1924, but it had not yet reached a general vote, and Dickinson hoped it would be ratified at the 1927 annual meeting. He let the AGS proposal lapse after the society passed a broader resolution calling for the removal of restrictions on birth control in the postal laws. (Dickinson to MS, May 27, 1927 [LCM 32:108B].)

235. To Hugh de Selincourt

Sanger returned to Europe on July 8 to finish final preparations for the World Population Conference, held August 31–September 2. Her role in organizing the conference was hailed enthusiastically in the closing addresses, and she declared it a success despite the fact that she yielded to pressure from delegates (all male) to omit any discussion of birth control and to refrain from participating in official conference meetings or discussions. She remained in Switzerland throughout the fall to edit the conference proceedings, rest, and take sight-seeing trips through the Alps. (MS, Proceedings of the World Population Conference, *356, 361–62; MS,* Autobiography, *383–88; MS to Raymond Pearl, Sept. 26, 1927 [*MSM *C4:423]; 1927 Calendar [LCM 2:653–61].)*

[*Geneva, Switzerland*]
Sept 22 [*1927*]

Hugh dear—

Yes it must have been heavenly having the King at Sand Pit.[1] What luck! Ah me, you are at last catching up with fate & I hope she will continue to cast luck & happiness your way. The Conference went over with a "bang" Juliet is at the Mayfair Hotel in London get her down to Sand Pit & make her tell you all about it.[2]

Then it is just possible that my Squire may also be in London this week end at the Same Hotel.[3] Surely if you send a note to him there & tell him that Bridget[4] will come & fetch him unless he promises to visit Sand Pit at once, I am sure he would adore being wanted th'o he'l bluff it off as th'o he has no time for such nonsense.

He went away so as to leave me absolutely alone for a while. He was such a darling all thr'u the conference & then at the end he seemed to regret the work put into it, because he had not realized that b.c. was not to be to the front in it at all.[5] The Scientists were not very courageous I'll admit and the Catholic influence was strongly felt.

Then some of those upon whom I had relied to stand by in the time of war—failed & compromised—so it goes.[6]

I am now working on the papers & editing the discussion for the final volume[7] & find it ↑a↓ great satisfaction to blue pencil the opinions I don't like Revenge.

How are you Hugh dear? Also where & how is Harold— He never writes a word, horrid man.[8] But you are mixing these days aren't you? Did Havelock dance? Nothing surprises me these days so I enquire. Keep J. N. as long as you can. Plan out a weeks tour where the sun shines arrange every thing, take the whole family but don't let him get too fat.

I'm going to the mountain top for a week to dream.[9] Love ever

Margaret

ALS Lader (*MSM* C4:429–31). Letterhead of the Hôtel De L'Écu.

1. Ellis said of his trip to Sand Pit that "everyone was very sweet & nice." However, the visit did not heal his breach with de Selincourt. (Ellis to MS, Sept. 10, 1924 [LCM 4:1241–42]; Grosskurth, *Havelock Ellis,* 355–57.)

2. Rublee had arrived in Europe in July to serve as unofficial treasurer of the World Population Conference and help with other administrative details. Back in London, she looked into investing in the production of a new diving suit. (MS to Rublee, Apr. 8, 1927, and Slee to MS, Sept. 26, 1927 [*MSM* C4:338, S3:943].)

3. Slee arrived from Paris on September 24 and stayed at the Mayfair. (Slee to MS, Sept. 23, 1927 [*MSM* S3:906].)

4. Bridget, the de Selincourts' daughter, was now sixteen.

5. As early as 1926, MS knew that to attract influential scientists (including conference president Sir Bernard Mallett), she had to exclude substantive discussion of birth control. ("Notes of Conference between C. C. Little, Margaret Sanger & C. F. Chance," June 9, 1926 [*MSM* C14:416].)

6. MS had not anticipated that the World Population Conference advisory committee would refuse to include her name and those of the female staff, as well as any reference to the ABCL, on the program. She had depended on Clarence Little and Raymond Pearl to handle this, but they supported the advisory committee. (MS, *Autobiography,* 385–87.)

7. Though MS initially projected two or more volumes, the proceedings were published in a single volume.

8. Harold Child wrote to MS from the de Selincourts' two days later to say he had been ill and depressed. (Child to MS, Sept. 24, 1927 [*MSM* S3:911].)

9. From September 26 to October 4, MS took a "cure" at the Clinique Générale Beaulieu in Geneva. Seeking relief from constipation, she underwent a treatment program that included a diet heavy in fruits and seeds, colon massage, and regular enemas. (1927 Calendar [LCM 2:655–56]; MS to Slee, Sept. 27 and 30, 1927 [*MSM* S3:949 and 977].)

236. To J. Noah Slee

Clinique [*Geneva, Switzerland*]
Monday noon. [*October 3, 1927*]

Dearest One:

Your letter of Saturday just came: Its many directions I'll follow out & attend to.[1]

The end of your letter startles me into ponderous thought & sadness. When you say, "Its difficult for me to get over a bruise to my ideals & faith in you".[2]————— If that is your feeling about the matter then I am lost in amazement. Your bruised faith over what? A few cross words in retaliation to being called humiliating names, ↑by the man I loved↓ why darling Noah you are not trying to see both sides at all. You are able only to see your own side where you see yourself as perfect & abused. If you still feel hurt, god knows I should feel crushed from the same thing! For I have seen some traits & growing tendencies that are far from "ideal" crop up here & there in your character which did I not adore & worship your every hair would "bruise" & "beat" my "faith" in God himself—

But life is full of growth & understanding. I am full of love; my nature is gentle & tender; I am unassuming, humble but honest & frank.

I am not aggressive, but I will not be bullied or dominated over!

My unassuming manner falsly gives people the idea ~~of~~ ↑that↓ they can "boss" or "dominate" me. Then they try it and are disappointed & chagrined because I ↑then↓ say what I think. This is really what has happened darling Noah in our lives. You forget what you do, to cause, the outburst. You never realize that your very set ways can be irritating to a creative person. Well God help us both——— I do not want to go, to Paris now![3] What is the use? We had better remain where we are until you want me more than anything else. Also until your desire to have me & my love is greater than your "bruised & beaten faith" I can not be happy if my love for you is only tolerated while underneath your kisses is a "hurt feeling & lost faith." No dear Noah you have touched my pride & my spirit. My love for you has been too glorious & whole souled, to soil it now by pretense. My love has been far deeper in me (I can see now) than yours has ever been— All the discoveries of a new person in you, sometimes surprises & disappointed have been insignificant & feeble before the force of my love for you, while yours is evidentially superficial, depending upon smiles & constant poise. Well, I can only say I want to die! devotedly & Faithfully for ever.

Margaret.

[*Written at top of first page*] yes watch came, no monogram yet arrive from Paris

---

ALS MSP, MN-SSC (*MSM* S4:37–42). A note attached by MS at a later date reads, "These letters of ours seem frequently to have [*expressed*] quarrels,— J. Noah had a quick cruel, tongue— He tried to 'show off' his power by trite remarks in front of other people. Never when alone at first I was silent & decided to separate. But to my surprise he remarked 'why don't you come back at me'——— I hated to—but I did—and how. M. S."

1. Slee listed various tasks they both needed to complete, including exchanging currency and attending to mail. (Slee to MS, Oct. 1, 1927 [*MSM* S4:15–24].)

2. Slee actually wrote, "It's difficult for me to get over a bruise to my ideals & faith in your undying love which was so beaten twice by you. God help me to understand your many sided nature." He also expressed disappointment that MS canceled her plans to join him in London.

3. MS arrived in Paris on October 5. Slee joined her the next day, but she had a cold and was "in bed all day" on the sixth and seventh and was "depressed" on the eighth. She returned to Geneva on October 11. (1927 Calendar [LCM 2:655–56].)

237. To Juliet Barrett Rublee

During the many months Sanger was abroad, the ABCL's executive committee, led by its chair, Eleanor Jones, increased the power of the board of directors at the expense of the president. Jones and the board worked to secure the ABCL's financial base by creating annual memberships and requiring that affiliated state leagues contribute 25 percent of their fees to the national. The board continued lobbying for state bills in New York, New Jersey, and Connecticut and sent more organizers into the field, but it did not launch any new initiatives. One casualty of Jones's new leadership style was Anne Kennedy, whom the board essentially dismissed on November 2. This decision led to a bitter split between those board members supportive of Jones's policies and Sanger loyalists.

[*Geneva, Switzerland*]
Nov 4. [*1927*]

Juliet darling—

Such a nice letter was yours about Mexico etc. Certainly I shall not mention it to J. N. until all is settled.[1]

Poor old Anne!! She was all set to return to U.S.A. hoping to make it up with Mrs J & the B of D— and wanting to do Federal work until my return in the spring.[2] Had some good "tips" & contacts prepared for a possible hearing. She was leaving for Paris at 11 AM today & after a few days there on to London with Emily.[3]

Last night about eight oclock I had a cable from Mrs Delafield saying "unanimous decision of B of D. meeting Nov 3. No opening field or office for Mrs Kennedy"!!![4] Practically a <u>dismissal</u>. I was aghast—and uncertain what to do. Should I let Anne go back & with you F. B. A. Mrs Day, Dr Vaughan fight for her or just let it go—[5]

Anyway I went & called her on the 'phone & asked her to postpone her trip today & to come down early to see me.

Needless to say she was crushed to despair hurt, and felt she had been dealt a blow. Where were you darling?[6] Did you know about it? What happened to bring it up? The Cooper report was unfair to Anne & Mrs Jones letter to me admitted an error.[7] I am at a loss to know just what to do but I think you should find out what caused such a ruthless action and if you are really going to resign <u>do it for Anne</u> as her friend and because you do not agree with their action. It would be a fine gesture in Annes direction & a right one. Unless of course there is some reason I can not guess.

I know Annes failings & good points— I have said I do not think she is at her best in an office, in fact she is not a good executive at all, but the other qualities which are useful to us are not only good but superb. She has cost the organization a lot [*of*] money to educate her. Now she is able to repay that cost.

Don't read this letter to anyone—I shall write Mrs Delafield & Mrs J—[8] Then please attend the meetings & speak up.

Don't allow Dr Stones narrow selfish views to color the account of the Conference.[9] It was the biggest boost for b.c. ever done in Europe. The enemy is terrorized at the momentum. My love darling dear ever to you. Devotedly ever

Margaret

ALS JRP, NhD (*MSM* C4:471). Letterhead of the World Population Conference.

1. The letter disclosing Rublee's plans to join her husband in Mexico was not found.

2. Anne Kennedy's troubles began in 1926 when Jones criticized her fieldwork in the Midwest and West, accusing her of extravagance and exaggerating her successes. Kennedy claimed that four board members were conspiring against her, but she resisted their directives and pressure to resign. She told MS: "You are still president and it is only on your authority that I can pass in my resignation." From May to November 1, 1927, she assisted MS in Geneva on the World Population Conference and its proceedings. After the conference's office closed, Kennedy sought a new ABCL assignment. (Kennedy to MS, May 5, 1927, Jones to MS, Nov. 21, 1927, and MS to Delafield, Nov. 16, 1927 [LCM 8:1311, 1228, and 169].)

3. Emily was Anne Kennedy's daughter, who was attending theatrical school in London, with financial help from Slee. (MS to Rublee, Nov. 8, 1927, and Kennedy to MS, Nov. 14, 1927 [*MSM* C4:47 and LCM 8:1274].)

4. See Delafield to MS, Nov. 3, 1927 (LCM 8:169).

5. She was referring to Frances Ackermann, Katharine Day, and John Vaughan, all board members.

6. Rublee did not attend the November 2 meeting. She had returned to the United States in October and remained in her Cornish, New Hampshire, home most of the fall and early winter, recuperating from an undisclosed illness. (Juliet Rublee to MS, Nov. 16 and Dec. 6–7, 1927 [LCM 10:59 and 66].)

7. Jones had asked ABCL medical director James Cooper to follow up on some of the claims Kennedy made in her report, and he had found that many of the clinics Kennedy said were established were nonexistent. Jones's letter was not found. (For an extract of Cooper's report to MS, Sept. 20, 1927, see LCM 24:62.)

8. MS may not have wanted Rublee to know that she and Jones had discussed the probability that Kennedy would leave the ABCL in July 1927. While MS protested the executive board's action to Jones and Delafield, she did not overrule the board. Instead, she encouraged Rublee's protests and offered Kennedy sympathy and financial aid. (MS to Delafield, Nov. 16, 1927, Kennedy to MS, Nov. 14, 1927, and Jones to MS, July 8, 1927, Nov. 21, 1927, and Jan. 4, 1928 [LCM 8:170, 1274, 1236, and 1228, 24:64]; MS to Rublee, Nov. 8, 1927 [*MSM* C4:475].)

9. A week earlier, MS wrote, "Dr Stone was silly to give the impression that she gave. It was not a B.C. Conference & was never intended to be one. All those like Stone, Cox & Bland who hoped it would turn into one were keenly critical." (MS to Rublee, Oct. 31, 1927 [*MSM* C4:460].)

238. *To Grant Sanger*[1]

[*Berlin, Germany*]
Nov 29. [*1927*]

Darling Grant:

When I arrived here this morning from London I found your two letters. Certainly I shall be careful not to mention what you write, especially any thing concerning personal matters.[2]

You are very wise to consider carefully any invitations not because of "matrimonial" compromises, but because of social obligations. I should not hesitate to accept hospitality to a house party where other fellows were going or in certain cases where they were not but that is where you need to be very thoughtful.

Anyway if you had any doubts—you were as well off not to accept. It is rotten luck—to have to make an excuse but you made it in advance of the day & I hope sufficiently in advance for them to get someone else.

I am glad Stuart invited Helena[3] that was good of him, because it is his big year & because they played & fought together as children—then she may not be a—beauty—but she has a mind.

Your attraction to a girl is normal & usual. Its what they call in London "S.A." ↑(sex Appeal or sex attraction).↓ Then after a week or two your brain begins to work & you take an inventory—consequently the reaction. It's a safe guide! At your age—you are mentally beyond the average girl—four or five years later you will find mental equality. Then the friendship will blossom.

It is dear of you to write me so frankly. I hope you always will know that I am the one to understand—you have a father a godfather—and a step father but I doubt if any of them know as much about themselves as you do about yourself.

Stuart is level headed with girls—especially since [*Sam?*] Brown gave him a "run" & landed him in debt. He will be the bachelor—not you—

Was the girls brother in Dr Slocums Sanatorium?[4] If so beware:————

Yes we are meeting various people—[5] At Geneva especially we met people from every where now at Berlin we will be getting ready for the Suvretta House St Moritz where we shall be Dec 15th.[6]

It is good news about your marks! Pater was thrilled about math.

Did Stuart get his "Y" I wonder.[7] Perhaps not.

You will have good sport at Quebec.[8] I trust the sprain is over & left no weak spots. Please get it on paper what your Dentist will charge— So I shall know where we are at. Pater is out of that charge. So do go easy & be convinced of the necessity won't you.

I had dinner in London with Prof Julian Huxley & his wife.[9] Did you know that Mrs Wells died? H. G. always asks about you.[10]
Pater sends [*written along right margin*] his love & so do I. Ever devotedly

Mother

ALS MSP, MN-SSC (*MSM* S4:166–70). Letterhead of the Hotel Adlon.

1. Grant entered Princeton (class of 1931) in September 1927.

2. Grant had mentioned his girlfriend, Helen Seward, in two letters. (Grant Sanger to MS, Nov. 13 and 14, 1927 [*MSM* S4:110 and 118].)

3. Stuart, a twenty-four-year-old Yale senior, had probably invited one of his childhood friends, Helena Archibald, who was the daughter of Adelaide G. Archibald, a Sanger family friend. (Grant Sanger to MS, Nov. 13, 1927 [*MSM* S4:110].)

4. In his November 13 letter, Grant had reported meeting Seward while she was visiting her brother at Craig House Sanitarium, a psychiatric institution in Beacon, New York, founded by MS's neighbor and friend, the psychiatrist Clarence Jonathan Slocum (1873–1950). Both Grant and Stuart sometimes worked at Craig House. (*New York Times*, Jan. 29, 1950.)

5. MS arrived in Germany on November 29 at the invitation of Agnes Smedley and the Association of German Medical Women, for whom she gave a series of lectures and met with German birth control advocates and feminists from December 6 through December 9. She left for Frankfurt on December 11 to see Dr. Hertha Riese's marriage advice center, before returning to Zurich on December 14. (Agnes Smedley, "Sanger Comes to Berlin," *BCR*, Feb. 1928, 50–66; 1927 Calendar [LCM 2:659].)

6. MS and Slee reached Suvretta House, an opulent St. Moritz ski hotel famous for its royal and celebrity guests, on December 15. (1927 Calendar [LCM 2:660].)

7. Stuart had earned an athletic letter for football at Yale.

8. Grant and Stuart planned to spend their Christmas holidays there. (Grant Sanger to MS, Nov. 25, 1927 [*MSM* S4:150].)

9. Sir Julian Sorrell Huxley (1887–1975) was a British zoologist, philosopher, and pioneer in the study of genetics, evolution, and animal behavior. Huxley was one of a younger generation of eugenicists whose "evolutionary humanism" sought to discover whether many of the race, class, and ethnic assumptions of eugenic theorists could be verified scientifically. He married Marie Juliette Baillot in 1919. (*DNB;* Garland E. Allen, "Julian Huxley and the Eugenical View of Human Evolution," in *Julian Huxley: Biologist and Statesman of Science,* ed. C. Kenneth Waters and Albert Van Helden [Houston, 1992], 193–222.)

10. Amy (Jane) Catherine Robbins Wells (?–1927), the second wife of H. G. Wells, died of cancer on October 6. Grant had met Wells in 1922. (Smith, *H. G. Wells,* 385–86.)

239. *To Edith How-Martyn*

[*St. Moritz, Switzerland*]
Feb 1—[*1928*]

Edith dearest:

Before your letter came I had already made the plunge & had a note from Lady Aster that as soon as she was rested & I was well we would meet.[1]

Today I had another note[2] that she would hunt me up before dinner at six a phone call asking me if I was well enough to come to her room I was & from her 'phone I sensed she was to give me 20 minutes— Well I went & found her in bed with cold cream all over her face—her windows wide open in a most unAmerican fashion & we started right in to laugh together as if our spirits were old friends laughter does tell you know especially that mellow rich spontaneous laughter of an experienced soul & well trained mind.

Well she talked & we laughed for ten minutes over nothing at all, & then she asked me straight out if I believed in B.C. I said I had no reservations that it was my religion. She said she did not know enough about it to take sides, but wanted to know—

Then she asked questions about Prostitute—I said I was not interested in their part in B.C. questions because they had all knowledge & access to abortion—it was the poor slave mother I was wanting to help, & that the Gov of G.B. had the greatest opportunity of reaching the lowest elements through the M & C.W. Centers[3] I told her of the pessary etc & our clinic in N.Y. & then her sister came in Mrs Brandt.[4]

I had not met her th'o knew who she was & have seen her skating. She sat down & began—she believed in B.C. for the insane, feebleminded & incurables but that was all— I said that was good, but there were six more places where it should be applied—then I gave her the others—& she moved along two more accepting the T.B. heart & kidney diseased mothers—& subnormal children mothers also,—[*illegible*] but that seemed to [*be*] her limit.

Lady Aster (Nancy) was against sterilization but wanted to know more & suggested we take luncheon together or go for a night ride & talk, (an hour & a half had ↓gone)↑. I found her facinating & stimulating & wished I could inspire her to come in on B.C. she is certainly more interested than she was, in fact she said why this is really very interesting its far deeper than I had any idea of.

She can be reached I know now the thing is how to push the interest.

I like her very much—she is genuine, frank, honest. I am glad I sent the note & I think she is not sorry to have given the time. She sees no one, she says so it was very good of her really to see me. She looks tired & needs the rest.

She is Anti-Catholic thank God.[5] So she & I were one on many things. She said she would arrange to see me in London. You do know I plan to be there a few days before I sail.[6] All love Edith dear are you well?[7]

Margaret

ALS Palmer (*MSM* C4:564–69). Letterhead of the Suvretta House. Dark original.

1. The letter was not found. Lady Nancy Astor was also staying at Suvretta House. (See MS to How-Martyn, Jan. 25, 1928 [*MSM* C4:555].)
2. The letter was not found.
3. This was a reference to Britain's maternity and child welfare centers. The Ministry of Health strenuously opposed efforts to allow contraceptive services to be dispensed in these centers. Individual medical officers of health could legally offer birth control services, but few did. (Leathard, *Fight for Family Planning*, 35.)
4. Phyllis Langhorne Brand (1880–1937) was a social reformer who moved to London in 1915 after divorcing her first husband. She married the banker Robert H. Brand in 1917. (*New York Times*, Jan. 21, 1937.)
5. Astor was an ardent Christian Scientist, whose anti-Catholic views were widely known. (Sykes, *Nancy*, 139–41, 247–48.)
6. MS lunched with Lady Astor in London on February 22, then left for Paris. She sailed for New York City on March 7, 1928, aboard the SS *Ile de France*. (MS to Rublee, Feb. 23 and 25, 1928 [*MSM* C4:581 and 583]; 1928 Calendar [LCM 2:679–80].)
7. How-Martyn, who had been helping MS with the World Population Conference, had been unable to work for several months after contracting scarlet fever. She was back at work by February 1928, helping MS promote international birth control. (MS, *My Fight*, 378–79, 382; How-Martyn to MS, Jan. 2, 8, and 15, 1928 [*MSM* S4:232, 240, and 261].)

240. From Havelock Ellis

*Having achieved her own financial security, Sanger sought to ease the burdens of friends, particularly Ellis. Sanger wrote to Françoise Lafitte on January 22, "When I see Harold Cox and all the men in the world who write, having the details done for them by a capable secretary, in order to save the energy & strength of the writer, I froath at the mouth to think that our dear Havelock toils over details of proof reading, indexes, etc etc which could easily be done for him. I want terribly to give him a Secretary for his 70th birthday & for the rest of his blessed life—and I would love it if you would be that Secretary. I do not know how to ask him to accept this, and so I come to you Françoise dear to ask your help. I have £300 a year that is doing nothing. It is not much I know, but perhaps for half time you would be able to make that do, and then be free for translations or what ever else you may wish to take on." Ellis was ambivalent about the offer and told Lafitte not to rush into leaving her teaching post. But after Sanger arrived in London on February 22, she and Lafitte persuaded him to accept. (MS to Lafitte, Jan. 22 and 26, 1928, and Lafitte to MS, Jan. 30, 1928 [*MSM *S4:277 and 284; LCM 3:162]; Grosskurth, *Havelock Ellis*, 396.)*

Broadstairs, Kent. [*England*]
2 Feb/28

I have your beautiful letter, Margaret Dear, with your wonderful Birthday greetings. What you are proposing is so generous & overwhelming that I feel powerless to say anything. But I certainly do not feel that I can say NO. Françoise ran down here on Saturday, giving notice by telegram, to talk to me about it. And if I wanted to say NO she might kill me! (Faith Oliver,[1] who went to see her a few days ago, writes me that never has she seen F. so radiant & happy.)

The wonderful thing is the [*marvelously*] "Providential" way in which your beautiful proposal comes at the present time. Of course there is no available person who could help me so much, & in such various ways, as Françoise, since my work is very special & I am, any way, a difficult person. For some time, ever since her illness,[2] though she is now in good health, Françoise has felt severely the strain of teaching, & we have often talked about how she could change her way of life & perhaps help me. But, with her boys[3] to educate, that move seemed too full of anxious responsibilities. Then, only last month, Mneme Kirkland, who has always been near to give an eye to my household arrangements & send on my correspondence when necessary, gave up her flat at Brixton as her husband has now retired. Her father, also, my old friend Dr Barker Smith, now 82, has suddenly broken down in health.[4] In November he went with Françoise & me for a few days to Ipswich & was as youthful & active as ever. Now he is confined to bed, Mneme has left her husband to come & nurse him, & he is not expected to live long. So I should soon be left completely alone at Brixton which nowadays is not a prospect I find pleasant. If Françoise is enabled to live near & be at hand all my difficulties are settled.

I do not agree that she is "wasted" at school. She is a beautiful & helpful influence there, & is much loved. I do not like the idea of her breaking off <u>all</u> connection there, & I hope it will not be necessary.

As for me, I seem busier than ever, so there is plenty for [*Secretary*] to do!

No more at present, wonderful woman, but my dear love,

Havelock.

[*Written along left margin of last page*] You call this my <u>70</u>th birthday. But <u>I</u> call it 69th only! I was born in 1859.

ALS MSP, DLC (LCM 5:14–17).

1. Faith Oliver (1897?–?), a schoolteacher who had befriended Ellis, had a year-long affair with him in 1926 and sustained a correspondence with him for years. (Grosskurth, *Havelock Ellis*, 349–53.)

2. Lafitte had undergone a hysterectomy in 1925. (Grosskurth, *Havelock Ellis,* 314.)

3. François Lafitte was her son by an American syndicalist, and Paul was her son by her Russian husband, Serge Cyon. (Grosskurth, *Havelock Ellis,* 276.)

4. Mneme (Amy) Smith Kirkland (1869?–?), the daughter of Ellis's old friend John Barker Smith (1846?–1928), a British chemist and the author of several books on pharmaceuticals and esoteric philosophy, was a nurse. Her sporadic sexual affair with Ellis beginning in 1898 caused Edith Ellis to attempt suicide. Though Smith married in 1916, she remained close to Ellis, caring for him when he was ill. (Grosskurth, *Havelock Ellis,* 55–56, 158–63, 265, 397; Brome, *Havelock Ellis,* 113–16, 178–79.)

241. *From Client*

Some contraceptives, including cervical caps, jellies, and douching solutions, were advertised in women's magazines and tabloids and were available in department stores and pharmacies, through mail order houses, or direct from their manufacturers. In large cities, some manufacturers even hired door-to-door saleswomen. However, when commercially marketed, contraceptives were often given euphemistic names and described as "feminine hygiene" products to obscure their real purpose, which may have made it difficult for some women to locate the specific items Sanger noted in Family Limitation. *(Amy Sarch, "Dirty Discourse: Birth Control Advertising in the 1920s and 1930s," Ph.D. diss., University of Pennsylvania, 1984, 105–6, 112–13, 124.)*

Athens, Georgia
February 29, 1928

Dear Miss Sanger,

It certainly must be far easier to have perscriptions filled in New York than in these southern cities! We have tried drug store after drug store—none of them has the Mizpath[1] pessary; Patrick's Drug Store here doesn't have the Aseptikan suppositories[2] and when given the composition the druggist at the Normal Pharmacy promised to fill it and send to the house the following morning—I waited a day or so and when my husband asked him about it he said the boy must have misplaced the order and that they didn't have some of the ingredients anyway—so. At the U-Save-it drug dept. in Albany, we [*know*] the Dr. in charge, Mr. Morcock was told the equivalent of the Aseptikan would be filled but that we were to be most strongly advised against anything containing salicylic acid—and you recall it contains 2 grains; so efforts there were of no avail last month.

In your "Family Limitation"—source, St. Louis, I believe[3] if I remember correctly—you give a suppository prescription the French peasants make up:: gelatine, water, glycerine, b. of quinine but how much is 2 grammes? Also the one of 10 grains boric acid, 20 cocoa butter does not state how much to each suppositiory nor whether it or the French one are 3—min. or 20 minutes required for introduction into the vagina.[4]

Quite a list of questions, isn't this? but we have one baby and are trying so hard to wait three years before the next one and to be perfectly frank, this one wasn't quite five months of age when I was certain another was on the way, but it proved a mistake.

Since you advise a good pessary, I prefer using one, but please tell me the name of a drug store in New York, Jacksonville, Atlanta or somewhere where [*one*] may be bought which is a Mizpath for $2.00—and I would appreciate it thoroughly if you'd go to all the trouble to give the information asked above.

Many thanks to you, I am Sincerely,

Mrs. [*Name omitted*]

TLS ABCLR, MH-H (*MSM* C4:587). Letterhead of the Albany Chamber of Commerce. In the interest of privacy, the editors have omitted the author's name. A handwritten note at the top by James Cooper reads, "wrote to her after Albany mtg— JFC Apr 10 1928."

1. This was the Mizpah cervical cap.

2. This was a spermicide made from a cocoa butter base, with chinosol, quinine, salicylic, and boric acid as active ingredients. The suppositories were inserted into the vagina, where they melted, forming an oily coating over the mouth of the uterus while the active ingredients killed the sperm. By 1928, cocoa butter was being replaced by glycerine and gelatin, which made the suppositories less messy and smell better. In large cities, a wide variety was still available "from almost any druggist," though birth control reformers recommended diaphragms used with jellies as more effective. (*Family Limitation,* 1st ed., 1914 [LCM 129:189]; Cooper, *Technique of Contraception,* 83–87.)

3. This was probably a reference to a St. Louis edition of *Family Limitation,* printed during MS's 1916 tour (not found).

4. In the first edition of *Family Limitation,* MS had noted that these were made using one part gelatine, two parts water, five parts glycerine, and one-half part quinine. To make the suppository, the ingredients were to be mixed into a paste, spread out and allowed to solidify, and then cut into two-gram pieces. MS included a boric acid and cocoa butter recipe, along with recipes for three other suppositories, two of which included the time required between the insertion of the suppository and intercourse. Later editions included variations on these recipes. (*Family Limitation,* 1914 [*MSM* S76:842].)

242. *To Mary Boggs East*[1]

[*New York, N.Y.*]
March 26, 1928.

Dear Mrs. East:

It was very nice to have yours of March 14th upon my return from Europe,[2] and I take great pleasure in getting in touch with you again.

As to your question concerning the old Birth Control league and its revival,[3] it is hard for me to say what should be done. Usually I find in such groups that it is better to inject new blood and to let the old ones die out, but I remember that you had a very good, enthusiastic, generous, fighting group some years ago. Why not call a small group meeting at your home and see what prospects there are for an aggressive campaign?

Mrs. Oakes Ames[4] was at our office a few days ago, but, unfortunately, I missed seeing her, for I should have had more intimate knowledge of the situation in your state. It might be possible to send some of our organizers to see you and to advise with you if you wished it, for some of us are very keen to see Massachusetts take a stand in this matter.

As to the question of a small active group accomplishing more quietly than a large noisy group, I am rather inclined to believe that the noise is necessary—especially in the first stages of education. As to accomplishment in legislative work, a small active group working quietly would certainly be better, but with your Catholic element who are aggressively stubborn and obstinate, I think it would be best to gather to your group numbers as fast as they can be coralled for the sake of an aggressive showing. This is just my opinion, prompted perhaps by feeling rather than clear thinking, so just take it for what it is worth; but no matter what method you decide upon, be prepared for a hard fight with clear heads in the lead.

Please extend my best regards to Dr. East. I hope he has already received the Proceedings of the Conference.[5] Do let me know if anything that we can do can help you get started again. Most cordially,

Margaret Sanger [*signed*]

TLS PPLMR, MN-SSC (*MSM* S4:407). Letterhead of the ABCL.

1. Mary Lawrence Boggs East (1881–1960), the wife of the genetics professor Edward Murray East, had been one of the founders of the Massachusetts Birth Control League (MBCL) and its executive secretary. (CA Death Index; Ames, "Margaret Sanger's Influence," 3.)
2. The letter was not found. MS had returned to New York City on March 13.
3. The MBCL, which had evolved out of the 1916 Van Kleeck Allison Defense Committee, dissolved in 1920 from lack of support. It was revived in 1928, after the February arrest of Dr. Antoinette Konikow for lecturing on birth control, when East and several other former MBCL members formed an Emergency Defense Committee. The committee was renamed the Birth Control League of Massachusetts in May 1928. (MS to Charles and Bessie Drysdale, Aug. 9, 1916, note 25, herein; Preliminary Inventory, 1985 [PPLMR].)
4. Blanche Ames Ames (1878–1969), a suffragist, botanical illustrator, and inventor, had cofounded the MBCL in 1916. (*NAW*)
5. Edward East's paper "Food and Population" was published in the *Proceedings of the World Population Conference*, 85–91.

243. *From Client*[1]

Bklyn. N.Y.
March. [*28?*] 1928.

Dear Mrs Sanger:-

It isn't a very pleasant subject I'm writing on, but I feel like I must talk to some one of my terrible experiences and my present circumstances.

If you keep any kind of records you will find I was a patient of Dr. Bocker in 1924. That was a few months after I had my second baby. (oldest is 7 yrs now.) I came to your Dr. for information and rec'd a rubber cap which I could never use, couldn't be placed & didn't fit. Everything went alright until September 1926 when a Dr. said I was again pregnant, this 3rd boy was born last June ↑1927↓. When he was 3 months old I came to your place again, determined to get help if I could, didn't come sooner because I have no way of getting to N.Y with 3 children and no place to leave them while I am out. Anyway, I was fitted with another rubber cap[2] which was said to "fit better" also the jelly with it, was shown how to place cap etc. I went home happy to think my troubles & fears were over and at last I could place confidence in a good cause like yours. Have been having periods twice a month in Nov & Dec. last year, then the regular 6 day period in last part of Jan. running into Feb. then I expected it last of Feb. or first of March surely but to this date nothing yet. Have been to a Specialist 3 times, first visit he said I am flowing too much and nothing wrong except for a fibrous uterus[3] second visit he said I am delayed and the raw spot could cause delay. Now on third visit he tells me I am pregnant and that the rubber cap I used has irritated the growth and caused it to swell and become inflamed, also that I must have an operation which won't come under two hundred dollars.

You can't imagine my feelings, I have no mother to go to, no relations at all, a few friends are down on me because I had the 3rd one but said then if I ever get so again they wouldn't ever speak to me. My husband refuses to use protectors, children are playthings when not crying & while babies but wouldn't get up for them at night. Has no tho't of responsibilities, like cards, movies, other outside company etc. I am a wreck inwardly from so many children—all unwanted but the first so I have more love for him than the others because I had to have them, not because I wanted to.

Now I plan to seek legal advice, as to a separation with allowance for myself & oldest, my husband dislikes this one because he resembles me, I am not a Jew. The others are darker and more like him. I feel like an out cast, like a leper, no friends, no money, no future worth seeing. Dear Mrs Sanger, if this letter reaches your attention as I earnestly hope & pray it will, won't you write me a line to encourage me a tiny bit, my burden is heavy and for the sake of this boy I must go on no matter how rough the journey, he needs me. I do wish you had time to make personal calls, would be so pleased with a visit from you, but if you are kind enough to reply I would appreciate it. I became a life member & took magazine for some time,[4] giving it to a girl I knew, but I hope you will excuse me from any further payments, the "prevention" can be of no value to me; This month I am married just eight years, but it seems like a life time to me. Nothing but trouble, a man who don't care either way and not even a friend I can talk to. I am going to visit one in Ridgewood and 2 in Newark—where my home was—and say Goodbye to them, for I'll never be able to see them any more, they said they wouldn't look at me and thats my encouraging future.

Anyway I realy hope that the A.B.C.L. will some day get the right thing to help people like me, something that realy & truly will prevent unwanted children. I have your book "Woman & the New Race", its good & true only doesn't go far enough.

Hoping I may receive some reply, and kindest regards to you, Sincerely yours,

[*Name omitted*]

ALS MSP, DLC (LCM 32:320–24). In the interest of privacy, the editors have omitted the author's name.

1. The author wrote another letter directly to the ABCL/CRB signed "a discontented member," complaining, "Prevention, Ideas, they are far from safe, all I can see is a big money making plan. . . . Birth Control League is a failure." (Client to ABCL, Mar. 28, 1928 [LCM 32:319].)

2. In 1924, the CRB recommended a variety of pessaries, but by 1927, the Ramses pessary was the one most often prescribed. (See breakdown of 1924 "experimental series" in Cooper, *Technique of Contraception,* 174–76, 133.)

3. Uterine fibromyomas, or fibroids, are benign tumors in the muscle of the uterus that often cause excessive menstrual bleeding. Fibroids are more likely to appear during women's childbearing years, though their cause is unknown. (Gordon Macpherson, ed., *Black's Medical Dictionary* [New York, 1999], 574.)

4. ABCL "life members" paid a dollar and signed an endorsement slip. They constituted the vast majority of the ABCL's approximately 37,000 members until 1928, when this category was replaced by three membership classes: annual (paying two dollars per year), contributing (twenty-five dollars per year), and sustaining (a hundred dollars per year). (MS to Friend, n.d., and ABCL By-Laws, ca. 1928 [*MSM* S61:246 and 42].)

244. *To Client*

[*New York, N.Y.?*]
April 3, 1928.

Dear Mrs. [*name omitted*]:

Your letter has come to me[1] and I am grieved more than words can tell you of your condition.

I wish I could know more about your case and what Doctor fitted you and advised you.[2]

Could you come over to see me? Bring the children—if necessary—and I will pay your fare. Only be sure to let me know the day you come, so [*I'll*] be in my office to see you.

You must not be discouraged. Your friends must be joking, for they could not turn from you because of another baby!! Besides, your doctor may be wrong. Why did he not know your condition earlier?

Do come over here next week—one day if you can—I'd like to talk over the case. Regretfully & Sympathetically,

---

TLcy MSP, DLC (LCM 32:326). In the interest of privacy, the editors have omitted the recipient's name. Carbon smears.

1. See Client to MS, March 28?, 1928, herein.
2. By 1928, the CRB had four staff doctors and had treated over a thousand clients. Though she could have accessed the client's history card at the CRB, MS may have wished to hear the patient's version of her clinic visits. (MS, "A Program of Contraceptive Research," June 5, 1928 [*MSM* S61:203].)

245. *To Grant Sanger*

[*New York, N.Y.?*]
April 18—28

Grant dearest:

If you can forgive this penciled letter I'll get this off to you while sitting here in bed writing my "speech" for tonight.[1]

Now as to the question of joining a church— In our way you already belong to the Episcopal Church as you were baptized in that Church when a year old in Hastings on [*Hudson*]. That really makes you a member of the church I believe—[2]

When I was a growing girl I had the same desires—I wanted to join the church of the friends I knew—but later when I went to a Methodist School[3] & had to go to Episcopal Services a long way from the school I often wished I had not joined any church, but had been free to attend any services I wished—

I once had a strong impulse to go forward in a Methodist prayer meeting & join that Church—but a good friend held me back by saying "that preacher is working up the emotions of us all—I won't go up tonight—lets think it over." So I did—& she was right.

There is an age when certain boys & girls from 15 to 21—often want to attach themselves to some church— If they want it very hard I say go to it—no harm can come of it.

I have outgrown the need of Church by my interest in Philosophy, Psychology & Humanity.

Very often I find the Church narrows & limits the mental horizon of a person—when in reality it should broaden & deepen. Karl Reiland has issued a new creed for the church & I agree with it absolutely.[4] Even he finds the old creed limiting—

I have no objection to your joining the church & being confirmed. It rather startled me at first. For I've been a Free Thinker[5] for so many years that it was natural to hope you & Stuart[6] had in some way taken on or absorbed the same viewpoint—

However now that I think it over I agree with you to do it, if you want to. If you go in for Science you will doubtless find a constant Challenge to the church in your discoveries but it makes both more interesting so go ahead & do as you are urged to do—only be sure you really do want to—

You might talk ↑it over with↓ K. R.[7] when he is at Willowlake in June—Glad you will be home early. All for now—forgive pencil please— Have you spent <u>all</u> the money Pater sent you for allowance, car fares etc??? I wrote you that $50 is due you on clothes of which $30 was sent you yesterday—

Yes you must pay your debts yourself now— But you might have earned more than $100 at the Lake[8]—anyhow love ever & always

Mother

ALS MSP, MN-SSC (*MSM* S4:424–27). Letterhead of the World Population Conference struck out by MS.

1. The speech was not found, nor was the event identified.
2. Grant had asked his mother about being confirmed in the Episcopal church. MS had all three children christened over the protests of William Sanger. (Grant Sanger to MS, Apr. 15, 1928, and William Sanger to MS, Dec. 8, 1914 [*MSM* S4:416, S1:305]; Hersey, "Margaret Sanger," 86.)
3. MS was referring to Claverack College.
4. On March 18 at St. George's Episcopal Church in New York City, where he was rector, Reiland had introduced the first of his "new creeds"—a revision of the Apostle's Creed, which he found to be an "inadequate expression of Christian faith." Reiland claimed that he was not repudiating older creeds but was reinterpreting and modernizing them. (*New York Times,* Mar. 19, 1928.)
5. There is no evidence that MS had any affiliation with any freethinkers' group, but she did, like her father, reject religious authority and dogma.
6. Stuart was not formally affiliated with any church at this time.
7. K. R. was Karl Reiland.
8. Grant worked at a summer camp in Stratford, New Hampshire, though MS had hoped he would again work at Craig House, near Willowlake. (Grant Sanger to MS, Apr. 15, 1928 [*MSM* S4:416].)

246. Dream

NY. (Grosvenor) [*N.Y.*]
April 18 [*1928*]

I dreamed again that I was holding a chamber for a baby while he did his "duties" then I followed B. S.[1] about in a very warm passionate desire for him—but he was spiritually cold tho physically aroused.

Someone came into the room a man tall, straight, very handsome, strong looking with arms folded on chest I had pushed BS away from me, when this stranger entered, I do not know who he was.

AD MSP, MN-SSC (*MSM* S70:254). Written by MS at the top right: "copy."

1. She was referring to William Sanger.

247. To Juliet Barrett Rublee

*On her return in March, Sanger found that the ABCL board, led by Eleanor Jones, resisted her attempts to resume her authority at the expense of the now more powerful executive committee, by delegating duties to individual board members. Frustrated by their intransigence, she attempted to pull out as early as mid-April, when she unsuccessfully tried to persuade Charlotte Delafield to fill out her presidential term. By this time, Sanger's primary interest was in the CRB, which she wanted to run as a separate entity. She asserted that the clinic was not actually a part of the ABCL, a claim the board dismissed. For Sanger, the last straw came when the board impudently offered her the right to run the CRB for two years, provided she accept responsibility for funding it. (ABCL Board Minutes, Feb. 14, Apr. 10, and May 8, 1928 [*MSM *S61:124 and 130, *LCM *28:10]; Charlotte Delafield to MS, Apr. 16 and May 24, 1928 [*LCM *8:182 and 185].)*

[*New York, N.Y.*]
May 17 [*1928*]

Juliet beloved:

No word from you since your dear voice called me on the 'phone at Beacon. Where & How are you?[1] Do write— Did you get my letter?[2]

Anyway here goes this one— I am resigning on June 12 as President—!! At last darling it had to be.

The spirit, the love, the trust necessary for me to do my best is gone. I can not work in an atmosphere of rules & regulations—[3]

So I am taking up the Research Dept for two years & ↑shall↓ run it & finance it & expand it as I see fit. Frances Ackerman is going on my Committee & resigning as Treas & from the Board—[4]

All is done pleasantly & without friction. I am giving "Health" as the reason & "going on with other work".

The B of D. wants other women & have two new ones[5] to take vacancies as soon as some of us get off. I am expanding the Clinic & it looks lovely—twenty two sessions a week & harmony & love prevail—That's the atmosphere for growth. Now darling thats all. What about you? Shall you remain away much longer? How is George liking it?

New York is dull & dirty.

Mrs Blagden is back from Europe.[6] We miss you horribly— Its tragic to have you away— Met Mrs Brush & Mr Brush[7] will be in town today—you should be here— He is giving $500,000 foundation [*sons*] memory,[8] eugenics etc. AK is on the job to get some of that for B.C.[9] Love ever

Margaret

ALS JRP, NhD (*MSM* C4:637–39). Letterhead of the Grosvenor.

1. Rublee was in Mexico City, where her husband had recently been appointed legal adviser to the American embassy, serving under Ambassador Dwight Morrow. (MS to Rublee, Apr. 28, 1928, and Rublee to MS, May 20, 1928 [*MSM* C4:624, S4:470].)
2. The letter was not found.
3. This was probably a reference to the board's request that MS adhere to its now more formal decision-making procedures and internal fiscal policies. (ABCL Board Minutes, Feb. 14, Apr. 10, and May 8, 1928 [*MSM* S61:124 and 130, LCM 28:10].)
4. Ackermann, one of Anne Kennedy's defenders, had kept MS apprised of the board's doings in a series of long, troubled letters. In writing "my Committee," MS was referring to the group of wealthy women who supported the CRB and later became its board of managers. (See Ackermann to MS, Nov. 3–13 and Dec. 13, 1927, and CRB Board of Managers Minutes, 1929–32 [LCM 7:657–73 and 34:486–518].)
5. Helen Prentiss Converse Thorpe, the wife of the Wall Street broker Warren Thorpe, filled a board vacancy in May; the board proposed several other members in February 1929, including Florence Haskell Corliss Lamont, the wife of the financier Thomas Lamont, and Leslie Tompkins, both of whom joined. (ABCL Board Minutes, May 8, 1928, and Feb. 13, 1929 [LCM 28:10 and 21].)
6. Mabel Whitney Blagden (Sabin) (1875–1968), the wife of the stockbroker Dexter Blagden, was a member of the ABCL national council (1921–23) and the board of directors (1924–38). In the disputes between MS and Jones, she often voted with Jones; after MS resigned, Blagden became a vice-president. (*New York Times,* July 16, 1968; Ackermann to MS, Feb. 23, 1929 [LCM 7:704].)
7. Dorothy Hamilton Brush (1894–1968) was a Cleveland-born socialite who had married Charles F. Brush Jr. (1893–1927), a cousin of Juliet Rublee, in 1917. After meeting MS in 1921 at the First American Birth Control Conference, she was determined to open a birth control clinic in Ohio. Brush got her husband to pledge five thousand dollars to establish the Cleveland Maternal Health Association (CMHA) shortly before his death. "Mr. Brush" is a reference to her father-in-law (Rublee's uncle), Charles Francis Brush Sr. (1849–1929), the developer of practical arc lighting systems and cofounder of the Brush Electric Company. He devoted much of his life to inventions, research, and

promoting eugenics. (*ANB;* Reed, *Birth Control Movement and American Society,* 291–92; Meyer, "Birth Control Policy," 110–12.)

8. In 1928, Charles F. Brush Sr. established the Brush Foundation in his son's memory. It provided grants for eugenics and population control and subsidized the CMHA. (Reed, *Birth Control Movement and American Society,* 291–92; Meyer, "Birth Control Policy," 67, 110–12.)

9. In February 1928, Anne Kennedy went to Cleveland to help Brush and Hortense Shepard form the CMHA. (Kennedy to MS, Jan. 10, 1928 [LCM 8:1270].)

248. Open Letter to Patrick Cardinal Hayes[1]

[*New York, N.Y.*]
[*May 28, 1928*]

My attention has just been called to your statement to the delegates at the 18th Annual Convention of the Catholic Press Association,[2] reported in the New York Evening Sun of May 25th, 1928.

You are quoted as saying, in your welcome to the delegates on behalf of the Diocese of New York, that you are "in full agreement that the church should be kept out of politics— And at the same time let us have the Catholic press keep out of politics."[3]

The American Birth Control League, Inc. is deeply interested in this statement. Every year the League sponsors a bill at Albany which, if passed, would permit physicians to give Birth Control advice to married persons.[4] Every year the only opposition comes from the Roman Catholic Church, through the Dioceses of Albany and New York, and from the Associated Catholic Charities of the state of New York.[5]

When our representatives were interviewing members of Congress at Washington two years ago, they found Catholics, directed by the National Catholic Welfare Council, lobbying against any change in the Federal law governing the distribution or importation of Birth Control information or materials.[6]

Does your statement mean that in future the Catholic Church will keep out of politics where legislation on Birth Control is concerned, and will your Church cease its policy of intimidation of those members of Congress and of the New York Legislature who do not think as you do, but who have been threatened, in the past, with defeat if they voted for our bills?

We entirely agree with your reported statement that "the church should be kept out of politics." Is the statement attributed to you correct, and what does it imply? Many thousands of married people in New York State are interested in your answer.

TL MSP, DLC (LCM 130:425). This letter was never published.

1. Hayes had been elevated to cardinal on March 24, 1924.

2. Founded in 1911, the Catholic Press Association, made up of Catholic and lay magazine and newspaper publishers, worked closely with the National Catholic Welfare Council (NCWC). Their annual convention was held at New York City's Knights of Columbus Hotel on May 24. (Mary Lonan Reilly, *A History of the Catholic Press Association, 1911–1968* [Metuchen, N.J., 1971], 23, 34].)

3. Hayes called for the church to "leave politics to others," a theme reiterated at the convention. (*New York Sun,* May 25, 1928.)

4. The ABCL sponsored a series of bills in the New York State Assembly, including Rosenman (1923), Boyle (1924, 1925), Gedney (1927), and Olsen (1928), all of which died in committee. ("New York State Bills," n.d. [LCM 27:446].)

5. The New York Catholic church was an extremely well-organized opponent of birth control. MS held the Albany and New York City dioceses responsible for the 1921 Town Hall raid, the 1922 attempt in Syracuse to prohibit birth control discussion, and the 1923 suppression of her Albany lecture. They also opposed her legislative efforts through vehement denunciations of birth control by the Archdiocesan Council of Catholic Women. (Dienes, *Law, Politics, and Birth Control,* 93; "A Calling of the Clan," *BCR,* Mar. 1923, 59–60].)

6. Anne Kennedy reported that the NCWC followed up on every visit by ABCL workers to congressmen. ("News Notes," *BCR,* Apr. 1926, 137.)

249. *To Juliet Barrett Rublee*

[*New York, N.Y.*]
June 1. [*1928*]

Beloved Juliet:

Your dear letter of May 24th came yesterday as I was on my way to N.Y for the day.[1] I am glad to have word at last that some of my letters to you have been received. The first one I wrote[2] was sent while you were en route to Mexico trusting you would receive it shortly after your arrival. I have all your letters I think you are adorable to write so fully. I love to know all about your doings.

As to the resignation—what a precious dear you are—I shall present it with my own. Its form is quite correct you Francie[3] & I all resigning at once looks like collusion. Certainly it is impossible for me to work with all the restrictions they have made. Mrs J—[4] dominates and plays politics, gets her ideas entrenched before she comes to meetings, ↑she↓ sees that Mrs D—[5] or Mrs B—[6] suggest them while she argues in favor & defends them. Its too obvious to be clever. Its really stupid because a child could see through it all.

Its not the way I work or can work— The discussion is biased before it begins. Anyway it will be a relief to hand it over. I feel the same way—absolute relief. Thank you darling for your willingness to come on the committee.[7] I accept and shall put your name down for that.

Do you think you will stay down there forever? Darling—darling—you do not deserve financial worries. Won't the tide ever turn in your favor?[8] Do you keep in touch with Unity?[9] Perhaps its too simple for you to accept seriously, but its simplicity has won me to believe in its methods. Try—try try!

A letter from Harold saying I did not read his letter correctly. That he was not in New York (letter postmarked NY). & sent letter at Panama Canal—but said he was going home ~~via~~ without stopping ~~at~~ off etc.[10]

I can't get it at all, but I'll look up his letter & see how I could have misread its meaning.

Have you seen the new book on Havelock by Houston Peterson? Its worth reading. I am reviewing it for the B.C.R.[11]

Long & lovely letters continue to come from Hugh.[12] He is a joy on earth in my life, the bright spot keeping fresh my faith hope & love in humanity I am working on the book of letters & love to see it take shape under my eye.[13]

H. G. has brought out a book on Catherine (Jane).[14] He has written a stunning introduction to the book; well worth reading. I went on a diet of orange juice for two weeks and lost only five pounds but looked like twenty one, color came back—felt like a new person. I'm back on vegetables ~~again~~ ↑now↓ but long to try it again.

Love to George and tons to my adorable Juliet. Devotedly

Margaret

ALS JRP, NhD (*MSM* C4:662–65). Letterhead of the Grosvenor.

1. No May 24 letter from Rublee was found; possibly it was Rublee to MS, May 20, 1928 (*MSM* S4:470).
2. MS to Rublee, Apr. 28, 1928 (*MSM* C4:624).
3. Neither Rublee's nor Ackermann's letter of resignation was found.
4. Mrs. J was Eleanor Dwight Jones.
5. This was a reference to Charlotte Delafield, who considered herself MS's friend but supported Jones's more professional management style and Anne Kennedy's dismissal. (Delafield to MS, Apr. 16, 1928 [LCM 8:182].)
6. This was probably Mabel Blagden, who, according to Frances Ackermann, was the "worst—poisoned by Mrs. J— she now outdoes her." (Ackermann to MS, Feb. 11, 1927 [LCM 22:96].)
7. She was referring to the CRB.
8. Rublee, suffering from depression and loneliness, had also recently lost part of her fortune to a fraudulent money manager. (Rublee to MS, May 20, 1928, and MS to Rublee, July 10 and 13, 1928 [*MSM* S4:470, C4:694 and 701].)
9. Unity School of Christianity was a religious movement founded in Kansas City, Missouri, with theological and historical links to Christian Science. MS periodically contacted Unity's prayer ministry and received its devotional magazine, the *Daily Word.* (Daniel G. Reid, *Dictionary of Christianity in America* (Downers Grove, Ill., 1990), 1204–5; Silent Unity to MS, Mar. 14, 1951, and Lois R. Nelson to Unity, Apr. 30, 1951 [*MSM* S34:77 and 420].)

10. The letters were not found.

11. Houston Peterson (1897–1981), a philosophy professor and author, published *Havelock Ellis: Philosopher of Love* (1928). (*New York Times,* May 20, 1981; for MS review, see "Havelock Ellis," *BCR,* July 1928, 210 [*MSM* S71:142].)

12. See, for instance, Hugh de Selincourt to MS, Apr. 12–May 19, 1928 (*MSM* S4:411–68).

13. Later that year, MS published *Motherhood in Bondage,* an edited collection of approximately four hundred client letters describing their bleak economic and reproductive situations. Mary Sumner Boyd assisted MS in assembling the letters; her analysis of 250,000 such letters is included in the appendix.

14. *The Book of Catherine Wells* (1928), edited by H. G. Wells, was a collection of her writings.

250. To ABCL Board of Directors

[*New York, N.Y.*]
June 8, 1928.

To the Board of Directors:

I hereby present to you my resignation as president of the American Birth Control League.

When in 1914 I commenced my campaign for the recognition and legalization of Birth Control education, I decided that there were four main steps by which this goal could be reached. The first to awaken the consciousness of the American public to the idea and the necessity of contraception; the second was to bring the discussion of Birth Control out of the abyss of prurient silence to which it had been condemned by prejudice and convention—to bring the doctrine out into the sunlight of frank and open discussion; the third necessary step was to awaken the interest and effect the alliance of scientists and doctors which would eventuate in the perfecting of a practical and hygienic technique; while the fourth and large step would aim at the establishment of clinics and the creation of a research department.

After fourteen years of incessant and apparently endless effort, we have accomplished a great deal in these various fields. If our work is not yet completed, it is through no lack of organized effort on the part of this League. In fact we may say that all four of our fundamental aims are closer to realization that anyone ten years ago could have believed possible.

I believe, however, that the research work through clinics needs direction and organization and I want to give what time I have to this branch of the work, both here and abroad. I have already started a clinic in Berlin under the auspices and direction of a medical group. This is set in the heart of the workers' section—Neukolln—and has at its head the chief of the Health Department of that district—Dr. Schmienke.[1] This group will test out all appliances known in Germany and will cooperate with the New York Clinic in its undertakings and follow our lead in the future.

There is also now established in the University of Edinburgh a department on Contraceptive Research under Dr. F. A. E. Crew, Chief of the Department of Zoology.[2] This is a great step forward when one considers the difficulty of getting eminent scientists to work in the field of contraception. Dr. Crew has imported a first-class scientist from Germany, Dr. Wiesner, to do this work,[3] and Dr. Crew looks to some of us to help him carry on. This I have promised to do.

During my absence of almost two years, doubtless it was found necessary to restrict and to prohibit the powers of the President. In such restriction there often lurks a danger—the danger of curtailing the initiative of individuals and deadening that creative interest which is essential to successful leadership. Continued growth in the future still depends, as it has in the past, upon that dynamic energy which is released by profound interest, devotion and whole-souled conviction and faith.

In offering my resignation as President of the American Birth Control League, I do so fully confident that its progress will not be impeded or its activities slackened by any lack of these motive powers. What some call fanaticism is never dangerous to the life of such an organization as this one. Apathy and languid convictions are. I am offering my resignation fully convinced that the work will go on as before—even that new life, new people and new energies may be brought into it.

I know that all of our Directors have demonstrated their powers of cooperation and their loyalty to our ideals. It is especially gratifying to me to realize at this time that some of you, who are still active in the League, have stood by me since those early days, twelve or thirteen years ago, when it took more than the usual courage and grit to face the ridicule and condemnation which confronted anyone who openly advocated Birth Control. The loyalty and faith of Mrs. Rublee[4] and Mrs. Delafield[5] have always strengthened my courage, and I wish to thank them both for their long years of devotion to the cause.

I also wish to thank Mrs. Ackermann[6] for her steadfast devotion and hard work as treasurer and bookkeeper of the League. In those days when we could not afford a bookkeeper, it was Mrs. Ackermann who did that drudgery in her "leisure" time.

With gratifying confidence that the American Birth Control League has reached a stage of maturity and organization at which it need no longer depend upon its first president, I hereby tender my resignation to its Board of Directors.[7] Respectfully submitted,

Margaret Sanger [*signed*]

TLS PPFAR, MN-SSC (*MSM* S4:494–95); for a transcribed copy, see *MSM* C4:670. Letterhead of the ABCL. A handwritten note, probably by Juliet Rublee, at the top of the first page reads, "Year in which Margaret Sanger resigned from ABC League."

1. The clinic opened on July 1, 1928, operated by the Committee for Birth Control, a small group of gynecologists, health administrators, and birth control advocates organized by Agnes Smedley. Both the committee and clinic were inspired by MS's 1927 Berlin trip, and she and Slee subsidized the clinic. Richard Schmincke (?–1939) was a Neukölln city councilman, a Communist Party member, and the health commissioner. (Atina Grossmann, *Reforming Sex: The German Movement for Birth Control and Abortion Reform, 1920–1950* [New York, 1995], 51–53, 264*n*89.)

2. Francis Albert Eley Crew (1886–1973) was a University of Edinburgh medical researcher and eugenicist credited with making the study of genetics respectable. The director of the Animal Breeding Research Department, where he studied the commonalities between human and animal breeding, Crew was convinced that declining fertility was linked to population density and nutrition rather than to contraceptive use. He had asked MS for help in raising funds for research on the problems of fecundity and fertility. (*London Times,* May 30 and June 2, 1973; for Crew-MS letters between Dec. 1927 and June 1928, see *MSM* C4:298 and LCM 19:981–1000, 14:805; Soloway, *Birth Control,* 270.)

3. Bertold Paul Wiesner (1901– ?), an Austrian sex-physiologist who was working on developing a method of determining pregnancy, was hired by Crew in 1928 to head a pregnancy diagnosis station in the Department of Animal Breeding. His research focused on finding ways to prevent conception by inhibiting the implantation of fertilized eggs in the womb, as well as preventing the production of spermatozoa. (Margaret Deacon, "The Institute of Animal Genetics at Edinburgh—The First Twenty-five Years," unpublished report, [University of Edinburgh Library]; MS to Wiesner, Apr. 20, 1928 [LCM 19:998].)

4. The board accepted Rublee's resignation as vice-president but asked her to reconsider her resignation from the board. (ABCL Board Minutes, June 12, 1928 [LCM 28:11].)

5. Delafield's name was proposed as president, but she declined. Eleanor Dwight Jones was elected. (ABCL Board Minutes, June 12, 1928 [LCM 28:11].)

6. Ackermann's resignation as treasurer was accepted, but she, too, was asked to remain on the board. The board voted to ask Slee to take the treasurer's post and named Helen Thorpe as assistant treasurer. (ABCL Board Minutes, June 12, 1928 [LCM 28:11].)

7. This letter of resignation was accepted by the board at its June 12 meeting. MS remained on the ABCL board.

Bibliography

Full citations for sources that appear only once in the volume are in the endnotes. Those mentioned more than once are listed below. For those items that also appear on the Sanger microfilm, reel and frame citations follow the entry.

Abbott, Leonard. "The Conviction of William Sanger." *Mother Earth,* Oct. 1915, 268–71.

Aldred, Guy. *No Traitor's Gate: The Life and Times of Guy Aldred, 1957–1963.* Vol. 3. Glasgow, 1963.

Ames, Blanche. "Margaret Sanger's Influence." In "Our Margaret Sanger," 1959 manuscript, edited by Erma Brown, Dorothy Brush, Mesako Ledward, and Ellen Watumull. Margaret Sanger Papers, Sophia Smith Collection, Smith College. (*MSM* S77:729).

Avrich, Paul. *Anarchist Voices: An Oral History of Anarchism in America.* Princeton, N.J., 1995.

———. *Modern School Movement: Anarchism and Education in the United States.* Princeton, N.J., 1980.

Banks, Olive, ed. *Biographical Dictionary of British Feminists.* New York, 1985–90.

Benn, J. Miriam. *Predicaments of Love.* London, 1992.

Berkman, Alexander. *Prison Memoirs of an Anarchist.* New York, 1912.

"Birth Control in Ohio." *Birth Control Review,* Dec. 1922, 243.

"Birth Control in Syracuse." *Birth Control Review,* Apr. 1924, 100–101.

Birth Control—What It Is, How it Works, What It Will Do: Proceedings of the First American Birth Control Conference. New York, 1921.

Björkman, Frances Maule. "Light Ahead." *Birth Control Review,* Dec. 1919, 9–10.

Bloch, Iwan. *The Sexual Life of Our Time in Its Relation to Modern Civilization.* 1908. Reprint, New York, 1928.

Boyer, Paul S. *Purity in Print: The Vice-Society Movement and Book Censorship in America.* New York, 1968.

Brissenden, Paul. *The I.W.W.: A Study of American Syndicalism.* New York, 1919.

Brodie, Janet Farrell. *Contraception and Abortion in Nineteenth-Century America.* Ithaca, N.Y., 1994.

Brome, Vincent. *Havelock Ellis, Philosopher of Sex: A Biography.* London, 1979.

Brownlow, Kevin. *Behind the Mask of Innocence.* Berkeley, Calif., 1992.

Buhle, Mari Jo. *Women and American Socialism, 1870–1920.* Urbana, Ill., 1981.

Buhle, Mari Jo, Paul Buhle, and Dan Georgakas, eds. *Encyclopedia of the American Left.* New York, 1990.

Caldwell, Jonathan Taylor. *Come Dungeons Dark.* Barr, Ayrshire, 1988.

Carlson, Peter. *Roughneck: The Life and Times of Big Bill Haywood.* New York, 1983.

Chen, Constance M. *"The Sex Side of Life": Mary Ware Dennett's Pioneering Battle for Birth Control and Sex Education.* New York, 1996.

Chesler, Ellen. "Interview with Grant Sanger," Aug. 1976. Oral History Project on the History of Women in the Population Control and Abortion Movements, Schlesinger Library, Radcliffe Institute for Advanced Study, Harvard University.

———. *Woman of Valor: Margaret Sanger and the Birth Control Movement in America.* New York, 1992.

"Children of a Strike." *Survey* 27 (Feb. 4, 1912): 1791.

"The Conviction of Alexander Scott." *International Socialist Review* 14 (July 1913): 10–11.

Cooper, James F. *Technique of Contraception: The Principles and Practice of Anti-Conceptional Methods.* New York, 1928.

Crawford, Anne et al., eds. *The Europa Biographical Dictionary of British Women.* Detroit, 1989.

D'Emilio, John, and Estelle Freedman. *Intimate Matters: A History of Sexuality in America.* New York, 1997.

Dennett, Mary Ware. *Birth Control Laws.* New York, 1926.

Dickinson, Robert Latou. "Contraception: A Medical Review of the Situation." *American Journal of Obstetrics and Gynecology* 8 (Nov. 1924): 583–604.

Dienes, C. Thomas. *Law, Politics, and Birth Control.* Urbana, Ill., 1972.

Dubofsky, Melvyn. *We Shall Be All: A History of the Industrial Workers of the World.* 2d ed. Urbana, Ill., 1988.

Eastman, Max. *Love and Revolution: My Journey through an Epoch.* New York, 1964.

Ellis, Havelock. *My Life: Autobiography of Havelock Ellis.* Boston, 1939.

———. "The Objects of Marriage." *Birth Control Review,* Apr. 1917, 3–4, 8.

———. *Sex in Relation to Society.* Vol. 6 of *Studies in the Psychology of Sex.* Philadelphia, 1913.

Falk, Candace, Stephen Cole, and Sally Thomas, eds. *Emma Goldman: A Guide to Her Life and Documentary Sources.* Alexandria, Va., 1995.

Fawcett, James Waldo. *Jailed for Birth Control: The Trial of William Sanger.* New York, 1917.

Fishbein, Leslie. *Rebels in Bohemia: The Radicals of* The Masses, *1911–1917.* Chapel Hill, N.C., 1982.

Golin, Steve. *The Fragile Bridge: The Paterson Silk Strike, 1913.* Philadelphia, 1988.

Gordon, Linda. *Woman's Body, Woman's Right: A Social History of Birth Control in America.* 1976. Reprint, New York, 1977.

Gray, Madeline. *Margaret Sanger: A Biography of the Champion of Birth Control.* New York, 1979.

Grosskurth, Phyllis. *Havelock Ellis: A Biography.* New York, 1980.

Hall, Ruth. *Passionate Crusader: The Life of Marie Stopes.* New York, 1977.
Haste, Cate. *Keep the Home Fires Burning.* London, 1977.
Haywood, William D. *Bill Haywood's Book: The Autobiography of William D. Haywood.* 1929. Reprint, New York, 1977.
Hersey, Harold B. "Margaret Sanger: The Biography of the Birth Control Pioneer." 1938 manuscript. New York Public Library.
———. "The Vision." *Birth Control Review,* Mar. 1921, 15.
Himes, Norman E. *Medical History of Contraception.* 1936. Reprint, New York, 1970.
Ishimoto, Shidzue. *Facing Two Ways: The Story of My Life.* 1935. Reprint, Stanford, Calif., 1984.
Katz, Sherry Jeanne. "Dual Commitments: Feminism, Socialism, and Women's Political Activism in California, 1890–1900." Ph.D. diss., University of California at Los Angeles, 1991.
Kevles, Daniel J. *In the Name of Eugenics: Genetics and the Uses of Human Heredity.* Cambridge, 1995.
Kisch, Enoch Heinrich. *Sexual Life of Woman in Its Physiological and Hygienic Aspects.* New York, 1928.
Kreiger, Nancy. "Queen of the Bolsheviks: The Hidden History of Marie Equi." *Radical America* 17 (Sept.–Oct. 1983): 55–73.
Lader, Lawrence. *The Margaret Sanger Story and the Fight for Birth Control.* 1955. Reprint, Westport, Conn., 1973.
Larson, Edward J. *Sex, Race, and Science: Eugenics in the Deep South.* Baltimore, 1995.
Leaming, Barbara. *Katharine Hepburn.* New York, 1995.
Leathard, Audrey. *Fight for Family Planning: The Development of Family Planning Services in Britain, 1921–1974.* London, 1980.
Ledbetter, Rosanna. *A History of the Malthusian League, 1877–1927.* Columbus, Ohio, 1976.
Lee, Erma Conkling, ed. *Biographical Cyclopaedia of American Women.* Vol. 2. New York, 1925.
Luhan, Mabel Dodge. *Movers and Shakers.* 1936. Reprint, Alburquerque, 1985.
Lydon, James. *The Making of Ireland: From Ancient Times to the Present.* London, 1998.
Lynch, Patrick. "Pennsylvania Anthracite: A Forgotten IWW Venture, 1906–1916." M.A. thesis, Bloomsburg State College, Bloomsburg, Penn., 1974.
Marashio, Paul. "Interview with Horace Rublee," Apr. 19, 1980. Juliet Rublee Papers, Dartmouth College.
McCann, Carole. *Birth Control Politics in the United States, 1916–1945.* Ithaca, N.Y., 1994.
McClearey, Kevin E. "The Noonday Devil: Margaret H. Sanger's 1916 American Lecture Tour." 1999 manuscript. In author's possession.
McLaren, Angus. *Birth Control in Nineteenth-Century England.* New York, 1978.
———. *A History of Contraception from Antiquity to the Present Day.* Oxford, 1990.
Meckel, Richard. *Save the Babies: American Public Health Reform and the Prevention of Infant Mortality, 1850–1920.* Baltimore, 1990.
Meyer, Jimmy Elaine. "Birth Control Policy, Practice and Prohibition in the 1930's: The Maternal Health Association of Cleveland, Ohio." Ph.D. diss., Case Western Reserve University, 1993.
"Outline of Legislative Work in Albany." *Birth Control Review,* May 1921, 11–12.
Preston, William. *Aliens and Dissenters: Federal Suppression of Radicals, 1903–1933.* 2d ed. Urbana, Ill., 1994.
Rabban, David. *Free Speech in Its Forgotten Years.* Cambridge, 1997.

Reed, James. *The Birth Control Movement and American Society: From Private Vice to Public Virtue.* 1978. Reprint, Princeton, N.J., 1983.

Report on Strike of Textile Workers in Lawrence, Mass. in 1912. 62d Cong., 2d sess., 1912, S. Doc. 870.

Roosevelt, Theodore. "Race Decadence." *Outlook,* Apr. 8, 1911, 763–79.

Rose, June. *Marie Stopes and the Sexual Revolution.* London, 1992.

Sanger, Alexander C. "Margaret Sanger: The Early Years, 1910–1917." M.A. thesis, Princeton University, 1969.

Sanger, Margaret. "The Aim." *Woman Rebel,* Mar. 1914, 1. (*MSM* C16:515).

———. *Autobiography.* New York, 1938.

———. "Clinics, Courts and Jails." *Birth Control Review,* Apr. 1918, 3–4. (*MSM* S70:795).

———. "Editorial." *Birth Control Review,* June 1925, 163–64. (*MSM* S71:28).

———. "Editorial." *Birth Control Review,* Mar. 1921, 3–4.

———. *Family Limitation.* [New York], 1914. (*MSM* S76:848).

———. *Happiness in Marriage.* New York, 1926.

———. "London Birth Control Meetings." *Birth Control Review,* Sept. 1920, 7–8. (*MSM* C16:144).

———. *Motherhood in Bondage.* New York, 1928.

———. *My Fight for Birth Control.* New York, 1931.

———. "The New Feminists." *Woman Rebel,* Mar. 1914, 1–2. (*MSM* C16:515).

———. *The Pivot of Civilization.* New York, 1922.

———. "Portet and Ferrer." *Modern School,* Nov.–Dec. 1916, 136, Jan. 1917, 157, Feb. 1917, 184. (*MSM* C16:93, 100, 104).

———. "A Statement of Facts—An Obligation Fulfilled." *Birth Control Review,* Aug. 1918, 3–4. (*MSM* S70:798).

———. "The War against Birth Control." *American Mercury,* June 1924, 231–36. (LCM 129:647). Reprinted as "The Fight against Birth Control," *Birth Control Review,* Sept. 1924, 245–48, 269.

———. *Woman and the New Race.* New York, 1920.

———. "Woman and War." *Birth Control Review,* June 1917, 5. (*MSM* S70:790).

———. ed. *The Case for Birth Control: A Supplementary Brief and Statement of the Facts.* New York, 1917.

———. *Proceedings of the World Population Conference.* Geneva, 1927.

Schwartz, Judith. *Radical Feminists of Heterodoxy: Greenwich Village, 1912–1940.* Norwich, Vt., 1986.

Shorter, Edward. *A History of Women's Bodies.* New York, 1982.

Smith, David C. *H. G. Wells, Desperately Mortal: A Biography.* New Haven, Conn., 1986.

Soloway, Richard A. *Birth Control and the Population Question in England, 1877–1930.* Chapel Hill, N.C., 1982.

———. *Demography and Degeneration: Eugenics and the Declining Birth Rate in Twentieth-Century Britain.* 1990. Reprint, Chapel Hill, N.C., 1995.

Stopes, Marie Carmichael. *Contraception (Birth Control): Its Theory, History and Practice, a Manual for the Medical and Legal Profession.* London, 1924.

———. *Married Love.* London, 1918.

Sykes, Christopher. *Nancy: The Life of Lady Astor.* London, 1972.

Taylor, A. J. P. *English History, 1914–1945.* Oxford, 1965.

Traxel, David. *An American Saga: The Life and Times of Rockwell Kent.* New York, 1980.

Tripp, Linda. *The I.W.W. and the Paterson Strike of 1913.* Urbana, Ill., 1987.
U.S. Bureau of the Census. *Fourteenth Census of the United States, 1920.* Washington, D.C., 1920.
———. *Thirteenth Census of the United States, 1910.* Washington, D.C., 1910.
U.S. Children's Bureau. *Results of a Field Study in Johnstown, Pa., Based on Births in One Calendar Year.* Infant Mortality Series, No. 3. Washington, D.C., 1915.
U.S. Code of Laws, United States Statutes at Large, 1909. Washington, D.C., 1926.
Van Voris, Jacqueline. "Olive Byrne Richard Interview." Nov. 25, 1977, manuscript. Margaret Sanger Papers, Unfilmed Portion, Sophia Smith Collection, Smith College.
Voge, Cecil I. B. *The Chemistry and Physics of Contraceptives.* London, 1933.
Vreeland, Francis McLennan. "The Process of Reform with Especial Reference to Reform Groups in the Field of Population." Ph.D. diss., University of Michigan, 1929.
Watson, Steve. *Strange Bedfellows: The First American Avant-Garde.* New York, 1991.
Wexler, Alice. *Emma Goldman: An Intimate Life.* New York, 1984.
Who's Who of American Women. 9th ed. Chicago, 1958.
Young, Louise M. *In the Public Interest: The League of Women Voters, 1920–1970.* New York, 1989.

Index

Page numbers in **bold** indicate main biographical information; numbers in ***bold italics*** indicate that the reference is to the text of a document by or to the individual or organization cited.

ESTHER KATZ is the director and editor of the Margaret Sanger Papers Project and an associate professor (adjunct) of history at New York University.

CATHY MORAN HAJO is the assistant director and editor of the Margaret Sanger Papers and a doctoral candidate in history at New York University.

PETER C. ENGELMAN is the assistant editor of the Margaret Sanger Papers Project, a writer, and an archivist.

University of Illinois Press
1325 South Oak Street
Champaign, IL 61820-6903
www.press.uillinois.edu